Lecture Notes in Computer Science 16289

Founding Editors

Gerhard Goos
Juris Hartmanis

Editorial Board Members

Elisa Bertino, *Purdue University, West Lafayette, IN, USA*
Wen Gao, *Peking University, Beijing, China*
Bernhard Steffen, *TU Dortmund University, Dortmund, Germany*
Moti Yung, *Columbia University, New York, NY, USA*

The series Lecture Notes in Computer Science (LNCS), including its subseries Lecture Notes in Artificial Intelligence (LNAI) and Lecture Notes in Bioinformatics (LNBI), has established itself as a medium for the publication of new developments in computer science and information technology research, teaching, and education.

LNCS enjoys close cooperation with the computer science R & D community, the series counts many renowned academics among its volume editors and paper authors, and collaborates with prestigious societies. Its mission is to serve this international community by providing an invaluable service, mainly focused on the publication of conference and workshop proceedings and postproceedings. LNCS commenced publication in 1973.

Josef Kittler · Hongkai Xiong · Jian Yang ·
Xilin Chen · Jiwen Lu · Weiyao Lin · Jingyi Yu ·
Weishi Zheng
Editors

Pattern Recognition and Computer Vision

8th Chinese Conference, PRCV 2025
Shanghai, China, October 15–18, 2025
Proceedings, Part XVIII

Editors
Josef Kittler
University of Surrey
Guildford, UK

Jian Yang
Nanjing University of Science and Technology
Nanjing, Jiangsu, China

Jiwen Lu
Tsinghua University
Beijing, China

Jingyi Yu
ShanghaiTech University
Shanghai, China

Hongkai Xiong
Shanghai Jiao Tong University
Shanghai, China

Xilin Chen
Chinese Academy of Sciences
Beijing, China

Weiyao Lin
Shanghai Jiao Tong University
Shanghai, China

Weishi Zheng
Sun Yat-sen University
Guangzhou, China

ISSN 0302-9743 ISSN 1611-3349 (electronic)
Lecture Notes in Computer Science
ISBN 978-981-95-5763-9 ISBN 978-981-95-5764-6 (eBook)
https://doi.org/10.1007/978-981-95-5764-6

© The Editor(s) (if applicable) and The Author(s), under exclusive license to Springer Nature Singapore Pte Ltd. 2026

This work is subject to copyright. All rights are solely and exclusively licensed by the Publisher, whether the whole or part of the material is concerned, specifically the rights of translation, reprinting, reuse of illustrations, recitation, broadcasting, reproduction on microfilms or in any other physical way, and transmission or information storage and retrieval, electronic adaptation, computer software, or by similar or dissimilar methodology now known or hereafter developed.
The use of general descriptive names, registered names, trademarks, service marks, etc. in this publication does not imply, even in the absence of a specific statement, that such names are exempt from the relevant protective laws and regulations and therefore free for general use.
The publisher, the authors and the editors are safe to assume that the advice and information in this book are believed to be true and accurate at the date of publication. Neither the publisher nor the authors or the editors give a warranty, expressed or implied, with respect to the material contained herein or for any errors or omissions that may have been made. The publisher remains neutral with regard to jurisdictional claims in published maps and institutional affiliations.

This Springer imprint is published by the registered company Springer Nature Singapore Pte Ltd.
The registered company address is: 152 Beach Road, #21-01/04 Gateway East, Singapore 189721, Singapore

If disposing of this product, please recycle the paper.

Preface

Welcome to the proceedings of the Eighth Chinese Conference on Pattern Recognition and Computer Vision (PRCV 2025), held in Shanghai, China.

PRCV is formed from the combination of two distinguished conferences: CCPR (Chinese Conference on Pattern Recognition) and CCCV (Chinese Conference on Computer Vision). Both have consistently been the top-tier conference in the fields of pattern recognition and computer vision within China's academic field. Recognizing the intertwined nature of these disciplines and their overlapping communities, the union into PRCV aims to reinforce the prominence of the Chinese academic sector in these foundational areas of artificial intelligence and enhance academic exchanges. Accordingly, PRCV is jointly sponsored by China's leading academic institutions: the China Society of Image and Graphics (CSIG), the Chinese Association for Artificial Intelligence (CAAI), the China Computer Federation (CCF), and the Chinese Association of Automation (CAA).

PRCV's mission is to serve as a comprehensive platform for dialogues among researchers from both academia and industry. While its primary focus is to encourage academic exchange, it also places emphasis on fostering ties between academia and industry. With the objective of keeping abreast of leading academic innovations and to showcase the most recent research breakthroughs, pioneering thoughts, and advanced techniques in pattern recognition and computer vision, esteemed international and domestic experts were invited to present keynote speeches, introducing the most recent developments in these fields.

PRCV 2025 was hosted by Shanghai Jiao Tong University. From our call for papers, we received 2370 full submissions. Each paper underwent rigorous double-blind reviews by at least three experts, either from our dedicated Program Committee or from other qualified researchers in the field. After thorough evaluations, 692 papers were selected for the conference, comprising 66 oral presentations and 626 posters, maintaining an acceptance rate of 29.20%.

Our heartfelt gratitude goes out to our keynote speakers: Mohammed Bennamoun from the University of Western Australia, Pascal Fua of the École Polytechnique Fédérale de Lausanne, Abdulmotaleb El Saddik of the University of Ottawa, Ivan Laptev from Mohamed bin Zayed University of Artificial Intelligence, Moncef Gabbouj from Tampere University, and Long Quan from Hong Kong University of Science and Technology.

We give sincere appreciation to all the authors of submitted papers, the members of the Program Committee, the reviewers, and the Organizing Committee. Their combined efforts have been instrumental in the success of this conference. A special acknowledgment to our sponsors and organizers of various special forums; their support made the conference a success. We also express our thanks to Springer for taking on the publication.

We hope these proceedings will be both enlightening and enjoyable for all readers.

Jiwen Lu
Weiyao Lin
Jingyi Yu
Weishi Zheng

Organization

General Chairs

Josef Kittler	University of Surrey, UK
Hongkai Xiong	Shanghai Jiao Tong University, China
Jian Yang	Nanjing University of Science and Technology, China
Xilin Chen	Institute of Computing Technology, Chinese Academy of Sciences, China

Program Committee Chairs

Jiwen Lu	Tsinghua University, China
Weiyao Lin	Shanghai Jiao Tong University, China
Jingyi Yu	ShanghaiTech University, China
Weishi Zheng	Sun Yat-sen University, China

Organizing Chairs

Cairong Zhao	Tongji University, China
Wei Jia	Hefei University of Technology, China
Tao Chen	Fudan University, China
Ziyang Zheng	Shanghai Jiao Tong University, China

Publicity Chairs

Xiang Bai	Huazhong University of Science and Technology, China
Mingkui Tan	South China University of Technology, China
Lifang Wu	Beijing University of Technology, China
Lei Zhu	Tongji University, China

International Liaison Chairs

Mingming Cheng	Nankai University, China
Cewu Lu	Shanghai Jiao Tong University, China
Xiaojun Chang	University of Science and Technology of China, China

Tutorial Chairs

Zhanyu Ma	Beijing University of Posts and Telecommunications, China
Jiaying Liu	Peking University, China
Ran He	Institute of Automation, Chinese Academy of Sciences, China

Workshop Chairs

Zhaoxiang Zhang	Institute of Automation, Chinese Academy of Sciences, China
Wangmeng Zuo	Harbin Institute of Technology, China
Ruiping Wang	Institute of Computing Technology, Chinese Academy of Sciences, China
Jufeng Yang	Nankai University, China

Doctoral Forum Organizing Chairs

Si Liu	Beijing University of Aeronautics and Astronautics, China
Yan Huang	Institute of Automation, Chinese Academy of Sciences, China
Liquan Shen	Shanghai University, China

Special Session Chairs

Yueqi Duan	Tsinghua University, China
Chenjia Bai	Institute of AI (TeleAI), China Telecom, China

Publication Chairs

Xuyao Zhang	Institute of Automation, Chinese Academy of Sciences, China
Limin Wang	Nanjing University, China
Yansong Tang	Tsinghua Shenzhen International Graduate School, China

Sponsorship Chairs

Zechao Li	Nanjing University of Science and Technology, China
Xi Li	Zhejiang University, China
Zhijun Fang	Donghua University, China
Junchi Yan	Shanghai Jiao Tong University, China
Shugong Xu	Xi'an Jiaotong-Liverpool University, China

Exhibitions Chairs

Qi Wang	Northwestern Polytechnical University, China
Man Zhang	Beijing University of Posts and Telecommunications, China
Dan Zeng	Shanghai University, China

Contest Chairs

Jingkuan Song	Tongji University, China
Yonglu Li	Shanghai Jiao Tong University, China
Xiaopeng Zhang	Huawei Technologies, China

Registration Chairs

Xue Yang	Shanghai Jiao Tong University, China
Huabin Liu	Shanghai Jiao Tong University, China
Duoduo Xue	Shanghai Jiao Tong University, China

Website Chairs

Yu Zhou	Nankai University, China
Nuowen Kan	Shanghai Jiao Tong University, China
Huanyu He	Shanghai Jiao Tong University, China

Contents

Object Detection, Tracking and Identification

FlowDet: Overcoming Perspective and Scale Challenges in Real-Time End-to-End Traffic Detection

Zixing Wang[1] and Yuhang Zhao[2(✉)]

[1] Chinese Academy of Medical Sciences and Peking Union Medical College, Beijing 100730, China
s2023002057@pumc.edu.cn

[2] CICT Mobile Communication Technology Co., Ltd., Beijing 100191, China
ewanzhao@163.com

Abstract. End-to-end object detectors offer a promising NMS-free para-digm for real-time applications, yet their high computational cost remains a significant barrier, particularly for complex scenarios like intersection traffic monitoring. To address this challenge, we propose **FlowDet**, a high-speed detector featuring a decoupled encoder optimization strategy applied to the DETR architecture. Specifically, FlowDet employs a novel **Geometric Deformable Unit (GDU)** for traffic-aware geometric modeling and a **Scale-Aware Attention (SAA)** module to maintain high representational power across extreme scale variations. To rigorously evaluate the model's performance in environments with severe occlusion and high object density, we collected the **Intersection-Flow-5k** dataset, a new challenging scene for this task. Evaluated on Intersection-Flow-5k, FlowDet establishes a new state-of-the-art. Compared to the strong RT-DETR baseline, it **improves AP^{test} by 1.5% and ${AP_{50}}^{test}$ by 1.6%**, while simultaneously **reducing GFLOPs by 63.2% and increasing inference speed by 16.2%**. Our work demonstrates a new path towards building highly efficient and accurate detectors for demanding, real-world perception systems. The Intersection-Flow-5k dataset is available at https://github.com/AstronZh/Intersection-Flow-5K.

1 Introduction

Real-time traffic flow monitoring at urban intersections is a cornerstone of modern Intelligent Transportation Systems (ITS). Deploying accurate and efficient object detectors on resource-constrained edge devices is paramount for enabling proactive traffic management and automated safety protocols. However, this application domain exposes a fundamental dilemma in current object detection paradigms. On one hand, CNN-based detectors, epitomized by the YOLO series [5,7,8,10–12], achieve exceptional inference speed but rely on Non-Maximum Suppression (NMS). This post-processing step becomes an Achilles'

© The Author(s), under exclusive license to Springer Nature Singapore Pte Ltd. 2026
J. Kittler et al. (Eds.): PRCV 2025, LNCS 16289, pp. 3–16, 2026.
https://doi.org/10.1007/978-981-95-5764-6_1

heel in crowd-ed intersections, where it frequently fails, erroneously suppressing valid detections of densely packed or occluded vehicles [2,12].

On the other hand, Transformer-based end-to-end detectors like DETR [18] eliminate the NMS bottleneck via set-based prediction. Yet, their prohibitive computational complexity and slow convergence, stemming from global self-attention mechanisms, have historically precluded real-time deployment [19]. While recent models like RT-DETR have made significant strides in bridging this efficiency gap [22], they remain general-purpose architectures. They are not explicitly engineered to tackle the trifecta of challenges endemic to traffic surveillance: **1) severe perspective distortion**, **2) extreme object scale variations**, and **3) persistent, complex inter-object occlusions**, which are well-documented challenges in modern datasets [1,3].

To bridge this critical gap, we propose **FlowDet**, a high-speed end-to-end detection framework specifically engineered for the rigors of traffic intersection monitoring. Our framework is distinguished by two synergistic innovations designed to directly counteract the aforementioned challenges. First, a **Geometric Deformable Unit (GDU)** that moves beyond standard deformable convolutions [19] by adaptively learning traffic-aware sparse sampling points. This allows the model to intrinsically model geometric transformations and focus on discriminative, non-occluded vehicle parts. Second, a **Scale-Aware Attention (SAA)** mechanism that efficiently processes vast scale disparities through a dual-branch architecture, dedicating parallel pathways to capture both fine-grained local details and broad global context, offering an efficient alternative to classical feature pyramids [4].

Concurrently, to catalyze research and establish a standardized evaluation platform for this challenging domain, we introduce the **Intersection-Flow-5K** dataset. This comprehensive scene, comprising 6,928 high-resolution images with over 406,000 meticulously annotated bounding boxes, is the first of its kind specifically focused on complex intersection scenarios. As demonstrated in Fig. 1, extensive experiments show that FlowDet not only establishes a new state-of-the-art on this benchmark and others like COCO [24], but also maintains the computational efficiency requisite for practical edge deployment.

Our contributions are summarized as follows:

- **A novel and efficient end-to-end framework, FlowDet**, specifically designed to address the key challenges of intersection monitoring. It sets a new state-of-the-art in detection accuracy while maintaining real-time, edge-compatible performance.
- **Two synergistic technical innovations**: the **GDU** for adaptive modeling of perspective and occlusion, and the **SAA** module for robust detection across extreme scale variations.
- **A new comprehensive scene, Intersection-Flow-5K**, densely annotated with over 400K instances. It serves as a benchmark to facilitate systematic evaluation and foster future research in intersection traffic surveillance.

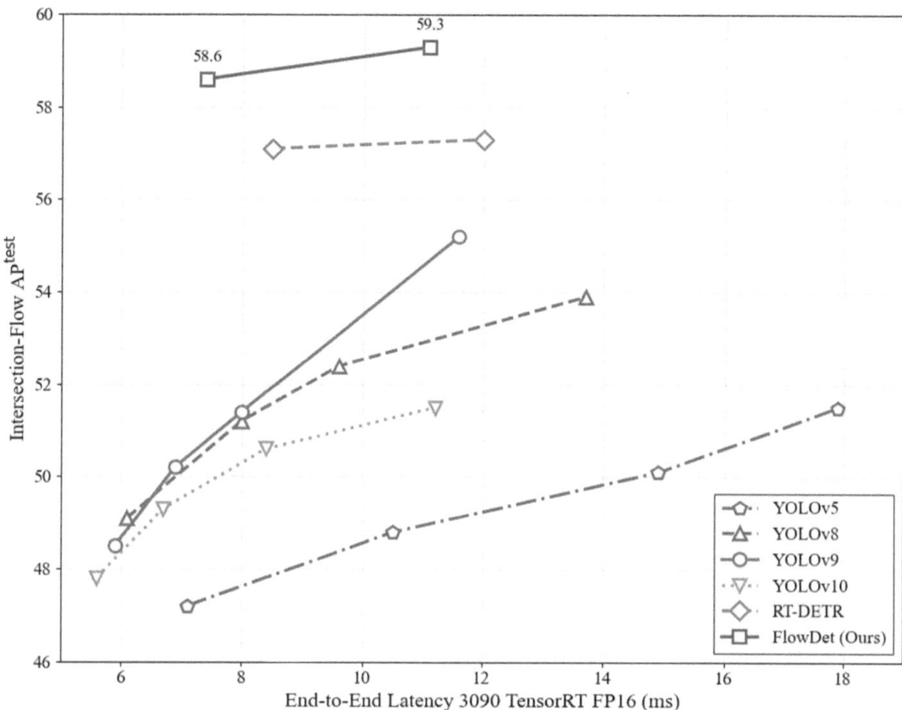

Fig. 1. Performance comparison on the Intersection-Flow-5K dataset. FlowDet establishes a new state-of-the-art Pareto curve, achieving superior accuracy at real-time speeds compared to advanced detectors like YOLOv9 [11] and RT-DETR [22].

2 Related Work

2.1 CNN-Based Real-Time Detection

The YOLO (You Only Look Once) family of detectors has become synonymous with real-time object detection since its initial version introduced a pioneering one-stage CNN architecture [5]. Through continuous evolution, the YOLO series has consistently outperformed other one-stage approaches, such as SSD [6], and established dominance in practical applications. This development trajectory has encompassed a wide range of architectural innovations, including both anchor-based and anchor-free paradigms, to achieve strong trade-offs between speed and accuracy. The series continues to advance the state-of-the-art with its most recent iterations [7–12].

The success of YOLO architectures largely stems from efficient feature aggregation mechanisms and backbone designs. Cross Stage Partial (CSP) connections [13] have proven particularly effective in YOLO architectures, enabling efficient gradient flow while reducing computational redundancy. CSP networks partition feature maps into two parts, with one part undergoing a series of operations while the other maintains identity connections, ultimately concatenating both parts to create rich feature representations with improved efficiency.

However, these advanced real-time detectors produce numerous overlapping bounding boxes and require Non-Maximum Suppression (NMS) post-processing, which introduces latency bottlenecks in dense scenarios typical of traffic intersections. This fundamental limitation motivates the exploration of end-to-end detection approaches that eliminate post-processing requirements.

2.2 End-to-End Detection and Efficient Attention

Vision Transformers have revolutionized computer vision by using self-attention mechanisms from natural language processing [14]. Since the introduction of ViT for image classification [15], subsequent works have enhanced transformer architectures by incorporating convolutional layers, introducing pyramid feature maps, and improving locality through various design innovations [16,17].

DETR [18] introduced groundbreaking end-to-end object detection using Transformers, framing detection as a set prediction problem to eliminate NMS dependency. However, early transformer-based detectors suffered from high computational complexity and slow convergence, limiting practical deployment. Subsequent improvements, such as Deformable DETR [19], focused on improving convergence speed, reducing computational overhead, and improving detection accuracy through architectural innovations [20,21].

Efficient attention mechanisms aim to reduce the quadratic complexity of standard multi-head self-attention (MSA). Representative approaches in computer vision include spatial reduction attention [17], local window attention [16], and various hybrid mechanisms. However, existing methods typically focus on either local or global attention patterns within individual layers, leading to suboptimal performance when handling extreme scale variations. Some approaches attempt to address this limitation by introducing additional global tokens or mixing local attention with convolutional operations, but often suffer from inefficient implementations that cannot fully leverage modern hardware acceleration.

RT-DETR [22] achieved a critical breakthrough by designing an Efficient Hybrid Encoder with optimized query selection mechanisms, successfully bringing end-to-end detection into real-time domains. This advancement established a strong foundation for practical transformer-based detection systems, demonstrating through direct comparisons [22] that careful architectural design can overcome traditional efficiency limitations of attention-based approaches.

3 Methodology

To address the challenges inherent in intersection traffic monitoring, we introduce **FlowDet**, a detection framework that enhances feature representation through traffic-specific innovations. The framework integrates two core components: a **Progressive Adaptive Feature Cascade (PAFC)** module featuring our novel **GDU**, and a **SAA** module designed for extreme scale variation handling.

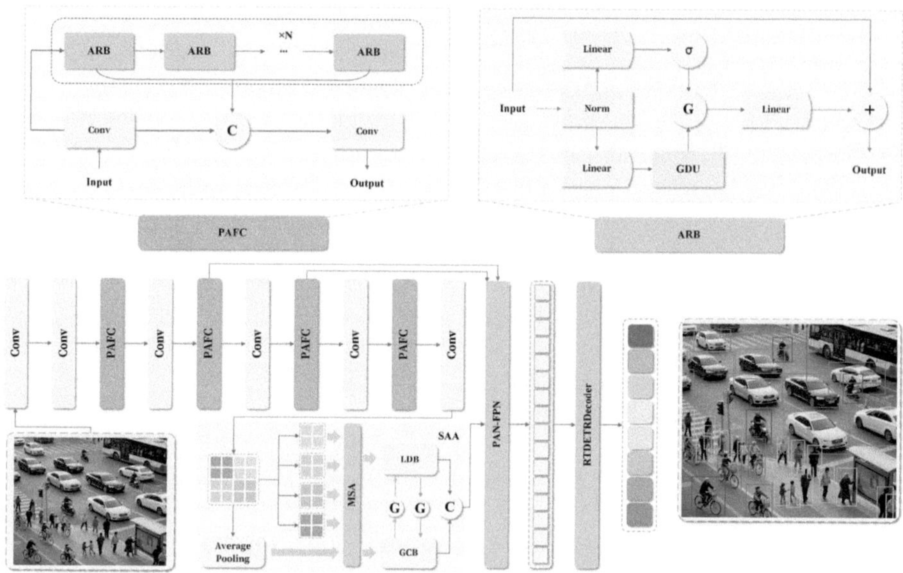

Fig. 2. Overall architecture of FlowDet. The framework integrates PAFC with GDU in the backbone and SAA in the encoder for efficient traffic object detection.

The synergistic design significantly elevates detection accuracy and robustness while preserving real-time performance essential for practical deployment. Figure 2 illustrates the complete architecture.

3.1 PAFC with Geometric Deformable Unit

Intersection traffic monitoring presents unique geometric challenges due to **perspective distortion** caused by fixed camera viewpoints, where vehicles exhibit significant shape variations and spatial transformations across different image regions. Standard backbone architectures are constrained by static convolution operations, limiting their ability to model these geometric variations effectively. The PAFC module addresses this through specialized **Adaptive Refinement Blocks (ARBs)** that progressively refine features while dynamically adjusting receptive fields to accommodate perspective-induced deformations.

The PAFC architecture employs cross-stage partial connections for efficient information flow:

$$\mathbf{Y}_0, \mathbf{Y}_1 = \text{Split}\left(Conv(\mathbf{X})\right) \tag{1}$$

$$\mathbf{Y}_i = \text{ARB}_\text{i}(\mathbf{Y}_{i-1}), \quad \text{for } i \in \{2, \ldots, n\} \tag{2}$$

$$\mathbf{Y}_\text{PAFC} = \mathcal{F}_\text{fusion}\left(\bigoplus_{i=0}^{n} \mathcal{W}_i \mathbf{Y}_i\right) \tag{3}$$

Unlike standard deformable convolutions that learn unconstrained 2D offsets, the GDU disentangles the modeling of complex geometric transformations. It features two parallel deformable convolution branches, termed Horizontality and Verticality, which learn spatial offsets primarily along their respective principal axes. This specialized design more effectively captures the systematic shearing and foreshortening effects prevalent in traffic surveillance imagery.

A critical component of the GDU is the modulation term $\psi(\|\Delta\mathbf{p}_k^{\mathrm{geo}}\|_2)$, as shown in Eq. (4). This term dynamically re-weights the contribution of each sampled point based on the magnitude of its learned offset ($\Delta\mathbf{p}_k^{\mathrm{geo}}$). This allows the model to prioritize stable, nearby points (small offsets) while cautiously sampling from distant, potentially noisy locations (large offsets), significantly improving the robustness of the feature representation.

The GDU operation is formulated as:

$$\mathrm{GDU}(\mathbf{X};\mathbf{p}_0)=\sum_{k\in\mathcal{K}}\omega_k^{\mathrm{geo}}\cdot\mathbf{X}(\mathbf{p}_0+\mathbf{p}_k+\Delta\mathbf{p}_k^{\mathrm{geo}})\cdot\psi(\|\Delta\mathbf{p}_k^{\mathrm{geo}}\|_2) \tag{4}$$

The geometric offset prediction incorporates both local and global context to **address perspective distortion systematically**:

$$\{\Delta\mathbf{p}_k\}_{k\in\mathcal{K}}=\mathcal{F}_{\mathbf{offset}}(\mathrm{DWConv}(\mathbf{X}))\cdot\sigma \tag{5}$$

Here, DWConv (Depth-wise Separable Convolution[25]) is used to efficiently capture spatial patterns for offset prediction without significant computational overhead. The scaling factor σ modulates the magnitude of the offsets, ensuring training stability.

3.2 Scale-Aware Attention (SAA)

Traffic monitoring demands simultaneous processing across extreme scale variations, from **distant vehicles occupying minimal pixel areas to nearby large objects**. Traditional attention mechanisms face fundamental trade-offs between capturing fine-grained local texture details essential for small object detection and modeling global contextual relationships necessary for scene understanding. The SAA module employs a **dual-branch architecture with adaptive gate-controlled fusion** to decouple these processes while maintaining computational efficiency (Fig. 3).

The SAA processes input features through specialized branches with **learnable gate mechanisms** that adaptively balance local and global information:

$$\mathbf{F}_{\mathrm{out}}=\mathcal{F}_{\mathrm{fusion}}(\mathrm{LDB}(\mathbf{F}_{\mathrm{in}}),\mathrm{GCB}(\mathbf{F}_{\mathrm{in}}),\mathcal{W}_{\mathrm{gate}}(\mathbf{F}_{\mathrm{in}})) \tag{6}$$

Local Detail Branch (LDB) for Small Object Optimization Our Local Detail Block (LDB) first partitions the input feature map into non-overlapping

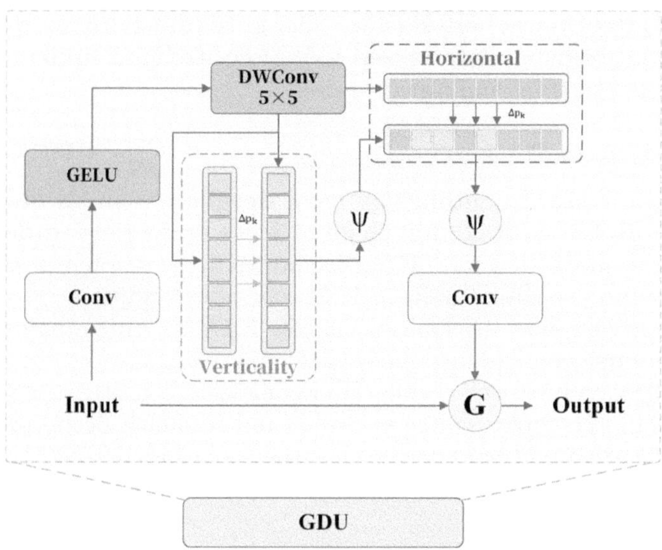

Fig. 3. GDU within Adaptive Refinement Unit. The learned geometric-aware spatial offsets enable adaptive modeling for traffic objects with varying perspective characteristics.

windows. Within each window, we apply self-attention enhanced by our specific Local Position Encoding to effectively model local geometric relationships.

$$\text{WindowAttn}(\mathbf{W}) = \text{Softmax}\left(\frac{\mathbf{Q}_{\text{window}}\mathbf{K}_{\text{window}}^T}{\sqrt{d_k}} + \text{LPE}_{\text{specific}}\right)\mathbf{V}_{\text{window}} \quad (7)$$

The processed windows are then merged back to form the final output feature map. This windowed attention mechanism ensures computational efficiency while preserving the high spatial resolution crucial for localizing small, distant vehicles. By focusing on a constrained local context, the LDB excels at discriminating fine-grained features, such as vehicle contours and lights, which are vital for small object detection.

Global Context Branch (GCB) for Scene Understanding The Global Context Branch models long-range dependencies and **scene-level contextual relationships** through spatial reduction attention:

$$\text{GlobalAttn}(\mathbf{F}) = \text{Softmax}\left(\frac{\mathbf{Q}_{\text{global}}\mathbf{K}_{\text{global}}^T}{\sqrt{d_k}} + \text{GPE}_{\text{scene}}(\mathbf{F})\right)\mathbf{V}_{\text{global}} \quad (8)$$

GCB employs global position encodings ($\text{GPE}_{\text{scene}}$) that capture **inter-object spatial relationships and scene structure**, enabling robust detection in cluttered environments with complex occlusion patterns.

Adaptive Gate-Controlled Fusion The **gate mechanism dynamically balances local texture details and global contextual information** based on spatial characteristics and object scales:

$$\mathcal{F}_{\text{fusion}} = \mathbf{F}_{\text{local}} \odot (1 - \mathcal{W}_{\text{gate}}) + \mathbf{F}_{\text{global}} \odot \mathcal{W}_{\text{gate}} + \mathbf{F}_{\text{cross}} \tag{9}$$

where $\mathcal{W}_{\text{gate}}$ learns to **emphasize local details for small objects while prioritizing global context for large objects and scene understanding**. The cross-scale interaction term $\mathbf{F}_{\text{cross}}$ facilitates information exchange between branches, ensuring coherent multi-scale feature representation.

This adaptive fusion mechanism enables SAA to **automatically adjust attention focus**: emphasizing fine-grained local texture patterns when processing small/distant objects, while leveraging global contextual relationships for understanding complex traffic scenarios and resolving occlusions. The gate weights are learned end-to-end, allowing the model to develop traffic-specific attention strategies optimized for intersection monitoring challenges.

4 Intersection-Flow-5K Dataset

Traffic intersection monitoring presents unique challenges inadequately addressed by existing benchmarks. Infrastructure-based cameras observe persistent occlusion patterns, extreme scale variations, and complex illumination conditions that differ fundamentally from ego-centric driving datasets. To address these limitations, we introduce **Intersection-Flow-5K**, a specialized benchmark designed for real-world traffic surveillance evaluation.

Table 1. Intersection-Flow-5K Dataset Statistics

Category	Train	Val	Test	Total
Images	5,483	722	723	6,928
Vehicle	190,417	23,450	23,978	237,845
Bus	2,816	315	322	3,453
Bicycle	23,396	2,771	3,051	29,218
Pedestrian	19,005	2,250	2,459	23,714
Engine	642	74	80	796
Truck	7,749	881	916	9,546
Tricycle	1,610	225	200	2,035
Obstacle	82,190	8,902	9,059	100,151
Total Objects	**327,825**	**38,868**	**40,065**	**406,758**

The dataset construction involved systematic sampling from urban intersections, comprising 6,928 high-resolution images (1920 × 1080) with over 406,000 annotations across 8 categories. Table 1 presents comprehensive statistics demonstrating balanced representation across training, validation, and test splits. The annotation protocol mandates labeling of heavily occluded objects (up to 75% occlusion) and extremely small objects (minimum 15×15 pixels), essential for realistic traffic monitoring evaluation.

Figure 4 illustrates four critical scenarios that characterize intersection monitoring challenges. The nighttime glare scenario demonstrates direct headlight interference that saturates sensors and obscures nearby objects. The vehicle occlusion scenario shows persistent blockage where large vehicles systematically obscure smaller traffic participants in adjacent lanes. The small object scenario captures distant vehicles at minimal pixel resolutions, testing detection capabilities at extreme scales. The ideal scenario provides baseline comparison under optimal visibility conditions. These scenarios establish comprehensive evaluation protocols for traffic-specific detection algorithms.

Fig. 4. Intersection-Flow-5K captures a spectrum of critical challenges in traffic surveillance, including (a) sensor saturation from nighttime glare, (b) complex inter-object occlusion, (c) extreme scale variation with distant objects, and (d) baseline ideal conditions.

5 Experiments

All experiments are conducted on RTX 3090 GPUs under TensorRT FP16 precision with batch size 1. We adopt unified 640×640 input resolution for fair comparison across all methods. Training employs AdamW optimizer with learning rate 1e-4, weight decay 1e-4, and cosine scheduling over 200 epochs (Tables 2 and 3).

5.1 Comparison with State-of-the-Art Methods

We compare FlowDet against representative methods from real-time and end-to-end detection paradigms, organizing results into complementary tables for clarity.

Table 2. Comparison with Real-Time Detection Models. All methods use unified 640 × 640 input resolution for fair comparison under identical experimental conditions.

Method	Epochs	Params (M)	GFLOPs	FPS	AP^{test}	AP^{test}_{50}	AP^{test}_S	AP^{test}_L
YOLOv5-L	400	46	109	67	50.1	68.8	19.1	72.3
YOLOv5-X	400	86	205	56	51.5	70.2	20.3	73.8
YOLOv8-L	400	43	165	104	52.4	71.7	20.0	87.4
YOLOv8-X	400	68	257	73	53.9	73.1	29.5	74.3
YOLOv9-C	400	25	102	125	51.4	70.5	18.9	86.9
YOLOv9-E	400	57	189	86	55.2	73.8	25.5	88.0
YOLOv10-L	400	24	120	119	50.6	69.8	19.5	74.2
YOLOv10-X	400	29	160	89	51.5	70.5	18.4	74.9
Faster-RCNN	600	42	180	18	45.2	65.1	25.4	60.5
Faster-RCNN	600	60	247	14	46.8	67.0	27.0	62.1
FlowDet	**200**	**15**	**50**	**136**	**58.6**	**82.3**	**34.2**	**89.0**
FlowDet-L	**200**	**21**	**78**	**90**	**59.3**	**83.1**	**35.4**	**89.7**

FlowDet demonstrates superior performance across all metrics. Compared to RT-DETR-R50, our method achieves **1.5% AP^{test} improvement** (58.6% vs 57.1%) and **1.6% AP^{test}_{50} enhancement** (82.3% vs 80.7%) while reducing computational cost by **63.2%** (50.0 vs 136.0 GFLOPs) and increasing inference speed by **16.2%** (136 vs 117 FPS). Performance improvements are particularly pronounced for small objects (AP^{test}_S: 34.2% vs 31.0%), critical for traffic monitoring where distant vehicles must be detected reliably.

5.2 Comprehensive Ablation Studies

We conduct extensive ablation studies to validate component contributions and analyze design choices.

The primary ablation demonstrates that both SAA and PAFC contribute significantly to performance improvement. SAA alone achieves 1.2% AP^{test} improvement while reducing latency by 0.5 ms. PAFC provides 1.1% AP^{test} enhancement and 0.7 ms latency reduction. Combined, they yield 1.5% AP^{test} improvement and 1.1 ms latency reduction (Tables 4, 5 and 6).

Weight sensitivity analysis reveals that balanced local/global processing achi-eves optimal performance, particularly for small object detection (AP^{test}_S:

Table 3. Comparison with End-to-End Detection Models. All transformer-based methods evaluated under identical experimental protocols and hardware configurations.

Method	Epochs	Params (M)	GFLOPs	FPS	AP^{test}	AP_{50}^{test}	AP_S^{test}	AP_L^{test}
DETR-DC5	500	41	187	10	47.5	67.3	25.8	66.2
DETR-DC5	500	60	253	7	49.1	68.9	27.4	67.8
Deformable-DETR	300	40	173	15	52.8	72.5	33.1	68.3
DAB-Deformable-DETR	300	48	195	12	53.9	73.4	34.0	69.5
Efficient-DETR	150	35	210	25	50.8	70.5	30.1	67.9
Efficient-DETR	150	54	289	17	52.1	71.8	31.5	69.3
RT-DETR-R50	200	42	136	117	57.1	80.7	31.0	85.0
RT-DETR-R101	200	76	259	83	57.3	81.4	32.1	87.2
FlowDet	**200**	**15**	**50**	**136**	**58.6**	**82.3**	**34.2**	**89.0**
FlowDet-L	**200**	**21**	**78**	**90**	**59.3**	**83.1**	**35.4**	**89.7**

Table 4. Component-wise Ablation Analysis

ID	Backbone	Attention	Latency (ms)	AP^{test} (%)	AP_{50}^{test} (%)
1	ResNet-50	AIFI	8.5	57.1	80.7
2	ResNet-50	**SAA**	8.0	58.3	81.9
3	**PAFCNet**	AIFI	7.8	58.2	82.1
4	**PAFCNet**	**SAA**	**7.4**	**58.6**	**82.3**

Table 5. SAA Branch Weight Sensitivity Analysis

Local Weight	Global Weight	AP^{test} (%)	AP_{50}^{test} (%)	AP_S^{test} (%)	AP_L^{test} (%)
0.3	0.7	57.8	81.2	32.1	88.4
0.4	0.6	58.1	81.6	33.2	88.7
0.5	0.5	58.6	82.3	34.2	89.0
0.6	0.4	58.3	82.0	33.8	88.9
0.7	0.3	57.9	81.4	33.1	88.6

34.2%). This validates our adaptive fusion mechanism that dynamically adjusts branch contributions.

The window size analysis demonstrates that 2×2 windowing provides an optimal trade-off between local detail capture and computational efficiency. Smaller windows (1×1) lack sufficient context for effective local feature learning, while larger windows (4×4, 8×8) introduce excessive computational overhead without proportional accuracy gains.

Table 6. Local Detail Attention Window Size Analysis

Window Size	Latency (ms)	AP_S (%)	AP_M (%)	AP_L (%)	Overall AP (%)
1×1	6.8	32.1	59.2	88.7	58.1
2×2	7.4	34.2	59.5	89.0	58.6
4×4	8.9	33.8	58.9	88.4	58.3
8×8	11.2	32.5	57.8	87.9	57.7

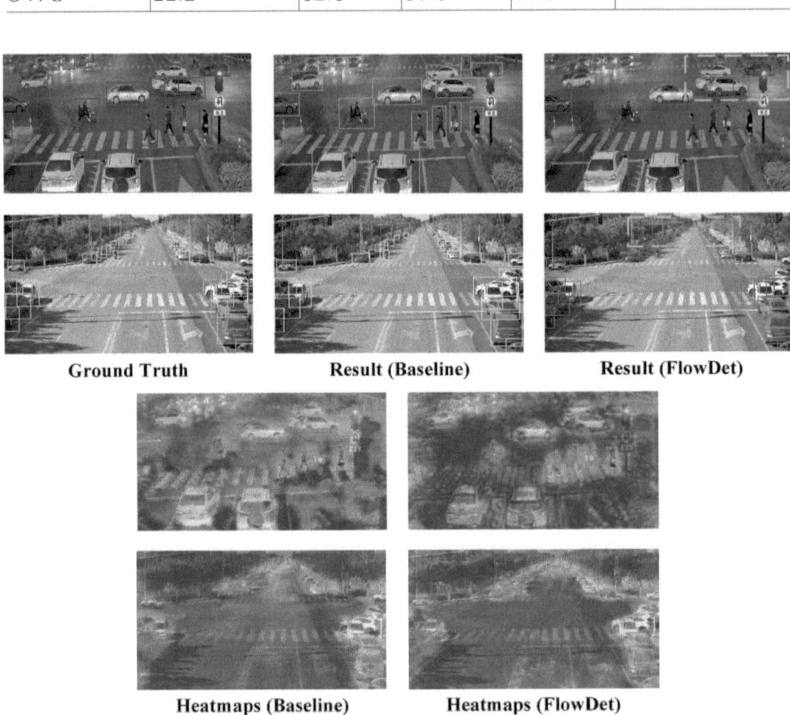

Fig. 5. Qualitative comparison showcasing FlowDet's superior attention mechanism and detection performance. **Top row (Occlusion):** In challenging scenarios with severe inter-object occlusion, FlowDet precisely focuses on visible vehicle parts, leading to robust detection. **Bottom row (Small Objects):** For distant, low-resolution targets, our model maintains a tight attention focus, demonstrating its resilience to extreme scale variations. FlowDet's refined geometric and scale-aware modeling results in more accurate and reliable detections in both cases.

5.3 Qualitative Analysis and Visualization

Figure 5 provides qualitative analysis of FlowDet's performance in challenging scenarios. The vehicle occlusion scenarios demonstrate FlowDet's ability to detect partially occluded objects through improved context understanding and geometric modeling capabilities. The attention heatmaps reveal that our SAA mechanism effectively focuses on relevant object regions while suppressing background noise. In small object scenarios, FlowDet consistently detects distant vehicles that baseline methods miss, validating the effectiveness of our scale-aware attention design. The improved attention patterns demonstrate that our dual-branch architecture successfully captures both local details necessary for small object detection and global context required for understanding scene structure and object relationships.

6 Conclusion

This work presents FlowDet, a novel approach for real-time traffic flow detection that enhances DETR architecture through specialized innovations for intersection monitoring. Our framework integrates two key components: the Geometric Deformable Unit enabling adaptive geometric modeling for traffic objects with varying characteristics, and the Scale-Aware Attention module providing efficient multi-scale processing through dual-branch architecture. Comprehensive evaluation on the newly introduced Intersection-Flow-5K dataset demonstrates significant improvements: 1.5% AP^{test} improvement and 63.2% computational reduction compared to RT-DETR baseline while maintaining 136 FPS real-time performance. The method shows particular strength in small object detection (34.2% AP_S^{test} vs 31.0% baseline), crucial for traffic monitoring applications. Our traffic-specific optimizations make FlowDet suitable for deployment in resource-constrained edge computing scenarios typical of traffic infrastructure, providing practical value for intelligent transportation systems.

References

1. Yu, F., et al.: BDD100K: a diverse driving dataset and challenges for open-vocabulary object detection and tracking. In: Proceedings of the IEEE/CVF Conference on Computer Vision and Pattern Recognition, pp. 2636–2645 (2020)
2. Bodla, N., Singh, B., Chellappa, R., Davis, L.S.: Soft-NMS–improving object detection with one line of code. In: Proceedings of the IEEE International Conference on Computer Vision, pp. 5561–5569 (2017)
3. Caesar, H., et al.: nuScenes: a multimodal dataset for autonomous driving. In: Proceedings of the IEEE/CVF Conference on Computer Vision and Pattern Recognition, pp. 11621–11631 (2020)
4. Lin, T.Y., Dollár, P., Girshick, R., He, K., Hariharan, B., Belongie, S.: Feature pyramid networks for object detection. In: Proceedings of the IEEE Conference on Computer Vision and Pattern Recognition, pp. 2117–2125 (2017)
5. Redmon, J., Divvala, S., Girshick, R., Farhadi, A.: You only look once: unified, real-time object detection. In: Proceedings of the IEEE Conference on Computer Vision and Pattern Recognition, pp. 779–788 (2016)
6. Liu, W., et al.: SSD: single shot multibox detector. In: Leibe, B., Matas, J., Sebe, N., Welling, M. (eds.) ECCV 2016. LNCS, vol. 9905, pp. 21–37. Springer, Cham (2016). https://doi.org/10.1007/978-3-319-46448-0_2
7. Redmon, J., Farhadi, A.: YOLOv3: an incremental improvement. arXiv preprint arXiv:1804.02767 (2018)

8. Bochkovskiy, A., Wang, C.Y., Liao, H.Y.M.: YOLOv4: optimal speed and accuracy of object detection. arXiv preprint arXiv:2004.10934 (2020)
9. Ge, Z., Liu, S., Wang, F., Li, Z., Sun, J. YOLOX: exceeding YOLO series in 2021. arXiv preprint arXiv:2107.08430 (2021)
10. Wang, C.Y., Bochkovskiy, A., Liao, H.Y.M.: YOLOv7: trainable bag-of-freebies sets new state-of-the-art for real-time object detection. In: Proceedings of the IEEE/CVF Conference on Computer Vision and Pattern Recognition, pp. 7464–7475 (2022)
11. Wang, C.Y., Yeh, I.H., Liao, H.Y.M.: YOLOv9: learning what you want to learn using programmable gradient information. arXiv preprint arXiv:2402.13616 (2024)
12. Wang, A., et al.: YOLOv10: real-time end-to-end object detection. arXiv preprint arXiv:2405.14458 (2024)
13. Wang, C.Y., Liao, H.Y.M., Wu, Y.H., Chen, P.Y., Hsieh, J.W., Yeh, I.H.: CSPNet: a new backbone that can enhance learning capability of CNN. In: Proceedings of the IEEE/CVF Conference on Computer Vision and Pattern Recognition Workshops, pp. 390–391 (2020)
14. Vaswani, A., et al.: Attention is all you need. In: Advances in Neural Information Processing Systems, pp. 5998–6008 (2017)
15. Dosovitskiy, A., et al.: An image is worth 16 × 16 words: transformers for image recognition at scale. arXiv preprint arXiv:2010.11929 (2020)
16. Liu, Z., et al.: Swin transformer: hierarchical vision transformer using shifted windows. In: Proceedings of the IEEE/CVF International Conference on Computer Vision, pp. 10012–10022 (2021)
17. Wang, W., et al.: Pyramid vision transformer: a versatile backbone for dense prediction without convolutions. In: Proceedings of the IEEE/CVF International Conference on Computer Vision, pp. 568–578 (2021)
18. Carion, N., Massa, F., Synnaeve, G., Usunier, N., Kirillov, A., Zagoruyko, S.: End-to-end object detection with transformers. In: Vedaldi, A., Bischof, H., Brox, T., Frahm, J.-M. (eds.) ECCV 2020. LNCS, vol. 12346, pp. 213–229. Springer, Cham (2020). https://doi.org/10.1007/978-3-030-58452-8_13
19. Zhu, X., Su, W., Lu, L., Li, B., Wang, X., Dai, J.: Deformable DETR: deformable transformers for end-to-end object detection. arXiv preprint arXiv:2010.04159 (2020)
20. Liu, S., et al.: DAB-DETR: dynamic anchor boxes are better queries for DETR. arXiv preprint arXiv:2201.12329 (2022)
21. Yao, Z., Ai, J., Li, B., Zhang, C.: Efficient DETR: improving end-to-end object detector with dense prior. arXiv preprint arXiv:2104.01318 (2021)
22. Zhao, Y., et al.: DETRs beat YOLOs on real-time object detection. In: Proceedings of the IEEE/CVF Conference on Computer Vision and Pattern Recognition, pp. 8587–8596 (2024)
23. Ren, S., He, K., Girshick, R., Sun, J.: Faster R-CNN: towards real-time object detection with region proposal networks. In: Advances in Neural Information Processing Systems, pp. 91–99 (2015)
24. Lin, T.-Y., et al.: Microsoft COCO: common objects in context. In: Fleet, D., Pajdla, T., Schiele, B., Tuytelaars, T. (eds.) ECCV 2014. LNCS, vol. 8693, pp. 740–755. Springer, Cham (2014). https://doi.org/10.1007/978-3-319-10602-1_48
25. Chollet, F.: Xception: deep learning with depthwise separable convolutions. In: Proceedings of the IEEE Conference on Computer Vision and Pattern Recognition, pp. 1251–1258 (2017)

MIRaSeg: Exploring mmWave Radar and Low Resolution Infrared Sensor Fusion for Robust Human Semantic Segmentation

Xiangjie Tang[1], Ruili Shi[1], Shuai Wang[1], Zeyu Zhang[1], Bin Wang[1,2], Zhiqiang Li[3], and Shuai Wang[1(✉)]

[1] Southeast University, Nanjing, China
{213223671,ruilishi,shuaiwang_iot,zeyuzhang_iot,shuaiwang}@seu.edu.cn, wangbin8@xcmg.com

[2] State Key Laboratory of Intelligent Manufacturing of Advanced Construction Machinery, Xuzhou, China

[3] Nanjing Tongke Technology Development Co., Ltd., Nanjing, China

Abstract. Human semantic segmentation is increasingly important in various human sensing scenarios such as motion analysis. However, traditional visual methods raise privacy concerns, while RF methods suffer from multi-path reflections or sparse signals. This paper introduces MIRaSeg, a novel multi-modal human semantic segmentation system that fuses millimeter-wave radar and the low-resolution infrared sensor. Specifically, we carefully design a unique feature extraction and fusion network to enhance human semantic segmentation of millimeter-wave point clouds using low-resolution infrared heatmap information. We construct a 400,000 frame activity dataset from 34 volunteers, the experiments show that MIRaSeg achieved an average accuracy of 83.21%, all of which outperformed the state-of-the-art methods.

Keywords: Human semantic segmentation · mmWave Radar · Low-resolution infrared sensor

1 Introduction

Accurate identification and segmentation of human semantic information, including body parts such as the head, torso, and limbs, is crucial for various human sensing applications. For example, in motion analytics, precise limb detection enables accurate posture estimation and training guidance to enhance athletic performance [3]. In smart elderly care, targeted semantic body part segmentation improves reliability of fall detection [15], while in virtual reality, accurate limb segmentation forms the foundation for natural interaction [21].

Current human semantic segmentation methods can be categorized into three modalities: vision-based, depth-based, and RF-based. Vision-based

© The Author(s), under exclusive license to Springer Nature Singapore Pte Ltd. 2026
J. Kittler et al. (Eds.): PRCV 2025, LNCS 16289, pp. 17–32, 2026.
https://doi.org/10.1007/978-981-95-5764-6_2

approaches [33] employ deep neural networks to segment human images captured by cameras, but their accuracy suffers from occlusion, image blur, and lighting variations. Privacy concerns also limit camera use in sensitive areas such as bathrooms and bedrooms. Another widely used approach is the depth-based method, which processes dense point clouds or depth images obtained from LIDAR [35] or depth camera [20]. However, this approach requires expensive hardware and substantial computational resources, which has not yet become mainstream. With the development of radio-frequency (RF) technology, wireless sensing methods [22,28] represented by commercial millimeter-wave (mmWave) radar [2,24] are widely applied in human sensing scenarios. These methods exhibit robustness in low-light environments and offer privacy protection as well as low cost [19]. Although research on human semantic segmentation based on mmWave radar has made several progress [8,29], these methods remain constrained by limited radar performance, resulting in sparse point clouds and missing human reflection information.

Since a single modality cannot complete tasks well, the idea of multi-modality emerged. Infrared modality is often used to complement visual semantics [4,13] due to its characteristic of containing heat information. Its privacy-protecting feature also supports its combined use with mmWave radar. The low-resolution infrared sensor is a very low-cost sensor that complements the semantic information of mmWave point clouds. It can provide information on human body contours and heat [9,25] with just 64 pixels. It can help supplement the semantics of certain body parts missing in sparse mmWave point clouds and also distinguish living bodies. However, the fusion of multiple modalities also presents many challenges. The 2D infrared heatmaps are difficult to align and match with the 3D mmWave point cloud in space. And none of the existing feature fusion algorithms can extract and integrate the human motion information contained in mmWave point clouds and the human body temperature information contained in infrared data.

To overcome these challenges, we propose MIRaSeg, a novel human semantic segmentation system based on mmWave radar and low-resolution infrared fusion. Our solution integrates: (1) dedicated feature extraction networks - an improved PointNet incorporating attention mechanisms and LSTM (Long Short-Term Memory) networks for point cloud processing, coupled with Gaussian pyramid and bilinear interpolation methods alongside ResNet for infrared heatmap processing; (2) a Non-Local Network (NLN) [31] based fusion module that establishes cross-modal correlations to achieve complementary modality integration; (3) a multi-task learning output module that jointly optimizes semantic segmentation and pose estimation, using structural pose information to guide network learning. Our main contributions are summarized as follows:

- We propose MIRaSeg, a novel mmWave radar and low-resolution infrared fusion human semantic segmentation system, which uses infrared heatmap features to complement mmWave point cloud information to enhance environmental robustness. It can be widely applied in various scenarios in the field of human sensing. Due its privacy protection and low-cost characteristics, MIRaSeg can be widely used in various human sensing scenarios.

- We establish a multi-modal feature fusion scheme based on two parallel NLN networks to effectively fuse the features of two modalities: mmWave point cloud and infrared heatmap.
- We collect 400,000 frames of radar-infrared datasets from 34 volunteers in three scenarios. Further experimental results show that MIRaSeg achieves 83.21% human semantic segmentation performance, which has significant advantages over existing methods.

2 Related Works

Human body semantic segmentation technology first distinguishes human-related data from the background, and then precisely identifies different parts of the human body such as the head, arms, and legs in sensor data. The following will focus on introducing several commonly used data modalities in human body semantic segmentation, and analyze how to carry out semantic segmentation based on these modalities, and discuss their respective advantages and limitations.

Human semantic segmentation based on the visual modality takes images and videos as research objects and is currently the most mainstream research direction in human semantic segmentation. Traditional methods mainly rely on manual feature extraction and traditional machine learning algorithms such as support vector machines [14] and random forests to carry out human semantic segmentation work. With the advancement of deep learning technology, the research on human semantic segmentation has entered a new era. Xia et al. [32] proposed an efficient framework for human semantic segmentation in complex multi-person images. POSTURE [6] proposes an pose guided unsupervised domain adaptation for human body part segmentation.

Due to the privacy issues that RGB cameras may cause, some studies choose to use depth modalities for human semantic segmentation. Depth modality refers to the three-dimensional depth information of a scene obtained through depth camera or Lidar, aiming to supplement the spatial distance perception information lacking in the visual modality. Huang et al. [12] proposed a Modality Adaptation pipeline via Feature Difference Learning, which ultimately achieves depth human parsing based on only depth images. LiDARCapV2 [35] proposes a method for capturing human motion and performing human parsing from LiDAR point clouds.

With the vigorous development of radio frequency (RF) technology [5,7,10,17,18,27,30,34,36] in the field of IoT, some research has also begun to use RF technology for the semantic segmentation of the human body. Song et al. [26] proposed a segmentation system capable of capturing the temporal topological coupling features to achieve semantic segmentation of human bodies in mmWave point clouds. mmParse [29] implicitly enhanced the structural feature representation of sparse mmWave point clouds through the pose estimation task, proposed a cross-task attention mechanism, achieved efficient fusion of heterogeneous features, and ultimately realized accurate human semantic segmentation.

3 Preliminary

3.1 Principles of mmWave Radar

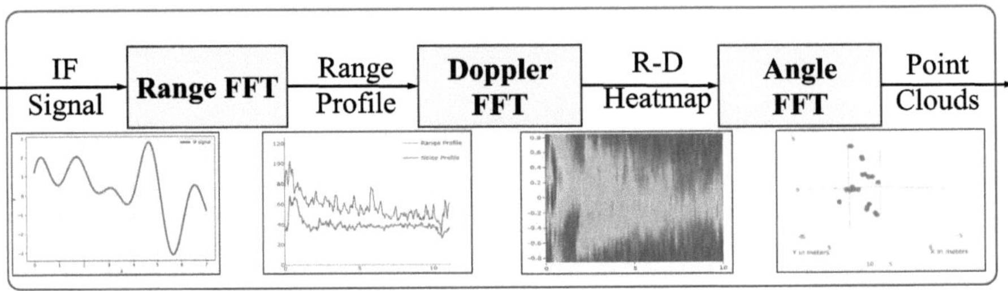

Fig. 1. mmWave Radar workflow.

mmWave radar is a sensor based on Frequency Modulated Continuous Wave (FMCW) technology. The core of FMCW is the continuous waveform signal with a linearly varying frequency over time, called a "chirp". These signals are emitted by the transmitting antenna (TX). When signals encounter obstacles, they are reflected back to the radar. Once received by the receiving antenna (RX), these reflected signals are mixed with the original transmitted signals to generate an intermediate frequency (IF) signal. Through the processing of this IF signal, the mmWave radar can measure the distance, relative velocity, and reflected intensity of the object. Figure 1 displays the workflow of IWR6843-ODS mmWave radar [2], produced by Texas Instruments, which is used in our system. The on-board processor accepts ADC data of IF signal as input from mmWave front end and then performs Range and Doppler FFT followed by non-coherent detection using CFAR. Finally, the angle is estimated using 3D FFT and the detected points represent the point cloud data.

3.2 Low-Resolution Infrared Sensor

In this work, we aim to integrate a low-resolution infrared sensor as an additional input to compensate for the lack of semantic information in the single-modality mmWave radar, thereby we employ the AMG8833 low-resolution infrared sensors [1] for synchronous perception during the experiment. The sensor's core consists of a 64-pixel infrared thermal imaging array and signal processing circuitry, which outputs 8×8 temperature pixel matrices (i.e., infrared heatmaps) to provide additional semantic information such as body contours to supplement the mmWave modality. Moreover, similar to the mmWave radar, the infrared sensor does not capture any visual information, which means MIRaSeg can be deployed in privacy-sensitive environments such as bedrooms.

4 System Design

4.1 Overview

To achieve fine-grained human semantic segmentation, we propose MIRaSeg, whose overall architecture is shown in Fig. 2. MIRaSeg takes point clouds collected by the mmWave radar and 8×8 infrared heatmaps captured by the low resolution infrared sensor as input and ultimately performs semantic segmentation of the human body (such as head, torso, left arm, etc.). From a system perspective, MIRaSeg consists of four core components: mmWave point cloud feature extraction, low-resolution infrared heatmap feature extraction, multi-modal feature aggregation, and human semantic output based on multi-task learning.

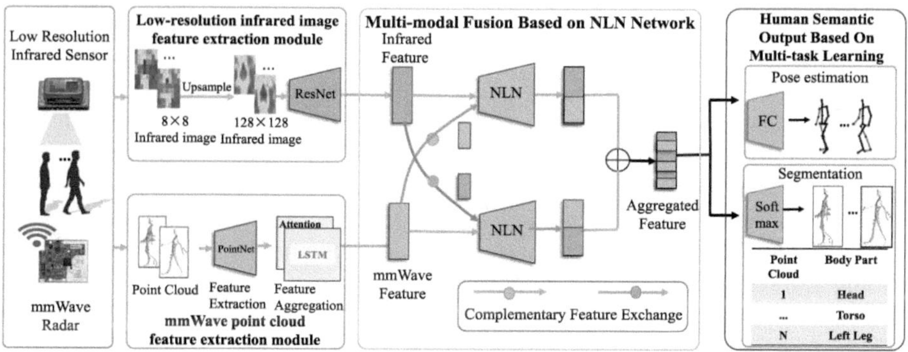

Fig. 2. MIRaSeg architecture.

After acquiring the two modal data perceived from the human body, the mmWave point cloud feature extraction module and low-resolution infrared heatmap feature extraction module independently extract high-dimensional features from mmWave point clouds and low-resolution infrared heatmaps, respectively. High-dimensional features extracted by each module are aggregated via a NLN based architecture, where both self-attention and mutual-attention mechanisms are implemented to enable cross-modal feature complementation. Ultimately, the aggregated features will be input into the human semantic output module based on multi-task learning to achieve pose estimation and human semantic segmentation.

4.2 mmWave Point Cloud Feature Extraction Module

As shown in Fig. 3, the mmWave point cloud feature extraction module takes the continuous mmWave radar point cloud frames collected by the mmWave radar as input and ultimately outputs high-dimensional point features. Specifically, we construct a two-layer shared-weight MLP based PointNet [23], which maps

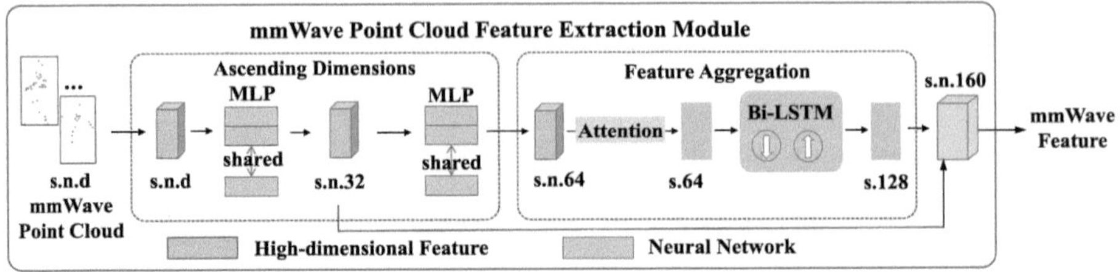

Fig. 3. mmWave point cloud feature extraction module architecture.

5D point clouds into a high-dimensional feature space. For each point cloud $P_{i,t}$ in the point cloud set P_t of frame t, the first MLP layer outputs: $e_{i,t} = MLP_1(p_{i,t}; \theta_e)$ where θ_e denotes the learnable parameters, and $\dim(e_{i,t}) = 32$. This feature is then processed by the second MLP layer: $h_{i,t} = MLP_2(e_{i,t}; \theta_h)$ with $\dim(h_{i,t}) = 64$, producing the final high-dimensional representation of a single point.

To aggregate point-wise features into frame-level representations, we design a feature aggregation network based on self-attention mechanisms and Bidirectional Long Short-Term Memory (Bi-LSTM). For each point cloud, an attention function is constructed using Softmax and linear layers, generating weighted sums of all point features. The aggregated features are then processed by the Bi-LSTM network to encode temporal dependencies, effectively supplementing current frame information with historical context while mitigating missing body-part observations. This network outputs a 128-dimensional feature B_t. Finally, B_t is concatenated with the 32-dimensional point features from the ascending dimensions stage, producing the 160-dimensional output R_t as the final representation from the mmWave point cloud feature extraction module.

4.3 Low-Resolution Infrared Heatmap Feature Extraction Module

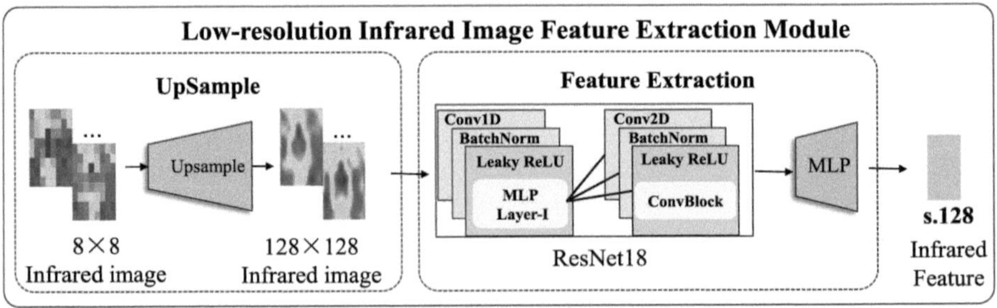

Fig. 4. Low-resolution infrared heatmap feature extraction module architecture.

The input of this module is an 8×8 infrared heatmap, and the output is high-dimensional infrared features. Due to the low resolution of infrared thermal images, directly feeding them into feature extraction networks fails to capture sufficient human semantic information. To solve this, we employ a Gaussian pyramid-based bilinear interpolation fusion algorithm to upsample input images. We first upsample the 8×8 pixel image to 128×128 resolution using bilinear interpolation. Subsequently, we apply four iterative cycles of 5×5 Gaussian filter ($\sigma = 5$) to generate a 128×128 infrared heatmap representing the top layer of the Gaussian pyramid. Finally, we perform weighted fusion between the bilinear interpolated image and the pyramid-reconstructed image to produce the final 128×128 infrared heatmap (Fig. 4).

To extract infrared features from the upsampled heat map, we employ a pre-trained ResNet18 network. In the output stage, the feature maps are flattened and processed through a MLP to obtain the final results. Let $o_t$denote the flattened feature vector. The MLP computation can be expressed as $V_t = MLP_1(O_t; \theta_t)$, V_t represents the high-dimensional infrared features encoded by this module. The output features have a dimension of 128, encapsulating both thermal distribution and body contour information, thereby providing effective infrared modality information for subsequent multi-modal feature fusion.

4.4 Multi-modal Fusion Based on NLN Network

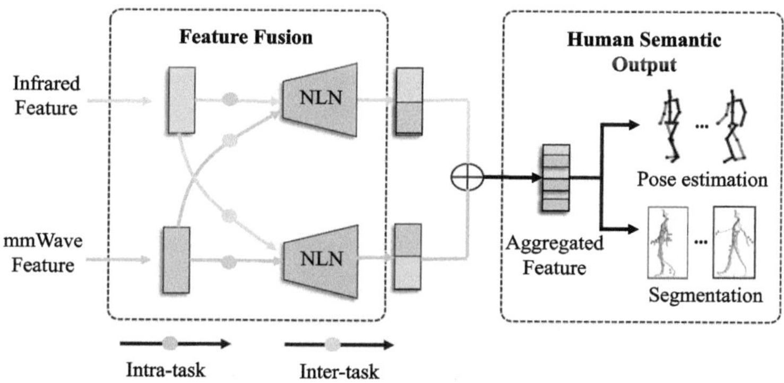

Fig. 5. Multi-modal fusion based on NLN network.

To effectively utilize infrared modality information to supplement the semantics of mmWave point clouds and address the issues of sparsity and multi-path reflection in them, we carefully design a multi-modal feature fusion module based on NLN with self-attention and mutual attention mechanisms. As shown in Fig. 5, when the mmWave features and infrared features are input into the fusion module, they will be processed by two parallel NLN respectively. The principle of the NLN network is based on nearest neighbor search to obtain local feature information of different modalities. Therefore, by using two parallel NLN networks to interact bidirectionally, complementary information from the two different modalities can be utilized.

We employ learnable projection matrices W_q and W_k to map mmWave features R_t and infrared features V_t into unified Query and Key spaces, respectively represented as: Q_i and K_j, where i, j denote feature indices. We compute the cosine similarity $S_{i,j}$ between the two feature vectors as:

$$S_{i,j} = \frac{Q_i \cdot K_j}{\|Q_i\| \|K_j\|} \tag{1}$$

After obtaining the similarity matrix, MIRaSeg employs a K-nearest neighbors (KNN) strategy to select top k relevant infrared features for each mmWave feature $R_{t,j}$, forming a neighbor set M_i. These selected features are then aggregated via a learnable weight matrix W_M and combined with the original mmWave features, achieving cross-modal information fusion:

$$R_t' = \sum_{i \in N} (R_{t,i} + \frac{1}{K} \sum_{j \in M_i} W_M V_{t,j}) \tag{2}$$

where N is the dimensionality of the mmWave features, M_i contains the indices of the top k infrared features most similar to the ith mmWave feature, W_m corresponds to a trainable weighting matrix, $V_{t,j}$ indicates the jth infrared feature vector at time step t, and R_t' signifies the representation of the fused mmWave feature augmented with infrared data. Similarly, each infrared feature can also be matched with its top-k relevant mmWave features through a symmetric process. Infrared features enhanced with mmWave data can be expressed as V_t'. Finally, a weighted averaging operation combines the enhanced features of two modalities into a unified representation:

$$F_{fusion} = \alpha R_t' + (1 - \alpha) V_t' \tag{3}$$

This fusion module combines the spatial information of mmWave radar with the thermal information of infrared sensor, providing a more complete semantic representation for downstream human semantic segmentation tasks.

4.5 Human Semantic Segmentation Based on Multi-task Learning

The multi-task learning module takes the fusion feature F_{fusion} as input. Finally, MIRaSeg adopts a multi-task learning framework to simultaneously train two tasks: pose estimation and human semantic segmentation. The pose estimation task can guide the network to learn the structural prior knowledge of the human body, which can be used as strong supervision signals to help the semantic segmentation task identify the boundaries and semantic categories of different parts of the human body more accurately [32]. Therefore, to achieve joint training of multiple tasks, we propose two loss functions. The first loss function L_H measures the error between the predicted and ground-truth categories for each point, while the second loss function L_p quantifies the discrepancy between estimated skeletal key points and their actual positions.

The objective of the human body semantic segmentation task is to minimize the discrepancy between the predicted category and the true category for each point. For segmenting the point cloud into K distinct anatomical regions, we employ the cross-entropy loss function in Eq. 4, where N denotes the number of points and K represents the number of categories. y_k^n is an indicator function that takes the value 1 if the nth sample belongs to class k, and 0 otherwise. $p(\widehat{y}_k^n)$ represents the predicted probability of the nth sample belonging to category k.

$$L_H = -\frac{1}{N}\sum_{n=1}^{K}\sum_{k=1}^{K} y_k^n \log p(\widehat{y}_k^n) \tag{4}$$

The loss of Mean Squared Error (MSE) measures the discrepancy between the predicted positions of the skeletal key points and their actual positions. Assuming there are M skeletal key points in total, we employ the loss function as Eq. 5, where $\hat{p}_m$ and p_m denote the predicted position and ground-truth position of the mth skeletal point.

$$L_P = \frac{1}{M}\sum_{m=1}^{M} ||\hat{p}_m - p_m|| \tag{5}$$

The final joint loss function is formulated as:

$$L = \gamma L_H + \beta L_P \tag{6}$$

where hyperparameters γ and β balance the relative importance of the two tasks.

5 Implementation

5.1 Hardware Setup

The data acquisition system consists of three devices: a low-resolution infrared camera AMG8833 for capturing infrared heatmaps of subjects, an Azure Kinect DK device equipped with depth sensors and RGB cameras for acquiring high-resolution 3D human meshes, and an IWR6843-ODS mmWave radar for capturing mmWave point clouds generated by subject movement.

5.2 Data Collection Setup

We recruit 34 volunteers for data collection and design three common daily scenarios: (1) Corridor environment: A 4.0 m × 2.0 m area containing chairs, tables, and distant metal cabinets that introduce radar signal interference. (2) Conference room environment: A more confined 3.0 m × 1.8 m space with metal partitions, a conference table, and walls that may cause multi-path effects and noise in mmWave signals. (3) Outdoor lawn environment: A 4.5 m × 3.0 m open area without obstructions (Fig. 6).

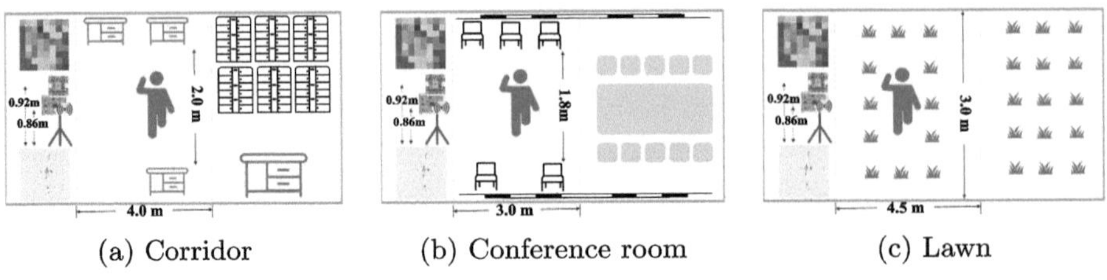

Fig. 6. Data collection scenarios.

During data collection, subjects moved freely within a designated area in front of the radar and performed natural arm movements (e.g. swinging, stretching, waving). The radar was mounted on a stand at a height of 0.86 m, capturing mmWave point clouds at 10 frames per second (FPS) as subjects moved. The low-resolution infrared sensor, also fixed on a stand at 0.92 m, recorded thermal images at 6 FPS. To acquire high-quality human semantic labels, we used a Kinect as the motion capture device, positioning it at 0.9 m above the ground to record 3D human meshes at 15 FPS. We have collected a total of more than 400,000 frames of human activity data. After that, we divide the data into samples of length 20 frames, and use 80% of the data for model training and the remaining 20% for validation.

6 Evaluation

6.1 Evaluation Setup

For evaluating semantic segmentation task, we adopt three standard evaluation metrics [23]:

Mean Accuracy (mAcc): Defined as the average proportion of correctly classified point clouds across all body parts, representing classification accuracy.

Mean Intersection over Union (mIoU): Computes the overlap between predicted and ground-truth segmentation regions, reflecting segmentation completeness.

Mean Dice Coefficient (mDice): Measures the similarity between predicted and ground-truth segmentations, indicating segmentation precision.

MIRaSeg is a novel multi-modal system that integrates infrared heatmap and mmWave point cloud. There are no existing multi-modal learning models based on these two modalities. So we compare MIRaSeg with four state-of-the-art single-modal mmWave point cloud processing models, including PointNet [23], PointCNN [16], P4Transformer [11], and mmParse [29].

6.2 Overall Performance

Table 1 presents a performance comparison between MIRaSeg and other existing methods on our self-built dataset. It demonstrates that our proposed MIRaSeg outperforms all competing approaches in all evaluation metrics, validating its effectiveness. Specifically, MIRaSeg achieves an mAcc of 83.21%, an mIoU of 80.27% and an mDice of 82.03%. Notably, among existing single-modality models, mmParse delivers the best mAcc (82.03%) for human semantic segmentation but still falls short of our multi-modal fusion framework. These results confirm that low-resolution infrared features in our system provide complementary semantic cues to millimeter-wave point clouds, significantly enhancing segmentation accuracy compared to single-modal approaches.

Table 1. Performance comparison on human semantic segmentation.

Model	mAcc(%)	mIoU(%)	mDice(%)
PointNet [23]	79.37	75.62	77.61
PointCNN [16]	81.14	77.57	79.24
P4Transformer [11]	77.11	74.15	75.63
mmParse [29]	82.03	79.10	81.33
MIRaSeg	**83.21**	**80.27**	**82.03**

6.3 Qualitative Analysis

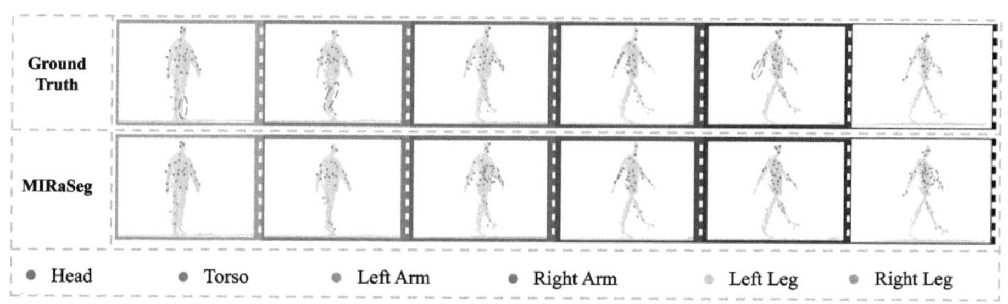

Fig. 7. Qualitative analysis results of MIRaSeg on freely walking subjects.

As illustrated in Fig. 7, the experiment employs color-coded point clouds to annotate semantic labels of different body parts, where the first row displays ground-truth segmentation labels generated from Kinect Mesh and the second row presents our system's output. The visualization reveals that partial point cloud absence occurs in certain frames due to specular reflections on human surfaces and temporary limb motion cessation during movement. For instance, the red-circled regions indicate undetected areas in mmWave point clouds. Nevertheless, our method achieves precise body part segmentation, demonstrating high consistency with ground-truth labels for the head, torso, and limbs. Only minor prediction errors occur at elbow-torso junctions, as marked by blue circles. Consequently, our system's segmented point clouds closely approximate the ground truth.

6.4 Sensitivity Analysis

We analyze the segmentation results of MIRaSeg in different environments and for different body parts (Table 2).

Table 2. Body part segmentation performance.

Body Part	mAcc (%)	mIoU (%)	mDice (%)
Head	87.61	85.27	86.43
Torso	88.93	86.31	87.21
Left Arm	81.18	78.07	80.06
Right Arm	80.04	77.21	79.13
Left Leg	80.61	77.43	79.71
Right Leg	80.23	77.33	79.64
Average	**83.21**	**80.27**	**82.03**

In terms of body part segmentation, the torso and head have the highest accuracy rate (close to 90%). A detailed analysis reveals that this is due to the large reflective area and high mmWave signal intensity of these two parts. In contrast, the limbs (arms and legs) have a relatively low segmentation accuracy because of their high joint degrees of freedom and significant specular reflection effect during movement. At the same time, they are more prone to occlusion, which further exacerbates the sparsity of point cloud data (Table 3).

Table 3. Environmental segmentation performance.

Scenario	mAcc (%)	mIoU (%)	mDice (%)
Corridor	83.51	80.52	82.57
Meeting Room	81.92	79.03	81.03
Outdoor Lawn	85.62	81.43	83.52

From the operational principles of mmWave radar and the infrared sensor, their sensing capabilities are susceptible to environmental interference. We experimentally validate the robustness of MIRaSeg across diverse environmental conditions. The mAcc in the corridor, meeting room and outdoor lawn are 83.51%, 81.92% and 85.62%, demonstrating good robustness. The mIoU and mDice also show a similar trend.

6.5 Ablation Studies

To systematically evaluate the contribution of each component, we conduct comprehensive ablation studies by comparing four model variants: (1) Full: the complete system with all modules; (2) w/o IR: removing the infrared heatmap feature extraction module while maintaining mmWave point cloud processing; (3) N2C: replacing the parallel NLN based feature fusion with direct feature concatenation; (4) w/o Pose: eliminating the pose estimation task from the multi-task learning framework while preserving the semantic segmentation pipeline. The quantitative results of these ablation experiments are presented in Table 4.

Table 4. Ablation study results.

Model	mAcc(%)	mIoU(%)	mDice(%)
w/o IR	75.83	72.59	74.78
N2C	76.31	73.52	74.98
w/o Pose	76.47	73.74	75.27
Full System	**83.21**	**80.27**	**82.03**

The ablation results demonstrate performance degradation when removing the infrared modality, with mAcc, mIoU, and mDice decreasing by 7.38%, 7.68%, and 7.25%. This confirms the infrared module's role in enhancing semantic information from sparse point clouds and improving segmentation accuracy. For multi-modal feature fusion, the NLN demonstrates superior performance over direct feature concatenation by establishing precise semantic correlations between 3D point clouds and 2D infrared heatmaps. Quantitative comparisons reveal that NLN's attention mechanism better preserves complementary features compared to naive concatenation. The performance decline observed when removing the pose estimation module (w/o Pose) verifies its importance. The pose estimation branch enhances system robustness through two mechanisms: (1) modeling long-range dependencies via skeletal constraints to mitigate local point cloud deficiencies caused by specular reflections; (2) temporal integration of body part information across frames. These capabilities prove valuable when handling sparse and discontinuous mmWave point clouds.

7 Conclusion

We proposed a human semantic segmentation system based on mmWave radar point cloud with low-resolution infrared sensor fusion, called MIRaSeg. Our method first fuses mmWave radar point cloud with low-resolution infrared sensor images for human sematic segmentation. We have designed unique feature extraction modules for mmWave radar point clouds and infrared heatmaps respectively, and developed an NLN with self-attention and mutual-attention for the fusion of features from the two modalities. We conduct extensive experiments on MIRaSeg using our self-constructed multi-modal dataset and ultimately achieve superior performance compared to current advanced single millimeter-wave radar modality methods under multiple human semantic segmentation standards.

Acknowledgements. This work is partially supported by the National Natural Science Foundation of China (Grants No. 62272098, and U24B20152), the Natural Science Foundation of Jiangsu Province (Grants No. BK20241274).

References

1. Amg8833 infrared sensor. https://industrial.panasonic.com/ww/products/pt/grid-eye/models/AMG8833
2. Iwr6843isk-ods. https://www.ti.com.cn/tool/cn/IWR6843ISK-ODS
3. An, S., Ogras, U.Y.: Mars: mmwave-based assistive rehabilitation system for smart healthcare. ACM Trans. Embed. Comput. Syst. (TECS) **20**(5s), 1–22 (2021)
4. Chen, M., Cheng, Y., He, X., Wang, X., Aze, Y., Xiang, J.: Simplefusion: a simple fusion framework for infrared and visible images. In: Chinese Conference on Pattern Recognition and Computer Vision (PRCV), pp. 49–63. Springer, Cham (2024)
5. Cui, K., et al.: Correlation-aware cross-modal attention network for fashion compatibility modeling in UGC systems. ACM Trans. Multimed. Comput. Commun. Appl. (2024)
6. Dutta, A., et al.: Posture: pose guided unsupervised domain adaptation for human body part segmentation. CoRR (2024)
7. Fan, X., Gong, W., Liu, J.: I2tag: RFID mobility and activity identification through intelligent profiling. ACM Trans. Intell. Syst. Technol. (TIST) **9**(1), 1–21 (2017)
8. Feng, Y., Dai, S., Zhang, Q., Wang, Z., Zhang, X., Zhou, Y.: M3pose: multi-person 3D pose estimation using sparse millimeter-wave radar point clouds. In: Chinese Conference on Pattern Recognition and Computer Vision (PRCV), pp. 504–517. Springer, Cham (2024)
9. Gochoo, M., et al.: Novel IoT-based privacy-preserving yoga posture recognition system using low-resolution infrared sensors and deep learning. IEEE Internet Things J. **6**(4), 7192–7200 (2019)
10. Gong, W., Cao, L., Zhu, Y., Zuo, F., He, X., Zhou, H.: Federated inverse reinforcement learning for smart ICUs with differential privacy. IEEE Internet Things J. **10**(21), 19117–19124 (2023)
11. Hang, Z., Wang, Y., Huang, S.: P4 transformer: towards unified programming for the data plane of software defined network. In: 2021 IEEE 45th Annual Computers, Software, and Applications Conference (COMPSAC), pp. 544–551. IEEE (2021)
12. Huang, S., et al.: Modality adaptation via feature difference learning for depth human parsing. Comput. Vis. Image Underst. **247**, 104070 (2024)
13. Jie, Y., Chen, Y., Li, X., Yi, P., Tan, H., Cheng, X.: Fufusion: fuzzy sets theory for infrared and visible image fusion. In: Chinese Conference on Pattern Recognition and Computer Vision (PRCV), pp. 466–478. Springer, Cham (2023)
14. Kim, K., Oh, C., Sohn, K.: Non-parametric human segmentation using support vector machine. IEEE Trans. Consum. Electron. **62**(2), 150–158 (2016)

15. Li, W., et al.: Real-time fall detection using mmwave radar. In: 2022 IEEE International Conference on Acoustics, Speech and Signal Processing (ICASSP), ICASSP 2022, pp. 16–20. IEEE (2022)
16. Li, Y., Bu, R., Sun, M., Wu, W., Di, X., Chen, B.: Pointcnn: convolution on x-transformed points. In: Advances in Neural Information Processing Systems, vol. 31 (2018)
17. Lin, J., Zhang, Z., Shi, R., Wang, S., Wang, S.: Personnel detection via reinforcement learning-based dynamic parameter optimization with vehicle-mounted ultra-wideband. In: International Conference on Intelligent Computing, pp. 522–533. Springer, Cham (2025)
18. Liu, R., et al.: Real-time mmwave radar human sensing testbed. In: Proceedings of the 30th Annual International Conference on Mobile Computing and Networking, pp. 1787–1789 (2024)
19. Liu, R., et al.: Mission: mmwave radar person identification with RGB cameras. In: Proceedings of the 22nd ACM Conference on Embedded Networked Sensor Systems, pp. 309–321 (2024)
20. Martínez-González, A., Villamizar, M., Canévet, O., Odobez, J.M.: Real-time convolutional networks for depth-based human pose estimation. In: 2018 IEEE/RSJ International Conference on Intelligent Robots and Systems (IROS), pp. 41–47. IEEE (2018)
21. Mei, L., et al.: mmspyvr: Exploiting mmwave radar for penetrating obstacles to uncover privacy vulnerability of virtual reality. Proc. ACM Interact. Mob. Wearable Ubiquit. Technol. **8**(4), 1–29 (2024)
22. Meng, L., et al.: Minipi: a multi-scale neural network based impulse radio ultra-wideband radar indoor personnel identification method. In: Chinese Conference on Pattern Recognition and Computer Vision (PRCV), pp. 537–548. Springer, Cham (2022)
23. Qi, C.R., Su, H., Mo, K., Guibas, L.J.: Pointnet: deep learning on point sets for 3D classification and segmentation. In: Proceedings of the IEEE Conference on Computer Vision and Pattern Recognition, pp. 652–660 (2017)
24. Shi, R., Wang, S., Liu, R., Jiang, W., Wang, S.: mmhat: 3D human arm tracking with joint learning using dynamic mmwave point cloud. In: 2024 20th International Conference on Mobility, Sensing and Networking (MSN), pp. 57–64. IEEE (2024)
25. Shi, R., Wang, S., Xu, Z.D., Wang, S., Zhou, X., Su, Y.: Cmpir: cross-modal pose image reconstruction via style-semantic fusion. CCF Trans. Pervasive Comput. Interact. 1–15 (2025)
26. Song, P., Mei, L., Cheng, H.: Human semantic segmentation using millimeter-wave radar sparse point clouds. In: 2023 26th International Conference on Computer Supported Cooperative Work in Design (CSCWD), pp. 1275–1280. IEEE (2023)
27. Sun, K., et al.: Wuloc: achieving extremely long-range high-precision localization via wi-fi-uwb connection. Proc. ACM Interact. Mob. Wearable Ubiquit. Technol. **9**(1), 1–24 (2025)
28. Wang, F., Zhou, S., Panev, S., Han, J., Huang, D.: Person-in-wifi: fine-grained person perception using wifi. In: Proceedings of the IEEE/CVF International Conference on Computer Vision, pp. 5452–5461 (2019)
29. Wang, S., Cao, D., Liu, R., Jiang, W., Yao, T., Lu, C.X.: Human parsing with joint learning for dynamic mmwave radar point cloud. Proc. ACM Interact. Mob. Wearable Ubiquit. Technol. **7**(1), 1–22 (2023)
30. Wang, S., Zeng, Y., Jain, V., Pathak, P.: Umusic: in-car occupancy sensing via high-resolution uwb power delay profile. In: Proceedings of the 23rd ACM Conference on Embedded Networked Sensor Systems, pp. 116–129 (2025)

31. Wang, X., Girshick, R., Gupta, A., He, K.: Non-local neural networks. In: Proceedings of the IEEE Conference on Computer Vision and Pattern Recognition, pp. 7794–7803 (2018)
32. Xia, F., Wang, P., Chen, X., Yuille, A.L.: Joint multi-person pose estimation and semantic part segmentation. In: Proceedings of the IEEE Conference on Computer Vision and Pattern Recognition, pp. 6769–6778 (2017)
33. Yang, B., Yu, C., Liu, J., Gao, C., Sang, N.: Graph-based scale-aware network for human parsing. In: Chinese Conference on Pattern Recognition and Computer Vision (PRCV), pp. 279–290. Springer, Cham (2019)
34. Yuan, L., Xiong, C., Chen, S., Gong, W.: Embracing self-powered wireless wearables for smart healthcare. In: 2021 IEEE International Conference on Pervasive Computing and Communications (PerCom), pp. 1–7. IEEE (2021)
35. Zhang, J., Mao, Q., Shen, S., Wen, C., Xu, L., Wang, C.: Lidarcapv 2: 3D human pose estimation with human-object interaction from lidar point clouds. Pattern Recogn. **156**, 110848 (2024)
36. Zhou, Z., Wang, F., Yu, J., Ren, J., Wang, Z., Gong, W.: Target-oriented semi-supervised domain adaptation for wifi-based har. In: IEEE INFOCOM 2022-IEEE Conference on Computer Communications, pp. 420–429. IEEE (2022)

Towards Robust Infrared Wildlife Multi-object Tracking with Temperature-Aware Modeling

Ziqing Han[1], Ting Zhang[1], Zhaoying Liu[1](✉), Yuxiang Zhang[1], and Qian Liu[2]

[1] Beijing University of Technology, No. 100 Ping Leyuan, Chaoyang District, Beijing 100124, China

[2] Beijing Institute of Control and Electronic Technology, No. 15 Xinjiangongmen Road, Haidian District, Beijing 100091, China

Abstract. Infrared multi-object tracking (MOT) is essential for applications such as wildlife monitoring and nighttime surveillance. To address the problems of low robustness in infrared tracking and the scarcity of high-quality datasets, we propose a novel strategy that integrates infrared temperature characteristics with visual appearance information. Specifically, we introduce a temperature-guided attention module based on physical inversion. It leverages a remote-sensing radiance model to estimate surface temperature from brightness temperature, guiding the encoder to focus on thermally salient regions and enhancing the representation of low-texture targets. Furthermore, we propose a temporal heat conduction mechanism to enhance the temporal consistency of thermal features, ensuring more stable association across frames. In addition, we design a temperature-aware association method (TAM), which dynamically constructs a matching weight matrix by integrating temperature scores, trajectory uncertainty, and appearance similarity, aiming to improve the association stability in scenarios with occlusions and appearance ambiguity. Moreover, we construct a high-quality infrared wildlife MOT dataset IRWT, and standardize the formats of two existing infrared MOT datasets. Comparisons with five state-of-the-art MOT methods demonstrate that our approach achieves leading performance on the IRWT dataset. Evaluations on two additional non-animal infrared datasets further confirm its generalization and practical applicability.

Keywords: Infrared Multi-Object Tracking · Infrared Wildlife Tracking Dataset · Temperature Inversion Attention · Temperature-aware association module

1 Introduction

Multi-object tracking of wildlife is essential for studying habitats, activity patterns, and population dynamics. It aids in species conservation, biodiversity monitoring, and protected area management. Infrared imaging, with its long-range,

© The Author(s), under exclusive license to Springer Nature Singapore Pte Ltd. 2026
J. Kittler et al. (Eds.): PRCV 2025, LNCS 16289, pp. 33–47, 2026.
https://doi.org/10.1007/978-981-95-5764-6_3

all-weather, and light-independent capabilities, enables reliable monitoring in complex environments, ideal for wildlife tracking and ecological research.

Current deep learning-based multi-object tracking methods are generally classified into three paradigms: Tracking-by-Detection (TBD), Joint Detection and Tracking (JDT), and Joint Detection and Embedding (JDE). TBD methods separate detection and tracking into independent stages, ByteTrack [1] reduces trajectory loss during occlusion by combining high and low-confidence detections, while OC-SORT [2] improves tracking stability by using trajectory direction consistency and observation smoothing. These methods are simple, efficient, and widely used in visible-light tracking.

JDT methods adopt end-to-end architectures to jointly model object detection and temporal association, eliminating the need for a separate data association module. Representative methods such as TransTrack [3] extend detection queries into trajectory queries for cross-frame modeling, while GTR [4] and TrackFormer [5] incorporate memory mechanisms and parallel decoding to improve trajectory continuity and target discrimination.

JDE methods simultaneously extract identity embedding features during the detection process, sharing a common backbone between the detection and ReID modules to enhance cross-task collaboration and computational efficiency. Representative methods like JDE [6] and FairMOT [7] integrate embedding heads into the detection branch to unify detection and association. Subsequent studies have introduced various improvements to better decouple and coordinate these tasks.

However, most existing tracking methods are designed for visual RGB images. In contrast, infrared imagery lacks color information, has limited resolution, and weak texture details, leading to blurred object boundaries and increased tracking challenges. When applied to infrared imagery, certain MOT models tend to exhibit degraded robustness, increased identity ambiguities, and suboptimal occlusion handling, attributable to the inherent modality gap between thermal and visual domains. To address this, RISTrack [9] introduces multigranularity feature fusion and virtual trajectory modeling, achieving some success in infrared ship tracking. However, existing methods often overlook "temperature variation", a key property of infrared imagery, and most feature enhancement strategies focus on high-level semantics or post-processing, lacking effective guidance at shallow feature levels.

To overcome these limitations, we construct an infrared wildlife multi-object tracking dataset, and propose a novel strategy that combines infrared temperature characteristics with visual appearance cues. Specifically, we incorporate a physics-based temperature-guided attention mechanism, previously developed in our earlier work, and embed it into the encoder of the tracking network. This module leverages a remote sensing radiance transfer model to invert brightness temperature into surface temperature, generating multi-scale thermal saliency maps to guide the network's attention toward thermally prominent regions, thereby enhancing target recognition capabilities. To further enhance the temporal consistency of thermal features, we introduce a temporal heat conduction that mimics physical heat diffusion across adjacent frames by applying local smoothing to the previous frame's surface temperature map before integrating it with the current frame. This encourages stable temperature representations and strengthens the network's ability to maintain robust associations across time.

We further introduce a temperature-aware matching strategy. Based on temporal thermal consistency, we dynamically construct an association weight matrix by integrating predicted temperature trends and appearance similarity, enabling adaptive feature weighting during matching. Compared to traditional approaches that rely solely on appearance or spatial features, our method incorporates a physically interpretable "thermal signal", offering a new perspective for infrared MOT.

The main contributions of this paper are summarized as follows:

(1) We propose a strategy that combines infrared temperature characteristics and appearance features, enabling physics-guided region-aware representation during feature extraction. Furthermore, we introduce a temporal thermal conduction mechanism that models the temperature evolution trends of tracked targets, enhancing the robustness of association in complex and occluded scenarios.
(2) We propose a temperature-aware association module for infrared images that enhances target discrimination in texture-deficient and appearance-ambiguous scenes. To the best of our knowledge, this is the first work to directly integrate physical temperature features into an association module for infrared multi-object tracking.
(3) We construct and release a high-quality infrared wildlife MOT dataset captured in a real wildlife zoo environment. Additionally, we curate five datasets and standardize the formats of two, conducting systematic evaluations on representative MOT frameworks to support future benchmarking and method development.

2 Related Work

2.1 Joint Detection and Embedding

The JDE paradigm offers a unified framework that performs both object detection and appearance embedding within a single network, enabling efficient multi-object tracking. Compared to traditional TBD and JDT methods, JDE demonstrates superior adaptability and robustness in infrared scenarios, characterized by weak textures, low contrast, and ambiguous appearance cues. While TBD suffers from identity switches in low-texture environments and JDT faces high computational demands, JDE strikes a balance between speed and accuracy, making it well-suited for infrared tracking.

In this study, we adopt SimpleTrack [8] as our baseline, a refined version of the JDE method designed to enhance both accuracy and computational efficiency. SimpleTrack introduces three key improvements: a bottom-up feature fusion mechanism, a novel Embedding and GIoU (EG) matrix for better association, and a lightweight retrieval strategy to recover missed targets. We extend this framework with thermal-aware attention and association mechanisms for infrared tracking.

2.2 Association Strategies

In multi-object tracking tasks, association strategies play a central role in ensuring temporal consistency of targets across frames. Early methods such as SORT [10] primarily rely on motion prediction and spatial position for data association. They use a Kalman filter to predict object trajectories and construct a matching matrix based on the Intersection over Union distance, with the optimal assignment solved via the Hungarian algorithm. OC-SORT [2] introduces Observation-Centric Momentum, which enhances matching robustness by modeling the directionality of object motion, thereby improving occlusion recovery. Hybrid-SORT [11] further incorporates weak spatial cues such as object height and detection confidence into the matching mechanism, proposing techniques like Height Modulated IoU and Tracklet Confidence Modeling to address IoU failure cases under occlusion scenarios.

Beyond positional cues, appearance features serve as more stable discriminative information, playing a crucial role in long-term tracking and re-identification. DeepSORT [13] is the first to combine appearance embeddings with positional matching. Subsequent approaches such as FairMOT [7] and CSTrack [12] introduce various improvements in feature fusion strategies and backbone architectures to enhance the joint representation of detection and re-identification. Moreover, GHOST [14] applies an Exponential Moving Average to update trajectory features, improving target consistency. Deep OC-SORT [15] integrates motion direction, spatial cues, and appearance features through a multi-stage matching process, significantly boosting occlusion recovery performance.

However, these association strategies are almost exclusively developed for visible-spectrum imagery and fail to take into account the physically meaningful characteristics of infrared data.

3 The Proposed Method

We propose a strategy that integrates infrared temperature characteristics with object appearance features. The method performs joint optimization at both the feature modeling and data association levels, fully leveraging thermal physical information from infrared imaging and deep appearance representations. Our overall framework is illustrated in Fig. 1.

The proposed framework consists of three main components: an encoder for multi-scale feature extraction, a decoder for joint object detection and identity embedding, and a matching module for data association. In the encoder, we introduce a Temperature-Inversion Attention Module (TIAM) to highlight thermally salient regions and guide the network to focus on infrared targets. To improve the temporal consistency of thermal features, we further propose a temporal heat conduction mechanism (THCM), which simulates local heat diffusion across adjacent frames to smooth temperature representations over time. For data association, we propose a Temperature-Aware Matching (TAM) strategy. Built upon conventional IoU and ReID feature fusion, TAM introduces target temperature scoring to dynamically adjust the matching weights. This improves association robustness in complex tracking scenarios.

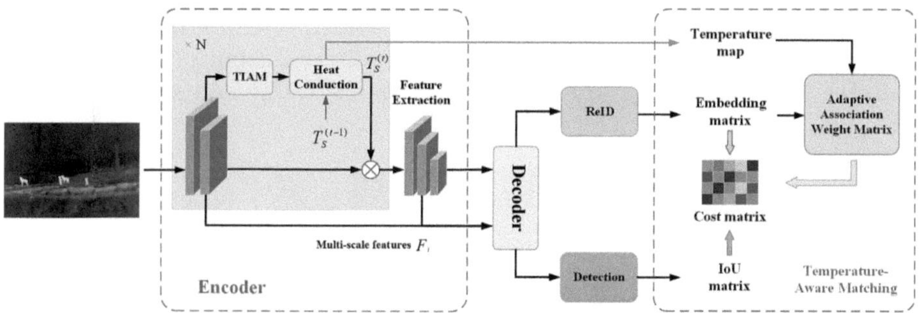

Fig. 1. Temperature-Inversion Guided infrared multi-object tracking pipeline.

3.1 Temperature-Inversion-Based Multi-object Tracking

To enhance the ability of perceiving thermal targets during the feature encoding stage, we introduce a Temperature-Inversion Attention Module (TIAM), which is integrated into the encoder of the tracking framework. This module is inspired by land surface temperature inversion theory from the remote sensing domain and is designed as a learnable attention mechanism that guides the network to focus on thermally salient target regions. The structure of TIAM is illustrated in Fig. 2.

The TIAM module is based on the Mono-Window algorithm, with the specific inversion formula given in Equation (1), where α denotes atmospheric transmittance, β represents surface emissivity, and T_a is the mean atmospheric temperature. Constants K_1 and K_2 are inversion coefficients, and B_T denotes the brightness temperature. To ensure adaptability to varying scenes and image characteristics, the physical parameters involved, including the inversion coefficients K_1, K_2, α and β are designed as trainable tensors. These parameters are automatically optimized during network training without the need for external meteorological data or radiometric calibration tables.

$$T_s = \frac{K_1\alpha^2(1-\beta) + B_T[K_2\alpha^2(1+\beta)+1] - T_a[\alpha^2(\beta-1) - \alpha\beta + 1]}{\alpha\beta} \tag{1}$$

After normalization, the temperature map is used as a spatial attention map and fused with the original features via channel-wise weighting, enhancing the feature representations. This process improves the network's response to weak thermal signals, reduces background interference, and aligns with the principles of infrared imaging, enhancing foreground-background separability and interpretability.

TIAM is embedded into multiple stages of the encoder to capture temperature-guided information at different scales, as shown by the blue regions in Fig. 1. At each stage, convolutional operations and TIAM work together to support global context and local thermal enhancement. In the JDE paradigm, where detection and ReID share a common encoder, TIAM strengthens target activation in detection while improving feature discriminability and consistency for ReID, thus enhancing cross-frame association stability and accuracy.

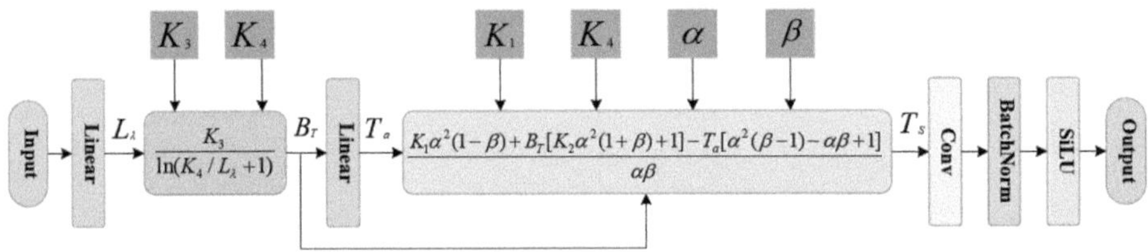

Fig. 2. Structure diagram of TIAM module.

To enhance the temporal stability of temperature-related features in infrared images, we propose a temporal heat conduction mechanism (THCM), which simulates the physical process of thermal diffusion to improve consistency in temperature representation across adjacent frames.

Let $T_s^{(t-1)}$ denote the surface temperature map from the previous frame obtained by TIAM, and $T_s^{(t)}$ the current one. We first apply a spatial diffusion operation to $T_s^{(t-1)}$ to simulate the intra-region heat propagation:

$$T_{smooth}^{(t-1)} = G_k * T_s^{(t-1)} \tag{2}$$

where G_k is a depthwise convolution kernel of size $k \times k$, used to perform local temperature smoothing. The smoothed previous temperature map is then linearly fused with the current frame's temperature map to generate a temporally consistent representation:

$$T = (1-\alpha) \cdot T_s^{(t)} + \alpha \cdot T_{smooth}^{(t-1)} \tag{3}$$

Here, $\alpha \in [0, 1]$ is a balancing factor that controls the degree of diffusion, regulating the fusion between current and historical temperatures.

3.2 Temperature-Aware Matching(TAM)

In infrared multi-object tracking, temperature information of target regions shows stable and distinguishable physical properties. To improve matching in dynamic environments, we propose a dynamic weighting mechanism combining temperature evolution trends and visual features. This approach adjusts appearance matching weights by integrating target trajectory temperature evolution with current infrared data, enhancing physical consistency and temporal stability.

Temperature changes of the same target across adjacent frames are stable, while different targets show larger thermal discrepancies due to species, radiation, or occlusions. We model the historical temperature sequence to assess the physical consistency between the current detection and historical trajectory.

Specifically, at frame t, the temperature sequence corresponding to a historical trajectory is denoted as $T_i = \{T_i^{t-k}, \ldots, T_i^{t-1}\}$. Assuming that the infrared radiation change of the target within a short time period follows a linear trend, we employ least squares fitting to model the temporal evolution, obtaining the temperature slope a_i and variance σ_i^2. The predicted temperature at the next frame is given by $\hat{T}_i^{t+1} = T_i^t + a_i$.

For the current candidate detection box D_j, we extract the average infrared temperature T_j^d of the detected region and calculate the current deviation $\Delta_{\text{cur}} = |T_i^t - T_j^d|$ and the predicted deviation $\Delta_{\text{pred}} = |\hat{T}_i^{t+1} - T_j^d|$. To evaluate the confidence of the trend consistency, we introduce a temperature reliability factor:

$$w_i = \exp\left(-\frac{\Delta_{\text{pred}}^2}{\sigma_i^2 + \epsilon}\right) \tag{4}$$

This factor is then used to construct the thermal consistency deviation term, which jointly considers the historical prediction error and current thermal deviation:

$$D_{\text{temp}} = \text{normalize}\left(w_i \cdot \Delta_{\text{pred}} + (1 - w_i) \cdot \Delta_{\text{cur}}\right) \tag{5}$$

Meanwhile, to account for inter-frame thermal fluctuations, we use the current deviation Δ_{cur} to construct a thermal stability modulation factor:

$$w_{\text{temp}} = \exp\left(-\lambda \cdot \Delta_{\text{cur}}\right) \tag{6}$$

When the target temperature remains stable across frames, this factor stays high, ensuring thermal consistency. However, during occlusion recovery, abrupt changes, or misassociation, it lowers the thermal weight to reduce mismatches. To adjust the importance of appearance features during association, we generate an adaptive modulation weight based on temperature deviation and appearance distance:

$$W = \gamma \cdot D_{\text{emb}} + (1 - \gamma) \cdot w_{\text{temp}} \cdot D_{\text{temp}} \tag{7}$$

This formulation fuses appearance information and physical consistency via a weighted strategy, which mitigates the misleading effects of visual cues under drastic thermal changes or occlusions. The final association cost is computed as:

$$C = W \cdot D_{\text{emb}} + D_{\text{iou}} \tag{8}$$

where D_{emb} and D_{iou} represent the appearance embedding distance and the spatial IoU distance, respectively. $\gamma \in [0, 1]$ is a hyperparameter that adjusts the relative importance of thermal and visual cues. To prevent instability, the weight matrix W is constrained within a fixed range.

4 The Proposed Infrared Wildlife Tracking Dataset

Compared to infrared single-object tracking, publicly available infrared multi-object tracking datasets are limited, and existing datasets often have inconsistent formats and differ from mainstream model input requirements, necessitating additional preprocessing. For example, CAMEL [16] includes diverse targets, but only provides XML annotations with identity labels and suffers from imprecise bounding boxes and missing category information. A dataset for infrared time-sensitive target detection and tracking for air-ground application (TSDT) [17] focuses on vehicle tracking with per-frame identity labels, supporting studies on time-sensitive target detection. For maritime scenes, SFIST [9], XMCMT [18] and short-wave infrared ocean multi-object tracking dataset (SWIRT) [19][1] provide infrared footage of ships and nearshore targets, but SFIST requires reorganization before use. BIRDSAI [20] is one of the few datasets involving wildlife. However, it has limited resolution and visibility, and many frames contain blurred or minuscule targets. Although it includes full tracking annotations, its storage format still demands additional processing. At present, there remains a lack of high-quality infrared multi-object tracking datasets specifically designed for wildlife monitoring.

To address the lack of multi-object real-world datasets in natural infrared tracking scenarios, we construct Infrared Wildlife Tracking Dataset (IRWT), a dedicated infrared video dataset for multi-object tracking of wildlife. Captured in a wildlife park, the dataset reflects animals' natural behavior under authentic ecological conditions. It features high realism and diversity, aiming to support practical applications of thermal infrared tracking in ecological monitoring and behavior analysis.

The dataset contains 33 video sequences with over 17,000 frames, covering 20 common wildlife species. Detailed information about each sequence is provided in Table 1. All videos were recorded using infrared cameras, preserving typical thermal imaging characteristics and enabling the model to learn more robust spatiotemporal feature representations. Each frame was manually annotated, and the annotations were organized in the MOTChallenge format to ensure

[1] The dataset is from Center for Optics Research and Engineering of Shandong University.

Table 1. Detailed information of sequences in the IRWT dataset.

Seq	Frame Length	Boxes	Track num	Target Category	Seq	Frame Length	Boxes	Track num	Target Category
1	1274	1697	5	Elephant	18	249	1232	8	Goat, Person
2	299	661	7	Lion	19	149	282	7	Deer, Person
3	474	685	2	Lion	20	474	1137	4	Lion
4	549	602	11	Crane	21	474	1101	8	Ostrich
5	99	113	2	Ox	22	1399	2263	11	Ostrich
6	229	913	8	Alpaca	23	674	999	6	Leopard
7	724	1225	4	Camel	24	424	1548	4	Hyena
8	449	636	3	Horse	25	399	940	7	Horse
9	874	523	12	Ox, Bird	26	349	515	3	Kangaroo
10	374	832	13	Ox	27	249	196	1	Kangaroo
11	424	1058	5	Bird	28	549	1525	8	Crocodile
12	199	471	8	Bear, Person	29	449	642	6	Horse, Donkey, Ox
13	1624	6887	41	Deer, Person	30	449	639	14	Horse, Dog, Ox,
14	674	1090	6	Wolf					Person, Chicken
15	779	1162	5	Lion	31	224	303	2	Ox
16	147	622	5	Ox, Person	32	249	323	6	Bird
17	779	2115	6	Goat	33	849	3773	13	Donkey, Person

compatibility with existing tracking models. The label files include 2D bounding boxes, identity IDs, and class labels for each target, making the dataset well-suited for supervised training in multi-object detection and tracking tasks.

In addition, we placed particular emphasis on preserving key visual challenges within the dataset, explicitly retained and highlighted complex scenarios such as occlusions, small-object tracking, and dense target distributions, providing a challenging infrared benchmark.

Figure 3 shows examples from the dataset under three typical conditions. The left column displays standard scenes with clear target boundaries and distinct infrared features, featuring multiple animals in natural states. The middle column presents occlusions, where targets are partially hidden by natural elements. The right column shows small-object scenarios, where targets are sparse, small, and occupy minimal image space, posing challenges for detection and identity preservation. Different colored bounding boxes represent different identities.

Fig. 3. Representative samples from the proposed IRWT dataset.

5 Experimental Results

5.1 Dataset

To assess the robustness and generalization of our proposed infrared multi-object tracking method, we conduct experiments on three datasets. We utilize IRWT dataset, proposed in this study, for wildlife tracking in ecological environments, and to further validate our method, we also employ other widely used datasets: TSDT [17] and SFIST [9]. The dataset in TSDT, captured with UAV-mounted infrared sensors, presents long-range views, small targets, and significant background clutter, posing challenges for airborne tracking. SFIST includes maritime infrared sequences recorded under varying conditions, where targets exhibit weak texture, variable size, and frequent occlusions.

Additionally, we provide an overview of existing infrared multi-object tracking datasets in Table 2. While these datasets are useful, they vary in format. To ensure fair evaluation and facilitate reuse, we have converted SFIST and TSDT into a unified format compatible with the MOTChallenge benchmark.

5.2 Experimental Results and Analysis

To evaluate the effectiveness of the proposed temperature-guided infrared multi-object tracking method, we conducted experiments on three representative infrared datasets. The evaluation metrics employed in this study are consistent with [21,22]. Results are demonstrated in Table 3, where red for the best performance and blue for the second-best, with all TBD-based methods using the same detector for fairness.

On the IRWT dataset, which focuses on real-world wildlife tracking, our method achieves the best overall performance, with a HOTA of 44.82, IDF1 of 60.78, and MOTA of 52.50. It also reaches competitive results in AssA

Table 2. Overview of existing infrared multi-object tracking datasets.

Datasets	Num of sequences	Max frames	Min frames	Total frames	Image size	Num of classes	Object classes
CAMEL [16]	24	2008	197	16184	336*245	4	Person, Bicycle Dog, Vehicles
SFIST [9]	20	1299	141	10178	1920*1080	1	Ship
BIRDSAI [20]	32	7957	142	40661	519*698	10	Person, animals
SWIRT [19]	2	927	640	1529	640*512	1	Vessel
TSDT [17]	87	250	250	21750	480*640	1	Vehicles
IRWT	33	1624	99	17717	576*704	21	Person, animals

(45.57) and maintains a relatively low number of ID switches (25), outperforming strong baselines such as ByteTrack, OC-SORT, and Hybrid-SORT. These results demonstrate that the proposed temperature-guided mechanism can effectively enhance detection robustness and identity preservation in low-texture, occlusion-prone ecological scenes. The improvement benefits from the temperature-inversion attention module (TIAM), which enhances the network's focus on thermally salient regions, and the temperature-aware matching strategy, which dynamically adjusts association weights based on thermal reliability. The relatively stable background and pronounced thermal contrast in many scenes further enable the model to fully leverage temperature cues, highlighting the advantage of physically grounded guidance for medium-scale infrared targets in dynamic, low-visibility environments.

To further evaluate the generalization capability of the proposed method, we conducted experiments on two non-wildlife datasets, which demonstrated its effectiveness as well. On the SFIST maritime dataset, our method again outperforms all others. We achieved the highest HOTA (49.03), IDF1 (60.17), and AssA (45.84), with a relatively low ID switch count (22). This indicates that our approach is highly stable and resilient, even in maritime scenarios where weak thermal contrast and complex backgrounds are common challenges. On the TSDT dataset, our method achieved generally good results, indicating stable identity association and strong generalization ability across different infrared scenarios. It exceeded most trackers in metrics such as HOTA(63.27) and IDF1(84.29), showing notable improvements in detection and identity preservation.

It is worth noting that although the TBD paradigm has become mainstream in multi-object tracking and performs well in visible-light scenarios, our experiments reveal that JDE paradigm still holds strong potential and adaptability for infrared multi-object tracking tasks. JDE models enable joint modeling of contextual information and feature consistency, ensuring stable identity tracking even under frequent occlusion, poor contrast, and weak appearance features in infrared imagery.

Table 3. Experimental results on datasets IRWT, SFIST and TSDT.

Dataset	Model	HOTA↑	DetA↑	AssA↑	MOTA↑	IDF1↑	MOTP↑	IDs↓
IRWT	FairMOT	41.72	39.37	44.41	48.25	56.22	77.47	**20**
	SimpleTrack	42.05	42.23	42.05	50.77	55.99	77.06	30
	ByteTrack	44.42	43.99	45.19	51.76	57.79	77.45	48
	OC-SORT	44.69	42.43	**47.54**	49.61	57.26	**79.39**	55
	Hybrid-SORT	44.72	**44.73**	45.13	52.02	57.65	78.44	55
	Ours	**44.82**	44.30	45.57	**52.50**	**60.78**	77.33	25
SFIST	FairMOT	36.13	51.37	25.57	58.77	36.82	79.00	**12**
	Hybrid-SORT	43.62	54.67	35.06	54.89	42.50	82.82	213
	OC-SORT	43.95	54.37	35.81	55.54	43.33	**82.95**	148
	ByteTrack	48.34	**55.16**	42.46	59.46	59.46	50.67	89
	SimpleTrack	48.69	52.53	45.21	**65.24**	59.60	77.82	23
	Ours	**49.03**	52.53	**45.84**	65.13	**60.17**	77.80	22
TSDT	ByteTrack	47.81	36.56	62.98	47.11	63.98	68.73	18
	SimpleTrack	61.50	55.87	67.81	72.50	80.86	76.81	32
	FairMOT	62.58	**63.07**	62.32	**81.42**	81.05	75.96	84
	Hybrid-SORT	62.71	56.56	69.69	71.64	79.47	78.37	70
	OC-SORT	63.19	56.79	**70.45**	72.15	80.06	**78.40**	56
	Ours	**63.27**	57.49	69.79	74.80	**84.29**	76.87	**17**

Table 4. Ablation experiments on the IRWT dataset.

TIAM	THCM	TAM	HOTA↑	IDF1↑	AssA↑	DetA↑	MOTA↑
			42.05	55.99	42.05	42.23	50.77
✓			44.00	56.83	44.72	43.48	51.88
✓	✓		44.75	60.53	45.59	44.15	52.35
✓		✓	44.27	59.33	**45.75**	43.07	52.33
✓	✓	✓	**44.82**	**60.78**	45.57	**44.30**	**52.50**

5.3 Ablation Studies

To further validate the individual and combined contributions of the proposed modules, we conducted ablation experiments on the IRWT dataset. We sequentially incorporated Temperature-Inversion Attention Module(TIAM), the temporal heat conduction mechanism (THCM), and Temperature-Aware Matching (TAM) strategy into the baseline model.

As shown in Table 4, adding TIAM enhances the model's robustness in detecting low-texture targets and improves embedding feature discriminability by focusing on thermally salient regions. Introducing THCM further strengthens temporal consistency by simulating heat conduction across frames, smoothing temperature cues. The inclusion of TAM optimizes the association stage by dynamically adjusting matching weights based on target states, reducing errors from occlusion and appearance ambiguity. Parts of the visualization results are shown in Fig. 4(a) and (b).

When all modules are combined, the model achieves the best results across all metrics, with HOTA of 44.82, IDF1 of 60.78, and MOTA of 52.50, outperforming configurations with fewer modules. These results highlight the stability and effectiveness of thermal information in improving feature representation and data association.

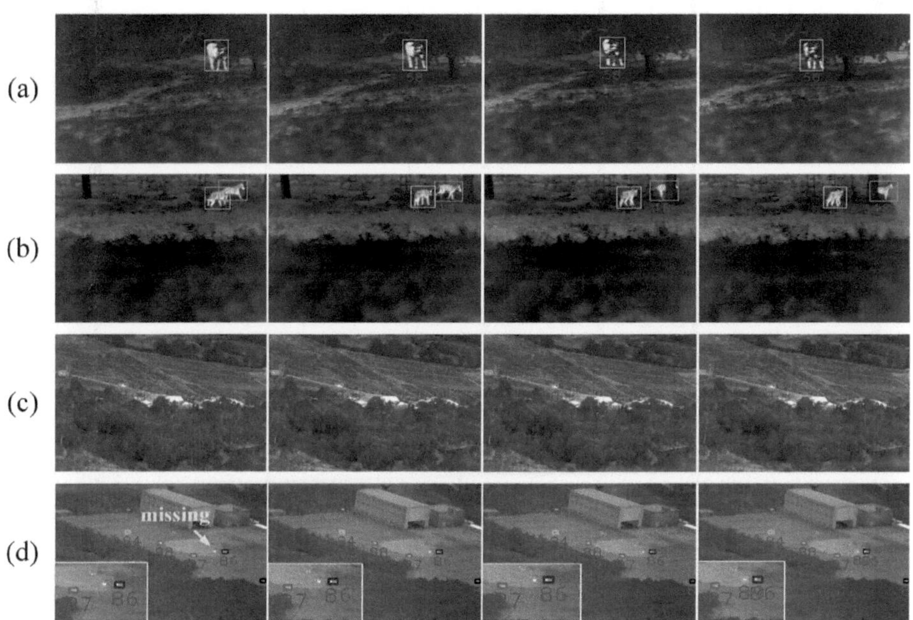

Fig. 4. Examples of the visual results.

5.4 Limitations

Although the proposed method performs well overall, we observed limitations when tested on the TSDT dataset. As shown in Fig. 4(d), detection and association performance were limited under these conditions due to the small size and low thermal contrast of the targets, as well as the sensitivity of the temperature-guided attention to background thermal noise. These results suggest that further improvements are needed for environments with higher detection demands.

6 Conclusion

This paper addresses the challenges of multi-object tracking of wildlife in infrared images and systematically proposes a solution from dataset construction to algorithm optimization. We propose an infrared tracking strategy that integrates temperature characteristics with appearance features. The temperature-inversion attention mechanism enhances detection and re-identification by focusing on thermally salient regions, while the heat-conduction-based temporal module improves feature consistency across frames. Additionally, a temperature-aware association strategy is designed to boost matching accuracy under occlusion and appearance ambiguity. Finally, we release a high-quality infrared wildlife tracking dataset, addressing the gap in data for real ecological scenarios. In the future, enhancing detection capabilities and improving motion modeling could be potential directions for further exploration.

Acknowledgement. This work is supported by the National Natural Science Foundation of China (U23A20357, 61806013, 61906005) and the General Project of Science and Technology Plan of Beijing Municipal Education Commission (KM202110005028).

References

1. Zhang, Y., et al.: ByteTrack: multi-object tracking by associating every detection box. In: European Conference on Computer Vision, pp. 1–21. Springer, Cham (2022). https://doi.org/10.1007/978-3-031-20047-2_1
2. Cao, J., Pang, J., Weng, X., Khirodkar, R., Kitani, K.: Observation-centric SORT: rethinking SORT for robust multi-object tracking. In: Proceedings of the IEEE/CVF Conference on Computer Vision and Pattern Recognition (CVPR), pp. 9686–9696. IEEE (2023). https://doi.org/10.1109/CVPR52729.2023.00934
3. Sun, P., et al.: TransTrack: multiple object tracking with transformer. arXiv preprint arXiv:2012.15460 (2020)
4. Zhou, X., Yin, T., Koltun, V., Krähenbühl, P.: Global tracking transformers. In: Proceedings of the IEEE/CVF Conference on Computer Vision and Pattern Recognition, pp. 8771–8780 (2022). https://doi.org/10.1109/CVPR52688.2022.00857
5. Meinhardt, T., Kirillov, A., Leal-Taixé, L., Feichtenhofer, C.: TrackFormer: multi-object tracking with transformers. In: Proceedings of the IEEE/CVF Conference on Computer Vision and Pattern Recognition, pp. 8844–8854 (2022). https://doi.org/10.1109/CVPR52688.2022.00864
6. Wang, Z., Zheng, L., Liu, Y., Li, Y., Wang, S.: Towards real-time multi-object tracking. In: European Conference on Computer Vision, pp. 107–122. Springer, Cham (2020). https://doi.org/10.1007/978-3-030-58621-8_7
7. Zhang, Y., Wang, C., Wang, X., Zeng, W., Liu, W.: FairMOT: on the fairness of detection and re-identification in multiple object tracking. Int. J. Comput. Vis. **129**, 3069–3087 (2021)
8. Li, J., Ding, Y., Wei, H.L., Zhang, Y., Lin, W.: SimpleTrack: rethinking and improving the JDE approach for multi-object tracking. Sensors **22**(15), 5863 (2022)
9. Wu, P., et al.: RISTrack: robust infrared ship tracking with modified appearance feature extraction and matching strategy. IEEE Trans. Geosci. Remote Sens. **61**, 1–14 (2023)
10. Bewley, A., Ge, Z., Ott, L., Ramos, F., Upcroft, B.: Simple online and realtime tracking. In: 2016 IEEE International Conference on Image Processing (ICIP), pp. 3464–3468. IEEE (2016). https://doi.org/10.1109/ICIP.2016.7533003

11. Yang, M., et al.: Hybrid-SORT: weak cues matter for online multi-object tracking. In: Proceedings of the AAAI Conference on Artificial Intelligence, vol. 38, no. 7, pp. 6504–6512 (2024). https://doi.org/10.1609/aaai.v38i7.28471
12. Chen, Y., Ding, S., Guo, J., Yang, C., Li, L.: CSTrack: a comprehensive and concise vision transformer tracker. In: Chinese Conference on Pattern Recognition and Computer Vision (PRCV), pp. 120–132. Springer, Singapore (2023). https://doi.org/10.1007/978-981-99-8555-5_1
13. Wojke, N., Bewley, A., Paulus, D.: Simple online and realtime tracking with a deep association metric. In: 2017 IEEE International Conference on Image Processing (ICIP), pp. 3645–3649. IEEE (2017). https://doi.org/10.1109/ICIP.2017.8296962
14. Seidenschwarz, J., Brasó, G., Castro Serrano, V., Elezi, I., Leal-Taixé, L.: Simple cues lead to a strong multi-object tracker. In: Proceedings of the IEEE/CVF Conference on Computer Vision and Pattern Recognition (CVPR), pp. 13813–13823. IEEE (2023). https://doi.org/10.1109/CVPR52729.2023.01327
15. Maggiolino, G., Ahmad, A., Cao, J., Kitani, K.: Deep OC-SORT: multi-pedestrian tracking by adaptive re-identification. In: 2023 IEEE International Conference on Image Processing (ICIP), pp. 3025–3029. IEEE (2023). https://doi.org/10.1109/ICIP49359.2023.10222576
16. Gebhardt, E., Wolf, M.: CAMEL dataset for visual and thermal infrared multiple object detection and tracking. In: 2018 15th IEEE International Conference on Advanced Video and Signal Based Surveillance (AVSS), pp. 1–6. IEEE (2018). https://doi.org/10.1109/AVSS.2018.8639094
17. Fu, R., et al.: A dataset for infrared time-sensitive target detection and tracking for air-ground application. China Sci. Data **7**(2), 206–221 (2022). https://doi.org/10.11922/11-6035.csd.2021.0085.zh1
18. Ding, J., Li, W., Pei, L., Yang, M., Tian, A., Yuan, B.: Novel pipeline integrating cross-modality and motion model for nearshore multi-object tracking in optical video surveillance. Eng. Appl. Artif. Intell. **127**, 109387 (2024). https://doi.org/10.1109/TITS.2024.3373370
19. Li, Y., Zhao, X., Liu, Z., et al.: Short-wave infrared ship target instance segmentation and multi-object tracking dataset. Center for Optics Research and Engineering, Shandong University (2024). http://www.gxzx.sdu.edu.cn/info/1133/3180.htm. Accessed 30 June 2025
20. Bondi, E., et al.: BIRDSAI: a dataset for detection and tracking in aerial thermal infrared videos. In: Proceedings of the IEEE/CVF Winter Conference on Applications of Computer Vision, pp. 1747–1756 (2020). https://doi.org/10.1109/WACV45572.2020.9093284
21. Leal-Taixé, L., Milan, A., Schindler, K., Cremers, D., Reid, I., Roth, S.: Tracking the trackers: an analysis of the state of the art in multiple object tracking. arXiv preprint arXiv:1704.02781 (2017)
22. Luiten, J., et al.: Hota: a higher order metric for evaluating multi-object tracking. Int. J. Comput. Vis. **129**(3), 548–578 (2021)

FINet: Detecting Camouflaged Objects Using Frequency-Aware Information

Chengfeng Zhu[1], Zeming Liu[1], Qing Zhang[1(✉)], and Xuefeng Wu[2]

[1] Shanghai Institute of Technology, Shanghai, China
zhangqing0329@gmail.com
[2] Jiaxing Intermediate People's Court, Zhejiang, China

Abstract. Camouflaged object detection (COD) is a pixel-level task that aims to accurately identify and segment camouflaged objects from scenes exhibiting similar visual properties. Currently, most methods utilize the RGB domain to represent and learn the content of the scene. However, these methods struggle to capture subtle camouflage cues. To address this issue, we propose a novel frequency-aware COD method to promote the collaborative learning between frequency domain and RGB domain information. Specifically, we propose the frequency-aware fusion module (FFM) to integrate multi-scale features from the perspective of frequency information, consisting of a frequency learning module (FLM) and a frequency decomposition unit (FDU). Our FFM explores the distinct roles of different frequency components to emphasize global semantics for capturing camouflaged objects and discard irrelevant information for mitigating interferences. Experiments demonstrate that our FINet exhibits superiority and effectiveness compared to existing representative methods.

Keywords: Camouflaged object detection · Frequency information · Pixel-level segmentation · Multi-level integration

1 Introduction

Camouflaged object detection (COD) aims to identify and segment objects that are usually embedded in their environment. Camouflaged objects are not easily noticeable visually since they typically have similar colors, textures, or shapes to their surroundings, making COD a more challenging task compared to the general pixel-level prediction tasks (*e.g.*, salient object detection and semantic segmentation) that mostly utilizing distinctive characteristics. COD can be applied to a variety of vision applications, such as medical image analysis (*e.g.*, polyp segmentation and lung infection detection), surface defect detection and agriculture pest detection.

In recent years, various deep learning-based camouflaged object detection approaches [4,5,25,30] have been explored to identify the positions of potential

C. Zhu and Z. Liu—These authors contributed equally to this work.

© The Author(s), under exclusive license to Springer Nature Singapore Pte Ltd. 2026
J. Kittler et al. (Eds.): PRCV 2025, LNCS 16289, pp. 48–61, 2026.
https://doi.org/10.1007/978-981-95-5764-6_4

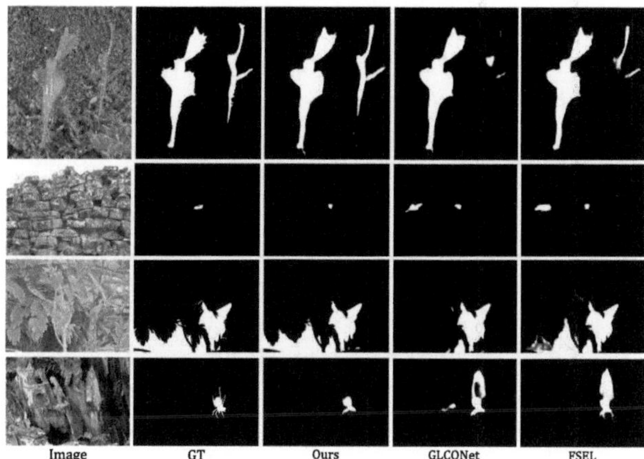

Fig. 1. Visual comparison of different models in challenging scenarios, including multiple objects, small objects, occlusion, highly similar foreground and background. Compared to non-frequency-based model GLCONet [25] and frequency-based model FSEL [24], our model produce more high-quality predictions.

camouflaged objects and capture inconspicuous details. For example, Pang *et al.* [23] propose a hybrid-scale network which mimics the behavior of humans when observing vague images, *i.e.*, zooming in and out. Xing *et al.* [29] design a three-stage architecture called search-amplify-recognize, in which the search and amplify parts aim to roughly locate and magnify the object, and the recognize part fine segments the object. In addition, various COD benchmark datasets [5, 13, 20] are constructed for model training. Although these previous methods have significantly advanced the field, they still tend to produce inaccurate and incomplete predictions in some complex scenarios, such as objects with ambiguous boundaries, occlusion, multiple objects, and small objects, as illustrated in Fig. 1. We argue that this failure may be attributed to the limitation of RGB domain, which hinder the ability to distinguish camouflaged objects from visually similar backgrounds resulting in the difficulty of distinguishing the camouflaged objects from visually similar backgrounds.

To address the deficiencies associated with RGB domain-based COD approaches, frequency information has been introduced into the COD task [1, 17, 24, 28, 35, 37] to enhance the localization and segmentation of camouflaged objects. Modeling camouflaged object cues in frequency domains has exhibited potential in overcoming the inherent challenges of the COD task, which requires a powerful representation capability to discern subtle cues that differentiate camouflaged objects from their background. For example, Cong *et al.* [1] propose learnable and separable frequency perception mechanism driven by the semantic hierarchy in the frequency domain. He *et al.* [7] address the intrinsic similarity of foreground and background by decomposing the features into different frequency bands using learnable wavelets. Existing frequency-based COD methods often indiscriminately utilize frequency cues, neglecting the fact that different frequency components play distinct roles in identifying camouflaged objects with well-defined boundaries.

In this paper, we propose a novel FINet for camouflaged object detection, which explores different components in the frequency domain to effectively emphasize the learning of the positions and details of camouflaged objects, thereby enhancing the network's ability to segment these objects in complex scenarios. Specifically, we design a frequency-aware fusion module (FFM) consisting of a frequency learning module (FLM) and a frequency decomposition unit (FDU), which integrates distinct yet related multi-scale features to alleviate the limitations associated with scale-specific representation. This module aims to learn feature representation of different frequency components, thereby retaining important information for distinguishing camouflaged object cues and discarding irrelevant interferences. As illustrated in Fig. 1, our proposed network generates more coherent camouflaged objects with clear boundaries in different scenarios.

In summary, the main contributions of this paper are as follows:

- We propose a novel camouflaged object detection network, called FINet, which utilize the frequency information to compensate for the deficiencies of the RGB domain, thereby effectively locating the positions of concealed objects and delineating fine-grained details for high-quality predictions.
- We design a frequency-aware fusion module to integrate multi-scale RGB domain features by excavating different components in the frequency domain to differentiate subtle yet important camouflage cues.
- Extensive experiments on public and widely-used benchmarks demonstrate the effectiveness of our proposed network across four evaluation metrics.

2 Related Works

2.1 Camouflaged Object Detection

COD has shown a rapid development trend in recent years. Numerous approaches [23,25,32–34,36,38] have been proposed to enhance detection accuracy and efficiency, including multi-scale feature aggregation [23], multi-stage strategy [4,11], multi-task learning [14,20], boundary guidance [19,26] and depth information [27]. Jia *et al.* [11] propose an iterative refinement framework to use multi-stage strategy to realize segmentation, amplification and iteration. Sun *et al.* [26] propose a boundary-guided network, which uses edge semantics to facilitate the network to capture details. In [27], depth information is integrated to unearth subtle visual cues for distinguishing concealed objects from the background, and a large-scale RGB-D agricultural concealed object datasets is compiled. In [8], a high-resolution iterative feedback network is introduced to extract the informative and high-resolution representations for tackling the degradation issue of segmentation details. Yin *et al.* [31] present a simple masked

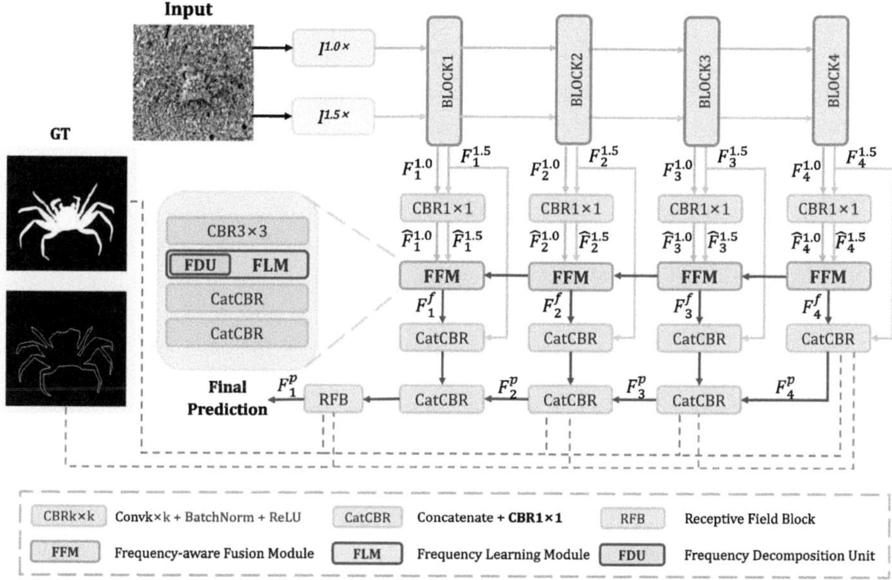

Fig. 2. Overview of the proposed FINet. Our network employs the frequency-aware fusion module (FFM), which consists of a frequency learning module (FLM) and a frequency decomposition unit (FDU), to excavate subtle camouflage cues in the frequency domain, and generates the final prediction in a coarse-to-fine manner.

separable attention which divides the attention heads into three groups and discovers the foreground and background regions by separately computing their attention scores via predicted maps. Unlike the previous methods merely using RGB domain information, we excavate discriminative camouflage cues from the perspective of frequency domain.

2.2 Frequency Learning

The frequency domain is very important for signal analysis, and it has recently been introduced into camouflaged object detection. Sun *et al.* [24] extended global frequency features to different applications, involving multi-receptive fields perception, transformer, and reverse attention. Cong *et al.* [1] use octave convolution to capture frequency domain information and fuse multi-level frequency features through adjacent-layer connections. Although existing methods [7,17,28,35] have achieved promising results, they often indiscriminately rely on frequency features from specific levels and overlook the distinctiveness of different frequency components. Differently, we explore the inner relationship between different frequency components and subtle camouflage cues, enabling the network to accurately segment the camouflaged objects from the complex scenarios.

3 Proposed Method

The architecture of our proposed FINet is illustrated in Fig. 2. Inspired by the previous works [22,23], we leverage multi-scale cues from the input image I by incorporating both the main scale and a auxiliary scale, empirically defined as 1.0× and 1.5×, respectively. These scales $I^{1.0\times}$ and $I^{1.5\times}$ are processed through a pre-trained backbone encoder to extract multi-level and multi-scale features, denoted as $F_i^{1.0}$ and $F_i^{1.5}$ ($i = \{1, 2, 3, 4\}$). To optimize computational efficiency, a 1×1 convolutional layer is applied to these features to reduce the channel number to 128, which results in the refined features $\hat{F}_i^{1.0}$ and $\hat{F}_i^{1.5}$ ($i = \{1, 2, 3, 4\}$). Subsequently, the refined feature $\hat{F}_i^{1.0}$ and its corresponding auxiliary feature $\hat{F}_i^{1.5}$ are fed into the frequency-aware fusion module (FFM) to capture discriminative camouflaged object features from the perspective of the frequency domain, yielding frequency-enhanced features F_i^f. To emphasize fine-grained information, the auxiliary scale feature $\hat{F}_i^{1.5}$ is integrated with the corresponding frequency-enhanced feature F_i^f within the decoder. Furthermore, to enhance local details, we additionally apply a receptive field block [15] at the shallowest level. The feature decoding is conducted progressively in a coarse-to-fine manner to produce side-output features F_i^p. Finally, two forms of supervisions, namely a object mask prediction and an edge mask prediction, are applied at each level to ensure the network effectively learns the localization and fine details of camouflaged objects.

3.1 Frequency-Aware Fusion Module (FFM)

Unlike previous works that primarily integrate cross-level and cross-scale information from the RGB domain, we propose the frequency-aware fusion module (FFM) to explore how to represent cross-scale features from the frequency domain and then fuse them effectively. This module allows the network to discern subtle differences between camouflaged objects and their background, thereby producing discriminative camouflaged object features.

As shown in Fig. 3, a convolutional layer is applied to the features $\hat{F}_i^{1.0}$ and $\hat{F}_i^{1.5}$, respectively, to reduce the channel number by half. Then, these channel-reduced features are processed through the frequency learning module (FLM) to generate frequency-enhanced features $F_a^{1.0}$ and $F_a^{1.5}$. This process can be formulated as:

$$F_a^t = \mathrm{FLM}(\mathrm{Conv}_3(\hat{F}_i^t)) \tag{1}$$

where $t \in \{1.0, 1.5\}$, FLM(·) denotes our FLM, and $\mathrm{Conv}_k(\cdot)$ denotes a $k \times k$ convolutional layer.

After that, to address potential deficiencies at the current level, we introduce the output feature F_{i+1}^f from the FFM of the adjacent deep level and fuse it with the frequency-enhanced features to obtain discriminative camouflaged object features F_i^f. This fusion process is defined as:

$$F_b = \mathrm{Conv}_3(\mathrm{Cat}(F_a^{1.0}, \mathrm{D}(F_a^{1.5}))) \tag{2}$$

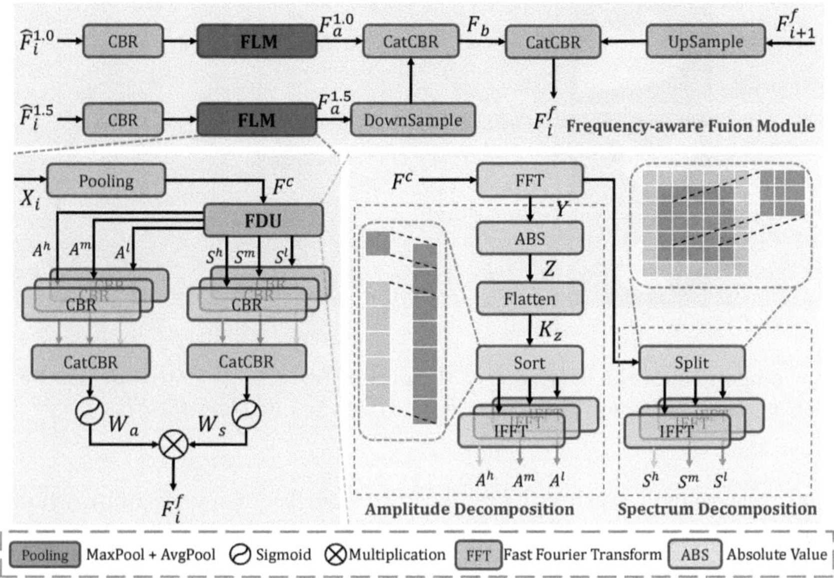

Fig. 3. The details of our frequency-aware fusion module (FFM) consisting of a frequency learning module (FLM) and a frequency decomposition unit (FDU).

$$F_i^f = \text{Conv}_3(\text{Cat}(\text{U}(F_{i+1}^f), F_b)) \tag{3}$$

where D(·) is the downsampling operation, U(·) indicates the upsampling operation, and Cat(·) represents the concatenation operation. Figure 4 displays the heatmaps of the outputs generated by our FFMs at different levels. It can be observed that from (c) to (f), our network FINet progressively highlights the complete camouflaged objects with well-defined boundaries while effectively suppressing irrelevant backgrounds. This observation underscores the effectiveness of our FFM in distinguishing subtle differences against visually similar backgrounds.

3.2 Frequency Learning Module (FLM)

Our frequency learning module (FLM) is designed to perceive camouflaged objects that blend seamlessly into their environments from the perspective of the frequency domain. The details of our FLM are shown in Fig. 3.

Specifically, given the input feature X_i, we apply both maximum pooling and average pooling to smooth the feature, thereby eliminating potential negative impacts on subsequent processing:

$$F^c = \text{AvgPool}(X) + \text{MaxPool}(X) \tag{4}$$

where AvgPool(·) and MaxPool(·) denote the average pooling and maximum pooling operations, respectively.

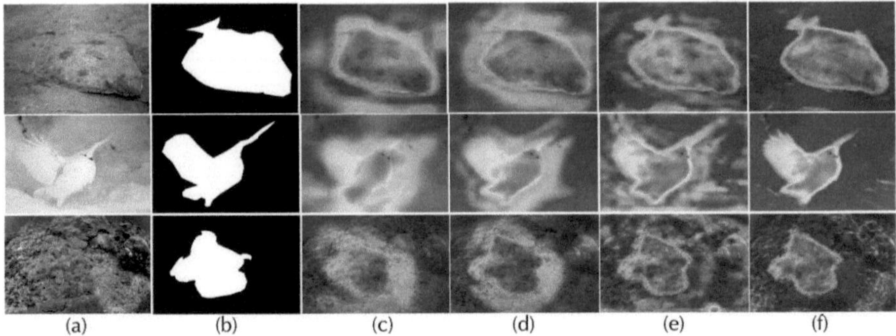

Fig. 4. Comparison of the heatmaps of the output features generated by our FFMs at different levels. (a) Image, (b) GT, (c) F_4^f, (d) F_3^f, (e) F_2^f, and (f) F_1^f.

Next, the refined feature F^c is fed into the frequency decomposition unit (FDU) to produce various frequency information, including spectrum features (*i.e.*, low-frequency feature S^l, mid-frequency feature S^m, and high-frequency feature S^h) as well as amplitude features (*i.e.*, low-amplitude feature A^l, mid-amplitude feature A^m, and high-amplitude feature A^h). We then integrate these spectrum features and amplitude features to obtain weight maps W_s and W_a. This process can be formulated as:

$$W_s = \sigma(\text{Conv}_3(Cat(\text{Conv}_3(S^l), \text{Conv}_3(S^m), \text{Conv}_3(S^h)))) \tag{5}$$

$$W_a = \sigma(\text{Conv}_3(Cat(\text{Conv}_3(A^l), \text{Conv}_3(A^m), \text{Conv}_3(A^h)))) \tag{6}$$

where $\sigma(\cdot)$ represents the sigmoid activation function.

Finally, the weight maps are integrated with the input feature X to guide the proposed network to focus on learning the important information of camouflaged objects:

$$F_f = W_s \otimes W_a \otimes X \tag{7}$$

where $\otimes$ is the element-wise multiplication. In this way, the network can effectively locate potential camouflaged objects and capture imperceptible details from the frequency domain perspective.

3.3 Frequency Decomposition Unit (FDU)

We propose the frequency decomposition unit (FDU) to model feature representation in the frequency domain. As shown in Fig. 3, we perform a two-dimensional Fast Fourier Transform (FFT) on the input feature F^c. To facilitate frequency component analysis, we perform frequency domain centering on the FFT results, yielding a spectrum Y.

The FDU consists of two parallel branches: the spectrum decomposition branch and the amplitude decomposition branch, which independently extract frequency features $\{S^l, S^m, S^h\}$ and amplitude features $\{A^l, A^m, A^h\}$.

In the amplitude decomposition branch, we derive the amplitude information $Z \in \mathbb{R}^{C \times H \times W}$ from the spectrum:

$$Z(u, v) = |Y(u, v)| \tag{8}$$

where $|\cdot|$ represents the modulus of a complex number, and u and v are frequency variables, with H, W and C representing the height, width and channel number, respectively. Next, the amplitude information Z is flatten, resulting in a feature map $K_z \in \mathbb{R}^{C \times HW}$, and sorted in descending order. We then retain the top $\alpha_1\%$, top $\alpha_2\%$ and bottom $\alpha_3\%$ of the feature map K_z, and employ the Inverse Fast Fourier Transform (IFFT) to convert these frequency domain components to the spatial domain, yielding low-amplitude feature A^l, mid-amplitude feature A^m and high-amplitude feature A^h, respectively.

In the frequency decomposition branch, we segment the spectrum Y into distinct components. To be specific, the central 40% square region of the spectrum Y is extracted as the low-frequency component; the ring-shaped region covering 40%–80% of the spectrum Y is defined as the mid-frequency component; and the outermost ring constitutes the high-frequency component. These components are then processed through IFFT to produce frequency features S^l, S^m, and S^h, respectively.

3.4 Loss Function

In this paper, we introduce a hybrid loss function $\mathcal{L}_{total}$ to supervise the predictions of camouflaged objects and their boundaries at each level of our proposed network. For the camouflaged object predictions, the loss function is composed of a weighted binary cross-entropy loss (ℓ_{bce}^{w}) and the weighted intersection over union loss (ℓ_{iou}^{w}):

$$\mathcal{L}_o = \ell_{bce}^{w} + \ell_{iou}^{w} \tag{9}$$

For the camouflaged boundary predictions, we utilize the dice loss (ℓ_{dice}^{w}), which is effective in addressing the challenges posed by the imbalance between positive and negative samples. Consequently, the total loss function of the proposed network FINet is defined as follows:

$$\mathcal{L}_{total} = \sum_{i=1}^{4} \left(\frac{1}{2^i} \mathcal{L}_o(P_o^i, G_o) + 2\ell_{dice}^{w}(P_e^i, G_e) \right) \tag{10}$$

where P_o^i and P_e^i represent the object prediction map and the boundary prediction map at the i-th level, and G_o and G_e are the ground truth of the object and the boundary, respectively.

4 Experiment

4.1 Experiment Setup

Implementation Details. All experiments are conducted on an NVIDIA L20 GPU using the PyTorch framework. The proposed model adopts the pretrained PVTv2 as the backbone. The batch size is set to 8 during training. We employ the AdamW optimizer with an initial learning rate of 8e-5 and a weight decay factor of 0.05. To adjust the learning rate dynamically, we implement the CosineAnnealingLR scheduler, configured with a maximum number of iterations $T_{max} = 30$ and a minimum learning rate 1e-6. To prevent overfitting, the input images are randomly flipped, and resized to a resolution of 384×384. The entire training process is conducted over 60 epochs.

Table 1. Performance of different methods on benchmark datasets. The top two results are highlighted **bold** and *underline*.

Method	Pub./Year	CAMO				COD10K				NC4K			
		S_m ↑	wF_β ↑	MAE ↓	E_m ↑	S_m ↑	wF_β ↑	MAE ↓	E_m ↑	S_m ↑	wF_β ↑	MAE ↓	E_m ↑
SINetV2 [4]	TPAMI'22	0.822	0.743	0.070	0.884	0.815	0.680	0.037	0.864	0.847	0.770	0.048	0.901
FEDER [7]	CVPR'23	0.799	0.733	0.073	0.873	0.822	0.715	0.032	0.901	0.846	0.787	0.044	0.913
EVP [16]	CVPR'23	0.833	0.756	0.067	0.896	0.837	0.712	0.032	0.877	-	-	-	-
FSPNet [10]	CVPR'23	0.857	0.799	0.050	0.919	0.851	0.735	0.026	0.900	0.879	0.816	0.035	0.923
FPNet [1]	MM'23	0.851	0.802	0.056	0.912	0.850	0.755	0.029	0.909	-	-	-	-
HINet [8]	AAAI'23	0.849	0.809	0.055	0.910	0.868	0.806	0.023	0.936	0.874	0.834	0.037	0.928
SDRNet [6]	KBS'24	0.871	0.826	0.049	0.924	0.871	0.785	0.023	0.928	0.889	0.842	0.032	0.934
VSCode [18]	CVPR'24	0.873	0.820	0.046	0.928	0.869	0.780	0.023	0.929	0.891	0.841	0.032	0.939
PRNet [9]	TCSVT'24	0.872	0.831	0.050	0.927	0.874	0.799	0.022	0.939	0.891	0.848	0.031	0.939
RISNet [27]	CVPR'24	0.870	0.827	0.050	0.922	0.873	0.799	0.025	0.927	0.882	0.834	0.037	0.926
CamoFormer [31]	TPAMI'24	0.873	0.831	0.046	0.931	0.869	0.786	0.023	0.931	0.892	0.847	0.030	0.941
GLCONet [25]	TNNLS'24	0.880	0.849	0.038	0.940	0.863	0.783	0.023	0.929	0.887	0.847	0.030	0.942
SAE [12]	TCE'24	0.885	0.847	0.040	0.941	0.872	0.791	0.022	0.931	0.892	0.849	0.030	0.940
FSEL [24]	ECCV'24	0.885	0.851	0.040	0.942	0.877	0.800	0.021	0.928	0.893	0.853	0.030	0.941
FINet	Ours	**0.896**	**0.865**	**0.035**	**0.949**	**0.888**	**0.822**	**0.019**	**0.943**	**0.900**	**0.865**	**0.028**	**0.946**

Datasets. We evaluate our network on three publicly widely-used COD benchmarks, including CAMO [13], COD10K [5], and NC4k [20]. CAMO contains 1,250 images, divided into 1,000 images for training and 250 for testing. COD10K contains 5,066 images with high-quality pixel-level labels, which is further split into 3,040 images for training and 2,026 images for testing. NC4K is another large-scale dataset, comprising a total of 4,121 images.

Evaluation Metrics. We use four evaluation metrics to assess the performance of our method, including S-measure (S_m) [2], weighted F-measure (wF_β) [21], mean absolute error (MAE), E-measure (E_m) [3].

4.2 Comparisons with State-of-the-Arts

To evaluate our FINet, we compare it with several competing methods. The results of all these methods are either provided by the authors or generated using their released codes. As shown in Table 1, FINet consistently surpasses the competing methods across all datasets, demonstrating a significant performance advantage. Specifically, on the COD10K dataset, FINet achieves a 1.3% rise in S_m, a 2.8% increase in wF_β, a 1.6% boost in E_m, and a 9.5% improvement in MAE compared to the recently published frequency-based method FSEL [24].

We display the visual comparison results of our FINet and some state-of-the-art methods in Fig. 5. The predictions of our network are closer to the ground truth across various scenarios, including occlusion, small objects, multiple objects, large objects and objects with unclear boundaries. For example, in the first row, all competing methods fail to capture the fine structures of the camouflaged objects, whereas FINet successfully segments the unobstructed regions of the target object, demonstrating its sensitivity to subtle details. In the fifth and sixth rows, most methods exhibit false detections, mistakenly segmenting non-camouflaged regions. In contrast, FINet accurately identifies and segments target objects, validating the effectiveness of frequency-domain guidance in excavating useful information and mitigating distractions.

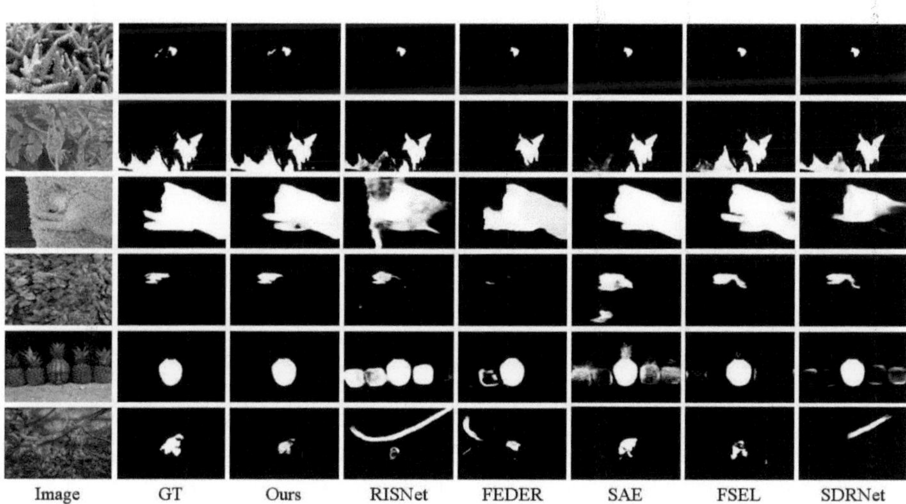

Fig. 5. Visual comparisons of prediction maps produced by our FINet and some competing approaches.

4.3 Ablation Studies

Effectiveness of Key Components. To validate the effectiveness of each proposed modules, we conduct ablation experiments on the FFM, FLM, and FDU.

We replace the FFM with concatenation and convolution to construct a network denoted as "w/o FFM". Additionally, we construct a network "w/o FLM" by removing the FLM from our proposed network. Furthermore, we remove the FDU from our network to construct a network denoted as "w/o FDU". As shown in Table 2, our model, FINet, consistently outperforms the other networks, indicating that each key component contributes to the performance of our network.

Table 2. Quantitative comparison of ablation studies of key components. The top results are highlighted **bold**.

Method	CAMO				COD10K				NC4K			
	$S_m \uparrow$	$wF_\beta \uparrow$	MAE $\downarrow$	$E_m \uparrow$	$S_m \uparrow$	$wF_\beta \uparrow$	MAE $\downarrow$	$E_m \uparrow$	$S_m \uparrow$	$wF_\beta \uparrow$	MAE $\downarrow$	$E_m \uparrow$
w/o FFM	0.888	0.851	0.040	0.933	0.883	0.819	0.021	0.936	0.893	0.861	0.030	0.935
w/o FLM	0.888	0.857	0.039	0.935	0.885	0.820	0.020	0.937	0.895	0.863	0.029	0.937
w/o FDU	0.893	0.863	0.037	0.936	0.886	0.820	**0.019**	0.939	0.898	**0.865**	0.029	0.939
FINet	**0.896**	**0.865**	**0.035**	**0.949**	**0.888**	**0.822**	**0.019**	**0.943**	**0.900**	**0.865**	**0.028**	**0.946**

Effectiveness of Our FDU. In our FDU, we explore the frequency information within the spectrum branch and the amplitude branch. By removing one branch, we construct networks denoted as "w/o spectrum" and "w/o amplitude", respectively. As shown in Table 3, the networks "w/o spectrum" and "w/o amplitude" are inferior to our network, confirming that each branch of the FDU helps to emphasize important camouflage cues, thereby improving the performance of our network.

Table 3. Comparison of ablation studies on our FDU. The top results are highlighted **bold**.

Method	CAMO				COD10K				NC4K			
	$S_m \uparrow$	$wF_\beta \uparrow$	MAE $\downarrow$	$E_m \uparrow$	$S_m \uparrow$	$wF_\beta \uparrow$	MAE $\downarrow$	$E_m \uparrow$	$S_m \uparrow$	$wF_\beta \uparrow$	MAE $\downarrow$	$E_m \uparrow$
w/o spectrum	0.892	0.859	0.037	0.935	0.887	0.820	**0.019**	0.940	0.899	0.861	0.029	0.936
w/o amplitude	0.895	**0.865**	0.037	0.936	0.887	0.821	**0.019**	0.938	0.898	0.864	**0.028**	0.938
FINet	**0.896**	**0.865**	**0.035**	**0.949**	**0.888**	**0.822**	**0.019**	**0.943**	**0.900**	**0.865**	**0.028**	**0.946**

Effectiveness of Auxiliary Scale. In our model, we use the main scale image and its 1.5× auxiliary scale as multi-scale inputs to capture hierarchical information from both the RGB domain and the frequency domain. To validate the effectiveness of this strategy, we remove the auxiliary scale input. As shown in Table 4, our network significantly performs better than the network merely using the main scale (⑥). This implies that our multi-scale strategy effectively captures more camouflage cues for segmenting target objects. Furthermore, we vary the scales of the auxiliary inputs to verify the rationale behind our configuration. From Table 4, we observe that our FINet achieves superior performance compared to other results (①-⑤), indicating that our configuration effective captures and leverages complementary information across different scales.

Table 4. Comparison of experimental results of input images. "AS" means the auxiliary scale. The top results are highlighted **bold**.

No.	AS	CAMO				COD10K				NC4K			
		$S_m \uparrow$	$wF_\beta \uparrow$	MAE $\downarrow$	$E_m \uparrow$	$S_m \uparrow$	$wF_\beta \uparrow$	MAE $\downarrow$	$E_m \uparrow$	$S_m \uparrow$	$wF_\beta \uparrow$	MAE $\downarrow$	$E_m \uparrow$
①	0.5	0.880	0.838	0.043	0.924	0.866	0.777	0.024	0.922	0.890	0.842	0.031	0.930
②	0.75	0.889	0.854	0.038	0.934	0.873	0.792	0.022	0.931	0.892	0.849	0.030	0.933
③	1.25	0.885	0.852	0.041	0.932	0.884	0.813	0.020	0.937	0.898	0.861	0.029	0.938
④	1.75	0.891	0.860	0.037	0.937	0.885	0.819	0.020	0.942	0.897	0.863	0.029	0.941
⑤	2	0.893	0.863	0.036	0.938	0.884	**0.822**	**0.019**	0.942	0.896	0.861	**0.028**	0.940
⑥	✗	0.883	0.844	0.041	0.929	0.874	0.794	0.022	0.928	0.894	0.853	0.030	0.935
⑦ (Ours)	1.5	**0.896**	**0.865**	**0.035**	**0.949**	**0.888**	**0.822**	**0.019**	**0.943**	**0.900**	**0.865**	**0.028**	**0.946**

Effectiveness of Our Decoder. To assess the effectiveness of our decoder architecture, we conduct ablation experiments by removing the short connection ("w/o $F_i^{1.5}$") and the edge supervision ("w/o edge"). From Table 5, with the inclusion of the short connection and the edge supervision, the performance improves.

Table 5. Comparison of experimental results of our decoder. The top results are highlighted **bold**.

Method	CAMO				COD10K				NC4K			
	$S_m \uparrow$	$wF_\beta \uparrow$	MAE $\downarrow$	$E_m \uparrow$	$S_m \uparrow$	$wF_\beta \uparrow$	MAE $\downarrow$	$E_m \uparrow$	$S_m \uparrow$	$wF_\beta \uparrow$	MAE $\downarrow$	$E_m \uparrow$
w/o edge	0.891	0.860	0.038	0.936	0.886	0.821	0.020	0.941	0.899	0.863	0.029	0.938
w/o $F_i^{1.5}$	0.893	0.861	0.036	0.943	0.887	0.818	0.020	0.939	**0.901**	0.864	**0.028**	0.939
FINet	**0.896**	**0.865**	**0.035**	**0.949**	**0.888**	**0.822**	**0.019**	**0.943**	0.900	**0.865**	**0.028**	**0.946**

5 Conclusions

In this paper, we propose a FINet for camouflaged object detection, which introduces the frequency-aware fusion (FFM), consisting of a frequency learning module (FLM) and a frequency decomposition unit (FDU). These proposed modules facilitate dynamic cross-domain feature alignment and integration, effectively emphasizing subtle camouflage cues while mitigating irrelevant distractions. Extensive experimental results demonstrate that our FINet achieves superior performance across three widely-used benchmark datasets. In the future, we will focus on exploring knowledge distillation techniques to reduce the computational complexity associated with the multi-scale strategy.

References

1. Cong, R., Sun, M., Zhang, S., Zhou, X., Zhang, W., Zhao, Y.: Frequency perception network for camouflaged object detection. In: The 31st ACM International Conference on Multimedia, pp. 1179–1189 (2023)

2. Fan, D.P., Cheng, M.M., Liu, Y., Li, T., Borji, A.: Structure-measure: a new way to eval foreground maps. In: IEEE International Conference on Computer Vision, pp. 4548–4557 (2017)
3. Fan, D.P., Gong, C., Cao, Y., Ren, B., Cheng, M.M., Borji, A.: Enhanced-alignment measure for binary foreground map evaluation. In: International Joint Conference on Artificial Intelligence, pp. 698–704 (2018)
4. Fan, D.P., Ji, G.P., Cheng, M.M., Shao, L.: Concealed object detection. IEEE Trans. Pattern Anal. Mach. Intell. 6024–6042 (2022)
5. Fan, D.P., Ji, G.P., Sun, G., Cheng, M.M., Shen, J., Shao, L.: Camouflaged object detection. In: 2020 IEEE/CVF Conference on Computer Vision and Pattern Recognition, pp. 2774–2784 (2020)
6. Guan, J., Fang, X., Zhu, T., Qian, W.: Sdrnet: camouflaged object detection with independent reconstruction of structure and detail. Knowl.-Based Syst. 112051 (2024)
7. He, C., et al.: Camouflaged object detection with feature decomposition and edge reconstruction. In: 2023 IEEE/CVF Conference on Computer Vision and Pattern Recognition, pp. 22046–22055 (2023)
8. Hu, X., et al.: High-resolution iterative feedback network for camouflaged object detection. In: AAAI Conference on Artificial Intelligence, pp. 881–889 (2023)
9. Hu, X., Zhang, X., Wang, F., Sun, J., Sun, F.: Efficient camouflaged object detection network based on global localization perception and local guidance refinement. IEEE Trans. Circuits Syst. Video Technol. 5452–5465 (2024)
10. Huang, Z., et al.: Feature shrinkage pyramid for camouflaged object detection with transformers. In: 2023 IEEE/CVF Conference on Computer Vision and Pattern Recognition, pp. 5557–5566 (2023)
11. Jia, Q., Yao, S., Liu, Y., Fan, X., Liu, R., Luo, Z.: Segment, magnify and reiterate: Detecting camouflaged objects the hard way. In: 2022 IEEE/CVF Conference on Computer Vision and Pattern Recognition, pp. 4703–4712 (2022)
12. Kang, K., et al.: Shrink and expose: locate edge coarse-to-fine for camouflaged object detection. IEEE Trans. Consum. Electron. (2024)
13. Le, T.N., Nguyen, T.V., Nie, Z., Tran, M.T., Sugimoto, A.: Anabranch network for camouflaged object segmentation. Comput. Vis. Image Understand. 45–56 (2019)
14. Li, A., Zhang, J., Lv, Y., Liu, B., Zhang, T., Dai, Y.: Uncertainty-aware joint salient object and camouflaged object detection. In: 2021 IEEE/CVF Conference on Computer Vision and Pattern Recognition, pp. 10066–10076 (2021)
15. Liu, S., Huang, D., Wang, Y.: Receptive field block net for accurate and fast object detection. In: European Conference on Computer Vision, pp. 404–419 (2018)
16. Liu, W., Shen, X., Pun, C.M., Cun, X.: Explicit visual prompting for low-level structure segmentations. In: 2023 IEEE/CVF Conference on Computer Vision and Pattern Recognition, pp. 19434–19445 (2023)
17. Liu, Z., Deng, X., Jiang, P., Lv, C., Min, G., Wang, X.: Edge perception camouflaged object detection under frequency domain reconstruction. IEEE Trans. Circuits Syst. Video Technol. 10194–10207 (2024)
18. Luo, Z., et al.: Vscode: general visual salient and camouflaged object detection with 2D prompt learning. In: 2024 IEEE/CVF Conference on Computer Vision and Pattern Recognition, pp. 17169–17180 (2024)
19. Lyu, Y., Zhang, H., Li, Y., Liu, H., Yang, Y., Yuan, D.: UEDG: uncertainty-edge dual guided camouflage object detection. IEEE Trans. Multimed. 4050–4060 (2024)
20. Lyu, Y., et al.: Simultaneously localize, segment and rank the camouflaged objects. In: 2021 IEEE/CVF Conference on Computer Vision and Pattern Recognition, pp. 11586–11596 (2021)

21. Margolin, R., Zelnik-Manor, L., Tal, A.: How to eval foreground maps? In: 2014 IEEE/CVF Conference on Computer Vision and Pattern Recognition, pp. 248–255 (2014)
22. Pang, Y., Zhao, X., Xiang, T.Z., Zhang, L., Lu, H.: Zoom in and out: a mixed-scale triplet network for camouflaged object detection. In: 2022 IEEE/CVF Conference on Computer Vision and Pattern Recognition, pp. 2150–2160 (2022)
23. Pang, Y., Zhao, X., Xiang, T.Z., Zhang, L., Lu, H.: Zoomnext: a unified collaborative pyramid network for camouflaged object detection. IEEE Trans. Pattern Anal. Mach. Intell. 9205–9220 (2024)
24. Sun, Y., Xu, C., Yang, J., Xuan, H., Luo, L.: Frequency-spatial entanglement learning for camouflaged object detection. In: European Conference on Computer Vision, pp. 343–360 (2024)
25. Sun, Y., Xuan, H., Yang, J., Luo, L.: Glconet: learning multisource perception representation for camouflaged object detection. IEEE Trans. Neural Netw. Learn. Syst. (2024)
26. Sun, Y., Wang, S., Chen, C., Xiang, T.Z.: Boundary-guided camouflaged object detection. In: International Joint Conferences on Artificial Intelligence Organization, pp. 1335–1341 (2022)
27. Wang, L., Yang, J., Zhang, Y., Wang, F., Zheng, F.: Depth-aware concealed crop detection in dense agricultural scenes. In: 2024 IEEE/CVF Conference on Computer Vision and Pattern Recognition, pp. 17201–17211 (2024)
28. Xie, C., Xia, C., Yu, T., Li, J.: Frequency representation integration for camouflaged object detection. In: The 31st ACM International Conference on Multimedia, pp. 1789—-1797 (2023)
29. Xing, H., Gao, S., Wang, Y., Wei, X., Tang, H., Zhang, W.: Go closer to see better: camouflaged object detection via object area amplification and figure-ground conversion. IEEE Trans. Circuits Syst. Video Technol. 5444–5457 (2023)
30. Yang, F., et al.: Uncertainty-guided transformer reasoning for camouflaged object detection. In: 2021 IEEE/CVF International Conference on Computer Vision, pp. 4126–4135 (2021)
31. Yin, B., et al.: Camoformer: masked separable attention for camouflaged object detection. IEEE Trans. Pattern Anal. Mach. Intell. (2024)
32. Zhang, C., Wu, J., Zhang, Q., Zhai, Y., Pang, Y.: Retrospective memory for camouflaged object detection. arXiv preprint arXiv:2506.15244 (2025)
33. Zhang, C., Zhang, Q., Wu, J.: Rethinking camouflaged object detection via foreground-background interactive learning. In: 2025 IEEE International Conference on Acoustics, Speech and Signal Processing, ICASSP 2025, pp. 1–5 (2025)
34. Zhang, C., Zhang, Q., Wu, J., Pang, Y.: Cgcod: class-guided camouflaged object detection. arXiv preprint arXiv:2412.18977 (2024)
35. Zhao, Y., Zhang, Q., Li, Y.: Frequency learning network with dual-guidance calibration for camouflaged object detection. In: Asian Conference on Computer Vision, pp. 235—-251 (2024)
36. Zhao, Y., Zhang, Q., Li, Y.: Camouflaged object detection with CNN-transformer harmonization and calibration. In: ICASSP 2025-2025 IEEE International Conference on Acoustics, Speech and Signal Processing (ICASSP), pp. 1–5 (2025)
37. Zhong, Y., Li, B., Tang, L., Kuang, S., Wu, S., Ding, S.: Detecting camouflaged object in frequency domain. In: 2022 IEEE/CVF Conference on Computer Vision and Pattern Recognition, pp. 4494–4503 (2022)
38. Zhuang, C., Zhang, Q., Zhang, C., Yuan, X.: Boundary-and-object collaborative learning network for camouflaged object detection. Image Vis. Comput. 105596 (2025)

DFA-Net: Detection-Guided Feature Aggregation Network for Vehicle Re-identification

Can Ping[1,2], Leixiao Li[1,2,3], Dongjiang Liu[1,2,3](✉), Hao Lin[4], and Ming Yan[1,2]

[1] Inner Mongolia University of Technology, Inner Mongolia Autonomous Region, Huhhot 010080, China
lileixiao@imut.edu.cn

[2] Inner Mongolia Key Laboratory of Beijing Cyberspace Security, Inner Mongolia Autonomous Region, Hohhot 010080, China

[3] Inner Mongolia Autonomous Region Software Service Engineering Technology Research Center Based on Big Data, Inner Mongolia Autonomous Region, Hohhot 010080, China

[4] Tianjin University of Technology, Tianjin 300384, China

Abstract. Vehicle Re-identification is designed to locate and match specific vehicles from images or videos captured by a set of non-overlapping cameras. This technology has broad application prospects in intelligent transportation systems, urban security, and autonomous driving. In recent years, methods based on convolutional neural networks have made significant progress in the field of vehicle re-identification. However, existing methods still have shortcomings in dealing with background information interference and attribute feature extraction. To address these issues, we propose a vehicle re-identification method called Detection-Guided Feature Aggregation Network (DFA-Net). DFA-Net first performs vehicle detection and image cropping using YOLO to eliminate interference from non-target regions. Then, it employs two attribute classification networks as attribute feature extractors to extract the color and type features of vehicles, respectively. Finally, it introduces a Spatial Attribute Gating Fusion (SAGF) module to dynamically fuse the global features and attribute features of vehicles through learnable spatial weights. Experiments on the Veri-776 and VehicleID datasets show that DFA-Net has increased the mAP by an average of 8.01% on the Veri-776 dataset and by 9.93% on the VehicleID dataset. These results demonstrate the robustness and superiority of DFA-Net in the task of vehicle re-identification.

Keywords: Vehicle Re-Identification · Feature Fusion · Attribute Features

1 Introduction

Vehicle re-identification is an important task in computer vision, which aims to recognize the same vehicle from different viewpoints or at different times using images or videos captured by surveillance cameras [1]. This technology has broad application prospects in fields such as intelligent transportation systems [2], urban security [3], and autonomous driving [4].

© The Author(s), under exclusive license to Springer Nature Singapore Pte Ltd. 2026
J. Kittler et al. (Eds.): PRCV 2025, LNCS 16289, pp. 62–75, 2026.
https://doi.org/10.1007/978-981-95-5764-6_5

The attribute information of vehicles (such as color, type, and model) has unique advantages in the task of vehicle re-identification. These attributes are typically unaffected by environmental factors such as lighting and angle, and thus possess high stability and discriminability. Therefore, many researchers have used vehicle attribute information as a supplement to global features to enhance the feature representation capability. However, existing methods still have some shortcomings. Most current methods rely on the entire image for Re-ID modelling, ignoring the interference of a large amount of irrelevant background information in the image. Moreover, many methods that use attribute features for vehicle re-identification depend on the labeled attribute information of vehicles. When some samples in the dataset lack attribute labels, these samples cannot be normally used for vehicle re-identification.

To address the aforementioned issues, we propose a vehicle re-identification method called Detection-guided Feature Aggregation Network (DFA-Net). To tackle the problem of background information interference, we first detect the vehicle in the vehicle image and then crop the image, using only the cropped vehicle main body image for re-identification. To address the issue of missing attribute labels in the dataset samples, we designed and pre-trained two attribute classification networks, and then removed the classification layers to use them for attribute feature extraction. This approach effectively solved the problem of vehicles lacking attribute information due to insufficient data annotations. Finally, we introduce a Spatial Attribute Gating Fusion (SAGF) module to dynamically allocate the weights of color and type features, thereby improving the feature representation capability by fusing global and attribute features through this module. The main contributions of this paper include:

- DFA-Net effectively removes background noise and reduces the interference caused by background information in vehicle re-identification through the preprocessing steps of vehicle detection and image cropping.
- Two attribute classification networks are trained, and their model weights are frozen and classification layers removed to transform these networks into efficient feature extractors, fully utilizing the attribute information of vehicles.
- A feature fusion module based on SAGF is designed to effectively integrate global features, color features, and type features.
- Extensive experiments are conducted on the Veri-776 and VehicleID datasets, verifying the effectiveness and robustness of the proposed method.

2 Related Works

In recent years, with the rapid development of deep learning technology, methods based on convolutional neural networks have made significant progress in the field of vehicle re-identification. These methods primarily rely on the extraction and matching of global features, capturing the overall appearance information of vehicles through pre-trained deep models. However, methods that solely depend on global features have limitations when dealing with vehicles that have similar appearances, especially in the presence of significant background information interference. To overcome this limitation, many researchers have begun to explore methods that integrate local features [5–10]. Integrating local features on the basis of global features can enhance the model's ability to learn subtle differences. However, focusing too much on local details may embed irrelevant information, such as background, into the global features, which is detrimental to vehicle re-identification.

Vehicle attribute features, as stable semantic information, can effectively alleviate problems such as the similarity in appearance of different vehicles and the difficulty of cross-view matching. They also provide clear semantic guidance in feature fusion, which helps construct a more structured feature representation space. In recent years, researchers have fully explored the use of vehicle attribute information in the task of vehicle re-identification. References [11–13] directly utilize the attribute annotations in the dataset to generate descriptive texts for vehicles and train the model using both the descriptive texts and visual features. References [14, 15] extracted vehicle attribute features through attribute feature extraction networks and concatenated them with global features, using the concatenated features for vehicle re-identification. These methods effectively utilized the discriminability of attribute features to enhance the performance of vehicle re-identification. However, with the wide variety of vehicle attribute information, treating all attribute information as equally important and feeding it into the model increases the computational complexity of the model and may lead to information redundancy and decreased model generalization ability. To address this issue, references [16–21] used different feature weights to implement the concatenation of attribute features or element-wise addition of feature vectors, thereby improving the representation ability of vehicle features. These studies have shown that incorporating attribute features on the basis of global features can effectively improve the accuracy and robustness of vehicle re-identification.

Despite the significant progress made by existing methods in the task of vehicle re-identification, they still have shortcomings in dealing with background information interference and multi-feature fusion. DFA-Net aims to reduce the interference of background information and achieve effective fusion of global and attribute features, thereby enhancing the performance of vehicle re-identification.

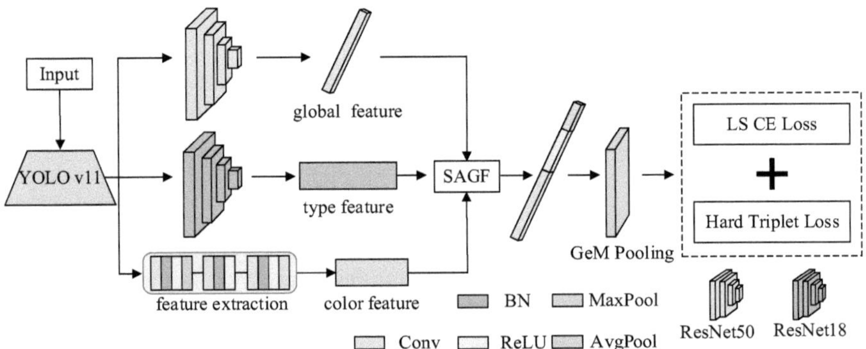

Fig. 1. Architecture of the DFA-Net

3 Methodology

DFA-Net first employs a pre-trained YOLO v11 [22] model for vehicle detection and subsequently crops the images based on the detection results to eliminate background interference. Following this, two attribute feature classification models are trained to extract the color and type features of vehicles, respectively. After the training is completed, the classification layers are removed, and these models are utilized as feature extractors. Finally, the SAGF module is used to fuse the global features, attribute features, and type features. The overall architecture of the model is shown in Fig. 1.

3.1 Vehicle Detection

In existing vehicle re-identification datasets, images are mostly cropped from surveillance videos and then manually annotated. These images have two significant issues. First, the images contain not only vehicle information but also a large amount of irrelevant background information, and in some samples, the background even includes other unrelated vehicles. Second, since the sample images are cropped from surveillance videos, samples of the same identity often have high background similarity, which may cause existing vehicle re-identification algorithms to overly rely on background information during feature extraction.

To overcome these issues, we introduce a vehicle detection preprocessing step based on YOLOv11. Specifically, we first train the YOLO model using a portion of samples from the MS COCO dataset and some samples from the VeRi dataset. By combining these two datasets, the trained YOLO model is capable of accurately detecting vehicles in the vehicle re-identification datasets. During the vehicle detection phase, the trained YOLO model is applied to each image in the vehicle re-identification dataset. The original images are then cropped according to the detected vehicle bounding boxes to extract the main body of the vehicles. The cropped images serve as the input to the vehicle re-identification model. This process not only removes background noise but also reduces the interference of background information to the vehicle re-identification model. The process of vehicle detection and cropping using YOLOv11 is illustrated in Fig. 2.

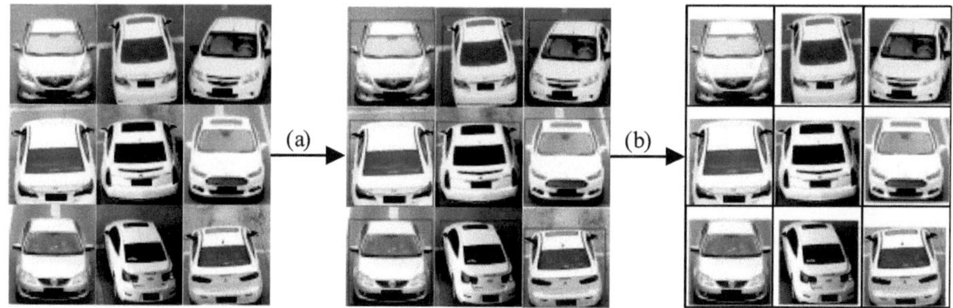

Fig. 2. Vehicle Detection and Image Cropping Using YOLO. The vehicle images are from the VehicleID dataset. (a) shows the process of vehicle detection using the YOLOv11 model, and (b) shows the process of cropping the sample images based on the vehicle detection results.

3.2 Vehicle Attribute Feature Extraction

Color Feature Extraction of Vehicles

We first trained a vehicle color classification model. The feature extractor of this model consists of convolutional layers, batch normalization layers, ReLU activation layers, max-pooling layers, average pooling layers, and a flatten layer. The color classifier employs a two-layer fully connected network. After training, we removed the classification and flattening layers and retained the remaining part as the vehicle color feature extractor. The overall structure of this module is shown in Fig. 3.

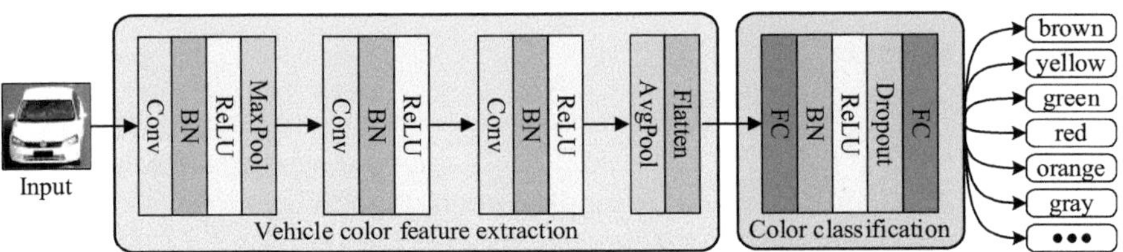

Fig. 3. The process of vehicle color classification.

After training the vehicle color classification model, the Flatten layer and the color classification layer at the end of the network are removed. The vehicle color feature f_{color} can be represented as:

$$f_{color} = GAP(RBC(RBC(P_{\max}(RBC(I))))) \tag{1}$$

where $RBC(\cdot) = \mathrm{Re}LU(BN(Conv(\cdot)))$, GAP denotes Global Average Pooling, BN refers to the BatchNorm layer, $Conv$ refers to the Convolution layer, $P_{\max}$ denotes the max-pooling layer, and I represents the input image.

Vehicle Type Feature Extraction

We employed the ResNet18 model as the base architecture and trained it with a classification layer appended. After training, the fully connected layer was removed, and the ResNet18 model was utilized as a vehicle type feature extractor. For an input image I, the vehicle type feature extractor outputs f_{type}. By adopting this training method, even if the dataset lacks attribute annotations for vehicles in the future, we can still use the pre-trained model to extract the color and type features of vehicles.

Loss Function

During the training process of the vehicle attribute classification model, to enhance the model's generalization and robustness, we utilized the Label Smoothing Cross-Entropy Loss to optimize the model, with the label smoothing parameter ϵ set to 0.1.

3.3 Vehicle Re-identification

Global Feature Extraction

We adopted the R50 mentioned in [23] as the baseline network, with ResNet50-IBN serving as the backbone network. In this network, the output of the fourth layer of ResNet50 is utilized as the global feature. For an input image I, the backbone network extracts a global feature map $f_g \in R^{c \times h \times w}$, where c, h and w are channels, height and width of f_g, respectively. The network is capable of transforming vehicle images into global features rich in semantic information. These features not only encompass the appearance information of the vehicle but also include visual features under different lighting conditions, poses, and backgrounds, thereby providing a powerful feature representation capability for the task of vehicle re-identification.

Spatial Attribute Gating Fusion

To fully utilize the attribute information of vehicles and dynamically fuse the global features, color features, and type features, we propose a feature fusion method called SAGF. SAGF introduces a gating mechanism to achieve collaborative optimization between vehicle attribute features and global features, thereby enhancing the performance of vehicle re-identification. The network structure of SAGF is illustrated in Fig. 4.

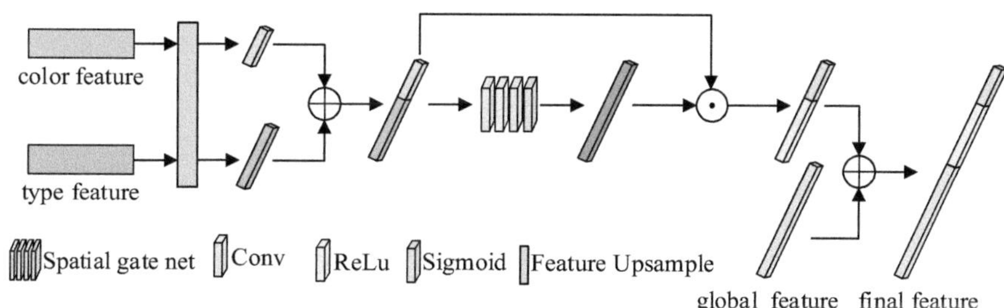

Fig. 4. The architecture of the SAGF network fuses the color feature, type feature, and global feature through a gating mechanism and attribute feature transformation layers.

Since the vehicle color feature $f_{color} \in R^{C_c \times 1 \times 1}$ and attribute feature $f_{type} \in R^{C_t \times 1 \times 1}$ have low spatial resolution and cannot be directly fused with the global feature, we first upsample the vehicle attribute features to the same spatial dimension as the global feature. The upsampling operation is performed through a 1×1 convolutional kernel for feature mapping, followed by bilinear interpolation to expand the feature to the target spatial size. The upsampled vehicle color feature and attribute feature are denoted as $f_{up\_color} \in R^{C_c \times h \times w}$ and $f_{up\_type} \in R^{C_t \times h \times w}$, respectively.

The spatial gating network takes the concatenated attribute features $f_{attr} \in R^{(C_c + C_t) \times h \times w}$ as input and generates spatial gating coefficients $G \in R^{N \times h \times w}$, where $N = 2$, representing the number of attribute features (color and type). The specific implementation is as follows:

$$f_{attr} = [f_{\text{up\_color}}, f_{up\_type}] \tag{2}$$

$$G = \sigma(conv2(\text{Re}LU(conv1(f_{attr})))) \tag{3}$$

Here, $conv1$ and $conv2$ represent different convolutional layers, and σ denotes the sigmoid activation function. The output gating tensor contains two spatial attention maps: the color gate G_c and the type gate G_t.

Next, we utilize the spatial gating to perform spatially weighted fusion of the attribute features, enhancing the response of relevant regions:

$$\widetilde{F_c} = f_{up\_color} \odot G_c \tag{4}$$

$$\widetilde{F_t} = f_{up\_type} \odot G_t \tag{5}$$

where $\odot$ is an element-wise product operation.

Finally, we concatenate the global feature with the gated color feature and type feature to form the final feature representation.

$$f_{\text{fuse}} = [f_g, \widetilde{F_c}, \widetilde{F_t}] \tag{6}$$

To further enhance the discriminative power and robustness of the features, we applied Generalized Mean Pooling to the fused feature f_{fuse}, drawing on relevant work in FastReID [24]. Generalized Mean Pooling adjusts the pooling operation through a learnable parameter p, which can flexibly emphasize or suppress different parts of the feature map, effectively handling subtle differences in vehicle appearance.

Loss Function

We employed the Label Smoothing Cross-Entropy Loss and the hard mining Triplet Loss as the optimization objectives for the model. The Label Smoothing Cross-Entropy Loss, by introducing a smoothing mechanism, effectively mitigates the overfitting issue that may arise during the training process with the traditional cross-entropy loss function and enhances the model's robustness to noisy data. The label smoothing hyperparameter ϵ as set to 0.1. The hard mining Triplet Loss, by selecting hard positive and negative samples, enhances the model's ability to distinguish between different vehicle identities in the feature space. The margin was set to 0.1.

4 Experiments

4.1 Vehicle Re-identification Datasets

The Veri-776 dataset [25] is a vehicle re-identification dataset collected from surveillance cameras in real traffic environments. It contains 51,035 images of 776 distinct vehicles, with the number of samples per vehicle ranging from 2 to 18. The training set of this dataset consists of 37,778 images from 576 vehicles, while the test set comprises 11,579 images from 200 vehicles. To evaluate the performance of models, the test set is further divided into a query set containing 1,678 images and a gallery set containing 11,579 images. Additionally, the Veri-776 dataset categorizes vehicle colors into 10 types (such as yellow, white, etc.) and vehicle types into 9 categories (such as SUV, MPV, etc.).

The VehicleID dataset [26] is a widely used vehicle re-identification dataset, containing 221,763 images of 26,267 vehicles, with only front and rear views included. The dataset provides three test subsets of different sizes: the small test subset consists of 6,493 images from 800 vehicles, the medium test subset comprises 13,377 images from

1,600 vehicles, and the large test subset contains 19,777 images from 2,400 vehicles. Additionally, the VehicleID dataset provides detailed annotations for vehicle colors and models. Vehicle colors are categorized into 7 types, such as black and blue, and vehicle models are divided into 250 models, including Audi Q5 and Mercedes-Benz S.

4.2 Implementation Details

Vehicle Detection

During the training process of the vehicle detection model, we initially attempted to train YOLO v11 using the KITTI [27] autonomous driving dataset and the SODA10M [28] vehicle detection dataset. However, the detection performance was not satisfactory. Upon in-depth analysis, we found that the KITTI and SODA10M datasets were collected through in-vehicle surveillance, whereas the vehicle re-identification datasets were captured by surveillance cameras. There are significant differences in visual features between the two, resulting in poor adaptability of the model to the vehicle re-identification datasets.

To improve this situation, we trained YOLO v11 using samples of the categories car, bus, and truck from the MS COCO dataset [29]. This improvement significantly enhanced the vehicle detection performance of the model on the VeRi-776 and VehicleID datasets. However, upon further analysis of the undetected vehicle samples in the two datasets, we found that the probability of detecting vehicles of the type truck was relatively low. After detailed analysis, we believe this may be due to the significant differences in the proportions of different vehicle types in the MS COCO dataset. In the MS COCO dataset, the proportion of cars is as high as 73.4%, while the proportions of buses and trucks are 10.8% and 15.8%, respectively.

To address this issue, we manually annotated the bounding boxes for some samples of the types bus and truck in the VeRi-776 dataset and combined these annotated samples with the samples of the categories car, truck, and bus from the MS COCO dataset to train YOLO v11. In this process, we do not aim to classify vehicles but focus solely on the vehicle detection task. Therefore, all labels are uniformly annotated as "Vehicle." It should be noted that the VeRi-776 dataset we used includes parts of the training and validation sets and is only used for the vehicle detection stage, not for the subsequent vehicle re-identification task, so there is no leakage of test set information.

Moreover, in the vehicle re-identification datasets, some sample images contain multiple vehicles, which contradicts the objective of the vehicle re-identification task. To address this issue, during vehicle detection, if multiple samples are detected in an image, we calculate the area ratio of each vehicle's bounding box in the image and retain only the vehicle with the largest area ratio as the detection target, as illustrated in Fig. 5.

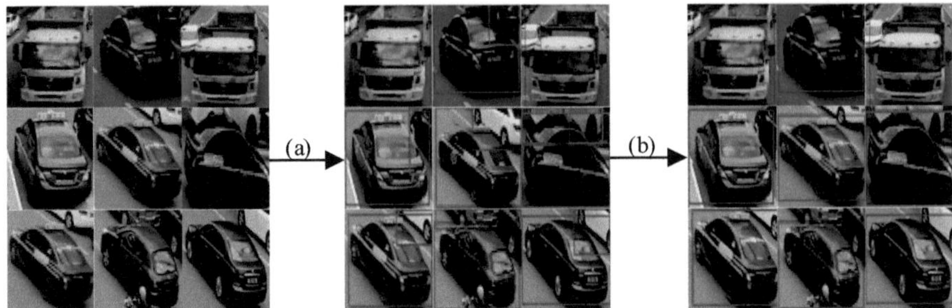

Fig. 5. Some samples in the dataset contain multiple vehicles, and these images are from the VeRi-776 dataset. (a) shows the results of YOLO v11 detecting multiple vehicles when the sample image contains more than one vehicle, and (b) illustrates the process of YOLO v11 selecting samples based on the largest box area ratio.

Attribute Classification

The color classifier employs a two-layer fully connected network, which includes batch normalization (BN) and a 30% Dropout rate. In the Veri-776 dataset, the number of color categories is 10, in the VehicleID dataset, the number of color categories is 7. During training, we conducted 30 epochs of training, employing the OneCycleLR scheduler to dynamically adjust the learning rate. The maximum learning rate was set to 2×10^{-4}, with the learning rate increase phase occupying 15% of the total training steps. The smoothing coefficient for the Label Smoothing Cross-Entropy Loss was set to 0.15.

The type classifier employs a linear classification layer for classification. In the Veri-776 dataset, the number of type categories is 9; in the VehicleID dataset, the number of model categories is 250. During the training of vehicle type classification, we used a two-stage training method to extract features. In the pre-training stage, we initialized the network with the pre-trained ResNet18 weights from ImageNet. To stabilize the training process and reduce the computational burden, we froze the first three blocks of ResNet18 and trained only the last block and the classification layer for 30 epochs. Subsequently, we unfroze the entire ResNet18 network and trained it for another 30 epochs. Additionally, we applied an early stopping mechanism during training to prevent overfitting of the model.

After training the vehicle color and type classifiers, we removed the classification layers and froze the remaining network layers to use them for extracting vehicle color and type features.

Vehicle Re-identification

In the process of vehicle re-identification, we do not directly use the attribute labels in the dataset. Instead, we use a pre-trained vehicle attribute feature extraction network to extract vehicle attribute features, which are then dynamically fused with the global vehicle features. With this approach, vehicle re-identification can be performed normally even if some samples in the dataset lack attribute labels. For the extraction of global features, we utilized ResNet50-IBN as the backbone network, initializing it with weights pre-trained on ImageNet. The input images were resized to 256×256 pixels. When constructing training batches, we referred to the PK sampling strategy mentioned in [23, 24], which samples based on the number of images per identity in each dataset. In the Veri-776 dataset, P = 6 and K = 8, resulting in batches of 48, meaning each batch consisted of images from 6 different identities, with 8 images sampled from each identity. On the VehicleID dataset, P = 32 and K = 4, resulting in batches of 128. The model was trained for 130 epochs on each dataset, using the Adam optimizer. During training, a hybrid learning rate scheduling strategy combining linear warmup and multi-step decay was employed. The learning rate was warmed up from 0.0 and linearly increased to 1×10^{-4} during the first 10 epochs, followed by a decay within a fixed number of epochs. All experiments were conducted on two NVIDIA TESLA V100S GPUs using the PyTorch deep learning framework.

4.3 Evaluation Metrics

We utilized mAP and Rank-n as evaluation metrics. mAP comprehensively considers the precision and recall of the algorithm, effectively measuring the overall performance of the model in retrieval tasks. mAP is calculated by averaging the precision over all query samples, thereby providing a comprehensive performance assessment. Rank-n denotes the probability of correctly matching the target vehicle within the top n positions of the similarity ranking list. Commonly used metrics include Rank-1 and Rank-5, which represent the probability of matching the target vehicle in the first image and within the first five images of the similarity ranking list, respectively.

4.4 Ablation Studies

Ablation Study of Key Steps

The ablation studies on key steps include the impact of cropping on vehicle color classification, the impact of cropping on vehicle type classification, and the impact of different training strategies for ResNet18 on vehicle type classification. The experimental results are shown in Fig. 6. Figure 6(a) illustrates the effect of cropping on the performance of vehicle color classification. The experimental results indicate that on the VeRi-776 dataset, the color classification accuracy increased from 91.26% to 92.95% after using the cropping operation. On the VehicleID dataset, the color classification accuracy increased from 93.02% to 94.21% after using the cropping operation. The single-stage training directly utilizes the pre-trained ResNet18 weights from ImageNet and trains with all parameters unfrozen. The two-stage training method involves initially training only the last block and the classification layer for 30 epochs, after which all parameters are unfrozen for further training. Figure 6(b) and (c) respectively show the impact of single-stage and two-stage training strategies on vehicle type classification performance. The experimental results demonstrate that on both datasets, the two-stage training strategy based on transfer learning achieved an average improvement of 1.3% in vehicle type recognition accuracy compared to the single-stage end-to-end training strategy. Additionally, the datasets using the cropping operation achieved an average improvement of 1.05% in vehicle type recognition accuracy compared to those without cropping.

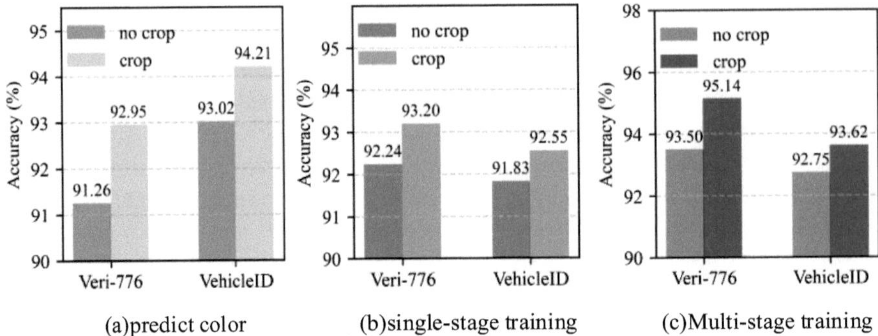

Fig. 6. Ablation study of key steps. (a) shows the impact of image cropping on the accuracy of vehicle color classification. (b) shows the impact of image cropping on the accuracy of type classification using single-stage training of ResNet18. (c) shows the impact of image cropping on the accuracy of type classification using two-stage training of ResNet18.

Ablation Studies on Feature Levels

We conducted comparative experiments on two different datasets to investigate the impact of different feature fusion strategies on vehicle re-identification performance. Specifically, we evaluated the effects of using global features alone, concatenating color features alone, concatenating type features alone, concatenating both color and type features, and ultimately fusing all three features using the SAGF module. The experimental results are shown in Table 1. The results indicate that concatenating color and type features with global features significantly improves model performance. Particularly, when the SAGF module is used to fuse all three features, the model achieves the best performance. Compared to using only the baseline network, the use of the SAGF module to fuse all three features resulted in an increase of 2.82% in mAP, and 0.54% in Rank-5 on the VeRi-776 dataset. On the VehicleID dataset, mAP increased by 1.24%, Rank-1 by 0.89%, and Rank-5 by 1.67%. Moreover, compared to simply concatenating the three features, the SAGF module also showed improvements in all metrics on both datasets, highlighting its crucial role in optimizing the feature fusion process.

Table 1. Ablation analysis of different fusion methods for two attribute features and global features. The absence of the SAGF module indicates the use of direct concatenation only. The VehicleID dataset uses the small validation set.

DateSet	global	color	type (model)	SAGF	mAP	Rank-1	Rank-5
Veri-776	√	×	×	×	81.15	96.96	97.63
	√	√	×	×	82.40	95.62	98.12
	√	×	√	×	82.87	95.35	97.87
	√	√	√	×	83.19	95.81	98.05
	√	√	√	√	83.97	97.01	98.17

(continued)

Table 1. *(continued)*

DateSet	global	color	type (model)	SAGF	mAP	Rank-1	Rank-5
VehicleID	√	×	×	×	89.18	94.82	96.29
	√	√	×	×	90.14	95.00	97.13
	√	×	√	×	89.92	95.23	97.27
	√	√	√	×	90.16	95.34	97.62
	√	√	√	√	90.42	95.71	97.96

4.5 Comparison with State-of-the-Art Methods

To comprehensively validate the effectiveness of our proposed vehicle re-identification algorithm, we conducted performance comparisons on two widely used datasets: Veri-776 and VehicleID. The comparison results are shown in Table 2.

In this performance comparison, we focused primarily on the performance of methods that integrate vehicle attribute features in the task of vehicle re-identification. As can be seen from Table 2, our baseline model has already achieved a high level of performance. On the Veri-776 dataset, DFA-Net's mAP increased by an average of 8.01%, Rank-1 by 1.12%, and Rank-5 by 0.45%. On the VehicleID (small) dataset, DFA-Net's mAP increased by an average of 9.93%, Rank-1 by 9.11%, and Rank-5 by 3.74%. These results indicate that DFA-Net excels in integrating vehicle attribute features, significantly enhancing the performance of vehicle re-identification. This further validates the effectiveness and superiority of our proposed method.

Table 2. Comparison with state-of-the-art on Veri-776 and VehicleID

Model	Veri-776			VehicleID (Small)		
	mAP	Rank-1	Rank-5	mAP	Rank-1	Rank-5
AIVR-Net [16]	64.9	87.6	–	61.9	83.7	–
Sun.et al. [17]	68.83	92.94	96.88	–	–	–
AGNet [18]	71.59	95.61	96.6	74.05	71.15	83.78
PATReId [19]	79.00	96.00	–	82.10	90.10	–
AttributeNet [20]	80.1	96.9	–	85.8	**95.9**	**99.0**
ASSEN [21]	81.7	97.3	**98.8**	–	86.0	**97.8**
VAT [30]	80.4	**97.5**	98.7	89.9	84.5	–
Baseline [23]	81.15	96.96	97.63	89.18	94.82	96.29
ours	**83.97**	97.01	98.17	**90.42**	95.71	97.96

5 Conclusions

In this work, we propose a vehicle re–identification method, DFA-Net, which aims to enhance the performance of vehicle re-identification by integrating global features with vehicle attribute features (color and type). Through a series of experiments, DFA-Net has achieved significant performance improvements on two widely used datasets, Veri-776 and VehicleID. In future work, we plan to further optimize this method in two directions: on the one hand, exploring the use of semantic segmentation techniques to precisely extract vehicle foreground information to reduce background interference and enhance feature discriminability; on the other hand, further introducing local features on the basis of integrating global and attribute features to enhance feature representation capabilities, thereby further improving the performance of vehicle re-identification.

Acknowledgments. This work was supported by the National Natural Science Foundation of China (No. 62362055), National Key Research and Development Program of China (No. 2023YFB2703900), Program for Young Talents of Science and Technology in Universities of Inner Mongolia Autonomous Region (No. NJYT22084, No. NJYT24035), Inner Mongolia Natural Science Foundation (No. 2023MS06008), Scientific research projects of universities directly under the Inner Mongolia Autonomous Region (No. JY20220061, No. JY20230119, No. JY20230019), Science and Technology Plan Project of Inner Mongolia (No. 2024SKYPT0012), Ordos Key R&D Program Projects (No. YF20232328).

References

1. Zapletal, D., Herout, A., et al.: Vehicle re-identification for automatic video traffic surveillance. In: 29th IEEE Conference on Computer Vision and Pattern Recognition (CVPR), pp. 1568–1574 (2016)
2. Liu, S., Huang, S., Xu, X., Lloret, J., Muhammad, K.: Efficient visual tracking based on fuzzy inference for intelligent transportation systems. IEEE Trans. Intell. Transp. Syst. **24**, 15795–15806 (2023)
3. Yar, H., Khan, Z.A., Ullah, F.U.M., Ullah, W., Baik, S.W.: A modified YOLOv5 architecture for efficient fire detection in smart cities. Expert Syst. Appl. **231** (2023)
4. Sun, C., Wang, Y., Deng, Y., Li, H., Zhou, R., Guo, J.: Efficient vehicle-infrastructure collaborative perception based on vehicle re-identification and mini-ICP algorithm. IEEE Trans. Intell. Transp. Syst. **25**, 6927–6937 (2024)
5. Zhang, X., Zhang, R., Cao, J., Gong, D., You, M., Shen, C.: Part-guided attention learning for vehicle instance retrieval. IEEE Trans. Intell. Transp. Syst. **23**, 3048–3060 (2022)
6. Liang, Y., Gao, Y., Shen, Z.Y.: Transformer vehicle re-identification of intelligent transportation system under carbon neutral target. Comput. Ind. Eng. **185** (2023)
7. Li, M., Huang, X., Zhang, Z., et al.: Self-supervised geometric features discovery via interpretable attention for vehicle re-identification and beyond. In: 18th IEEE/CVF International Conference on Computer Vision (ICCV), pp. 194–204 (2021)
8. Shen, F., Xie, Y., Zhu, J., Zhu, X., Zeng, H.: GiT: graph interactive transformer for vehicle re-identification. IEEE Trans. Image Process. **32**, 1039–1051 (2023)
9. Lee, S., Woo, T., Lee, S.H.: Multi-attention-based soft partition network for vehicle re-identification. J. Comput. Des. Eng. **10**, 488–502 (2023)

10. Sun, Y., Lu, J., Li, M., Ren, G., Ma, J.: Vehicle re-identification with a pose-aware discriminative part learning model. In: 7th Chinese Conference on Pattern Recognition and Computer Vision, pp. 251–265 (2024)
11. Zhang, X., Ling, Y.N., Li, K.G., Shi, W.M., Zhou, Z.: Multimodality adaptive transformer and mutual learning for unsupervised domain adaptation vehicle re-identification. IEEE Trans. Intell. Transp. Syst. **25**, 20215–20226 (2024)
12. Li, S., Sun, L., Li, Q.: CLIP-ReID: exploiting vision-language model for image re-identification without concrete text labels. In: 37th AAAI Conference on Artificial Intelligence (AAAI)/35th Conference on Innovative Applications of Artificial Intelligence/13th Symposium on Educational Advances in Artificial Intelligence, pp. 1405–1413 (2023)
13. Ding, L., et al.: Text-to-image vehicle re-identification: multi-scale multi-view cross-modal alignment network and a unified benchmark. IEEE Trans. Intell. Transp. Syst. **25**, 7673–7686 (2024)
14. Huang, Y., et al.: Dual domain multi-task model for vehicle re-identification. IEEE Trans. Intell. Transp. Syst. **23**, 2991–2999 (2022)
15. Tumrani, S., Deng, Z., Lin, H., Shao, J.: Partial attention and multi-attribute learning for vehicle re-identification. Pattern Recogn. Lett. **138**, 290–297 (2020)
16. Zhang, H., Kuang, Z., Cheng, L., Liu, Y., Ding, X., Huang, Y.: AIVR-Net: attribute-based invariant visual representation learning for vehicle re-identification. Knowl.-Based Syst. **289** (2024)
17. Sun, X.M., et al.: Vehicle re-identification method based on multi-attribute dense linking network combined with distance control module. Front. Neurorobot. **17** (2024)
18. Wang, H., Peng, J., Chen, D., Jiang, G., Zhao, T., Fu, X.: Attribute-guided feature learning network for vehicle reidentification. IEEE Multimedia **27**, 112–121 (2020)
19. Kishore, R., Aslam, N., Kolekar, M.H.: PATReId: pose apprise transformer network for vehicle re-identification. IEEE Trans. Emerg. Top. Comput. Intell. **8**, 3691–3702 (2024)
20. Quispe, R., Lan, C., Zeng, W., Pedrini, H.: AttributeNet: attribute enhanced vehicle re-identification. Neurocomputing **465**, 84–92 (2021)
21. Li, H., Li, C., Zheng, A., Tang, J., Luo, B.: Attribute and state guided structural embedding network for vehicle re-identification. IEEE Trans. Image Process. **31**, 5949–5962 (2022)
22. Khanam, R., Hussain, M.: YOLOv11: an overview of the key architectural enhancements. Arxiv, arXiv:2410.17725 (2024)
23. Almeida, E., Silva, B., Batista, J., et al.: Strength in diversity: multi-branch representation learning for vehicle re-identification. In: IEEE 26th International Conference on Intelligent Transportation Systems (ITSC), pp. 4690–4696 (2023)
24. He, L., et al.: FastReID: a Pytorch toolbox for general instance re-identification. In: 31st ACM International Conference on Multimedia (MM), pp. 9664–9667 (2023)
25. Liu, X.C., Liu, W., Mei, T., Ma, H.D.: PROVID: progressive and multimodal vehicle reidentification for large-scale urban surveillance. IEEE Trans. Multimedia **20**, 645–658 (2018)
26. Liu, H.Y., Tian, Y.H., Wang, Y.W., Pang, L., Huang, T.J.: Deep relative distance learning: tell the difference between similar vehicles. In: 2016 IEEE Conference on Computer Vision and Pattern Recognition (CVPR), pp. 2167–2175 (2016)
27. Geiger, A., Lenz, P., Urtasun, R.: Are we ready for autonomous driving? The KITTI vision benchmark suite. In: 2012 IEEE Conference on Computer Vision and Pattern Recognition, pp. 3354–3361 (2012)
28. Han, J., et al.: SODA10M: a large-scale 2D self/semi-supervised object detection dataset for autonomous driving. arXiv:2106.11118 (2021)
29. Lin, T.-Y., et al.: Microsoft COCO: common objects in context arXiv:1405.0312 (2014)
30. Yu, Z., Pei, J., Zhu, M., Zhang, J., Li, J.: Multi-attribute adaptive aggregation transformer for vehicle re-identification. Inf. Process. Manage. **59** (2022)

SOD-SRB: A General Super-Resolution Auxiliary Branch for Small Object Detection

Yao Dong[1,2], Huiying Xu[1,2(✉)], Xinzhong Zhu[1,2,3], Yang Liu[4], Yunzhong Si[1,2], Wenhao Zhang[1,2], and Hongbo Li[3]

[1] Zhejiang Key Laboratory of Intelligent Education Technology and Application, Zhejiang Normal University, Jinhua 321004, Zhejiang, China
{dongyao,xhy,zxz,siyunzhong,zwh2012918201}@zjnu.edu.cn

[2] School of Computer Science and Technology, Zhejiang Normal University, Jinhua 321004, Zhejiang, China

[3] Beijing Geekplus Technology Co., Ltd, Beijing, China
jason.li@geekplus.com

[4] School of Mathematical Sciences, Zhejiang Normal University, Jinhua 321004, Zhejiang, China
liuyang@zjnu.edu.cn

Abstract. The primary challenge in detecting small objects stems from their inherently limited size, necessitating strategies such as enlarging the size of input images or feature maps. In this regard, researchers often employ super-resolution (SR) techniques. While existing methods can partially address this issue, several bottlenecks remain: 1) It is challenging to mitigate the high computational overhead associated with high-resolution (HR) images or feature maps while enhancing detection performance. 2) There is a distinct separation between the SR network and the detection network in terms of architecture design. To overcome these, we first establish a design concept of an SR network tailored for small object detection (SOD) and propose the SR Auxiliary Branch for SOD (SOD-SRB) with bidirectional semantic information matching. We use ablation experiments to validate the rationality of our method. Comparative experimental results indicate that SOD-SRB outperforms the state-of-the-art (SOTA) SR auxiliary branch designed for SOD and can enhance the detection performance of baseline across various detectors on different small object datasets.

Keywords: SR Auxiliary Branch · Small Object Detection · Bidirectional Semantic Information Matching

1 Introduction

Currently, deep convolution neural networks (CNNs) have achieved significant advancements across various domains, particularly in object detection. However,

Y. Dong and H. Xu—These authors contributed equally to this work.

© The Author(s), under exclusive license to Springer Nature Singapore Pte Ltd. 2026
J. Kittler et al. (Eds.): PRCV 2025, LNCS 16289, pp. 76–91, 2026.
https://doi.org/10.1007/978-981-95-5764-6_6

challenges persist in SOD. To extract richer semantic information, CNN architectures are often designed with multiple stages. As the number of stages increases, the resolution of feature maps diminishes, which is detrimental to SOD. From a perspective of information bottleneck, the sparse nature of semantic information in small objects leads to a gradual loss of critical discriminative features as input images undergo abstraction and compression of multiple layers. This results in misjudgments during the high-level semantic reasoning phase of the model. To address this issue, researchers introduce the super-resolution technique.

It is observed that the representation of small objects in high-level networks is not as differentiated as that of large objects. Perceptual GAN [1] first introduces GAN in SOD to enhance the structural correlation between small and large objects. The discriminator of GAN [2] can help the generator generate realistic HR images, and adjust the representation of small objects by using realistic HR images, which can compensate for the mutual information between the high-level network and the input to a certain extent. Some subsequent studies [3–5] expand the application of GAN in SOD based on this idea. However, all the proposed models have complex training operations, and most even require additional training for the GAN. Although study [6] has proposed an architecture of end-to-end training, the generator in GAN contains a heavy SR network, and all the above studies have not dealt with the large computational overhead it brings.

To reduce the computational load of the SR network, some research adopts the idea of the auxiliary branch. Liu et al. proposed ESRTMDet [7], which jointly trains an SR network and an object detection network, removing the SR network during inference. However, their method includes an SR module embedded in the main branch, which increases the size of the feature map and multiplies the computational load of the subsequent network. Although SuperYOLO [8] also increases the size of feature maps and reduces the number of model stages, its SR method fully combines the auxiliary branch to address the issue of excessive computation of the SR network. However, the SR method of SuperYOLO is still flawed. Its SR target is not task-driven [9], meaning it may not effectively compensate for the information the input is intended to express. As a result, the mutual information between the high-level network and the output may not increase, thereby weakening the generalization ability of the network. Additionally, research [5] indicates that in feature-level SR, the low-resolution (LR) feature and the SR target differ too much in their relative receptive fields, which can greatly mislead the model. However, SuperYOLO overlooks this issue and uses the HR image directly as the SR target.

This paper introduces a simple and effective design for a general SR auxiliary branch. In this design, High-Resolution Feature Extractor (HFE) accurately extracts HR features as SR targets by aligning LR features based on semantic information, while Super-Resolution Feature Generator (SFG) employs Depthwise Separable Channel Extender (DCE) to convert LR features into SR features and preserve the information of the LR features. Since the role of the auxiliary branch is to guide the main branch in retaining effective information during forward propagation, SFG is less complex than traditional SR networks. It performs only channel information aggregation and upsampling for LR features, with the main branch responsible for adjusting the semantic information. Considering the specificity of the object detection task, critical information that significantly influences the output of the model is typically concentrated in the vicinity of the target region. In SR networks, pixel-wise loss functions are commonly employed. However, due to the relatively small number of pixels occupied by small objects in an image, their influence on the overall loss is diminished. Consequently, we introduce a weighting strategy to enhance the contribution of small objects. Furthermore, to mitigate the elevated training cost associated with the SR auxiliary branch, we propose a greedy training strategy. Under this strategy, the forward propagation and gradient return of the auxiliary branch are triggered solely when the loss of the main branch decreases. This method significantly reduces training time without compromising the accuracy of detection.

In summary, the contributions of this paper are as follows:

- For the first time, we establish a design concept of the SR network in SOD and propose SOD-SRB, which is comprehensively implemented using the auxiliary branch method. We provide a rigorous explanation and validation that SR targets must maintain high accuracy and that the integrity of LR features should be preserved during the SR process to make the semantic information align between the two networks.
- We introduce Small Object Weighting Loss (SOW Loss) to direct the focus of the network toward small objects.
- We propose a greedy training strategy to improve the training efficiency of the model incorporating SOD-SRB.

2 Related Work

We review two types of super-resolution techniques adopted in small object detection.

2.1 GAN

Li et al. first apply GAN [2] to SOD and propose Perceptual GAN [1]. This method enhances the feature representation of small objects by using the generator, making it more similar to that of large objects, which improves detection performance. Later, Bai et al. develop a multi-task GAN framework [3] and introduce an image-level SR module. This module generates HR object proposal regions, capturing more feature details of small objects, thus optimizing detection performance. Building on this, Bai's team proposes a model [10] for tiny face detection. The model uses the generator to restore high-resolution facial images, while the discriminator assesses both the authenticity of the image and the face category, offering new insights for SOD. Furthermore, Noh et al. introduce a novel method [5] based on feature-level SR. They directly supervise the

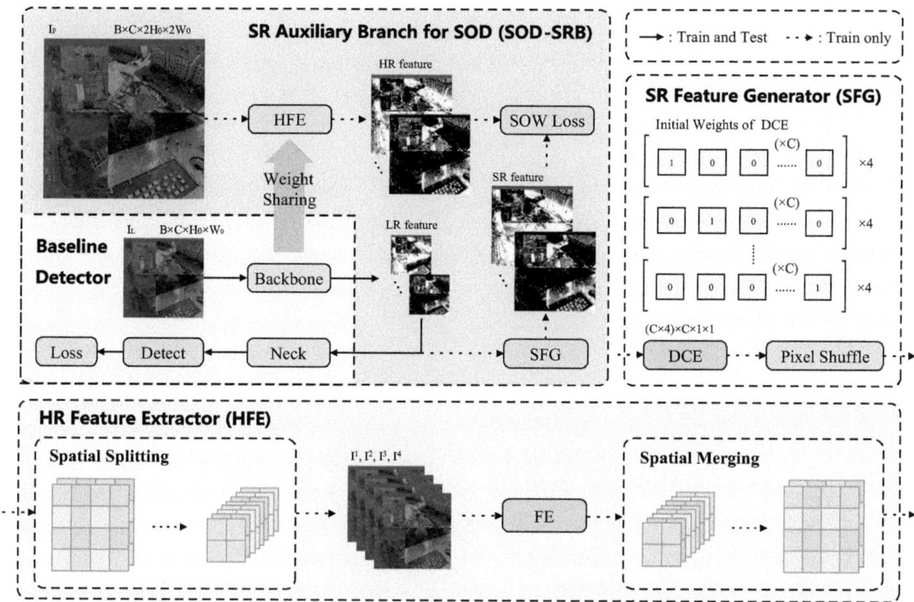

Fig. 1. Illustration of overall model architecture containing SOD-SRB. SOD-SRB can accept multiple layers of the backbone as input, each corresponding to a distinct group of features. Only one group is shown here for illustration purposes.

training of the super-resolution network using high-resolution features, which significantly improves the stability of model training. Numerous similar studies [11–13] suggest that GAN, as an SR technique, holds significant potential in enhancing the performance of the SOD model. However, the models that incorporate GANs typically involve more complex training processes, with substantial computational resource demands during both training and inference, resulting in less efficient models.

2.2 SR Auxiliary Branch

The existing researches [14,15] show that an SR network without GAN can also effectively assist the model in detecting small objects. These networks simplify the architecture significantly compared to GANs, but still face the bottleneck of high computational complexity. The current mainstream lightweight solutions primarily use auxiliary branch architectures to implement SR networks. In some researches [8,16–18], by integrating low-level detail features and high-level semantic features from the backbone network, a composite feature map is created for the SR network, with the original HR image as the SR target. This kind of method essentially continues the traditional SR technology paradigm, leading to a significant separation between the enhancement of features and the task of object detection. In contrast, the other method [7,19] constructs SR features for the feature maps of specific levels and uses the HR features of the corresponding layers as the optimization targets. By establishing a hierarchical feature mapping relationship, the cooperation between the SR network and the detection model is initially achieved. However, existing research still has clear limitations in key design aspects, lacks in-depth analysis of the SR network mechanism, and fails to establish a deep connection between an SR auxiliary branch and a detection model. In this paper, we abandon the traditional design concept of the SR network and tightly integrate the proposed SR auxiliary branch into the detection network from the perspective of bidirectional semantic information matching.

3 Method

The design of SOD-SRB is founded on three key principles: (1) SR targets are accurate; (2) SR features retain the information of LR features to the greatest extent possible; (3) The SR network focuses on small target regions. Due to the generalization of SOD-SRB, there are various options for selecting the main branch. Therefore, this paper does not provide an example of a baseline detector for discussion. Figure 1 shows the overall architecture of the model, including proposed HFE, SFG, and SOW Loss. Among them, the HR features$\{F_i\}_{i\in[1,m]}$, LR features$\{L_i\}_{i\in[1,m]}$ and SR features $\{S_i\}_{i\in[1,m]}$ each have m parts, corresponding m stages in the backbone.

3.1 HFE

The ideal model output closely aligns with the accurate target, and the key aspect of HFE design is ensuring the accuracy of the SR target. The following will be discussed from two perspectives.

On one hand, the relative receptive field (RRF) of SR targets must align with that of LR features. Otherwise, the information perceived by the same target in the original image may not correspond, and this mismatch becomes more noticeable as the size of an object decreases. This issue has been partially addressed by researchers [5], who proposed using dilated convolution instead of regular convolution. However, this method lacks rigorous calculations and merely enlarges the absolute receptive field (ARF) of the SR target to make the RRF of SR targets approximate the RRF of LR features. In HFE, I_F is divided into four spatially arranged copies, each having the same size as I_L, labeled as $\{I^1, I^2, I^3, I^4\}$. The spatial splitting f_{sp} is defined as

$$\begin{aligned} f_{sp}(x) = x[::2, ::2], x[1::2, ::2], \\ x[::2, 1::2], x[1::2, 1::2]. \end{aligned} \tag{1}$$

The four images are fed into the feature extractor (FE) that has the same structure as the backbone, resulting in $4m$ feature maps $\{\{F_i^1, F_i^2, F_i^3, F_i^4\}\}_{i\in[1,m]}$. Finally, these feature maps are merged into $\{F_i\}_{i\in[1,m]}$ using the inverse operation of spatial splitting, spatial merging f_{sm}. For simplicity, let's take stage 1 as an example. The regions of coordinate $\{(x, y) \mid a \leq x \leq b, c \leq y \leq d\}$

in $L_1, F_1^1, F_1^2, F_1^3, F_1^4$ are represented by $D_{L_1}, D_{F_1^1}, D_{F_1^2}, D_{F_1^3}, D_{F_1^4}$, respectively. Correspondingly, region D_{F_1} in F_1 equals $\{(\mathrm{x}, \mathrm{y}) \mid 2\mathrm{a} \leq \mathrm{x} \leq 2\mathrm{b}, 2\mathrm{c} \leq \mathrm{y} \leq 2\mathrm{d}\}$. Based on the information above, we can derive

$$I_F = f_{sm}\left(I^1, I^2, I^3, I^4\right), \tag{2}$$

$$F_1 = f_{sm}\left(F_1^1, F_1^2, F_1^3, F_1^4\right), \tag{3}$$

$$D_{F_1} = f_{sm}\left(D_{F_1^1}, D_{F_1^2}, D_{F_1^3}, D_{F_1^4}\right). \tag{4}$$

Since L_1, F_1^1, F_1^2, F_1^3, F_1^4 are obtained through networks with the same structure, the ARF of D_{L_1}, $D_{F_1^1}$, $D_{F_1^2}$, $D_{F_1^3}$, $D_{F_1^4}$ are identical, as are the relative positions of their perceived regions. Then the ARF of F_1 can be calculated as

$$\begin{aligned} ARF_{D_{F_1}} &= \mathrm{Area}\left(f_D\left(D_{F_1}\right)\right) \\ &= \mathrm{Area}\left(f_{sm}\left(f_D\left(D_{F_1^1}\right), ..., f_D\left(D_{F_1^4}\right)\right)\right) \\ &= \sum_{i=1}^{4} ARF_{D_{F_1^i}} = \sum_{i=1}^{4} ARF_{D_{L_1}} = 4\, ARF_{D_{L_1}}, \end{aligned} \tag{5}$$

where f_D is a function to calculate the region of the receptive field. The RRF ratio between F_1 and L_1 can be calculated as

$$\frac{RRF_{D_{F_1}}}{RRF_{D_{L_1}}} = \frac{ARF_{D_{F_1}} / \left(2H_0 * 2W_0\right)}{ARF_{D_{L_1}} / \left(H_0 * W_0\right)} = 1. \tag{6}$$

On the other hand, SR targets must be supervised by the downstream task. The SR target functions to correct LR features using its richer information, compensating for lost mutual information during forward propagation between the network and the output. Without supervision, there is no guarantee that the information carried by SR targets fulfills the requirements of the task. Therefore, we share the weights of the backbone with FE, ensuring that their weights remain the same across each forward propagation. At this stage, we achieve the alignment of semantic information between SR targets and LR features. Notably, designed in this way, HFE can be easily applied to different models with minimal code modifications during migration.

3.2 SFG

The scales of SR targets are twice that of LR features, so LR features need to be upsampled by a factor of two. Since SFG is removed during inference, it should not be designed like a traditional SR network. Unlike traditional SR networks, the goal of SFG is not to reconstruct LR features to resemble SR targets. Instead, it aims to transmit information about SR targets to the main branch. SFG serves as an intermediary and should minimize the disruption to LR features. Therefore, we propose DCE to increase the dimensionality while ensuring the integrity of the information of LR features.

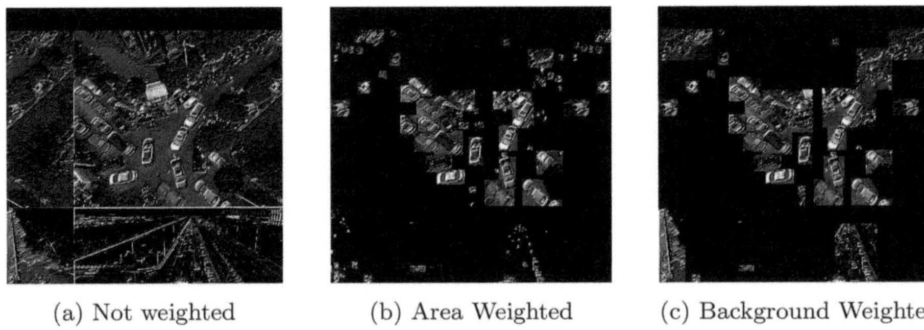

(a) Not weighted (b) Area Weighted (c) Background Weighted

Fig. 2. Visualization of weight matrix on the feature maps.

Taking $L_1 \in \mathcal{R}^{C_1 \times H_1 \times W_1}$ as an example, we treat each channel as an independent unit to preserve the invariance of the spatial structure, which allows us to represent L_1 as $\{L_1^i\}_{i \in [1, C_1]}$. We then perform a linear transformation to aggregate and extend the dimension of L_1, resulting in $L_1' \in \mathcal{R}^{4C_1 \times H_1 \times W_1}$ which is defined as

$$L_1' = \left\{ \sum_{i=1}^{C_1} a_{ij} L_1^i \right\}_{j \in [1, 4C_1]}, \tag{7}$$

where $a_{ij} \in \mathcal{R}$ is a learnable parameter. Each channel of a feature map emphasizes different information, and channel aggregation allows for comprehensive utilization of existing data, ensuring that S_1 minimizes redundancy and preserves as much information of L_1 as possible. Next, L_1' is divided into four groups, each with a length of C_1 along the channel. These groups are then combined spatially to achieve $2\times$ upsampling.

However, our upsampling method is still unstable at this stage, as the meaning of the information in the space dimension of S_1 at the initial state is unclear. This means that the information emphasis of S_1 does not align with that of L_1 on the same channel, or that the information of S_1 may lack emphasis. This can mislead the training of the SR network, undermining its foundation. Therefore, we fixed the initial value of a_{ij}, ensuring that L_1' in the initial state is equal to four instances of L_1 concatenated on the channel. In this case, S_1 can be viewed as the result of nearest neighbor interpolation of L_1. By guiding with accurate F_1, the semantic information of S_1 will consistently align with L_1. To enable SFG to generate S_1 with more detailed and F_1-aligned features, L_1 will be driven to retain more fine-grained features (Fig. 2).

3.3 SOW Loss

To enhance the fine-grained features retained by L_1, with a focus on improving the representation of small objects, we propose a weighting strategy in the loss function of the SR network based on three key characteristics of small objects. The weight matrix is visualized in Fig. 3.

First, small objects occupy a small area in the image, leaving most areas of the image ineffective for detection models. Since the pixel-wise loss treats each pixel equally, areas with little useful information dominate the LR features because of their larger area. To address this, we define the weight matrix $W_{\mathrm{so}} \in \mathcal{R}^{H \times W}$ to help the network focus on the target region. Let $w^{ij} \in \mathcal{R}$ represent the pixel value of W_{so} at position (i,j). The weight matrix is preliminarily defined as

$$w^{ij} = \begin{cases} 1, (i,j) \in \bigcup_n^N bbox_n \\ 0, \text{ other} \end{cases}, \tag{8}$$

where $bbox_n$ represents the region of the nth truth box, with a total of N boxes.

In real-world scenarios, the scales of different objects often vary significantly, and the same kind of object can also exhibit noticeable changes in scale depending on the distance. To balance the importance of objects at different scales, smaller objects should be assigned higher weights. Therefore, we establish a threshold that defines the boundaries of small objects.

$$threshold = 32 \times \frac{\sqrt{H \times W}}{640}. \tag{9}$$

This means that 32 pixels are divided by the downsampling multiples. Next, we define $bbox(i,j)$ to represent the region of the truth box that the point (i,j) belongs to, and calculate the weight of the region of the truth box as

$$f_w(i,j) = e^{-\frac{\sqrt{\text{Area }(bbox(i,j))}}{threshold}} + 1. \tag{10}$$

Considering that small objects will be concentrated in some special areas, which are more significant than general backgrounds and can be used to supplement the contextual information of the small objects. To identify these areas, we apply a clustering algorithm to group all the truth boxes. Specifically, we apply DBSCAN [20] to treat the center point of each truth box as a core point and define the domain scope as

$$\varepsilon = 38 \times \frac{\sqrt{H \times W}}{640}. \tag{11}$$

The core points and their neighboring points are grouped into clusters, resulting in N clusters. Then, the special region can be defined as

$$background = \bigcup_n^N \mathrm{MBR}\left(c_n, bbox_n\right) - \bigcup_n^N bbox_n, \tag{12}$$

where c_n represents the region of the nth cluster, and MBR is the calculation of the minimum bounding rectangle. Finally, we define the weight matrix as

$$w^{ij} = \begin{cases} f_w(i,j), (i,j) \in \bigcup_n^N bbox_n \\ 1, (i,j) \in background \\ 0, \text{ other} \end{cases}. \tag{13}$$

Similar to traditional SR networks, we incorporate the pixel-wise loss into our SOW Loss, which is designed based on the Mean Squared Error (MSE) [21] and is defined as

$$L_{\text{SOW}} = \sum_{i=1}^{m} \text{MSE}\left(S_i * W_{so_i}, F_i * W_{so_i}\right). \tag{14}$$

The total loss for the model is defined as

$$L_{\text{model}} = \alpha L_{\text{SOW}} + L_{\text{main}} , \tag{15}$$

where α is a constant coefficient, set to 0.1 in this paper, and L_{main} represents the loss of the main branch.

3.4 Training

We train both the main branch and the auxiliary branch simultaneously. The auxiliary branch contains large-sized feature maps, which lead to low calculation efficiency and significantly increase training time. To address this issue, we propose a greedy training strategy. Taking into account the unique aspects of HFE design, the better the performance of the model during training, the higher the quality of the SR targets. Naturally, we introduce the greedy strategy, enabling the auxiliary branch only when the performance of the model improves. However, it is not recommended to verify the model after each backpropagation. Considering that generally, a lower loss in the detection part of L_{main} indicates better detection performance. We use the detection loss, L_{det}, instead of mAP and other evaluation metrics to assess the performance of the model. Finally, after the current batch completes the forward propagation of the main branch, if L_{det} is lower than that of the previous batch, or if the current batch is the first one, we forward propagate the auxiliary branch and include L_{SOW} in the total loss of the model.

4 Experiments

In this section, we perform extensive experiments on SOD-SRB across multiple models. All experiments are conducted on a single NVIDIA GeForce RTX 3090 GPU, with the hyperparameters following the default configuration of the baseline. Unless otherwise specified, the model is trained from scratch for 300 epochs with a batch size of 16, while the input image sizes for the main and auxiliary branches are set to 640×640 and 1280×1280, respectively, with the LR feature layers configured as the first three downsampling layers of the main branch for each experiment.

4.1 Datasets

We use four small object datasets for verification, namely VisDrone2019 [22], Tsinghua-Tencent (TT) 100K 2021 [23], AI-TOD [24], and VEDAI [25]. The training sets of these datasets contain 6,417, 6,105, 11,214, and 1,089 images, while the verification sets contain 548, 3,065, 2,804, and 121 images, respectively.

Table 1. Influence of accuracy of the SR targets on model performance on VisDrone2019 validation set.

Method	mAP_{50} (%)	mAP (%)
DRRF mismatch	33.1	19.3
Not task-driven	33.8	19.7
Ours	**34.4**	**20.1**

Table 2. Influence of the design concept of SFG on model performance on VisDrone2019 validation set.

Method	mAP_{50} (%)	mAP (%)
EDSR	34.1	19.7
No initialization	33.6	19.7
Ours	**34.4**	**20.1**

Table 3. Influence of different weighting methods on model performance on VisDrone2019 validation set. "Fixed-n" means the fixed weight for the target region is set to n, while the weight for other regions is 0. "Only background" indicates that both the target and background regions are weighted to 1.

Method	mAP_{50} (%)	mAP (%)
Not weighted	34.1	19.8
Fixed-1	34.0	19.8
Fixed-1.5	33.9	19.7
Fixed -2	34.0	19.7
Only area	34.1	19.8
Only background	34.1	20.0
Area and background	**34.4**	**20.1**

Table 4. Comparison between different pixel-wise loss functions on VisDrone2019 verification set.

Method	mAP_{50} (%)	mAP (%)
L1	33.8	19.6
L2	34.1	19.8
SOW Loss	**34.4**	**20.1**

4.2 Ablation Study

We use YOLOv8n [32] as the baseline detector to assess the impact of each component of SOD-SRB by adding and removing design elements on VisDrone2019.

HFE. We test two factors that affect the accuracy of SR targets in Table 1. For DRRF mismatches, we remove Spatial Splitting and directly feed HR images into FE. For SR targets that are not task-driven, we make FE and the backbone no longer share weights. The experimental results show that both of them mislead model training and that ensuring the accuracy of the SR targets can effectively improve the detection accuracy of the model.

SFG. SFG transforms the traditional design of the SR method by shifting the focus from increasing the similarity of SR features restoration to ensuring the integrity of LR feature information transmission. As shown in Table 2, we validate the rationality of this transformation by introducing EDSR [26]. Additionally, as observed, the spatial information alignment initialization of the parameters of DCE can significantly enhance the robustness and accuracy of the model.

Table 5. Influence of greedy training strategy on model performance on VisDrone2019 verification set. Training time includes the time for verification after each epoch of training.

Method	mAP_{50} (%)	mAP (%)	Training time/h
w.o.	34.2	19.8	28.7
Greedy training	**34.4**	**20.1**	**15.8**

Table 6. Comparison with SR auxiliary branch of SuperYOLO on VEDAI verification set. "SR" refers to the SR auxiliary branch of SuperYOLO.

Method	mAP_{50} (%)
SuperYOLO-SR	79.2
SuperYOLO	79.6
SuperYOLO-SR+ours	**80.6**

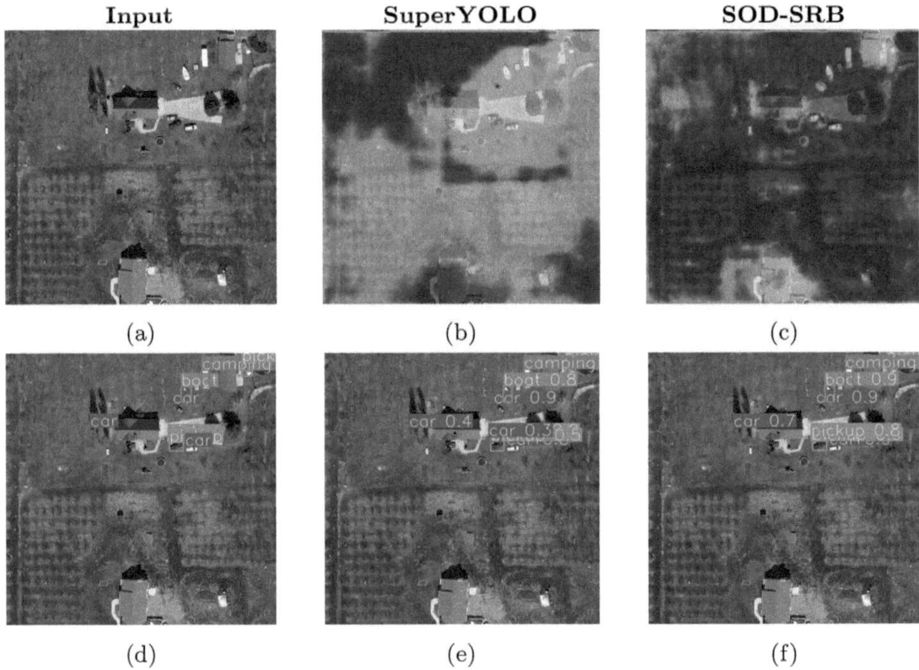

Fig. 3. Visual results on SuperYOLO. (a) Input. (d) Ground truth. (b) and (c) are attention visualizations generated using Grad-CAM [36] for 'layer 4,8' on SuperYOLO and SuperYOLO with SOD-SRB. (e) and (f) are detection results on SuperYOLO and SuperYOLO with SOD-SRB.

SOW Loss. Table 3 shows that fixed weighting slightly decreases accuracy because context information helps supplement the limited features of small objects, thereby improving their representation ability. Emphasizing only the target region while ignoring other areas is too extreme. The accuracy of the model with area weighting is improved, demonstrating the effectiveness of area weighting. Background weighting further improves accuracy, highlighting the importance of context information and the effectiveness of background weighting.

Table 7. Comparison of different detectors with their own applying SOD-SRB on three SOD datasets. "SR" refers to SOD-SRB.

Method	VisDrone2019		TT 100K 2021		AI-TOD	
	mAP_{50} (%)	mAP (%)	mAP_{50} (%)	mAP (%)	mAP_{50} (%)	mAP (%)
YOLOv5s	32.5	17.6	93.8	67.9	47.0	18.2
YOLOv5s+SR	**33.3**	**18.0**	**94.5**	**69.0**	**47.6**	**19.1**
YOLOv7n	35.7	18.2	91.4	63.0	15.0	5.3
YOLOv7n+SR	**36.7**	**18.8**	**93.8**	**66.2**	**18.7**	**6.7**
YOLOv8n	33.0	19.0	92.8	67.6	36.1	15.6
YOLOv8n+SR	**34.4**	**20.1**	**93.3**	**68.6**	**38.0**	**16.6**
RetinaNet	10.2	6.0	65.3	36.0	**10.5**	3.3
RetinaNet+SR	10.2	**6.1**	**65.7**	**36.7**	10.4	**3.4**
Faster R-CNN	20.4	12.3	52.7	38.1	11.2	4.9
Faster R-CNN+SR	**20.8**	**12.6**	**54.5**	**39.0**	**11.8**	**5.2**
YOLOv12n	32.9	19.3	92.2	67.4	33.8	14.5
YOLOv12n+SR	**34.0**	**19.7**	**92.4**	**67.6**	**34.3**	**15.0**
RemDet-tiny	37.0	21.9	92.9	67.7	36.0	15.1
RemDet-tiny+SR	**38.0**	**22.5**	**93.1**	**67.9**	**37.3**	**15.3**
YOLOv13n	32.5	18.9	-	-	-	-
YOLOv13n+SR	**32.9**	**19.1**	-	-	-	-

It is noted that the accuracy of the area-weighted and unweighted models is the same, challenging to demonstrate the role of prominent target features in detecting small objects. Therefore, we conduct the "Only background" experiment to verify this. Additionally, the results in Table 4 show that SOW Loss is more effective as a loss function for an SR network in SOD.

Greedy Training Strategy. In Table 5, we compare the influence of using or not using a greedy training strategy on training efficiency. The results show that if the SR network discards parts of the batch with reduced detection effect during training, the model can reduce the training time by approximately 45% while maintaining the original detection accuracy.

4.3 Comparisons of Different Models

Comparison with SOTA SR Auxiliary Branch for SOD. Table 6 compares the SOTA SR auxiliary branch for SOD, which is the SR auxiliary branch of SuperYOLO. We select VEDAI, the dataset used in the ablation experiment of SuperYOLO and set the LR feature layer to layers 4 and 8 consistent with SuperYOLO, using default configurations of SuperYOLO for all settings. The results show that SOD-SRB outperforms SuperYOLO by 1% in mAP_{50}, establishing it as the new SOTA SR auxiliary branch. As shown in Fig. 3, SuperYOLO can focus more on small objects with the assistance of SOD-SRB.

Comparison on Different Baseline Detectors. To validate the general applicability of SOD-SRB, we perform experiments using 6 baseline detectors. Among them, Faster R-CNN [27], RetinaNet [28] are implemented on MMDetection3.3.0 [29], using ResNet50 and FPN, with pre-trained weights and a "1×" schedule for fine-tuning over 12 epochs. For Faster R-CNN, we modify the batch size to 4. Given the suboptimal detection performance of RetinaNet under its default configuration, we adjust the learning rate to 0.0025 and the batch size to 2 for RetinaNet. The remaining experiments are conducted using the official codebases of the models.

Table 7 summarizes the experimental results. SOD-SRB positively impacts the baseline detector across three small object datasets with varying characteristics. Specifically, SOD-SRB achieves a maximum mAP increase of 1.1%, 3.2%, 1%, and 0.7% for the classic one-stage detectors YOLOv5s [30], YOLOv7n [31], YOLOv8n, and RetinaNet, respectively. Notably, our SR auxiliary branch is also applicable to two-stage detectors, yielding a maximum 0.9% mAP increase for Faster R-CNN. Additionally, we conducted experiments on current advanced detectors and SOD-SRB still improves the detection accuracy for YOLOv12n [34], RemDet-tiny [33] and YOLOv13n [35]. It should be emphasized again that all components of our SR method are removed during inference, meaning that the number of parameters and computations remains the same as the baseline in every experiment. The experiments demonstrate the wide applicability and reliable practicality of SOD-SRB.

5 Conclusion

This paper elaborates on the design concept of an SR network in small object detection for the first time and proposes SOD-SRB, a general SR auxiliary branch. Specifically, we propose HFE to extract accurate SR targets that match LR features in semantic information. Additionally, we introduce SFG, which employs a depthwise separable aggregation and extension method with initial spatial alignment for upsampling while protecting the integrity of the information of the LR features. In the loss function, we highlight features of small objects and filter the context information. Finally, we introduce a greedy training strategy that improves training efficiency. In terms of performance, SOD-SRB outperforms the current state-of-the-art SR auxiliary branch. Regarding generalization, the SOD-SRB can be applied to both one-stage and two-stage detectors and enhance the performance of advanced object detectors. We hope this study offers new insights into the application of super-resolution technology for small object detection.

References

1. Li, J., Liang, X., Wei, Y., Xu, T., Feng, J., Yan, S.: Perceptual generative adversarial networks for small object detection. In: Proceedings of IEEE Conference on Computer Vision and Pattern Recognition, pp. 1951–1959 (2017). https://doi.org/10.1109/CVPR.2017.211
2. Goodfellow, I.J., et al.: Generative adversarial nets. In: Advances in Neural Information Processing Systems, vol. 27, pp. 2672–2680 (2014)
3. Bai, Y., Zhang, Y., Ding, M., Ghanem, B.: SOD-MTGAN: small object detection via multi-task generative adversarial network. In: Ferrari, V., Hebert, M., Sminchisescu, C., Weiss, Y. (eds.) ECCV 2018. LNCS, vol. 11217, pp. 210–226. Springer, Cham (2018). https://doi.org/10.1007/978-3-030-01261-8_13
4. Pang, Y., Cao, J., Wang, J., Han, J.: JCS-net: joint classification and super-resolution network for small-scale pedestrian detection. IEEE Trans. Inf. Forensics Secur. **14**(12), 3322–3331 (2019). https://doi.org/10.1109/TIFS.2019.2916592
5. Noh, J., Bae, W., Lee, W., Seo, J., Kim, G.: Better to follow, follow to be better: towards precise supervision of feature super-resolution. In: Proceedings of IEEE International Conference on Computer Vision, pp. 9724–9733 (2019). https://doi.org/10.1109/ICCV.2019.00982
6. Rabbi, J., Ray, N., Schubert, M., Chowdhury, S., Chao, D.: Small-object detection in remote sensing images with end-to-end edge-enhanced GAN. Remote Sens. **12**(9), 1432 (2020). https://doi.org/10.3390/rs12091432
7. Liu, F., et al.: ESRTMDet: an end-to-end super-resolution enhanced real-time rotated object detector. IEEE J. Sel. Top. Appl. Earth Obs. Remote Sens. **16**, 4983–4998 (2023). https://doi.org/10.1109/JSTARS.2023.3278295
8. Zhang, J., Lei, J., Xie, W., Fang, Z., Li, Y., Du, Q.: SuperYOLO: super resolution assisted object detection. IEEE Trans. Geosci. Remote Sens. **61**, 5605415 (2023). https://doi.org/10.1109/TGRS.2023.3258666
9. Haris, M., Shakhnarovich, G., Ukita, N.: Task-driven super resolution: object detection in low-resolution images. arXiv:1803.11316 (2018)
10. Bai, Y., Zhang, Y., Ding, M., Ghanem, B.: Finding tiny faces in the wild with generative adversarial network. In: Proceedings of IEEE Conference on Computer Vision and Pattern Recognition, pp. 21–30 (2018). https://doi.org/10.1109/CVPR.2018.00010
11. Wang, H., Wang, J., Bai, K., Sun, Y.: Centered multi-task generative adversarial network for small object detection. Sensors **21**(15), 5194 (2021). https://doi.org/10.3390/s21155194
12. Ren, K., Gao, Y., Wan, M., Gu, G., Chen, Q.: Infrared small target detection via region super resolution generative adversarial network. Appl. Intell. **52**(10), 11725–11737 (2022). https://doi.org/10.1007/s10489-021-02955-6
13. Courtrai, L., Pham, M.T., Lefevre, S.: Small object detection in remote sensing images based on super-resolution with auxiliary GANs. Remote Sens. **12**(19), 3152 (2020). https://doi.org/10.3390/rs12193152
14. Hu, L., Hu, L., Chen, M.: Edge-enhanced infrared image super-resolution reconstruction model under transformer. Sci. Rep. **14**, 15585 (2024). https://doi.org/10.1038/s41598-024-66302-8
15. Zou, H., et al.: Rescaling-assisted super-resolution for medium-low resolution remote sensing ship detection. Remote Sens. **14**(11), 2566 (2022). https://doi.org/10.3390/rs14112566

16. Berardini, D., Migliorelli, L., Galdelli, A., Marin-Jimenez, M.J.: Edge artificial intelligence and super-resolution for enhanced weapon detection. Eng. Appl. Artif. Intell. **140**, 109684 (2025). https://doi.org/10.1016/j.engappai.2024.109684
17. Nan, G., Zhao, Y., Fu, L., Ye, Q.: Object detection by channel and spatial exchange for multimodal remote sensing imagery. IEEE J. Sel. Top. Appl. Earth Obs. Remote Sens. **17**, 8581–8593 (2024). https://doi.org/10.1109/JSTARS.2024.3388013
18. Baldini, C., et al.: Improving real-time detection of laryngeal lesions using super-resolution enhanced YOLO. Comput. Methods Programs Biomed. **260**, 108539 (2025). https://doi.org/10.1016/j.cmpb.2024.108539
19. Liu, J., Zhang, J., Ni, Y., Chi, W., Qi, Z.: Small-object detection in remote sensing images with super-resolution perception. IEEE J. Sel. Top. Appl. Earth Obs. Remote Sens. **17**, 15721–15734 (2024). https://doi.org/10.1109/JSTARS.2024.3452707
20. Ester, M., Kriegel, H.P., Sander, J., Xu, X.: A density-based algorithm for discovering clusters in large spatial databases with noise. In: Proceedings of International Conference on Knowledge Discovery and Data Mining, pp. 226–231 (1996)
21. Zhao, H., Gallo, O., Frosio, I., Kautz, J.: Loss functions for image restoration with neural networks. IEEE Trans. Comput. Imaging **3**(1), 47–57 (2017). https://doi.org/10.1109/TCI.2016.2644865
22. Zhu, P., et al.: Detection and tracking meet drones challenge. IEEE Trans. Pattern Anal. Mach. Intell. **44**(11), 7380–7399 (2021)
23. Zhu, Z., Liang, D., Zhang, S., Huang, X., Li, B., Hu, S.: Traffic-sign detection and classification in the wild. In: Proceedings of IEEE Conference on Computer Vision and Pattern Recognition (2016)
24. Wang, J., Yang, W., Guo, H., Zhang, R., Xia, G.S.: Tiny object detection in aerial images. In: Proceedings of International Conference on Pattern Recognition, pp. 3791–3798 (2021)
25. Razakarivony, S., Jurie, F.: Vehicle detection in aerial imagery: a small target detection benchmark. J. Vis. Commun. Image Represent. **34**, 187–203 (2016). https://doi.org/10.1016/j.jvcir.2015.11.002
26. Lim, B., Son, S., Kim, H., Nah, S., Lee, K.M.: Enhanced deep residual networks for single image super-resolution. In: Proceedings of IEEE Conference on Computer Vision and Pattern Recognition Workshop, pp. 1132–1140 (2017). https://doi.org/10.1109/CVPRW.2017.151
27. Ren, S., He, K., Girshick, R., Sun, J.: Faster R-CNN: towards real-time object detection with region proposal networks. In: Advances in Neural Information Processing Systems, vol. 28, pp. 91–99 (2015)
28. Lin, T.Y., Goyal, P., Girshick, R., He, K., Dollar, P.: Focal loss for dense object detection. IEEE Trans. Pattern Anal. Mach. Intell. **42**(2), 318–327 (2020). https://doi.org/10.1109/TPAMI.2018.2858826
29. Chen, K., et al.: MMDetection: open MMLab detection toolbox and benchmark. arXiv:1906.07155 (2019)
30. Jocher, G.: Ultralytics YOLOv5 (2020). https://github.com/ultralytics/yolov5
31. Wang, C.Y., Bochkovskiy, A., Liao, H.Y.M.: YOLOv7: trainable bag-of-freebies sets new state-of-the-art for real-time object detectors. In: Proceedings of IEEE Conference on Computer Vision and Pattern Recognition, pp. 7464–7475 (2023). https://doi.org/10.1109/CVPR52729.2023.00721
32. Jocher, G.: Ultralytics YOLOv8 (2023). https://github.com/ultralytics/ultralytics
33. Li, C., Zhao, R., Wang, Z., Xu, H., Zhu, X.: RemDet: rethinking efficient model design for UAV object detection. arXiv:2412.10040 (2024)

34. Tian, Y., Ye, Q., Doermann, D.: YOLOv12: attention-centric real-time object detectors. arXiv:2502.12524 (2025)
35. Lei, M., Li, S., Wu, Y., et al.: YOLOv13: real-time object detection with hypergraph-enhanced adaptive visual perception. arXiv:2506.17733 (2025)
36. Selvaraju, R.R., Cogswell, M., Das, A., Vedantam, R., Parikh, D., Batra, D.: Grad-CAM: visual explanations from deep networks via gradient-based localization. In: Proceedings of the IEEE International Conference on Computer Vision, pp. 618–626 (2017)

Road Disease Detection Algorithm Based on Multiscale Feature Fusion and Receptive Field Enhancement

Zhihao Xue[1], Zunwang Ke[1], Gang Wang[2(✉)], Shijie Xu[1], Yugui Zhang[3], Menghui Shen[1], and Zhiyu Wu[1]

[1] College of Software, Xinjiang University, Urumqi 830046, China
[2] School of Computing and Data Engineering, NingboTech University, Ningbo 315100, Zhejiang, China
wanggangnit@nit.zju.edu.cn
[3] Institute of Semiconductors, Chinese Academy of Sciences, Beijing 100083, China

Abstract. The precise detection of road diseases, which is the core of modern road maintenance, is of great Significance for ensuring the safe operation of road infrastructure. However, existing algorithms have problems such as inaccurate positioning, missed detection, and false detection in scenarios such as low-contrast textures, small-sized defects, and complex background interference. To address the aforementioned problems, this study proposes a road disease detection algorithm, ECD-YOLO, which is based on multiscale feature fusion and an extended receptive field. First, the multiscale feature fusion module (EMSC) is employed to fully integrate features of different scales, thereby enhancing the perception of texture features. Second, a compound receptive field enhancement module (CRFB) is introduced to expand the perception of context information through dilated convolution and enhance the recognition ability of small targets. Finally, by utilizing the Dynamic Task Collaborative Detection Head (DTAD), task decomposition alignment is achieved through shared convolution and dynamic feature selection, thereby effectively reducing the impact of complex backgrounds on detection accuracy. Tests were conducted on the RDD2022, MEdDatasetV4, and vq840 datasets. The experimental results show that the algorithm proposed in this study improves the mAP metric by 2.5%, 1.8%, and 1.4% compared to the benchmark model. The results show that the proposed algorithm has significant advantages for road disease detection.

Keywords: Road Disease Detection · Object Detection · Multi-scale Feature Fusion · Enhancement of the Receptive Field

1 Introductory

Roads are a vital form of infrastructure closely tied to the national economy and the well-being of people's livelihoods. With the expansion of the road network,

© The Author(s), under exclusive license to Springer Nature Singapore Pte Ltd. 2026
J. Kittler et al. (Eds.): PRCV 2025, LNCS 16289, pp. 92–106, 2026.
https://doi.org/10.1007/978-981-95-5764-6_7

the task of road maintenance has become increasingly arduous. Road surface diseases not only affect driving comfort and service life but also pose a threat to driving safety. Timely detection of diseases and assessment of road conditions are of great Significance for road maintenance management and extension of service life [1].

Currently, pavement disease detection methods are primarily categorized into two types: traditional methods and methods based on deep learning. Traditional methods rely on manual detection or image segmentation techniques, such as multi-image multi-resolution detection, multi-feature manifold learning, and matrix factorization methods, as well as region-growing feature methods. However, these methods have obvious limitations in complex road conditions. Mainly due to the lack of a unified feature modeling approach, feature extraction is incomplete, detection results are unstable, and it is challenging to achieve comprehensive and accurate identification and localization of different types of pavement defects.

To overcome problems such as limited feature extraction ability and poor generalization of traditional methods, researchers have gradually shifted their research focus to deep learning techniques. Deep learning relies on a multi-layer neural network structure and can automatically learn high-level semantic features from data, thereby avoiding the cumbersome manual feature design process. It has stronger nonlinear modeling capabilities and the ability to adapt to complex scenarios. Therefore, it shows significant performance advantages in the task of pavement disease detection [2,3]. In recent years, single-stage detection algorithms, such as the You Only Look Once (YOLO) [4] series, have covered the entire image pixel by pixel by utilizing candidate boxes of different sizes. Wibowo et al. proposed YOLOv7-MOD [5], which integrates a deformable convolutional layer and employs soft NMS to reduce the number of parameters and enhance the accuracy of target detection.

The current detection algorithm faces the following key technical difficulties. Firstly, under complex lighting and weather conditions (as shown in Fig. 1a), road diseases typically exhibit low contrast with the background, resulting in insufficiently prominent features and making it difficult to distinguish them accurately. Secondly, the vehicle-mounted camera system is limited by the shooting distance, and its feature expression ability for long-distance small-scale diseases (as shown in Fig. 1b) is also limited. In addition, the texture similarity between the pavement repair marks, oil stains, watermarks, and other interfering substances (as shown in Fig. 1c) and the real disease significantly increases the risk of false-positive detection. These challenges significantly limit the detection capabilities of existing detection algorithms.

To address the aforementioned issues in road disease detection, this paper proposes a novel algorithm for road disease detection, which combines multiscale feature fusion and receptive field enhancement. Our main contributions are as follows:

1. We designed a multiscale feature fusion module. Through multiscale parallel convolution, the model's ability to extract texture features and structural

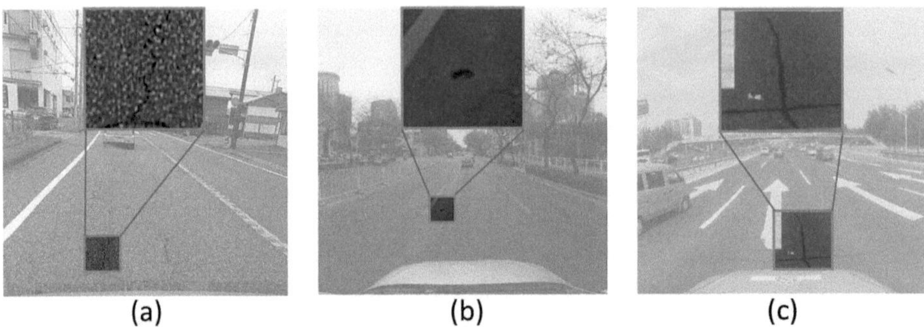

Fig. 1. (a) low contrast disease, (b) small target disease, (c) complex background interference.

information about road diseases is enhanced. Combined with the spatial context awareness mechanism, the texture awareness ability is enhanced, effectively addressing the similarity issue between road diseases and background colors.

2. We introduce a receptive field enhancement module. The multiscale receptive field feature pyramid is constructed using dilated convolution and combined with a residual connection to retain the original spatial details, thereby enhancing the detection performance of subtle diseases under long-distance shooting by a vehicle-mounted camera and improving the model's resolution ability for diseases of small targets.
3. We propose the dynamic task collaborative detection head. Through shared convolution, task alignment, and spatial probability guidance, the task interaction ability is enhanced, the focus on disease characteristics is achieved, and the interference of complex backgrounds is reduced.

2 Related Work

Road Disease Detection. In the field of road disease detection, the current mainstream algorithms are still insufficient in terms of their ability to distinguish targets under complex background interference and their detection capability for small targets. The current research is mainly divided into two aspects. One aspect is the detection of road defects based on data augmentation methods. For example, in 2022, HOU Yue et al. [6] adopted a data depth enhancement method that combines WGAN-GP with the Poisson transfer algorithm to enhance road surface images. Wang et al. [7] proposed the MC-YOLO method, which includes image preprocessing, utilizing MobileNetV2 [8] as the backbone network to accelerate detection and incorporate an attention module to enhance accuracy. Cao et al. proposed MCS-YOLO [9] through methods such as adding a coordinate concern module, adding a small target detection layer, and introducing the Swin Transformer structure.

On the other hand, it is based on the model to improve the detection of road diseases. Wang J.et al. introduced an improved YOLOv5 pavement detection method, GSC-YOLOv5 [10], to enhance the detection ability for small cracks. Kang et al. [11] proposed a method for detecting, locating, and quantifying disease areas. Ni et al. [12] introduced a three-stage bridge road damage and lane location method based on YOLOv7 and improved LaneNet. In 2024, Li et al. [13] introduced modules such as CrackConv, ADSample, CAS, MSConv, and MSHead to improve the problem of crack feature extraction. Yue Li et al. proposed RDD-YOLO [14], which presents a new attention mechanism and convolutional network for crack detection. In 2025, YingJie DU et al. proposed the LEE-YOLO model [15] and presented a real-time network system, which improved pavement assessment. Wei Wang et al. proposed the YOLO-RD model [16], introducing the SOM module to enhance the detection of small-scale diseases and the MAF module to improve robustness in complex environments.

Multi-scale Feature Fusion. In the field of computer vision, low-level feature maps contain rich spatial information and detailed features; however, they are noisy and lack strong semantic content. The high-level feature map has strong semantics and anti-interference capabilities, but it has low resolution and lacks detail perception. To leverage the advantages of both, multiscale feature fusion has become a key technology for improving detection accuracy, widely used in image recognition and object detection tasks. Current feature fusion structures are primarily categorized into two types: parallel multi-branch and serial multi-branch. In the parallel structure, Liu et al. [17], referring to the Inception structure, introduced dilated convolutions of different scales to simulate the human eye receptive field and improve detection accuracy. Based on FPN, PANet further incorporates a bottom-up path aggregation module to enhance the upward transmission of low-level edge information, albeit at the expense of introducing high computational overhead. To improve efficiency, BiFPN [18] combines skip connection and bidirectional aggregation path to achieve lighter and more efficient feature fusion. For dense object detection tasks, CEDNet [19] further enhances the ability to express multiscale information by guiding the learning of low-level features. MFF-YOLO [20] achieves efficient cross-layer feature interaction by introducing dilated convolution and separable convolution structures. Gpc-net [21] enhances the complementarity between shallow details and high-level semantic information by introducing a global attention module into pyramid features and combining multiscale feature fusion with global context information. These methods lay a solid foundation for the continuous evolution of multiscale feature fusion technology.

3 Method

3.1 Network Architecture

In this chapter, we present the overall architecture of our algorithm. Figure 2 shows the overall architecture of the algorithm. In the Backbone part, the Multiscale feature fusion module (EMSC) is introduced during feature extraction, fusing image features of different scales by segmenting the input and performing parallel convolution processing, thereby enhancing the algorithm's perception of different scales. After the processed image enters the Neck part, it undergoes convolution and upsampling. Finally, through three Extended Receptive Field modules (CRFB) modules, the receptive field of the algorithm is expanded by using dilated convolution to improve the detection ability of small targets. After entering the Dynamic Task Collaborative Detection Head (DTAD), shared convolution [13] and task alignment were employed to construct classification and regression branches, respectively, to reduce interference from complex backgrounds.

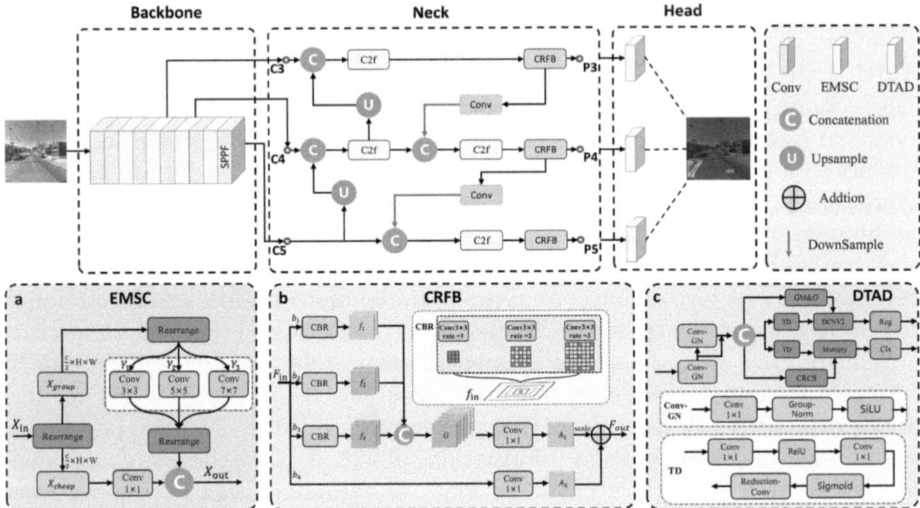

Fig. 2. The overall architecture diagram is mainly composed of three parts: Backbone, Neck, and Head, where a, b, and c represent the EMSC, CRFB, and DTAD modules, respectively.

3.2 Multi-scale Feature Fusion

Aiming to address the issue of low contrast between the background and disease in road disease detection, existing studies primarily employ methods based on the attention mechanism (such as the SE module [22]), which achieves feature channel enhancement and inhibition through global average pooling [23] and dynamic learning of channel weights via a fully connected layer. However, this method weakens fine-grained spatial information in complex road scenes, resulting in the loss of local texture features, and it is difficult to distinguish between background and diseased targets.

To address the issue of low contrast between the background and disease in road disease detection, we introduce the Efficient Multiscale Convolution (EMSC) module. In Fig. 2a, the module combines multiscale convolution and grouped convolution dimensionality reduction strategies to perceive local texture information and structure contours. We divide the input feature maps $X \in \mathbb{R}^{H \times W \times C}$ into two groups in the channel dimension:

$$X_{cheap}, X_{group} = Split(X_{in}) \tag{1}$$

where, X_{cheap} and X_{group} respectively represent the results after splitting the feature maps X_{in}. One group X_{cheap} does nothing for low-complexity feature preservation. The other X_{group} performs convolution operations of different channels through multiscale grouped convolution for texture feature extraction. The module employed a channel grouping strategy, dividing the input feature map into three branches based on the channel dimension. The first branch captured local detail features, such as disease edges and texture, through a 3×3 convolution. In the middle branch, 5×5 convolution was used to extract medium-scale structural information. The final branch uses a 7×7 convolution to capture a wider range of context associations with the following formula:

$$Y_k = Conv_{i \times i} \left(rearrange \left(X_{group} \right) [k] \right), k = 1, 2, 3; i = 3, 5 \tag{2}$$

$$X_{group}^{out} = rearrange(Y_1, Y_2, Y_3) \tag{3}$$

where rearrange means to rearrange the data. Y_k denote the group k. i denotes the size of the standard convolution kernel. X_{group}^{out} represents the output after multi-scale convolution. Finally, we concatenate the channels and integrate the feature maps using a 1×1 convolution:

$$X_{out} = Conv_{1 \times 1} \left(Concat \left(X_{cheap}, X_{group}^{out} \right) \right) \tag{4}$$

where *Concat* denotes the channel splicing operation. $Conv_{1 \times 1}$ denotes the 2D convolution with kernel size 1 for tuning the number of channels and enhancing the nonlinearity.

3.3 Complex Sensory Wildness Enhancement

In the road surface situation captured by the onboard camera, the road diseases are from far to near, which leads to a large number of small targets in the detection. To enhance the model's perception ability for small objects on road surface diseases, existing methods primarily improve the detection performance of small objects by enhancing context correlation or introducing an attention mechanism [24]. However, these methods still have a high miss rate in detecting small objects.

To further reduce the missed detection rate of small targets, we designed a novel Compound Receptive Field enhancement module named the Compound Receptive Field Block (CRFB). CRFB mainly consists of three parallel CBR branches and one input feature transform. Among them, branches b_1, b_2 and b_3 focus on feature capture for small, medium and large receptive fields, respectively. Firstly, the input feature map f_{in} undergoes two consecutive 1×1 convolutions and batch normalization operations in each branch for channel compression. Subsequently, it goes through a *RelU* activation function and a normalization operation. Then, as shown in Fig. 2b, in the CBR module in part b, each branch continues to stack convolution operations with different expansion rates, as well as the *RelU* activation functions, to obtain context information at different scales. The output feature f_{out} can be formally expressed as:

$$f_{out} = \sum_{i=1}^{3} \left(f_i \cdot \delta(FC_2^i(\sigma(FC_1^i GAP(f_i))))\right), i = 1, 2, 3 \tag{5}$$

$$f_i = Conv_{3\times3}^{r_j}(\sigma(DConv_{1\times1}(f_{in}))), j = 1, 2, 3 \tag{6}$$

Among them, GAP represents the global average pooling. FC_i^1 indicates that two layers are fully connected to extract channel dependencies. δ represents the Sigmoid activation to generate channel weights. $Conv_{3\times3}^{r_j}$ means that a 3×3 dilated convolution with expansion rate j is used. $DConv_{1\times1}$ indicates that depthwise separable convolutions are used to compress the channel. $\sigma(\cdot)$ is the nonlinear activation function *RelU*. Then, the outputs f_1, f_2 and f_3 of the three branches are concatenated and fused in the channel dimension to obtain G, and integrated into a unified output feature map A_1 through a 1×1 convolutional layer. In addition, in order to retain the key information of the input feature map and enhance the training stability of the model, CRFB introduces the residual connection mechanism, which directly adds the F_{in} input to the fused result after a 1×1 convolution transformation. The final output feature F_{out} is expressed as follows:

$$F_{out} = \sigma(\alpha \cdot Conv_{1\times1}(G) + Conv_{1\times1}(F_{in})) \tag{7}$$

Here, α is the learnable scaling factor *scale*.

3.4 Dynamic Task-Aligned Detection Head

The YOLO original detection head divides the detection task into two separate branches: category prediction and position regression, which enhances the feature learning ability. However, the lack of effective information exchange and cooperation between the two branches limits the model to deal with complex and variable detection scenarios. It has little effect on the anti-interference of a complex background, which can easily lead to false detection.

To better mitigate the interference of complex backgrounds on Detection accuracy, a new Detection Head module, the Dynamic Task-Aligned Detection Head (DTAD), is proposed to achieve more accurate detection performance. As shown in Fig. 2c, the overall structure of DTAD is demonstrated. The module is mainly composed of four parts: a shared feature extraction sub-network, a task alignment module, a dynamic deformable alignment module, and a spatial attention guidance module. Specifically, the input feature map first undergoes two shared convolution blocks to extract a common representation, and the intermediate layer features are concatenated to form richer semantic features, which provide a high-quality feature basis for subsequent decoupling. Subsequently, it is fed into the classification branch and the regression branch, respectively. In the classification branch, a spatial attention guidance module is introduced to guide the network in focusing on potential disease regions, thereby enhancing the response of classification features to these regions. In the regression branch, the dynamic deformable convolution is introduced to dynamically adjust the sampling position according to the extracted offset and mask information, thereby improving the model's ability to model irregular object boundaries. Finally, the output of DTAD can be formalized as follows.

$$Y = [S \cdot DFL(Conv_{1\times1}(F_{reg}))||\delta(Conv_{1\times1}(F_{cls})] \tag{8}$$

where S represents the learnable scale factor, DFL is the distributed focus regression decoder to ensure the accuracy of detection results, $||$ represents the channel dimension splicing operation, and the final output is the classification probability combining bounding box regression and attention guidance.

4 Experimental Results and Analysis

4.1 Datasets

In this paper, three publicly available road disease detection datasets are used to verify the model's performance. The main dataset is RDD2022 [28], released by the University of Tokyo, which covers 23,767 road images from China, Japan, Norway, and the United States. Four typical diseases, including longitudinal cracks (D00), transverse cracks (D10), cracks (D20), and potholes (D40), are identified and screened out. It is divided into a training set (16,637 images), validation set (4,753 images), and test set (2,377 images) according to the ratio of 7:2:1. The supplementary data set includes MEdDatasetV4 [29], which contains 3,449 640×640 vehicle images covering multiple types of diseases such as cracks and pock-holes, which is suitable for verifying the robustness of the model in actual complex scenes. The vq840 [30] dataset provides 2,000 vehicle-mounted view images containing disease samples under various lighting and road conditions to test the model's cross-scene adaptation ability. The three groups of data sets ensure the effectiveness and comprehensiveness of model training and evaluation from multiple dimensions.

4.2 Experimental Setup

In this experiment, a high-performance computing environment was used for model training and testing. The hardware configuration included: Ubuntu 22.04.5 operating system, Intel Core i9-9900K processor, and NVIDIA RTX 4090D 24 GB graphics card. The software environment was based on Python 3.8, CUDA 12.2, and PyTorch 1.13.1 framework. The training parameters were set to 100 epochs with a batch size of 16 and 8 data-loading workers. We used the Adam optimizer ($\beta_1 = 0.9$, $\beta_2 = 0.999$) for parameter updates, with an initial learning rate of 0.001, and optimized the model using the cross-entropy loss function. This configuration provided stable hardware support and efficient training performance for the experiments.

4.3 Evaluation Metrics

The evaluation of algorithm performance is primarily considered from two aspects: computational complexity and detection accuracy. Among them, in terms of detection accuracy, the following indicators are usually adopted for comprehensive evaluation: Precision, Recall, and Mean Average Precision (mAP) are used as indicators to evaluate the road detection model and are introduced respectively as follows:

$$Precision = \frac{TP}{TP + FP} \tag{9}$$

$$Recall = \frac{TP}{TP + FN} \tag{10}$$

$$AP = \frac{1}{n_{pos}} \sum_{r=1}^{n_{pos}} (precision(r) \times recall(r)) \tag{11}$$

$$mAP = \frac{1}{n} \sum_{c=1}^{n} AP(c) \tag{12}$$

Among them:*Precision* represents the accuracy rate. *TP* represents the number of correctly detected diseases. *FP* represents the number of non-diseased targets detected. *Recall* indicates the recall rate. *FN* represents the number of disease targets that have not been correctly detected. *AP* represents the average value of all categories. Where n_{pos} is the number of positive instances in the real situation. In contrast, $precision(r)$ and $recall(r)$ are, respectively, the precision value and recall rate at the (r)th instance retrieved. Where n is the total number of categories or classifications. mAP represents the mean average accuracy rate of all categories.

4.4 Comparative Experiment

To verify the superiority of the algorithm in road disease detection, the proposed algorithm in this paper is compared with current mainstream algorithms on the RDD2022 [28] dataset, and the experimental results are presented in Table 1. Compared to the baseline model, our algorithm improves the precision, recall, and mAP by 2.8%, 0.7%, and 2.5% respectively without increasing the number of parameters. The proposed algorithm outperforms the latest advanced methods, such as RDD-YOLO [14] (2024) and YOLO12n [27] (2025), in terms of detection accuracy.

At the same time, to verify the model's detection effect on different datasets, this paper conducts experiments on two datasets: MEdDatasetV4 [29] and vq840 [30]. The experimental results are presented in Table 1 below. Compared to the baseline model, the proposed algorithm achieves a 4.4% increase in precision, a 2.2% increase in recall rate, and a 2.8% increase in mAP, in the MEdDatasetV4 [29] dateset. Additionally, compared to the baseline model, the average precision increases by 1.5%, the recall increases by 0.3%, and the mAP increases by 1.4%, in the vq840 [30] dateset. From the results of each evaluation index on the three datasets, the proposed algorithm outperforms the comparison methods in both detection accuracy and robustness without increasing the number of parameters, fully reflecting its advantages in detection accuracy.

Table 1. Comparative experimental results across datasets. (Red: Best) Among them, A, B, and C represent the datasets RDD2022, MEdDatasetV4, and vq840 respectively.

Dataset	Model	Precision	Recall	mAP@0.5	mAP@0.5:0.95	Params
A	Baseline [32]	61.6	49.2	52.7	27.2	3.00
	Faster R-CNN [31]	54.3	44.2	45.5	23.0	41.57
	Efficientdet-do [18]	52.6	43.1	40.1	21.2	3.90
	YOLOv10n [25]	56.6	46.3	49.2	25.4	2.26
	YOLO11n [26]	62.0	47.8	52.5	27.1	2.58
	RDD-YOLO [14]	63.2	49.3	54.6	28.9	2.55
	YOLO12n [27]	58.0	46.3	49.2	25.3	2.55
	Ours	64.4	49.9	55.2	29.3	2.90
B	Baseline [32]	34.8	32.4	26.3	11.1	3.00
	Faster R-CNN [31]	28.3	27.3	20.4	10.0	41.57
	Efficientdet-do [18]	29.2	28.0	22.5	10.3	3.90
	YOLOv10n [25]	30.0	27.9	23.4	10.0	2.26
	YOLO11n [26]	35.3	33.3	26.8	11.2	2.58
	RDD-YOLO [14]	38.0	32.1	27.1	10.4	2.55
	YOLO12n [27]	36.5	32.4	25.9	10.3	2.55
	Ours	39.2	34.6	28.1	11.2	2.90
C	Baseline [32]	55.0	40.8	41.5	22.5	3.00
	Faster R-CNN [31]	33.8	30.0	26.6	13.5	41.57
	Efficientdet-do [18]	42.4	30.0	29.1	14.2	3.90
	YOLOv10n [25]	44.8	33.8	39.4	11.5	2.26
	YOLO11n [26]	44.6	37.6	37.4	19.6	2.58
	RDD-YOLO [14]	54.5	40.4	41.5	22.3	2.55
	YOLO12n [27]	50.8	39.8	41.1	20.9	2.55
	Ours	56.5	41.1	42.9	22.5	2.90

Figure 3 shows the comparison of visual detection results of different models on the three datasets. Through horizontal comparison, it can be seen that the proposed algorithm exhibits better detection performance on the three datasets of RDD2022 [28], MEdDatasetV4 [29], and vq840 [30]. Specifically, compared with other comparison algorithms, this method has a significant improvement in the positioning accuracy and detection accuracy of road disease targets.

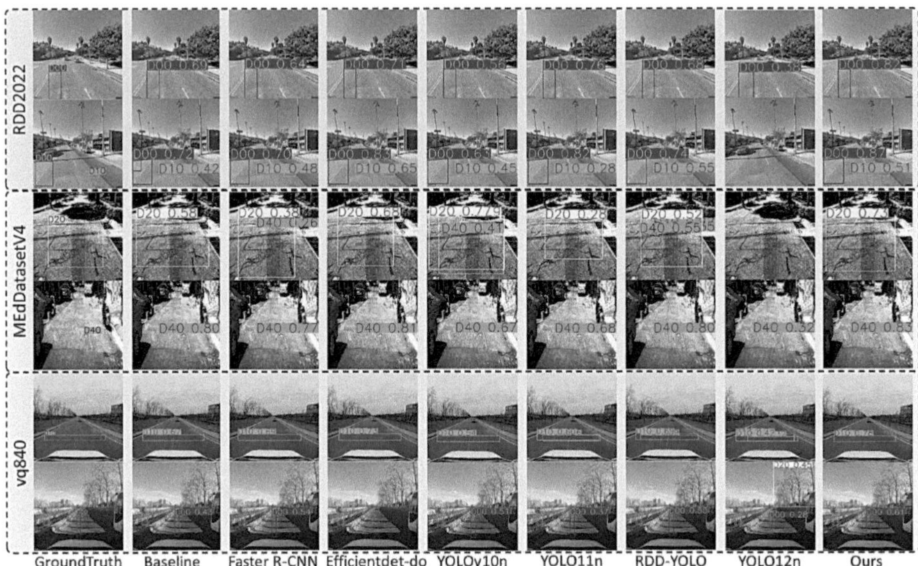

Fig. 3. Experimental visualizations were compared on three datasets.

4.5 Ablation Experiment

In order to fully verify the detection performance of the proposed algorithm and verify the effectiveness of the three methods proposed in this paper. In this paper, the proposed EMSC, CRFB, and DTAD modules are individually or in combination validated on the RDD2022 [28] dataset, and the results are shown in Table 2. The EMSC module replaces the original feature extraction module, which extracts features on different convolution kernel sizes. The introduction of the EMSC module improves precision, recall, and mAP by 0.2%, 0.3%, and 0.2%, respectively, demonstrating the effectiveness of the module. By adding the CRFB module, the model's precision, recall, and mAP increase by 0.2%, 0.7%, and 1.2%, respectively. Using the new detection head, DTAD, the model's precision, recall, and mAP are increased by 1.6%, 0.5%, and 2%, respectively. Experiments show that the detection effect is more accurate after the introduction of a DTAD detection head. In the combination improvement, the feature extraction module in the baseline model is replaced by EMSC, the CRFB module is added before detection, and a new detection head, DTAD, is added to obtain the new model presented in this paper. The experimental results show that the precision, recall, and mAP of the model are improved by 2.8%, 0.7%, and 2.5%, respectively. This indicates that the improved network structure yields a significant improvement in disease detection accuracy compared to the baseline model.

Table 2. Ablation study results of different modules. (Red: Best)

Group	EMSC	CRFB	DTAD	Precision	Recall	mAP@0.5	mAP@0.5:0.95
1	×	×	×	61.6	49.2	52.7	27.2
2	√	×	×	61.7	49.5	52.9	27.4
3	×	√	×	61.8	49.9	53.8	28.3
4	×	×	√	63.2	49.2	54.7	29.1
5	√	√	×	61.8	49.7	53.9	28.5
6	√	×	√	62.6	49.9	54.2	28.6
7	×	√	√	62.8	49.8	54.8	29.2
8	√	√	√	64.4	49.9	55.2	29.3

4.6 Heat Map Visualization

To more intuitively demonstrate the effectiveness of the proposed model in road disease detection, this paper analyses the heat map visualization of the model's detection focus area based on a real-world road surface image, as shown in Fig. 4. We can see from the figure that Baseline [32] has obvious shortcomings when dealing with small-scale cracks or subtle diseases. It is often difficult to accurately focus on the target area, and the detected diseases are often larger than the size of the disease itself. Especially in scenes with dense disease or complex backgrounds, it is easy to miss or misdiagnose. In contrast, the proposed model can better focus on fine-grained target areas such as cracks and spalling under the same input, has stronger target sensitivity and alignment ability, and shows higher detection accuracy. This fully verifies the effectiveness and advantages of the proposed algorithm in the actual road disease detection task.

Fig. 4. The heat map visualization results of the baseline model and the algorithm proposed in this paper on different datasets.

5 Conclusion

In this paper, an advanced road disease detection algorithm is proposed to address the challenges of low contrast interference, small targets that are difficult to detect, and excessive background interference information in road disease detection. Firstly, the EMSC module reduces background interference through an efficient parallel multiscale convolution structure. Secondly, with the help of the multi-branch dilated convolution mechanism, the CRFB module enhances the model's ability to extract features from different receptive fields, thereby improving the recognition of small target diseases. Finally, the DTAD detection head effectively suppresses the interference of complex backgrounds by introducing shared convolution, task alignment, and spatial probability guidance. The Mean Average Precision (mAP) of our algorithm on the datasets RDD2022 [28], MEd-DatasetV4 [29], and vq840 [30] is 55.2%, 28.1%, and 42.9%, respectively. The results show that the proposed algorithm outperforms existing mainstream methods in terms of detection accuracy, small target recognition, and anti-interference ability. It shows better detection accuracy.

Although current algorithms have demonstrated superior performance in road disease detection, they still face challenges of high computational complexity and insufficient detection stability under extreme lighting conditions. Future research will focus on optimizing the computational efficiency of the model, enhancing the algorithm's adaptability under various lighting conditions, and exploring new methods to reduce the demand for labeled data, thereby promoting the practical application of this technology in mobile terminal intelligent road inspection systems.

Acknowledgements. This work is supported by the Ningbo Key R&D Program under Grant No. 2023Z231, and the Natural Science Foundation of the Xinjiang Uygur Autonomous Region 2024D01C53, and the Special Project of the Key Research and Development Task of the Xinjiang Uygur Autonomous Region under Grant 2022B02052-3, and Finance Science and Technology Project of Xinjiang Uyghur Autonomous Region under Grant 2023B01029-1.

References

1. Ai, D., Jiang, G., Lam, S.-K., He, P., Li, C.: Computer vision framework for crack detection of civil infrastructure–a review. Eng. Appl. Artif. Intell. **117**, 105478 (2023)
2. Du, Z., Yuan, J., Xiao, F., Hettiarachchi, C.: Application of image technology on pavement distress detection: a review. Measurement **184**, 109900 (2021)
3. Yang, G., et al.: Datasets and processing methods for boosting visual inspection of civil infrastructure: a comprehensive review and algorithm comparison for crack classification, segmentation, and detection. Constr. Build. Mater. **356**, 129226 (2022)

4. Sohan, M., Sai Ram, T., Rami Reddy, C.V.: A review on YOLOv8 and its advancements. In: Jacob, I.J., Piramuthu, S., Falkowski-Gilski, P. (eds.) ICDICI 2023. Algorithms for Intelligent Systems, pp. 529–545. Springer, Singapore (2024). https://doi.org/10.1007/978-981-99-7962-2_39
5. Wibowo, A., Trilaksono, B.R., Hidayat, E.M.I., Munir, R.: Object detection in dense and mixed traffic for autonomous vehicles with modified YOLO. IEEE Access **11**, 134866–134877 (2023)
6. Hou, Y., et al.: Research and comparison of intelligent detection methods of pavement distress based on deep data augmentation. J. Beijing Univ. Technol. **48**(6), 622–634 (2022)
7. Wang, X., Hao, X., Wang, K.: MC-YOLO-based lightweight detection method for nighttime vehicle images in a semantic web-based video surveillance system. Int. J. Semant. Web Inf. Syst. (IJSWIS) **19**(1), 1–18 (2023)
8. Sandler, M., Howard, A., Zhu, M., Zhmoginov, A., Chen, L.-C.: Mobilenetv2: inverted residuals and linear bottlenecks. In: Proceedings of the IEEE Conference on Computer Vision and Pattern Recognition, pp. 4510–4520 (2018)
9. Cao, Y., Li, C., Peng, Y., Ru, H.: MCS-YOLO: a multiscale object detection method for autonomous driving road environment recognition. IEEE Access **11**, 22342–22354 (2023)
10. Wang, J., Gao, X., Liu, Z., Wan, Y.: GSC-YOLOv5: an algorithm based on improved attention mechanism for road creak detection. In: 2023 IEEE 12th Data Driven Control and Learning Systems Conference (DDCLS), pp. 1664–1671. IEEE (2023)
11. Kang, D., Benipal, S.S., Gopal, D.L., Cha, Y.-J.: Hybrid pixel-level concrete crack segmentation and quantification across complex backgrounds using deep learning. Autom. Constr. **118**, 103291 (2020)
12. Ni, Y., Mao, J., Fu, Y., Wang, H., Zong, H., Luo, K.: Damage detection and localization of bridge deck pavement based on deep learning. Sensors **23**(11), 5138 (2023)
13. Zhang, X., et al.: LDConv: linear deformable convolution for improving convolutional neural networks. Image Vis. Comput. **149**, 105190 (2024)
14. Li, Y., Yin, C., Lei, Y., Zhang, J., Yan, Y.: RDD-YOLO: road damage detection algorithm based on improved You Only Look Once version 8. Appl. Sci. **14**(8), 3360 (2024)
15. Du, Y., Cheng, Q., Liu, X., Xu, J., Yi, Y.: Enhancing road maintenance through cyber-physical integration: the LEE-YOLO model for drone-assisted pavement crack detection. IEEE Trans. Intell. Transp. Syst. (2025)
16. Wang, W., et al.: YOLO-RD: a road damage detection method for effective pavement maintenance. Sensors **25**(5), 1442 (2025)
17. Liu, S., Huang, D., Wang, Y.: Receptive field block net for accurate and fast object detection. In: Ferrari, V., Hebert, M., Sminchisescu, C., Weiss, Y. (eds.) ECCV 2018. LNCS, vol. 11215, pp. 404–419. Springer, Cham (2018). https://doi.org/10.1007/978-3-030-01252-6_24
18. Tan, M., Pang, R., Le, Q.V.: Efficientdet: scalable and efficient object detection. In: Proceedings of the IEEE/CVF Conference on Computer Vision and Pattern Recognition, pp. 10781–10790 (2020)
19. Zhang, G., Li, Z., Tang, C., Li, J., Hu, X.: CEDNet: a cascade encoder-decoder network for dense prediction. Pattern Recogn. **158**, 111072 (2025)
20. Li, G., Cao, H., Wang, H., Guo, W., Gong, C.: MFF-YOLO: multiscale feature fusion network for small ship detection in night scenes. In: ECAI (2024)

21. Shan, Z., et al.: GPA-net: no-reference point cloud quality assessment with multi-task graph convolutional network. IEEE Trans. Visual. Comput. Graph. (2023)
22. Hu, J., Shen, L., Albanie, S., Sun, G., Wu, E.: Squeeze-and-excitation networks. arXiv preprint arXiv:1709.01507 (2019)
23. Lee, W., Ham, B., Kim, S.: Maximizing the position embedding for vision transformers with global average pooling. Proc. AAAI Conf. Artif. Intelli. **39**(17), 18154–18162 (2025)
24. Roy, A., Sarkar, S., Ghosal, S., Kaplun, D., Lyanova, A., Sarkar, R.: A wavelet guided attention module for skin cancer classification with gradient-based feature fusion. In: 2024 IEEE International Symposium on Biomedical Imaging (ISBI), pp. 1–4 (2024)
25. Wang, A., et al.: YOLOv10: real-time end-to-end object detection. In: Advances in Neural Information Processing Systems, vol. 37, pp. 107984–108011 (2024)
26. Khanam, R., Hussain, M.: YOLOv11: an overview of the key architectural enhancements. arXiv preprint arXiv:2410.17725 (2024)
27. Tian, Y., Ye, Q., Doermann, D.S.: YOLOv12: attention-centric real-time object detectors. arXiv preprint arXiv:2502.12524 (2025)
28. Arya, D., Maeda, H., Ghosh, S.K., Toshniwal, D., Sekimoto, Y.: RDD2022: a multi-national image dataset for automatic road damage detection. Geosci. Data J. **11**(4) (2024)
29. grades: MEdDatasetV4 Dataset. Roboflow Universe, Roboflow (2023). Open Source Dataset (2023). https://universe.roboflow.com/grades/meddatasetv4
30. project-j0yrp: vq840 Dataset. Roboflow Universe, Roboflow (2024). Open Source Dataset (2024). https://universe.roboflow.com/project-j0yrp/-vq840
31. Ren, S., He, K., Girshick, R., Sun, J.: Faster R-CNN: towards real-time object detection with region proposal networks. IEEE Trans. Pattern Anal. Mach. Intell. **39**(6), 1137–1149 (2017)
32. Varghese, R., Sambath, M.: YOLOv8: a novel object detection algorithm with enhanced performance and robustness. In: 2024 International Conference on Advances in Data Engineering and Intelligent Computing Systems (ADICS) (2024)

Bounding Box-Derived Mask Guidance Network for Accurate Surface Defect Detection

Lisha Cui[1,2,3], Xin Ma[1], Fengye Tian[1], Qianqian Tong[4], Xiaoheng Jiang[1,2,3], and Mingliang Xu[1,2,3](✉)

[1] School of Computer and Artificial Intelligence, Zhengzhou University, Zhengzhou 450001, China
{ielscui,iexhjiang,iexumingliang}@zzu.edu.cn

[2] Engineering Research Center of Ministry of Education on Intelligent Swarm Systems, Zhengzhou University, Zhengzhou 450001, China

[3] National Supercomputing Center in Zhengzhou, Zhengzhou 450001, China

[4] Computer Science Department, University of North Carolina at Greensboro, Greensboro, NC 27410, USA
q_tong@uncg.edu

Abstract. Surface defect detection is a critical technology in the field of intelligent manufacturing, playing a significant role in improving product quality. The core task of typical object detectors is to achieve defect classification and localization through bounding box annotations. However, due to the multi-scale nature of surface defects and the complexity of the background, the inherent information sparsity in the supervision signals of bounding box labels often makes it difficult for models to accurately locate defect positions and identify the categories. To address this issue, we propose a Bounding Box-Derived Mask Guidance Network for Accurate Surface Defect Detection (BDMGNet). During the training phase, BDMGNet first generates Bounding Box-Derived Masks (BDM) from object bounding boxes and enhances the backbone network's localization capability for object regions by incorporating an Auxiliary Segmentation Guidance Subnetwork (ASGS). Additionally, a Preference Dynamic Weight Averaging (PDWA) strategy is introduced to optimize the model's attention allocation for detection tasks. During the inference phase, the ASGS can be pruned and thus improve defect detection accuracy without increasing the original model's parameter count or complexity. Notably, the ASGS exhibits high generality and adaptability, functioning as a plug-and-play module for all object detection networks while maintaining the original model's inference speed and effectively improving accuracy. Experimental results on the NEU-DET, DeepPCB,

M. Xu—This work was supported in part by the China Postdoctoral Science Foundation under Grant 2021TQ0301, in part by the National Natural Science Foundation of China under Grant 62106232, 62172371, and U21B2037, in part by the National Key Research and Development Program of China under Grant 2021YFB3301500. We also thank the National Supercomputing Center in Zhengzhou for providing the computational resources.

© The Author(s), under exclusive license to Springer Nature Singapore Pte Ltd. 2026
J. Kittler et al. (Eds.): PRCV 2025, LNCS 16289, pp. 107–121, 2026.
https://doi.org/10.1007/978-981-95-5764-6_8

and GBC-DET datasets demonstrate that BDMGNet achieves significant performance improvements across series baseline models, validating the effectiveness and universality of the proposed method.

Keywords: Surface defect detection · Semantic label generation · Multi-task learning · Auxiliary segmentation guidance · Industrial inspection

1 Introduction

Surface defect detection is a critical technology in intelligent manufacturing, playing a vital role in ensuring product quality, improving production efficiency, and reducing manufacturing costs. In recent years, with the rapid development of deep learning, neural network-based methods have become the mainstream solution for industrial surface defect detection. Among them, the YOLO algorithm [1], as a representative model in object detection, has been widely applied in industrial defect detection tasks due to its efficiency and accuracy. The core idea of YOLO series [1–3] are to formulate object detection as a single regression problem, directly predicting bounding boxes and class probabilities from input images, enabling end-to-end fast detection.

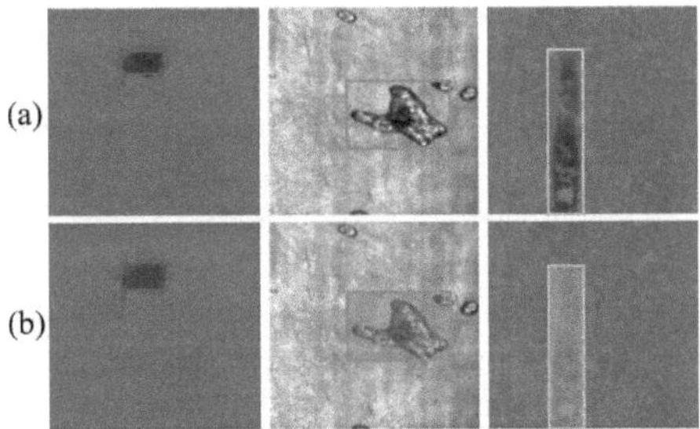

Fig. 1. (a) Bounding box labels; (b) Bounding box mask labels.

Recent YOLO-based improvement methods primarily focus on designing more effective feature extraction modules and adopting feature enhancement mechanisms to improve the network's feature representation capability, emphasizing critical features while suppressing irrelevant ones. Specifically, some studies [11] employ multi-scale convolutional kernel combinations to obtain richer feature representations. Additionally, several studies [12,13] introduce various attention mechanisms to enable the network to adaptively focus on key feature regions.

However, industrial defect detection faces significant challenges due to large scale variations, low contrast, and the limited representation capacity of conventional bounding box supervision (Fig. 1(a)), which provides sparse spatial signals that hinder discriminative feature extraction and precise regression. In contrast,

2D bounding box masks (Fig. 1(b)) offer dense spatial information and contour cues, enabling more accurate defect localization and shape perception.

Based on the observation, we propose the Bounding Box-Derived Mask Guidance Network (BDMGNet) that introduces a Bounding Box-Derived Mask (BDM) mechanism by transforming box coordinates into enriched 2D supervision signals through morphological processing. Meanwhile, we design a plug-and-play Auxiliary Segmentation Guidance Subnetwork (ASGS) that injects spatial constraints via weight sharing and enables multi-scale feature enhancement while remaining removable during deployment. During training we propose a Preference Dynamic Weight Averaging (PDWA) strategy that dynamically optimizes loss weights between detection and segmentation tasks based on evolving feature distributions and task difficulty, ensuring balanced optimization without compromising primary detection objectives. In summary, the contributions of this work are as follows:

- We propose a Bounding Box-Derived Mask (BDM) generation mechanism that produces corresponding two-dimensional masks with positional and categorical information from ground-truth bounding box labels, providing more precise guidance for feature learning.
- We propose a plug-and-play Auxiliary Segmentation Guidance Subnetwork (ASGS) that effectively injects the spatial constraint information from BDM into the backbone network to enhance perception capability for defect regions. During deployment, ASGS can be seamlessly integrated through pruning to improve accuracy without modifying the baseline model.
- We propose a Preference Dynamic Weight Averaging (PDWA) strategy that dynamically adjusts the weights between detection and segmentation tasks based on task difficulty and feature distribution during training. This ensures the model focuses on critical detection tasks while avoiding optimization bias.
- Extensive experiments are conducted on both the public defect dataset (NEU-DET, DeepPCB) and our self-collected Green Battery Case Detection dataset (GBC-DET). The results demonstrate that BDMGNet can effectively improve the accuracy of defect detection while maintaining strong generalization capability.

2 Related Work

2.1 Defect Detection

The advancement of industrial automation has heightened the demand for efficient surface defect recognition, prompting researchers to develop improved detection methods. Attention mechanisms have shown particular promise, with [8] combining spatial and channel attention for precise feature localization and [9] enhancing feature saliency across hierarchical maps. Concurrently, multi-scale approaches have advanced significantly: [10] achieved 80.6% mAP50 using deformable convolutions (though limited by speed), [11] improved tiny defect detection through scale-aware alignment. [7] further demonstrate progress through innovative combinations of attention mechanisms and feature transformation techniques, though real-time industrial deployment remains challenging.

Despite these advancements, whether through attention mechanisms or enhanced multi-scale feature extraction, such improvements often come at the cost of increased model complexity, reduced processing speed, and higher computational demands. Moreover, while these methods optimize models by seeking richer feature representations or emphasizing key features, they fail to explicitly guide the model on which regions should be prioritized.

2.2 Deep Supervision

Deep supervision [14,15] introduces intermediate prediction layers, while other auxiliary approaches use meta-information to guide feature learning. For instance, [16] applied instance-level supervision to pyramidal features to reduce semantic gaps, [17] utilized depth-aware supervision for 3D detection, and [18] extended Mask R-CNN [6] with auxiliary branches for transformation maps and segmentation - though at increased computational cost. While such supervision enhances model capability without parameter growth, acquiring auxiliary labels (e.g., depth/segmentation maps) often requires additional resources.

3 Method

3.1 Motivation

In object detection, models must precisely map images to spatial coordinates and category labels. Traditional bounding box supervision (x,y,w,h,c) suffers from inherent information sparsity, where (x,y) denotes box center, (w,h) represents dimensions, and c indicates the object class. This coarse supervision yields two fundamental limitations: (1) gradient updates only affect global box parameters, ignoring internal feature distributions; (2) the loss provides vague directional guidance without shape modeling capacity.

Conversely, 2D mask supervision delivers denser gradient feedback through pixel-wise annotation, enabling precise contour modeling and internal structure learning. As demonstrated by Mask R-CNN's RoIAlign-enhanced segmentation branch [6], such supervision significantly boosts detection performance.

However, this mask-based supervision faces serious challenges in industrial defect detection scenarios. The most prominent issue is that existing industrial defect detection datasets typically only provide bounding box annotations without precise pixel-level mask labels. Obtaining high-quality mask supervision requires substantial manual annotation costs. Moreover, simply adding segmentation auxiliary branches introduces problems like increased model complexity and multi-task optimization difficulties.

Based on the above analysis, we propose a bounding box-derived mask guidance network for accurate surface defect detection. By introducing an auxiliary BDM branch, we leverage the dense spatial supervision signals to enhance object detection performance.

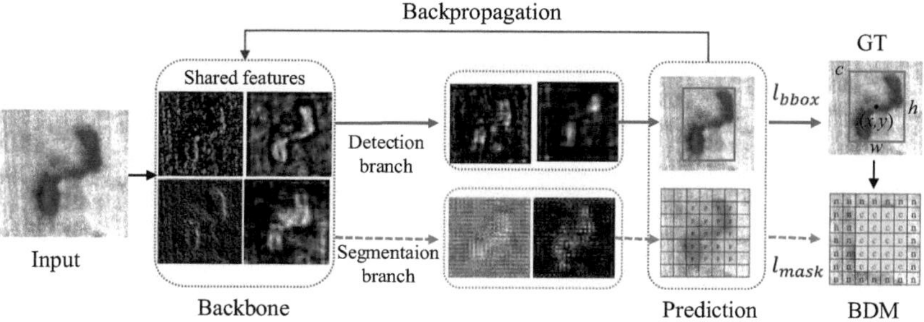

Fig. 2. Framework schematic of bounding box-derived mask guidance network.

3.2 Framework

The overall framework of our model is illustrated in Fig. 2. We first employ a shared backbone network where both the detection branch and segmentation branch utilize the same feature maps, enabling collaborative feature representation learning. The detection branch focuses on object localization and classification tasks, while the segmentation branch is responsible for predicting bounding box mask. The BDM is generated based on the annotated regions of ground-truth bounding boxes and their corresponding object categories.

During training, the detection branch learns semantic features by comparing its predictions with ground-truth bounding box labels. Simultaneously, the segmentation branch captures fine-grained spatial distribution information supervised by BDM labels. The dual-branch cooperative training mechanism facilitates the progressive integration of spatial details into the shared feature maps through backpropagation, thereby enhancing detection performance.

Specifically, the boundary distribution information learned by the segmentation branch is encoded into the shared features via gradient backpropagation. This process enriches the spatial contextual cues available to the detection task, ultimately optimizing detection performance. Notably, the auxiliary segmentation branch only operates during the training phase and can be completely removed via pruning during deployment. This design enables the model to maintain inference speed while improving detection accuracy.

3.3 Bounding Box-Derived Mask (BDM)

For object detection tasks, networks are required to accurately identify both the location and scale of object regions. However, conventional one-dimensional labels (*e.g.*, bounding box coordinates and class labels) provide limited information, making it challenging to precisely localize object regions during backpropagation. In contrast, semantic segmentation labels offer richer spatial information. To address this, we propose a method that converts bounding box labels into pixel-level masks to enhance supervisory signals. The generated masks are referred to as Bounding Box-Derived Mask (BDM).

Specifically, given an input image R^{H*W} with its corresponding ground-truth label (x, y, w, h, c) (assuming n object classes, $c \in [0, n-1]$). The mask is generated by assigning pixel values inside the box to the corresponding class label c, while the background regions to n, which can be formally represented as:

$$M_c(u,v) = \begin{cases} c, & \text{if } (u,v) \in \mathcal{B}(x,y,w,h) \\ n, & \text{otherwise} \end{cases} \tag{1}$$

where $M_c(u,v)$is the mask value at coordinates (u,v), and B(x,y,w,h) is the rectangular region defined by the bounding box.

BDM offers a computationally efficient alternative to conventional semantic segmentation by transforming 1D detection labels into 2D supervisory signals without additional annotation overhead, significantly enhancing spatial distribution learning through the hard-assignment function that enforces intra-rectangle class consistency while uniformly labeling external regions as background. This approach provides stable gradient propagation, particularly beneficial for small defect detection, by introducing a rectangular prior that serves as specialized regularization, where the uniform class distribution simultaneously mitigates label noise-induced gradient fluctuations and maintains balanced training weights across varying object scales.

3.4 Auxiliary Segmentation Guidance Subnetwork

For clarity, we use YOLOv11 as the baseline to illustrate the proposed network architecture, as illustrated in Fig. 3(a). Specifically, the ASGS first shares the backbone network of the main branch by taking B5 from the main branch as input. During the feature prediction phase, multi-scale prediction features of the detection neck are fused with correspondingly sized decoded features from ASGS. For instance, P4 serves as partial input to A5 to achieve cross-task feature interaction. The decoding modules of ASGS at different stages are shown in Fig. 3(b) and (c). When hierarchical cross-task feature interaction is required (A4 and A5 in Fig. 3(a)), the basic structure is presented in Fig. 3(b). For instance, B5 is first upsampled through transposed convolution, then concatenated with the corresponding features P4 in the detection neck after processing through the feature extraction module C3K2, and finally passed through another C3K2 module, which can be formulated as:

$$A5 = C3K2(concat(C3K2(transconv(B5)), P4)) \tag{2}$$

For A1, A2, and A3 in Fig. 3(a), the specific operation is shown in Fig. 3(c). The input $A_i(i = 4, 3, 2)$ undergoes feature map expansion through transposed convolution followed by feature learning via a C3K2 module, which can be defined as:

$$A_{i-1} = C3K2(transconv(A_i)), (i = 4, 3, 2) \tag{3}$$

During feature extraction, the dual-branch network uses pixel-level supervision to cluster same-category features while separating different categories,

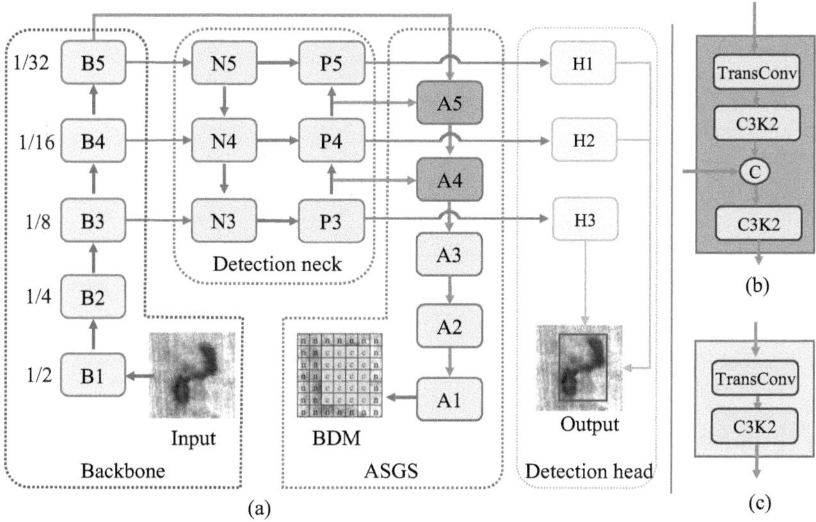

Fig. 3. The network architecture of proposed BDMGNet based on YOLOv11.

enhanced by BDM's foreground-background discrimination that suppresses background features via regularization. In feature mapping, hierarchical cross-task interaction combines main branch predictions with ASGS decoder layers, where BDM's pixel-level labels enforce category-specific feature encoding. This explicit supervision simplifies feature optimization by directly mapping object features to their categories while suppressing background interference.

3.5 Preference Dynamic Weight Averaging

To address the optimization imbalance caused by gradient magnitude differences between semantic segmentation and object detection losses in multi-task learning, we propose a PDWA strategy based on the Dynamic Weight Average (DWA) method [19] to ensure the optimization process better enhances the performance of the primary object detection task.

The conventional DWA method dynamically adjusts weights by calculating the rate of change for each task's loss:

$$r_k(t) = \frac{L_k(t-1)}{L_k(t)} \tag{4}$$

where $L_k(t)$ denotes the loss value of task k at t, and $r_k(t)$ reflects the descent rate of task k. $r_k(t) > 1$ indicates successful learning for the task; otherwise, the task faces learning difficulties. Based on this, DWA calculates dynamic weights according to the rate of change in each task's loss:

$$w_k(t) = \frac{K \cdot e^{r_k(t)/T}}{\sum\limits_i e^{r_i(t)/T}} \tag{5}$$

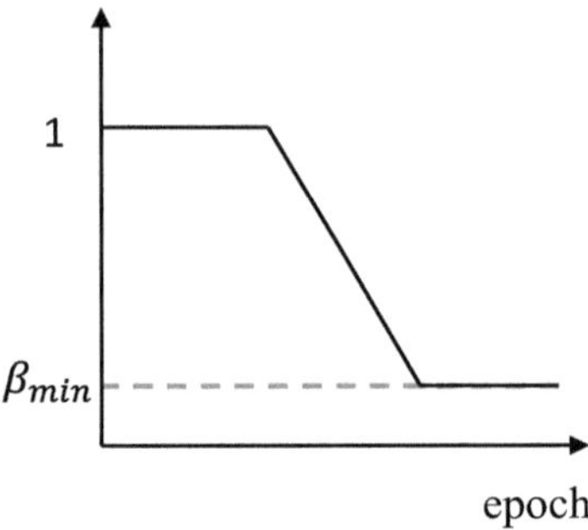

Fig. 4. Evolution of β from equation (7) across training epochs.

where K represents the number of tasks and T denotes the temperature coefficient.

The conventional DWA tends to allocate more weights to difficult-to-learn tasks and achieve inter-task balance. However, since our objective is to optimize the performance of the main branch through the auxiliary branch, we propose the PDWA strategy by introducing a preference coefficient s_k, constructing new multi-task loss weights λ_k:

$$\lambda_k = w_k(t) \cdot s_k \tag{6}$$

For the object detection loss weight, we fix the preference coefficient s_{bbox} to 1, while for the ASGS loss weight, the preference coefficient s_{mask} is dynamically adjusted during training. Specifically, we initially set a fixed s_{mask} value, and when the network approaches convergence, we gradually reduce the segmentation task weight according to the following formula:

$$s_{mask} = \alpha \cdot \beta_{epoch} \tag{7}$$

where α is the adjustment coefficient, and β_{epoch} satisfies the condition shown in Fig. 4.

Additionally, a minimum value β_{min} is set for β_{epoch} to ensure the auxiliary branch maintains a persistent influence. The overall loss function is defined as:

$$L_{total} = \lambda_{bbox} * l_{bbox} + \lambda_{mask} * l_{mask} \tag{8}$$

where l_{bbox} and l_{mask} are the loss functions for the object detection and segmentation tasks, respectively. This design enables the network to fully learn shared feature representations during the initial training phase while progressively focusing more on optimizing the primary object detection task in later stages.

4 Experiment

4.1 Datasets and Experimental Parameters

NEU-DET [22] is a publicly available dataset focused on steel surface defect detection consisting of 1,800 images with 6 common defect types: *crazing*, *inclu-*

Table 1. Experiment results on NEU-DET and GBC-DET.

Model	NEU-DET		GBC-DET		Param.(M)
	mAP50(%)	mAP50:95(%)	mAP50(%)	mAP50:95(%)	
YOLOv5-n [2]	76.2	43.5	90.1	47.8	2.7
YOLOv5-n (+BDMG)	76.6 (+0.4)	43.6 (+0.1)	90.8 (+0.7)	49.4 (+1.6)	2.7
YOLOv5-s [2]	76.8	44.3	90.1	48.5	9.5
YOLOv5-s (+BDMG)	77.6 (+0.8)	44.6 (+0.3)	91.1 (+1.0)	50.0 (+1.5)	9.5
YOLOv8-n [3]	76.9	44.5	90.8	47.8	3.2
YOLOv8-n (+BDMG)	77.3 (+0.4)	44.9 (+0.4)	91.3 (+0.5)	48.9 (+1.1)	3.2
YOLOv8-s [3]	78.4	45.2	90.5	48.8	11.2
YOLOv8-s (+BDMG)	79.6 (+1.2)	45.9 (+0.7)	91.5 (+1.0)	48.9 (+0.1)	11.2
GELAN-s [20]	78.3	45.6	90.7	49.6	7.1
YOLOv9-s [20]	78.4 (+0.1)	45.9 (+0.3)	91.5 (+0.8)	50.0 (+0.4)	7.1
GELAN-s (+BDMG)	79.2 (+0.9)	46.5 (+0.9)	90.8 (+0.1)	50.1 (+0.5)	7.1
YOLOv11-n [21]	77.0	43.5	88.7	46.2	2.9
YOLOv11-n (+BDMG)	77.7 (+0.7)	44.2 (+0.7)	89.4 (+0.7)	47.9 (+1.7)	2.9
YOLOv11-s [21]	78.1	44.9	88.7	47.6	10.2
YOLOv11-s (+BDMG)	78.7 (+0.6)	45.2 (+0.3)	91.7 (+3.0)	49.7 (+2.1)	10.2
DERT [24]	77.4	43.9	89.6	48.5	41.0
DERT (+BDMG)	78.6 (+1.2)	45.0 (+1.1)	91.2 (+1.6)	49.8 (+1.3)	41.0

sion, *patches*, *pitted surface*, *rolled-in_scale*, and *scratches*. All images have a fixed resolution of 200×200 pixels. **Green Battery Case Defect Dataset (GBC-DET)** is a self-constructed dataset for new energy battery shell surface defects, comprising 4,350 images with 5 defect categories: *pit*, *smudge*, *R_angle*, *sand_hole*, and *wrinkle*. The images vary in resolution, including 320×320, 384×384, and 800×512 pixels. To further evaluate the generalization capability of our method across different industrial inspection scenarios, we additionally employ the **DeepPCB** [23]. It is a publicly available benchmark dataset designed for printed circuit board (PCB) defect detection. It consists of 1,500 image pairs, each containing a defect-free template image and a test image to be inspected, with a resolution of 640×640 pixels. The dataset provides annotations for 6 common PCB defect types: *missing hole*, *mouse bite*, *open circuit*, *short*, *spur*, and *spurious copper*. All defects are meticulously annotated at the pixel level with precise ground truth.

The experimental setup comprises an Ubuntu 20.04 LTS system with an NVIDIA RTX 3090 GPU (24 GB VRAM) and Intel i9-14900K CPU, using PyTorch 1.13.1 with CUDA 11.7 acceleration. We resize all images to 640 × 640 resolution and split them into training and validation sets in a ratio of 8:2. Model training employs SGD optimization (initial lr = 0.01) with cosine annealing (final lr = 0.0001, lrf = 0.01) over 300 epochs to ensure convergence.

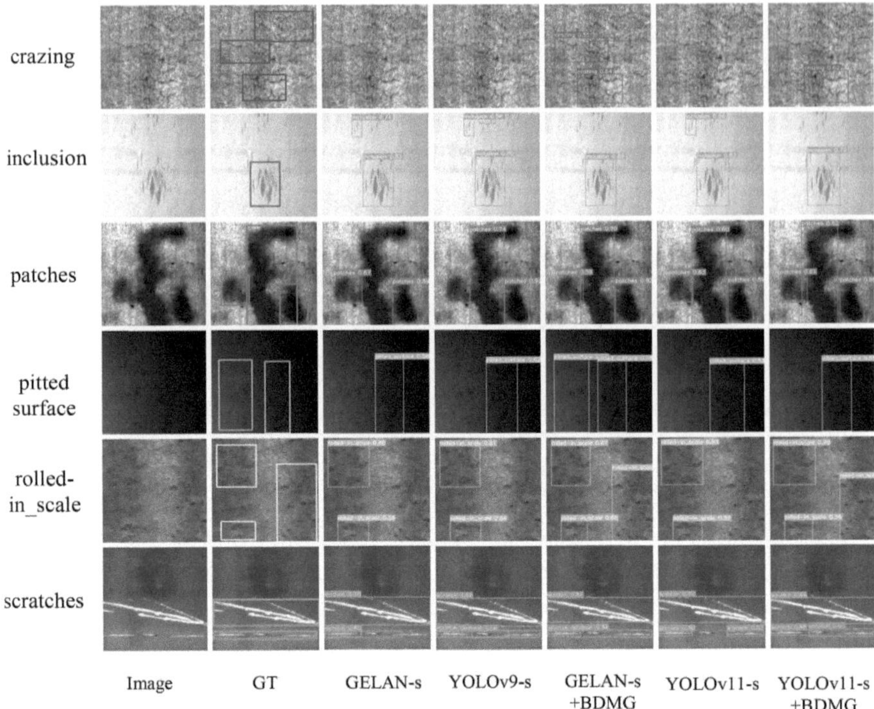

Fig. 5. Detection results of different models on NEU-DET dataset.

4.2 Quantitative Experiments

Table 1 presents the comparative experimental results of multiple YOLO-series models with the introduced BDMG. It is observed that all YOLO series demonstrate significant performance improvements after incorporating the BDMG on both the NEU-DET and GBC-DET datasets. Specifically, systematic enhancements are observed in both the mAP50 and mAP50:95 evaluation metrics. On the NEU-DET dataset, when using YOLOv8-s as the baseline model, mAP50 is improved by 1.2%. On the GBC-DET dataset, with YOLOv11-s as the baseline model, mAP50 and mAP50:95 are increased by 3% and 2.1%, respectively.

Figure 5 shows the visualization results on NEU-DET. It further demonstrate that BDMGNet can improve defect identification while reducing false detections, especially in complex multi-object scenarios. Figure 6 reveals BDMG-enhanced YOLOv11-s achieves better small-object detection and low-contrast defect recognition on GBC-DET.

To thoroughly investigate the influence of the BDMG on feature learning, we conduct qualitative analysis through feature heatmap visualization. As shown in Fig. 7, we compare the feature response maps of the YOLOv11-n model at three representative scales (1/8, 1/16, and 1/32). After BDMG integration, the activation contours of object regions become notably clearer across all

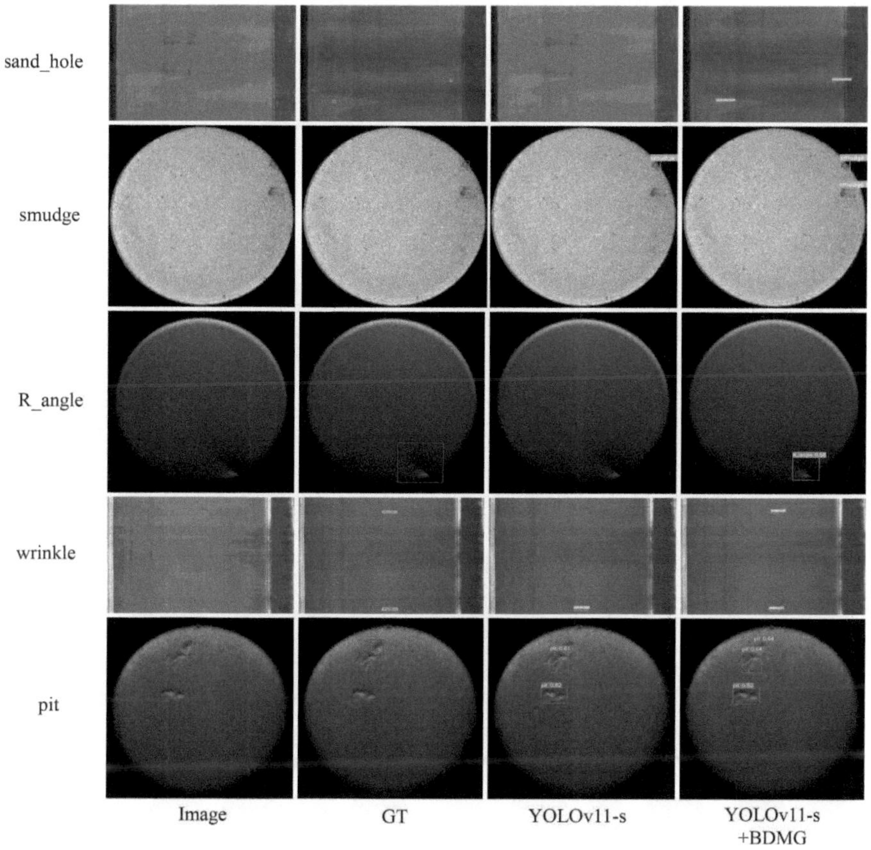

sand_hole
smudge
R_angle
wrinkle
pit
Image GT YOLOv11-s YOLOv11-s +BDMG

Fig. 6. The visualization results of YOLOv11-s and the proposed BDMGNet on GBC-DET dataset.

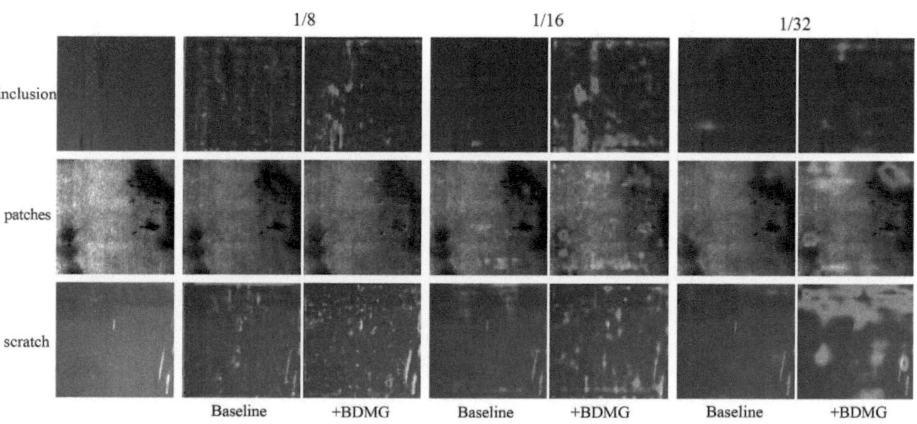

Fig. 7. Feature heatmaps corresponding to different-scale detection Heads.

Table 2. Experiment results on DeepPCB.

Model	mAP50(%)	mAP95(%)	Param.(M)
YOLOv11-s [21]	97.0	70.1	10.2
YOLOv11-s (+BDMG)	98.3 (+1.3)	73.9 (+3.8)	10.2
DERT [24]	96.5	69.9	41.0
DERT (+BDMG)	97.3 (+0.8)	72.3 (+2.4)	41.0

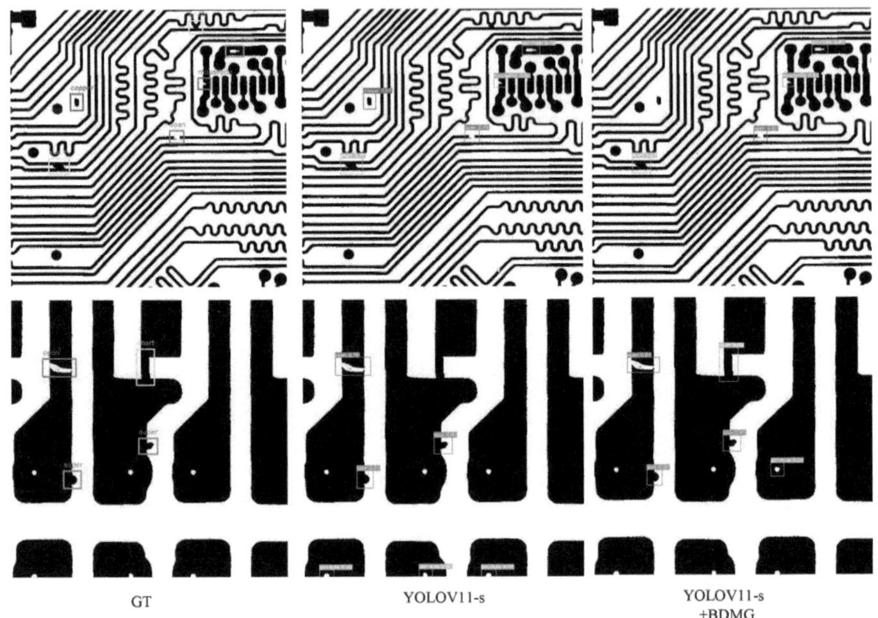

Fig. 8. The visualization results of YOLOv11-s and the proposed BDMGNet on DeepPCB dataset.

scales. The heatmap analysis reveals that the BDMG significantly enhances the model's multi-scale feature learning capability. By providing pixel-level supervision through its auxiliary branch, the BDMG enables the network to establish more precise feature representations.

As shown in Table 2, our method demonstrates excellent generalization in PCB inspection (a domain distinct from steel surface inspection), achieving optimal detection performance. It consistently improves all baseline models, setting a new state-of-the-art on this benchmark. Figure 8 qualitatively confirms these improvements: our detector locates various PCB defects more accurately with precise bounding boxes and fewer false positives.

4.3 Ablation Studies

To systematically validate the effectiveness of the proposed method, we conduct stepwise verification experiments on the auxiliary branch design, employing YOLOv11-s as the baseline model. Table 3 shows the comparison results under different auxiliary branch configurations: in the *Assistant branch* column, *bone* indicates that the auxiliary branch only connects to the backbone network to achieve basic feature sharing, while *bone+neck* represents the complete auxiliary network structure that synchronously transmits multi-level feature information from object detection predictions to the auxiliary branch. In the *segmask* column, binary masks (0,1) merely distinguish foreground and background information, whereas multi-class masks (0,n) further differentiate semantic information across different categories.

When upgrading the auxiliary branch from *bone* to *bone+neck*, the mAP50 metric increased by 1.9% with (0,1) masks and by 1.4% with (0,n) masks, demonstrating that multi-level feature fusion significantly enhances model performance. Furthermore, using (0,n) multi-class masks provided an additional 0.9% mAP50 improvement compared to (0,1) masks in the *bone+neck* configuration. Overall, the auxiliary branch achieved total gains of 3% in mAP50 and 2.1% in mAP50:95 relative to the baseline model.

Table 3. Ablation study on ASGS

Assistant Branch	Segmask	mAP50	mAP50:95
–	–	88.7	47.6
bone	(0,1)	88.9 ± 0.2	47.8 ± 0.1
bone	(0,n)	90.3 ± 0.3	48.1 ± 0.2
bone+ neck	(0,1)	90.8 ± 0.2	48.5 ± 0.2
bone+ neck	(0,n)	91.7 ± 0.1	49.7 ± 0.2

Table 4. Ablation study on PDWA

Model	Optimization	s_{mask}	mAP50	mAP50:95
YOLOv11-s	–	–	88.7	47.6
+BDMG	–	0.5	89.1 ± 0.3	46.9 ± 0.5
+BDMG	DWA	0.5	90.1 ± 0.1	48.5 ± 0.3
+BDMG	DWA	0.05	89.6 ± 0.2	47.9 ± 0.1
+BDMG	PDWA	0.5	91.7 ± 0.2	49.7 ± 0.3

For the PDWA strategy, systematic validation is conducted with key parameters fixed at $\beta_{min} = 0.1$ and $s_{bbox} = 1$. As shown in Table 4, comparative analysis between PDWA and DWA reveal that the PDWA strategy provides a 1.6% accuracy improvement over traditional DWA. Specifically, controlled experiments with DWA's s_{mask} set to 0.5 versus 0.05 confirm PDWA's superiority in weight adjustment range (from maximum to minimum values), where PDWA achieves 2.6% higher mAP50 and 2.8% higher mAP50:95 compared to non-PDWA approaches, collectively demonstrating the effectiveness and adaptability of the PDWA strategy for the object tasks in this study.

5 Conclusion

In this paper, we propose an innovative surface defect detection network that enhances feature learning by converting bounding boxes into pixel-level masks and implementing a collaborative training mechanism between segmentation and detection branches, coupled with dynamic weight optimization. The proposed BDMGNet maintains the original model efficiency by removing the auxiliary branch during deployment. In the future work, we will focus on the issues of degraded mask quality for overlapping objects and suboptimal multi-task optimization, suggesting improvements in robust mask generation and training strategies.

References

1. Redmon, J.: You only look once: unified real-time object detection. In: Proceedings of the IEEE Conference on Computer Vision and Pattern Recognition, pp. 779–788. IEEE, Las Vegas (2016)
2. Jocher, G.: YOLOv5 release v7.0 (2022). https://github.com/ultralytics/yolov5/releases/tag/v7.0. Accessed 7 Mar 2022
3. Jocher, G.: YOLOv8 release v8.1.0 (2024). https://github.com/ultralytics/ultralytics/releases/tag/v8.1.0. Accessed 7 Mar 2024
4. Hu, J., Shen, L., Albanie, S., Sun, G., Wu, E.: Squeeze-and-excitation networks. IEEE Trans. Pattern Anal. Mach. Intell. **42**(8), 2011–2023 (2020)
5. Woo, S., Park, J., Lee, J.-Y., Kweon, I.S.: CBAM: convolutional block attention module. In: Ferrari, V., Hebert, M., Sminchisescu, C., Weiss, Y. (eds.) ECCV 2018. LNCS, vol. 11211, pp. 3–19. Springer, Cham (2018). https://doi.org/10.1007/978-3-030-01234-2_1
6. He, K., et al.: Mask R-CNN. IEEE Trans. Pattern Anal. Mach. Intell. **40**(3), 650–662 (2018)
7. Wang, Q., Wu, B., Zhu, P., et al.: ECA-Net: efficient channel attention for deep convolutional neural networks. In: Proceedings of the IEEE/CVF Conference on Computer Vision and Pattern Recognition, pp. 11534–11542. IEEE, Seattle (2020). https://doi.org/10.3390/math10101750
8. Li, T., Ren, J., Yang, Q., et al.: Defect detection algorithm for battery cell casings based on dual-coordinate attention and small object loss feedback. Processes **12**(3), 601 (2024). https://doi.org/10.3390/pr12030601
9. Zhao, Z.-Q., Zheng, P., Xu, S.-T., et al.: Object detection with deep learning: a review. IEEE Trans. Neural Netw. Learn. Syst. **30**(11), 3212–3232 (2019)
10. Hao, R., Lu, B., Cheng, Y., Li, X., Huang, B.: A steel surface defect inspection approach towards smart industrial monitoring. J. Intell. Manuf. **32**(7), 1833–1843 (2021)
11. Yu, X., Lyu, W., Zhou, D., Wang, C., Xu, W.: ES-net: efficient scale-aware network for tiny defect detection. IEEE Trans. Instrum. Meas. **71**, 1–14 (2022)
12. Chen, B., Liu, Y., Zhang, Z., Lu, G., Kong, A.W.K.: TransAttUnet: multi-level attention-guided U-net with transformer for medical image segmentation. IEEE Trans. Emerg. Top. Comput. Intell. **8**(1), 55–68 (2024). https://doi.org/10.1109/TETCI.2023.3309626
13. Yi, H., Liu, B., Zhao, B., Liu, E.: Small object detection algorithm based on improved YOLOv8 for remote sensing. IEEE J. Sel. Top. Appl. Earth Observ. Remote Sens. **17**, 1734–1747 (2024). https://doi.org/10.1109/JSTARS.2023.3339235
14. Lee, C.-Y., Xie, S., Gallagher, P., Zhang, Z., Tu, Z.: Deeply-supervised nets. In: Artificial Intelligence and Statistics, pp. 562–570. PMLR, San Diego (2015)

15. Szegedy, C., Liu, W., Jia, Y., et al.: Going deeper with convolutions. In: Proceedings of the IEEE/CVF Conference on Computer Vision and Pattern Recognition, pp. 1–9. IEEE, Boston (2015)
16. Guo, C., Fan, B., Zhang, Q., Xiang, S., Pan, C.: AugFPN: improving multi-scale feature learning for object detection. In: Proceedings of the IEEE/CVF Conference on Computer Vision and Pattern Recognition, pp. 12595–12604. IEEE, Seattle (2020)
17. Huang, K.-C., Wu, T.-H., Su, H.-T., Hsu, W.H.: MonoDTR: monocular 3D object detection with depth-aware transformer. In: Proceedings of the IEEE/CVF Conference on Computer Vision and Pattern Recognition, pp. 4012–4021. IEEE, New Orleans (2022)
18. Levinshtein, A., Sereshkeh, A.R., Derpanis, K.: DATNet: dense auxiliary tasks for object detection. In: Proceedings of the IEEE/CVF Winter Conference on Applications of Computer Vision, pp. 1419–1427. IEEE, Snowmass (2020)
19. Liu, S., Johns, E., Davison, A.J.: End-to-end multi-task learning with attention. In: IEEE/CVF Conference on Computer Vision and Pattern Recognition, pp. 1871–1880. IEEE, Salt Lake City (2018). https://arxiv.org/abs/1803.10704
20. Wang, C.-Y., Yeh, I.-H., Liao, H.-Y.M.: YOLOv9: learning what you want to learn using programmable gradient information. arXiv preprint arXiv:2402.13616 (2024). http://arxiv.org/abs/2402.13616
21. Khanam, R., Hussain, M.: YOLOv11: an overview of the key architectural enhancements. arXiv preprint arXiv:2410.17725 (2024). https://arxiv.org/pdf/2410.17725
22. He, Y., Song, K., Meng, Q., et al.: An end-to-end steel surface defect detection approach via fusing multiple hierarchical features. IEEE Trans. Instrum. Meas. **69**(4), 1493–1504 (2020). https://doi.org/10.1109/TIM.2019.2915404
23. Liu, Y., Shen, Z., Lin, L., et al.: DeepPCB: a deep learning approach to PCB defect detection. In: 2018 IEEE International Conference on Computer Vision (ICCV) Workshops, pp. 1965–1972 (2018). https://doi.org/10.1109/ICCVW.2018.00243
24. Carion, N., Massa, F., Synnaeve, G., Usunier, N., Kirillov, A., Zagoruyko, S.: End-to-end object detection with transformers. In: Vedaldi, A., Bischof, H., Brox, T., Frahm, J.-M. (eds.) ECCV 2020. LNCS, vol. 12346, pp. 213–229. Springer, Cham (2020). https://doi.org/10.1007/978-3-030-58452-8_13

MDS-YOLO: Small Target Detection Algorithm in UAV Aerial Images Based on Multi-scale Feature Fusion

Haihe Shi, Shenglin Chen, Wen Xu, Peng Fan, Zuchang Yu, and Yanwen Qu(✉)

Jiangxi Normal University, Jiangxi Nanchang 330022, China
qu_yw@jxnu.edu.cn

Abstract. To address the low detection accuracy caused by irregular target shapes, large scale variations, and dense distributions in UAV aerial images, this paper proposes a multi-scale feature fusion algorithm for small-target detection. First, to better represent irregular targets, a feature extraction structure combining deformable convolution with a multi-branch fusion module is designed. Then, to counter the feature loss and inadequate contextual information for small targets amidst large scale variations, a dynamic adaptive feature pyramid network is constructed by integrating high-resolution detection heads and dynamic weighting mechanisms. To resolve missed detections of overlapping targets in dense scenes, which is a common flaw of standard suppression methods, a strategy combining SoftNMS and DIoU is proposed. Finally, model pruning is applied for lightweight deployment. Experimental results on the VisDrone2019 dataset demonstrate that the lightweight model achieves 48.3% $mAP_{0.5}$ and 32.0% $mAP_{0.5:0.95}$, representing substantial improvements over YOLOv8s, validating both the effectiveness and efficiency of the proposed method.

Keywords: Aerial images · Feature fusion · Bidirectional feature pyramid · Small object detection · Non-maximum suppression

1 Introduction

In recent years, Unmanned Aerial Vehicles (UAVs) have gained widespread application in agricultural monitoring, disaster rescue, urban planning, and other fields due to their advantages of low cost and high maneuverability [8]. This has spurred an urgent demand for efficient and accurate analysis techniques of UAV aerial images, among which object detection is a core technology.

Object detection algorithms have evolved from two-stage to one-stage approaches. Early representative two-stage works include R-CNN [6], Fast R-CNN [5], and Faster R-CNN [16]. These algorithms achieve high accuracy through the strategy of "first generating region proposals then classifying them", but suffer from high computational complexity. In contrast, one-stage algorithms

© The Author(s), under exclusive license to Springer Nature Singapore Pte Ltd. 2026
J. Kittler et al. (Eds.): PRCV 2025, LNCS 16289, pp. 122–135, 2026.
https://doi.org/10.1007/978-981-95-5764-6_9

represented by SSD [12], RetinaNet [11], and YOLO [15] eliminate the region proposal generation step, achieving faster detection speeds and striking a better balance between speed and accuracy.

Challenges become more complex during UAV aerial photography. As shown in Fig. 1, varying viewpoints cause object rotation/deformation, changes in flight altitude lead to significant scale differences, and densely distributed targets are prone to cause missed detections due to non-maximum suppression (NMS). To address these, researchers have proposed various solutions. Li et al. [10] proposed the DASSF model, aggregating multi-scale contextual information by adding Adaptive Spatial Feature Fusion (ASFF) and upsampling modules to the feature fusion network. Gong et al. [7] improved the fusion mechanism in FPN by designing fusion factors to control the fusion weights of adjacent feature layers, demonstrating its effectiveness depending on the absolute size of targets. Zhang et al. [21] proposed FFCA-YOLO, designing feature fusion and context attention modules to enhance feature extraction capabilities for tiny targets through cross-channel interaction and spatial attention mechanisms. Zhang et al. [20] proposed MMF-YOLO, incorporating a multi-branch cross-scale feature fusion module to capture and fuse features with different characteristics in parallel. Chen et al. [2] designed a High-level Screening Feature Pyramid Network (HS-FPN) to filter features of targets at different scales, enhancing the model's expressive power. Zhu et al. [24] proposed TPH-YOLOv5, improving small target detection capability by adding a high-resolution detection head and a Transformer prediction head, but at the cost of significantly reduced inference speed. The RSSO [18] model alleviated the misalignment between feature maps and Regions of Interest (RoI) caused by object rotation by introducing a region proposal feature alignment module. TS4Net [23] proposed a two-stage sample selection strategy to optimize rotated bounding box regression through finer-grained screening of positive and negative samples.

Fig. 1. The drone aerial sample images from the VisDrone dataset showcase scenes with complex variations in occlusion, background, lighting, and other factors.

In summary, Although existing UAV aerial image object detection algorithms have made progress, key issues remain: complex feature fusion modules are computationally intensive and difficult to deploy on UAV platforms; feature representation for targets with large scale differences (especially small targets) is inadequate; when recognizing multi-form targets (particularly dense and rotated objects), model structures are complex and miss rates are high; in dense scenes, traditional post-processing methods easily suppress valid detection boxes erroneously. To address this, this paper proposes MDS-YOLO, a multi-scale feature fusion-based small target detection algorithm for UAV aerial images, which systematically solves the above problems through co-design of network architecture and post-processing strategy:

1) Multi-branch Feature Fusion Module is designed. It uses a deformable convolution branch to adaptively align and extract features of irregular objects, while fusing decomposed and dilated convolution branches to capture diverse spatial information. This enhances robustness to geometric deformations and improves feature representation accuracy.
2) Dynamic Adaptive Feature Pyramid Network is constructed. Detection capability for tiny targets is strengthened by adding a higher-resolution detection head. A cross-scale weighted fusion mechanism is introduced, utilizing dynamically generated weights to regulate feature fusion ratios from different levels, ensuring effective retention and enhancement of small target details in deep networks.
3) DIoU [22] combined with Soft-NMS [1] replaces the original NMS [14]. This softly suppresses overlapping boxes rather than discarding them. It utilizes DIoU's center-point distance metric to more accurately judge spatial relationships between boxes, significantly reducing erroneous suppression of valid detection boxes in dense scenes.
4) The Layer-adaptive Magnitude-based Pruning (LAMP) [9] method is cited, significantly reducing parameters and computational complexity while maintaining model accuracy without substantial drop.

The remainder of this paper is organized as follows: Sect. 2 elaborates on the proposed method, Sect. 3 presents the experimental results, Sect. 4 provides the conclusion.

2 Method

2.1 Overview

Although YOLO11 demonstrates advantages in parameter efficiency, YOLOv8 has become the predominant object detection framework in industrial applications due to its superior detection accuracy and robust performance. When addressing challenges in UAV aerial scenarios—including diverse target morphologies, significant scale variations, and dense distributions—the original YOLOv8 still exhibits limitations. To overcome these constraints, this paper proposes the MDS-YOLO model (architecture illustrated in Fig. 2)

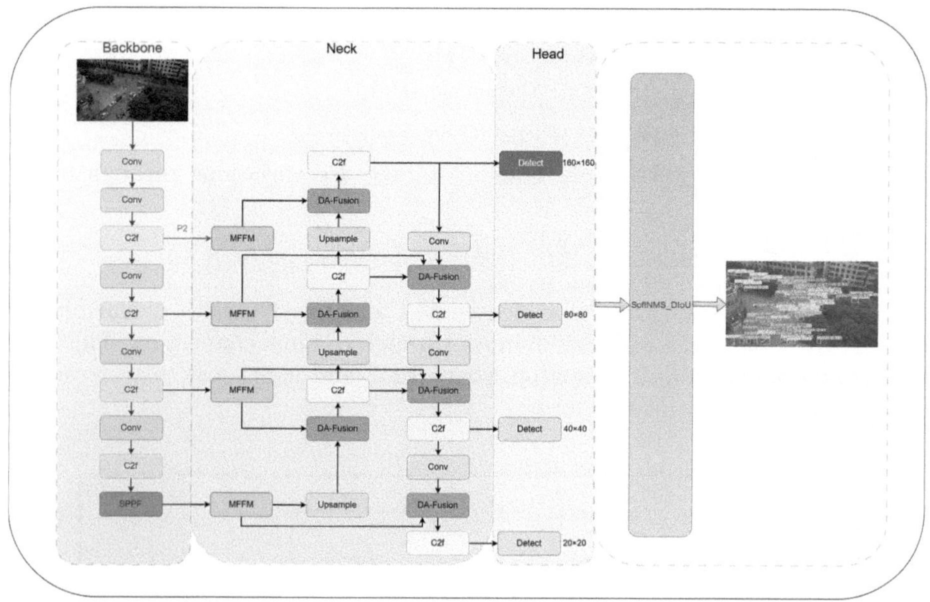

Fig. 2. The network structure of MDS-YOLO.

2.2 Multi-branch Feature Fusion Module

In deep convolutional networks, reduced feature map resolution facilitates high-level semantics but loses fine-grained details crucial for UAV aerial scenarios with irregular deformations, scale variations, and background similarity. To address this, we propose the Multi-branch Feature Fusion Module (MFFM), deployed at backbone-to-neck transfer nodes as shown in Fig. 3.

Given input feature map $F_{\text{in}} \in \mathbb{R}^{C_{\text{in}} \times H \times W}$, MFFM first adjusts channels via 1×1 convolution:

$$X = f_{\text{in}}(F_{\text{in}}) \in \mathbb{R}^{C_{\text{out}} \times H \times W} \tag{1}$$

X is then processed in parallel through four branches.

Deformable Convolution Branch: Employs deformable convolution (DCN) to adapt to target geometric deformations through learnable offsets:

$$\Delta \mathbf{p} = f_{\text{offset}}(X) \tag{2}$$

$$X_1 = f_{\text{dcn}}(X, \Delta \mathbf{p}) \tag{3}$$

where f_{offset} generates offsets via standard convolution.

Factorized Convolution Branch: Maintains large receptive field with reduced complexity by factorizing 3×3 convolution:

$$X_2 = f_{1\times3}\left(f_{3\times1}\left(f_{1\times1}(X)\right)\right) \tag{4}$$

Each convolution includes BatchNorm and ReLU.

Dilated Convolution Branch: Expands receptive field without computational increase:

$$X_3 = f_{\text{dilate}}(f_{1\times1}(X)) \tag{5}$$

where f_{dilate} uses 3×3 dilated convolutions with rate r.

Multi-scale Pooling Branch: Handles target size variations through multi-kernel pooling:

$$X_4 = \text{MaxPool}_{5\times5}(f_{1\times1}(X)) + \text{MaxPool}_{9\times9}(f_{1\times1}(X)) \tag{6}$$

Branch outputs are channel-concatenated and fused via 1×1 convolution f_{fusion}, then combined with original input through residual connection. This integrates deformation-adaptive, spatial, contextual, and multi-scale features while maintaining computational efficiency.

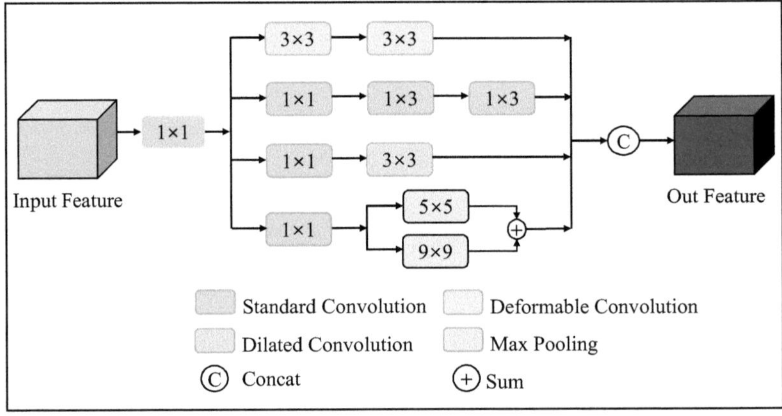

Fig. 3. Structure of MFFM

2.3 Dynamic Adaptive Fusion Bidirectional Feature Pyramid Network

In UAV aerial image object detection, varying flight altitudes and viewing angles cause images to contain numerous small targets with drastic scale variations. While the PAN+FPN structure in YOLOv8 integrates multi-level features, it relies on simple concatenation for fusion, inadequately highlighting small target information under severe scale changes in UAV contexts.

We propose the Dynamic Adaptive Fusion Feature Pyramid Network (DAFPN). First, by incorporating shallow feature map P2, we build a 160×160 detection head to utilize detail-rich shallow features and mitigate small target loss in deep networks. Second, inspired by the Bidirectional Feature Pyramid Network (BiFPN) [17], we add cross-connections between top-down and bottom-up paths, breaking PAN+FPN's unidirectional flow limitation. Finally, improving the Fast Normalized Fusion (FNF) of BiFPN, we introduce the Dynamic

Adaptive Fusion (DAF) module to replace neck concatenation. DAF resolves FNF's static weight limitation by dynamically generating fusion weights based on input feature content.

The fusion process is defined as:

$$w_i' = \frac{w_i}{\epsilon + \sum_j w_j} \tag{7}$$

where w_i is the learnable base weight for the i-th feature map, w_i' is normalized weight, and ϵ is a small constant.

Subsequently, compute dynamic weights. Sum all input features x and process them through a Dynamic Conv module to generate dynamic weights D_w:

$$D_w = \text{Sigmoid}\left(\text{DynamicConv}\left(\sum_i x_i\right)\right) \tag{8}$$

Final output O combines weights with residual connection:

$$O = \sum_i \left(w_i' \cdot x_i \cdot (1 + D_{w_i})\right) \tag{9}$$

where x_i is the i-th input, D_{w_i} is its dynamic weight component. This enables efficient multi-scale feature flow while dynamically adjusting fusion based on target characteristics, preserving small target features in complex backgrounds and improving detection performance.

2.4 Post-processing Enhancement Algorithm

In UAV aerial image object detection tasks, densely distributed and mutually occluded targets are common. Traditional Non-Maximum Suppression (NMS) employs a hard threshold strategy, which easily erroneously deletes valid overlapping detection boxes, leading to degraded detection performance. To address this, this paper proposes SoftNMS_DIoU, which replaces the traditional IoU with DIoU (Distance Intersection over Union) under the soft suppression framework of SoftNMS, to enhance detection accuracy in dense scenarios.

The traditional NMS algorithm first sorts candidate boxes in descending order of confidence, retains the highest-scoring box, then calculates the Intersection over Union (IoU) values with the remaining boxes. If the IoU exceeds a threshold, the box is considered redundant and removed, ultimately retaining high-confidence, non-redundant detection boxes. For highly overlapping prediction boxes, the traditional NMS algorithm adopts a "hard threshold" strategy: for a candidate box b_i, if its IoU with the highest-scoring detection box M exceeds a preset threshold N_t, its score s_i is directly set to zero, thus being completely suppressed. Its mathematical expression is:

$$s_i = \begin{cases} 0, & \text{IoU}(M, b_i) \geq N_t \\ s_i, & \text{IoU}(M, b_i) < N_t \end{cases} \tag{10}$$

SoftNMS replaces hard threshold suppression with a Gaussian decay strategy, effectively alleviating missed detections in dense targets by gradually reducing scores. Its mathematical expression is:

$$s_i = s_i e^{-\frac{\text{IoU}(M,b_i)^2}{\sigma}}, \forall b_i \notin D \tag{11}$$

In this formula, the score of candidate box b_i decreases in a Gaussian function manner as its IoU with M increases. The parameter σ controls the decay rate.

However, traditional IoU only considers overlap area while ignoring positional relationships, leading to insensitivity to the spatial distribution of boxes. As shown in Fig. 4, This paper combines DIoU with SoftNMS. DIoU adds an additional penalty term to traditional IoU, which directly measures the normalized distance between the centers of predicted and ground truth boxes. Its mathematical expression is:

$$\text{DIoU} = \text{IoU} - \frac{\rho^2(b, b^{gt})}{c^2} \tag{12}$$

where $\rho^2(b, b^{gt})$ represents the Euclidean distance between centers of predicted box b and ground truth box b^{gt}, and c^2 is the diagonal length of the smallest enclosing region that can contain both boxes.

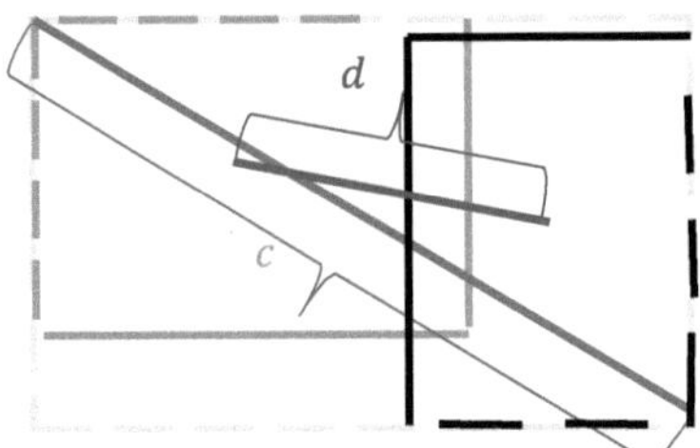

Fig. 4. DIoU loss for bounding box regression, c is the diagonal length of the smallest enclosing box covering two boxes, and $d = \rho(b, b^{gt})$ is the distance of central points of two boxes.

Combining DIoU with SoftNMS forms SoftNMS_DIoU, which considers both overlap area and center distance when attenuating confidence scores. DIoU effectively distinguishes boxes with different spatial distributions, reducing false suppression caused by SoftNMS's sole reliance on IoU.

2.5 Pruning Algorithm

The proposed multi-branch feature fusion and dynamic adaptive feature pyramid network enhance detection accuracy but increase computational complexity (GFLOPs), hindering UAV real-time deployment. To achieve lightweight models while maintaining performance, we introduce Layer-Adaptive Magnitude-based

Pruning (LAMP). Traditional magnitude-based pruning methods use uniform pruning rates or global thresholds, ignoring layer-wise parameter redundancy and sensitivity, often leading to over-pruned critical layers and performance degradation (Fig. 5).

$$\begin{bmatrix} u_1 \\ u_2 \\ u_3 \\ \cdots \end{bmatrix} \begin{bmatrix} v_1 \\ v_2 \\ v_3 \\ \cdots \end{bmatrix} \longrightarrow \begin{bmatrix} \frac{u_1^2}{u_1^2} \\ \frac{u_2^2}{u_1^2+u_2^2} \\ \frac{u_3^2}{u_1^2+u_2^2+u_3^2} \\ \cdots \end{bmatrix} \begin{bmatrix} \frac{v_1^2}{v_1^2} \\ \frac{v_2^2}{v_1^2+v_2^2} \\ \frac{v_3^2}{v_1^2+v_2^2+v_3^2} \\ \cdots \end{bmatrix} \longrightarrow \begin{bmatrix} \frac{u_1^2}{u_1^2} & \frac{v_1^2}{v_1^2} \\ \frac{u_2^2}{u_1^2+u_2^2} & \emptyset \\ \emptyset & \emptyset \\ \cdots & \cdots \end{bmatrix}$$

Fig. 5. The LAMP score is the square of the weight magnitude, normalized by the sum of all "surviving weights" in the layer. The left panel shows sorted Weight Magnitudes, the middle panel represents the LAMP score, and the right panel illustrates Global Pooling and Pruning.

LAMP is an efficient unstructured pruning method that adaptively assigns layer-wise sparsity via an importance scoring mechanism. Its core insight is that weight importance should be evaluated within layer context rather than solely by absolute magnitude. The LAMP score is defined as:

$$\text{score}(u; W) = \frac{(W[u])^2}{\sum_{v \geq u} (W[v])^2} \tag{13}$$

where $W[u]$ is the target weight and $W[v]$ denotes weights in the same layer with magnitudes no less than $W[u]$, adaptively assessing relative importance within local context.

The LAMP procedure comprises: (1) Computing LAMP scores for all prunable parameters; (2) Globally ranking scores and removing lowest-ranked weights; (3) Fine-tuning the sparse network to recover performance. This approach automatically determines optimal layer-wise sparsity, enabling efficient model compression while preserving detection accuracy, yielding the lightweight L-MDS-YOLO model.

3 Experiment Results

3.1 Datasets

Two challenging public datasets for small object detection are adopted: VisDrone2019 [3] and TinyPerson [19].

VisDrone2019 contains UAV aerial images from 14 Chinese cities under diverse scenarios and weather conditions. It includes 10 categories (pedestrian, car, etc.), with small targets defined by aspect ratio below 0.1. The dataset is split into 6471 training, 548 validation, and 1610 test images.

TinyPerson focuses on long-range tiny pedestrian detection with 72,651 annotated bounding boxes. Covering maritime and terrestrial scenes under varied weather, it contains two categories: maritime person and terrestrial person. Data is split in 8:1:1 ratio: 1288 training, 161 validation, and 161 test images.

3.2 Experimental Environment and Configuration

The experiments were conducted on an Ubuntu operating system using Python 3.8 compiler, PyTorch 1.10.0 deep learning framework, and CUDA 11.3 parallel computing platform. Hardware configuration included an NVIDIA RTX 4090D GPU and AMD EPYC 9754 128-core processor. Experimental parameters were set to 200 training epochs, batch size of 8, input image size of 640×640 pixels, initial learning rate of 0.01, learning rate momentum of 0.937, SGD optimizer, with default values for other parameters.

3.3 Evaluation Metrics

To comprehensively evaluate the performance of the proposed algorithm, precision (P), recall (R), mean average precision (mAP), model parameters (Params), giga floating-point operations (GFLOPs), and model size were adopted as evaluation metrics.

3.4 Experiment Results and Analysis

Feature Fusion Comparative Experiment. To validate the effectiveness of dynamic adaptive fusion, a comparative experiment on feature fusion methods was designed. Results are shown in Table 1 (FNF: Fast Normalized Fusion; DAF: Dynamic Adaptive Fusion; P2: 160×160 small object detection head). The experimental results indicate that compared to the Concat connection in YOLOv8 which achieved only 39.1 $\mathrm{mAP}_{0.5}$, DAF slightly outperforms FNF, verifying the effectiveness of dynamic weight generation. After adding the P2 small object detection head, the recall (R) of FNF+P2 and DAF+P2 increased by 3.7% and 8.4% respectively, confirming its critical role in small object detection. The DAF+P2 combination achieves optimal performance across all metrics, significantly improving accuracy while maintaining lightweight design (13% parameter reduction), particularly for small object detection.

Post-processing Algorithm Comparative Experiment. To validate the superiority of the proposed SoftNMS_DIoU post-processing method, a comparative experiment was conducted. Results are shown in Table 2. Key findings: SoftNMS significantly improves $\mathrm{mAP}_{0.5}$ to 44.7 by gradually decaying scores of overlapping boxes (instead of zeroing); SoftNMS_DIoU outperforms other IoU variants ($\mathrm{mAP}_{0.5}$ to 45.6, $\mathrm{mAP}_{0.5:0.95}$ to 30.2) by considering both overlap area and center distance during confidence attenuation, demonstrating the effectiveness of DIoU.

Table 1. Performance Comparison of Different Feature Fusion Methods.

Fusion Method	P (%)↑	R (%)↑	$mAP_{0.5}$ ↑	$mAP_{0.5:0.95}$ ↑	Params (M)↓
Concat	50.8	37.9	39.1	23.4	11.14
FNF	51.1	38.7	39.9	24.1	10.24
DAF	50.5	39.3	40.2	24.3	10.32
FNF+P2	52.7	42.4	43.4	26.2	**9.59**
DAF+P2	**55.2**	**47.7**	**44.4**	**26.8**	9.69

Table 2. Performance Comparison of Post-processing Methods.

Post-processing Method	$mAP_{0.5}$ ↑	$mAP_{0.5:0.95}$ ↑
NMS	39.1	23.4
SoftNMS	44.7	24.1
SoftNMS_MPDIoU	45.2	29.9
SoftNMS_GIoU	45.3	30.0
SoftNMS_DIoU	**45.6**	**30.2**

Ablation Study. To validate the effectiveness of improved modules (A: MFFM, B: DAFPN, C: SoftNMS_DIoU), ablation experiments were conducted on the YOLOv8s baseline. Results in Table 3 show: Adding A improves $mAP_{0.5}$ by 0.9%; B boosts $mAP_{0.5}$ by 5.3% and enhances small object detection; C increases $mAP_{0.5}$ by 6.5%, solving missed detections in dense scenes. A+B improves 6%, A+C reaches 46.4% (+7.3%), B+C reaches 47.6% (+8.5%). Full model A+B+C achieves 48.6% (+9.5%), validating module synergy.

Table 3. Ablation Results (A: MFFM, B: DAFPN, C: SoftNMS_DIoU).

A	B	C	$mAP_{0.5}$ ↑	$mAP_{0.5:0.95}$ ↑	Params (M)↓	GFLOPs↓	Model Size (MB)↓
×	×	×	39.1	23.4	11.1	**28.7**	21.4
✓	×	×	40.0	23.9	11.6	31.2	23.7
×	✓	×	44.4	26.8	9.69	36.8	19.8
×	×	✓	45.6	30.2	11.1	28.7	21.4
✓	✓	×	45.1	27.5	10.6	47.2	21.9
✓	×	✓	46.4	30.7	11.6	31.2	23.7
×	✓	✓	47.6	31.3	**9.69**	36.8	**19.8**
✓	✓	✓	**48.6**	**32.0**	10.6	47.2	21.9

Detection Algorithm Comparison Experiment. To verify the performance of L-MDS-YOLO, it was compared with mainstream object detection models (e.g., Faster R-CNN, RetinaNet) and YOLO series algorithms (e.g., YOLOv5s, YOLOv8s) on the VisDrone2019 and Tiny Person datasets. All experiments were conducted in the same environment, and the results are shown in Tables 4 and 5.

L-MDS-YOLO achieved the best performance on the VisDrone2019 dataset ($mAP_{0.5} = 48.3\%$, $mAP_{0.5:0.95} = 32.0\%$), significantly outperforming YOLOv8s and other algorithms. Meanwhile, it has a lightweight model (Params = 2.2M), reducing computational costs. On the Tiny Person dataset, L-MDS-YOLO also performed excellently ($mAP_{0.5} = 40.7\%$, $mAP_{0.5:0.95} = 18.5\%$), with significantly lower parameters and model size than comparative algorithms, demonstrating its advantages in UAV aerial small object detection tasks.

Table 4. Results on VisDrone2019 Dataset.

Methods	$mAP_{0.5}\uparrow$	$mAP_{0.5:0.95}\uparrow$	Params (M)↓	GFLOPs↓	Model Size (MB)↓
TOOD [4]	47.2	30.4	32.0	199	–
Faster R-CNN [18]	45.1	27.7	41.4	208	108
RetinaNet [11]	38.8	24.3	36.5	210	–
RTMDet-tiny [13]	28.7	23.3	4.9	**8.03**	–
YOLOv5s	34.5	19.0	7.1	16.0	14.4
YOLOv7-tiny	31.1	19.3	6.1	13.3	12.3
YOLOv8s	39.1	23.4	11.1	28.7	21.4
YOLOv10s	38.2	22.9	8.1	24.8	16.5
YOLO11s	38.9	23.3	9.4	21.6	19.2
L-MDS-YOLO (Ours)	**48.3**	**32.0**	**2.2**	26.0	**4.7**

Table 5. Results on TinyPerson Dataset.

Methods	$mAP_{0.5}\uparrow$	$mAP_{0.5:0.95}\uparrow$	Params (M)↓	GFLOPs↓	Model Size (MB)↓
TOOD [4]	23.1	8.9	32.0	199	–
Faster R-CNN [18]	13.6	5.7	41.4	208	108
RetinaNet [11]	11.4	4.1	36.5	210	–
RTMDet-tiny [13]	17.5	6.4	4.9	**8.03**	–
YOLOv5s	19.9	6.4	7.1	16.0	14.4
YOLOv7-tiny	12.8	3.4	6.1	13.3	12.3
YOLOv8s	21.2	7.7	11.1	28.7	21.4
YOLOv10s	19.4	6.8	8.1	24.8	16.5
YOLO11s	21.1	7.7	9.4	21.6	19.2
L-MDS-YOLO (Ours)	**40.7**	**18.5**	**2.2**	26.0	**4.7**

Algorithm Visualization Analysis. To intuitively verify the superiority of the L-MDS-YOLO algorithm, visualization results on different scenes of the VisDrone2019 dataset are shown. As shown in Fig. 6(a), the original YOLOv8s fails to detect distant tiny people and vehicles, while the improved algorithm detects more. As shown in Fig. 6(b), in low-light nighttime environments, the original algorithm has detection shortcomings, whereas the improved algorithm maintains high accuracy. As shown in Fig. 6(c), for dense and overlapping targets, the original algorithm has missed detections and false positives, which the improved algorithm effectively resolves with more accurate recognition.

(a) Detection comparison in complex scenarios

(b) Detection comparison in low-light scenarios

(c) Detection comparison in dense scenarios

Fig. 6. Visual comparison results of the proposed method vs. baseline across different challenging scenarios. Each subfigure shows the baseline result (left) and our improved result (right).

4 Conclusion

In this paper, we propose MDS-YOLO, a multi-scale feature fusion- based algorithm for drone small object detection, addressing challenges of tiny size, irregular shapes, insufficient features, and dense occlusion. The key contributions are summarized as follows:

(1) A multi-branch feature extraction module is designed, combining deformable convolution, factorized convolution, dilated convolution, and multi-scale pooling to capture irregular target features; (2) A Dynamic Adaptive Fusion (DAF) is introduced in the high-resolution detection head (P2) to enhance detail retention for small objects; (3) The detection pipeline is optimized by combining SoftNMS and DIoU, reducing missed detections in dense scenes. (4) LAMP pruning is further demonstrated for lightweight model deployment, achieving real-time performance on edge devices.

On the VisDrone2019 dataset, the $mAP_{0.5}$ reached 48.3% with a parameter count of only 2.2M. The proposed algorithm significantly outperforms YOLOv8s and other mainstream algorithms in terms of both detection accuracy and model complexity, demonstrating its superiority and practicality in the task of small object detection in UAV aerial imagery.

References

1. Bodla, N., Singh, B., Chellappa, R., Davis, L.S.: Soft-NMS–improving object detection with one line of code. In: Proceedings of the IEEE International Conference on Computer Vision, pp. 5561–5569 (2017)
2. Chen, Y., et al.: Accurate leukocyte detection based on deformable-DETR and multi-level feature fusion for aiding diagnosis of blood diseases. Comput. Biol. Med. **170**, 107917 (2024)
3. Du, D., et al.: VisDrone-DET2019: the vision meets drone object detection in image challenge results. In: Proceedings of the IEEE/CVF International Conference on Computer Vision Workshops (2019)
4. Feng, C., Zhong, Y., Gao, Y., Scott, M.R., Huang, W.: TOOD: task-aligned one-stage object detection. In: 2021 IEEE/CVF International Conference on Computer Vision (ICCV), pp. 3490–3499. IEEE Computer Society (2021)
5. Girshick, R.: Fast R-CNN. In: Proceedings of the IEEE International Conference on Computer Vision, pp. 1440–1448 (2015)
6. Girshick, R., Donahue, J., Darrell, T., Malik, J.: Region-based convolutional networks for accurate object detection and segmentation. IEEE Trans. Pattern Anal. Mach. Intell. **38**(1), 142–158 (2015)
7. Gong, Y., Yu, X., Ding, Y., Peng, X., Zhao, J., Han, Z.: Effective fusion factor in FPN for tiny object detection. In: Proceedings of the IEEE/CVF Winter Conference on Applications of Computer Vision, pp. 1160–1168 (2021)
8. Kim, P., Youn, J.: Performance evaluation of an object detection model using drone imagery in urban areas for semi-automatic artificial intelligence dataset construction. Sensors (Basel, Switzerland) **24**(19), 6347 (2024)
9. Lee, J., Park, S., Mo, S., Ahn, S., Shin, J.: Layer-adaptive sparsity for the magnitude-based pruning. arXiv preprint arXiv:2010.07611 (2020)
10. Li, H., Qu, H.: DASSF: dynamic-attention scale-sequence fusion for aerial object detection. In: Didyk, P., Hou, J. (eds.) International Conference on Computational Visual Media, vol. 15663, pp. 212–227. Springer, Singapore (2025). https://doi.org/10.1007/978-981-96-5809-1_12

11. Lin, T.Y., Goyal, P., Girshick, R., He, K., Dollár, P.: Focal loss for dense object detection. In: Proceedings of the IEEE International Conference on Computer Vision, pp. 2980–2988 (2017)
12. Liu, W., et al.: SSD: single shot MultiBox detector. In: Leibe, B., Matas, J., Sebe, N., Welling, M. (eds.) ECCV 2016. LNCS, vol. 9905, pp. 21–37. Springer, Cham (2016). https://doi.org/10.1007/978-3-319-46448-0_2
13. Lyu, C., et al.: RTMDet: an empirical study of designing real-time object detectors. arXiv preprint arXiv:2212.07784 (2022)
14. Neubeck, A., Van Gool, L.: Efficient non-maximum suppression. In: 18th International Conference on Pattern Recognition, ICPR'06, vol. 3, pp. 850–855. IEEE (2006)
15. Redmon, J., Divvala, S., Girshick, R., Farhadi, A.: You only look once: unified, real-time object detection. In: Proceedings of the IEEE Conference on Computer Vision and Pattern Recognition, pp. 779–788 (2016)
16. Ren, S., He, K., Girshick, R., Sun, J.: Faster R-CNN: towards real-time object detection with region proposal networks. IEEE Trans. Pattern Anal. Mach. Intell. **39**(6), 1137–1149 (2016)
17. Tan, M., Pang, R., Le, Q.V.: EfficientDet: scalable and efficient object detection. In: Proceedings of the IEEE/CVF Conference on Computer Vision and Pattern Recognition, pp. 10781–10790 (2020)
18. Wang, J., Shao, F., He, X., Lu, G.: A novel method of small object detection in UAV remote sensing images based on feature alignment of candidate regions. Drones **6**(10), 292 (2022)
19. Yu, X., Gong, Y., Jiang, N., Ye, Q., Han, Z.: Scale match for tiny person detection. In: Proceedings of the IEEE/CVF Winter Conference on Applications of Computer Vision, pp. 1257–1265 (2020)
20. Zhang, Q., Zhang, H., Lu, X.: Adaptive feature fusion for small object detection. Appl. Sci. **12**(22), 11854 (2022)
21. Zhang, Y., Ye, M., Zhu, G., Liu, Y., Guo, P., Yan, J.: FFCA-YOLO for small object detection in remote sensing images. IEEE Trans. Geosci. Remote Sens. **62**, 1–15 (2024)
22. Zheng, Z., Wang, P., Liu, W., Li, J., Ye, R., Ren, D.: Distance-IoU loss: faster and better learning for bounding box regression. In: Proceedings of the AAAI Conference on Artificial Intelligence, vol. 34, pp. 12993–13000 (2020)
23. Zhou, J., Feng, K., Li, W., Han, J., Pan, F.: TS4Net: two-stage sample selective strategy for rotating object detection. Neurocomputing **501**, 753–764 (2022)
24. Zhu, X., Lyu, S., Wang, X., Zhao, Q.: TPH-YOLOv5: improved YOLOv5 based on transformer prediction head for object detection on drone-captured scenarios. In: Proceedings of the IEEE/CVF International Conference on Computer Vision, pp. 2778–2788 (2021)

A Fog Text Detection Network with Visual-Language Models and Fog Feature Decoupling

Gang Zhou(✉), Zhaoxi Liu, Jiakun Tian, Xinyi Chen, Li Zhang, and Zhenhong Jia

Key Laboratory of Signal Detection and Processing, Department of Computer Science and Technology, Xinjiang University, Xinjiang, China
gangzhou_xju@126.com

Abstract. Despite the significant success of deep learning-based scene text detection methods, detecting text under adverse weather conditions, particularly in foggy weather, remains a challenge due to poor visibility. In this paper, we propose a novel fog text detection network that integrates visual-language models and fog feature decoupling. Specifically, we leverage the popular CLIP model to embed textual information into the detection network, achieving cross-modal assist scene text detection. In addition, we introduce a fog feature decoupling module that learns to extract fog-related factors from the visual style. By alternately optimizing the fog feature decoupling module and the text detection model, the gap between normal images and foggy images is progressively reduced, allowing the model to learn fog-invariant features. Experimental results demonstrate that our method outperforms existing approaches on real-world foggy scene text detection datasets.

Keywords: Scene text detection · Visual-language model · Fog feature decoupling

1 Introduction

Scene text detection is a crucial preliminary step in scene text reading, focused on accurately locating text within images. Due to its practical applications in areas such as scene understanding, autonomous driving, and photo translation, it has been an active research field for many years. While existing text detection methods have demonstrated excellent performance in high quality images, their effectiveness typically diminishes significantly under adverse weather conditions. Foggy environments, in particular, pose a challenge for text detection as the suspended particles in the air absorb and scatter light, making it more difficult to extract features from the images. To address this issue, several approaches have been proposed. For instance, FTDNet [1], which builds upon DBNet [2], enhances detection performance in foggy conditions by integrating a multi-task

© The Author(s), under exclusive license to Springer Nature Singapore Pte Ltd. 2026
J. Kittler et al. (Eds.): PRCV 2025, LNCS 16289, pp. 136–147, 2026.
https://doi.org/10.1007/978-981-95-5764-6_10

(a) DBNet (b) FTDNet (c) Ours (d) GT

Fig. 1. The detection effect of several algorithms in the real-world foggy scene, where the blue rectangular box represents the detection area. (Color figure online)

learning model that includes image defogging. However, as illustrated in Fig. 1, challenges such as missed detections still persist under foggy conditions.

We observe that most existing text detection algorithms predominantly rely on visual information, failing to fully leverage multimodal data and optimize feature extraction for foggy images [3–7]. To overcome these limitations, we propose a novel text detection model that integrates a visual-language model with fog feature decoupling. Unlike single modal text detection algorithms, our approach utilizes cross-modal information from visual, semantic, and textual domains to enhance performance. This is motivated by two key advantages of CLIP [8]: (1) The pre-trained multimodal model CLIP demonstrates exceptional performance across a variety of downstream tasks by leveraging both visual and linguistic knowledge [9–11]. (2) Scene text in natural images typically contains rich character-level information, which aligns well with CLIP's capabilities. Hence, we utilize cross-modal information from the visual and textual domains to enhance text detection performance, refining coarse-grained text regions within image embeddings.

To further address foggy conditions, we introduce a fog feature decoupling module along with a corresponding fog feature loss function to help the model learn effectively. During training, we adopt an alternating strategy across different modules, enabling the network to decouple fog features into fog-invariant and fog-dependent components, while allowing the detection network to learn fog-invariant features. This approach effectively mitigates the impact of variations in foggy regions, improving detection performance under foggy conditions. Similar to the concept of FIFO [12], our method accounts for the presence of differentiate weather domain attributes, which we refer to as the fog domain.

The contributions of our paper are as follows:

- We propose a novel fog text detection network combining visual language model and fog feature decoupling. Compared with TCM [13] and conventional single-mode text detection algorithms, our focus is to effectively combine CLIP model and fog decoupling module and apply them to text detection in foggy scenarios.
- A fog feature decoupling module is introduced in this paper, which can decouple fog features into fog dependent features and fog invariant features, effectively improving the generalization ability of the model in different fog domains.

- A large number of experiments on synthetic fog datasets and natural fog image datasets demonstrate the excellent performance of our method.

2 Proposed Method

The overall framework of our proposed fog text detection network, which integrates a visual language model with fog feature decoupling, is illustrated in Fig. 2. The framework primarily consists of a CLIP-enhanced text detector and a fog feature decoupling module. In this work, the text detector is based on DBNet, with the CLIP visual language model incorporated to leverage textual knowledge and improve detection performance. During the training process, the text detector and the fog feature decoupling module are alternately trained in each mini-batch. The fog feature decoupling module separates the fog features into fog-invariant and fog-related components, which are subsequently utilized by the text detector and the fog feature decoupling module, respectively.

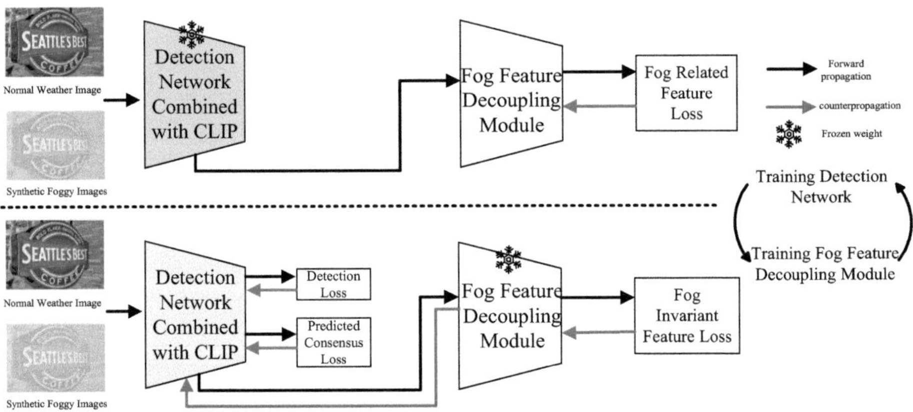

Fig. 2. Overall framework of algorithm.

2.1 Text Detection Model Combined with CLIP

The architecture of the text detector used in this paper is illustrated in Fig. 3. We extract the image features of the input image through the image encoder, and encode the input textual features into text embedding through the pre-trained CLIP text encoder. In this paper, the components of the detector, excluding the backbone network, feature pyramid network, and detection head, are referred to as the transformation module for converting CLIP into a text detection network (Change Model, CM). This corresponds to the dashed part in Fig. 3.

Inspired by TCM, this paper introduces a hint generator to generate hint vectors. Unlike the CLIP model, which uses templates such as "A photo of a

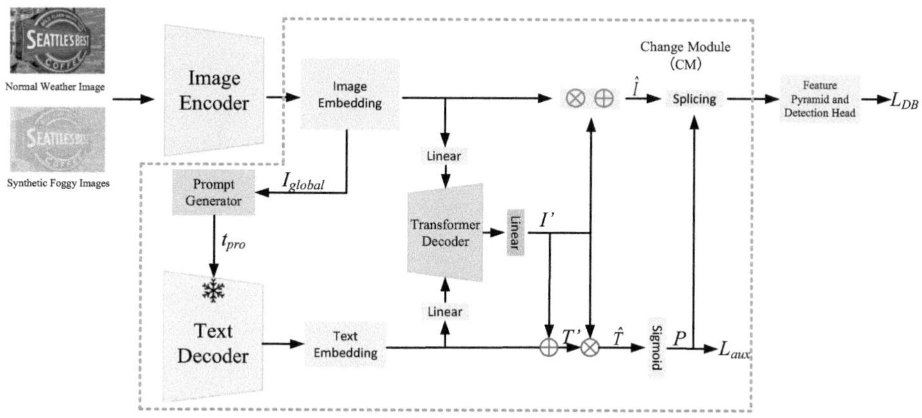

Fig. 3. Detection network combined with CLIP.

object", this article predefined the discrete language prompt as "Text". The tip t_{pro} for final use consists of learnable tip $[c_1,..., c_n]$ and pre-defined tip t_{pre} for the CLIP model. The predefined tip t_{pre} is defined as follows:

$$t_{pre} = WordEmbedding\,(Text) \in R^D \tag{1}$$

where, $WordEmbedding\,(\cdot)$ represents the predefined prompt "Text" class. D is the embedding dimension of the word, set to 512.

This paper adds a learnable prompt $[c_1,..., c_n]$ for learning. n indicates the number of tips that can be learned and is set to 4. Therefore, the text encoder input prompt t_{pro}. The definition is as follows:

$$t_{pro} = [c_1, ..., c_n, t_{pre}] \in R^{(n+1)\times D} \tag{2}$$

CLIP networks have the capability to directly respond to text inputs, allowing the feature information contained in the text embedding T to be interpreted as coarse-grained text area information generated by the text encoder. After being processed by the Transformer Decoder, the text embedding T and image embedding I undergo feature refinement, resulting in the generation of fused image-text multimodal features. The process can be expressed as:

$$I' = TransformerDecoder\,(Q = I, K = T, V = T) \in R^C \tag{3}$$

during training, this paper uses an auxiliary loss to minimize the intersection of P and text area labels Cross Entropy:

$$L_{aux} = \sum_i \sum_j y_{ij} \log\left(P_{iy}\right) + \left(1 - y_{iy}\right) \log\left(1 - P_{iy}\right) \tag{4}$$

here, The y_{ij} and P_{ij} respectively belong to the text of the instance pixels (i, j) label and prediction probability. Auxiliary loss is used to enhance the image encoder's perception of the text region during training. The loss of the detector part L_{DET} is:

$$L_{DET} = L_{DB} + \lambda L_{aux} \tag{5}$$

here, we set λ to 1 using the same scaling factor as in TCM. The introduction of L_{aux} effectively integrates textual and visual information, significantly improving the accuracy of mapping text to its corresponding regions in the image, and alleviating the issue of image blurriness under foggy conditions.

2.2 Fog Feature Decoupling

Research in FIFO [12] has shown that the Gram matrix is not suitable for accurately quantifying the impact of fog, as it is influenced by other stylistic factors and image content beyond fog. Therefore, this paper introduces a fog feature decoupling module and an associated loss function to more accurately capture fog-related factors from the Gram matrix of feature maps, effectively separating them from fog-invariant features. Instead of directly utilizing the original feature map from the detection network, the fog feature decoupling module inputs the overall style representation of the feature map, focusing more on the image's style by filtering out some content information. In this paper, we employ the Gram matrix of the feature map as the style representation, as it provides richer style information compared to other methods, such as channel-level feature statistics [14].

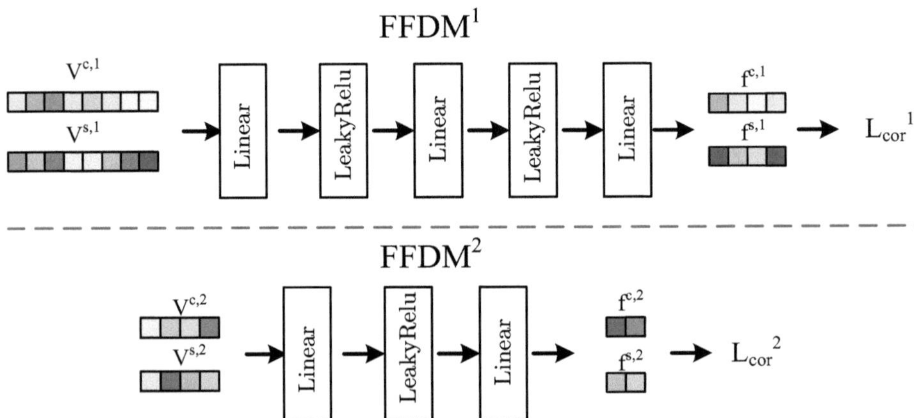

Fig. 4. Fog feature decoupling module.

The structure of fog feature decoupling module is shown in Fig. 4. It consists of two parts. FFDM^1 and FFDM^2 represent the fog feature decoupling module of layer 1 and layer 2 respectively, which are connected with Backbone's layer 1 and layer 2. $\text{V}^{c,i}$ and $\text{V}^{s,i}$ represent the upper triangular vectorization form of the Gram matrix of the feature graph from the normal weather image c and the fog image s, respectively. $f^{c,i}$ and $f^{s,i}$ represent $V^{c,i}$ and $V^{s,i}$ fog related features generated by the fog feature decoupling module.

As shown in Fig. 2, when the weights of the training detection network and the fog feature decoupling module are frozen, this paper adopts the fog invariant feature loss L_{inv} to make the detection network learn the fog invariant feature:

$$L_{inv}^{i}\left(f^{c,i}, f^{s,i}\right) = \frac{1}{4l_i^2 d_i^2} \sum_{j=1}^{l_i} \left(f^{c,i}, f^{s,i}\right)^2 \tag{6}$$

in the above formula, l_i and d_i respectively represent the spatial dimensions of the fog related features and the feature map of layer i of the detection network. Since the fog images are synthesized from normal weather, the detection network should have the same prediction results for the corresponding images of two different fog domains. Therefore, when the weight of the fog feature decoupling module is frozen and the detection network is trained, this paper uses the feature consistency loss L_{con} loss to strengthen the alignment of the network to the two prediction results:

$$L_{con}\left(B^c, B^s\right) = \sum_{p} KL\left(B_p^c, B_p^s\right) \tag{7}$$

B^c and B^s represent differentiable binary graphs of the detection head's prediction of normal images and fog images respectively. KL(.) represents KL divergence., where p is pixel value index feature consistency loss further strengthens the network's learning ability of fog invariant features.

When fog feature decoupling module and the detector are frozen, we utilize fog related feature loss L_{cor} to make FFDM learn fog related features:

$$\begin{aligned} L_{cor^i} = \sum_{(a,b)\in(c,s)} & \left\{ In(a,b)\left[CosDis\left(f^{a,i}, f^{b,i}\right) - m\right]^2 \right. \\ & \left. + (1 - In(a,b))\left[m - CosDis\left(f^{a,i}, f^{b,i}\right)\right]^2 \right\} \end{aligned} \tag{8}$$

$CosDis(.)$ represents the cosine distance, and m is set to 0.1. In the training process of the network, (c, s) represents the fog domain composed of normal weather and fog images, and (a, b) represents the fog domain to which the features output by the feature decoupling module in each mini-batch belong. The $In\,(a, b)$ is an indicator function that returns 1 when a and b belong to the same fog domain (not including cases from the same image), and 0 otherwise.

The total loss L of the network is:

$$L = \begin{cases} L_{cor} \\ L_{DEF} + L_{inv} + \lambda L_{con} \end{cases} \tag{9}$$

in the experiment, λ is set to 0.01. The fog-invariant loss encourages the detection network to learn fog-invariant features by minimizing the MSE distance between image features across different fog domains. Simultaneously, the fog feature decoupling module learns fog-related features by minimizing the cosine distance of image features within the same fog domain while maximizing the cosine distance between features from different fog domains. To achieve this, the following training strategies are implemented: when the detector and the fog feature decoupling module are frozen, the fog feature decoupling module is activated for training, with the fog-related feature loss L_{cor} guiding the process. When the detector is activated for training, the weights of the fog feature decoupling module are frozen, and the entire network is trained using L_{DEF}, L_{inv}, and L_{con}.

3 Experimental Results and Analysis

3.1 Experimental Detail

The datasets used in the experiment were NFT and SFT [1], and the network was trained by the Ranger optimizer. The SFT dataset is a mixed Chinese-English dataset comprising 2,400 training images and 948 test images. It is a synthetic foggy dataset generated using an atmospheric light scattering model, with the images selected from the ICDAR 2015 [15], 2017 MLT [16], 2017 RCTW [17], 2019 MLT [18], and 2019 LSVT [19] datasets. The NFT dataset, which we compiled, contains 787 real-world foggy images. The initial learning rate of the detection network training combined with CLIP is set to 1×10^{-3}, but the learning rate of the Backbone part is set to 1×10^{-4}. The backbone weight of the detection network is initialized by the image encoder of CLIP model, and the weight parameter of the text encoder is initialized by the text encoder of CLIP model. The learning rate of the fog feature decoupling module is 5×10^{-5}, and the weight provided by FIFO is used for initialization.

3.2 Experimental Result

The comparison results are shown in Table 1. Compared with other methods, the method proposed in this paper has advantages of at least 2.1%, 1.3%, 1.8% and 1.6%, 1.5% and 1.6% in the precision, recall rate and F-scores of the two datasets. Compared with FTDNet, the proposed method incorporates not only image information but also textual information extracted by the CLIP model. Moreover, the method introduces a fog feature decoupling module, enabling the detection network to learn fog-invariant features and further reduce the negative impact of fog. The multi-task network structure used in FTDNet is inherently constrained by the correlation between image defogging and text detection, making its gradient updates suboptimal for foggy scene text detection. In contrast, the proposed method addresses this issue by alternately training the detector and the fog feature decoupling module. As shown in Fig. 5 and Fig. 6, the proposed method significantly reduces missed and false detections in both real and synthetic foggy scenes.

Table 1. Comparison of the proposed method to the state-of-the-art on the NFT and SFT datasets.

Methods	NFT			SFT		
	R	P	F	R	P	F
PSE [20]	0.670	0.823	0.739	0.590	0.731	0.653
PAN [21]	0.675	0.850	0.752	0.601	0.755	0.669
DB [2]	0.682	0.830	0.749	0.613	0.732	0.667
CT [7]	0.681	0.858	0.759	0.611	0.766	0.679
I3CL [22]	0.697	0.861	0.770	0.639	0.770	0.698
FTDNet [1]	0.717	0.860	0.782	0.652	0.778	0.709
Ours	**0.739**	**0.874**	**0.801**	**0.668**	**0.794**	**0.725**

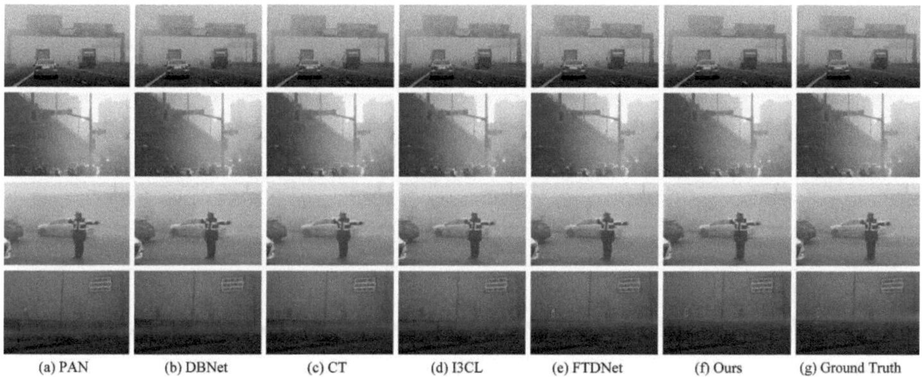

Fig. 5. Visualization results of various methods on real fog images.

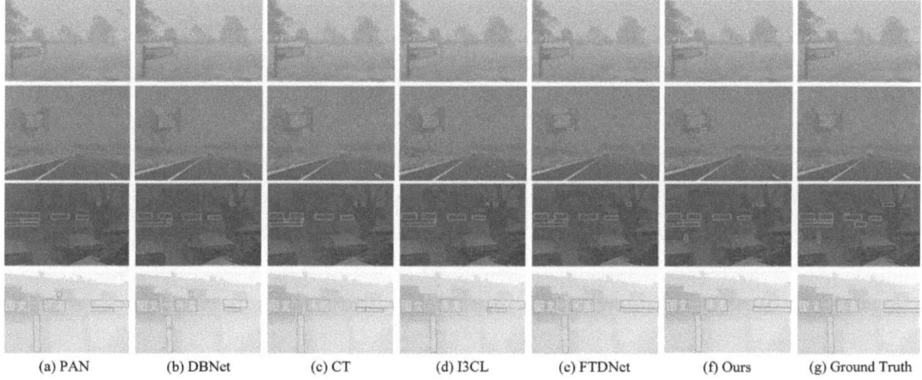

Fig. 6. Visualization results of various methods on synthetic fog images.

3.3 Ablation Study

This section describes the ablation tests conducted to verify the effectiveness of the combination of CLIP and detector and the fog decoupling module proposed in this paper. As shown in Table 2, the optimal combination of CM, FFDM and L_{con} was determined through experiments in this paper.

In the second row, we added the CM to DBNet, resulting in a 1.4% and 2.1% improvement in F-scores on the NFT and SFT datasets, respectively. In the third and fourth rows, we compared the CM with the cross-modal fusion modules in DenseCLIP [23] and TCM [13]. Both DenseCLIP and TCM leverage the CLIP model to achieve information exchange and fusion between text and image modalities. Unlike TCM, our approach employs more advanced feature fusion techniques. The CM utilizes six 4-head bidirectional Transformer Decoder layers to enable thorough interaction between image and text embeddings. After generating the image-text features, the CM further refines them through operations such as adaptive weighted addition, dot product summation, and channel-wise concatenation to produce image-to-text and text-to-image corresponding features. In the sixth row, we introduced the FFDM, which led to a 3.5% and 4.4% increase in F-scores compared to the DBNet. The last row represents our complete model, showing a 5.2% and 5.8% improvement in F-scores on the NFT and SFT datasets, respectively, compared to DBNet.

Table 2. Ablation study on various modules of our approach on the NFT and SFT datasets.

Methods	NFT			SFT		
	R	P	F	R	P	F
DBNet	0.682	0.831	0.749	0.614	0.732	0.667
DBNet+CM (wo L_{aux})	0.694	0.848	0.763	0.623	0.769	0.688
DBNet+DenseCLIP [23]	0.693	0.846	0.761	0.627	0.751	0.683
DBNet+TCM [13]	0.697	0.862	0.770	0.628	0.783	0.696
DBNet+CM (w L_{aux})	0.701	0.864	0.774	0.629	0.783	0.697
DBNet+FFDM	0.727	0.852	0.784	0.629	0.760	0.688
DBNet+L_{con}	0.691	0.831	0.754	0.620	0.733	0.672
DBNet+CM+FFDM	0.733	0.874	0.797	0.659	0.790	0.718
DBNet+FFDM+L_{con}	0.729	0.852	0.786	0.650	0.771	0.706
DBNet+CM+FFDM+L_{con}	**0.739**	**0.874**	**0.801**	**0.668**	**0.794**	**0.726**

This section also investigates the impact of different learning rates. The cross-modal feature fusion part of CM and the detection head of the detector adopt the original learning rate from DBNet, while different learning rate settings are applied to the image encoder and text encoder of the model. This subsection provides an explanation of these settings. Table. 3 shows the model performance

Table 3. Ablation Study on Different Learning Rates. IF denotes the learning rate coefficient for the image encoder, TF denotes the learning rate coefficient for the text encoder, and the values in the table represent the F1-Score on NFT under different combinations of learning rate.

Learning Rate Settings for Encoder		IF		
		0	0.1	1.0
TF	0	59.639	**80.115**	78.941
	0.1	58.672	79.255	78.050
	1.0	56.592	77.648	77.126

under various combinations of learning rates for the image encoder and text encoder. The results indicate that using a lower learning rate for the image encoder and freezing the text encoder yields the optimal configuration for training the entire model. When a learning rate of 1.0 is directly applied to both encoders, a performance drop is observed. The model performs best when the text encoder parameters are frozen. This suggests that freezing the text encoder stabilizes the training process, whereas fine-tuning the text encoder disrupts the parameter distribution of the model and impairs the generalization ability of CLIP. The CLIP model has been pre-trained on 400 million large-scale data, endowing it with substantial prior knowledge. The core function of CM is to guide the utilization of CLIP's pre-learned knowledge through cross-modal feature fusion, enhancing the model's perception of text regions. According to the experimental results, this goal can be achieved by moderately fine-tuning only the image encoder of CLIP, which maximally preserves the generalization capability of CLIP.

4 Conclusion

This paper presents a text detection network tailored for foggy scenes, which enhances detection performance by integrating cross-modal information and decoupling fog features. The CLIP model is employed to leverage both textual and visual information, and their interaction is facilitated through a proposed conversion module, thereby improving the model's ability to perceive text regions. Additionally, by decoupling fog features, these features are separated into fog-invariant characteristics and fog-related features. This enables the network to learn fog-invariant features, thereby improving its generalization ability under foggy conditions. Experimental results and analysis demonstrate that the proposed method outperforms previous approaches.

Acknowledgement. This work was supported by the National Natural Science Foundation of China (No. 62166040, No. 62261053), the Tianshan Talent Training Project, the Technology Innovation Team Program (2023TSYCTD0012), and the Basic Research Business Expense Project of Universities in Xinjiang Uygur Autonomous Region under Grant XJEDU2025P009.

References

1. Tian, J., Zhou, G., Liu, Y., Deng, E., Jia, Z.: FTDnet: joint semantic learning for scene text detection in adverse weather conditions. In: Fink, G.A., Jain, R., Kise, K., Zanibbi, R. (eds.) ICDAR 2023. LNCS, vol. 14191, pp. 137–154. Springer, Cham (2023). https://doi.org/10.1007/978-3-031-41734-4_9
2. Liao, M., Wan, Z., Yao, C., Chen, K., Bai, X.: Real-time scene text detection with differentiable binarization. In: Proceedings of the AAAI Conference on Artificial Intelligence, vol. 34, pp. 11474–11481 (2020)
3. Long, S., Qin, S., Panteleev, D., Bissacco, A., Fujii, Y., Raptis, M.: Towards end-to-end unified scene text detection and layout analysis. In: Proceedings of the IEEE/CVF Conference on Computer Vision and Pattern Recognition, pp. 1049–1059 (2022)
4. Baek, Y., Lee, B., Han, D., Yun, S., Lee, H.: Character region awareness for text detection. In: Proceedings of the IEEE/CVF Conference on Computer Vision and Pattern Recognition, pp. 9365–9374 (2019)
5. Dai, P., Zhang, S., Zhang, H., Cao, X.: Progressive contour regression for arbitrary-shape scene text detection. In: Proceedings of the IEEE/CVF Conference on Computer Vision and Pattern Recognition, pp. 7393–7402 (2021)
6. Liao, M., Pang, G., Huang, J., Hassner, T., Bai, X.: Mask TextSpotter V3: segmentation proposal network for robust scene text spotting. In: Vedaldi, A., Bischof, H., Brox, T., Frahm, J.-M. (eds.) ECCV 2020. LNCS, vol. 12356, pp. 706–722. Springer, Cham (2020). https://doi.org/10.1007/978-3-030-58621-8_41
7. Sheng, T., Chen, J., Lian, Z.: Centripetaltext: an efficient text instance representation for scene text detection. In: Advances in Neural Information Processing Systems, vol. 34, pp. 335–346 (2021)
8. Radford, A., et al.: Learning transferable visual models from natural language supervision. In: International Conference on Machine Learning, pp. 8748–8763. PMLR (2021)
9. Wan, Q., Ji, H., Shen, L.: Self-attention based text knowledge mining for text detection. In: Proceedings of the IEEE/CVF Conference on Computer Vision and Pattern Recognition, pp. 5983–5992 (2021)
10. Song, S., et al.: Vision-language pre-training for boosting scene text detectors. In: Proceedings of the IEEE/CVF Conference on Computer Vision and Pattern Recognition, pp. 15681–15691 (2022)
11. Xue, C., Zhang, W., Hao, Y., Lu, S., Torr, P.H., Bai, S.: Language matters: a weakly supervised vision-language pre-training approach for scene text detection and spotting. In: Avidan, S., Brostow, G., Cissé, M., Farinella, G.M., Hassner, T. (eds.) ECCV 2022. LNCS, vol. 13688, pp. 284–302. Springer, Cham (2022). https://doi.org/10.1007/978-3-031-19815-1_17
12. Lee, S., Son, T., Kwak, S.: Fifo: learning fog-invariant features for foggy scene segmentation. In: 2022 IEEE. CVF Conference on Computer Vision and Pattern Recognition (CVPR), pp. 18889–18899 (2022)
13. Yu, W., Liu, Y., Hua, W., Jiang, D., Ren, B., Bai, X.: Turning a clip model into a scene text detector. In: Proceedings of the IEEE/CVF Conference on Computer Vision and Pattern Recognition, pp. 6978–6988 (2023)
14. Ulyanov, D.: Instance normalization: the missing ingredient for fast stylization. arXiv preprint arXiv:1607.08022 (2016)
15. Karatzas, D., et al.: ICDAR 2015 competition on robust reading. In: 2015 13th International Conference on Document Analysis and Recognition (ICDAR), pp. 1156–1160. IEEE (2015)

16. Nayef, N., et al.: ICDAR2017 robust reading challenge on multi-lingual scene text detection and script identification-RRC-MLT. In: 2017 14th IAPR International Conference on Document Analysis and Recognition (ICDAR), vol. 1, pp. 1454–1459. IEEE (2017)
17. Shi, B., et al.: ICDAR2017 competition on reading Chinese text in the wild (RCTW-17). In: 2017 14th IAPR International Conference on Document Analysis and Recognition (ICDAR), vol. 1, pp. 1429–1434. IEEE (2017)
18. Nayef, N., et al.: ICDAR2019 robust reading challenge on multi-lingual scene text detection and recognition—RRC-MLT-2019. In: 2019 International Conference on Document Analysis and Recognition (ICDAR), pp. 1582–1587. IEEE (2019)
19. Sun, Y., et al.: ICDAR 2019 competition on large-scale street view text with partial labeling-RRC-LSVT. In: 2019 International Conference on Document Analysis and Recognition (ICDAR), pp. 1557–1562. IEEE (2019)
20. Wang, W., et al.: Shape robust text detection with progressive scale expansion network. In: Proceedings of the IEEE/CVF Conference on Computer Vision and Pattern Recognition, pp. 9336–9345 (2019)
21. Wang, W., et al.: Efficient and accurate arbitrary-shaped text detection with pixel aggregation network. In: Proceedings of the IEEE/CVF International Conference on Computer Vision, pp. 8440–8449 (2019)
22. Du, B., Ye, J., Zhang, J., Liu, J., Tao, D.: I3CL: intra-and inter-instance collaborative learning for arbitrary-shaped scene text detection. Int. J. Comput. Vision **130**(8), 1961–1977 (2022)
23. Rao, Y., et al.: Denseclip: language-guided dense prediction with context-aware prompting. In: Proceedings of the IEEE/CVF Conference on Computer Vision and Pattern Recognition, pp. 18082–18091 (2022)

Collaborative Perception and Dual-Stage Decoder Network for Camouflaged Object Detection

Zhenjie Ji[1], Yanjiao Shi[1(✉)], Qing Zhang[1], and Qiangqiang Zhou[2]

[1] Shanghai Institute of Technology, Shanghai 201418, China
Shiyanjiao616@163.com

[2] Jiangxi Normal University, Nanchang 330022, China

Abstract. In recent years, Vision Transformers have achieved impressive results in camouflaged object detection (COD). However, two major challenges remain: limited perception capability and insufficient feature propagation in the decoder stage. Addressing these limitations is crucial for enhancing detection accuracy. To this end, we propose a novel camouflaged object detection network based on collaborative perception and a dual-stage decoder architecture, referred to as collaborative perception and dual-stage decoder network (CPDDNet). Specifically, a Coordinate-window collaborative attention (CWCA) module is introduced to jointly exploit global contextual information and local structural cues. In addition, we design a dual-stage decoder structure to enhance multi-level semantic feature fusion and spatial detail recovery. Extensive experiments on four widely-used COD datasets across sixteen evaluation metrics demonstrate that our method outperforms state-of-the-art approaches in both accuracy and robustness.

Keywords: Camouflaged Object detection · Deep learning · Computer Vision

1 Introduction

Camouflaged object detection (COD) [4] is an important subtask of semantic segmentation [17], aiming to identify objects in natural images that exhibit high visual similarity to their surrounding backgrounds. Unlike traditional salient object detection or semantic segmentation tasks, COD presents unique challenges, as camouflaged objects often blend into their environments in terms of texture, color, and shape. These objects usually lack obvious boundaries or salient features, significantly increasing the difficulty of detection. COD has broad application prospects in areas such as wildlife protection and medical image analysis.

This work is supported by grants from the National Natural Science Foundation of China (No. 62262030), and Jiangxi Provincial Natural Science Foundation (No. 20232BAB202021).

© The Author(s), under exclusive license to Springer Nature Singapore Pte Ltd. 2026
J. Kittler et al. (Eds.): PRCV 2025, LNCS 16289, pp. 148–161, 2026.
https://doi.org/10.1007/978-981-95-5764-6_11

In recent years, Vision Transformers have achieved significant progress in various visual recognition tasks due to their powerful global modeling capabilities. These architectures have also been introduced into COD frameworks to enhance global perception. However, existing Transformer-based COD methods still suffer from two key limitations. First, although Transformers excel at capturing global context, they struggle to model fine-grained local details—such as edge structures and subtle texture changes—leading to blurred boundaries and missed targets. Second, mainstream decoder architectures often suffer from limited feature-level propagation and insufficient integration between shallow spatial features and deep semantic representations.

To address the first limitation, we adopt a hybrid Transformer backbone, such as scale-aware modulation Transformer (SMT) [15], which combines the strengths of CNNs and Transformers and is well-suited to COD-specific vision tasks. In addition, we design a coordinate-window collaborative attention (CWCA) module to enhance the perception capability of the backbone. CWCA strengthens global perception while compensating for the limited local modeling capacity of Transformers. To address the second limitation, we redesign the decoder structure to enable effective hierarchical feature fusion. Our main contributions can be summarized as follows:

- We propose CPDDNet, a novel camouflaged object detection network that integrates a newly designed CWCA module and a dual-stage decoder. Extensive experiments on four widely used COD benchmarks show that our method outperforms 10 state-of-the-art competitors across multiple evaluation metrics.
- We design a CWCA mechanism that effectively integrates coordinate attention and window-based attention. These components guide each other during training, enhancing the global perception ability of the Transformer backbone while improving local feature modeling.
- We propose a novel dual-stage decoder architecture, which performs two decoding processes to refine and integrate hierarchical features. The final prediction is obtained by fusing the outputs from both decoding stages.

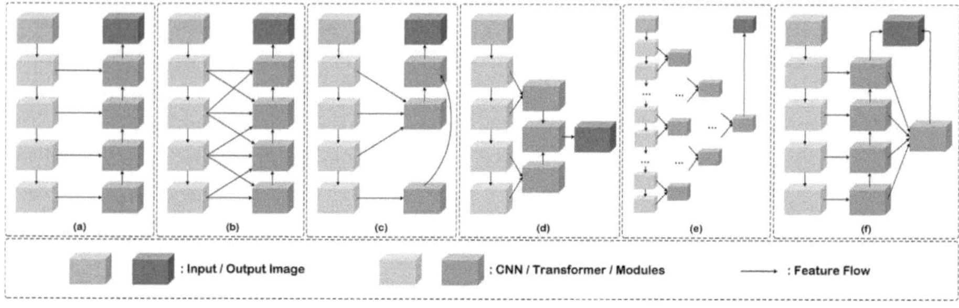

Fig. 1. Different types of decoder architectures.

2 Related Work

2.1 Recent Advanced Camouflaged Object Detection Networks

COD methods have achieved increasingly precise and refined segmentation results, with the field witnessing rapid methodological diversification. For instance, FSPNet [11] refines contextual representations by leveraging a progressive shrinkage hierarchical decoding scheme, which facilitates the generation of globally enhanced positional features from neighboring transformer layers. Meanwhile, GLCONet [25] formulates a collaborative optimization framework based on multi-source perception, featuring a decoder architecture that integrates cross-layer aggregation with reverse supervision strategies. To tackle the ambiguity between foreground and background, CamoFocus [12] introduces a supervised mask-driven foreground-background modulation mechanism that effectively disentangles camouflaged regions. SARNet [26] presents a three-stage search-amplify-recognize paradigm to sequentially enhance object localization and recognition. Recently, PRBE-Net [28] simultaneously generates coarse region and fine boundary cues by integrating multi-level features using a well-designed Region and boundary exploration module.

2.2 Decoder Architecture

Reviewing the decoder designs in downstream tasks of semantic segmentation reveals five commonly adopted architectural patterns: (a) U-shaped decoders [21,24,33], (b) densely integrated decoders [30], (c) feedback refinement decoders [29,31], (d) decoupled high-low level feature decoders [5], and (e) pyramid contraction decoders [11], as illustrated in Fig. 1. Specifically, the U-shaped decoder is the most widely used structure, capable of progressively restoring fine object details in a bottom-up manner. The densely integrated decoder is designed to alleviate the negative influence of large-scale resolution differences during feature fusion, improving overall decoding performance. The feedback refinement decoder independently enhances the top-level semantic features and subsequently merges them with features from other layers to improve localization and segmentation accuracy. In addition, some approaches explicitly separate the decoding of high-level and low-level features, achieving promising performance in COD. More recently, methods such as FSPNet [11] have adopted a pyramid contraction decoding structure, which incrementally reconstructs camouflaged information via hierarchical feature compression and expansion. In contrast to the aforementioned mainstream designs, we propose a novel dual-stage decoder architecture, as depicted in Fig. 1(f). This architecture not only facilitates bottom-up detail recovery, but also introduces an additional feature aggregation phase to compensate for semantic information loss that typically occurs during top-down propagation. By integrating the prediction maps generated from both decoding stages, our decoder is capable of producing finer and more precise segmentation results, particularly suited for detecting camouflaged objects with high fidelity.

3 Method

The overall architecture of our proposed CPDDNet is illustrated in Fig. 2. It mainly consists of three key components: an encoder, a collaborative perception module, and a dual-stage decoder. The encoder adopts the hybrid Transformer backbone SMT, which is responsible for extracting multi-level semantic features. To enhance global perception while compensating for SMT's limited ability to capture local details, we introduce a coordinate-window collaborative attention (CWCA) mechanism. This module strengthens the encoder's global modeling capacity and reinforces local structural sensitivity. The dual-stage decoder is composed of two sequential decoding stages. In the first stage, we employ the fourier fusion convolutional mixer (FFCM) [7] for enhanced feature integration, followed by a U-shaped decoding structure. This design allows high-level semantic features to effectively guide low-level spatial representations, generating four prediction maps at different scales. In the second stage, a global frequency-aware wavelet (GFW) module is introduced to fuse features across all hierarchical levels. This compensates for the semantic information degradation often encountered in traditional U-shaped decoders. The second stage produces an additional prediction map that benefits from globally harmonized features. Finally, the ultimate prediction map is obtained by a weighted fusion of the lowest-level prediction from the first stage and the output prediction from the second stage, resulting in more accurate and fine-grained camouflaged object detection.

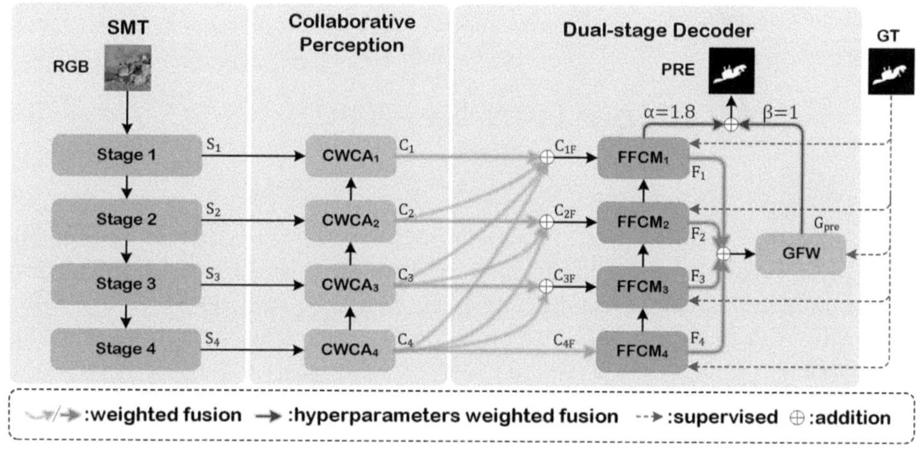

Fig. 2. The overall architecture of the proposed CPDDNet.

For the encoder of our network, we employ SMT, a vision Transformer-based backbone, to model the global contextual information of camouflaged objects. Given an input image $I \in \mathbb{R}^{H \times W \times 3}$, SMT extracts hierarchical features across four stages, denoted as Stage 1 to Stage 4, with corresponding outputs $S_i, (i = 1, 2, 3, 4)$, as illustrated in Fig. 2. In this hierarchy, higher-stage features represent deeper semantic information with reduced spatial resolution, whereas lower-stage features retain higher resolution and richer fine-grained details.

3.1 Coordinate-Window Collaborative Attention

For each output C_i of the coordinate-window collaborative attention (CWCA) module, it is obtained by integrating C_{i+1} and S_i, except for C_4, which is generated solely from S_4. This process can be formally described as follows:

$$C_i = \begin{cases} CWCA_i\left(S_i, C_{i+1}\right), \ i = 1, 2, 3 \\ CWCA_i\left(S_i\right), \ i = 4 \end{cases} \tag{1}$$

Before applying attention for feature perception, we first concatenate and fuse features from different levels to ensure that higher-level features can effectively guide the lower-level representations. Given that SMT is a relatively lightweight Transformer backbone, we enhance both its global perception capacity and local modeling ability during the collaborative perception phase, as illustrated in Fig. 3 under global context perception and local window-aware perception. At this stage, two attention weight components, f_{ca} and f_{wa} are generated. To balance their influence on the feature representation, we adopt a cross-interference and mutual-guidance strategy to facilitate collaborative learning, as depicted in Fig. 3 under cross-interference and guidance. This process can be mathematically formulated as follows:

$$f = Conv3\left(Concat\left(split\left(S_i\right), split\left(G_{i+1}\right)\right)\right) \tag{2}$$

$$f_{ca} = CA(f)\ ; f_{wa} = WA(f) \tag{3}$$

$$G_i = f \otimes \left(AS\left(f_{ca}\right) \odot f_{wa} + AS\left(f_{wa}\right) \odot f_{ca}\right) \tag{4}$$

where, $Conv3(\cdot)$ denotes a 3×3 convolutional layer; $Concat(\cdot)$ represents the channel-wise concatenation operation; $split(\cdot)$ refers to the operation of splitting the feature map into two halves along the channel dimension; $Ca(\cdot)$ denotes the coordinate attention module [9]; and $Wa(\cdot)$ indicates the window attention module [16].

3.2 Dual-Stage Decoder

Before decoding, we first perform a top-down adaptive weighted fusion of the feature maps from the collaborative perception stage. This process can be formalized as:

$$C_{iF} = \begin{cases} C_i, \ i = 4 \\ C_i + \sum_{i+1}^{4} UP\left(PW\left(C_{i+1}\right)\right), \ i = 1, 2, 3 \end{cases} \tag{5}$$

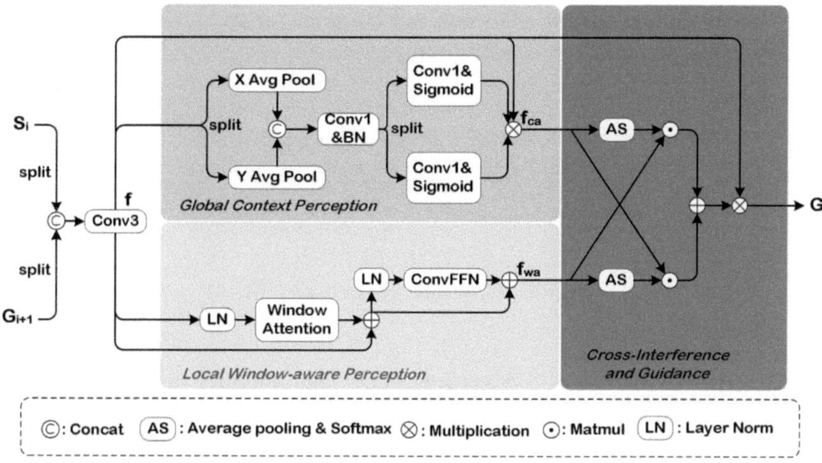

Fig. 3. Structure of each CWCA.

where $PW(\cdot)$ represents the pointwise convolution layer and $UP(\cdot)$ refers to the upsampling operation.

To address the limitation of conventional U-shaped decoders—specifically, the partial loss of high-level semantic information—we redesign the decoder into a dual-stage architecture, as illustrated in Fig. 2. In the first stage, features are enhanced using the FFCM and then decoded through a U-shaped structure. In the second stage, outputs from all levels of the first stage are adaptively weighted and fused, followed by the application of GFW to perform high- and low-frequency decomposition across the entire feature map. The refined features are then independently decoded. Both stages produce a total of five intermediate prediction maps (F_1, F_2, F_3, F_4 and G_{pre}), all of which are supervised by the ground truth (gt). The final prediction map is obtained through a hyperparameter-weighted fusion of G_{pre} and F_1. According to extensive experiments, the optimal comprehensive performance is achieved when the coefficients α and β in Fig. 2 are set to 1.8 and 1, respectively.

Fused Fourier Convolution Mixer. As the decoding module in the first stage, we employ the FFCM, which provides global feature enhancement to ensure that high-level semantic features can effectively guide low-level representations in a layer-wise manner. The structure of FFCM is illustrated in Fig. 4. Prior to applying FFCM for feature enhancement, we first perform hierarchical feature fusion, which can be formulated as:

$$F_i = f + MLP(FFCM(f)),\ f = Conv1\left(Concat\left(G_{iF}, F_{i+1}\right)\right) \tag{6}$$

where $Conv1(\cdot)$ denotes a 1×1 convolutional layer.

Subsequently, global feature enhancement is performed via FFCM, followed by feature transformation through a multilayer perceptron (MLP). The final output is obtained by adding the residual connection to the enhanced features. This process can be mathematically expressed as:

Fig. 4. Structure of each FFCM.

Global Frequency-Aware Wavelet. For the decoder module in the second stage, we design a GFW module, which performs low-frequency and high-frequency wavelet convolutions on the feature map based on the full input and output dimensions of the model. This approach enhances local features with a larger receptive field at a relatively low computational cost. The structure of GFW is shown in Fig. 5.

We first perform a weighted summation of the four feature maps from the first decoding stage and adjust the number of channels to 4, resulting in a unified feature map F. The map F is then decomposed into high-frequency and low-frequency components using wavelet transform convolution, and mutual learning is performed between the two branches, yielding the high-frequency feature map F_h and the low-frequency feature map F_l. After aligning the spatial dimensions of F_h and F_l, they are summed together and the channel dimension is reduced to 1 to produce the final prediction map G_{pre} from the second decoding stage. This process can be formulated as:

$$F = Conv1\left(\sum_{i=1}^{4} F_i\right) \tag{7}$$

$$\begin{cases} F_h = WTConv(Conv1(F)) + Conv3(UP(Conv1(Avgpool(F)))) \\ F_l = WTConv(Conv1(Avgpool(F))) + Conv3(Avgpool(Conv1(F))) \end{cases} \tag{8}$$

$$G_{pre} = Conv1\left(Conv1\left(F_h\right) + Conv1\left(UP\left(Conv1(F)_l\right)\right)\right) \tag{9}$$

where $WTConv(\cdot)$ denotes the wavelet convolution [6].

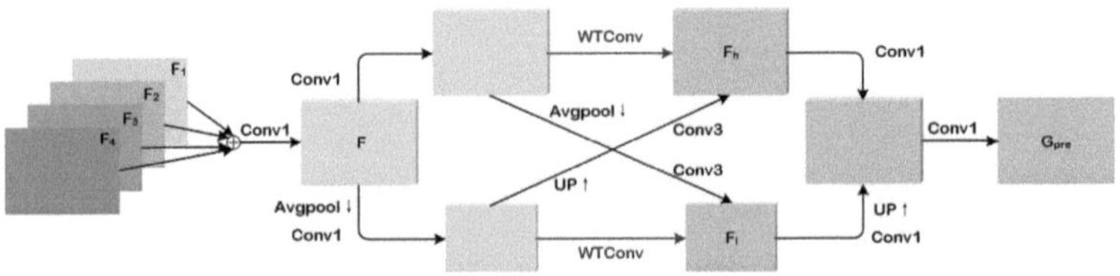

Fig. 5. Structure of GFW.

After obtaining the prediction maps from the two decoding stages, the final prediction map is generated through hyperparameter-weighted fusion of these maps, as shown in Fig. 2. This process can be described by the following equation:

$$PRE = \alpha \times F_1 + \beta \times G_{pre} \tag{10}$$

3.3 Loss Function

The same loss function is applied to all five prediction maps generated by the dual-stage decoder. We adopt a hybrid loss composed of binary cross-entropy (BCE) loss [2] and intersection over union (IoU) loss [20], along with a deep supervision strategy [14]. Ground truth supervises the four camouflaged prediction maps P_i. BCE loss improves pixel-level classification, refining boundaries and reducing errors. IoU loss enhances region overlap between prediction and ground truth. The combined loss enables the network to emphasize pixel precision and region-level accuracy, capturing more detailed foreground-background cues. The total loss L is defined as:

$$L = L_{BCE}\left(G_{pre}, G\right) + L_{IOU}\left(G_{pre}, G\right) + \sum_{i=1}^{4} L_{BCE}^{i}\left(F_i, G\right) + L_{IOU}^{i}\left(F_i, G\right) \tag{11}$$

where L_{BCE} represents the BCE loss, L_{IOU} is the IOU loss, and G is the ground truth.

4 Experiment

4.1 Experimental Setup

Datasets. For comprehensive performance evaluation and fair comparison, we validate our CPDDNet on four widely used COD benchmarks: Chameleon [23], COD10K [4], NC4K [18], and CAMO [13]. During training, we utilize a combined dataset consisting of 3,040 images from COD10K and 1,000 images from CAMO. For testing, we evaluate on the entire Chameleon and NC4K datasets, as well as the official test splits of COD10K and CAMO.

Evaluation Metrics and Experimental Detail. We adopt four widely used evaluation metrics, including mean absolute error (M) [22], mean F-measure [1], mean E-measure [3], and weighted F-measure [19]. Our model is implemented based on the PyTorch framework, with input images resized to 384×384. The optimizer is set to Adam with an initial learning rate of 1e−5. The model is trained for 300 epochs, with the learning rate reduced by an order of magnitude every 100 epochs. All training and inference processes are conducted on a workstation equipped with a single NVIDIA RTX 3080 Ti GPU.

Table 1. Quantitative comparison of our method with 10 state-of-the-art methods. The best two results are highlighted in red and green, respectively.

Methods	Publication & Year	Chameleon				COD10K-Test				NC4K				CAMO-Test			
		$M\downarrow$	$F_\beta uparrow$	$E_m uparrow$	$F_\omega uparrow$	$M\downarrow$	$F_\beta uparrow$	$E_m uparrow$	$F_\omega uparrow$	$M\downarrow$	$F_\beta uparrow$	$E_m uparrow$	$F_\omega uparrow$	$M\downarrow$	$F_\beta uparrow$	$E_m uparrow$	$F_\omega uparrow$
MFFN-R2	WACV, 23	0.021	0.871	0.963	0.852	0.028	0.782	0.917	0.745	0.042	0.827	0.888	0.791	-	-	-	-
MRRNet	TNNLS, 23	-	-	-	-	0.032	0.753	0.901	-	0.044	0.816	0.906	-	0.070	0.797	0.880	-
DINet	TMM, 24	-	-	-	-	0.031	0.761	0.903	0.744	0.043	0.824	0.909	0.820	0.068	0.790	0.874	0.790
FEDER-MIS	CVPR, 23	0.023	0.869	0.959	-	0.028	0.756	0.913	-	0.042	0.827	0.917	-	0.067	0.809	0.886	-
FSPNet	CVPR, 23	-	-	-	-	0.026	0.769	0.895	0.735	0.035	0.843	0.915	0.816	0.050	0.830	0.899	0.799
SARNet	TCSVT, 23	0.021	0.879	0.957	0.871	0.024	0.800	0.931	0.777	0.032	0.863	0.937	0.842	0.047	0.850	0.927	0.828
PRNet	TCSVT, 24	0.022	0.881	0.964	0.867	0.022	0.826	0.934	0.794	0.030	0.880	0.940	0.850	0.048	0.861	0.925	0.829
GLCONet-P	TNNLS, 24	-	-	-	-	0.022	0.796	0.930	0.794	0.031	0.856	0.939	0.846	0.042	0.861	0.939	0.847
CamoFocus-P2	WACV, 24	0.023	0.884	0.957	0.876	0.021	0.818	0.935	0.802	0.030	0.870	0.936	0.853	0.043	0.861	0.926	0.842
PRBE-Net	TMM, 25	0.020	-	0.951	0.878	0.021	-	0.932	0.793	0.031	-	0.931	0.845	0.045	-	0.928	0.837
Ours (CPDDNet-T)	-	0.019	0.893	0.970	0.885	0.021	0.832	0.941	0.804	0.029	0.885	0.914	0.856	0.044	0.875	0.937	0.846
Ours (CPDDNet-S)	-	0.017	0.896	0.967	0.888	0.019	0.844	0.949	0.821	0.026	0.892	0.951	0.869	0.039	0.886	0.947	0.863

Table 2. Parameters and computational complexity of all compared methods.

Methods	MFFN	MRRNet	DINet	FEDER	FSPNet	SARNet	PRNet	GLCONet	CamoFocus	PRBE-Net	CPDDNet-T	CPDDNet-S
Params (M)	36.554	71.99	30.836	-	273.79	47.20	12.74	91.35	-	-	13.96	25.00
FLOPs (G)	-	18.67	112.238	-	238.31	23.10	10.24	173.58	-	-	11.58	18.31

4.2 Performance Evaluation

Our model based on the SMT backbone is developed in two variants: CPDDNet-T and CPDDNet-S. The former is trained using the ultra-lightweight SMT-Tiny backbone, while the latter is trained using the more computationally intensive SMT-Small backbone. To demonstrate both the high performance and efficiency of our method, we compare it with ten state-of-the-art models proposed within the past three years, including (MFFN [32], MRRNet [27], DINetDINet [34], FEDER [8], FSPNet [11], SARNetSARNet [26], PRNet [10], GLCONet [25], CamoFocus [12], PRBE-Net [28]). The evaluation metrics and predicted maps for the compared models are either provided by the respective authors or reproduced based on their official code.

Quantitative Comparison. As shown in Table 1, our proposed COD model outperforms ten state-of-the-art methods in terms of evaluation metrics. Specifically, CPDDNet-S achieves superior performance across 15 out of 16 evaluation metrics on four benchmark datasets. Although CPDDNet-T does not reach the same level of performance as CPDDNet-S, it still delivers competitive results while being significantly more lightweight, as illustrated in Table 2. Table 2 summarizes the parameter count and computational complexity. In particular, CPDDNet-T requires only 11.58G FLOPs and contains 13.96M parameters, whereas CPDDNet-S demands 18.31G FLOPs and 25.00M parameters. Overall, CPDDNet achieves remarkable performance with minimal computational cost and model size.

Visual Comparison. We conduct an intuitive visual comparison between CPDDNet and three other state-of-the-art algorithms, as illustrated in Fig. 6. Specifically, the compared images are selected from the official datasets, each

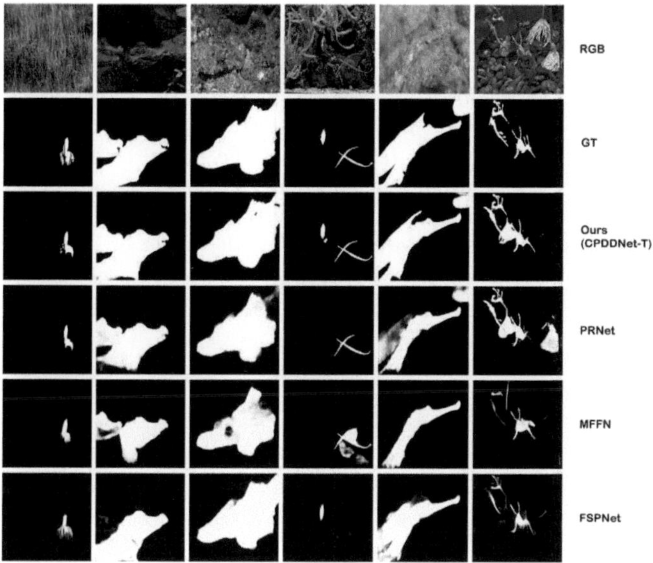

Fig. 6. Comparison of prediction maps between CPDDNet and the state-of-the-art models. RGB denotes the original color image, and GT represents the ground truth.

emphasizing different challenges. The first column shows occluded camouflaged objects; the second and third columns present large camouflaged targets; the fourth column focuses on small camouflaged targets; and the fifth and sixth columns depict multiple camouflaged objects. The predicted maps demonstrate that our method achieves significant improvements in both the localization and boundary segmentation of camouflaged objects compared to existing advanced approaches. As observed, the compared methods often fail to accurately locate camouflaged objects or produce coarse segmentation results. In contrast, our method is capable of more precise localization and finer segmentation of camouflaged targets.

4.3 Ablation Study

To validate the effectiveness and rationality of our model design, we conduct a series of ablation studies.

Effectiveness of CWCA, FFCM and GFW. We design a series of experiments to evaluate the effectiveness of CWCA, FFCM, and GFW. Starting from the baseline model (SMT-T) in experiment (a), we first assess its performance. Then, in experiment (b), CWCA is integrated into the model, followed by retraining and evaluation on the benchmark datasets. As shown in Table 3, the inclusion of CWCA consistently improves all evaluation metrics. Subsequently, in experiment (c), FFCM is incorporated into the model, further enhancing performance.

Table 3. Ablation experiments are conducted on two datasets to validate the effectiveness of the model. In experiment (a), the Baseline refers to using the lightweight SMT-T backbone for feature extraction and training, followed by a basic decoder to generate prediction maps. Experiments (b), (c), and (d) indicate the successive addition of CWCA, FFCM, and GFW, respectively, where experiment (d) corresponds to our proposed CPDDNet-T. Experiment (e) evaluates the model using only the prediction map from the first stage of the dual-stage decoder, while experiment (f) evaluates using only the prediction map from the second stage. Experiment (g) fuses the prediction maps from both stages of the decoder using a default weight of 1. The best results are highlighted in red.

Experiments	COD10K-Test				CAMO-Test			
	$M\downarrow$	F_{β}*uparrow*	E_{m}*uparrow*	F_{ω}*uparrow*	$M\downarrow$	F_{β}*uparrow*	E_{m}*uparrow*	F_{ω}*uparrow*
(a)	0.027	0.792	0.914	0.751	0.050	0.856	0.923	0.819
(b)	0.023	0.822	0.931	0.789	0.047	0.866	0.929	0.836
(c)	0.022	0.830	0.935	0.796	0.046	0.869	0.933	0.839
(d)	0.021	0.832	0.941	0.804	0.044	0.875	0.937	0.846
(e)	0.022	0.830	0.936	0.798	0.046	0.871	0.932	0.840
(f)	0.023	0.825	0.924	0.790	0.046	0.870	0.931	0.836
(g)	0.021	0.832	0.940	0.802	0.044	0.874	0.936	0.845

Finally, experiment (d) adds GFW to complete the proposed CPDDNet. This configuration achieves the best performance across all metrics. These experimental results validate the effectiveness of CWCA and GFW, as well as the correctness of incorporating FFCM into our model design.

Effectiveness of the Dual-Stage Decoder. We also conduct experiments to validate the effectiveness of the dual-stage decoder. As shown in Table 3, experiment (e) uses only the prediction map from the first stage of the dual-stage decoder; (f) uses only the prediction map from the second stage; (g) performs default-weight fusion of the prediction maps from both stages; and (d) applies hyperparameter-weighted fusion of the prediction maps from both stages. (The result of using only the original U-shaped decoder is already presented in experiment (c).) The final results indicate that employing both decoder stages outperforms using either stage individually, and further performance improvements are achieved through weighted fusion. It is worth noting that experiments (d), (e), (f), and (g) all use the same model weights without retraining, since the model architecture and supervision signals remain unchanged.

5 Conclusion

In this paper, we propose a novel solution to the major challenges faced by existing COD models, namely insufficient perceptual capability and inadequate feature transmission within decoders. By leveraging the unique design of CWCA and the dual-stage decoder, as well as the effective integration of FFCM, the proposed COD model CPDDNet achieves excellent performance across the four most widely adopted datasets, with extremely low computational cost and parameter count. Overall, CPDDNet surpasses the compared state-of-the-art methods. Future research may focus on further optimizing the architecture and decoder design, and exploring the potential for real-world deployment.

References

1. Achanta, R., Hemami, S., Estrada, F., Susstrunk, S.: Frequency-tuned salient region detection. In: 2009 IEEE Conference on Computer Vision and Pattern Recognition, pp. 1597–1604. IEEE (2009)
2. De Boer, P.T., Kroese, D.P., Mannor, S., Rubinstein, R.Y.: A tutorial on the cross-entropy method. Ann. Oper. Res. **134**, 19–67 (2005)
3. Fan, D.P., Gong, C., Cao, Y., Ren, B., Cheng, M.M., Borji, A.: Enhanced-alignment measure for binary foreground map evaluation. arXiv preprint arXiv:1805.10421 (2018)
4. Fan, D.P., Ji, G.P., Sun, G., Cheng, M.M., Shen, J., Shao, L.: Camouflaged object detection. In: Proceedings of the IEEE/CVF Conference on Computer Vision and Pattern Recognition, pp. 2777–2787 (2020)
5. Fan, D.-P., et al.: PraNet: parallel reverse attention network for polyp segmentation. In: Martel, A.L., et al. (eds.) MICCAI 2020. LNCS, vol. 12266, pp. 263–273. Springer, Cham (2020). https://doi.org/10.1007/978-3-030-59725-2_26
6. Finder, S.E., Amoyal, R., Treister, E., Freifeld, O.: Wavelet convolutions for large receptive fields. In: Leonardis, A., Ricci, E., Roth, S., Russakovsky, O., Sattler, T., Varol, G. (eds.) ECCV 2024. LNCS, vol. 15112, pp. 363–380. Springer, Cham (2024). https://doi.org/10.1007/978-3-031-72949-2_21
7. Gao, N., Jiang, X., Zhang, X., Deng, Y.: Efficient frequency-domain image deraining with contrastive regularization. In: Leonardis, A., Ricci, E., Roth, S., Russakovsky, O., Sattler, T., Varol, G. (eds.) ECCV 2024. LNCS, vol. 15099, pp. 240–257. Springer, Cham (2024). https://doi.org/10.1007/978-3-031-72940-9_14
8. He, C., et al.: Camouflaged object detection with feature decomposition and edge reconstruction. In: Proceedings of the IEEE/CVF Conference on Computer Vision and Pattern Recognition, pp. 22046–22055 (2023)
9. Hou, Q., Zhou, D., Feng, J.: Coordinate attention for efficient mobile network design. In: Proceedings of the IEEE/CVF Conference on Computer Vision and Pattern Recognition, pp. 13713–13722 (2021)
10. Hu, X., Zhang, X., Wang, F., Sun, J., Sun, F.: Efficient camouflaged object detection network based on global localization perception and local guidance refinement. IEEE Trans. Circuits Syst. Video Technol. **34**(7), 5452–5465 (2024)
11. Huang, Z., et al.: Feature shrinkage pyramid for camouflaged object detection with transformers. In: Proceedings of the IEEE/CVF Conference on Computer Vision and Pattern Recognition, pp. 5557–5566 (2023)
12. Khan, A., Khan, M., Gueaieb, W., El Saddik, A., De Masi, G., Karray, F.: Camofocus: enhancing camouflage object detection with split-feature focal modulation and context refinement. In: Proceedings of the IEEE/CVF Winter Conference on Applications of Computer Vision, pp. 1434–1443 (2024)
13. Le, T.N., Nguyen, T.V., Nie, Z., Tran, M.T., Sugimoto, A.: Anabranch network for camouflaged object segmentation. Comput. Vis. Image Underst. **184**, 45–56 (2019)

14. Lee, C.Y., Xie, S., Gallagher, P., Zhang, Z., Tu, Z.: Deeply-supervised nets. In: Artificial Intelligence and Statistics, pp. 562–570. PMLR (2015)
15. Lin, W., Wu, Z., Chen, J., Huang, J., Jin, L.: Scale-aware modulation meet transformer. In: Proceedings of the IEEE/CVF International Conference on Computer Vision, pp. 6015–6026 (2023)
16. Liu, X., Liu, J., Tang, J., Wu, G.: Catanet: efficient content-aware token aggregation for lightweight image super-resolution. In: Proceedings of the Computer Vision and Pattern Recognition Conference, pp. 17902–17912 (2025)
17. Long, J., Shelhamer, E., Darrell, T.: Fully convolutional networks for semantic segmentation. In: Proceedings of the IEEE Conference on Computer Vision and Pattern Recognition, pp. 3431–3440 (2015)
18. Lv, Y., et al.: Simultaneously localize, segment and rank the camouflaged objects. In: Proceedings of the IEEE/CVF Conference on Computer Vision and Pattern Recognition, pp. 11591–11601 (2021)
19. Margolin, R., Zelnik-Manor, L., Tal, A.: How to evaluate foreground maps? In: Proceedings of the IEEE Conference on Computer Vision and Pattern Recognition, pp. 248–255 (2014)
20. Máttyus, G., Luo, W., Urtasun, R.: Deeproadmapper: extracting road topology from aerial images. In: Proceedings of the IEEE International Conference on Computer Vision, pp. 3438–3446 (2017)
21. Pang, Y., Zhao, X., Xiang, T.Z., Zhang, L., Lu, H.: Zoom in and out: a mixed-scale triplet network for camouflaged object detection. In: Proceedings of the IEEE/CVF Conference on Computer Vision and Pattern Recognition, pp. 2160–2170 (2022)
22. Perazzi, F., Krähenbühl, P., Pritch, Y., Hornung, A.: Saliency filters: contrast based filtering for salient region detection. In: 2012 IEEE Conference on Computer Vision and Pattern Recognition, pp. 733–740. IEEE (2012)
23. Skurowski, P., Abdulameer, H., Błaszczyk, J., Depta, T., Kornacki, A., Kozieł, P.: Animal camouflage analysis: Chameleon database. Unpublished manuscript (2018). http://kgwisc.aei.polsl.pl/index.php/en/dataset/63-animal-camouflage-analysis
24. Siris, A., Jiao, J., Tam, G.K., Xie, X., Lau, R.W.: Scene context-aware salient object detection. In: Proceedings of the IEEE/CVF International Conference on Computer Vision, pp. 4156–4166 (2021)
25. Sun, Y., Xuan, H., Yang, J., Luo, L.: Glconet: learning multisource perception representation for camouflaged object detection. IEEE Trans. Neural Netw. Learn. Syst. (2024)
26. Xing, H., Gao, S., Wang, Y., Wei, X., Tang, H., Zhang, W.: Go closer to see better: camouflaged object detection via object area amplification and figure-ground conversion. IEEE Trans. Circuits Syst. Video Technol. **33**(10), 5444–5457 (2023)
27. Yan, X., Sun, M., Han, Y., Wang, Z.: Camouflaged object segmentation based on matching–recognition–refinement network. IEEE Trans. Neural Netw. Learn. Syst. (2023)
28. Yue, G., et al.: Progressive region-to-boundary exploration network for camouflaged object detection. IEEE Trans. Multimedia (2024)
29. Zhai, Q., Li, X., Yang, F., Chen, C., Cheng, H., Fan, D.P.: Mutual graph learning for camouflaged object detection. In: Proceedings of the IEEE/CVF Conference on Computer Vision and Pattern Recognition, pp. 12997–13007 (2021)
30. Zhang, P., Wang, D., Lu, H., Wang, H., Ruan, X.: Amulet: aggregating multi-level convolutional features for salient object detection. In: Proceedings of the IEEE International Conference on Computer Vision, pp. 202–211 (2017)

31. Zhao, X., Pang, Y., Zhang, L., Lu, H., Zhang, L.: Suppress and balance: a simple gated network for salient object detection. In: Vedaldi, A., Bischof, H., Brox, T., Frahm, J.-M. (eds.) ECCV 2020. LNCS, vol. 12347, pp. 35–51. Springer, Cham (2020). https://doi.org/10.1007/978-3-030-58536-5_3
32. Zheng, D., Zheng, X., Yang, L.T., Gao, Y., Zhu, C., Ruan, Y.: MFFN: multi-view feature fusion network for camouflaged object detection. In: Proceedings of the IEEE/CVF Winter Conference on Applications of Computer Vision, pp. 6232–6242 (2023)
33. Zhou, H., Xie, X., Lai, J.H., Chen, Z., Yang, L.: Interactive two-stream decoder for accurate and fast saliency detection. In: Proceedings of the IEEE/CVF Conference on Computer Vision and Pattern Recognition, pp. 9141–9150 (2020)
34. Zhou, X., Wu, Z., Cong, R.: Decoupling and integration network for camouflaged object detection. IEEE Trans. Multimedia **26**, 7114–7129 (2024)

MRM-RETrack: Hybrid Multi-scale Residual and Mamba for RGB-Event Tracking

Yuting He[1], Bin Fan[1], Zhexiong Wan[1], Zhiyuan Zhang[2], and Yuchao Dai[1](✉)

[1] School of Electronics and Information, Northwestern Polytechnical University, Xi'an 710129, China
daiyuchao@nwpu.edu.cn

[2] College of Electronic Science and Technology, National University of Defense Technology, Changsha 410073, China

Abstract. In recent years, RGB-event object tracking has achieved significant progress, demonstrating its increasingly enhanced perception and tracking capabilities in dynamic scenes. However, existing methods are predominantly based on CNN or Transformer architectures, which typically suffer from high computational complexity and memory overhead. The emerging Mamba architecture, while preserving the ability to model long-range dependencies, significantly reduces memory consumption, opening new avenues for the design of efficient tracking models. Nevertheless, current Mamba-based RGB-event tracking methods still face challenges such as insufficient feature learning and lack of cross-modal alignment, thereby impacting tracking accuracy and overall robustness. This paper proposes a novel RGB-event tracking framework, aiming to achieve high-performance, low-memory cross-modal object tracking. Specifically, we introduce a hierarchical local-global feature extraction strategy, integrating a Multi-Scale Residual Module (MSRM) and a Gated Mamba Module (GMM), to collaboratively enhance both fine-grained local feature extraction and long-range dependency capture. Furthermore, we develop an efficient Aligned Difference-Enhanced Mamba module (ADE-Mamba), which explicitly aligns complementary contextual features by focusing on inter-modal discrepancies. To further boost tracking performance, we design an adaptive dual-modal tracking head that dynamically adjusts and fuses the contributions from the RGB and event modalities, enabling precise target localization. Extensive experiments on multiple benchmark datasets demonstrate that our method exhibits superior performance in both short-term and long-term tracking tasks.

Keywords: Object Tracking · Event Camera · Mamba · Multimodal Fusion

1 Introduction

Visual object tracking is one of the most sought-after yet challenging research topics in computer vision [28]. This technology aims to locate the target by analyzing consecutive frames in a video sequence to achieve continuous tracking of the object's trajectory.

Supplementary Information The online version contains supplementary material available at https://doi.org/10.1007/978-981-95-5764-6_12.

© The Author(s), under exclusive license to Springer Nature Singapore Pte Ltd. 2026
J. Kittler et al. (Eds.): PRCV 2025, LNCS 16289, pp. 162–177, 2026.
https://doi.org/10.1007/978-981-95-5764-6_12

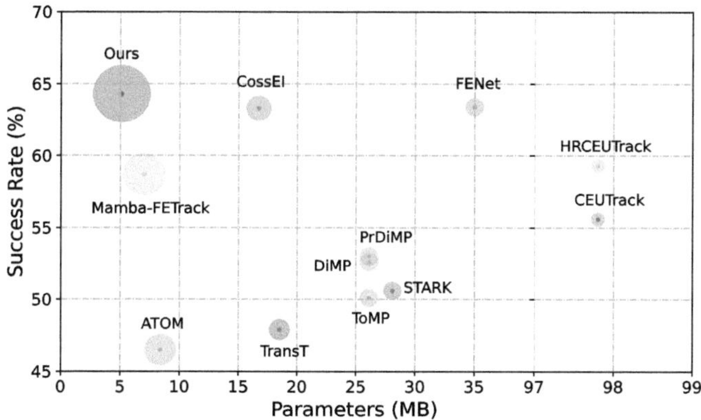

Fig. 1. Comparison between our tracker and advanced tracking methods on the FE108 dataset [46] in terms of parameter and success rate (SR). The bubble size is determined by the normalized ratio of success rate to parameter count, where a larger bubble reflects a better trade-off between model compactness and tracking performance.

Accurate object tracking, which enables the effective identification and monitoring of specific objects in complex environments, has driven the development of numerous methods. Most of these methods are developed based on RGB cameras [1,6,26,39,40], greatly promoting the development of the tracking field. However, single-modality object tracking still has a performance bottleneck. Especially in extreme scenarios, *e.g.*, low illumination or fast motion, these methods struggle due to a lack of motion cues.

Consequently, multimodal tracking techniques have emerged. In particular, the event camera outputs event streams asynchronously, which offers advantages such as high temporal resolution, high dynamic range, low latency, low redundancy, and low power consumption [18,31,42]. This makes fusing RGB and event data a promising approach to achieve robust object tracking. In recent years, research on RGB-E tracking has rapidly advanced, leading to the proposal of several key methods. For instance, FENet [46] introduces a cross-domain feature extractor to facilitate information interaction between the frame and event domains. Tang et al. [30] proposed CEUTrack, a unified vision transformer-based network designed for feature extraction, fusion, and tracking, concurrently introducing the COESOT dataset. While these methods have improved tracking performance, they also exhibit certain limitations. Specifically, early RGB-E tracking methods based on Convolutional Neural Networks (CNNs) [45,46] were limited by their local receptive fields, hindering their ability to effectively capture long-range dependencies. In contrast, tracking methods based on Vision Transformers (ViTs) [30,50] gained global modeling capabilities, but their self-attention mechanism incurs a quadratic computational complexity, which can negatively impact real-time performance. Recently, an emerging architecture based on the state space model (SSM) [21], *i.e.*, Vision Mamba (ViM) [49], with its strong long-range modeling capabilities and linear complexity, has become a compelling alternative to CNNs and ViTs. It has also been widely applied to various tasks, such as image classification [43], image reconstruction [41], image dehazing [47], and multimodal image fusion [36].

Against this backdrop, Huang et al. [24] pioneered the introduction of ViM into the RGB-E tracking task, proposing Mamba-FETrack, which strikes a balance between global receptive fields and computational efficiency. However, when applied to challenging tracking scenarios, Mamba-FETrack still faces two significant limitations. *Firstly*, the object tracking task demands a high sensitivity to fine-grained local information to accurately delineate object contours. Although Mamba excels in global modeling, it may fall short in efficiently capturing and utilizing key local discriminative features, potentially limiting its feature representation capabilities in complex scenarios. *Secondly*, Mamba-FETrack primarily relies on implicit cross-modal feature interaction to fuse complementary RGB and event information, but it may overlook explicit spatial alignment between modalities. This lack of alignment hinders the two modalities from achieving deeper synergistic enhancement, especially in extreme scenarios where the quality of one modality is severely degraded, consequently impacting the accuracy and stability of tracking.

To address the aforementioned limitations, we propose an effective and robust RGB-E tracking framework, named MRM-RETrack. *Firstly*, we design a hierarchical local-global feature extraction strategy. This strategy organically combines a multi-scale residual module with a gated Mamba module. The former is dedicated to deeply mining fine-grained local features at diverse scales, while the latter concentrates on efficiently capturing global contextual dependencies. Through this synergistic effect, our method can simultaneously enhance the perception of fine target details and the understanding of overall scene information. *Secondly*, we propose an efficient Alignment-Discrepancy Enhanced Mamba module (ADE-Mamba). It focuses on utilizing the inter-modal differences before modal interaction, explicitly aligning and amplifying their complementary semantic features to achieve more effective feature fusion. Furthermore, we introduce an adaptive dual-modal tracking head, which, after feature interaction, dynamically adjusts and explicitly fuses the contributions of the RGB and event modalities, thereby enhancing tracking robustness in dynamic scenarios. Experimental results demonstrate that by integrating two key architectural designs, our proposed approach achieves superior performance in both short-term and long-term tracking tasks, while also enjoying lower computational complexity, as shown in Fig. 1.

In summary, this paper makes contributions by

1) proposing a tractable RGB-E tracking framework, termed MRM-RETrack, which effectively captures local and global features and efficiently fuses RGB visual information with event-based motion cues via the alignment-discrepancy enhanced Mamba module;
2) developing a multi-scale residual module and a gated Mamba module to hierarchically capture fine-grained local structures and global contextual information, significantly enhancing the model's capability to represent target features in complex scenarios; and
3) designing an adaptive dual-modal tracking head, capable of explicitly adjusting contribution weights based on the information quality of each modality, thereby maximizing information utilization in dynamic scenarios.

2 Related Work

2.1 Visual Object Tracking

In the past few years, we have witnessed rapid advancements in visual object tracking, which has become an important research area in computer vision [5]. Currently, Siamese networks have gained significant attention due to their outstanding performance, and trackers based on deep Siamese networks have become increasingly popular. Among them, SiamFC [1] employs two identical fully convolutional network (FCN) branches for offline training and determines the target position via cross-correlation, achieving real-time performance. After vision transformer (ViT) successfully applied the transformer model to various image processing tasks [16,22,25,32], TransT [6] is the first to introduce it to tracking tasks. It effectively integrates the correlation between template and search features, thereby improving tracking performance. OSTrack [40] stacks transformer layers to create a pure transformer-based single-stream, one-shot object tracker. Linker [38] effectively utilizes short-term scene information provided by the reference region and introduces the reference enhancement module to improve object tracking accuracy. These tracking methods depend on strong visual cues but degrade significantly under extreme conditions like over-exposure or fast motion.

2.2 Event-Based Object Tracking

In recent years, the event camera, also known as the dynamic vision sensor (DVS), has emerged as a bionic visual sensor [4,18], representing a paradigm shift in the way visual information is acquired [19,27,48]. Each pixel of the event camera independently senses brightness changes and generates an "event" only when a change occurs, offering high temporal resolution, high dynamic range, and low power consumption, which are far beyond the capabilities of traditional RGB cameras [12–15,17]. Therefore, event-based tracking methods [35,44] demonstrate advantages in high-speed motion and challenging lighting conditions but often struggle with precise target localization and long-term stability due to the lack of rich visual texture information. Consequently, RGB-event object tracking methods [30,45,46,50,51] have emerged, aiming to combine the strengths of both modalities to enhance tracking robustness and accuracy.

Zhang et al. [46] proposed FENet, which features a novel cross-domain feature extractor (CDFI) that integrates features from two domains, enhancing tracking performance. Tang et al. [30] developed a transformer-based unified tracking framework that simultaneously handles feature extraction, interaction, and fusion. AFNet [45] is a multi-modal architecture for high-frame-rate object tracking. Using event-driven cross-modal alignment and cross-correlation fusion modules, it effectively improves tracking performance. CrossEI [8] leverages adaptive event sampling and a bidirectional fusion framework to explore the complementarity between event and image data, significantly improving tracking performance in complex environments.

2.3 Mamba-Based RGB-Event Tracking

Current mainstream tracking methods are primarily based on CNN and Transformer architectures. CNNs, which rely on local receptive fields, may result in the model's

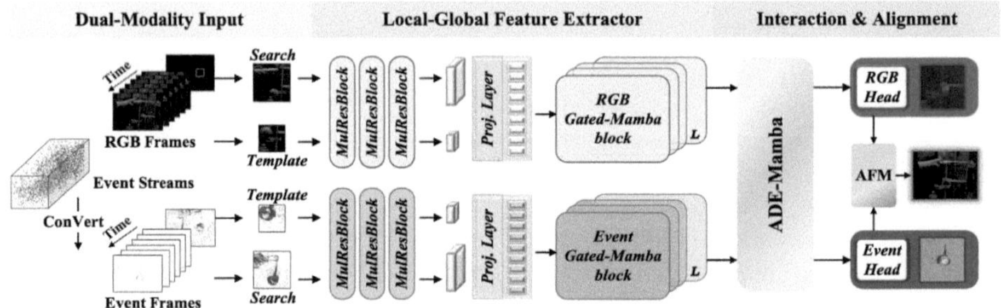

Fig. 2. Overview of the proposed RGB-event tracking architecture.

insufficient perception of global information. While Transformer can capture global context, its self-attention mechanism has a computational complexity that grows quadratically with the length of the context, limiting the practical application of tracking methods. Vision Mamba (ViM) [49] is based on a bidirectional state space model (SSM) and processes visual sequences through position embeddings, effectively solving the computational and storage challenges faced by transformers when dealing with high-resolution images. Therefore, Huang et al. [24] proposed the Mamba-FETrack, which effectively reduces the model's parameters. However, current research on Mamba-based RGB-event tracking is still in its early stages and faces two main challenges: first, these frameworks lack sufficient attention to local details; second, the lack of explicit spatial alignment between the two modalities limits the effectiveness of deeper synergistic enhancement between them. To address these issues, this paper designs a novel tracking framework that integrates local and global feature learning, dual-modality alignment and discrepancy enhancement, as well as inter-modal interaction. Moreover, we develop independent tracking heads for the RGB and event modalities, along with an adaptive fusion module, effectively improving the robustness of RGB-event tracking.

3 Approach

3.1 Framework Overview

To achieve efficient and robust object tracking in dynamic scenes, we propose MRM-RETrack, an RGB-event tracking framework that integrates local and global feature learning, as illustrated in Fig. 2. Feature quality directly impacts object tracking performance. Thus, we separately process RGB and event data based on a dual-modal Siamese network, extracting local details via the Multi-Scale Residual Module (MSRM) and then capturing global context through the Gated Mamba Module (GMM). Subsequently, the Alignment-Discrepancy Enhanced Mamba (ADE-Mamba) module is designed to explicitly align and fuse dual-modal features. Finally, features from RGB and event branches are processed by their respective tracking heads, and the outputs are dynamically weighted and fused by the Adaptive Fusion Module (AFM) according to modality quality, improving tracking accuracy.

3.2 Dual-Modality Input

We first describe the input configuration adopted in our framework. Following [24], the dual-modal inputs are divided into template and search regions. For the RGB modality, the template and search regions are defined as $\mathbf{z}_f \in \mathbb{R}^{H_z \times W_z \times 3}$ and $\mathbf{s}_f \in \mathbb{R}^{H_s \times W_s \times 3}$, respectively. For the event modality, the raw event streams are first converted into event frames [20] through preprocessing, with the corresponding template and search regions denoted as $\mathbf{z}_{ef} \in \mathbb{R}^{H_z \times W_z \times 3}$ and $\mathbf{s}_{ef} \in \mathbb{R}^{H_s \times W_s \times 3}$, respectively. These inputs are then fed into the feature extractor to obtain more effective feature representations and undergo further fusion analysis.

3.3 Local-Global Feature Extractor

In object tracking, local features capture fine details for precise contours, while global features model long-range dependencies to enhance context. To address Mamba's limitations in local feature extraction, we designed a framework combining the Multi-Scale Residual Module (MSRM) and the Gated Mamba Module (GMM), which work together to improve tracking performance. In the following, we introduce the design and principles of these modules.

Multi-scale Residual Module. Object tracking requires high sensitivity to fine-grained local information for accurate target delineation. In the single-modal branch, template and search patches from RGB and event data are separately processed by the Multi-Scale Residual Module (MSRM) to extract local features. MSRM consists of three stacked multi-scale residual blocks (MulResBlock, Fig. 3), each with 1×1, 3×3, and 5×5 convolutional layers that collaboratively extract and fuse multi-scale details.

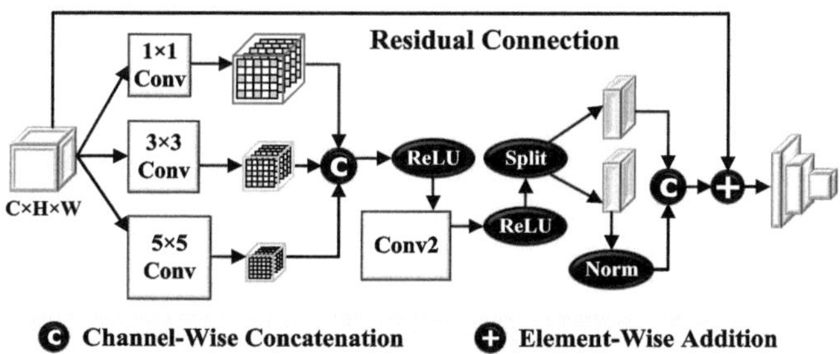

Fig. 3. Illustration of multi-scale residual block.

The specific process consists of four main steps: 1. *Multi-Scale Feature Extraction*: Input images are processed through parallel convolutional layers to extract features at different scales, which are then concatenated. 2. *Non-linear Transformation and Fusion*: The fused features are passed through a *LeakyReLU* activation function, followed by a second 3×3 convolution layer for further feature extraction. 3. *Feature Splitting and Concatenation*: The feature map is split into two parts, one undergoes instance normalization for stability, while the other remains unchanged to preserve original information. The features are then concatenated. 4. *Residual Connection*: Finally, a residual connection is introduced to mitigate the vanishing gradient problem, enhancing feature propagation and overall performance. The whole process can be expressed as:

$$\mathbf{x}_{scale_1} = \text{Conv}_{1\times1}(\mathbf{x}), \mathbf{x}_{scale_2} = \text{Conv}_{3\times3}(\mathbf{x}), \mathbf{x}_{scale_3} = \text{Conv}_{5\times5}(\mathbf{x}), \tag{1}$$

$$\mathbf{x}_{fuse} = [\mathbf{x}_{scale_1}, \mathbf{x}_{scale_2}, \mathbf{x}_{scale_3}], \mathbf{x}_1 = \gamma(\text{Conv}_{3\times3}(\gamma(\mathbf{x}_{fuse}))), \tag{2}$$

$$\mathbf{x}_{out_1}, \mathbf{x}_{out_2} = \langle \mathbf{x}_1 \rangle, \mathbf{x}_{out} = [Norm(\mathbf{x}_{out_1})], \tag{3}$$

where $\text{Conv}_{k\times k}$ denotes a $k \times k$ convolutional layer, $[\cdot]$ indicates channel-wise concatenation, $\langle\cdot\rangle$ denotes the channel-wise splitting operation, γ represents the $LeakyReLU$ activation function, and $Norm$ is the normalization.

Gated Mamba Module. To further capture contextual information, we introduce the Gated Mamba Module (GMM) as a global feature extractor. As shown in Fig. 2, single-modality templates and search tokens are first processed through the MSRM to extract local features. These local feature encodings are then input into the GMM to extract intra-modality global features. Specifically, GMM is composed of multiple stacked Gated Mamba Blocks (GMB) (where $L = 24$ [24]), with each GMB consisting of Vision Mamba (ViM) and Residual Gated Linear Unit (ResGLU). ViM is used for modeling long-range dependencies, while ResGLU refines and enhances the features. The combination of both effectively improves global representation ability and temporal modeling performance. With this structure, GMM can efficiently model the global context of both RGB and event modalities. Next, we will respectively introduce ViM and ResGLU.

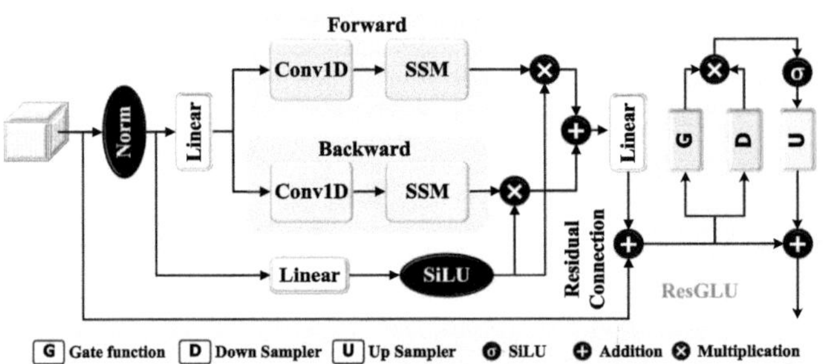

Fig. 4. Illustration of gated Mamba block.

ViM. The ViM block is illustrated in Fig. 4 (*left*). The input is first normalized to improve stability and convergence. The normalized features produce $\mathbf{z}$ and $\mathbf{x}$, with forward and backward scans on $\mathbf{x}$ enhancing temporal features. Using the state space model (SSM), forward and backward outputs are computed and dynamically merged to update the input and improve feature representation. Residual connections preserve the input to facilitate information flow. See supplementary materials for more details.

ResGLU. To further enhance the feature representation capability and training efficiency of the global feature extractor, we propose the residual gated linear unit (ResGLU) as an inter-layer adaptation mechanism. As shown in Fig. 4 (*right*), input features are downsampled to reduce complexity and processed by a linear gating mechanism using SiLU activation to generate gating signals. These signals modulate the features before upsampling to the original size. Residual connections improve gradient flow and training stability. ResGLU enhances feature representation and efficiency with minimal added complexity, improving tracking performance.

3.4 Interaction and Alignment

As previously mentioned, we adopt a dual-modal dual-branch structure, extracting local and global features through MSRM and GMM, respectively. The RGB modality provides rich texture information, while the event modality conveys motion cues, making them complementary in different scenarios. However, existing methods lack explicit spatial alignment during interaction, which limits deeper synergistic enhancement between the modalities. This issue becomes especially prominent when one modality degrades, significantly affecting tracking accuracy. To address this issue, we design the cross-modal alignment and interaction module ADE-Mamba (see Fig. 5), which achieves explicit alignment and information interaction between modalities. It consists of two stages: alignment-discrepancy enhancement and cross-modal interaction.

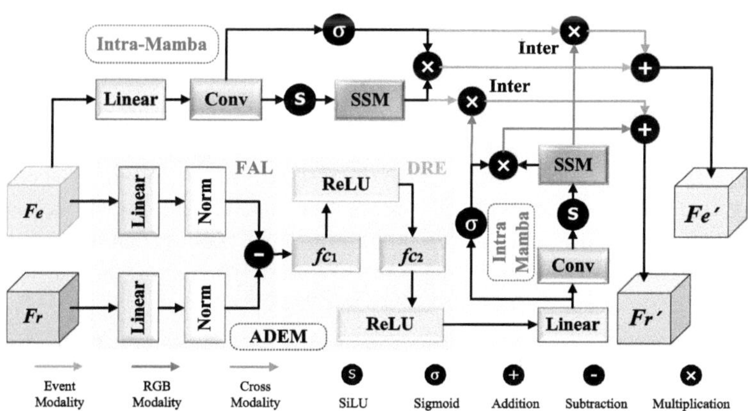

Fig. 5. Architecture of alignment-discrepancy enhanced Mamba module.

Alignment-Discrepancy Enhancement. The Alignment and Discrepancy Enhancement Module (ADEM) consists of two sequential steps: Feature Alignment Learning (FAL) and Discrepancy Representation Enhancement (DRE).

FAL Step. To facilitate effective interaction between RGB and event features, we propose an explicit feature alignment step. FAL first projects the features from both modalities into a shared feature space through linear transformations, followed by layer normalization to adjust their statistical distributions. Considering that the same object may exhibit differences across modalities, these differences often contain complementary and discriminative information. FAL further calculates the discrepancies between the features of the two modalities. Through this process, the alignment between features is achieved, providing a unified representation foundation for subsequent fusion.

DRE Step. After obtaining the difference representation, the DRE uses fully connected layers and nonlinear activation to further enhance the discrepancy. The fully connected layers strengthen the difference, while the nonlinear activation highlights the unique features of both modalities, enabling the model to better capture modality-specific attributes and improve robustness in complex tracking scenarios. In summary, the alignment and discrepancy enhancement process can be expressed as:

$$\hat{\mathbf{m}}_1 = Norm(\text{Linear}_1(\mathbf{m}_1)), \quad \hat{\mathbf{m}}_2 = Norm(\text{Linear}_1(\mathbf{m}_2)), \tag{4}$$

$$\mathbf{F}_d = \hat{\mathbf{m}}_1 - \hat{\mathbf{m}}_2, \quad \mathbf{F}'_d = \sigma(fc_1(\mathbf{F}_d)), \quad \mathbf{F}''_d = \sigma(fc_2(\mathbf{F}'_d)), \tag{5}$$

where $\mathbf{m}_1$ and $\mathbf{m}_2$ are the input features, they are first aligned to a shared space through linear transformation Linear and layer normalization ($Norm$). The feature difference $\mathbf{F}_d$ is then computed to capture complementary information, followed by enhancement using fully connected layers (fc) and nonlinear activation (σ, ReLU function).

Cross-Modal Interaction. After feature alignment and discrepancy enhancement, we introduce the Fusion Mamba module [23,24] to enable deep fusion of enhanced features from both modalities. As shown in Fig. 5, Fusion Mamba consists of Intra-Mamba for bidirectional modeling within each modality and Inter-Mamba for gated cross-modal interaction. The RGB modality provides rich texture and appearance details, while the event modality offers crucial motion cues in fast motion or low-light scenarios. By combining feature alignment with this interaction mechanism, the model effectively fuses complementary information from modalities. This process can be formulated as:

$$\mathbf{F}_{global} = FM(\mathbf{m}_1, \hat{\mathbf{m}}_2 + \mathbf{F}''_d), \tag{6}$$

where $\hat{\mathbf{m}}_2$ denotes the convolutional and normalized features, and $\mathbf{F}''_d$ represents the aligned and enhanced difference features used to improve cross-modal fusion. "FM" refers to Fusion Mamba [23], which combines RGB texture and event motion cues to enhance tracking robustness.

3.5 Adaptive Dual-Modal Tracking Head

Independent tracking heads allow each modality to adopt different strategies, enhancing the model's interpretability and flexibility. Therefore, we feed RGB and event features into separate tracking heads for prediction. Each tracking head [24] consists of four 3×3 convolutional layers (with BN-ReLU) and one 1×1 convolutional layer, outputting classification scores, center offsets, and bounding box sizes.

In addition, the model introduces an Adaptive Fusion Module (AFM) that dynamically adjusts the weights of the outputs from the RGB and event tracking heads based on their actual contributions, thereby further enhancing tracking accuracy. This fusion process reflects the dynamic coordination and alignment between the response maps, enabling explicit and effective fusion at the decision level based on the contributions of each modality. It can be mathematically expressed as:

$$\left(\mathbf{w}_{rgb}^{norm}, \mathbf{w}_{event}^{norm}\right) = \left(\frac{\mathbf{w}_{rgb}}{\mathbf{w}_{rgb} + \mathbf{w}_{event}}, \frac{\mathbf{w}_{event}}{\mathbf{w}_{rgb} + \mathbf{w}_{event}}\right), \tag{7}$$

$$\mathbf{y} = \left[\mathbf{w}_{rgb}^{norm}, \mathbf{w}_{event}^{norm}\right] \times \begin{pmatrix} \mathbf{y}_{rgb} \\ \mathbf{y}_{event} \end{pmatrix}, \tag{8}$$

where $\mathbf{w}_{rgb}^{norm}$ and $\mathbf{w}_{event}^{norm}$ are the normalized weights for RGB and event modalities, which are initially set to 0.5 and can be dynamically adjusted based on their contributions. $\mathbf{y}_{rgb}$ and $\mathbf{y}_{event}$ represent the individual outputs of each modality, and the final output $\mathbf{y}$ is the weighted combination of these results. With the dual-head design and independent modality processing, the model effectively leverages the strengths of both RGB and event inputs to track objects across a wide range of environments.

3.6 Loss Function

When training our model, three classic loss terms, *i.e.*, the focal loss, the $\mathcal{L}_1$ loss, and the GIoU loss, are employed. The overall loss can be expressed as:

$$\mathcal{L} = \lambda_1 \mathcal{L}_{focal} + \lambda_2 \mathcal{L}_{L_1} + \lambda_3 \mathcal{L}_{giou}, \tag{9}$$

where trade-off parameters λ_1, λ_2, and λ_3 are set to 1, 14, and 1, respectively, as in [24].

4 Experiment

4.1 Implementation Details

We implement the **MRM-RETrack** model in PyTorch, training it on two RTX 3090 GPUs with a batch size of 20. The AdamW optimizer is used with an initial learning rate of 4×10^{-4}, decaying by 10% every 40 epochs. The tracker is trained on the FELT, FE108, and FE240Hz datasets, with ablation experiments on FE108 and comparative experiments on all three datasets. Following [24], we primarily adopt three representative evaluation metrics to assess the model's performance: success rate (SR), precision rate (PR), and normalized precision rate (NPR).

4.2 Comparison on Public Benchmarks

Results on FE108 Dataset. The FE108 dataset is collected by Zhang et al. [46] using a grayscale DVS346 camera and consists of 108 videos, with 76 for training and 32 for testing. As shown in Table 1, we compare our results with 13 advanced trackers. Experimental results show that our model achieves 64.3% and 95.8% in SR and PR metrics, respectively. Compared to the CEUTrack method [30], the SR metric improves by 8.7%. Relative to the baseline model Mamba-FETrack [24], our approach achieves improvements of 5.6% in SR and 4.8% in the PR metrics. When evaluated against HRCEUTrack [51] and CrossEI [8], our method achieves improvements of 4.5% and 2.8% in the PR metric, respectively. In summary, these results validate the effectiveness of the proposed hierarchical local-global feature extraction and alignment strategies.

Results on FE240Hz Dataset. The FE240Hz dataset [45] has an annotation frequency of up 240 Hz, containing 71 training videos and 25 testing videos, with over 1.13 million annotations. As shown in Table 2, we compared our results with 9 advanced trackers. Experimental results indicate that our model achieves 63.6% and 93.0% in SR and PR metrics, respectively. Compared to the CrossEI [8] method, the SR metric improved by 4.2%. In addition, we have included the overlap precision at threshold T (OP_T) metric [46] to more comprehensively evaluate the model's performance at different overlap thresholds (0.5 and 0.7). In these evaluations, our model achieved 80.8% at the 0.5 threshold and 39.3% at the 0.7 threshold. These results further validate the superior performance of our model across multiple metrics, demonstrating the effectiveness of the proposed method in high-frame-rate tracking.

Table 1. Experimental results (%) on FE108 dataset [46].

Trackers	SiamRPN [26]	SiamBAN [7]	SiamFC++ [37]	KYS [3]	CLNet [11]	CMT-MDNet [34]	ATOM [9]
SR/ PR	21.8/33.5	22.5/37.4	23.8/39.1	26.6/41.0	34.4/55.5	35.1/57.8	46.5/71.3
Trackers	DiMP [2]	PrDiMP [10]	CEUTrack [30]	HRCEUTrack [51]	CrossEI [8]	Mamba-FETrack [24]	Ours -
SR/ PR	52.6/79.1	53.0/80.5	55.6/84.5	59.3/91.3	63.3/93.0	58.7/91.0	**64.3/95.8**

Table 2. Experimental results (%) on FE240Hz dataset [45].

Trackers	SR	$OP_{0.5}$	$OP_{0.7}$	PR
Stark-S [39]	52.4	64.3	24.5	83.2
CMT-MDNet [34]	53.2	68.2	30.2	78.8
FENet [46]	54.0	65.8	24.2	85.7
PrDiMP [10]	55.4	70.4	26.7	84.6
DiMP [2]	57.0	72.6	27.6	87.5
AFNet [45]	58.7	74.1	28.2	89.0
CrossEI [8]	59.4	74.6	28.8	92.3
Mamba-FETrack [24]	61.2	77.9	33.0	91.9
Ours	**63.6**	**80.8**	**39.3**	**93.0**

Table 3. Experimental results (%) on FELT dataset [33].

Trackers	SR	PR	NPR
PrDiMP [10]	43.8	59.6	52.0
DiMP [2]	43.5	55.1	52.2
ATOM [9]	36.2	45.9	43.3
TransT [6]	34.6	44.3	41.6
KYS [3]	33.1	42.4	39.7
OSTrack [40]	32.5	40.3	38.4
AFNet [45]	28.9	36.6	34.4
Mamba-FETrack [24]	43.5	55.6	51.9
Ours	**44.0**	**56.0**	**52.3**

Results on FELT Dataset. The FELT dataset, proposed by Wang et al. [33], is the first benchmark for long-term frame-event single-object tracking, consisting of 742 videos and 1,594,474 image-event pairs, split into 520 training and 222 test videos, each with at least 1,000 frames. As shown in Table 3, we report the results of 8 existing advanced trackers on the FELT dataset. The experimental results demonstrate that our method outperforms several advanced algorithms, including the CNN-based AFNet [45], the ViT-based OSTrack [40], and the Mamba-based Mamba-FETrack [24] tracking methods. Specifically, our method improves the PR metric by 19.4% compared to AFNet, the SR metric by 11.5% compared to OSTrack, and the NPR metric by 0.4% compared to Mamba-FETrack. These results show that our method, leveraging multi-scale residual blocks and the Mamba module, has strong potential for long-term object tracking.

4.3 Ablation Study

Influence of Key Component. To evaluate the effect of different components, we performed ablation experiments in Table 4. The results show that the introduction of MSRM significantly improves tracking performance, with SR, PR, and NPR metrics increasing by 2.7%, 3.9%, and 5.8%, respectively, highlighting the importance of fine-grained information. The addition of GMM further improves all metrics, demonstrating that the combination of the gating mechanism and Mamba enhances global feature representation. The ADE-Mamba module effectively facilitates cross-modal interaction, and the AFM module further boosts overall performance.

Influence of Different Input Combinations. Since asynchronous event streams cannot be directly fed into traditional neural networks, we explore classic event representations, including Event Frame [20] and Event Timesurface [29], and evaluate their effectiveness. As shown in Table 5, experiments with both single-modality and combined-modality inputs were conducted. The results indicate that after cross-modality interaction, the performance is consistently better than single-modality inputs, demonstrating that RGB and event modalities complement each other, capturing richer information. The combination of RGB and event frames achieves the best performance.

Influence of Depth in MSRM. We evaluated the impact of MSRM network depth on overall performance. As reported in Table 6, the experimental results indicate that the best performance was achieved with 3 layers of $MulResBlock$. As the network depth increased from 1 to 3 layers, performance improved, primarily due to the effective capture of local fine-grained information.

Influence of ADE-Mamba Sub-modules. We evaluate the impact of the key sub-modules within the ADE-Mamba module, specifically focusing on the FAL and the DRE Module. As shown in Table 7, removing both sub-modules significantly degrades performance. Adding the FAL module improves NPR by 1.2% and SR by 0.8% by aligning features from different modalities. Using only the DRE module increases PR by 0.9%, as it highlights the differences between modalities. When both FAL and DRE modules are used together, NPR improves significantly by 3.9%, demonstrating that their combination not only enhances feature alignment but also generates richer representations for subsequent interactions.

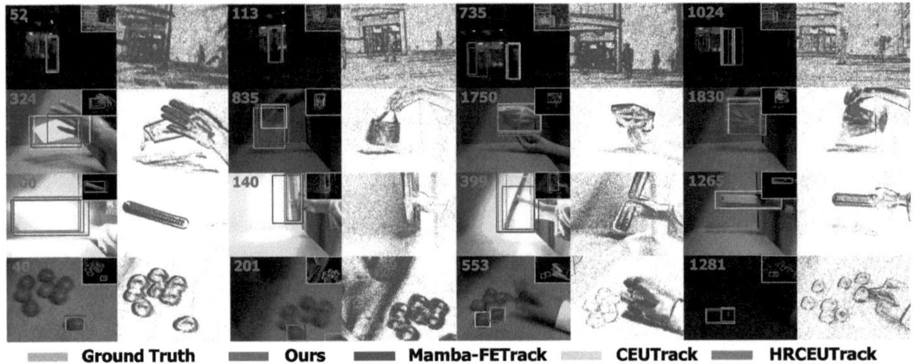

Fig. 6. Qualitative comparison results of our tracker with other SOTA trackers on the FELT dataset [33]. Event images are used for visual comparison.

Table 4. Ablation study on different components.

Method	SR (%)	PR (%)	NPR (%)
Baseline	58.7	91.0	62.9
+ MSRM	61.4	94.9	68.7
+ GMM	62.1	95.1	69.5
+ ADE-Mamba	63.8	95.2	71.6
+ AFM	**64.3**	**95.8**	**72.2**

Table 5. Ablation study on various input configurations.

Data Formulation	SR	PR	NPR
RGB Frame	45.8	72.9	50.4
Event Frame (EF)	58.6	91.5	62.1
Event TimeSurface (ETS)	59.3	92.1	62.5
RGB Frame & ETS	63.8	95.4	71.5
RGB Frame & EF	**64.3**	**95.8**	**72.2**

Table 6. Ablation study on the depth of MSRM.

Depth	SR	PR	NPR
1	61.5	93.8	69.0
2	61.9	94.1	69.8
3	**64.3**	**95.8**	**72.2**

Table 7. Ablation study on FAL and DRE modules.

FAL	DRE	SR	PR	NPR
×	×	61.3	94.5	68.3
✓	×	62.1	95.1	69.5
×	✓	62.1	95.4	69.5
✓	✓	**64.3**	**95.8**	**72.2**

Table 8. Evaluation of model efficiency.

Mamba-FETrack	Ours
Parameters	Parameters
7.0 MB	5.1 MB
Runtime	Runtime
66.4 ms	53.8 ms

Comparison on Efficiency. We compare our method with the representative Mamba-based baseline, Mamba-FETrack [24], to evaluate model efficiency. As shown in Table 8, our method achieves superior visual tracking performance while exhibiting a more lightweight model design (only 5.1 MB) and faster inference speed. This demonstrates that our method strikes a better balance between accuracy and efficiency.

4.4 Visualization

To intuitively demonstrate the effectiveness of MRM-RETrack, we compared its results with several advanced trackers on the FELT dataset [33]. As illustrated in Fig. 6, in challenging conditions, our predicted bounding boxes align more closely with the ground truth, showing better tracking performance. Additionally, we visualize the response weights of our method in the *supplementary material*, demonstrating that even under fast motion or low light, it generates strong responses at the target center.

5 Conclusion

In this paper, we propose MRM-RETrack, a novel RGB-event single object tracking framework that enhances cross-modal tracking performance while maintaining a lightweight model. By integrating local-global modeling, modality interaction, and dynamic fusion, the framework addresses the challenge of fine-grained local information extraction through MSRM and improves global feature representation with GMM. The ADE-Mamba module uses a joint alignment-discrepancy enhancement strategy to boost modality consistency and complementarity. Independent tracking heads and an adaptive fusion module allow dynamic adjustment of weights, enhancing tracking flexibility. Extensive experiments on FE108, FE240Hz, and FELT datasets validate the framework's effectiveness, demonstrating its robustness and potential in cross-modal tracking.

Acknowledgements. This work was supported in part by the National Natural Science Foundation of China (Nos. 62271410, 62401021), and the Fundamental Research Funds for the Central Universities (No. G2025KY05244).

References

1. Bertinetto, L., Valmadre, J., Henriques, J.F., Vedaldi, A., Torr, P.H.S.: Fully-convolutional Siamese networks for object tracking. In: Hua, G., Jégou, H. (eds.) ECCV 2016. LNCS, vol. 9914, pp. 850–865. Springer, Cham (2016). https://doi.org/10.1007/978-3-319-48881-3_56
2. Bhat, G., Danelljan, M., Gool, L.V., Timofte, R.: Learning discriminative model prediction for tracking. In: ICCV, pp. 6182–6191 (2019)
3. Bhat, G., Danelljan, M., Van Gool, L., Timofte, R.: Know your surroundings: exploiting scene information for object tracking. In: Vedaldi, A., Bischof, H., Brox, T., Frahm, J.-M. (eds.) ECCV 2020. LNCS, vol. 12368, pp. 205–221. Springer, Cham (2020). https://doi.org/10.1007/978-3-030-58592-1_13
4. Chang, Y., et al.: Towards HDR and HFR video from rolling-mixed-bit spikings. In: CVPR, pp. 25117–25127 (2024)
5. Chen, F., Wang, X., Zhao, Y., Lv, S., Niu, X.: Visual object tracking: a survey. Comput. Vis. Image Und. **222**, 103508 (2022)
6. Chen, X., Yan, B., Zhu, J., Wang, D., Yang, X., Lu, H.: Transformer tracking. In: CVPR, pp. 8126–8135 (2021)
7. Chen, Z., Zhong, B., Li, G., Zhang, S., Ji, R.: Siamese box adaptive network for visual tracking. In: CVPR, pp. 6668–6677 (2020)
8. Chen, Z., Wu, J., Dong, W., Li, L., Shi, G.: Crossei: boosting motion-oriented object tracking with an event camera. TIP **34**, 73–84 (2025)

9. Danelljan, M., Bhat, G., Khan, F.S., Felsberg, M.: Atom: accurate tracking by overlap maximization. In: CVPR, pp. 4660–4669 (2019)
10. Danelljan, M., Gool, L.V., Timofte, R.: Probabilistic regression for visual tracking. In: CVPR, pp. 7183–7192 (2020)
11. Dong, X., Shen, J., Shao, L., Porikli, F.: CLNet: a compact latent network for fast adjusting Siamese trackers. In: Vedaldi, A., Bischof, H., Brox, T., Frahm, J.-M. (eds.) ECCV 2020. LNCS, vol. 12365, pp. 378–395. Springer, Cham (2020). https://doi.org/10.1007/978-3-030-58565-5_23
12. Fan, B., Dai, Y., He, M.: Rolling shutter camera: modeling, optimization and learning. MIR **20**(6), 783–798 (2023)
13. Fan, B., Dai, Y., Li, H.: Rolling shutter inversion: bring rolling shutter images to high framerate global shutter video. TPAMI **45**(5), 6214–6230 (2022)
14. Fan, B., Dai, Y., Li, H.: Learning bilateral cost volume for rolling shutter temporal super-resolution. TPAMI **46**(5), 3862–3879 (2024)
15. Fan, B., Guo, Y., Dai, Y., Xu, C., Shi, B.: Self-supervised learning for rolling shutter temporal super-resolution. TCSVT **35**(1), 769–782 (2025)
16. Fan, B., Mao, Y., Dai, Y., Wan, Z., Liu, Q.: Joint appearance and motion learning for efficient rolling shutter correction. In: CVPR, pp. 5671–5681 (2023)
17. Fan, B., Wan, Z., Shi, B., Xu, C., Dai, Y.: Unified video reconstruction for rolling shutter and global shutter cameras. TIP **33**, 6821–6835 (2024)
18. Fan, B., Yin, J., Dai, Y., Xu, C., Huang, T., Shi, B.: Spatio-temporal interactive learning for efficient image reconstruction of spiking cameras. In: NeurIPS, pp. 21401–21427 (2024)
19. Gallego, G., et al.: Event-based vision: a survey. TPAMI **44**(1), 154–180 (2020)
20. Gehrig, M., Aarents, W., Gehrig, D., Scaramuzza, D.: DSEC: a stereo event camera dataset for driving scenarios. RA-L **6**(3), 4947–4954 (2021)
21. Gu, A., Goel, K., Ré, C.: Efficiently modeling long sequences with structured state spaces. arXiv preprint arXiv:2111.00396 (2021)
22. Guo, Y., He, M., Fan, B.: Grid-transformer for few-shot hyperspectral image classification. In: ICIP, pp. 755–759 (2023)
23. He, X., et al.: Pan-mamba: effective pan-sharpening with state space model. Inf. Fusion **115**, 102779 (2025)
24. Huang, J., Wang, S., Wang, S., Wu, Z., Wang, X., Jiang, B.: Mamba-FEtrack: frame-event tracking via state space model. In: Lin, Z., et al. (eds.) PRCV 2024. LNCS, vol. 15042, pp. 3–18. Springer, Singapore (2024). https://doi.org/10.1007/978-981-97-8858-3_1
25. Jin, Y., Zhang, L., Yan, S., Fan, B., Wang, B.: Boosting gaze object prediction via pixel-level supervision from vision foundation model. In: Leonardis, A., Ricci, E., Roth, S., Russakovsky, O., Sattler, T., Varol, G. (eds.) ECCV 2024. LNCS, vol. 15127, pp. 369–386. Springer, Cham (2024). https://doi.org/10.1007/978-3-031-72890-7_23
26. Li, B., Yan, J., Wu, W., Zhu, Z., Hu, X.: High performance visual tracking with Siamese region proposal network. In: CVPR, pp. 8971–8980 (2018)
27. Lou, H., Liang, J., Teng, M., Fan, B., Xu, Y., Shi, B.: Zero-shot event-intensity asymmetric stereo via visual prompting from image domain. In: NeurIPS, pp. 13274–13301 (2024)
28. Marvasti-Zadeh, S.M., Cheng, L., Ghanei-Yakhdan, H., Kasaei, S.: Deep learning for visual tracking: a comprehensive survey. IEEE T. Intell. Transp. **23**(5), 3943–3968 (2021)
29. Sironi, A., Brambilla, M., Bourdis, N., Lagorce, X., Benosman, R.: HATS: histograms of averaged time surfaces for robust event-based object classification. In: CVPR, pp. 1731–1740 (2018)
30. Tang, C., et al.: Revisiting color-event based tracking: a unified network, dataset, and metric. arXiv preprint arXiv:2211.11010 (2022)
31. Wan, Z., Dai, Y., Mao, Y.: Learning dense and continuous optical flow from an event camera. TIP **31**, 7237–7251 (2022)

32. Wang, B., Guo, C., Jin, Y., Xia, H., Liu, N.: Transgop: transformer-based gaze object prediction. In: AAAI, pp. 10180–10188 (2024)
33. Wang, X., et al.: Long-term frame-event visual tracking: benchmark dataset and baseline. arXiv preprint arXiv:2403.05839 (2024)
34. Wang, X., et al.: Visevent: reliable object tracking via collaboration of frame and event flows. IEEE Trans. Cybern. **54**(3), 1997–2010 (2023)
35. Wang, X., et al.: Event stream-based visual object tracking: a high-resolution benchmark dataset and a novel baseline. In: CVPR, pp. 19248–19257 (2024)
36. Xie, X., Cui, Y., Tan, T., Zheng, X., Yu, Z.: FusionMamba: dynamic feature enhancement for multimodal image fusion with mamba. Vis. Intell. **2**(1), 37 (2024)
37. Xu, Y., Wang, Z., Li, Z., Yuan, Y., Yu, G.: SiamFC++: towards robust and accurate visual tracking with target estimation guidelines. In: AAAI, pp. 12549–12556 (2020)
38. Xun, Z., et al.: Linker: learning long short-term associations for robust visual tracking. TMM **26**, 6228–6237 (2024)
39. Yan, B., Peng, H., Fu, J., Wang, D., Lu, H.: Learning spatio-temporal transformer for visual tracking. In: ICCV, pp. 10448–10457 (2021)
40. Ye, B., Chang, H., Ma, B., Shan, S., Chen, X.: Joint feature learning and relation modeling for tracking: a one-stream framework. In: Avidan, S., Brostow, G., Cissé, M., Farinella, G.M., Hassner, T. (eds.) ECCV 2022. LNCS, vol. 13682, pp. 341–357. Springer, Cham (2022). https://doi.org/10.1007/978-3-031-20047-2_20
41. Yin, J., Fan, B., Xu, C., Huang, T., Shi, B.: Spk2imgMamba: spiking camera image reconstruction with multi-scale state space models. In: WACV, pp. 9342–9352 (2025)
42. Yu, B., et al.: Active hyperspectral imaging using an event camera. In: CVPR, pp. 929–939 (2025)
43. Zhang, J., et al.: 2DMamba: efficient state space model for image representation with applications on giga-pixel whole slide image classification. In: CVPR, pp. 3583–3592 (2025)
44. Zhang, J., et al.: Spiking transformers for event-based single object tracking. In: CVPR, pp. 8801–8810 (2022)
45. Zhang, J., et al.: Frame-event alignment and fusion network for high frame rate tracking. In: CVPR, pp. 9781–9790 (2023)
46. Zhang, J., Yang, X., Fu, Y., Wei, X., Yin, B., Dong, B.: Object tracking by jointly exploiting frame and event domain. In: ICCV, pp. 13043–13052 (2021)
47. Zhang, R., Yang, Z., Pan, L.: DehazeMamba: large multi-modal model guided single image dehazing via mamba. Vis. Intell. **3**(1), 11 (2025)
48. Zhu, J., Wan, Z., Dai, Y.: Video frame prediction from a single image and events. In: AAAI, pp. 7748–7756 (2024)
49. Zhu, L., Liao, B., Zhang, Q., Wang, X., Liu, W., Wang, X.: Vision Mamba: efficient visual representation learning with bidirectional state space model. In: ICML, pp. 62429–62442 (2024)
50. Zhu, Y., et al.: CRSOT: cross-resolution object tracking using unaligned frame and event cameras. arXiv preprint arXiv:2401.02826 (2024)
51. Zhu, Z., Hou, J., Wu, D.O.: Cross-modal orthogonal high-rank augmentation for RGB-event transformer-trackers. In: ICCV, pp. 22045–22055 (2023)

Computational Photography, Sensing and Display Technology

Ultra Fast Automatic Exposure Target Estimation for Smartphone Platform

Chong Tang(✉), Lei Zhao, Chenlu Wei, Lei Pang, Pei Lv, Lei Zhang, Chen Chen, Wei Wang, and Ruirong You

UNISOC Technologies Co., Ltd., Shanghai, China
{chong.tang,michael.zhao,chenlu.wei,lei.pang,pei.lv,darren.zhang, chen.chen,sunny.wang,yoyo.you}@unisoc.com

Abstract. Modern methods primarily consider automatic exposure (AE) as an optimization problem based on metrics, which struggles with the challenge of defining a widely effective evaluation metric. In addition, the performance of the exposure algorithm is constrained by the mobile platform. Inspired by human perception, exposure preferences are greatly influenced by the environment and image content. We propose a novel and effective formulation for ultra fast exposure target estimation for smartphones' AE control across all scenarios. Specifically, we approach the automatic exposure target estimation as a self-adaptive regression problem, utilizing multivariate multiscale histograms and prior information. Initially, we calculate the global histogram of Y-RGB channels and the local histogram of the Y channel across multiple scales, while simultaneously obtaining environmental prior information through inline sensors or preprocessing. We then determine the desired exposure target for the photograph through self-adaptive regression. Ultimately, convergence control is conducted, and an appropriate exposure setting is selected from the exposure table to achieve the targeted exposure level. Extensive experiments on our datasets and real smartphones demonstrate that our method excels in both stability and consistency. Our method significantly reduces computational costs by using statistical histogram inputs instead of 2D images. This ultra-light model can even reach over 550 FPS based on TensorFlow Lite on the low-end smartphone CPU (2×A75 2.2G/6×A55 1.8G). Our model has the remarkable features of low power consumption, high frame rate and ultra-lightweight, thus it can be deployed to smartphones with a wide range of performance.

Keywords: Automatic exposure · target estimation · self-adaptive regression

1 Introduction

Automatic Exposure (AE) is a fundamental component in modern cameras and smartphones. It allows users to capture high-quality images with appropriate exposure levels in a variety of lighting scenarios [5].

© The Author(s), under exclusive license to Springer Nature Singapore Pte Ltd. 2026
J. Kittler et al. (Eds.): PRCV 2025, LNCS 16289, pp. 181–195, 2026.
https://doi.org/10.1007/978-981-95-5764-6_13

Traditionally, exposure levels are usually adjusted by optimizing a defined metric [8,18], such as gradient [4], and multiple weighted metrics [11,17]. Automatic exposure methods based on learning have also been developed in recent years [25]. Onzon et al. revisited auto-exposure control to boost HDR. A neural network was proposed for exposure selection, which was trained jointly end-to-end with an object detector and an image signal processing (ISP) pipeline [14]. Lee et al. proposed a camera exposure control framework that rapidly controls camera exposure while performing real-time processing by SAC reinforcement learning method [12]. Yang et al. proposed a reinforcement learning approach for real-time exposure control of a mobile camera based on the Markov Decision Process, which was trained through the Gaussian policy gradient in an end-to-end fashion [22]. In [24], an algorithm with asynchronously reinforced adversarial learning was developed for learning local exposures. A local exposure for each sub-image is automatically learned by virtue of the policy network sequentially, while the reward of learning is globally designed to strike a balance of overall exposures. Tomasi et al. explored a data-driven approach to account for environmental lighting changes by improving the quality of images [20]. The above methods have a common technical path, which is to supervise the model through high-level tasks such as visual odometry (VO), simultaneous localization and mapping (SLAM), or object detection. While these tasks are not significantly affected by slight variations in image brightness, subjective image quality assessment (IQA) is highly sensitive to it.

In addition, the scarcity of publicly accessible datasets is compounded by the limited scope of scenarios. Recent work [13] provided a dataset with intensive lighting for evaluating object detection and classification. For challenging environments, Tedla et al. captured and released a 4D dataset over a temporal sequence with moving objects, bright lights, and varying lighting. This dataset could be used on the designed platform to examine different AE algorithms and help develop better AE methods [19].

In previous methods, the optimization metric or reward is the critical component in automatic exposure. It struggles with the challenge of defining an evaluation metric that is widely effective across all scenarios. In [19], the user-defined target value (referred to as the key) is given as one constant. This wouldn't work in real cameras or smartphones. To address the aforementioned issues, a novel and effective formulation aimed at ultra fast automatic exposure target estimation on smartphones across various scenarios is proposed. The core contributions of our study can be summarized as follows:

- An automatic exposure target estimation formulation is proposed based on deep learning of dual branch networks, which treats the automatic exposure target estimation as a regression problem instead of an optimization problem.
- Multivariate multiscale histograms and prior information are processed as inputs to the dual branch network to improve inference speed and exposure accuracy.

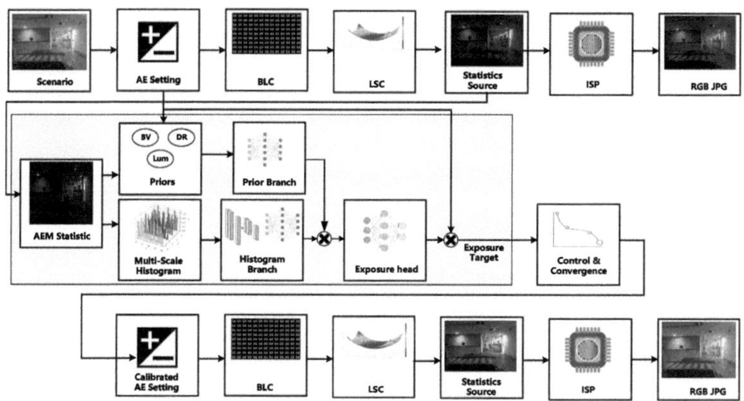

Fig. 1. The dual-channel automatic exposure target estimation algorithm based on multivariate multiscale histogram learning with prior information. The core contribution of this manuscript is in the shadow area.

- A raw image dataset has been collected, and our extensive experiments validate the effectiveness and advantages of the developed method, which enhances multiple exposure performances, such as stability and consistency.
- This is a low-power, high-frame-rate, ultra-lightweight exposure algorithm that is developed specifically for smartphone platforms.

2 Ultra Fast Dual Automatic Exposure Target Estimation

2.1 Method Overview

This paper introduces an innovative approach that uses multivariate multiscale histograms as inputs to the network model. In addition, our method takes into account environmental brightness, dynamic range, and current image brightness as prior information. This information is fed into the network model, enabling it to make differential adjustments to the exposure settings.

As illustrated in Fig. 1, the overall flowchart is presented. The initial exposure setting in automatic mode is arbitrary. The image sensor data is processed through black level correction (BLC), lens shading correction (LSC) and automatic exposure monitor (AEM). Then automatic exposure dual network outputs the exposure adjustment ratio. Finally, the new AE setting is calculated and applied for the next capture. This cycle continues until the image brightness stabilizes.

2.2 Ultra Fast Network Design

In the field of computer vision, 2D images are commonly used for model input, requiring network structures based on 2D convolution. Even the MobileNet family, designed for mobile platforms, cannot achieve ultra-fast inference on mobile

Table 1. Dual branch network structure.

Histogram Branch		filters	size	stride	output	Prior Branch		filters	output
0	input				M × 256	0	input		4
1	conv1d+bn1d+relu	64	4	4	64 × 64	1	fc+bn1d+relu	16	16
2	conv1d+bn1d+relu	128	4	2	128 × 31	2	fc+bn1d+relu	1024	1024
3	conv1d+bn1d+relu	256	3	2	256 × 15	3	fc+bn1d+relu	16	16
4	conv1d+bn1d+relu	512	3	2	512 × 7				
5	conv1d+bn1d+relu	512	3	2	512 × 3				
6	flatten				1536				
7	fc+bn1d+relu	1024			1024				
8	fc+bn1d+relu	16			16				
9	feature fusion								16
10	ln+fc+sigmoid	2			2				

CPUs [6,7,16]. Therefore, our model uses histograms as inputs and constructs a model based on 1D convolution.

The specific structure is shown in Table 1. Histogram branch mainly consists of five 1D convolutional layers and two fully connected layers, where M represents the number of input histograms, corresponding to the channel features. The input image of 8 bits results in a histogram length of 256. The prior branch and the exposure network mainly consists of fully connected layers. After fusing the output features, they pass through a fully connected layer to output the final exposure adjustment. In our algorithm, dual exposures are supported: short target exposure and safe target exposure. These dual exposures can improve the dynamic range in the image signal processor (ISP) pipeline.

2.3 AEM Statistics

The source raw image $I_R \in R^{H \times W \times 3}$ typically has a high resolution, commonly exceeding 12 megapixels. Directly using this raw image as a source for histogram statistics would increase computation time. Therefore, a statistical module must be designed to reduce the image's resolution and bit depth while preserving brightness and color information.

Assuming the number of divided windows is $N \times N$. It is necessary to select a center region of interest (ROI) that can be evenly divided by N for data statistics.

Within each window, pixel averaging is performed to obtain down-sampled 8-bit $N \times N$ images. In this implementation, N is set to 128.

2.4 Multivariate Multiscale Histogram

Histograms contain rich image information. In this manuscript, the histogram branch model requires a multivariate multi-scale histogram as input. The pro-

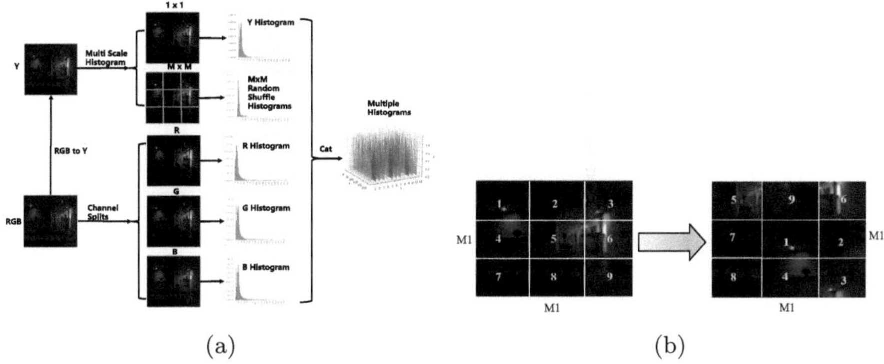

Fig. 2. Input Preprocessing. (a) Multivariate multi-scale histogram. (b) Multi-scale histogram division and random shuffle with $M_1 = 3$.

cessing flow is shown in Fig. 2a. The statistical map $I \in R^{N \times N \times 3}$ output by AEM needs to be transformed into luminance information $Y \in R^{N \times N}$.

In automatic exposure algorithms, it is necessary to consider not only the overall exposure level, but also whether there is severe overexposure or underexposure in local areas. Therefore, multi-scale histograms are adopted for more refined exposure control at different scales. For the luminance channel, various scales such as 1×1, $M_1 \times M_1, ..., M_n \times M_n$ are selected. Histogram statistics are performed within each window to obtain a total of $1 + \sum_{i=1}^{n} M_i^2$ histograms. By employing multi-scale histogram statistics, the algorithm captures both global and local exposure information, effectively balancing the exposure across different areas of the image.

During the training phase, regions of overexposure or underexposure are independent of their spatial locations. In our algorithm, we introduce **histogram shuffle**, where histograms at the same scale undergo a random reordering to augment the diversity and richness of the data, as depicted in Fig. 2b.

Additionally, for scenes with pure colors, relying solely on the luminance channel would result in the loss of color information. Consequently, global histogram statistics for the RGB channels are calculated separately.

Ultimately, the input data obtained for the histogram branch network is $X_{Hist} \in R^{(4+\sum_{i=1}^{n} M_i^2) \times 256}$.

2.5 Prior Information

For the same object, under different combinations of lighting and exposure settings, similar raw images can be obtained. The desired exposure levels can vary significantly with changes in lighting conditions. Consequently, relying solely on the raw image as input for the model is insufficient for differentiating scenes. Hence, it is necessary to incorporate prior information to gather as much relevant environmental and exposure information as possible.

Firstly, normalized image brightness level L is calculated as

$$L_{norm} = L/255 = Mean(Y)/255 \tag{1}$$

Then, normalized environmental brightness BV is estimated by APEX [10]

$$BV_{norm} = \left(LV_{cali} + 1.45 * ln \left(\frac{\frac{L}{T*G} \times 10^{11}}{BV_{cali}} \right) + 6 \right) /22 \tag{2}$$

where LV_{cali} and BV_{cali} represent calibrated physical quantities. T is the exposure time (ns), and G is the exposure gain. The range of BV value is [-6, 16] [3,15].

Additionally, dynamic range of scene is estimated based on global histogram H_y of the Y channel. Key brightness and dark thresholds are identified by a certain proportion, denoted as BH and BL respectively. The normalized environmental dynamic range is defined as

$$DR_{norm} = \frac{1}{ln(255/2)} ln(BH/BL), BL >= 2, BH >= BL \tag{3}$$

Based on the above information, the final input data for the prior branch network is obtained as follows,

$$X_{prior} = [BV_{norm}, DR_{norm}, L_{norm}, C] \tag{4}$$

where C is a constant for stability, usually $C = 0.5$.

2.6 Automatic Exposure and Loss

The histogram network and the prior network output features with same dimension, denoted as X_{21} and X_{22}. These features can be fused and feeded into automatic exposure target estimation network

$$X_3 = AutoExposureHead(X_{21} \times X_{22}) \tag{5}$$

Further dual exposure adjustment ratio is calculated as

$$Y = exp^{2Ln(\mu)(X_3 - 0.5)}, Y \in \left[\frac{1}{\mu}, \mu\right] \tag{6}$$

The brightness of Short GT and Safe GT images is represented as $L_{GT_{short}}$ and $L_{GT_{safe}}$. The brightness value of any initial state image is L_{input}. The short and safe learning objectives are formatted as

$$Y_{GT_{short}} = \frac{L_{GT_{short}}}{L_{input}}, Y_{GT_{safe}} = \frac{L_{GT_{safe}}}{L_{input}}, Y_{GT_{short}}, Y_{GT_{safe}} \in \left[\frac{1}{\mu}, \mu\right] \tag{7}$$

During the training stage, the Charbonnier loss is adopted as follows,

$$Loss = w_1\sqrt{(Y_{short} - Y_{GT_{short}})^2 + \epsilon^2} + w_2\sqrt{(Y_{safe} - Y_{GT_{safe}})^2 + \epsilon^2} \quad (8)$$

where w_1, w_2 are the loss weights for short and safe exposure loss, and ϵ is set to 1×10^{-3}

2.7 Network Inference

In this section, we demonstrate the process of obtaining results during inference. To enhance the precision and smoothness of exposure control during the inference phase, we use a moving average of exposure target values for a refined aggregation of exposure forecasts.

$$e_t = \gamma e_{t-1} + (1 - \gamma)Y \times L_{input} \quad (9)$$

where e_{t-1} and e_t are the exposure targets in the previous and current frame time, respectively. γ is the smoothing parameter.

3 Experiments

3.1 Experimental Setting

Datasets. To evaluate our approach, we first prepared datasets with raw images from underexposure to overexposure. The resolution of the raw images is 4000×3000, and the data depth is 14 bits. AEM statistics module generates low-resolution images of 128×128 with 8 bits, reducing storage needs from 24 MB to 66 KB per image. We've collected 303 data sets, comprising around 33K images, captured with multiple phones equipped with the IMX586 sensor. Firstly, the Short and Safe GTs are automatically labeled by virtue of our traditional AE algorithm. Then, these GTs are calibrated by evaluation experts with the ISP simulation tool from raw to JPG. The best imaging short and safe parameters would be our final GT. It seeks a balance between brightness and noise levels, as well as global and local brightness.

Evaluation Metrics. In the simulation experiment, the image from the test set serves as the initial frame, and the exposure target is calculated. The data frame closest to this target in the data sequence is then identified and used as input for subsequent iterations until full convergence is achieved. In the dataset, it is common for there to be only one GT frame. Therefore, we consider an exposure target within a $\pm 5\%$ margin of the GT as acceptable, as it does not significantly affect the final image quality in our ISP pipeline.

Assuming the number of images in the test set is denoted as N_a, and the number of images that have converged within the GT range in simulation is denoted as N_t, then the accuracy of the simulated exposure is calculated as

$$accuracy = N_t / N_a \times 100\% \quad (10)$$

Table 2. Hyperparameter settings for the neural network training.

Parameters	Description	Value
N	number of divided windows	128
n	scale size	1
M_1	scale value	3
μ	max ratio	5
w_1	short loss weight	0.5
w_2	safe loss weight	0.5
epoch	training epoch	2000
batchsize	training batches	128
num_worker	data loaders	16
lr	initial optimizer learning rate	0.1
eta_min	minimum learning rate	0.001
momentum	optimizer momentum	0.9
weight_decay	optimizer weight_decay	0.0005

Implementation Details. In the optimization process, we initially set the learning rate to 0.1 for the SGD optimizer. The learning rate is adjusted with a linear warmup from 0.01 to 0.1 and a cosine annealing policy from 0.1 to 0.001. Models are trained on PyTorch using an Nvidia RTX 3090 GPU. Hyperparameter settings are detailed in Table 2.

3.2 Ablation Study

Table 3. Ablation study results of removing a single key module compared to the full strateg

Prior Branch		✓	✓	✓	✓
RGB Histogram	✓		✓	✓	✓
Multi-Scale Histogram	✓	✓		✓	✓
Histogram Shuffle	✓	✓	✓		✓
Results	92.19%	94.39%	94.28%	93.99%	**97.05%**

Effectiveness of Prior Branch. The prior branch plays an essential role in accurate automatic exposure. Motivated by this, we propose a dual-branch network. To verify the effectiveness of the prior branch, we trained a model on our dataset without including the prior branch. The result is shown in Table 3. Accuracy on our test dataset decreases significantly by 4.86% without the prior branch, validating its effectiveness.

Table 4. Different configurations of multi-scale histograms.

Config	Accuracy	Delta
scale 1	94.28%	−2.77%
***scale 1-3**	**97.05%**	-
scale 1-3-5	96.52%	−0.53%
scale 1-3-5-7	95.97%	−1.08%

Effectiveness of RGB Histogram. Pure color scenes are challenging for automatic exposure. That often leads to contradictions and conflicts with other scenes and results in overexposure. Table 3 shows that the RGB histogram strategy leads to a 2.66% increase in accuracy.

Effectiveness of Multiscale Histogram. Multiscale histogram is a core component for accurate exposure. The performance of our method with only one global histogram would decrease significantly, as shown in Table 3. The multi-scale histogram technique could lead to a 3.06% increase in accuracy.

This raises the question of how many scales are needed to conduct automatic exposure target estimation. To discuss this question, we train the model using more configurations of scale to observe the model's performance. Results are depicted in Table 4. Here, scale 1-3 means two scales with the global histogram and local histograms of $M_1 = 3$, which is the optimal configuration in our method under the AEM size 128×128 . The best scale is related to the size of the AEM map. If the AEM is divided into small windows, there won't be enough pixel counts for histogram statistics.

Effectiveness of Histogram Shuffle. Histogram random shuffle is one policy for data augmentation, contributing to data diversity. Diverse datasets are essential for training robust models capable of generalizing well to unseen data. Results are shown in Table 3. The effectiveness of this strategy was confirmed through rigorous testing and analysis.

3.3 Simulation Results

In this experiment, several datasets were randomly selected to serve as the test set. This ensures that this group of data was not used for training, allowing for the evaluation of the model's generalization capability.

Figure 3-(a) shows a comparative simulation of sunny day data for cross-scenario validation. The green solid and dashed lines represent the current luminance calculated by the traditional AE and our AIAE algorithm, respectively. That shows a high degree of correlation between the two curves. However, there is a significant difference in the target calculated by our algorithm (ai-ae blue line) and traditional AE (ae purple line). The target calculated by our algorithm starts from the dark area and steadily rises, remaining stable in the mid-brightness and high-brightness regions. In contrast, the traditional AE exhibits more severe fluctuations during the transition from low to mid-brightness, which can affect the stability of exposure and the smoothness of transitions. Our model's target demonstrates smooth transitions and accurate exposure computations across various settings, highlighting its cross-scenario applicability and suitability for full-scene exposure. Additionally, the model maintains excellent smoothness and stability during transitions between low and high luminance.

Further cross-scenario exposure simulation comparisons were conducted on an overcast dataset, as shown in Fig. 3-(b). Examining the image transition curves reveals that our method provides smoother transitions than traditional AE, with fewer fluctuations in exposure values, ensuring stable exposure across all scenarios.

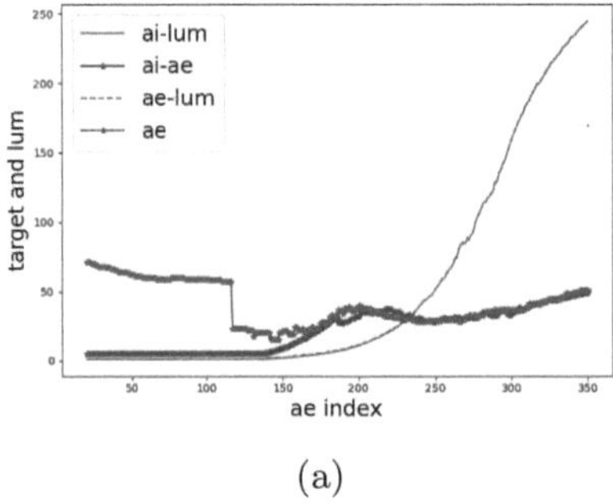

(a)

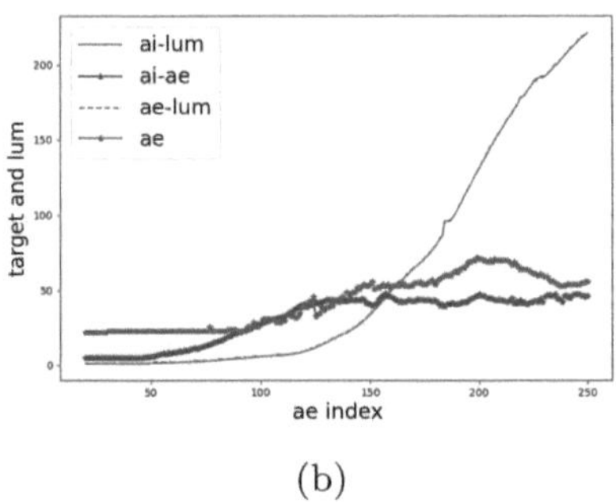

(b)

Fig. 3. Outdoor exposure comparison of traditional AE and our method. The blue ai-ae line and the purple ae line are the target curves of our method and traditional AE, respectively. The ai-lum and ae-lum lines are the luminance curves. (a) Outdoor exposure on a sunny day. (b) Outdoor exposure on a cloudy day. (Color figure online)

3.4 Mobile Phone Real Test

The proposed model is deployed on a mobile phone based on the TensorFlow Lite inference library. The phone is equipped with a low-end CPU (2×A75 2.2G/6×A55 1.8G). The model achieves an inference speed of 550 FPS (1.8 ms per frame) on this CPU, meeting the requirements for ultra-fast photography and video recording. Due to the fact that ISP is a system-level engineering, it's hard to compare our method with the AE algorithm in the references. Thus, in the following comparative experiments, the only ISP difference on the mobile phone is the traditional AE and our method (AIAE). Subsequently, the AIAE model is tested in laboratory lightbox scenes and natural scenes, respectively.

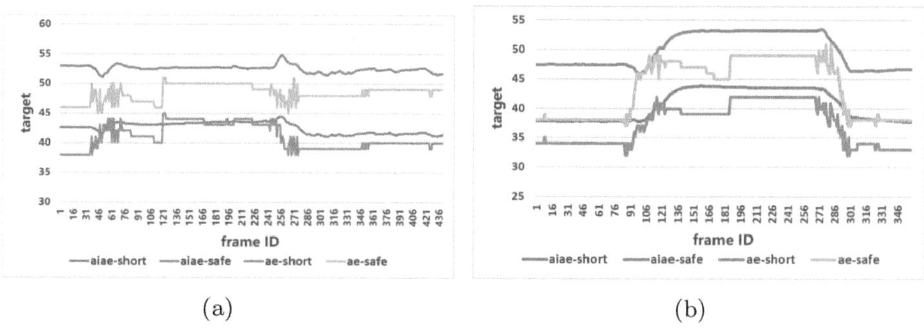

(a) (b)

Fig. 4. Laboratory highlighting testing of mobile phones. D65 is the international standard artificial daylight with a color temperature of 6500K. (a) Phone test under D65 300-1000-300 lux. (b) Phone test under D65 30-500-30 lux.

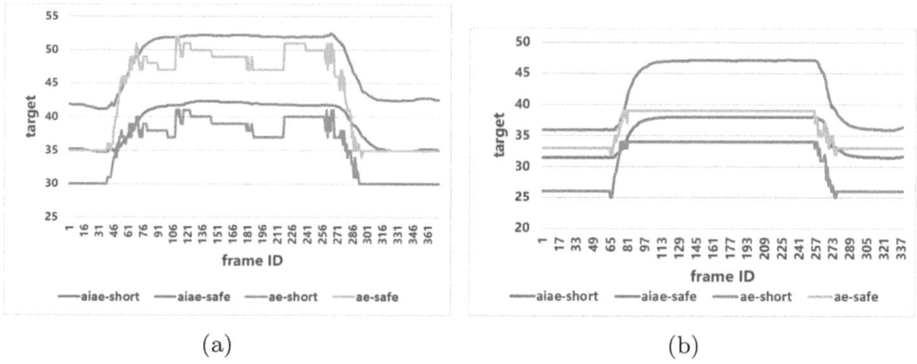

(a) (b)

Fig. 5. Laboratory low light testing of mobile phones. TL84 and LED are the abbreviations for Triphosphor Lamp P15 and Light Emitting Diode. (a) Phone test under TL84 10-250-250 lux. (b) Phone test under LED 5-30-5 lux.

Laboratory Lightbox Test. As shown in Figs. 4 and 5, our method is tested under four laboratory lightbox settings, representing high brightness, mid-to-high brightness, mid-to-low brightness, and low brightness environments, respectively. In each graph, the blue and orange solid lines represent the aiae-short and aiae-safe exposure targets of our method, while the gray and yellow solid lines represent the traditional ae-short and ae-safe exposure targets.

Under all lighting conditions, when experiencing changes in ambient brightness, the exposure target of our method shows much smoother and more stable variations compared to traditional AE, which has sharp fluctuations. This demonstrates that our model's exposure target stability is superior to that of traditional AE.

As shown in Fig. 4, during the middle phase, our model's exposure curve is nearly a horizontal straight line, while the traditional AE's exposure target curve shows fluctuations. Thus, our algorithm demonstrates superior consistency.

Table 5. IQA results of traditional AE and our method.

	IQA Mean Scores		Better Rate	
IQA Methods	AE	Ours	AE	Ours
QualiCLIP [1]	**0.4423**	0.4410	44.9%	**55.1%**
LIQE [26]	**2.115**	2.098	44.3%	**55.7%**
ARNIQA [2]	0.498	**0.500**	44.3%	**55.7%**
CLIPIQA(+) [21]	0.5292	**0.5299**	47.2%	**52.8%**
MANIQA [23]	0.3071	**0.3077**	38.6%	**61.4%**
MUSIQ [9]	36.226	**36.872**	48.3%	**51.7%**

(a)

(b)

Fig. 6. Outdoor greenery scene. (a) Captured by traditional AE. (b) Captured by our method.

Natural Scene Test. The developed model is able to capture photos in full natural scenes. Our model shows certain improvements over the traditional AE. There are 176 sets of images in total captured with AIAE and traditional AE, respectively. All images are evaluated by IQA methods [1,2,9,21,23,26]. IQA mean scores and better rates are listed in Table 5. The higher better rate means more image cases with higher IQA scores.

Additionally, our method could perform better in HDR scenarios. In Fig. 6, the left image shows more extensive overexposed areas in the sky, while the right image has a more reasonable exposure intensity for the sky. Additionally, both images show consistent brightness levels in the dark areas, indicating that our algorithm captures images with a superior dynamic range.

In Fig. 7, the left image shows significant overexposure of the fan area, while the right image provides a more suitable exposure for the fan section. Furthermore, the right image shows greater accuracy in color reproduction within the color bands area. Thus, the right exposure helps maintain proper automatic white balance and enhances color fidelity.

In summary, our method is characterized by its ability to suppress highlights and enhance lowlights, contributing to an expanded dynamic range in images.

(a)

(b)

Fig. 7. Indoor colorful scene. (a) Captured by traditional AE. (b) Captured by our method.

Moreover, our model ensures consistent scene imaging and significantly simplifies the parameter tuning process.

4 Conclusion

In this manuscript, a novel AE approach that integrates prior information and a multivariate multiscale histogram was introduced. The proposed formulation regarded AE as directly adjusting ratio regression based on inputs of prior information and multivariate multiscale histograms. Thus, the problems of efficiency were effectively addressed. Especially, the network design was capable of surpassing 550 FPS on smartphones with low-end CPUs. In addition, the proposed method demonstrated superior performance in exposure stability and consistency while ensuring the quality of the exposure effect.

However, our method does have some limitations. Customizing exposure target settings to individual preferences is not easily achievable. Additionally, the GT annotation process is complex and relies on traditional AE algorithms. These need to be further simplified and improved.

References

1. Agnolucci, L., Galteri, L., Bertini, M.: Quality-aware image-text alignment for real-world image quality assessment. arXiv preprint arXiv:2403.11176 (2024)
2. Agnolucci, L., Galteri, L., Bertini, M., Del Bimbo, A.: Arniqa: learning distortion manifold for image quality assessment. In: Proceedings of the IEEE/CVF Winter Conference on Applications of Computer Vision, pp. 189–198 (2024)
3. Banterle, F., Artusi, A., Debattista, K., Chalmers, A.: Advanced high dynamic range imaging. AK Peters/CRC Press (2017)
4. Bégin, M.A., Hunter, I.: Auto-exposure algorithm for enhanced mobile robot localization in challenging light conditions. Sensors **22**(3), 835 (2022)
5. Bernacki, J.: Automatic exposure algorithms for digital photography. Multimedia Tools and Appl. **79**(19), 12751–12776 (2020)

6. Howard, A., et al.: Searching for mobilenetv3. In: Proceedings of the IEEE/CVF International Conference on Computer Vision, pp. 1314–1324 (2019)
7. Howard, A.G., et al.: Mobilenets: Efficient convolutional neural networks for mobile vision applications. arXiv preprint arXiv:1704.04861 (2017)
8. Jayasuriya, S., Iqbal, O., Kodukula, V., Torres, V., LiKamWa, R., Spanias, A.: Software-defined imaging: a survey. In: Proceedings of the IEEE (2023)
9. Ke, J., Wang, Q., Wang, Y., Milanfar, P., Yang, F.: Musiq: multi-scale image quality transformer. In: Proceedings of the IEEE/CVF International Conference on Computer Vision, pp. 5148–5157 (2021)
10. Kerr, D.A.: Apex-additive system of photographic exposure. Issue **7**(2007.08), 04 (2007)
11. Kim, J., Cho, Y., Kim, A.: Exposure control using Bayesian optimization based on entropy weighted image gradient. In: 2018 IEEE International Conference on Robotics and Automation (ICRA), pp. 857–864. IEEE (2018)
12. Lee, K., Shin, U., Lee, B.U.: Learning to control camera exposure via reinforcement learning. In: Proceedings of the IEEE/CVF Conference on Computer Vision and Pattern Recognition, pp. 2975–2983 (2024)
13. Morawski, I., Chen, Y.A., Lin, Y.S., Dangi, S., He, K., Hsu, W.H.: Genisp: neural ISP for low-light machine cognition. In: Proceedings of the IEEE/CVF Conference on Computer Vision and Pattern Recognition, pp. 630–639 (2022)
14. Onzon, E., Mannan, F., Heide, F.: Neural auto-exposure for high-dynamic range object detection. In: Proceedings of the IEEE/CVF Conference on Computer Vision and Pattern Recognition, pp. 7710–7720 (2021)
15. Reinhard, E.: High dynamic range imaging. In: Computer Vision: a Reference Guide, pp. 1–6. Springer (2020)
16. Sandler, M., Howard, A., Zhu, M., Zhmoginov, A., Chen, L.C.: Mobilenetv2: inverted residuals and linear bottlenecks. In: Proceedings of the IEEE Conference on Computer Vision and Pattern Recognition, pp. 4510–4520 (2018)
17. Shin, U., Park, J., Shim, G., Rameau, F., Kweon, I.S.: Camera exposure control for robust robot vision with noise-aware image quality assessment. In: 2019 IEEE/RSJ International Conference on Intelligent Robots and Systems (IROS), pp. 1165–1172. IEEE (2019)
18. Tao, X., Jin, W., Yang, J., Li, S., Su, B., Wang, M.: Multi-integration time adaptive selection method for superframe high-dynamic-range infrared imaging based on grayscale information. Sensors **22**(11), 4258 (2022)
19. Tedla, S., Yang, B., Brown, M.S.: Examining autoexposure for challenging scenes. In: Proceedings of the IEEE/CVF International Conference on Computer Vision, pp. 13076–13085 (2023)
20. Tomasi, J., Wagstaff, B., Waslander, S.L., Kelly, J.: Learned camera gain and exposure control for improved visual feature detection and matching. IEEE Robot. Autom. Lett. **6**(2), 2028–2035 (2021)
21. Wang, J., Chan, K.C., Loy, C.C.: Exploring clip for assessing the look and feel of images. In: Proceedings of the AAAI Conference on Artificial Intelligence, vol. 37, pp. 2555–2563 (2023)
22. Yang, H., Wang, B., Vesdapunt, N., Guo, M., Kang, S.B.: Personalized exposure control using adaptive metering and reinforcement learning. IEEE Trans. Visual Comput. Graphics **25**(10), 2953–2968 (2018)
23. Yang, S., et al.: Maniqa: multi-dimension attention network for no-reference image quality assessment. In: Proceedings of the IEEE/CVF Conference on Computer Vision and Pattern Recognition, pp. 1191–1200 (2022)

24. Yu, R., Liu, W., Zhang, Y., Qu, Z., Zhao, D., Zhang, B.: Deepexposure: learning to expose photos with asynchronously reinforced adversarial learning. In: Advances in Neural Information Processing Systems, vol. 31 (2018)
25. Zhang, S., He, J., Zhu, Y., Wu, J., Yuan, J.: Efficient camera exposure control for visual odometry via deep reinforcement learning. IEEE Robot. Autom. Lett. (2024)
26. Zhang, W., Zhai, G., Wei, Y., Yang, X., Ma, K.: Blind image quality assessment via vision-language correspondence: a multitask learning perspective. In: IEEE Conference on Computer Vision and Pattern Recognition, pp. 14071–14081 (2023)

Fundamental Theory of Computer Vision

CurveViT: Exploring Efficient Vision Transformer with Frequency-Aware Curve Tokens

Rui Chen(✉) and Zheng Qin

Tianjin Key Laboratory of Imaging and Sensing Microelectronic Technology, School of Microelectronics, Tianjin University, Tianjin, China
{ruichen,zhengqin58}@tju.edu.cn

Abstract. Vision Transformers (ViTs) have achieved the excellent global modeling capability due to self-attention mechanism. Contrary to convolution operations, recent studies suggest that self-attentions behave like low-pass filters and enhancing their high-pass filtering capability can improve the performance of ViT-based models. While several attempts have been made to promote the high-frequency characteristics of ViTs, they have all faced the issue on how to find more generalized features. To handle this, we present a CurveViT that adaptively reconfigures the low- and high-frequency features. Especially, the spatial features are transformed into frequency domain to adaptively control the generation of a group of parameterized curves. We utilize the frequency-aware curve tokens as an effective complementation of multi-head self-attention to balance multi-band frequency components, which further enhance the representation ability of ViTs. Extensive experiments demonstrate the effectiveness of the proposed CurveViT and show that our method achieves significant improvements compared to the baseline models in typical vision tasks such as image classification, object detection, and semantic segmentation.

Keywords: Vision transformers · Token mixer · Frequency-aware curves · Curve tokens

1 Introduction

In the contemporary field of computer vision, the transformers [1–4] are successfully replacing the usage of Convolutional Neural Networks (CNNs). Benefiting from the excellent global modeling and data processing abilities, numerous follow-up models based on vision transformers have witnessed new state of the arts in a wide range of vision tasks such as image classification [5–7], object detection [8–10] and semantic segmentation [11–13].

Multi-Head Self-Attention (MHSA) is the main architecture of ViTs. The excellent performance of ViTs on various tasks is primarily attributed to the use of MHSA [14–17]. The self-attention modules of ViTs usually aggregate information between different spatial locations with high computation cost [18]. In

© The Author(s), under exclusive license to Springer Nature Singapore Pte Ltd. 2026
J. Kittler et al. (Eds.): PRCV 2025, LNCS 16289, pp. 199–214, 2026.
https://doi.org/10.1007/978-981-95-5764-6_14

practice, the standard ViT models can not effectively exploit the local structures as they split an image to a sequence of patches [19,20]. In order to further enhance the performance, the numerous variations of ViTs mainly focus on the development of spatial architectures of the token mixers by shifted windows [21], relative position encoding [22], refining attention maps [23], or incorporating the convolution [24]. The recent progress of ViTs enables adaptive feature extraction from global contexts and local windows [25,26]. However, a typical MHSA layer enforces the same global attention across all image patches without considering the characteristics of different underlying frequencies. When ViT scales up its depth, excessive low-pass filtering will smoothen feature maps to mostly preserve their low-frequency components [27]. Finding a good token mixer is challenging as it needs to scale with the sequence size and generalize to different patterns.

Some recent works try to improve the performance of ViTs with fourier transform or wavelet analysis [28–30]. It is also noticed that ViTs reduce high-frequency components while CNNs are better suited for filtering them [31]. When trained on image classification datasets, ViTs cannot exhibit bias towards texture information, which is the high-frequency element present in images. An irreversible loss of high-frequency information within the image causes an obvious decrease in the accuracy across different visual tasks [32]. Moreover, it is imperative to adapt the parameters of self-attention modules to better suit different datasets that embody distinct frequency characteristics [33]. The model performance can be successfully improved by enhancing high-pass filtering capability of MHSA, or by using a token mixer optimized from a filter perspective [34]. In addition, the complementarity of CNNs and ViTs exhibited in the frequency domain is explored for further improving the representations of the model [35,36]. But the relations between token mixers and the frequency bias of models have not been fully studied. A general-purpose global token mixing with the capability of retaining high-frequency information is still less explored.

In order to solve the aforementioned problems, we will strengthen the validity of frequency characteristics of ViT models from a new perspective of curve fusion. In this paper, we propose a plug-and-play module named Frequency-aware Curve Control Module (FCCM) and leverage it to derive a ViT model termed as CurveViT. First, we employ the discrete fourier transform to decompose the spatial outputs of MHSA into different frequency components. Then a Frequency Control Layer (FCL) is designed to learn a set of modulation parameters for reconfiguring the low- and high-frequency components of the intermediate features. Meanwhile, cooperated with a Curve Generation Layer (CGL), a group of frequency-aware curves are synthesized to boost the high-frequency components. Finally, a Feature Fusion Layer (FFL) is utilized to balance different token features, which can adapt to the input images with various frequency characteristics. The empirical study has revealed that our approach improves the feature representations across different datasets and continuously increases the model accuracy. Moreover, we verify the effectiveness of novel token mixers by conducting extensive experiments across diverse tasks and model scales.

Our contribution can be folded into following aspects:

- A novel token mixing module is proposed, which can be applied as a plugin to transformers, resulting in a significant improvement in the performance with only a negligible increase in computational cost.
- We present a frequency-domain modeling method for the dynamic relationship of token features, which contributes to adaptively capture the important frequency characteristics of different visual tokens.
- We introduce a generation method to synthesize the frequency-aware curves by systematically varying the frequency, amplitude, and phase of each basic waves. The proxy features extracted from geometric curves can enhance the representation ability of ViT models.

2 Related Work

2.1 Vision Transformers

Transformers have been first proposed for natural language processing (NLP), which utilize self-attention to learn the representations of the input sequence and relationships between different tokens [14]. By splitting images into a sequence of tokens, ViT [2] introduced a pure transformer backbone in image classification tasks and achieved remarkable performance. Thanks to the success of ViT, various remarkable ViT variants have been focusing on improving the tokenization, MHSA-based mixers and architectures to better suit vision tasks [3,13,25,37–39]. For example, CVT [24] accomplished a hierarchical transformer architecture by embedding the convolutions while maintaining the merits of CNNs and ViTs. Swin Transformer [21] presented a hierarchical architecture to model at various scales and shift at local windows, by which self-attention computation is restricted within windows to obtain linear computational complexity. MetaFormer [3] verified that a spatial pooling operator can achieve competitive performance on multiple vision tasks when replacing the self-attention. DETR [9] adopted an encoder-decoder architecture based on transformers to detect all objects in an end-to-end manner. SETR [11] utilized a pure transformer with gradually reduced spatial resolution to solve semantic segmentation problem. Segmenter [12] extended ViT to semantic segmentation by adopting a mask transformer decoder. TopFormer [13] modified ViTs to produce scale-aware semantic features for real-time segmentation. Despite that MHSAs play an essential role in the success of ViTs, some recent studies proposed to substitute MHSAs with Multi-Layer Perceptrons (MLPs) as token mixers, while achieving competitive performance [40,41].

2.2 Frequency-Domain Analysis of ViTs

The frequency domain analysis has been extensively studied in deep learning [42–44]. The low-frequency components correspond to global structures while the high frequencies focus on local details or fine textures. Recent work [29,31] revealed the low-pass characteristics of ViT structures because MHSAs spatially smoothen feature maps with self-attention weights. ViTs tend to reduce high-frequency components in the feature maps and almost only high-frequency components are preserved when the model going deeper [27]. Based on rigid theoretical analysis, Wang *et al.* [44] proposed to decompose a self-attention block into different frequency components and reweight feature maps on separate frequency bands. Pan *et al.* [34] presented to disentangle the self-attention layers into high- and low-frequency features. Bai *et al.* [33] proposed to augment the ability of ViTs to capture the high-frequency components by using adversarial training. Yun *et al.* [29] introduced a frequency-aware token mixer to capture high- and low-frequency components in a balanced manner.

2.3 Feature Augmentation for Models

In order to obtain high scores on different datasets, ViT models tend to require data augmentation for training or at test-time. The synthetic images computed by certain mathematical formulas can generate various types of geometric patterns and basic shapes, which are sufficient to acquire the necessary feature representations. In this context, FractalDB dataset [45] used the fractal geometry to automatically generate the different shapes and the paired labels for training. OFDB dataset [46] comprised images with more emphasis on contours and the training accuracy of these synthetic datasets has exceeded that of the human-annotated ImageNet. The dataset VisualAtom-21k [47] synthesized images from a mixture of sinusoidal waves to train models. Geoclidean [48] constituted a favorable geometric primitives for feature learning. To further enhance generalization and robustness performance, the complementary approaches are augmentation in the frequency domain [31,49]. Long *et al.* [50] introduced the spectrum saliency maps to adversarially perturb images in the frequency domain. Ryou *et al.* [51] proposed to leverage the mixup of frequency spectrum to train the networks for out-of-distribution images. Vaish *et al.* [28] utilized additive noise based on Fourier-basis functions to augment the robustness of models. These techniques have discovered capabilities beyond what visual augmentations can achieve and provide inspiration for our research. Our proposed method can take full advantages of the frequency-aware auxiliary features to enhance ViTs.

3 Proposed Method

3.1 CurveViT Architecture

In order to explore efficient vision transformer, we consider a mixture of spatial multi-head attention layers and frequency-domain layers. It has been evidenced that multi-head attention followed by fourier layers is more beneficial [5,7]. The basic idea behind our architecture is to learn long- and short-term interactions among frequency-aware geometric patterns. Moreover, the fourier transform is efficient in mixing the information of different tokens. We insert the proposed FCCMs behind self-attention and convolution (Conv) layers. The typical transformer architectures include vanilla- and hierarchical-style ViTs. We take a four-stage architecture as the backbone to introduce the basic CurveViT. The overall architecture of CurveViT is illustrated in Fig. 1. We sequentially stack a patch embedding layer, a positional embedding layer, MHSA module and FCCM to capture from local to global dependencies. FCCM mainly consists of the FCL, CGL and FFL. The network comprises four stages with a 2× downsampling rate. We obtain a patch embedding using a linear projection layer. The positional embedding employs a standard positional encoding layer. The Conv stem is used to obtain the global features with original frequency information. Then the output spatial features of MHSA are converted to extract main frequency components via a 2D discrete fourier transform. After generating the curve images, the learned geometric features are fused with the MHSA outputs.

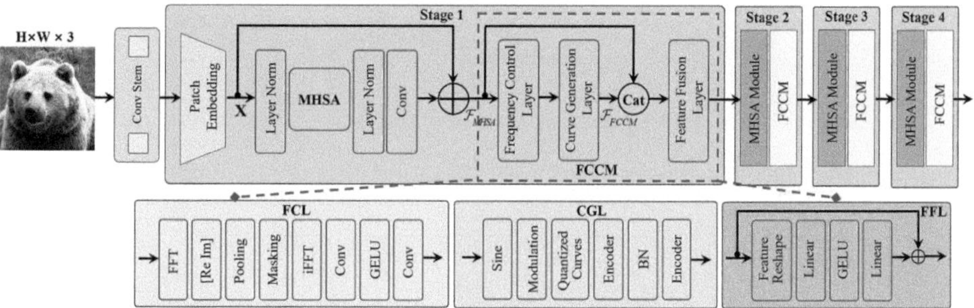

Fig. 1. The architecture details of the proposed CurveViT.

3.2 Frequency Control Layer

The structure of FCL is shown in Fig. 1. To adapt ViTs to vision tasks, we first split an image $\mathbf{I} \in \mathbb{R}^{H \times W \times 3}$ into a sequence of patches. Then all image patches are converted into token embeddings $\mathbf{X} \in \mathbb{R}^{N \times P^2 C}$ via a trainable linear layer. (H, W) is the original image size. C is the number of channels, P is the patch size, and N is the number of patches. The token sequence is fed into stacked MHSA modules and Conv layers. The self-attention (SA) in MHSA computes a set of queries $\mathbf{Q} = \mathbf{X}\mathbf{W}_Q$, keys $\mathbf{K} = \mathbf{X}\mathbf{W}_K$, values $\mathbf{V} = \mathbf{X}\mathbf{W}_V$, in which $\mathbf{W}_Q$, $\mathbf{W}_K$ and $\mathbf{W}_V \in \mathbb{R}^{P^2 C \times d}$ are trainable weights, and d denotes the attention head size. Formally, this process is represented as:

$$SA\left(\mathbf{X}\right) = \text{Softmax}\left(\mathbf{X}\mathbf{W}_Q(\mathbf{X}\mathbf{W}_K)^T \Big/ \sqrt{d}\right)\mathbf{X}\mathbf{W}_V. \tag{1}$$

MHSA involves a group of SA heads. The concatenation of h heads via a linear projection $\mathbf{W}_O$ is denoted as $MHSA\left(\mathbf{X}\right) = \left[SA_1\left(\mathbf{X}\right), \cdots, SA_h\left(\mathbf{X}\right)\right]\mathbf{W}_O$. With layer normalization (Norm) and skip connections, the output $\mathcal{F}_{MHSA} \in \mathbb{R}^{(N+1) \times D}$ of MHSA is written as follows:

$$\mathbf{X}' = \text{MHSA}\left(\text{Norm}\left(\mathbf{X}\right)\right), \tag{2}$$

$$\mathcal{F}_{MHSA} = \text{Conv}\left(\text{Norm}\left(\mathbf{X}'\right)\right) + \mathbf{X}. \tag{3}$$

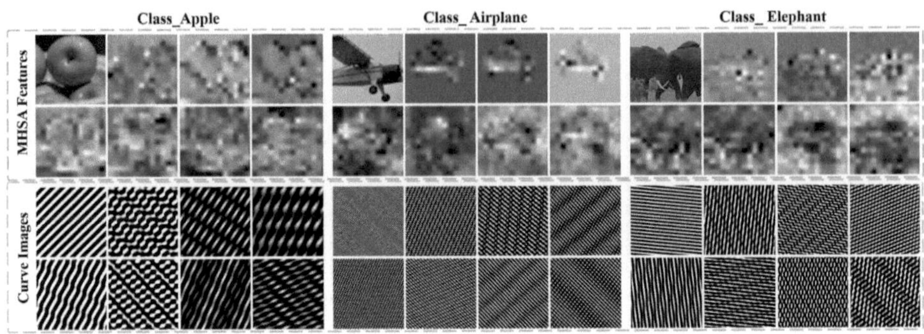

Fig. 2. Visualization of the MHSA features and the synthetic curves. The curve images are generated according to MHSA features.

MHSA would spatially smoothen feature maps with the self-attention weights when the ViT models go deeper. To supplement the high-frequency features, we transform original spatial features $\mathcal{F}_{MHSA}$ into a frequency domain to further control the generation of suitable frequency components. We can obtain the corresponding frequency representation via 2D discrete fourier transform:

$$\mathcal{D}\left(u,\ v\right) = \sum_{a=0}^{M-1}\sum_{b=0}^{N-1} \mathcal{F}_{MHSA}\left(a,\ b\right) e^{-j2\pi\left(\frac{u}{M}a+\frac{v}{N}b\right)}, \tag{4}$$

where M and N denote the height and width of the input features, respectively. j represents the imaginary unit. The frequency spectrum of feature maps can be calculated efficiently by using fast fourier transform (FFT) algorithm.

For the ease of post processing, we then transform the expression of $\mathcal{D}\left(u,\ v\right)$ by concatenating the real part Re and the imaginary part Im as $\bar{\mathcal{D}}\left(u,\ v\right)$. This frequency-based rearrangement would not change the spectrum information and makes the learning in frequency domain more efficient. We propose to apply a learnable frequency masking operation on $\bar{\mathcal{D}}\left(u,\ v\right)$ to further retain high-level frequency components about fine-grained local structures and the global contexts while suppressing the detrimental and sensitive ones. For masking, we first use the pooling operations to separately compress the information of each frequency component while the spectrum discriminability is still preserved. Then we use large convolution filters (e.g. 7×7) to learn the frequency masks $\mathcal{M}\left(\cdot\right)$. This masking processing is formulated as follows:

$$\bar{\mathcal{D}}_M = \bar{\mathcal{D}} \otimes \text{Sig}\left(\mathcal{M}\left(\left[\text{AvgPool}\left(\bar{\mathcal{D}}\right), \text{MaxPool}\left(\bar{\mathcal{D}}\right)\right]\right)\right), \tag{5}$$

where $\otimes$ is the Hadamard product between matrices. Sig $(\cdot)$ is a sigmoid function. AvgPool $(\cdot)$ and MaxPool $(\cdot)$ denote the average and max pooling operators, respectively. The spectrum squeeze via the masking operation is very computationally efficient and still has the ability to model discriminative information within a wide frequency range.

To enable the communication across frequency space and the designed curve space, we utilize the transferable frequency components of $\bar{\mathcal{D}}_M$ to obtain the control parameters of geometric curves. After removing irrelated frequency features, we feed $\bar{\mathcal{D}}_M$ into inverse FFT (iFFT) and Conv layers to infer the frequency-aware parameters of the corresponding curves. Then the output of FCL is given by:

$$\mathcal{C} = \text{Conv}\left(\text{iFFT}\left(\text{Re}\left(\bar{\mathcal{D}}_M\right), \ \ \text{Im}\left(\bar{\mathcal{D}}_M\right)\right)\right), \tag{6}$$

where $\mathcal{C}$ is the parameter set of the curves. FCL can provide stable and sufficient support for estimating the control parameters. When the different inputs dynamically change, the parameter values allow for the adaptive modulation.

3.3 Curve Generation Layer

The architecture of CGL is shown in Fig. 1. This layer is designed to generate the frequency-aware curve images, which would strengthen the frequency expression ability of ViT models. The vanilla multi-head self-attention branch communicates information among all tokens as the low-frequency mixer. On the other hand, the proposed CGL is taken as a parallel structure for adaptively generating the supplementary high-frequency components. The core idea behind the design of CGL is based on the fact that synthetic images can be used to pre-train models with high performance gain [45,47]. More importantly, our CGL can provide the additional frequency-aware geometric features as the augmentation of MHSA-based features, which are much more efficient than high-frequency components directly decomposed from the outputs of standard MHSA. The low- and high-level visual features trained on simple geometric shapes support the correct generalization [48]. Therefore, we propose to utilize a group of 2D Fourier functions as high-frequency curve tokens, from which the input-dependent geometric features are learned.

For aggregating particular frequency components more properly, we present Fourier-basis functions as the curve images to dynamically modulate the relationship between tokens. Examples of curve images are shown in Fig. 2. For simplicity, the sinusoidal wave function is used as a basic component and its parametric representation $\Phi_i\left(x, \ y\right)$ at position $\left(x, \ y\right)$ can be formulated as follows:

$$\Phi_i\left(x, \ y\right) = A_i \sin\left[2\pi n_i \left(x \cos\theta_i + y \sin\theta_i\right) - \varphi_i\right], \tag{7}$$

where i is the order number of base function $\{\Phi_i\}$. θ_i refers to the direction of propagation of a planar wave. The 2D sinusoidal function is determined by the specific amplitude A_i, the spatial frequency n_i and the phase shift φ_i.

Each curve token is modeled by the formula of Fourier series and consists of a group of the sinusoidal waves. To have a sufficient variety, we use the superposition of three sinusoidal waves to provide diverse high-frequency features to enhance the ViT representations. The k-th curve token E_k is generated by:

$$E_k(x,\ y) = B_k + \sum_{i=1}^{3} \Phi_i(x,\ y), \tag{8}$$

where B_k is a learned bias component. All channels of the output feature maps of FCL are utilized to generate the corresponding curve tokens $\{E_k\}_{k=1}^{K}$, where $K \in \mathbb{N}$ is the number of FCL channels. The contributions of the frequency components in MHSA and FCCM are not equal. The MHSA in CurveViT is mainly required to modulate the low-frequency components to capture the global spatial information, while FCCM is designed to amplify the high-frequency components to recover fine-grained features.

To capture the particular attributes for each input, we compute the parameter set of the curve tokens $\mathcal{C} = \{A,\ n,\ \theta,\ \varphi\}$ according to the FCL output. In practice, the parameters of a curve token are limited within different ranges to achieve the robust effect. We obtain the discrete curve image as the union set of the tokens. Finally, the output features of CGL are represented as:

$$\mathcal{F}_{FCCM} = \text{Encoder}\left(\bigcup_{k=1}^{K} E_k;\ \mathcal{C}\right), \tag{9}$$

where Encoder $(\cdot)$ is implemented via multiple Conv layers followed by batch normalization (BN). The amplitude $A \in \mathbb{R}$ is determined within the range $[0.1,\ 1]$. To incorporate more image structures, we quantize the direction angle θ into a discrete set of sample points, i.e. $\theta_i = 2\pi i/q\ (i = 0, \cdots, q-1)$. Here $q \in \mathbb{N}$ is the number of sample points. The size of the curve token is formulated as $T \times T$. Thereafter, the frequency $n \in \mathbb{N}$ is selected from the range $[T/16,\ T/2]$. To balance the model efficiency, we set $T = 16$ for natural images. The phase $\varphi \in \mathbb{R}$ varies within the range of $[0,\ \pi]$.

3.4 Feature Fusion Layer

To enhance information interaction across token features of MHSA and FCCM, we introduce a lightweight feature fusion layer (see Fig. 1). We aggregate the MHSA-based and geometric features at each stage, resulting in significant improvements in the representation ability of CurveViT. FFL involves concatenation (Cat) operator and then utilizes a MLP with the non-linear activation to capture essential features. Our FFL explicitly strengthens the relevant high-frequency signals, thereby enhancing the diversity of token features. Finally, the fusion process is expressed as:

$$\mathbf{Y} = \sigma\left(\text{Reshape}\left(\text{Cat}\left[\mathcal{F}_{MHSA},\ \mathcal{F}_{FCCM}\right]\right)\mathbf{W}_f\right), \tag{10}$$

where $\mathbf{W}_f$ is learnable parameters. Reshape $(\cdot)$ is used to rearrange feature tensors. $\sigma(\cdot)$ is activation function.

4 Experiments

4.1 Image Classification

Settings. We first evaluate the proposed CurveViT on the ImageNet-1K [52]. This widely-used dataset includes about 1.3M training images and 50K validation images, which cover 1,000 class categories. The Top-1 accuracy is reported on the validation set. We apply random cropping, random horizontal flipping, mixup [53], cutmix [54] and random erasing [55] for data augmentation. Based

Table 1. Performance of image classification on ImageNet-1K. "GFLOPs" are calculated with the resolution of 224 × 224.

Method	Token Mixer	Para	GFLOPs	Top-1 (%)
ResNet18 [56]	–	12	1.8	68.5
Deit-T [37]	Attention	6	1.3	72.2
PVT-T [8]	Attention	13	1.9	75.1
GFNet-T [7]	Conv	7	1.3	74.6
Swin-T [21]	Attention	29	4.5	81.3
LaViT-T [18]	Attention+Conv	10.9	1.6	79.2
RIFormer-S [26]	Attention+MLP	31	14.7	82.2
SPANet-S [29]	FFT	29	4.6	83.1
CurveViT-S (Ours)	Attention+FFT	31	4.6	84.3↑
ResNet50 [56]	–	26	4.1	78.5
Deit-S [37]	Attention	22	4.6	79.9
PVT-S [8]	Attention	25	3.8	79.8
GFNet-S [7]	Conv	25	4.5	80.0
Swin-S [21]	Attention	50	8.7	83.0
LaViT-S [18]	Attention+Conv	22.4	3.3	82.6
RIFormer-M [26]	Attention+MLP	56	25.9	83.4
SPANet-M [29]	FFT	42	6.8	83.5
CurveViT-M (Ours)	Attention+FFT	52	8.8	84.4↑
ResNet101 [56]	–	84	15.6	81.5
ViT-B [2]	Attention	87	17.6	81.8
Deit-B [37]	Attention	87	17.6	81.8
PVT-L [8]	Attention	61	9.8	81.7
GFNet-B [7]	Conv	43	7.9	80.7
Swin-B [21]	Attention	88	15.4	83.5
LaViT-B [18]	Attention+Conv	39.6	6.1	83.1
RIFormer-B [26]	Attention+MLP	73	34.1	83.7
SPANet-B [29]	FFT	76	12.0	84.0
CurveViT-L (Ours)	Attention+FFT	90	15.5	85.1↑

on the hierarchical architecture of Swin-transformer [21], we place one FCCM at each stage to design the structure of CurveViT. For comparison, we develop small (-S), medium (-M) and large (-L) versions of CurveViT with different sizes, which are evaluated by the number of parameters (M).

Implementation Details. We train the models using AdamW with momentum of 0.9 and weight decay of 5×10^{-2}. The batch size is set as 128 and the initial learning rate is initialized as 2×10^{-3}. The cosine schedule is used to decrease the learning rate. Label smoothing is set as 0.1. All models are trained for 300 epochs from scratch on eight Nvidia Tesla V100 GPUs (24G Memory).

Results. Table 1 shows that the CurveViT variants can achieve highly competitive performance compared with ResNets [56] and other transformer models mainly based on the convolution or self-attention. The introduction of FCCM only adds a small number of parameters and does not significantly affect GFLOPs. Only one FCCM is used at each stage and does not contribute much to the computational cost. The experimental results show that our models achieve the highest classification accuracy. Compared with SPANet-S, SPANet-M and SPANet-B, the Top-1 accuracy of models with the insertion of FCCM can increase 1.2%, 0.9% and 1.1% gains, respectively. In the case of the large model, our CurveViT-B achieves better performance than other state-of-the-art models, namely Swin-B, LaViT-B and RIFormer-B, despite having a similar number of parameters and GFLOPs. Similar results to those of the tiny and small cases are also observed for the compared models. With the frequency-aware control operation, all token features can be enhanced by aggregating the corresponding geometric features. By adopting FCCM, it is guaranteed that the derived models have the potential to achieve reasonable performance. Our CurveViT framework has demonstrated its capacity to obtain the significant improvements in down-stream tasks.

Table 2. Performance of object detection with RetinaNet, and object detection and instance segmentation with Mask R-CNN on COCO val2017. AP^b and AP^m denote bounding box AP and mask AP, respectively.

Backbone	RetinaNet 1×							Mask R-CNN 1×						
	Para	AP	AP_{50}	AP_{75}	AP_s	AP_m	AP_l	Para	AP^b	AP^b_{50}	AP^b_{75}	AP^m	AP^m_{50}	AP^m_{75}
ResNet50 [56]	38	36.3	55.3	38.6	19.3	40.0	48.8	44	38	58.6	41.4	34.4	55.1	36.7
PVT-S [8]	34	40.4	61.3	43.0	25.0	42.9	55.7	44	40.4	62.9	43.8	37.8	60.1	40.3
Swin-S [21]	39	41.5	62.1	44.2	25.1	44.9	55.5	48	42.2	64.6	46.2	39.1	61.6	42.0
SPANet-S [29]	38	43.3	63.7	46.5	25.8	47.7	57.0	48	44.7	65.7	48.8	40.6	62.9	43.8
CurveViT-S (Ours)	41	43.9↑	64.2	46.9	26.6↑	48.5↑	57.6↑	50	45.5↑	66.1	49.2	41.3↑	63.3	44.2
ResNet101 [56]	57	38.5	57.8	41.2	21.4	42.6	51.1	63	40.4	61.1	44.2	36.4	57.7	38.8
PVT-M [8]	54	41.9	63.1	44.3	25.0	44.9	57.6	64	42.0	64.4	45.6	39.0	61.6	42.1
Swin-M [21]	60	44.5	65.7	47.5	27.4	48.0	59.9	69	44.8	66.6	48.9	40.9	63.4	44.2
SPANet-M [29]	51	44.0	64.3	47.0	25.9	48.0	58.7	61	45.2	66.3	49.6	41.0	63.5	44.0
CurveViT-M (Ours)	62	45.8↑	66.2	48.1	28.4↑	48.8↑	60.6↑	71	46.3↑	67.3	50.2	42.5↑	64.1	45.0

4.2 Object Detection

Settings. We evaluate the model for object detection and instance segmentation tasks, which are performed on the COCO2017 dataset [57]. The models are trained on 118K training images and the performance is evaluated on the validation set with 5K images. The effectiveness of different backbones is validated by using two standard detectors, namely RetinaNet [58] and Mask R-CNN [59].

Implementation Details. We utilize the ImageNet-1K pre-trained weights to initialize the backbones, while Xavier initialization is utilized to initialize the newly added layers. We adopt AdamW for training with a batch size of 16 and an initial learning rate of 1×10^{-4}. Following usual practices [58,59], we adopted $1\times$ training schedule, in which the training duration is set to 12 epochs. The sides of training images are resized from 800 pixels to 1,333 pixels. For testing, the shorter sides of the images are also rescaled to 800 pixels.

Results. As shown in Table 2, FCCM-based models equipped with RetinaNet consistently outperform other comparable ResNets [56] and transformer-based counterparts. For the object detection task, the CurveViT variants can improve AP performance of 0.6 and 1.8 points in small (-S) and medium (-M) SPANet models, respectively. Similar results are observed for those models based on Mask R-CNN. For example, the medium model with the insertion of FCCM largely surpasses Swin-M in bounding box AP (1.5 point) and mask AP (1.6 point), respectively. It also achieves a good improvement in the instance segmentation task. The small ViT models with FCCM have a significant improvement in detecting large-sized objects. This is because the small ViT models have the relatively poor modeling capability, while CurveViT-S can utilize the frequency-aware geometric features to more accurately model global semantic relationships. Although relatively larger ViT models can model better global relationships, CurveViT-M also

Table 3. Performance of semantic segmentation on ADE20K. "GFLOPs" are calculated with the resolution of 512 × 512.

Backbone	Semantic FPN		
	Para	GFLOPs	mIoU (%)
ResNet50 [56]	29	45.6	36.7
PVT-S [8]	28	44.5	39.8
Swin-S [21]	32	46.1	41.5
SPANet-S [29]	32	46.0	45.4
CurveViT-S (Ours)	34	46.2	46.5↑
ResNet101 [56]	48	64.9	38.8
PVT-M [8]	48	60.6	41.6
Swin-M [21]	53	70.2	45.2
SPANet-M [29]	45	57.0	46.2
CurveViT-M (Ours)	55	70.3	47.1↑

enhances local discriminative information for each tokens via frequency domain analysis, enabling ViT models to establish the complete semantic information.

4.3 Semantic Segmentation

Settings. We select a challenging benchmark ADE20K [60] to evaluate the models for semantic segmentation, which requires the understanding of fine-grained details as well as the ability to analyze long-range interactions. This segmentation dataset includes 150 fine-grained semantic categories, which are allocated 20K training and 2K validation images. All the compared methods are evaluated as backbones equipped with semantic FPN framework [61] and measuring model performance in terms of mIoU.

Implementation Details. The backbone network is initialized with the Imagenet-1K pre-trained weights. The Xavier method is utilized to initialize the newly added layers. We train our models for 80K iterations with a batch size of 16. The models are optimized by employing the AdamW optimizer with an initial learning rate of 2×10^{-4}. The learning rate is decayed following the polynomial decay schedule with a power of 0.9. The images are randomly resized into 512×512 for training and are rescaled to the shorter side of 512 pixels for testing.

Results. As shown in Table 3, the insertion of FCCM can attain a significant improvement in the semantic segmentation task. FCCM-based models consistently outperform the models with backbones of CNN-based ResNets and other ViT models. After inserting FCCM, it has exhibited a significant improvement across model scales and improved the mIoU values of SPANet-S and SPANet-M models by 1.1% and 0.9%, respectively. These results demonstrate that the CurveViT variants can communicate the information among tokens based on the semantic information during the curve generation. At the same time, it better captures the global frequency-domain information.

Table 4. Ablation results for CurveViT on ImageNet-1K.

Ablation	Variants	Top-1(%)
—	Baseline	83.3
FCL	FCL and Pooling	83.9 (+0.6)
	Global Filtering and Pooling	83.5 (+0.2)
	MLP and Pooling	83.2 (-0.1)
CGL	CGL and Rescaling	84.4 (+1.1)
	HiLo Attention and Rescaling	83.8 (+0.5)
FFL	Addition	83.6 (+0.3)
	Concatenation	83.7 (+0.4)

4.4 Ablation Studies

To investigate the effectiveness of the proposed components, we individually integrate them into a baseline and train all variant models on ImageNet-1K. As the baseline, all FCLs and CGLs within the basic CurveViT are replaced with Conv layers, the addition operation is adopted to mix the features from short connections and all FFLs are removed. Table 4 reports the classification accuracy.

Frequency Control Layer. We first conduct the ablation by directly adding FCL module behind each transformer layer of the baseline to reweight the output feature maps. This module consists of a control layer and a pooling layer. Further, to verify the effects of the proposed FCL, we experimentally compare three different methods by replacing FCL with the discrete fourier transform (Global Filtering) and MLP. As evidenced by Table 4, FCL can improve model performance by Top-1 accuracy of 0.6%. The derived model with FCLs achieves highly competitive performance higher than the Global Filtering and MLPs with Top-1 accuracy of 0.4% and 0.7%, respectively. This is because FCLs can accurately reflect both the global relations and local structure information of the images.

Curve Generation Layer. The proposed CGL is used to discriminatively generate frequency-aware curves for enhancing the token features. We insert CGL into each stage of the baseline and then utilize the curve features to rescale the outputs of transformer layers. As shown in Table 4, we can find the model with CGLs is higher than the baseline by 1.1%. The results have demonstrated that the proposed CGL generalizes well to transformer-based backbones. When we replace each CGL with HiLo Attention, the performance gain increases by 0.5%. Frequency-based token mixers can benefit the generation of high-frequency textures with the guidance of CGLs.

Feature Fusion Layer. The feature fusion of MHSA and FCCM at each stage is also an important factor affecting the performance. When FFLs with addition operators are adopted for aggregation, the obvious performance increase of 0.3% is found. However, we have observed that FFLs with the concatenation operators are better for context aggregation and lead to an increase in performance to 83.7%. The results can be explained by the fact that restricting the combination of all possible token features would be sub-optimal during the training. Thus, we adopt the FFL with concatenation for the token fusion.

5 Conclusion

In this paper, we propose a novel ViT model to adaptively reconfigure frequency components of deep ViTs. Because high-frequency features tend to attenuate as the model deepens, we designed a heuristic scheme to insert FCCM after each stage of the ViT model to promote. By leveraging the synthesized curves, our token aggregation mechanism enables the optimal balance of high- and low-frequency components for visual features. Experimental results have demonstrated that our module can achieve significant improvements in multiple visual tasks after integrating into the ViT framework.

Acknowledgements. This work has been supported by the National Natural Science Foundation of China under Grant 62272341.

References

1. Huang, Z., Zhang, Z., Lan, C., Zha, Z.J., Lu, Y., Guo, B.: Adaptive frequency filters as efficient global token mixers. In: ICCV, pp. 6026–6036 (2023)
2. Dosovitskiy, A., et al.: An image is worth 16×16 words: transformers for image recognition at scale. In: ICLR, pp. 1–12 (2021)
3. Yu, W., et al.: MetaFormer is actually what you need for vision. In: CVPR, pp. 10809–10819 (2022)
4. Kacham, P., Mirrokni, V., Zhong, P.: PolySketchFormer: fast transformers via sketching polynomial kernels. In: ICML, pp. 1–12 (2024)
5. Si, C., Yu, W., Zhou, P., Zhou, Y., Wang, X., Yan, S.: Inception transformer. In: NeurIPS, pp. 1–12 (2022)
6. Baron, E., Zimerman, I., Wolf, L.: A 2-dimensional state space layer for spatial inductive bias. In: ICLR, pp. 1–12 (2024)
7. Rao, Y., Zhao, W., Zhu, Z., Lu, J., Zhou, J.: Global filter networks for image classification. In: NeurIPS, pp. 1–12 (2021)
8. Wang, W., et al.: Pyramid vision transformer: a versatile backbone for dense prediction without convolutions. In: ICCV, pp. 548–558 (2021)
9. Carion, N., Massa, F., Synnaeve, G., Usunier, N., Kirillov, A., Zagoruyko, S.: End-to-end object detection with transformers. In: Vedaldi, A., Bischof, H., Brox, T., Frahm, J.-M. (eds.) ECCV 2020. LNCS, vol. 12346, pp. 213–229. Springer, Cham (2020). https://doi.org/10.1007/978-3-030-58452-8_13
10. Koner, R., Jain, G., Jain, P., Tresp, V., Paul, S.: LookupViT: compressing visual information to a limited number of tokens. In: ECCV, pp. 1–17 (2024)
11. Zheng, S., et al.: Rethinking semantic segmentation from a sequence-to-sequence perspective with transformers. In: CVPR, pp. 6877–6886 (2021)
12. Strudel, R., Garcia, R., Laptev, I., Schmid, C.: Segmenter: transformer for semantic segmentation. In: ICCV, pp. 7242–7252 (2021)
13. Kim, M., Seo, P.H., Schmid, C., Cho, M.: Learning correlation structures for vision transformers. In: CVPR, pp. 18941–18951 (2024)
14. Vaswani, A., et al.: Attention is all you need. In: NeurIPS, pp. 1–12 (2017)
15. Xia, C., Wang, X., Lv, F., Hao, X., Shi, Y.: ViT-comer: vision transformer with convolutional multi-scale feature interaction for dense predictions. In: CVPR, pp. 5493–5502 (2024)
16. Bolya, D., Fu, C.Y., Dai, X., Zhang, P., Feichtenhofer, C., Hoffman, J.: Token merging: your ViT but faster. In: ICLR, pp. 1–12 (2023)
17. Hu, L., Liu, Y., Liu, N., Huai, M., Sun, L., Wang, D.: Improving interpretation faithfulness for vision transformers. In: ICML, pp. 1–11 (2024)
18. Zhang, S., Liu, H., Lin, S., He, K.: You only need less attention at each stage in vision transformers. In: CVPR, pp. 6057–6066 (2024)

19. Peng, Z., et al.: Conformer: local features coupling global representations for visual recognition. In: ICCV, pp. 357–366 (2021)
20. Pan, X., et al.: On the integration of self-attention and convolution. In: CVPR, pp. 805–815 (2022)
21. Liu, Z., et al.: Swin transformer: hierarchical vision transformer using shifted windows. In: ICCV, pp. 9992–1002 (2021)
22. Wu, K., Peng, H., Chen, M., Fu, J., Chao, H.: Rethinking and improving relative position encoding for vision transformer. In: ICCV, pp. 10013–10021 (2021)
23. Yun, S., Ro, Y.: SHViT: single-head vision transformer with memory efficient macro design. In: CVPR, pp. 5756–5767 (2024)
24. Wu, H., et al.: CVT: introducing convolutions to vision transformers. In: ICCV, pp. 22–31 (2021)
25. Han, D., et al.: Agent attention: on the integration of softmax and linear attention. In: ECCV, pp. 1–17 (2024)
26. Wang, J., et al.: RIFormer: keep your vision backbone effective but removing token mixer. In: CVPR, pp. 14443–14452 (2023)
27. Park, N., Kim, S.: How do vision transformers work. In: ICLR, pp. 1–12 (2022)
28. Vaish, P., Wang, S., Strisciuglio, N.: Fourier-basis functions to bridge augmentation gap: rethinking frequency augmentation in image classification. In: CVPR, pp. 17763–17772 (2024)
29. Yun, G., Yoo, J., Kim, K., Lee, J., Kim, D.H.: SPANet: frequency–balancing token mixer using spectral pooling aggregation modulation. In: ICCV, pp. 6090–6101 (2023)
30. Yao, T., Pan, Y., Li, Y., Ngo, C.W., Mei, T.: Wave-ViT: unifying wavelet and transformers for visual representation learning. In: ECCV, pp. 328–345 (2022)
31. Wang, S., Veldhuis, R., Brune, C., Strisciuglio, N.: What do neural networks learn in image classification? A frequency shortcut perspective. In: ICCV, pp. 1433–1442 (2023)
32. Dong, Y., et al.: FAN: Fourier analysis networks. In: NeurIPS, pp. 1–12 (2024)
33. Bai, J., Yuan, L., Xia, S.T., Yan, S., Li, Z., Liu, W.: Improving vision transformers by revisiting high-frequency components. In: ECCV, pp. 1–18 (2022)
34. Pan, Z., Cai, J., Zhuang, B.: Fast vision transformers with HiLo attention. In: NeurIPS, pp. 1–12 (2022)
35. Fan, Q., Huang, H., Chen, M., Liu, H., He, R.: RMT: retentive networks meet vision transformers. In: CVPR, pp. 5641–5651 (2024)
36. Venkataramanan, S., Ghodrati, A., Asano, Y.M., Porikli, F., Habibian, A.: Skip-attention: improving vision transformers by paying less attention. In: ICLR, pp. 1–13 (2024)
37. Touvron, H., Cord, M., Douze, M., Massa, F., Sablayrolles, A., Jegou, H.: Training data-efficient image transformers & distillation through attention. In: ICML, pp. 1–12 (2021)
38. Yuan, L., et al.: Tokens-to-token ViT: training vision transformers from scratch on ImageNet. In: ICCV, pp. 538–547 (2021)
39. Letourneau, P.D., et al.: PADRe: a unifying polynomial attention drop-in replacement for efficient vision transformer. In: NeurIPS, pp. 1–12 (2024)
40. Ramasinghe, S., Macdonald, L., Lucey, S.: On the frequency-bias of coordinate-MLPs. In: NeurIPS, pp. 1–12 (2022)
41. Tang, Y., et al.: An image patch is a wave: phase-aware vision MLP. In: CVPR, pp. 10925–10934 (2022)
42. Bu, Q., Huang, D., Cui, H.: Towards building more robust models with frequency bias. In: ICCV, pp. 4402–4411 (2023)

43. Ai, Y., Zhou, X., Huang, H., Zhang, L., He, R.: Uncertainty-aware source-free adaptive image super-resolution with wavelet augmentation transformer. In: CVPR, pp. 8142–8152 (2024)
44. Wang, P., Zheng, W., Chen, T., Wang, Z.: Anti-oversmoothing in deep vision transformers via the Fourier domain analysis: from theory to practice. In: ICLR, pp. 1–12 (2022)
45. Kataoka, H., et al.: Replacing labeled real–image datasets with auto-generated contours. In: CVPR, pp. 21200–21209 (2022)
46. Nakamura, R., Kataoka, H., Takashima, S., Martinez-Noriega, E.J., Yokota, R., Inoue, N.: Pre-training vision transformers with very limited synthesized images. In: ICCV, pp. 20303–20312 (2023)
47. Takashima, S., Hayamizu, R., Inoue, N., Kataoka, H., Yokota, R.: Visual atoms: pre-training vision transformers with sinusoidal waves. In: CVPR, pp. 18579–18588 (2023)
48. Hsu, J., Wu, J., Goodman, N.D.: Geoclidean: few-shot generalization in Euclidean geometry. In: NeurIPS, pp. 1–12 (2022)
49. Subramanian, A., Sizikova, E., Majaj, N.J., Pelli, D.G.: Spatial-frequency channels, shape bias, and adversarial robustness. In: NeurIPS, pp. 1–13 (2023)
50. Long, Y., et al.: Frequency domain model augmentation for adversarial attack. In: ECCV, pp. 549–566 (2022)
51. Ryou, D., Ha, I., Yoo, H., Kim, D., Han, B.: Robust image denoising through adversarial frequency mixup. In: CVPR, pp. 2723–2732 (2024)
52. Deng, J., Dong, W., Socher, R., Li, L.J., Li, K., Fei-Fei, L.: ImageNet: a large-scale hierarchical image database. In: CVPR, pp. 248–255 (2009)
53. Zhang, H., Cisse, M., Dauphin, Y.N., Lopez-Paz, D.: Mixup: beyond empirical risk minimization. In: ICLR, pp. 1–12 (2018)
54. Yun, S., Han, D., Oh, S.J., Chun, S., Choe, J., Yoo, Y.: CutMix: regularization strategy to train strong classifiers with localizable features. In: ICCV, pp. 6022–6031 (2019)
55. Zhong, Z., Zheng, L., Kang, G., Li, S., Yang, Y.: Random erasing data augmentation. In: AAAI, pp. 1–12 (2020)
56. He, K., Zhang, X., Ren, S., Sun, J.: Deep residual learning for image recognition. In: CVPR, pp. 770–778 (2016)
57. Lin, T.-Y., et al.: Microsoft COCO: common objects in context. In: Fleet, D., Pajdla, T., Schiele, B., Tuytelaars, T. (eds.) ECCV 2014. LNCS, vol. 8693, pp. 740–755. Springer, Cham (2014). https://doi.org/10.1007/978-3-319-10602-1_48
58. Lin, T.Y., Goyal, P., Girshick, R., He, K., Dollar, P.: Focal loss for dense object detection. In: ICCV, pp. 318–327 (2017)
59. He, K., Gkioxari, G., Dollar, P., Girshick, R.: Mask R–CNN. In: ICCV, pp. 2980–2988 (2017)
60. Zhou, B., et al.: Semantic understanding of scenes through the ADE20K dataset. IJCV **127**(3), 302–321 (2019)
61. Kirillov, A., Girshick, R., He, K., Dollar, P.: Panoptic feature pyramid networks. In: CVPR, pp. 6392–6401 (2019)

Adaptive Prototype Learning for Weakly Supervised Semantic Segmentation

Jiaqi Han[1], Xuezhuan Zhao[1,2,3,4(✉)], Lingling Li[1,3,5,6], Chaoliang Wang[1], and Suqiao Li[1]

[1] Zhengzhou University of Aeronautics, Henan 450046, Zhengzhou, People's Republic of China
[2] National Key Laboratory of Air-based Information Perception and Fusion, Henan 471000, Luoyang, People's Republic of China
zhaoxuezhuan@zua.edu.cn
[3] Aerospace Electronic Information Technology Henan Collaborative Innovation Center, Henan 401151, Zhengzhou, People's Republic of China
[4] Henan Province Artificial Intelligence Technology School-Enterprise Research and Development Center, Henan 450046, Zhengzhou, People's Republic of China
[5] Henan Province Multi-Modal Information Perception and Computing Engineering Research Center, Henan 450046, Zhengzhou, People's Republic of China
[6] Henan Province Aerospace Intelligent Technology and Systems International Joint Laboratory, Henan 450046, Zhengzhou, People's Republic of China

Abstract. Weakly Supervised Semantic Segmentation (WSSS) aims to perform pixel-level semantic segmentation using only image-level annotations. However, the sparse supervision and frequent co-occurrence of foreground and background regions make this task challenging. Most existing approaches rely on Class Activation Maps (CAMs) to generate pseudo-labels, which often suffer from false activations and limited accuracy, constraining further performance gains. To overcome these limitations, this paper proposes a novel framework, Adaptive Prototype Learning for Weakly Supervised Semantic Segmentation (CPDGL). Central to this approach is the Prototype Knowledge Refinement Module (PKRM), which constructs class prototypes from class tokens extracted by a Vision Transformer (ViT) and employs an Exponential Moving Average (EMA) mechanism to ensure stable and progressive prototype updates. Building upon this, the proposed Prototype Contrastive Loss ($\mathcal{L}_{PCL}$) encourages features to align closely with their corresponding class prototypes while enhancing inter-class separability, thereby improving category discriminability and semantic cohesion. To further strengthen local feature learning, the Local-Global Discriminative Fusion Module (LGDFM) is introduced, integrating fine-grained local semantics with global class-level information. Concurrently, a Local Consistency Contrastive Loss ($\mathcal{L}_{LCL}$) is introduced to suppress pseudo-label noise and improve the semantic consistency of local feature representations. Experimental results show that CPDGL achieves 72.5% and 71.8% MIoU on the PASCAL VOC

Supported by organization x.

© The Author(s), under exclusive license to Springer Nature Singapore Pte Ltd. 2026
J. Kittler et al. (Eds.): PRCV 2025, LNCS 16289, pp. 215–229, 2026.
https://doi.org/10.1007/978-981-95-5764-6_15

validation and test sets, and 42.5% on the MS COCO validation set, outperforming mainstream one-stage methods and demonstrating its effectiveness and generalization in WSSS.

Keywords: Weakly supervised semantic segmentation · Prototype learning · Contrastive learning

1 Introduction

To reduce the high cost and intensive labor associated with manual annotation in fully supervised semantic segmentation, recent research has explored the use of weak labels for training. In the task of WSSS, image-level supervision methods [1, 2] leverage classification labels to generate pseudo masks, which guide the model in learning pixel-level segmentation. Many approaches adopt CAMs [3] as initial pseudo labels, taking advantage of their strong object localization capabilities to identify target regions.

In recent years, numerous studies have investigated strategies for generating more effective CAMs. Chen et al. [4] reactivated converged CAMs by incorporating a softmax cross-entropy loss. Ru et al. [5] enhanced the representational capacity of CAMs by leveraging the ViT architecture [6]. While these methods have made notable progress, relying solely on image-level class labels continues to result in false activations within CAMs. To mitigate this issue, researchers have proposed prototype-aware approaches designed to capture the diversity and fine-grained attributes of object instances. Chen et al. [7] introduced an online prototype computation strategy, generating class-specific positive and negative prototypes from image-level labels during training. Tang et al. [8] proposed a feature distribution alignment method that aligns instance features with dense representations to enhance prototype awareness.

Although prototype-based methods have improved CAM quality to some extent, several critical challenges remain. Most existing approaches construct class prototypes by applying average pooling to the features across the entire image. While this global feature aggregation is straightforward to implement, it often neglects local structural details and fine-grained intra-class variations, making it difficult to fully capture the semantic diversity of a given class across different contexts. More importantly, as pixel-level feature distributions for each class are typically sparse within an image (as illustrated in Fig. 1(b2)), such coarse-grained prototype representations may inadvertently activate not only

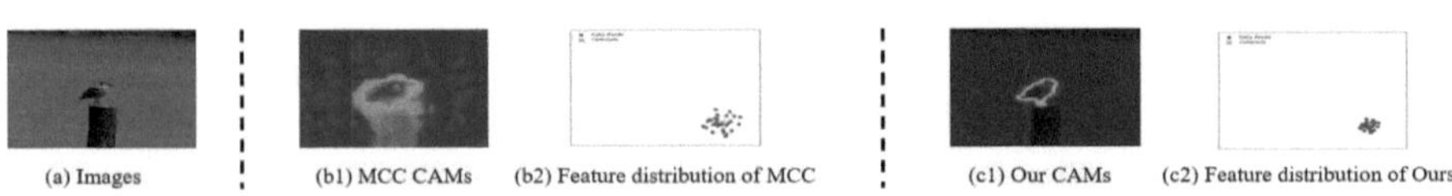

Fig. 1. Comparison of CAMs and Feature Distributions.

the correct foreground regions but also background areas with similar characteristics. This confusion between foreground and background is a key cause of the false activations frequently observed in CAMs (as shown in Fig. 1(b1)), ultimately degrading the quality of pseudo labels and hindering overall segmentation performance.

To achieve this, the model must not only extract common inter-class features from the global context—enhancing the overall understanding of target categories—but also mine fine-grained, discriminative features from local regions to better distinguish between visually similar classes. To this end, we propose a novel framework named CPDGL. Specifically, we introduce the PKRM, which utilizes class tokens to extract semantic information and dynamically updates class prototypes using an EMA mechanism. Additionally, a $\mathcal{L}_{PCL}$ is employed to refine class-specific feature representations and improve the discriminative power of the prototypes. Next, we design the LGDFM to integrate local discriminative features with global semantic cues, enabling the model to capture fine-grained intra-class variations. To further enhance the consistency between features and their corresponding prototypes, we introduce a $\mathcal{L}_{LCL}$. As illustrated in Fig. 1(c1) and 1(c2), the proposed framework effectively encourages the learning of compact, class-consistent foreground feature distributions, allowing class prototypes to activate target regions more accurately. The main contributions of this work are as follows:

- From the perspective of semantic modeling, this paper introduces a novel architecture called **Adaptive Prototype Learning for Weakly Supervised Semantic Segmentation (CPDGL)**.
- To construct discriminative and semantically rich class prototypes, this paper proposes the **Prototype Knowledge Refinement Module (PKRM)**. This module utilizes class tokens to capture global semantic information and introduces a **Prototype Contrastive Loss** ($\mathcal{L}_{PCL}$) to enhance inter-class separability while reinforcing intra-class consistency.
- To improve fine-grained modeling, we propose the **Local-Global Discriminative Fusion Module (LGDFM)**, which captures the complementary relationship between local discriminative features and global semantic information to highlight intra-class fine-grained variations. Additionally, the module enhances the consistency between features and class prototypes through the **Local Consistency Contrastive Loss** ($\mathcal{L}_{LCL}$).
- Experimental results demonstrate that the proposed framework significantly improves segmentation performance on the PASCAL VOC 2012 and MS COCO 2014 datasets, outperforming existing single-stage WSSS methods.

2 Related Work

Prototype Learning. Prototype Learning aims to guide feature representation learning by constructing class prototypes, thereby enhancing the model's understanding of class features and improving its segmentation ability. Chen et al. [9] explored the semantic relationships between pixels to extract spatial structure cues, identifying seed regions for each class and generating image-specific class prototypes to create Image-Specific CAM (IS-CAM). Du et al. [10] introduced a unified pixel-to-prototype contrastive learning framework that optimizes the pixel embedding space using prototype-based metric learning methods. Chen et al. [11] proposed Local Prototype CAM (LPCAM), which employs both discriminative and non-discriminative local prototypes to make the activation areas of target objects more comprehensive. Zhao et al. [12] developed the Prototype-based Secondary Discriminative Pixels Mining (PSDPM) framework, enabling class prototypes to activate more secondary discriminative pixels, thereby improving CAM completeness and class differentiation. While these methods enhance CAM discriminability within prototype-based learning frameworks, they often rely on fixed prototypes that struggle to adapt dynamically to complex backgrounds. In contrast, this paper introduces PKRM, which extracts semantic information using class tokens and dynamically optimizes class prototypes. By incorporating $\mathcal{L}_{PCL}$, PKRM improves both the discriminability and semantic consistency of the prototypes.

Contrastive Learning. Contrastive learning is a self-supervised approach that improves model discriminability by constructing positive and negative sample pairs, and has been widely adopted in weakly supervised semantic segmentation. Xie et al. [13] proposed cross-image foreground-background contrastive learning, leveraging unlabeled images to produce class-agnostic activation maps and identify reliable foreground regions. Zhou et al. [14] introduced semantic contrast to help models distinguish all potential object regions, enabling a more comprehensive understanding of object patterns. Ru et al. [15] developed the Patch Token Contrast (PTC) module, which supervises patch tokens via pseudo-token relationships derived from intermediate layers, yielding more accurate CAMs. Wu et al. [16] proposed Masked Collaborative Contrast (MCC), generating positive and negative pairs from masked local outputs and contrasting them with global features. While these methods alleviate false activations, they often struggle to suppress noise from incorrect labels. To address this, we introduce LGDFM, which fuses local and global information to capture intra-class variations. Coupled with $\mathcal{L}_{LCL}$, it enhances feature-prototype consistency, improves class discriminability, and effectively mitigates the impact of false labels.

3 Methodology

3.1 Framework Overview

This work proposes CPDGL, a comprehensive framework, as illustrated in Fig. 2. The ViT is employed as the backbone to extract both class tokens F and spatial feature maps from the input image. The class tokens F, serving as global semantic representations, are used to construct class prototypes P, which are dynamically updated using an EMA mechanism to enhance their stability and representational capacity. Based on these prototypes, $\mathcal{L}_{PCL}$ is introduced to improve category discriminability by encouraging samples to be closer to their respective prototypes while pushing them away from those of other classes. To further strengthen local semantic consistency, $\mathcal{L}_{LCL}$ is employed. It leverages CAM-guided region cropping to identify high-confidence positive pairs while mitigating the influence of noisy pseudo labels. In addition, a feature memory queue U is maintained to facilitate continuous contrastive learning and enhance boundary modeling. The final objective combines $\mathcal{L}_{cls}$, $\mathcal{L}_{PCL}$, $\mathcal{L}_{LCL}$, and $\mathcal{L}_{seg}$, effectively enhancing both segmentation performance and semantic consistency in WSSS tasks.

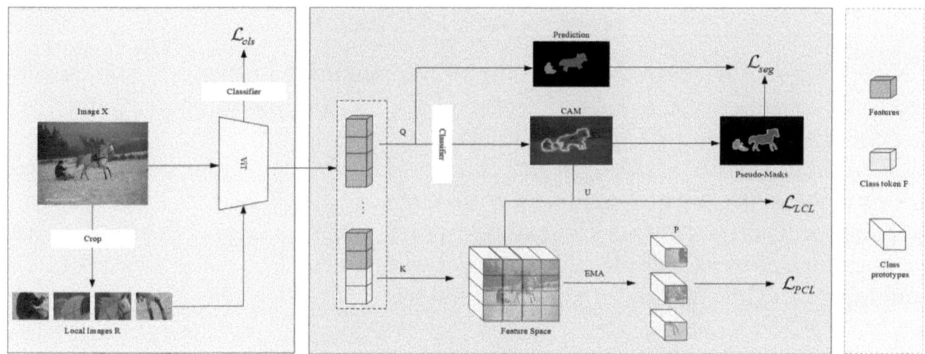

Fig. 2. Overall framework of CPDGL.

3.2 Prototype Knowledge Refinement Module

To address the limitations of traditional prototype construction methods—which typically rely on global or whole-image feature averaging and thus struggle to model the diversity and fine-grained semantic variations of the same class across different contexts—this paper proposes a class token-based PKRM mechanism. Specifically, for the input image X and its corresponding class label $Y = [y_1, y_2, \ldots, y_c] \in \{0,1\}^c$, the class token $F \in R^{D\times H\times W}$ for the current class is extracted from the backbone network E as the semantic embedding for that class. During the prototype update process, an EMA smoothing coefficient β is introduced to ensure that the class prototypes are updated smoothly in each training iteration, following the formula:

$$P_{t+1} = \beta \cdot P_t + (1-\beta) \cdot F_t \tag{1}$$

where, P_{t+1} denotes the updated class prototype; P_t is the current class prototype; F_t represents the current class feature representation, and t s the current training step. This mechanism effectively suppresses the bias caused by noise from individual samples, significantly enhancing the stability of semantic class representations, especially in the later stages of training.

To further address the prototype drift problem caused by imbalanced class frequency during training, a class counter N is introduced to record the occurrence frequency of each class within the current batch. This ensures that the update process is not dominated by single samples when a class appears infrequently. Additionally, to better capture intra-class diversity, a distributed feature aggregation strategy is employed. This strategy synchronizes and aggregates semantic tokens for each class across multiple processes, ensuring that each prototype update incorporates rich contextual information from diverse samples. The final class prototypes are computed using the following mean normalization strategy:

$$P_c = \frac{1}{N_c} \sum_{i=1}^{N_c} \frac{F_i^c}{||F_i^c||_2} \tag{2}$$

where, N_c denotes the number of samples belonging to class c in the current batch; F_i^c represents the feature vector of the ith sample in class c; and $|| \cdot ||$ denotes the vector normalization operation.

Building on this, a $\mathcal{L}_{PCL}$ is introduced. The primary goal is to minimize the distance between the feature F_i^c f the current sample and its corresponding category prototype P_i^c (positive sample pair), while maximizing the distance between the current sample and the prototypes of other categories (negative sample pair). The specific formula is as follows:

$$\mathcal{L}_{\text{PCL}} = -\sum_{i \in Y} \log \frac{\exp\left(\cos(F_i, P_i)/\tau\right)}{\sum_{j=1}^{C} \exp\left(\cos(F_i, P_j)/\tau\right)} \tag{3}$$

where, C denotes the total number of categories; $cos(\cdot)$ denotes the cosine similarity between feature vectors; F_i represents the category-specific feature of the current sample; P_i is the prototype vector corresponding to the sample's true category; P_j refers to the prototype vector of the jth non-target category; and τ is the temperature scaling parameter. This loss function encourages stronger similarity between features and their corresponding category prototypes, while explicitly suppressing similarity with prototypes of other categories. As a result, it significantly enhances the discriminative capacity of the prototypes and improves the semantic alignment and consistency of feature representations.

3.3 Local-Global Discriminative Fusion Module

To alleviate interference from background regions co-occurring with target objects, this paper introduces an LGDFM, leveraging global context and local details for robust feature representation. As shown in Fig. 3, the input image X is randomly cropped based on category-salient regions identified from CAMs. The cropped patches R_i form the local query set $Q = R_i$, while contrast samples $K = R_j$ are extracted from a memory queue of global views.

To ensure category relevance, a region-of-interest mask M is defined, where each pixel is labeled as uncertain (-1), background (0), and a specific category

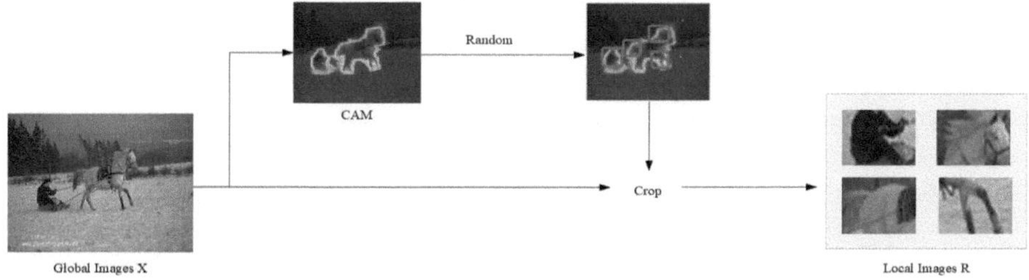

Fig. 3. Cropping Method Principle.

index (c). Foreground coordinates from M are used to sample crop centers:

$$C = \{(h_i, w_i) | M(h_i, w_i) > 0\} \tag{4}$$

$$R_i = X[h_i : h_i + \frac{s}{2}, w_i : w_i + \frac{s}{2}] \tag{5}$$

where, h_i and w_i the vertical and horizontal center coordinates of the ith cropped region, respectively. To support contrastive learning, features from Q and K are passed through a backbone and projection head to obtain:

$$q = Proj(f(Q)), k = \alpha \cdot Proj(f(K_{prev})) + (1 - \alpha) \cdot Proj(f(K)) \tag{6}$$

where, $f(\cdot)$ denotes the feature extraction function; $Proj(\cdot)$ represents the projection head, and α is the momentum update coefficient. The combined queue $U = q \cup k \cup Q$ provides the feature pool for contrastive learning.

A $\mathcal{L}_{LCL}$ is further introduced to suppress pseudo-label noise and enhance category discrimination. A similarity matrix $S(q, U)$ is computed, with invalid (uncertain) regions masked. To ensure high-confidence samples, a filtering strategy retains only those with similarity above the mean μ:

$$\mathcal{P}_q = \{k_i \in U \mid M(k_i) > 0, S^+(q, k_i) > \mu = \frac{1}{S^+(q)} \sum_{k_i \in U} S^+(q, k_i)\} \tag{7}$$

where $M(k_i)$ is a binary mask indicating whether k_i is a valid positive sample, and $S^+(q)$ denotes the set of similarity scores between q and all valid positive samples k_i in U. Only these reliable positive pairs contribute to the contrastive loss:

$$\mathcal{L}_{LCL} = -\frac{\tau}{\tau_0} \cdot \frac{1}{|S^+|} \sum_{k_i \in \mathcal{P}_q} \log \frac{\exp(S^+(q, k_i)/\tau)}{\sum_{k_j \in U} \exp(S(q, k_j)/\tau)} \tag{8}$$

where τ and τ_0 are the temperature parameters. By jointly modeling local discriminative regions and enforcing consistency through contrastive loss, this approach improves feature representation, reduces pseudo-label noise, and enhances segmentation quality.

3.4 Training Objectives

As illustrated in Fig. 2, the loss function of the proposed method consists of four components: $\mathcal{L}_{cls}$, $\mathcal{L}_{PCL}$, $\mathcal{L}_{LCL}$, and $\mathcal{L}_{seg}$. $\mathcal{L}_{cls}$ enhances the model's discriminative ability by encouraging each target class to form a distinct and compact cluster in the feature space. $\mathcal{L}_{PCL}$ reinforces class-wise feature separability by measuring the similarity between each sample and its corresponding class prototype, pulling same-class features closer while pushing others apart to improve generalization and intra-class consistency. $\mathcal{L}_{LCL}$ focuses on refining local feature representations by leveraging high-confidence positive sample pairs, thereby mitigating the adverse effects of noisy labels during training. Lastly, $\mathcal{L}_{seg}$ guides the model to generate accurate pixel-level predictions, enabling precise semantic understanding of image content. Together, these four loss terms collaboratively optimize classification accuracy, feature quality, and segmentation performance. The overall loss function is defined as:

$$\mathcal{L} = \mathcal{L}_{cls} + \lambda_1 \mathcal{L}_{PCL} + \lambda_2 \mathcal{L}_{LCL} + \lambda_3 \mathcal{L}_{seg} \tag{9}$$

Notably, unlike previous weakly supervised segmentation methods, this work dynamically adjusts the weights of individual loss terms based on the training stage, enabling a more stable and efficient optimization process.

4 Experiments

4.1 Experimental Settings

Datasets and Evaluation Metrics. The proposed method is evaluated on two widely used benchmark datasets: PASCAL VOC 2012 [17] and MS COCO 2014 [18]. For PASCAL VOC 2012, which includes 21 classes (20 object categories and 1 background), training is conducted on 10,582 image-level annotated images from the augmented set [19], while evaluation and testing use 1,449 and 1,456 pixel-level annotated images, respectively. Similarly, MS COCO 2014, comprising 81 classes (including background), provides 82,783 training images and 40,504 validation images. To assess the quality of localization maps, pseudo masks, and segmentation results, the Mean Intersection over Union (MIoU) is used as the evaluation metric.

Implementing Details. This work employs the ViT as the backbone to enhance global feature modeling. Training strategies are adapted to the scale of each dataset: for PASCAL VOC 2012, the model is trained for 20,000 iterations with a batch size of 4, while for the larger MS COCO 2014 dataset, training is extended to 80,000 iterations using the same batch size to capture richer category diversity. For optimization, the PolyWarmupAdamW optimizer is adopted, coupled with a multi-stage learning rate schedule that ensures stable learning in the early phases and effective convergence later on.

4.2 Comparisons with State-of-the-Art Methods

Performance of Semantic Segmentation. Table 1 presents the final segmentation performance of the proposed CPDGL method on the PASCAL VOC and MS COCO datasets. To thoroughly demonstrate its superiority, we compare it with both single-stage and multi-stage state-of-the-art approaches. Notably, CPDGL achieves MIoU scores of 72.5%, 71.8%, and 42.5% on the PASCAL VOC validation set, test set, and MS COCO validation set, respectively. Compared to the recent MCC method, it achieves improvements of 2.2%, 0.6%, and 0.2% respectively, clearly outperforming current mainstream single-stage methods. These results highlight CPDGL's enhanced segmentation capability, driven by its high-quality pseudo-label generation and more effective contrastive learning strategy.

Table 1. Semantic Segmentation Results. Sup. denotes the supervision type. $\mathcal{I}$: Image-level labels; $\mathcal{S}$: Saliency maps; $\mathcal{T}$: text-driven supervision from CLIP. Net. denotes the backbone network.

Methods	Sup.	Net.	VOC		COCO
			val (%)	test (%)	val (%)
Multi-stage WSSS methods					
Du et al. [10] CVPR'2022	$\mathcal{I}+\mathcal{S}$	DL-V2	72.6	73.6	–
Lin et al. [20] CVPR'2023	$\mathcal{I}+\mathcal{T}$	DL-V2	71.1	71.4	45.5
ReCAm [4] CVPR'2022	$\mathcal{I}$	DL-V2	68.4	68.2	45.0
VWL [21] IJCV'2022	$\mathcal{I}$	DL-V2	69.2	69.2	36.2
W-OoD [22] CVPR'2022	$\mathcal{I}$	WR38	70.7	70.1	–
MCTformer [2] CVPR'2022	$\mathcal{I}$	WR38	71.9	71.6	42.0
ESOL [23] NeurIPS'2022	$\mathcal{I}$	DL-V2	69.9	69.3	42.6
OCR [24] CVPR'2023	$\mathcal{I}$	WR38	72.7	72.0	42.5
ACR [25] CVPR'2023	$\mathcal{I}$	DL-V2	71.9	71.9	45.3
Single-stage WSSS methodes					
MBDA [26] TIP'2023	$\mathcal{I}+\mathcal{S}$	ResNet101	69.5	70.2	37.8
AFA [5] CVPR'2022	$\mathcal{I}$	MiT-B1	66.0	66.3	38.9
SLRNet [27] IJCV'2022	$\mathcal{I}$	WR38	67.2	67.6	35.0
TSCD [28] AAAI'2023	$\mathcal{I}$	MiT-B1	67.3	67.5	40.1
ToCo [15] CVPR'2023	$\mathcal{I}$	DeiT-B	69.8	70.5	41.3
MCC [16] WACV'2024	$\mathcal{I}$	DeiT-B	70.3	71.2	42.3
CPEWS [29] CMC'2025	$\mathcal{I}$	ViT-B	69.8	72.6	41.4
CPDGL	$\mathcal{I}$	**ViT-B**	**72.5**	**71.8**	**42.5**

In addition to the improvements in quantitative metrics, Fig. 4 presents a visual comparison of segmentation masks generated by the proposed CPDGL method, the MCC method, and ground truth annotations, offering intuitive insight into CPDGL's performance. As shown, CPDGL produces masks with clearer object boundaries and better suppression of background noise compared to MCC. Specifically, CPDGL yields smoother, more complete contours while effectively mitigating boundary blurring and reducing false activations in background regions. These improvements highlight CPDGL's ability to consistently capture target features and minimize background interference, resulting in more accurate weakly supervised semantic segmentation.

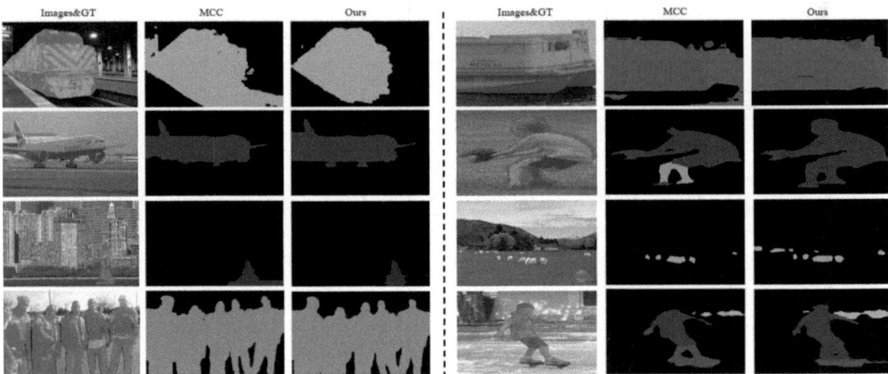

Fig. 4. Visualization of segmentation results on the PASCAL VOC 2012 and MS COCO 2014 datasets.

4.3 Ablation Studies

Component Analysis. This section systematically evaluates the practical contributions of each key component proposed in this work for the WSSS task. To quantify their individual and combined impact on model performance, we conduct ablation studies by progressively integrating each module. The following sections delve into the individual contributions of PKRM, $\mathcal{L}_{PCL}$, LGDFM, and $\mathcal{L}_{LCL}$ to the overall performance of the framework.

As shown in Table 2, the experimental results demonstrate the incremental performance gains achieved by each component of the proposed method. Starting from the baseline framework, the generated CAMs and segmentation results achieve MIoU scores of 67.8% and 66.6%, respectively. Introducing PKRM and $\mathcal{L}_{PCL}$ further enhances the discriminative power of class prototypes and semantic consistency, boosting segmentation accuracy to 69.5% MIoU. Building on this, the integration of LGDFM and $\mathcal{L}_{LCL}$ effectively captures the complementary relationship between global and local features, improving foreground-background discrimination. $\mathcal{L}_{LCL}$ also reinforces feature-prototype alignment, significantly suppressing noise in pseudo labels and improving CAM quality, pushing the MIoU to 70.5%.

Table 2. Ablation studies. M denotes the CAM performance and Seg. denotes the segmentation performance.

Baseline	PKRM	$\mathcal{L}_{PCL}$	LGDFM	$\mathcal{L}_{LCL}$	M (%)	Seg. (%)
✓	–	–	–	–	67.8	66.6
✓	✓	✓	–	–	71.2	69.5
✓	✓	✓	✓	✓	71.9	70.5

Model Performance Analysis. To thoroughly validate the effectiveness of the proposed CPDGL framework for WSSS, we conducted extensive evaluations on the PASCAL VOC 2012 validation set and compared its performance with two representative one-stage methods, MCC and ToCo. As illustrated in Fig. 5, CPDGL consistently demonstrates a stable and superior performance trajectory throughout the training process, indicating improved convergence speed and training robustness. Ultimately, CPDGL achieves a MIoU of 72.5% on the validation set, significantly surpassing MCC (69.4%) and ToCo (67.2%). These results underscore the enhancements in feature representation quality and pseudo-label reliability.

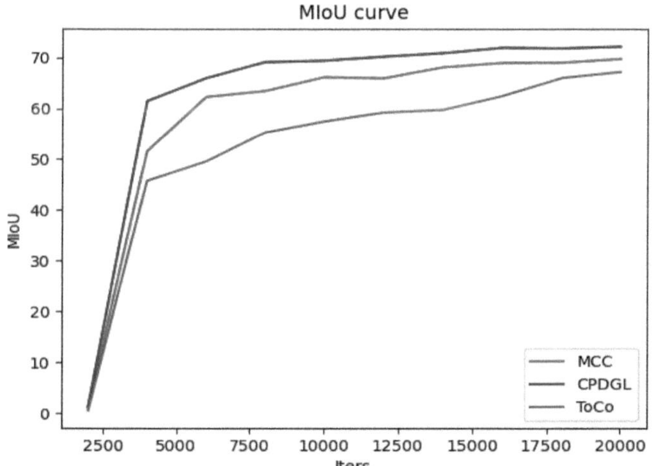

Fig. 5. Training curve comparison of CPDGL, MCC, and ToCo on the PASCAL VOC 2012 validation set.

Backbone Network Analysis. To comprehensively assess the generalization capability of the proposed CPDGL framework across different feature extractors, we conducted ablation experiments using two representative Transformer architectures: ViT-B and DeiT. As illustrated in Fig. 6, when ViT-B is used as the backbone, the model achieves a MIoU of 72.5% on the PASCAL VOC 2012 validation set, reflecting strong segmentation performance. When replaced with the more lightweight and parameter-efficient DeiT, performance shows a modest decline to 70.8%. This gap can be attributed to ViT-B's greater representational capacity and larger model size, which facilitate the generation of more stable and discriminative embeddings for prototype construction and contrastive learning.

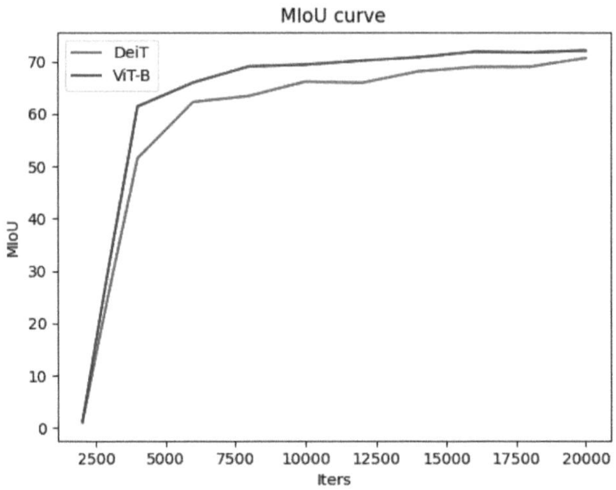

Fig. 6. Comparison of the MIoU curves between the DeiT and ViT-B models.

5 Conclusion

This paper introduces a novel CPDGL framework designed to tackle critical challenges in weakly supervised semantic segmentation, including low-quality pseudo-labels and inconsistent semantic representations. The proposed method focuses on two key aspects: enhancing class-level semantic consistency and improving the discriminative power of local features. To achieve this, the PKRM is introduced, which constructs dynamically stable semantic prototypes based on class tokens. Paired with the $\mathcal{L}_{PCL}$, this module effectively improves inter-class discriminability and semantic aggregation. Next, the LGDFM is employed to integrate discriminative local regions with global context, further strengthening the model's ability to capture fine-grained features. Additionally, the $\mathcal{L}_{LCL}$ is introduced to enhance the semantic consistency of local regions. Extensive experimental results on the PASCAL VOC 2012 and MS COCO 2014 datasets demonstrate that CPDGL outperforms existing mainstream one-stage methods, achieving superior segmentation performance and validating its effectiveness and generalization ability. Despite its strong performance, CPDGL still faces challenges such as limited prototype expressiveness and insufficient coverage of local views. Future research could explore integrating multi-modal information, uncertainty modeling, and graph-based prototype optimization strategies to further improve the model's performance and adaptability.

Acknowledgments. The study has been supported by funding from the following sources: Research Programs of Henan Science and Technology Department (232102210054,232102210033); Chongqing Natural Science Foundation (CSTB2023-NSCQ-MSX0070); Henan Province key research and development project (231111212000); Aviation Science Foundation (20230001055002); Supported by Henan Center for Outstanding Overseas Scientists (GZS2022011); Leading Innovative Talent of Zhongyuan (254000510017); National Natural Science Foundation of China Youth Science Fund Project (62202434); Henan Province Higher Education Young Backbone Teacher Project (2023GGJS111); Zhengzhou University of Aeronautics Scientific Research Team Program (23ZHTD01001); Graduate Education Innovation Program Fund of Zhengzhou University of Aeronautics (2025CX123).

References

1. Lee, J., Kim, E., Yoon, S.: Anti-adversarially manipulated attributions for weakly and semi-supervised semantic segmentation. In: Proceedings of the IEEE/CVF Conference on Computer Vision and Pattern Recognition (CVPR), pp. 4071–4080 (2021)
2. Xu, L., Ouyang, W., Bennamoun, M., Boussaid, F., Xu, D.: Multi-class token transformer for weakly supervised semantic segmentation. In: Proceedings of the IEEE/CVF Conference on Computer Vision and Pattern Recognition (CVPR), pp. 4310–4319 (2022)
3. Englebert, A., Cornu, O., De Vleeschouwer, C.: Poly-CAM: high resolution class activation map for convolutional neural networks. Mach. Vis. Appl. **35**(4), 89 (2024)
4. Chen, Z., Wang, T., Wu, X., Hua, X.-S., Zhang, H., Sun, Q.: Class re-activation maps for weakly-supervised semantic segmentation. In: Proceedings of the IEEE/CVF Conference on Computer Vision and Pattern Recognition (CVPR), pp. 969–978 (2022)
5. Ru, L., Zhan, Y., Yu, B., Du, B.: Learning affinity from attention: end-to-end weakly-supervised semantic segmentation with transformers. In: Proceedings of the IEEE/CVF Conference on Computer Vision and Pattern Recognition (CVPR), pp. 16846–16855 (2022)
6. Han, K., et al.: A survey on Vision Transformer. IEEE Trans. Pattern Anal. Mach. Intell. **45**(1), 87–110 (2022)
7. Chen, L., Lei, C., Li, R., Li, S., Zhang, Z., Zhang, L.: FPR: false positive rectification for weakly supervised semantic segmentation. In: Proceedings of the IEEE/CVF International Conference on Computer Vision (ICCV), pp. 1108–1118 (2023)
8. Tang, F., Xu, Z., Qu, Z., Feng, W., Jiang, X., Ge, Z.: Hunting attributes: context prototype-aware learning for weakly supervised semantic segmentation. In: Proceedings of the IEEE/CVF Conference on Computer Vision and Pattern Recognition (CVPR), pp. 3324–3334 (2024)
9. Chen, Q., Yang, L., Lai, J.-H., Xie, X.: Self-supervised image-specific prototype exploration for weakly supervised semantic segmentation. In: Proceedings of the IEEE/CVF Conference on Computer Vision and Pattern Recognition, pp. 4288–4298 (2022)

10. Du, Y., Fu, Z., Liu, Q., Wang, Y.: Weakly supervised semantic segmentation by pixel-to-prototype contrast. In: Proceedings of the IEEE/CVF Conference on Computer Vision and Pattern Recognition, pp. 4320–4329 (2022)
11. Chen, Z., Sun, Q.: Extracting class activation maps from non-discriminative features as well. In: Proceedings of the IEEE/CVF Conference on Computer Vision and Pattern Recognition, pp. 3135–3144 (2023)
12. Zhao, X., Yang, Z., Dai, T., Zhang, B., Xiao, J.: PSDPM: prototype-based secondary discriminative pixels mining for weakly supervised semantic segmentation. In: Proceedings of the IEEE/CVF Conference on Computer Vision and Pattern Recognition, pp. 3437–3446 (2024)
13. Xie, J., Xiang, J., Chen, J., Hou, X., Zhao, X., Shen, L.: Contrastive learning of class-agnostic activation map for weakly supervised object localization and semantic segmentation. arXiv preprint arXiv:2203.13505 (2022)
14. Zhou, T., Zhang, M., Zhao, F., Li, J.: Regional semantic contrast and aggregation for weakly supervised semantic segmentation. In: Proceedings of the IEEE/CVF Conference on Computer Vision and Pattern Recognition, pp. 4299–4309 (2022)
15. Ru, L., Zheng, H., Zhan, Y., Du, B.: Token contrast for weakly-supervised semantic segmentation. In: Proceedings of the IEEE/CVF Conference on Computer Vision and Pattern Recognition, pp. 3093–3102 (2023)
16. Wu, F., He, J., Yin, Y., Hao, Y., Huang, G., Cheng, L.: Masked collaborative contrast for weakly supervised semantic segmentation. In: Proceedings of the IEEE/CVF Winter Conference on Applications of Computer Vision, pp. 862–871 (2024)
17. Everingham, M., Van Gool, L., Williams, C.K.I., Winn, J., Zisserman, A.: The pascal visual object classes (VOC) challenge. Int. J. Comput. Vision **88**, 303–338 (2010)
18. Lin, T.-Y., et al.: Microsoft COCO: common objects in context. In: Fleet, D., Pajdla, T., Schiele, B., Tuytelaars, T. (eds.) ECCV 2014. LNCS, vol. 8693, pp. 740–755. Springer, Cham (2014). https://doi.org/10.1007/978-3-319-10602-1_48
19. Hariharan, B., Arbeláez, P., Bourdev, L., Maji, S., Malik, J.: Semantic contours from inverse detectors. In: 2011 International Conference on Computer Vision, pp. 991–998. IEEE, (2011)
20. Lin, Y., et al.: Clip is also an efficient segmenter: a text-driven approach for weakly supervised semantic segmentation. In: Proceedings of the IEEE/CVF Conference on Computer Vision and Pattern Recognition, pp. 15305–15314 (2023)
21. Ru, L., Du, B., Zhan, Y., Wu, C.: Weakly-supervised semantic segmentation with visual words learning and hybrid pooling. Int. J. Comput. Vision **130**(4), 1127–1144 (2022)
22. Lee, J., Oh, S.J., Yun, S., Choe, J., Kim, E., Yoon, S.: Weakly supervised semantic segmentation using out-of-distribution data. In: Proceedings of the IEEE/CVF Conference on Computer Vision and Pattern Recognition, pp. 16897–16906 (2022)
23. Li, J., Jie, Z., Wang, X., Wei, X., Ma, L.: Expansion and shrinkage of localization for weakly-supervised semantic segmentation. In: Advances in Neural Information Processing Systems, vol. 35, pp. 16037–16051 (2022)
24. Cheng, Z., et al.: Out-of-candidate rectification for weakly supervised semantic segmentation. In: Proceedings of the IEEE/CVF Conference on Computer Vision and Pattern Recognition, pp. 23673–23684 (2023)
25. Kweon, H., Yoon, S.-H., Yoon, K.-J.: Weakly supervised semantic segmentation via adversarial learning of classifier and reconstructor. In: Proceedings of the IEEE/CVF Conference on Computer Vision and Pattern Recognition, pp. 11329–11339 (2023)

26. Chen, T., Yao, Y., Tang, J.: Multi-granularity denoising and bidirectional alignment for weakly supervised semantic segmentation. IEEE Trans. Image Process. **32**, 2960–2971 (2023)
27. Pan, J., et al.: Learning self-supervised low-rank network for single-stage weakly and semi-supervised semantic segmentation. Int. J. Comput. Vision **130**(5), 1181–1195 (2022)
28. Xu, R., Wang, C., Sun, J., Xu, S., Meng, W., Zhang, X.: Self correspondence distillation for end-to-end weakly-supervised semantic segmentation. In: Proceedings of the AAAI Conference on Artificial Intelligence, vol. 37, no. 3, pp. 3045–3053 (2023)
29. Shao, X., Han, J., Li, L., Zhao, X., Yan, J.: CPEWS: contextual prototype-based end-to-end weakly supervised semantic segmentation. Comput. Mater. Continua **83**(1) (2025)

Federated Knowledge Distillation Based on Prompt for Matching Data Distribution

Yizhang Liu[1,2], Wenze Xu[3], Zixuan Xu[1], Tongtong Yuan[1(✉)], and Weihong Deng[2]

[1] Beijing University of Technology, 100 Pingleyuan, Beijing, China
{liu2004,xzxBjut}@emails.bjut.edu.cn, yuantt@bjut.edu.cn
[2] Mashang Consumer Finance Co., Ltd., Chongqing, China
weihong.deng@msxf.com
[3] The University of Sydney, Sydney, NSW 2006, Australia
wexu0327@uni.sydney.edu.au

Abstract. In the field of Federated Learning (FL), the differences in client-side data distribution pose a challenge of poor generalization of local models. Employing knowledge distillation methods allows the transmission of complex knowledge, referred to as dark knowledge, to client models. The global features within dark knowledge can assist clients in learning out-of-distribution knowledge, thereby enhancing the generalization ability of the federated system. To tackle issues caused by the difference in data distribution, we propose a Federated Knowledge Distillation approach that leverages a prompt generator to match data distribution in FL. Firstly, we develop a personalized visual prompt generator for image classification tasks. By implicitly handling the client's local data and training local models, this generator can effectively release data problems in distributed learning. Secondly, we utilize knowledge distillation to leverage the server's prediction probabilities, aiding clients in acquiring global out-of-self-distribution knowledge. Experiment results on three datasets with different data distributions across different sites demonstrate a significant improvement in the classification accuracy of FL models using this approach.

Keywords: Federated learning · Knowledge distillation · Visual prompt · Date heterogeneity

1 Introduction

Deep learning is currently widely applied across various sectors of society, with the training of high-quality deep learning models typically relying on vast and accessible data. However, many types of data contain sensitive private information, making it challenging to collect and centralize this dispersed data for model

Supported by Beijing University of Technology.

© The Author(s), under exclusive license to Springer Nature Singapore Pte Ltd. 2026
J. Kittler et al. (Eds.): PRCV 2025, LNCS 16289, pp. 230–243, 2026.
https://doi.org/10.1007/978-981-95-5764-6_16

training. To address this issue, privacy-preserving deep learning techniques are gaining increasing attention. Federated Learning (FL) [3,19] is a method for building machine learning models based on datasets distributed across multiple devices, effectively preventing data leakage and safeguarding local privacy data.

However, in FL, the data of each participating client, although independently distributed, does not follow the same sampling method. This heterogeneity in data distribution can affect the accuracy of the model after aggregation on the server side. Furthermore, there is a significant disparity between the data distribution of local models and the global data distribution [8,26]. Enhancing the generalization ability of the aggregated model on the global data is also a crucial factor limiting the performance of FL. We have found that incorporating image prompters and employing knowledge distillation in FL can more effectively utilize global knowledge, effectively addressing the issue of data distribution heterogeneity, and then improving the generalization performance of the aggregated model. Furthermore, inspired by some studies on knowledge distillation (KD) [20,27], we have discovered that transferring knowledge from the teacher model (aggregated model) to the student model (client) can enhance the model's generalization ability, thereby improving the generalization ability of the model after aggregation.

Integrating these aspects, we propose a method termed FDBP (Federated Distillation Based on Prompt), which leverages a prompt generator to guide the backbone networks of individual clients to focus on the structural characteristics of their local data. Simultaneously, a central server aggregates knowledge from all clients and serves as a teacher to distill and refine local models, thereby enhancing their generalization capabilities. Importantly, FDBP is not a simple combination of prompt generator and federated knowledge distillation. Rather, it establishes a collaborative framework in which these two components interact synergistically: the prompt generator facilitates personalized model adaptation to local data distributions, while federated knowledge distillation enables the transfer of global knowledge distilled from the aggregated model back to individual clients. This bidirectional exchange ensures that each client not only specializes in its local context but also benefits from the broader data diversity across the federation. As a result, the coordinated functioning of these components effectively mitigates the challenges posed by data heterogeneity in Federated Learning.

Our contributions are as follows:

- We introduce a prompt generator in client-side models to refine and train local models. This method aims to mitigate the impact of heterogeneous data distribution across clients.
- To better match data distribution, we introduce federated KD. Specifically, we distribute the logits aggregated from the global model to the clients to update and optimize the client models. This approach guides the training of client models, helping them learn global knowledge outside of their local distribution, thereby enhancing the generalization ability of the aggregated model.

- We conducted extensive experiments that validate the effectiveness of our proposed method, FDBP, showing superior performance compared to existing methods across different datasets with different data distribution settings.

2 Related Works

2.1 Data Heterogeneity in FL

In this paper, we focus on solving data heterogeneity in FL. FL, proposed by McMahan et al. [19], is designed for decentralized client-side learning. They introduced the standard algorithm FedAvg, which aggregates training local model parameters by averaging. However, the method does not achieve optimal solutions when the distributed data is heterogeneous. In recent years, numerous methods have been proposed to address the issue of data heterogeneity in FL. Wang et al. [25] presented the FedNova approach, which employs a normalized averaging method to eliminate objective inconsistencies and maintain fast error convergence. Acar et al. [4] proposed a method that assigns a dynamic regularizer for each device in each round, ensuring consistency between the global and device solutions at the limit. Fu et al. [2] introduced the FedDP algorithm which allocates weights based on the performance of data quality of each participant, thereby optimizing the performance of FL in the presence of data heterogeneity. Additionally, Pillutla et al. [21] presented a FL framework that depends on a super quantile-based learning objective, allowing the learning objective to capture tail statistics of error distributions on heterogeneous client devices.

2.2 Knowledge Distillation in FL

Employing knowledge distillation methods allows the transmission of complex knowledge, referred to as dark knowledge, to client models. Szegedy et al. [23] pointed out that using one-hot encoded labels might encourage a model to predict the probability of the target class as 1 and the probability of non-target classes as 0, leading to infinite logits for the target class in the softmax function. Therefore, in order to enhance the model's generalization ability, label smoothing involves distributing a portion of the target class label values to non-target classes. Zhao et al. [30] investigated the decoupling of logits into target and non-target class information and concluded that the non-target class information is crucial for the effectiveness of knowledge distillation. Zhang et al. [29] conducted a detailed analysis of the distillation process from the perspective of information quantification, indicating that reactive knowledge distillation often enables deep neural network models to learn more direct knowledge with a more stable optimization direction. Li et al. [13] utilized transfer learning and knowledge distillation to develop a universal framework for application in FL. Zhou et al. [31] proposed the distilled one-shot FL (DOSFL), significantly reducing communication costs through a weight-less and gradient-less design. Zhang et al. [28] introduced the FedFTG method, which alleviates the issue of direct model aggregation by using a data-free knowledge distillation method to fine-tune the global model in the server.

3 Methods

To address the issue of heterogeneous data distribution and the associated problem of model generalization, we propose a novel training model for FL. Firstly, we introduce a prompt generator in the client-side network to alleviate the problem of heterogeneous data distribution. Secondly, we develop a federated knowledge distillation algorithm to enhance the model's generalization ability.

3.1 Prompt Generator in FL

In some studies [5,24], visual prompts have been used to assist pre-trained visual models in performing downstream tasks effectively. By Prompt-based Learning [18], pre-trained models can receive prompts about the current task before executing it, enabling generalization to downstream transfer learning tasks without fine-tuning the entire model. Therefore, we add a parameterized prompt δ_i to the input image x, creating a prompt image $x + \delta_i$, which is then fed into the local network for training. We design a random-position visual prompt generator to generate random pixel patches. These patches are added to images at random positions to create prompt images. The selection of patch positions is random, and patches may be placed at different locations in different images. Subsequently, pixel-level operations are applied to these regions, such as altering pixel values, adding noise, or applying other image processing techniques. These specific image patches can be learned from local data during the training process.

We integrate a learnable prompt generator for each client model, whose task is to generate personalized visual prompts for each client based on the local data distribution. During the local training of FDBP, the generated personalized visual prompts are added to images as prior knowledge to assist the backbone network in completing the classification task. Each client includes a prompt generator, locally stored personalized learnable parameters, and a backbone network, and the server aggregates the backbone network parameters of each client. Since each prompt generator is trained on local data, it can effectively match the features of local data, alleviate data heterogeneity issues, and enhance the model's performance.

3.2 Federated KD

In this subsection, we introduce a federated distillation framework based on prompt generators, which utilizes the server to broadcast aggregated parameters representing global knowledge to generate global logits. These global logits are then used to guide the training of client models. The Federated KD framework is shown in Fig. 1.

We denote N clients as l_1, l_2, l_3, ..., l_n. Each client l_i learns a local model w_i on its local data D_i without exchanging raw data, where the loss function optimized by each client is denoted as $L_i(w_i)$, with $L_i(w_i)$ being the empirical loss of l_i. Each client trains its personalized model w_i by optimizing the problem

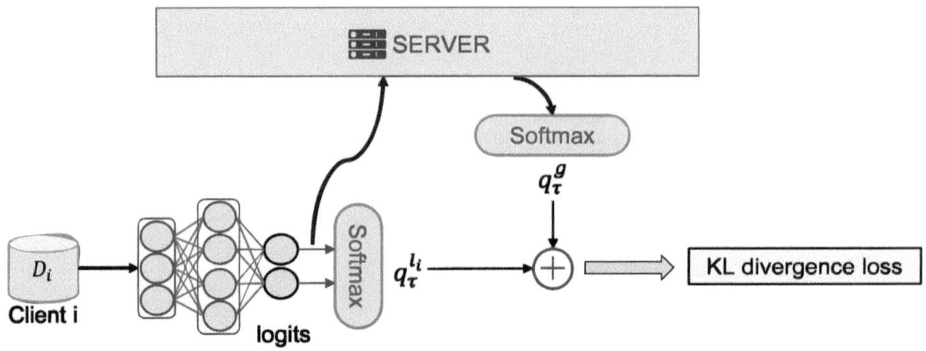

Fig. 1. Knowledge distillation in FL.

$L_i(w_i)$. As mentioned above, our goal is to learn personalized prompt generators δ_i and backbone networks w_i for each client. The prompt generator δ_i is also trained on local data. Our goal is to optimize $L_i(w_i, \delta_i)$, where L_i is the empirical loss of l_i. We adopt an alternating training approach, updating the prompt generator and backbone network of each client alternately. We first train the prompt generator using a fixed aggregation model to maximize the probability of correct labels, as shown in Eq. (1).

$$arg \min_{\delta_i} \mathcal{L}_i(w_i, \delta_i) = \mathbb{E}_{(x,y)\sim\mathcal{D}^i} \left[\ell_i \left(w_i; (x + \delta_i, y)\right)\right], \tag{1}$$

where y represents the target output. After optimizing the prompt generator on the client side, we freeze its parameters and then train the backbone network. During training, the optimization objective for the backbone network in each client l_i is as shown in Eq. (2).

$$arg \min_{w_i} \mathcal{L}_i(w_i, \delta_i) = \mathbb{E}_{(x,y)\sim\mathcal{D}^i} \big[\ell_i \big(w_i; (x + \delta_i, y)\big)\big] \tag{2}$$

In FL, the student model refers to the local model, denoted by l for local clients, while the teacher model represents the global model, denoted by g for the global server. The distillation framework is illustrated in Fig. 1, where each local client utilizes local data for simultaneous training, makes prediction outputs, and then updates the model parameters based on the gradient of the loss function. The locally updated model parameters are uploaded to the server for aggregation, and after aggregation, the server distributes the updated parameters back to the clients. The clients generate global predictions q_τ^g based on the parameters received from the server, then calculate the KL divergence between the global predictions q_τ^g and the local model predictions $q_\tau^{l_i}$, combining them with the cross-entropy loss (CE) between the local predictions of each client and the ground truth labels to form the client's loss function. The loss function ℓ_i defined for each client is shown in Eq. (3).

$$\ell_i = CE(q^{l_i}, y) + \beta \cdot KL\big(q_\tau^{l_i}, q_\tau^g\big), \tag{3}$$

where q^{l_i} represents the logits predicted by client l_i, y represents the true labels, $q_\tau^{l_i}$ and q_τ^{g} respectively represent the softmax-activated outputs of the client and the server model passed down, where the activation temperature is τ. The parameter β is used to adjust the weight of the KL loss, balancing the learning of global knowledge and local data to prevent over-reliance on local data or global knowledge.

Algorithm 1. Federated distillation algorithm based on prompt generator

Input: Number of communication rounds T, clients $\{l_1, \ldots, l_N\}$, dataset $D = \{D_i\}$, the set of clients sampled for communication in round t: $l^{(t)} \subset l$, number of training epochs for clients el, learning rate for client backbone network η_1, number of training epochs for prompt generator ep, learning rate η_2, initialize the prompt generator parameters δ_i for client l_i.

Initialize the client network w_0.

for $t = l \ldots T_l$ **do**

Server samples clients $l^{(t)}$ and broadcasts $\tilde{w}^{(t)} \leftarrow w^{(t)}$

for each client $l \in l^{(t)}$ in parallel **do**

for prompt generator training rounds: stepse $= 1 \ldots ep$ **do**

for batch $i = 1$ to B **do**

$$\delta_i^t \leftarrow \delta_i^t - \eta_g \nabla \ell_i(w_i^t; (x + \delta_i, y))$$

end for

end for

end for

Upload $\tilde{w}_k^t$ to the server

Server aggregation: $\delta^{(t+1)} \leftarrow \sum_{k=1}^{N} \frac{|\mathcal{D}^i|}{|\mathcal{D}|} \delta_k^{(t)}$

end for

for $t = T_l + 1 \ldots T$ **do**

Server samples clients $l^{(t)}$ and broadcasts $\widetilde{w}^{(t)} \leftarrow w^{(t)}$

for each client $l \subset l^{(t)}$ in parallel **do**

for prompt generator training steps $e = 1 \ldots ep$ **do**

for batches $j = 1 \ldots B$ **do**

$\tilde{w}_k^{(t)} \leftarrow \tilde{w}_k^{(t)} - \gamma \nabla_w \mathcal{L}(\tilde{w}_k^{(t)}; [\mathcal{D}^k]_j)$

end for

end for

end for

Upload $\tilde{w}_k^t$ to the server

Server aggregation: $w^{(t+1)} \leftarrow \sum_{k=1}^{N} \frac{|\mathcal{D}^i|}{|\mathcal{D}|} \tilde{w}_k^{(t)}$

end for

Server outputs: w_T

The strategy for the server-side aggregation of network parameters uploaded by clients is represented by Eq. (4), where t denotes the training round, $|\mathcal{D}^i|$ represents the size of the local dataset D_i of client l_i, $|\mathcal{D}|$ represents the total size of all client datasets, and N represents the number of clients. In this strategy, the server aggregates the parameters from each client by performing a weighted sum based on the size of the local data each client possesses, thus taking into account the variations in the sizes of different client datasets.

$$w^{t+1} \leftarrow \sum_{k=1}^{N} \frac{|\mathcal{D}^i|}{|\mathcal{D}|} w_k^t. \tag{4}$$

After aggregating the parameters, the server then sends them back to the individual clients. As a result, clients can utilize the distilled knowledge to enhance the performance of their local networks. The overall algorithm is shown in Algorithm 1.

3.3 Training Procedure

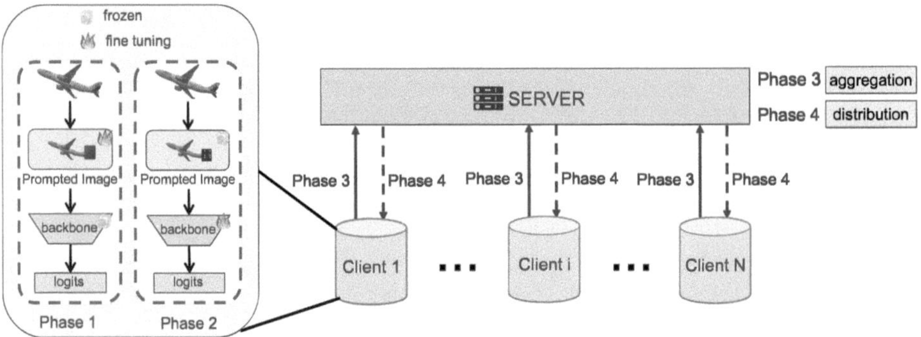

Fig. 2. Training framework for FDBP.

The training process of combining the prompt generator with FL mainly includes four steps, as shown in Fig. 2:

- Each client freezes the entire backbone network (i.e., no parameter updates, but continues to output predictions), and uses their local data to update the prompt generator's parameters, as shown in phase (1) of Fig. 2.
- After a specified number of rounds of training the prompt generator at each client will be frozen, and the images guided by prompts are used as inputs to the client's backbone network for training and parameter updates. This is illustrated in phase (2) of Fig. 2.
- Clients upload the trained network parameters to the server after several rounds of training, and the server performs aggregation operations. This is depicted in phase (3) of Fig. 2.

- The server broadcasts the aggregated parameters to all clients, and after updating the parameters, clients obtain new prediction results. They compute distillation loss by combining global logits knowledge received from the server with local logits predictions. This process helps in updating the local network parameters. This is explained in phase (4) of Fig. 2.

4 Experiments

4.1 Datasets

We use CIFAR-10, CINIC-10, and Camelyon17 datasets separately to validate our method. We use PyTorch along with NVIDIA GeForce RTX 3090 for training the data.

CIFAR-10 [11] consisted of 10 categories of RGB color images. Each image has a size of 32×32, with 6000 images per category. The dataset is divided into training and test sets in a 5:1 ratio. CINIC-10 [7] is a dataset for image classification. It has a total of 270,000 images, constructed from two different sources: ImageNet and CIFAR-10. Camelyon17 [6] is a dataset for classifying histopathology images of cancerous breast tissue. It includes 450,000 histopathology images with different stains from 5 different hospitals. Each hospital is considered a client, and images from different clients exhibit heterogeneous appearances. The CAMELYON17 dataset is a large-scale dataset designed for the evaluation of algorithms in breast cancer metastasis detection in lymph node tissue using whole-slide histopathology images (WSIs). The dataset poses significant challenges due to its high image resolution, domain variability between institutions, and the highly imbalanced nature of normal versus tumor tissue. CAMELYON17 supports a wide range of research applications, including cancer detection, segmentation, and grading, and has become a benchmark for machine learning models in computational pathology.

4.2 Implementation Details

We explored various prompt sizes p, where the number of parameters scales as Cp^2, with C denoting the number of image channels. Following the findings in prior work [14], which demonstrated that $p = 4$ yields optimal performance, we adopted the same setting in our study. Specifically, we validated the effectiveness of this configuration on the CIFAR-100 dataset, as shown in Table 1, and observed that setting $p = 4$ consistently achieved the best performance under our proposed method. Considering both classification accuracy and computational efficiency—minimizing the overhead introduced by the Cp^2 parameter count—we selected $p = 4$ as the default setting in all subsequent experiments.

For CAMELYON17 dataset, which is sourced from different hospital sites for the FL framework, we just use similar settings with HarmoFL. In the Camelyon17 dataset, we conduct 100 rounds of model training at different communication frequencies (uploading once every several rounds), using a cross-entropy

Table 1. Comparison of different prompt sizes on classification accuracy

Method	CIFAR-100		
	$p = 4$	$p = 15$	$p = 20$
FDBP	30.30	29.93	29.87

loss function and SGD optimizer with a learning rate set to 1e-3. Local clients communicate with the server after each training iteration, totaling 600 communication rounds, with the local client network frozen during the first 100 rounds of communication.

For the CINIC-10 and CIFAR-10 datasets, we distribute the data to 100 clients and randomly sample 10% of the clients. We employ a sharding-based independent and identically distributed strategy, sorting data based on labels, dividing them into equally-sized and non-overlapping shards, and controlling data heterogeneity through the number of shards s per user. During training, we use a momentum SGD optimizer with an initial learning rate of 0.1, momentum set to 0.9, learning rate decay factor of 0.99 per round, and weight decay factor of 1e-5. Each local client communicates with the server after every 5 training iterations, totaling 250 communication rounds. During the first 50 communication rounds, the local client's network is frozen for alternate training.

4.3 Comparisons on Camelyon17 Dataset

Table 2. Experiment on the influence factor of prompter for Camelyon17

Method	Breast Cancer Histology Image Classification(Accuracy)					
	A	B	C	D	E	Avg.
FedAvg [19]	91.10	83.12	82.06	87.49	74.78	83.71
FedProx [16]	91.03	82.88	82.78	87.07	74.93	83.74
FedNova [25]	90.99	82.97	82.40	86.93	74.86	83.61
FedAdam [9]	87.45	80.38	76.89	89.27	77.86	82.37
FedBN [17]	89.35	90.25	94.16	94.04	68.87	87.33
MOON [15]	88.92	83.52	84.71	90.02	67.79	82.99
HarmoFL [1]	96.17	93.60	95.54	95.58	96.50	95.48
HarmoFL + Prompter	97.02	95.50	95.74	95.89	96.93	96.22
FDBP	97.32	95.73	95.84	96.09	97.32	96.62

To comprehensively evaluate the effectiveness of our proposed method, FDBP, we conducted extensive experiments on the Camelyon17 dataset for the task of image classification. Table 2 presents the classification accuracy across five clients (denoted A–E) and the corresponding average accuracy.

We first compare the baseline methods, including FedAvg [19], FedProx [16], FedNova [25], FedAdam [9], FedBN [17], and MOON [15]. These methods exhibit moderate performance, with average accuracies ranging from 82.37% to 87.33%.

Subsequently, we investigate HarmoFL [1], a recent method tailored for non-IID federated learning scenarios. HarmoFL achieves a substantial performance boost with an average accuracy of 95.48%, outperforming all the baseline methods by a large margin. We further enhance HarmoFL by introducing a prompt generator, resulting in the "HarmoFL + Prompter" variant. This variant leverages prompts inserted at random positions in the image to guide the model's learning process. The addition of the prompt generator yields a noticeable improvement, increasing the average accuracy to 96.22%, which is 0.74% higher than HarmoFL.

Finally, our proposed method FDBP achieves the best performance among all compared methods. FDBP attains an average classification accuracy of 96.62% across all clients, with consistent improvements observed on each individual client. Specifically, FDBP outperforms "HarmoFL + Prompter" on all sites, demonstrating the robustness and generalizability of our approach. Compared to the original HarmoFL, FDBP improves the average accuracy by 1.14%, highlighting the effectiveness of our design. These results validate the superiority of FDBP in addressing data heterogeneity and improving federated learning performance on challenging medical image classification tasks.

4.4 Comparisons on CIFAR-10 and CINIC-10 Datasets

Table 3. Comparison of the accuracy of different algorithms on various datasets with the Non-IID Partition Strategy: Sharding

Method	Non-IID Partition Strategy: Sharding			
	CIFAR-10			CINIC-10
	s = 2	s = 3	s = 5	s = 2
FedAvg [19]	40.14	51.10	57.17	39.64
FedCury [22]	44.52	49.00	54.61	40.45
FedProx [16]	41.48	51.65	56.88	41.47
FedNova [25]	42.62	52.03	62.14	42.55
SCAFFOLD [10]	44.60	54.26	65.74	42.66
MOON [15]	38.51	50.47	56.69	37.07
FedNTD [12]	52.61	58.18	64.93	48.07
FDBP	54.35	61.12	68.27	49.88

For CIFAR-10 and CINIC-10 datasets We adopt a sharding-based data partitioning strategy to achieve independent and identically distributed (IID) data distribution, which is described as follows: The data is sorted by labels and divided into equal-sized, non-overlapping shards. The heterogeneity of the data is controlled by the number of shards s assigned to each client. Specifically, each shard contains $|D|/(N \times s)$ samples of the same class, where D is the total size of the dataset, N is the total number of clients, and s is the number of shards per client. In this strategy, since the size of the local dataset for each client is the same, only the heterogeneity of the data distribution is considered.

In comparative experiments, we test the proposed method FDBP using the CIFAR-10 and CINIC-10 datasets, comparing the results with other FL algorithms as shown in Table 3. In the experiments, we process the datasets by setting different numbers of shards s. The shard-based partitioning strategies for CIFAR-10 and CINIC-10 follow the setting used in FedNTD [12], which also adopts this approach for non-IID simulations. This consistency ensures a fair comparison and makes the results directly comparable, thereby justifying our choice and aligning with prior work. The results indicate that our method exhibited superior performance, achieving higher accuracy than other algorithms. For instance, on the CIFAR-10 dataset, when s was set to 2, 3, and 5, our method achieved accuracy rates of 54.35%, 61.12%, and 68.47%, respectively; on the CINIC-10 dataset, with $s = 2$, our accuracy reached 49.88%.

These experimental results demonstrate the effectiveness of prompt generators and knowledge distillation in guiding network training optimization, benefiting from the learnability of the prompt generator, enabling it to learn the distinctive features of heterogeneous data present in each client.

4.5 Ablation Study

To assess the contribution of the prompter module in our proposed FDBP framework, we conduct an ablation study on the Camelyon17 dataset. Specifically, we evaluate two variants: (1) the full model (FDBP), and (2) FDBP without the structured prompter component, denoted as *HarmoFL + Prompter*. In the ablated version, prompts are inserted at random positions without using our dedicated prompt generator.

As shown in Table 2, both variants outperform the baseline models. Notably, the full FDBP achieves the highest average accuracy of 96.62%, improving upon HarmoFL [1] by 1.14%. Removing the structured prompter leads to a drop in performance (96.22% average accuracy), confirming the effectiveness of our prompt generation strategy in enhancing model generalization across clients.

These results underscore the significance of the prompter component in our framework, demonstrating that it effectively enhances generalization across heterogeneous client data. This improvement contributes substantially to the superior performance of FDBP in federated histology image classification.

4.6 Discussion

The above experimental results clearly demonstrate the effectiveness of the proposed method. A key component contributing to this success is the generative prompter, which plays a critical role in enhancing the model's adaptability and performance. Specifically, the generative prompter enables the model to efficiently learn and utilize task-specific information, acting as a bridge between the core model and the new tasks, thereby improving the overall generalization and effectiveness of the system.

In terms of the additional time overhead introduced by incorporating new network modules, we emphasize that our generative prompter is designed to be lightweight, only adding Cp^2 parameters. This makes the computational overhead introduced by the module negligible, ensuring that the overall system remains efficient and scalable even as new tasks or data are introduced.

Moreover, we acknowledge that the current design of the generative prompter is relatively simple, focusing on demonstrating the concept and its feasibility. Recognizing its pivotal role in the proposed method, we plan to further refine and expand the design of the generative prompter in future work. This includes exploring more sophisticated prompt generation schemes, and potentially incorporating dynamic, adaptive, or data-dependent prompt designs to further enhance task-specific adaptability and model performance.

5 Conclusion

This paper focuses on addressing issues such as heterogeneous client data distribution in collaborative training models for FL. It is found that many existing algorithms do not consider the characteristics of data from distributed clients. Therefore, a personalized visual prompt generator for image classification tasks was constructed to implicitly represent the local data information of clients and provide this information to local models to aid in completing classification tasks. Additionally, by using knowledge distillation, clients are assisted in learning global features to improve model generalization ability, enabling models trained in distributed environments to better adapt to different client data. This method effectively handles data heterogeneity in distributed learning. In comparative experiments with various algorithms, our method consistently achieved the best performance. Our future work will involve expanding this method to other tasks, such as image segmentation, and object recognition.

References

1. Jiang, M., Wang, Z., Dou, Q.: Harmofl: Harmonizing local and global drifts in federated learning on heterogeneous medical images. In: Proceedings of the AAAI Conference on Artificial Intelligence, vol. 36. https://doi.org/10.1609/aaai.v36i1.19993
2. Fu, S., Zhao, X., Yang, C., Fang, Z.: Data heterogeneous federated learning algorithm for industrial entity extraction. Displays **80**, 102504 (2023). https://doi.org/10.1016/j.displa.2023.102504
3. Du, J., et al.: Federated learning using model projection for multi-center disease diagnosis with non-IID data. Neural Networks **178**, 106409 (2024). https://doi.org/10.1016/j.neunet.2024.106409

4. Acar, D.A.E., Zhao, Y., Navarro, R.M., Mattina, M., Whatmough, P.N., Saligrama, V.: Federated learning based on dynamic regularization (2021)
5. Bahng, H., Jahanian, A., Sankaranarayanan, S., Isola, P.: Exploring visual prompts for adapting large-scale models (2022)
6. Bándi, P., et al.: From detection of individual metastases to classification of lymph node status at the patient level: the camelyon17 challenge. IEEE Trans. Med. Imaging **38**(2), 550–560 (2019). https://doi.org/10.1109/TMI.2018.2867350
7. Darlow, L.N., Crowley, E.J., Antoniou, A., Storkey, A.J.: Cinic-10 is not imagenet or cifar-10 (2018)
8. Jia, Y., et al.: Dapperfl: domain adaptive federated learning with model fusion pruning for edge devices. In: Globerson, A., et al. (eds.) Advances in Neural Information Processing Systems, vol. 37, pp. 13099–13123. Curran Associates, Inc. (2024)
9. Ju, L., Zhang, T., Toor, S., Hellander, A.: Accelerating fair federated learning: adaptive federated adam. IEEE Trans. Mach. Learn. Commun. Networking **2**, 1017–1032 (2024). https://doi.org/10.1109/TMLCN.2024.3423648
10. Karimireddy, S.P., Kale, S., Mohri, M., Reddi, S., Stich, S., Suresh, A.T.: SCAFFOLD: stochastic controlled averaging for federated learning. In: III, H.D., Singh, A. (eds.) Proceedings of the 37th International Conference on Machine Learning. Proceedings of Machine Learning Research, vol. 119, pp. 5132–5143. PMLR (2020)
11. Krizhevsky, A., Hinton, G., et al.: Learning multiple layers of features from tiny images (2009)
12. Lee, G., Jeong, M., Shin, Y., Bae, S., Yun, S.Y.: Preservation of the global knowledge by not-true distillation in federated learning. In: Koyejo, S., Mohamed, S., Agarwal, A., Belgrave, D., Cho, K., Oh, A. (eds.) Advances in Neural Information Processing Systems, vol. 35, pp. 38461–38474. Curran Associates, Inc. (2022)
13. Li, D., Wang, J.: FedMD: heterogenous federated learning via model distillation (2019)
14. Li, G., Wu, W., Sun, Y., Shen, L., Wu, B., Tao, D.: Visual prompt based personalized federated learning. Trans. Mach. Learn. Res. (2024)
15. Li, Q., He, B., Song, D.: Model-contrastive federated learning. In: Proceedings of the IEEE/CVF Conference on Computer Vision and Pattern Recognition (CVPR), pp. 10713–10722 (2021)
16. Li, T., Sahu, A.K., Zaheer, M., Sanjabi, M., Talwalkar, A., Smith, V.: Federated optimization in heterogeneous networks. In: Dhillon, I., Papailiopoulos, D., Sze, V. (eds.) Proceedings of Machine Learning and Systems, vol. 2, pp. 429–450 (2020)
17. Li, X., Jiang, M., Zhang, X., Kamp, M., Dou, Q.: FedBN: federated learning on non-IID features via local batch normalization (2021)
18. Liu, P., Yuan, W., Fu, J., Jiang, Z., Hayashi, H., Neubig, G.: Pre-train, prompt, and predict: a systematic survey of prompting methods in natural language processing. ACM Comput. Surv. **55**(9) (2023). https://doi.org/10.1145/3560815
19. McMahan, B., Moore, E., Ramage, D., Hampson, S., y Arcas, B.A.: Communication-efficient learning of deep networks from decentralized data. In: Singh, A., Zhu, J. (eds.) Proceedings of the 20th International Conference on Artificial Intelligence and Statistics. Proceedings of Machine Learning Research, vol. 54, pp. 1273–1282. PMLR (2017)
20. Peng, B., et al.: Correlation congruence for knowledge distillation. In: Proceedings of the IEEE/CVF International Conference on Computer Vision (ICCV) (2019)
21. Pillutla, K., Laguel, Y., Malick, J., Harchaoui, Z.: Federated learning with superquantile aggregation for heterogeneous data. Mach. Learn. **113**(5), 2955–3022 (2024)

22. Shoham, N., et al.: Overcoming forgetting in federated learning on non-IID data (2019)
23. Szegedy, C., Vanhoucke, V., Ioffe, S., Shlens, J., Wojna, Z.: Rethinking the inception architecture for computer vision. In: Proceedings of the IEEE Conference on Computer Vision and Pattern Recognition (CVPR) (2016)
24. Tan, A.Z., Yu, H., Cui, L., Yang, Q.: Towards personalized federated learning. IEEE Trans. Neural Networks Learn. Syst. **34**(12), 9587–9603 (2023). https://doi.org/10.1109/TNNLS.2022.3160699
25. Wang, J., Liu, Q., Liang, H., Joshi, G., Poor, H.V.: Tackling the objective inconsistency problem in heterogeneous federated optimization. In: Larochelle, H., Ranzato, M., Hadsell, R., Balcan, M., Lin, H. (eds.) Advances in Neural Information Processing Systems, vol. 33, pp. 7611–7623. Curran Associates, Inc. (2020)
26. Wang, K., Ding, Z., So, D.K.C., Ding, Z.: Age-of-information minimization in federated learning based networks with non-IID dataset. IEEE Trans. Wireless Commun. **23**(8), 8939–8953 (2024). https://doi.org/10.1109/TWC.2024.3357208
27. Yang, Z., Li, Z., Zeng, A., Li, Z., Yuan, C., Li, Y.: ViTKD: practical guidelines for vit feature knowledge distillation (2022)
28. Zhang, L., Shen, L., Ding, L., Tao, D., Duan, L.Y.: Fine-tuning global model via data-free knowledge distillation for non-IID federated learning. In: Proceedings of the IEEE/CVF Conference on Computer Vision and Pattern Recognition (CVPR), pp. 10174–10183 (2022)
29. Zhang, Q., Cheng, X., Chen, Y., Rao, Z.: Quantifying the knowledge in a DNN to explain knowledge distillation for classification. IEEE Trans. Pattern Anal. Mach. Intell. **45**(4), 5099–5113 (2023). https://doi.org/10.1109/TPAMI.2022.3200344
30. Zhao, B., Cui, Q., Song, R., Qiu, Y., Liang, J.: Decoupled knowledge distillation. In: Proceedings of the IEEE/CVF Conference on Computer Vision and Pattern Recognition (CVPR), pp. 11953–11962 (2022)
31. Zhou, Y., Pu, G., Ma, X., Li, X., Wu, D.: Distilled one-shot federated learning (2021)

Multi-stage Image Inpainting Method Based on Lightweight GAN Inversion

Xiaowen Zhang, Ting Wang(✉), and Hongyang Wang

Chengdu University of Information Technology, Chengdu 610225, Sichuan, China
wangting@cuit.edu.cn

Abstract. Image inpainting, as a crucial task in computer vision, continues to face challenges such as insufficient inpainting accuracy and high computational cost, particularly when dealing with large and complex missing regions. To address these issues, this paper proposes a multi-stage image inpainting method based on lightweight Generative Adversarial Network (GAN) inversion. Built upon a lightweight hypernetwork, the proposed approach incorporates a multi-stage encoded feature fusion strategy to enhance contextual information integration. Additionally, a diversity regularization network is designed to ensure structural and stylistic consistency between the restored regions and the original image. Extensive experiments on datasets such as CelebA-HQ and Places2 demonstrate the superior performance of our method. It not only outperforms existing approaches in terms of objective metrics and subjective visual quality but also significantly reduces model parameters and improves inference efficiency, offering strong practical value.

Keywords: Generative Adversarial Networks · Image Inpainting · GAN Inversion · Lightweight Architecture

1 Introduction

With the rapid development and widespread application of deep learning, particularly the emergence of generative adversarial network (GAN) [1] in the field of computer vision, image inpainting has made significant progress. GAN, known for their powerful generative capabilities, can automatically learn to produce images that conform to specific patterns from random noise. However, their standard operation remains inherently one-way, generating data from latent space without the ability to map real data back to it. To overcome this limitation, GAN inversion reverses the process by taking real data such as an image and mapping it into the GAN's latent space. This identifies the corresponding latent code that enables the generator to reconstruct the original input, effectively bridging the gap between generation and analysis while allowing bidirectional data manipulation. Among various latent representations, the $\mathcal{W}$ and W^+ spaces in StyleGAN [2] are particularly notable. Unlike traditional approaches,

© The Author(s), under exclusive license to Springer Nature Singapore Pte Ltd. 2026
J. Kittler et al. (Eds.): PRCV 2025, LNCS 16289, pp. 244–258, 2026.
https://doi.org/10.1007/978-981-95-5764-6_17

GAN inversion-based inpainting methods [3] are capable of preserving contextual and structural information more effectively. They generate visually natural and semantically coherent results by leveraging both global structure and local texture features. However, most existing methods rely on iterative optimization to retrieve the most suitable latent code. Although these approaches offer high accuracy, they incur substantial computational overhead and result in long inference times. These observations highlight two major limitations in current inpainting approaches, namely, poor inpainting performance in large-area damaged regions and the trade-off between inpainting accuracy and computational efficiency.

To address these challenges, we propose a multi-stage image inpainting method based on lightweight GAN inversion. The method employs a lightweight hypernetwork to achieve accurate and natural inpainting while maintaining computational efficiency. To maximize the recovery of feature information from damaged regions, a multi-stage encoding feature fusion strategy is introduced, which integrates semantic features from visible regions through a multi-level residual convolutional network and a dynamic gating mechanism. Additionally, a diversity regularization network, incorporating ResNet-style skip connections [4], is designed to ensure stylistic and structural consistency between restored and intact regions.

The effectiveness of the proposed method is validated on several public benchmark datasets. Experimental results show that it consistently outperforms existing mainstream methods in both objective metrics and subjective visual quality. Moreover, the proposed framework significantly reduces the number of parameters, thereby enhancing inference speed and practical applicability.

The main contributions of this work are as follows.

- A lightweight hypernetwork is introduced that effectively reduces model complexity while maintaining high inpainting quality.
- A multi-stage encoded feature fusion strategy is proposed to enhance the reconstruction of complex structures and large-area damaged regions.
- A diversity regularization network is designed to enable high-quality and flexible style inpainting.
- The proposed model is shown to exhibit excellent fidelity and reconstruction performance in both qualitative and quantitative evaluations.

2 Related Works

2.1 Image Inpainting Method Based On GAN Inversion

Traditional image inpainting algorithms, such as block matching-based methods [5], can maintain local texture consistency, but struggle to reconstruct coherent global semantic structures. The reliance of CNN-based approaches on low-dimensional bottleneck features often leads to the loss of high-frequency details. As a result, the inpainting regions may exhibit blurry textures or semantic inconsistencies [6]. To mitigate these limitations, recent deep learning approaches have introduced attention mechanisms and Transformer architectures to enhance feature representation. However, they are limited by the deterministic coding mode, making it difficult to generate diverse and reasonable inpainting results in situations involving large-area occlusion and other situations [7].

In contrast, the deep feature space of GANs exhibits unique semantic disentanglement properties. For instance, intermediate layers of StyleGAN encode fine-grained textures, such as hair orientation, while its latent space governs global attributes like age or facial pose [8]. These characteristics have inspired GAN inversion-based inpainting methods, which project damaged images into the latent space of a pretrained generator and utilize its learned priors to reconstruct semantically plausible content. Yu et al. [9] achieved detail-level inpainting by optimizing multi-scale latent codes under perceptual loss constraints. However, this approach suffers from high computational overhead. To address this limitation, Wang et al. [10] introduced a dual-path collaborative framework that integrates a primary inpainting network with an auxiliary inversion network. This design ensures that the restored content aligns not only with local contextual cues but also with the global distribution learned by the generative model.

As the boundaries of generative techniques continue to expand, research has shifted from pure inpainting toward more diverse and controllable generation tasks. These scenarios require not only preserving the integrity of original content but also imaginatively expanding beyond it, placing higher demands on the controllability of generation models. For example, Cheng et al. [11] proposed a latent space diversity enhancement strategy that inverts input images into the latent space of BigGAN, and manipulates latent codes along specific semantic directions to generate multiple contextually consistent extrapolations.

2.2 Hypernetwork

Previous GAN inversion usually uses an encoder to map the input image feature information to the specified latent space to generate the initial latent code, and then optimizes the latent code through different optimization algorithms, so as to balance the quality of the inverted image and the computational efficiency of the model [12]. For instance, the IDInvert framework [13] and the PTI framework [14] have enhanced the quality of image inversion and semantic preservation capabilities. Despite this, such methods require the simultaneous training of encoders and optimization algorithms, and each image needs to be optimized or fine-tuned. Therefore, a large number of parameters need to be processed, the implementation complexity is relatively high, and there is a relatively high computational cost.

In GAN inversion tasks, deep learning frameworks with non-shared parameters offer high representation performance, but at the cost of increased parameter count and computational overhead. In contrast, parameter sharing can significantly reduce the number of model parameters, but may limit the representational capacity of the network. Hypernetworks, which generate the parameters of a larger network using a smaller network, provide a trade-off between shared and non-shared parameter paradigms. Originally introduced as neural networks that output the weights of another target network [15], hypernetworks offer a promising solution to alleviate the issue of excessive model parameters.

In the context of GAN inversion, hypernetworks are introduced to optimize the latent code processing stage, thereby improving the semantic consistency and reconstruction accuracy of the inversion results. However, conventional hypernetwork designs often suffer from high computational and memory costs, as they typically generate weights for each convolutional layer of the generator. This design introduces considerable redundancy in both spatial and channel dimensions, leading to large parameter sizes and inefficient inference.

To address these issues, we propose a lightweight hypernetwork architecture that efficiently learns the variation patterns of image attributes while reducing redundant computational overhead. This approach significantly improves the inversion efficiency and scalability while maintaining the expressive capacity of the model.

3 Method

In our paper, we proposed a multi-stage image inpainting method based on lightweight GAN inversion. The model structure is shown in Fig. 1. First, the damaged image is input into an encoder and mapped to the W^+ latent space of StyleGAN to extract semantic features [16]. The encoder adopts a feature pyramid structure and can extract image features at different levels, which correspond to the coarse, medium, and fine features in StyleGAN. At the same time, a diversified regularization network is designed, as shown in Fig. 1.d. First, random noise is sampled from the Gaussian distribution $z \sim N(0, 1)$ and inputted into the generator G after processing by the mapper to generate an initial random image. Subsequently, the image and the random mask generate a damaged image. Finally, the damaged image, random mask and random noise are simultaneously input into the encoder E for processing to obtain a random latent code W^r. Next, the encoded features W^h and the random latent code W^r after dynamic fusion by the lightweight hypernetwork are aligned through the intermediate reconstruction network to drive the StyleGAN generator to output the initial inpainting image. Finally, the generated content is seamlessly merged with the undamaged area of the original image marked by the mask through the unmasking operation to form a high-quality inpainting result. Next, we will provide a detailed description of our method specifics.

3.1 Multi-stage Coding Feature Fusion Strategy

To obtain semantically richer and spatially finer feature representations, a multi-stage encoded feature fusion strategy is proposed. As shown in Fig. 1.a, during the initial phase, the input image I is element-wise multiplied with a binary mask M and normalized to generate the damaged image I_D. Then, we used our previously proposed lightweight hypernetwork to map the damaged image into the

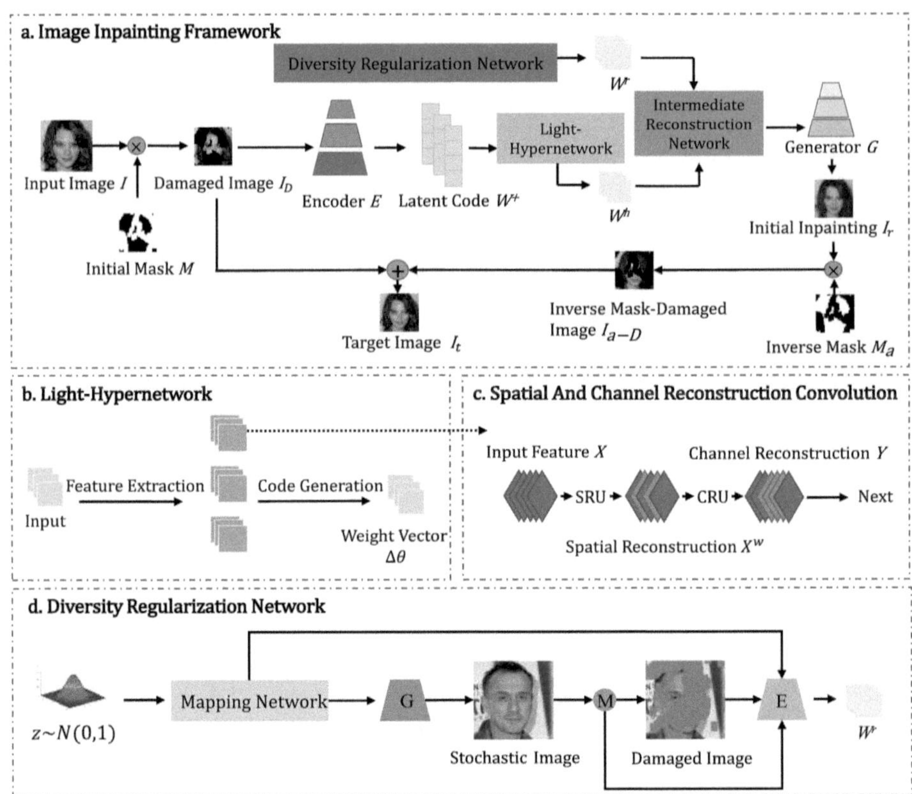

Fig. 1. Overview of the proposed multi-stage image inpainting framework based on lightweight GAN inversion.

W^+ latent space of StyleGAN to obtain an accurate latent space representation in a short time.

In the middle stage, an intermediate reconstruction module is designed in the middle to obtain more accurate visible information about the damaged image, as shown in Fig. 2. It consists of a multi-level residual convolutional encoder coupled with a dynamic gating mechanism. As depicted in Fig. 2.a, the multi-level residual convolutional encoder consists of four convolutional layers, grouped into two residual sub-blocks via skip connections. Each sub-block preserves the original feature representations while introducing localized enhancements. The two sub-blocks are subsequently merged into a secondary residual block through hierarchical residual aggregation, facilitating progressive inpainting of missing regions and fidelity preservation of intact content.

To enable more effective feature fusion, a dynamic gating mechanism is introduced. As illustrated in Fig. 2.b, given an input feature map x, a learnable gating matrix $k \in R^{C \times H \times W}$ is computed to adaptively assign spatially varying weights based on the input content. At the same time, by introducing a loss function to constrain the alignment between the generated features and the true distribution, combined with adversarial training to enhance the ability to generate high-frequency details, it is ensured that in the feature reconstruction process of the damaged area, the missing information can be effectively filled, and the fused features remain semantically consistent.

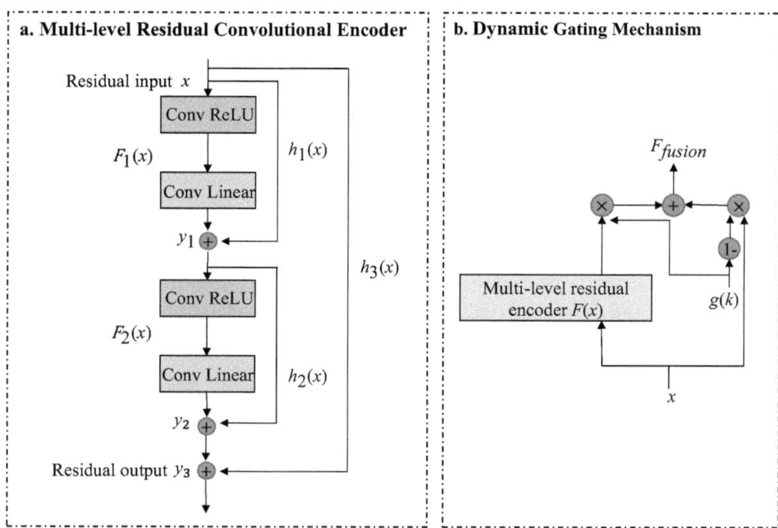

Fig. 2. The flowchart of the intermediate reconstruction module. This module contains a multi-level residual convolution module and a dynamic gating mechanism. **a.** Given an input x, the residual function $F_i(x)$ outputs y_1 and y_2, and y_3 represents the final residual feature, which combines fine-grained details and high-level semantic features. **b.** F_{fusion} represents the fusion feature of the final output, and $F(x)$ is the potential encoding feature tensor mapped by the residual encoder.

3.2 Lightweight Hypernetwork

To reduce the overall model complexity while maintaining the quality of image inpainting, a lightweight hypernetwork was designed in the overall framework based on the design idea of a low-parameter GAN inversion framework based on a hypernetwork proposed in our previous work [17]. This hypernetwork learns residual weight perturbations to update convolutional layers in the pretrained StyleGAN generator. Denoting the convolutional weights as $\theta_{conv} = (\theta_1, \ldots, \theta_N)$, the hypernetwork predicts residuals $\Delta\theta_j$ for each layer j (Eq. (1)). W_z and b_z are the weights and bias parameters of the hypernetwork. W_o and b_o are the weights and bias parameters used to generate the network parameters of this framework. The updated generator weights are denoted as $\widehat{\theta}_{conv} = (\theta_1 + \Delta\theta_1, \ldots, \theta_N + \Delta\theta_N)$.

$$\Delta\theta_j = H(z) = W_o \cdot \text{ReLU}\left(W_z \cdot z + b_z\right) + b_o \tag{1}$$

Prior to weight computation, identity-specific features are extracted to enhance facial domain representation. ArcFace [18] is used to capture the identity features of the face. It is concatenated with the input initial latent code W^+ and finally outputs the feature map f_c where c represents the input channel.

To enhance computational efficiency, a set of multi-channel parallel computation modules is incorporated following the feature map extraction stage, as shown in Fig. 1.b. As shown in Eq. (2), a shared parameter set w_i is utilized across N channels, enabling simultaneous processing of multiple feature maps through parallel operations. This parallel structure not only accelerates the computation by exploiting concurrency but also introduces parameter sharing, which significantly reduces the number of trainable parameters.

$$\Delta\theta = \sum_{i=1}^{N} (f_c \odot w_i) \tag{2}$$

To further mitigate feature redundancy, SCConv is referenced in the design of the hypernetwork, which comprises a Spatial Reconstruction Unit (SRU) and a Channel Reconstruction Unit (CRU). As shown in Fig. 1.c, given the feature X, the SRU is used to separate and reconstruct the features to obtain spatially refined features X^W. X^W is the feature information after fusing the features with higher and lower information content through cross reconstruction. Subsequently, the CRU performs a channel-wise splitting operation on the spatially refined feature X^W, dividing it into two subgroups and performing a transformation operation. In the final step, a fusion operation is performed to further eliminate channel redundancy and produce the final reconstructed feature representation Y.

3.3 Diversity Regularization Network

To achieve high-quality inpainting with diverse style variations, we design a diversity regularization network that leverages StyleGAN's latent space manipulation capabilities. By integrating this network with a skip connection mechanism [4], our approach not only enhances seamless blending between damaged and intact regions but also preserves the image's structural coherence while enabling rich style diversification. In this network, random noise z is input into the mapping network of StyleGAN, and then the KL divergence regularization term is introduced at the end to constrain the latent code W_{rand} to follow the standard normal distribution. The formula is shown in (3).

$$W_{rand} = \lambda_I \cdot KL\left(f_{mapper}(z) \| N(0, I)\right) \tag{3}$$

Among them, λ_1 is a hyperparameter that controls the weight of the regularization term. The function $f_{mapper}(z)$ maps the input random noise z to a latent code for subsequent image generation. Here, $N(0, I)$ represents a standard normal distribution with zero mean and identity covariance matrix I.

After generating the initial image, a random binary mask is applied to simulate image corruption. The structural features of the visible region are extracted by an encoder network and encoded into a content-aware latent representation, W_{encode}, which ensures the preservation of structural information during the inpainting. Notably, the dimensionality of W_{encode} is kept consistent with that of W_{rand}.

To achieve a balance between structure and style, we adaptively combine the style-constrained latent code W_{rand} with the structure-constrained latent code W_{encode}, resulting in a fused latent code W^r that integrates multiple style vectors, as defined in Eq. (4).

$$W^r = \alpha \cdot W_{\text{rand}} + (1 - \alpha)W_{\text{encode}} \tag{4}$$

Among them, the parameter α controls the contribution ratio of style and structure. Adjusting α, the stylization degree and structural fidelity of the inpainting result can be flexibly controlled. At the same time, in order to further solve the problem of seamless transition between damaged pixels and undamaged pixels in large-area damaged images, an encoder with a skip connection mechanism with the StyleGAN generator is trained by drawing on the skip connection idea of ResNet. The encoder can directly pass detailed features to enhance the image inpainting effect.

3.4 Loss Function

In our training process, we use a conventional combination of inpainting losses to ensure the accuracy of the restored pixels and the subjective perceptual quality of the image as defined in Eq. 5.

$$L = \lambda_{rec}L_{rec} + \lambda_{per}L_{per} + \lambda_{adv}L_{adv} + \lambda_{style}L_{style} \tag{5}$$

The reconstruction loss L_{rec} [19] is used to measure the pixel difference between the inpainting image and the original image. The perceptual loss L_{per} [20] is used to measure the difference in high-level semantic information between the restored image and the real image in the feature space. The adversarial loss L_{adv} [1] is used to guide the model output towards images that match the distribution of real images. The style loss L_{style} [21] is a loss function used to measure the style similarity of two images.

4 Experiment

4.1 Datasets And Indicators

For the face domain, we utilize the CelebA-HQ dataset [22], which consists of 30,000 high-resolution facial images with a resolution of 1024×1024. For natural scene inpainting, we introduce the Places2 dataset [23], covering 401 indoor and outdoor scene categories, each containing 5,000 to 30,000 samples.

Given the high complexity and annotation cost of real-world image degradation, this study adopts a mask synthesis strategy to construct the training dataset. The masks are sourced from the publicly released PConv dataset by

NVIDIA [24], which serves as the first standardized mask repository for irregular image inpainting.

Frechet Inception Distance (FID) [25], structural Similarity Index (SSIM) [26], Learning-based Perceptual Image Patch Similarity (LPIPS) [27] and Peak Signal-to-Noise Ratio (PSNR) [26], are used to quantitatively evaluate the image inpainting effect. Among them, FID measures the distribution difference between the generated image and the real image. SSIM reflects the structural similarity. LPIPS evaluates visual quality through perceptual features. PSNR measures the pixel difference and provides a logarithmic scale of the signal strength to noise ratio. The last three additional comparison indicators are runtime (Times), floating point operations (FLOPs), and number of overall model parameters (Params) under the Ubuntu 20.04 LTS system (using a single NVIDIA RTX A5000).

4.2 Baseline

To evaluate the performance of the proposed method in the field of image inpainting, the following five representative baselines were selected for comparison.

- LaMa [7] uses a lightweight U-Net structure, combined with Fourier convolution and gated convolution, to capture global information and enhance the learning ability of local features.
- CMT [28] uses the Transformer structure to gradually fill in missing areas through a continuous mask mechanism.
- CoordFill [29] models image inpainting as a mapping learning from coordinates to pixel values, and introduces a local implicit function and a multi-scale feature fusion mechanism.
- InvertFill [30] designs a new latent space based on GAN inversion, and proposes a pre-modulation network structure to enhance the semantic expression ability of the style vector using multi-scale reconstruction features.
- InViT [31] combines GAN inversion technology and Vision Transformer to restore missing content and capture global context information.
- ConFill [32] incorporates a Context-Adaptive Discrepancy (CAD) model. CAD enforces alignment between the intermediate distributions of known and unknown regions during the diffusion process, thereby progressively reducing discrepancies between generated and original images at each step and achieving contextually consistent completion.

4.3 Comparative Experiments

We conducted qualitative and quantitative comparisons of our method against others. The images were combined with mask images with occlusion ranges of 0%–20%, 20%–40%, and 40%–60% to generate damaged images for testing.

It is obvious from the numerical results in Table 1 that the overall performance of our method on the CelebA-HQ dataset and the Places2 dataset is

Fig. 3. Subjective comparison of inpainting results of different methods on the CelebA-HQ dataset.

better than that of other comparison methods. Specifically, on the CelebA-HQ dataset, LaMa restores overall image quality well under moderate damage but struggles with local structural consistency. CMT handles small-scale damage effectively, yet exhibits distribution mismatch with real images. CoordFill lacks global consistency under large occlusions. InvertFill fails to preserve structural and perceptual quality in complex scenes. InViT's performance drops significantly on large damaged areas.

As illustrated in Fig. 3, LaMa and CMT exhibit notable structural distortion when reconstructing key attributes such as eyes and facial symmetry under severe corruption. While CoordFill, InvertFill, and InViT yield visually plausible results at a coarse level, they fail to recover fine-grained details including hair texture and expression alignment. In contrast, our method preserves both global semantics and local fidelity, producing visually coherent and semantically consistent inpainting results.

Furthermore, the results on the Places2 dataset (Table 1, Fig. 4) demonstrate that our approach generalizes well beyond facial imagery. Even in diverse natural scenes with complex large-area corruption, the model restores textures and layouts that align with the original scene semantics, highlighting its robustness and scalability across domains.

4.4 Model Complexity Analysis

This section presents a comparative analysis of model complexity between the proposed image inpainting method and other GAN inversion-based inpainting approaches. The comparison focuses on three key aspects, including the number of parameters (Params), floating point operations (FLOPs), and inference

Fig. 4. Subjective comparison of inpainting results of different methods on the Places2 dataset.

time (Times). To ensure consistency across all experiments, evaluations were conducted using the same hardware environment with an NVIDIA A5000 GPU (24 GB memory). The detailed statistics are summarized in Table 2.

Based on Table 2 and the experiments, the proposed method reduces parameters, floating point operations, and inference time compared to traditional GAN inversion-based inpainting methods. This improved efficiency allows more tasks to be processed on the same hardware, making the method well-suited for scenarios requiring low latency and high performance. This was also proved in the subsequent ablation experiments.

4.5 Ablation Study

To evaluate the effectiveness of the proposed lightweight GAN inversion-based multi-stage image inpainting method, we conduct ablation studies on the CelebA-HQ dataset with mask ratios between 40% and 60% and adopted the same experimental settings as the comparative experiments. Three ablation experiments were designed as follows. (1) replacing the lightweight hypernetwork with a basic GAN inversion module (w/o light-hyper), (2) replacing the intermediate generation and reconstruction modules with the traditional StyleGAN generator (w/o gen-rec), and (3) eliminating the diversity regularization network (w/o diversity-net).

As shown in Table 3, our method achieves the best performance across all metrics, demonstrating improvements in both generation quality and computational efficiency. Among the three ablation settings, removing the intermediate generation module leads to the most significant degradation, with PSNR and SSIM dropping sharply, which highlights its crucial role in feature reconstruction

Table 1. Objective comparison of the inpainting results of different methods on the CelebA-HQ dataset and Places2 dataset. ↓ Indicates that lower values are better, while ↑ signifies that higher values are better.

Dataset	Indicators	Mask ratios	Methods						
			LaMa	CMT	CoordFill	InvertFill	InViT	ConFill	Ours
CelebA-HQ	FID ↓	0%–20%	6.572	9.547	7.563	7.712	6.550	7.08	**6.193**
		20%–40%	8.647	12.952	8.862	9.86	12.748	8.13	**7.451**
		40%–60%	21.445	22.306	20.974	21.54	22.673	**12.94**	20.827
	SSIM ↑	0%–20%	0.923	0.961	0.976	0.902	0.982	0.896	**0.987**
		20%–40%	0.852	0.907	0.872	0.819	0.915	0.854	**0.928**
		40%–60%	0.838	0.873	0.816	0.654	0.830	0.735	**0.894**
	LPIPS ↓	0%-20%	0.114	0.083	0.058	0.096	0.052	**0.034**	0.045
		20%–40%	0.137	0.117	0.107	0.127	0.120	**0.076**	0.077
		40%–60%	0.198	0.174	0.145	0.213	0.139	0.187	**0.132**
	PSNR ↑	0%–20%	32.533	33.446	33.286	34.628	35.011	-	**35.812**
		20%–40%	28.918	30.059	20.603	31.547	28.273	-	**33.822**
		40%–60%	24.365	25.492	25.624	27.163	23.992	-	**27.297**
Places2	FID ↓	0%-20%	13.212	4.881	5.492	9.294	5.962	8.91	**4.271**
		20%–40%	17.367	15.705	14.892	12.446	9.972	10.39	**8.208**
		40%–60%	25.844	33.194	27.365	22.363	28.890	**14.02**	21.084
	SSIM ↑	0%–20%	0.952	0.960	0.983	0.866	0.971	0.847	**0.987**
		20%–40%	0.873	0.869	0.895	0.749	0.888	0.812	**0.914**
		40%–60%	0.860	0.742	0.842	0.670	0.749	0.663	**0.872**
	LPIPS ↓	0%–20%	0.145	0.026	0.036	0.163	0.028	0.063	**0.021**
		20%–40%	0.123	0.128	0.084	0.235	0.096	0.120	**0.067**
		40%–60%	0.217	0.277	0.145	0.393	0.217	0.270	**0.128**
	PSNR ↑	0%–20%	32.165	33.651	29.627	31.051	34.126	-	**38.584**
		20%–40%	28.626	25.569	23.924	28.977	26.391	-	**29.750**
		40%–60%	25.410	21.136	22.076	24.822	21.663	-	**25.856**

Table 2. Objective comparison of the inpainting results of different methods on the CelebA-HQ dataset. ↓ Indicates that lower values are better.

Methods	Params (M) ↓	FLOPs (G) ↓	Times (s) ↓
InViT	89.6	183.11	0.23
InvertFill	105.9	235.95	0.41
Ours	**53.6**	**102.73**	**0.11**

and detail completion. Most importantly, removing the diversity regularization network causes a clear decline in perceptual and fidelity metrics, such as LPIPS and FID. To provide a more intuitive comparison, Fig. 5 presents representative

Table 3. Ablation experiment analysis. ↓ Indicates that lower values are better, while ↑ signifies that higher values are better.

Indicators	w/o light-hyper	w/o gen-rec	w/o diversity-net	Ours
LPIPS ↓	0.142	0.185	0.143	**0.136**
FID ↓	24.318	38.623	22.519	**20.822**
PSNR ↑	26.723	25.167	27.044	**27.296**
SSIM ↑	0.830	0.889	0.871	**0.894**
Params (M) ↓	96.7	-	-	**53.6**
FLOPS (G) ↓	214.41	-	-	**102.79**
Times (s) ↓	0.34	-	-	**0.11**

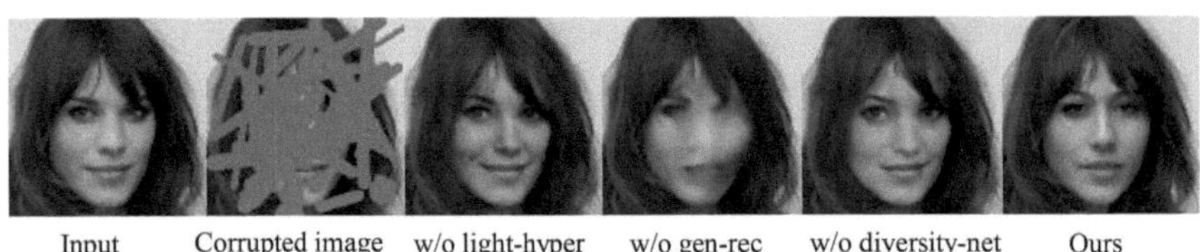

Fig. 5. Subjective comparison chart of ablation experiment.

subjective results. It can be observed that, while methods without the diversity regularization network produce relatively monotonous restorations, our method is able to generate results with distinct style tendencies in attributes such as skin tone and facial detail, while still maintaining structural consistency. This confirms that diversity regularization network plays a central role in controlling and enriching the stylistic attributes of the restored images.

5 Conclusion

This paper proposes a multi-stage image inpainting method based on a low-parameter GAN inversion framework, aiming to solve the problems of low inpainting quality and high computational resource consumption of existing methods when dealing with large and complex defect areas. By introducing a lightweight hypernetwork module, the parameter scale of the model is effectively compressed while maintaining high-fidelity semantic expression capabilities. A multi-stage encoding feature fusion module and a diversified regularization network are designed to enhance the semantic consistency and structural continuity in the inpainting task, so that the inpainting results have both structural fidelity and style diversity. Experimental results on the CelebA-HQ and Places2 datasets show that this method outperforms existing mainstream image inpainting methods in multiple evaluation indicators, while significantly reducing the number of model parameters and inference time, verifying its effective balance between inpainting quality and model efficiency. Future work will further explore the versatility and scalability of this framework in a wider range of scenarios.

Acknowledgments. This work was supported by the West Light Foundation of Chinese Academy of Sciences (Grant No. 202316), the key research and development project of Sichuan Provincial Department of Science and Technology (Grant No. 2024YFG00 12), and the demonstration Project for the Transfer and Transformation of Scientific and Technological Achievements in Sichuan Province (Grant No. 2024ZHCG0 027).

References

1. Goodfellow, I.J., et al.: Generative adversarial nets. In: Advances in Neural Information Processing Systems, vol. 27 (2014)
2. Karras, T., Laine, S., Aittala, M., Hellsten, J., Lehtinen, J., Aila, T.: Analyzing and improving the image quality of styleGAN. In: Proceedings of the IEEE/CVF Conference on Computer Vision and Pattern Recognition, pp. 8110–8119 (2020)
3. Lahiri, A., Jain, A.K., Agrawal, S., Mitra, P., Biswas, P.K.: Prior guided GAN based semantic inpainting. In: Proceedings of the IEEE/CVF Conference on Computer Vision and Pattern Recognition, pp. 13696–13705 (2020)
4. He, K., Zhang, X., Ren, S., Sun, J.: Deep residual learning for image recognition. In: Proceedings of the IEEE Conference on Computer Vision and Pattern Recognition, pp. 770–778 (2016)
5. Barnes, C., Shechtman, E., Finkelstein, A., Goldman, D.B.: Patchmatch: a randomized correspondence algorithm for structural image editing. ACM Trans. Graph. **28**(3), 24 (2009)
6. Li, J., Wang, N., Zhang, L., Du, B., Tao, D.: Recurrent feature reasoning for image inpainting. In: Proceedings of the IEEE/CVF Conference on Computer Vision and Pattern Recognition, pp. 7760–7768 (2020)
7. Suvorov, R., et al.: Resolution-robust large mask inpainting with Fourier convolutions. In: Proceedings of the IEEE/CVF Winter Conference on Applications of Computer Vision, pp. 2149–2159 (2022)
8. Xia, W., Zhang, Y., Yang, Y., Xue, J.H., Zhou, B., Yang, M.H.: Gan inversion: a survey. IEEE Trans. Pattern Anal. Mach. Intell. **45**(3), 3121–3138 (2022)
9. Yu, J., Lin, Z., Yang, J., Shen, X., Lu, X., Huang, T.S.: Generative image inpainting with contextual attention. In: Proceedings of the IEEE Conference on Computer Vision and Pattern Recognition, pp. 5505–5514 (2018)
10. Wang, W., Niu, L., Zhang, J., Yang, X., Zhang, L.: Dual-path image inpainting with auxiliary GAN inversion. In: Proceedings of the IEEE/CVF Conference on Computer Vision and Pattern Recognition, pp. 11421–11430 (2022)
11. Cheng, Y.C., Lin, C.H., Lee, H.Y., Ren, J., Tulyakov, S., Yang, M.H.: Inout: diverse image outpainting via GAN inversion. In: Proceedings of the IEEE/CVF Conference on Computer Vision and Pattern Recognition, pp. 11431–11440 (2022)
12. Bau, D., et al.: Inverting layers of a large generator. In: ICLR workshop, vol. 2, p. 4 (2019)
13. Zhu, J., Shen, Y., Zhao, D., Zhou, B.: In-domain GAN inversion for real image editing. In: Vedaldi, A., Bischof, H., Brox, T., Frahm, J.-M. (eds.) ECCV 2020. LNCS, vol. 12362, pp. 592–608. Springer, Cham (2020). https://doi.org/10.1007/978-3-030-58520-4_35
14. Roich, D., Mokady, R., Bermano, A.H., Cohen-Or, D.: Pivotal tuning for latent-based editing of real images. ACM Trans. Graph. (TOG) **42**(1), 1–13 (2022)

15. Ha, D., Dai, A., Le, Q.V.: Hypernetworks. arXiv preprint arXiv:1609.09106 (2016)
16. Karras, T., Laine, S., Aila, T.: A style-based generator architecture for generative adversarial networks. In: Proceedings of the IEEE/CVF Conference on Computer Vision and Pattern Recognition, pp. 4401–4410 (2019)
17. Wang, H., Wang, T., Xiang, D., Yang, W., Li, J.: Low-parameter GAN inversion framework based on hypernetwork. Multimedia Syst. **30**(4), 181 (2024)
18. Deng, J., Guo, J., Xue, N., Zafeiriou, S.: ArcFace: additive angular margin loss for deep face recognition. In: Proceedings of the IEEE/CVF Conference on Computer Vision and Pattern Recognition, pp. 4690–4699 (2019)
19. Zhao, H., Gallo, O., Frosio, I., Kautz, J.: Loss functions for image restoration with neural networks. IEEE Trans. Comput. Imaging **3**(1), 47–57 (2016)
20. Johnson, J., Alahi, A., Fei-Fei, L.: Perceptual losses for real-time style transfer and super-resolution. In: Leibe, B., Matas, J., Sebe, N., Welling, M. (eds.) ECCV 2016. LNCS, vol. 9906, pp. 694–711. Springer, Cham (2016). https://doi.org/10.1007/978-3-319-46475-6_43
21. Gatys, L.A., Ecker, A.S., Bethge, M.: A neural algorithm of artistic style. arXiv preprint arXiv:1508.06576 (2015)
22. Karras, T., Aila, T., Laine, S., Lehtinen, J.: Progressive growing of GANs for improved quality, stability, and variation. arXiv preprint arXiv:1710.10196 (2017)
23. Zhou, B., Lapedriza, A., Khosla, A., Oliva, A., Torralba, A.: Places: a 10 million image database for scene recognition. IEEE Trans. Pattern Anal. Mach. Intell. **40**(6), 1452–1464 (2017)
24. Liu, G., Reda, F.A., Shih, K.J., Wang, T.-C., Tao, A., Catanzaro, B.: Image inpainting for irregular holes using partial convolutions. In: Ferrari, V., Hebert, M., Sminchisescu, C., Weiss, Y. (eds.) ECCV 2018. LNCS, vol. 11215, pp. 89–105. Springer, Cham (2018). https://doi.org/10.1007/978-3-030-01252-6_6
25. Heusel, M., Ramsauer, H., Unterthiner, T., Nessler, B., Hochreiter, S.: GANs trained by a two time-scale update rule converge to a local Nash equilibrium. In: Advances in Neural Information Processing Systems, vol. 30 (2017)
26. Wang, Z., Bovik, A.C., Sheikh, H.R., Simoncelli, E.P.: Image quality assessment: from error visibility to structural similarity. IEEE Trans. Image Process. **13**(4), 600–612 (2004)
27. Zhang, R., Isola, P., Efros, A.A., Shechtman, E., Wang, O.: The unreasonable effectiveness of deep features as a perceptual metric. In: Proceedings of the IEEE Conference on Computer Vision and Pattern Recognition, pp. 586–595 (2018)
28. Ko, K., Kim, C.S.: Continuously masked transformer for image inpainting. In: Proceedings of the IEEE/CVF International Conference on Computer Vision, pp. 13169–13178 (2023)
29. Liu, W., Cun, X., Pun, C.M., Xia, M., Zhang, Y., Wang, J.: Coordfill: efficient high-resolution image inpainting via parameterized coordinate querying. In: Proceedings of the AAAI Conference on Artificial Intelligence, vol. 37, pp. 1746–1754 (2023)
30. Yu, Y., Zhang, L., Fan, H., Luo, T.: High-fidelity image inpainting with GAN inversion. In: Avidan, S., Brostow, G., Cissé, M., Farinella, G.M., Hassner, T. (eds.) ECCV 2022. LNCS, vol. 13676, pp. 242–258. Springer, Cham (2022). https://doi.org/10.1007/978-3-031-19787-1_14
31. Du, Y., Liu, H., He, S., Chen, S.: InViT: GAN inversion-based vision transformer for blind image inpainting. IEEE Access (2024)
32. Shamsolmoali, P., Zareapoor, M., Zhou, H., Felsberg, M., Tao, D., Li, X.: From missing pieces to masterpieces: image completion with context-adaptive diffusion. IEEE Trans. Pattern Anal. Mach. Intell. (2025)

Neural Collapse Violated: Why Dirty-Label Backdoor Samples Stand Out in Feature Space

Youjun Wang(✉)

School of Computer Science, Wuhan University, Wuhan 430072, China
youjunw1208@gmail.com

Abstract. Backdoor poisoning attacks (BPAs) compromise deep neural networks by creating poisoned training sets where adversaries strategically target a specific class. Models trained on such data correctly classify clean inputs but misclassify any trigger-embedded input as the targeted label. We expose a critical phenomenon contradicting Neural Collapse (NC): poisoned samples in dirty-label BPAs fail to collapse with genuine samples of their assigned target class, violating NC's core principle of intra-class variability collapse. Across diverse dirty-label attacks, our experiments show poisoned features persistently form distinct subclusters or outliers instead of merging into the clean target cluster. This inherent separation drastically reduces attack stealthiness, exposing poisoned samples as feature-space anomalies detectable by existing defenses. We provide a theoretical explanation for the phenomenon.

Keywords: Backdoor attack · Neural collapse

1 Introduction

Deep neural networks have achieved impressive performance in fields ranging from computer vision to natural language processing [4,14,28,31]. However, deep neural networks exhibit critical vulnerabilities to adversarial attacks, including adversarial examples [11,29] and data poisoning [3,22]. As deep learning is being increasingly applied in safety-critical scenarios where incorrect decisions may lead to serious consequences, ensuring the security and reliability of such systems has become a major concern [7].

The growing prominence of backdoor poisoning attacks (BPA), which exploit the model's learning mechanisms, further emphasizes the importance of building robust and trustworthy deep learning systems. BPA, especially dirty-label attacks can successfully compromise a model by merely adding a small partition of poisoned data to the training set. Dirty-label attacks insert crafted training samples containing specific triggers, such as square patches, and label them with a particular target class [12]. This leads a DNN trained on the poisoned dataset to capture not only the genuine patterns in the original data but also the fabricated

© The Author(s), under exclusive license to Springer Nature Singapore Pte Ltd. 2026
J. Kittler et al. (Eds.): PRCV 2025, LNCS 16289, pp. 259–270, 2026.
https://doi.org/10.1007/978-981-95-5764-6_18

association between the triggered samples and the designated target class. Consequently, the DNN exhibits malicious behavior when encountering test inputs containing the trigger, while continuing to perform normally on inputs without the trigger.

A wide range of methods have been proposed to improve the stealthiness of trigger samples and reduce their detectability in dirty-label attacks. Blended [6] introduces triggers by blending a translucent pattern into the entire image, making the trigger less visually salient while still effective. SIG [2] applies a sinusoidal signal perturbation to the image in the frequency domain, which remains imperceptible to the human eye but is easily recognized by the model. Additionally, Input-aware triggers [25] generate trigger patterns that adapt to the content of each image, thereby avoiding fixed or easily detectable patterns. Poison Ink [42] leverages imperceptible perturbations in the form of local texture alterations resembling real-world noise, effectively disguising the trigger as a natural image imperfection.

Neural collapse (NC) is a widely observed phenomenon during the terminal phase of neural network training [26]. According to the theory of NC [8,23], during standard training, the features of samples from the same class tend to converge to a common cluster, while features from different classes remain well separated. Although many previous works have focused on improving the stealthiness of trigger samples and reducing their detectability in dirty-label attacks, we observe that these attack methods commonly violate the principles of neural collapse. Specifically, the feature activations of poisoned samples are often noticeably distant from the clean feature cluster of the targeted class. This deviation leads to a significant reduction in stealthiness, as it introduces an abnormal **intra-class feature separation** as shown in Fig. 1 and Fig. 2. Based on this observation, we argue that monitoring the feature distribution of each class during training particularly checking for the phenomenon can serve as a strong indicator of potential poisoning in the dataset. To further support this observation, we provide a theoretical explanation that accounts for the separation between poisoned and clean feature clusters under dirty-label backdoor attacks.

1.1 Related Work

Related Work About Backdoor Attack. [34] propose the adaptability hypothesis to understand when and why a backdoor attack works for general learning models, including deep neural networks. [15] conduct a detailed analysis of BPAs in a two-layer convolutional neural network to explore how BPAs work. However, previous theoretical studies about BPAs have paid less attention to the intra-class feature separation.

Related Work About NC. NC provides a mathematical characterization of features and the last-layer classifier for deep neural networks during the terminal phase of neural network training. NC has been observed and applied in various settings, such as imbalanced learning [9,30,35–37], transfer learning [10,18,24], continual learning [38,39], learning for a large number of classes

[13], multi-label learning [17], regression [1], etc. Most of the studies adopt the unconstrained feature model (UFM) due to the network overparameterization, in which the features of the last layer are treated as free optimization variables. The rationale behind this model is that modern deep networks are extremely over-parameterized and expressive such that their feature mapping can be adapted to any training data [41]. However, this assumption overlooks the fact that the intrinsic structure of the input distribution should play a crucial role in shaping the representations learned by neural networks. To address this, we follow the approach of [27] by analyzing the training dynamics through momentum, in order to gain a more detailed understanding of how individual features are learned during training.

1.2 Organization and Contributions

In Sect. 2, we use experiments on multiple dirty-label attacks to demonstrate the existence of the intra-class feature separation phenomenon.

In Sect. 3, we show our theoretical model. In Sect. 4, we give our theories to explain the phenomenon. Our contributions can be summarized as follows:

- We reveal a common but previously overlooked anomaly in the training process of existing backdoor attacks under the dirty-label setting, which significantly reduces the stealthiness of poisoned samples.
- We provide a theoretical explanation for this phenomenon, offering insights into why and how the deviation occurs during feature learning.

1.3 Notations

We use $[n]$ to denote the set $\{1, 2, \ldots, n\}$. We use the notation f' to denote the derivative of the function f. Throughout this paper, we denote vectors by boldface lowercase letters, such as $\boldsymbol{v}$ and $\boldsymbol{u}$. We denote a Gaussian distribution with mean μ and variance σ^2 by $\mathcal{N}(\mu, \sigma^2)$. The $d \times d$ identity matrix is denoted by $\mathbf{I}_d$. The dot product (inner product) between vectors $\boldsymbol{a}$ and $\boldsymbol{b}$ is denoted by $\boldsymbol{a}^\top \boldsymbol{b}$. We denote the Euclidean norm (or L2-norm) of a vector by $\|\cdot\|_2$.

We use O, Θ and Ω to denote the standard asymptotic notations. We denote $f \leq O(g)$ if there exists x_0, $\alpha \in \mathcal{R}$ such that for all $x > x_0$, we have $f(x) \leq \alpha g(x)$. $f \geq \Omega(g)$ if there exists x_0, α such that for $x > x_0$, we have $f(x) \geq \alpha g(x)$. $f = \Theta(g)$ means that $f \geq \Omega(g)$ and $f \leq O(g)$. $f \leq o(g)$ means that for every $\alpha > 0$, there exists x_0 such that for all $x > x_0$ we have $f(x) \leq \alpha g(x)$.

2 Intra-class Feature Separation

We run experiments on CIFAR10, CIFAR100 using different dirty-label attack methods as shown in Fig. 1 and Fig. 2. We use BadNets [12], Blended [6], BppAttack [33], SIG [2], FTrojan [32], Input-aware [25], PoisonInk [42], ReFool [21],

TrojanNN [20], CTRL [16], SSBA [19] and Low-Frequency [40] backdoor attack methods.

As shown in Fig. 1 and Fig. 2, the features of poisoned samples form distinct clusters or outliers instead of merging into the clean target cluster.

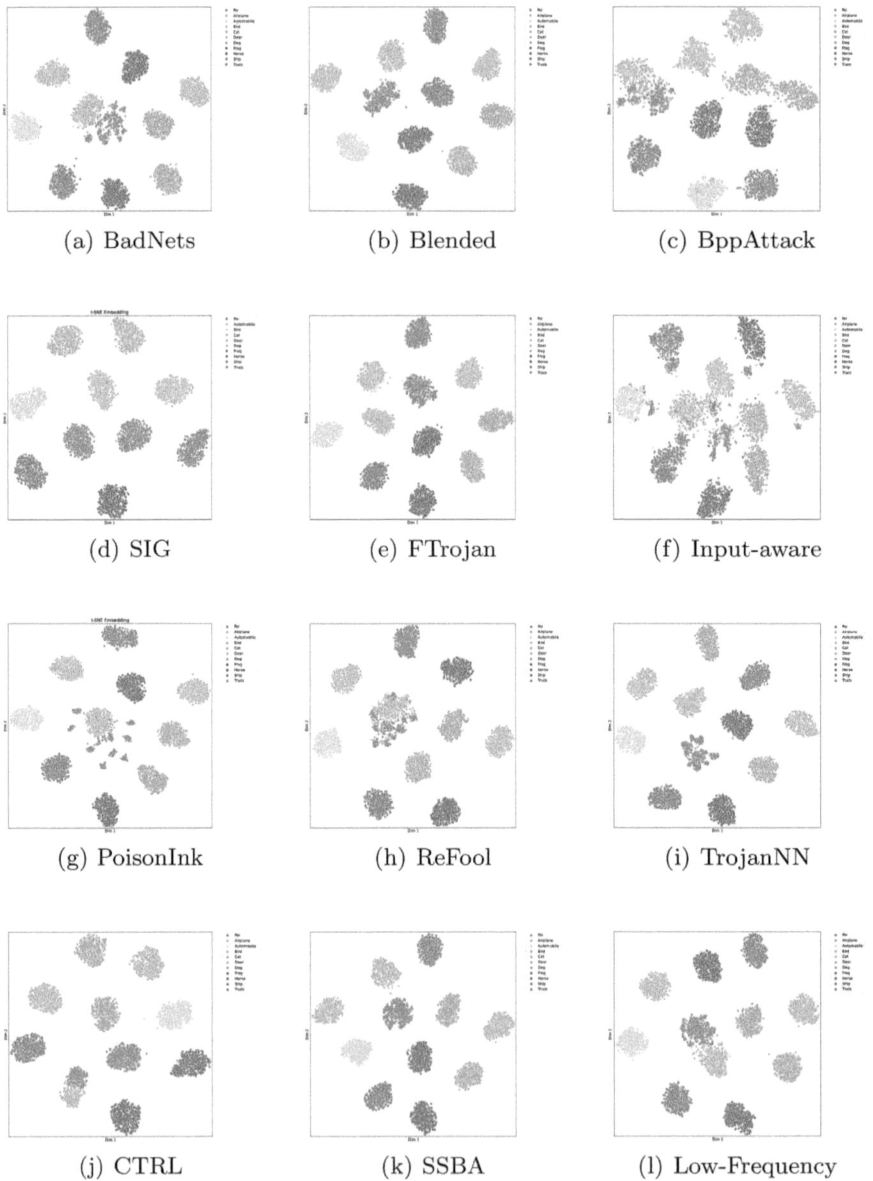

(a) BadNets (b) Blended (c) BppAttack

(d) SIG (e) FTrojan (f) Input-aware

(g) PoisonInk (h) ReFool (i) TrojanNN

(j) CTRL (k) SSBA (l) Low-Frequency

Fig. 1. T-SNE graph about backdoor attack on CIFAR10 dataset. The red points represent the poisoned sample points. (Color figure online)

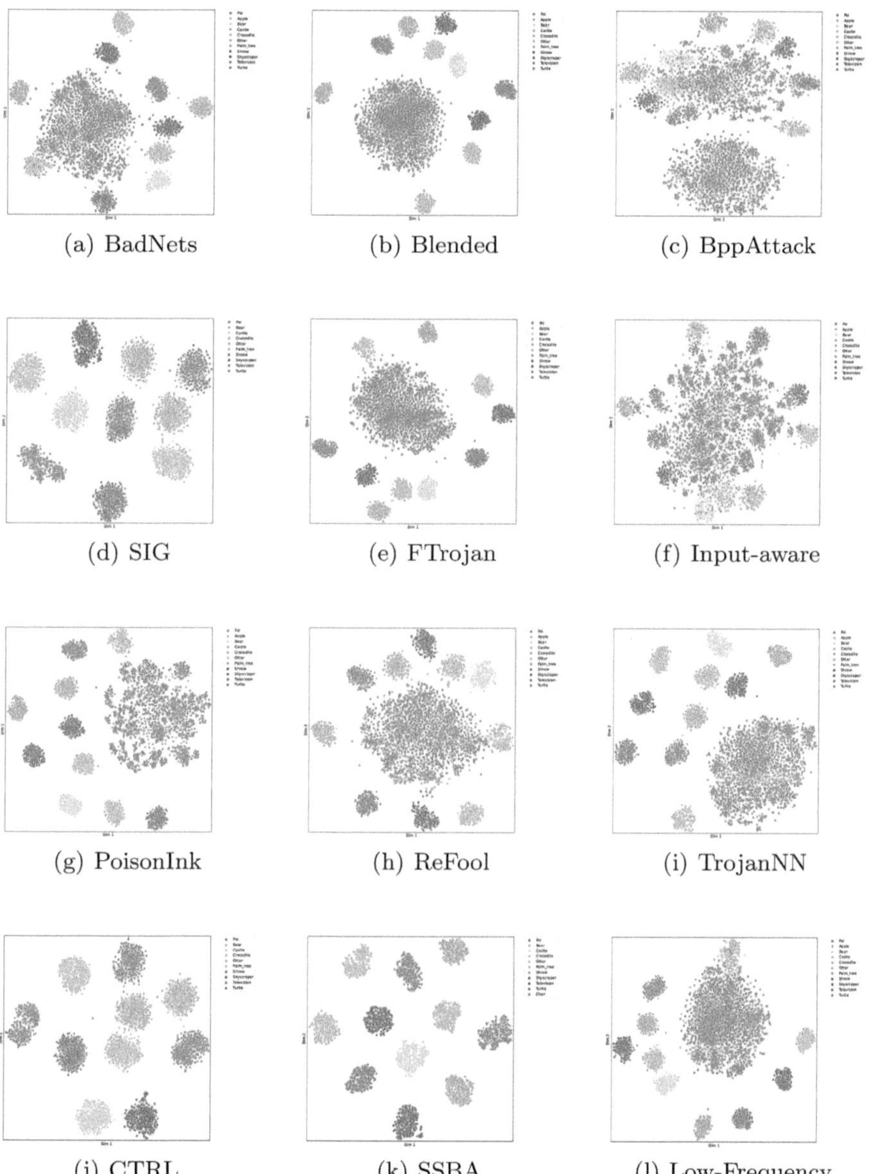

(a) BadNets (b) Blended (c) BppAttack

(d) SIG (e) FTrojan (f) Input-aware

(g) PoisonInk (h) ReFool (i) TrojanNN

(j) CTRL (k) SSBA (l) Low-Frequency

Fig. 2. T-SNE graph about backdoor attack on CIFAR100 dataset. The red points represent the poisoned sample points. For clearer visualization, we select embeddings from a subset of categories. (Color figure online)

This inherent separation drastically reduces attack stealthiness, exposing poisoned samples as feature-space anomalies detectable by existing defenses, for example, the Activation Clustering (AC) method [5].

3 Preliminaries

3.1 Data Model

Consider a binary classification problem. Our data model as defined below, is a simplified variation of the multi-view data distribution proposed in [27] for a binary classification task. We represent the inputs $\boldsymbol{x}$ as a collection of two non-overlapping patches $\boldsymbol{x} = (\boldsymbol{x}^1, \boldsymbol{x}^2) \in \mathbb{R}^{d\times 2}$, where each patch is a d-dimensional vector. We set the $\boldsymbol{x}^1$ as the feature patch and the $\boldsymbol{x}^2$ as the noise patch. Our data model is defined as follows:

Definition 1. *Given the sample number n, $\boldsymbol{u} \in \mathbb{R}^d$, $\mathcal{D}_\xi$. Now the dataset $\{\boldsymbol{z}_i = (\boldsymbol{x}_i, y_i) | i \in [n]\}$ is defined as follows:*

- *This dataset is balanced, with exactly half of the samples labeled as* 1 *and the other half as* -1 *(i.e., $\frac{n}{2}$ each).*
- *Given y_i, the feature patch is $y_i\boldsymbol{u}$ and the noise patch is $\boldsymbol{\xi}_i \sim \mathcal{D}_\xi$. So $\boldsymbol{x}_i = (y_i\boldsymbol{u}, \boldsymbol{\xi}_i)$.*

In our work, we assume $\mathcal{D}_\xi$ is $\mathcal{N}(0, \sigma_\xi^2\mathbf{I}_d)$ and $\|\boldsymbol{u}\|_2 = 1$. Next, we consider a dirty-label backdoor attack $\mathcal{A} : \mathcal{Z} \to \mathcal{Z}$. We inject the trigger into the second patch as shown in follows:

Definition 2. *Given the trigger vector $\boldsymbol{v} \in \mathbb{R}^d$ and target class y^{tar}, then for the sample $\boldsymbol{z}_i = (\boldsymbol{x}_i, y_i)$, $\mathcal{A}(\boldsymbol{z}_i)$ is defined as follows:*

$$\mathcal{A}(\boldsymbol{z}_i) = ((y_i\boldsymbol{u}, \boldsymbol{v}), y^{tar})$$

In this work, we assume that $y^{tar} = 1$ and apply $\mathcal{A}$ to samples with $y_i = -1$. We assume that $\boldsymbol{u} \perp \boldsymbol{v}$ and $1 < \|\boldsymbol{v}\|_2 \le O(\sigma_\xi)$. We denote the index set of samples with $\mathcal{I}$ and the index set of poisoned samples with $\mathcal{I}_p$. Let $\mathcal{I}_1$ and $\mathcal{I}_{-1}$ denote the index sets of samples labeled as 1 and -1 respectively. The number of poisoned samples is n_p. In the general case, $n_p \le o(n)$. In the general case, a lower bound on n_p is required to ensure that the dirty-label attack can succeed. In this paper, we assume that $n_p \ge \Omega(n/\|\boldsymbol{v}\|_2^2)$.

3.2 Network Model

Following [27], we use a patch-wise convolutional neural network architecture with C channels: let $\boldsymbol{W} = \{\boldsymbol{w}_1, \boldsymbol{w}_2, \ldots, \boldsymbol{w}_C\} \in \mathbb{R}^{d\times C}$ denote the first convolutional layer parameters. The second layer is linear layer and the weight of second layer is fixed as the all-one vector. The model is defined as:

$$F(\boldsymbol{W}, \boldsymbol{x}) = \sum_{c=1}^{C}\sum_{r=1}^{2} \sigma(\boldsymbol{w}_c^\top \boldsymbol{x}^r)$$

where

$$\sigma(z) = \begin{cases} \frac{1}{3}z^3 & \text{if } |z| \le 1 \\ z - \frac{2}{3} & \text{if } z \ge 1 \\ z + \frac{2}{3} & \text{if } z \le -1 \end{cases} \tag{1}$$

is the activation function. We adopt the logistic loss $\ell(F(\boldsymbol{W},\boldsymbol{x}),y) = -\mathbf{log}(1+\mathbf{exp}(-yF(\boldsymbol{W},\boldsymbol{x})))$ as the loss function. We use Gaussian initialization to initialize the network parameters, i.e., $\boldsymbol{w}_c(0) \sim \mathcal{N}(0,\sigma_0^2\mathbf{I}_d)$. We assume that the network is over-parameterized and n, d satisfy $n \leq o(\sqrt{d})$.

The feature $\boldsymbol{h}$ for the input $\boldsymbol{x}$ can be represented as

$$(\sum_{r=1}^{2}\sigma(\boldsymbol{w}_1^\top \boldsymbol{x}^r), \sum_{r=1}^{2}\sigma(\boldsymbol{w}_2^\top \boldsymbol{x}^r), \ldots, \sum_{r=1}^{2}\sigma(\boldsymbol{w}_C^\top \boldsymbol{x}^r))$$

which is a C-dimensional vector. We prove $\|\boldsymbol{h}_i - \boldsymbol{h}_j\| \gg \|\boldsymbol{h}_j - \boldsymbol{h}_k\|, \forall i \in \mathcal{I}_P, j,k \in \mathcal{I}_1$ to explain intra-class feature separation phenomenon.

3.3 Gradient Descent

We use the gradient descent (GD) algorithm to optimize $\boldsymbol{W}$. The loss $L(\boldsymbol{W}) = \frac{1}{n}\sum_{i=1}^{n}\ell(F(\boldsymbol{W},\boldsymbol{x}_i),y_i)$. Given the learning rate α, we can get the update rule for the $\boldsymbol{w}_c(t)$ at round t:

$$\begin{aligned} \boldsymbol{w}_c(t+1) &= \boldsymbol{w}_c(t) - \frac{\alpha}{n}\sum_{i=1}^{n}\ell'(F(\boldsymbol{x}_i),y_i)\nabla_{\boldsymbol{w}_c}\ell(F(\boldsymbol{x}_i,y_i)) \\ &= \boldsymbol{w}_c(t) - \frac{\alpha}{n}\sum_{i=1}^{n}\sum_{r=1}^{2} y_i\ell'(F(\boldsymbol{x}_i),y_i)\sigma'(\boldsymbol{w}_c^\top \boldsymbol{x}_i^r)\boldsymbol{x}_i^r \end{aligned} \tag{2}$$

So the $-\frac{n}{\alpha}(\boldsymbol{w}_c(t+1) - \boldsymbol{w}_c(t))$ can be represented as:

$$\begin{aligned} &\sum_{i=1}^{n}\sum_{r=1}^{2} y_i\ell'(F(\boldsymbol{x}_i),y_i)\sigma'(\boldsymbol{w}_c^\top \boldsymbol{x}_i^r)\boldsymbol{x}_i^r \\ &\quad= \sum_{i\in\mathcal{I}_p} -\ell'(F(\boldsymbol{x}_i),y_i)\sigma'(\boldsymbol{w}_c^\top \boldsymbol{u})\boldsymbol{u} + \sum_{i\in\mathcal{I}_p} y_i\ell'(F(\boldsymbol{x}_i),y_i)\sigma'(\boldsymbol{w}_c^\top \boldsymbol{v})\boldsymbol{v} \\ &\quad+ \sum_{i\notin\mathcal{I}_p} \ell'(F(\boldsymbol{x}_i),y_i)\sigma'(\boldsymbol{w}_c^\top \boldsymbol{u})\boldsymbol{u} + \sum_{i\notin\mathcal{I}_p} y_i\ell'(F(\boldsymbol{x}_i),y_i)\sigma'(\boldsymbol{w}_c^\top \boldsymbol{\xi}_i)\boldsymbol{\xi}_i \end{aligned} \tag{3}$$

From 3, we can conclude that

$$\begin{aligned} \frac{d\boldsymbol{w}_c^\top \boldsymbol{u}}{dt} &= -\frac{1}{n}\sum_{i=1}^{n} y_i\ell'(F(\boldsymbol{x}_i),y_i)\sigma'(\boldsymbol{w}_c^\top \boldsymbol{x}_i)\boldsymbol{w}_c^\top \boldsymbol{u} \\ &= \frac{1}{n}\sum_{i\in\mathcal{I}_p} \ell'(F(\boldsymbol{x}_i),y_i)\sigma'(\boldsymbol{w}_c^\top \boldsymbol{u})\|\boldsymbol{u}\|_2^2 - \frac{1}{n}\sum_{i\notin\mathcal{I}_p} \ell'(F(\boldsymbol{x}_i),y_i)\sigma'(\boldsymbol{w}_c^\top \boldsymbol{u})\|\boldsymbol{u}\|_2^2 \\ &- \frac{1}{n}\sum_{i\in\mathcal{I}_p} y_i\ell'(F(\boldsymbol{x}_i),y_i)\sigma'(\boldsymbol{w}_c^\top \boldsymbol{v})\boldsymbol{v}^\top \boldsymbol{u} - \frac{1}{n}\sum_{i\notin\mathcal{I}_p} y_i\ell'(F(\boldsymbol{x}_i),y_i)\sigma'(\boldsymbol{w}_c^\top \boldsymbol{\xi}_i)\boldsymbol{\xi}_i^\top \boldsymbol{u} \end{aligned} \tag{4}$$

At the initialization, $F(\boldsymbol{x}_i) = o(1)$, $\boldsymbol{w}_c(0)^\top \boldsymbol{u} = o(1)$ and $\ell' \approx -\frac{1}{2}$. We denote $f(t) = \boldsymbol{w}_c(t)^\top \boldsymbol{u}$. We can conclude that $f'(t) = (n - 2n_p)f(t)^2\|\boldsymbol{u}\|_2^2/2n$ when overlook the $\boldsymbol{\xi}_i$. The training dynamics can be viewed as an ODE. By solving the ODE equation, we have that when $t = \frac{2n}{(n-2n_p)\|\boldsymbol{u}\|_2^2 f(0)}$, $\boldsymbol{w}_c(t)^\top \boldsymbol{u} \geq \Omega(1)$, which means that $\boldsymbol{u}$ has been captured. Then we analysis the trigger vector $\boldsymbol{v}$. From 3, we have that:

$$\begin{aligned}
\frac{d\boldsymbol{w}_c^\top \boldsymbol{v}}{dt} &= -\frac{1}{n}\sum_{i=1}^{n} y_i \ell'(F(\boldsymbol{x}_i), y_i)\sigma'(\boldsymbol{w}_c^\top \boldsymbol{x}_i)\boldsymbol{w}_c^\top \boldsymbol{v} \\
&= \frac{1}{n}\sum_{i\in\mathcal{I}_P} \ell'(F(\boldsymbol{x}_i), y_i)\sigma'(\boldsymbol{w}_c^\top \boldsymbol{u})\boldsymbol{u}^\top \boldsymbol{v} - \frac{1}{n}\sum_{i\notin\mathcal{I}_P} \ell'(F(\boldsymbol{x}_i), y_i)\sigma'(\boldsymbol{w}_c^\top \boldsymbol{u})\boldsymbol{u}^\top \boldsymbol{v} \\
&\quad - \frac{1}{n}\sum_{i\in\mathcal{I}_P} y_i \ell'(F(\boldsymbol{x}_i), y_i)\sigma'(\boldsymbol{w}_c^\top \boldsymbol{v})\|\boldsymbol{v}\|_2^2 - \frac{1}{n}\sum_{i\notin\mathcal{I}_P} y_i \ell'(F(\boldsymbol{x}_i), y_i)\sigma'(\boldsymbol{w}_c^\top \boldsymbol{\xi}_i)\boldsymbol{\xi}_i^\top \boldsymbol{v}
\end{aligned} \tag{5}$$

We denote $g(t) = \boldsymbol{w}_c(t)^\top \boldsymbol{v}$. We can conclude that $g'(t) = n_p g(t)^2\|\boldsymbol{v}\|_2^2/2n$. When $t = \frac{2n}{n_p\|\boldsymbol{v}\|_2^2 g(0)}$, $\boldsymbol{w}_c(t)^\top \boldsymbol{v} \geq \Omega(1)$, which means that $\boldsymbol{v}$ has been captured. When $\|\boldsymbol{v}\|_2 \gg (\frac{(n-2n_p)f(0)}{n_p g(0)})^{\frac{1}{3}}\|\boldsymbol{u}\|_2$, the network captures the $\boldsymbol{v}$ first.

Next, we analyze the noise $\boldsymbol{\xi}$.

$$\begin{aligned}
\frac{d\boldsymbol{w}_c^\top \boldsymbol{\xi}_{i'}}{dt} &= -\frac{1}{n}\sum_{i=1}^{n} y_i \ell'(f(\boldsymbol{x}_i), y_i)\sigma'(\boldsymbol{w}_c^\top \boldsymbol{x}_i)\boldsymbol{w}_c^\top \boldsymbol{\xi}_{i'} \\
&= \frac{1}{n}\sum_{i\in\mathcal{I}_P} \ell'(f(\boldsymbol{x}_i), y_i)\sigma'(\boldsymbol{w}_c^\top \boldsymbol{u})\boldsymbol{u}^\top \boldsymbol{\xi}_{i'} - \frac{1}{n}\sum_{i\notin\mathcal{I}_P} \ell'(f(\boldsymbol{x}_i), y_i)\sigma'(\boldsymbol{w}_c^\top \boldsymbol{u})\boldsymbol{u}^\top \boldsymbol{\xi}_{i'} \\
&\quad - \frac{1}{n}\sum_{i\in\mathcal{I}_P} y_i \ell'(f(\boldsymbol{x}_i), y_i)\sigma'(\boldsymbol{w}_c^\top \boldsymbol{v})\boldsymbol{v}^\top \boldsymbol{\xi}_{i'} - \frac{1}{n}\sum_{i\notin\mathcal{I}_P}^{n} y_i \ell'(f(\boldsymbol{x}_i), y_i)\sigma'(\boldsymbol{w}_c^\top \boldsymbol{\xi}_i)\boldsymbol{\xi}_i^\top \boldsymbol{\xi}_{i'}
\end{aligned} \tag{6}$$

In this paper, we assume $\Omega(1) \leq \sigma_\xi \leq o(\frac{1}{\sigma_0 C^{3/2}})$ to ensure that the noise level remains constrained, thereby preventing it from overwhelming the learning of other features.

4 Main Results

Our theoretical analysis demonstrates that, during the initial training phase of the neural network, the model first captures the component $\boldsymbol{v}$, followed by the component $\boldsymbol{u}$. In the later stages of training, the term $\boldsymbol{w}_c(t)^\top \boldsymbol{v}$ grows at a faster rate than $\boldsymbol{w}_c(t)^\top \boldsymbol{u}$, which leads to intra-class feature separation. We provide our proof in the Appendix.

4.1 Initialization

Gaussian initialization is used to initialize the weights of the model, i.e., $\boldsymbol{w}_c(0) \sim \mathcal{N}(0, \sigma_0^2 \mathbf{I}_d)$ where $\sigma_0 \leq o(1)$. Since the initialization is random, we analyze the maximum values of $f(t)$ and $g(t)$ across different channels to reduce the impact of randomness.

Theorem 1. *The network parameters are initialized as* $\boldsymbol{w}_c(0) \sim \mathcal{N}(0, \sigma_0^2 \mathbf{I}_d)$. *With probability of (w.p.)* $1 - \frac{4C}{d} - \frac{4}{e^{C/4}}$, *the following holds:*

$$\|\boldsymbol{v}\|_2\sigma_0/2 \leq \mathbf{max}_{c\in[C]}|g(0)| \leq \sqrt{2\mathbf{log}(d)}\|\boldsymbol{v}\|_2\sigma_0$$

$$\|\boldsymbol{u}\|_2\sigma_0/2 \leq \mathbf{max}_{c\in[C]}|f(0)| \leq \sqrt{2\mathbf{log}(d)}\|\boldsymbol{u}\|_2\sigma_0$$

Theorem 1 implies $\mathbf{max}_{c\in[C]}g(0) = \widetilde{\Theta}(\sigma_0\|\boldsymbol{v}\|_2)$ and $\mathbf{max}_{c\in[C]}f(0) = \widetilde{\Theta}(\sigma_0\|\boldsymbol{u}\|_2)$.

4.2 Bound the Noise

To avoid interference from excessive noise in the learning of other features, we analyze the training momentum associated with noise components.

Theorem 2. *When* $t \leq o(\frac{n\sigma_0}{\alpha\sigma_\xi})$, *we have*

$$\forall i \in [n], |\boldsymbol{w}_c(t)^\top \boldsymbol{\xi}_i| \leq o(\sigma_0\sigma_\xi)$$

4.3 Initial Stage

In this stage, $\mathbf{max}_{c\in[C]}f(t)$ and $\mathbf{max}_{c\in[C]}g(t)$ are $o(1)$, and $\sigma'(x) = x^2$. Next, we analyze the training dynamics and prove that the networks capture $\boldsymbol{v}$ first in the initial stage.

Theorem 3. *When* $f(t) \leq O(C^{-1})$ *and* $|\boldsymbol{w}_c(t)^\top \boldsymbol{\xi}| \leq \widetilde{O}(\sigma_0\sigma_\xi)$, *the following holds*

$$\widetilde{\Omega}(\frac{\alpha\|\boldsymbol{u}\|_2^2 f(t)^2}{1 + e^{C^{-2}}}) \leq \Delta f(t) \leq \widetilde{O}(\alpha\|\boldsymbol{u}\|_2^2 f(t)^2)$$

We use Theorem 3 to bound the epoch t when the network captures $\boldsymbol{v}$ as shown in the following.

Theorem 4. *When* $f(t) \leq O(C^{-1})$ *and* $\boldsymbol{w}_c(t)^\top \boldsymbol{\xi} \leq \widetilde{O}(\sigma_0\sigma_\xi)$, *there exists* t_u,

$$\widetilde{\Omega}(\frac{1}{\alpha\sigma_0}) \leq t_u \leq \widetilde{O}(\frac{1 + \mathbf{exp}(C^{-2})}{\alpha\sigma_0})$$

such that $\mathbf{max}_{c\in[C]}f(t) = \Theta(C^{-1})$.

Theorem 5. *When* $g(t) \leq O(C^{-1/3})$ *and* $\boldsymbol{w}_c(t)^\top \boldsymbol{\xi} \leq \widetilde{O}(\sigma_0\sigma_\xi)$, *if* $n_p \geq O(n\sigma_\xi^3/\sqrt{d}\|\boldsymbol{v}\|_2^3)$, *the following holds:*

$$\Delta g(t) = \widetilde{\Theta}(\frac{n_p}{n}\alpha\|\boldsymbol{v}\|_2^2 g(t)^2)$$

We use Theorem 5 to bound the epoch t when the network captures $\boldsymbol{u}$ as shown in the following.

Theorem 6. *Suppose* $g(t) \leq O(C^{-1/3})$ *and* $\boldsymbol{w}_c(t)^\top \boldsymbol{\xi} \leq \widetilde{O}(\sigma_0 \sigma_\xi)$. *There exists* t_v,

$$\widetilde{\Omega}(\frac{n}{\alpha n_p \|\boldsymbol{v}\|_2^3 \sigma_0}) \leq t_v \leq \widetilde{O}(\frac{n}{\alpha n_p \|\boldsymbol{v}\|_2^3 \sigma_0})$$

such that $\mathbf{max}_{c \in [C]} g(t) = \Theta(C^{-1/3})$.

Since $n_p \geq \Omega(n/\|\boldsymbol{v}\|_2^3)$, $\frac{1}{\alpha\sigma_0} \geq \Omega(\frac{n}{\alpha n_p \|\boldsymbol{v}\|_2^3 \sigma_0})$. The network captures the $\boldsymbol{v}$ first. At $t = O(\frac{1+\mathbf{exp}(C^{-2})}{\alpha\sigma_0})$, intra-class feature separation has happened.

Theorem 7. *When* $t = t_u$,

$$\frac{\|\boldsymbol{h}_j - \boldsymbol{h}_k\|_2}{\|\boldsymbol{h}_i - \boldsymbol{h}_j\|_2} \leq o(1), \forall i \in \mathcal{I}_P, j, k \in \mathcal{I}_1$$

We prove the Theorem 7 by giving the lower bound, i.e., $\|\boldsymbol{h}_i - \boldsymbol{h}_j\|_2 > \mathbf{max}_{c \in [C]} g(t)^3 - 2\mathbf{max}_{c \in [C]} f(t)^3$. The order of the lower bound of $\|\boldsymbol{h}_i - \boldsymbol{h}_j\|_2$ is larger than the order of $\|\boldsymbol{h}_j - \boldsymbol{h}_k\|_2$.

4.4 Late Stage

In the late stage, we prove $\Delta g(t) \gg \Delta f(t)$ to explain that intra-class feature separation still exists in the late stage.

Theorem 8. *When* $t \geq \Omega(\frac{1+\mathbf{exp}(\mathbf{C}^{-2})}{\alpha\sigma_0})$, $\Delta g(t) \gg \Delta f(t)$.

Theorem 8 implies that $g(t) \gg f(t)$ in the late stage, which further keeps the intra-class feature separation. When $\Delta g(t) \gg \Delta f(t)$, $\mathbf{max}_{c \in [C]} g(t)^3 - 2\mathbf{max}_{c \in [C]} f(t)^3$ will keep the order at least and the order of $\|\boldsymbol{h}_j - \boldsymbol{h}_k\|_2$ remains the same. Consequently, the intra-class feature separation phenomenon still exists during the late stage of training.

5 Conclusion

In this work, we demonstrate intra-class feature separation across different dirty-label attack methods, which drastically reduces the stealthiness. By analyzing the training dynamics, we explain the phenomenon. The network first captures the trigger in the initial stage, besides the training dynamics about the trigger grow at a faster rate than the other features, which leads to the intra-class feature separation. Our theoretical analysis serves as an important reference for designing and detecting backdoor attacks in future research.

References

1. Andriopoulos, G., Dong, Z., Guo, L., Zhao, Z., Ross, K.W.: The prevalence of neural collapse in neural multivariate regression. CoRR (2024)
2. Barni, M., Kallas, K., Tondi, B.: A new backdoor attack in CNNS by training set corruption without label poisoning. In: ICIP (2019)
3. Biggio, B., Nelson, B., Laskov, P.: Poisoning attacks against support vector machines. In: ICML (2012)
4. Brown, T.B., et al.: Language models are few-shot learners. In: NeurIPS (2020)
5. Chen, B., et al.: Detecting backdoor attacks on deep neural networks by activation clustering. CoRR (2018)
6. Chen, X., Liu, C., Li, B., Lu, K., Song, D.: Targeted backdoor attacks on deep learning systems using data poisoning. CoRR (2017)
7. Dreossi, T., Donzé, A., Seshia, S.A.: Compositional falsification of cyber-physical systems with machine learning components. In: Barrett, C., Davies, M., Kahsai, T. (eds.) NFM 2017. LNCS, vol. 10227, pp. 357–372. Springer, Cham (2017). https://doi.org/10.1007/978-3-319-57288-8_26
8. Fang, C., He, H., Long, Q., Su, W.J.: Exploring deep neural networks via layer-peeled model: minority collapse in imbalanced training. Proc. Natl. Acad. Sci. (2021)
9. Fang, C., He, H., Long, Q., Su, W.J.: Layer-peeled model: toward understanding well-trained deep neural networks. Proc. Natl. Acad. Sci. (2021)
10. Galanti, T., György, A., Hutter, M.: On the role of neural collapse in transfer learning. In: ICLR (2022)
11. Goodfellow, I.J., Shlens, J., Szegedy, C.: Explaining and harnessing adversarial examples. In: ICLR (2015)
12. Tianyu, G., Dolan-Gavitt, B., Garg, S.: Badnets: identifying vulnerabilities in the machine learning model supply chain. CoRR (2017)
13. Jiang, J., et al.: Generalized neural collapse for a large number of classes. In: ICML (2024)
14. Krizhevsky, A., Sutskever, I., Hinton, G.E.: Imagenet classification with deep convolutional neural networks. In: NeurIPS (2012)
15. Li, B., Liu, W.: A theoretical analysis of backdoor poisoning attacks in convolutional neural networks. In: ICML (2024)
16. Li, C., et al.: An embarrassingly simple backdoor attack on self-supervised learning. In: ICCV (2023)
17. Li, P., Li, X., Wang, Y., Qu, Q.: Neural collapse in multi-label learning with pick-all-label loss. In: ICML (2024)
18. Li, X., et al.: Principled and efficient transfer learning of deep models via neural collapse. CoRR (2022)
19. Li, Y., Li, Y., Wu, B., Li, L., He, R., Lyu, S.: Invisible backdoor attack with sample-specific triggers. In: ICCV (2021)
20. Liu, Y., et al.: Trojaning attack on neural networks. In: NDSS (2018)
21. Liu, Y., Ma, X., Bailey, J., Lu, F.: Reflection backdoor: a natural backdoor attack on deep neural networks. In: Vedaldi, A., Bischof, H., Brox, T., Frahm, J.-M. (eds.) ECCV 2020. LNCS, vol. 12355, pp. 182–199. Springer, Cham (2020). https://doi.org/10.1007/978-3-030-58607-2_11
22. Mei, S., Zhu, X.: Using machine teaching to identify optimal training-set attacks on machine learners. In: Proceedings of the Twenty-Ninth AAAI Conference on Artificial Intelligence, 25–30 January 2015, Austin, Texas, USA (2015)

23. Mixon, D.G., Parshall, H., Pi, J.: Neural collapse with unconstrained features. In: Sampling Theory, Signal Processing, and Data Analysis (2022)
24. Munn, M., Dherin, B., Gonzalvo, J.: The impact of geometric complexity on neural collapse in transfer learning. CoRR (2024)
25. Nguyen, T.A., Tran, A.T.: Input-aware dynamic backdoor attack. In: NeurIPS (2020)
26. Papyan, V., Han, X.Y., Donoho, D.L.: Prevalence of neural collapse during the terminal phase of deep learning training. Proc. Natl. Acad. Sci. (2020)
27. Shen, R., Bubeck, S., Gunasekar, S.: Data augmentation as feature manipulation. In: ICML (2022)
28. Simonyan, K., Zisserman, A.: Very deep convolutional networks for large-scale image recognition. In: ICLR (2015)
29. Szegedy, C., et al.: Intriguing properties of neural networks. In: ICLR (2014)
30. Thrampoulidis, C., Kini, G.R., Vakilian, V., Behnia, T.: Imbalance trouble: revisiting neural-collapse geometry. In: NeurIPS (2022)
31. Vaswani, A., et al.: Attention is all you need. In: NeurIPS (2017)
32. Wang, T., Yao, Y., Xu, F., An, S., Tong, H., Wang, T.: An invisible black-box backdoor attack through frequency domain. In: Avidan, S., Brostow, G., Cissé, M., Farinella, G.M., Hassner, T. (eds.) ECCV 2022. LNCS, vol. 13673, pp. 396–413. Springer, Cham (2022). https://doi.org/10.1007/978-3-031-19778-9_23
33. Wang, Z., Zhai, J., Ma, S.: BPPattack: stealthy and efficient trojan attacks against deep neural networks via image quantization and contrastive adversarial learning. In: CVPR (2022)
34. Xian, X., et al.: Understanding backdoor attacks through the adaptability hypothesis. In: ICML (2023)
35. Xie, L., Yang, Y., Cai, D., He, X.: Neural collapse inspired attraction-repulsion-balanced loss for imbalanced learning. In: Neurocomputing (2023)
36. Yan, H., Qian, Y., Peng, F., Luo, J., Zhu, Z., Li, F.: Neural collapse to multiple centers for imbalanced data. In: NeurIPS (2024)
37. Yang, Y., Chen, S., Li, X., Xie, L., Lin, Z., Tao, D.: Inducing neural collapse in imbalanced learning: do we really need a learnable classifier at the end of deep neural network? In: NeurIPS (2022)
38. Yang, Y., Yuan, H., Li, X., Lin, Z., Torr, P.H.S., Tao, D.: Neural collapse inspired feature-classifier alignment for few-shot class-incremental learning. In: ICLR (2023)
39. Yu, L., Hu, T., Hong, L., Liu, Z., Weller, A., Liu, W.: Continual learning by modeling intra-class variation. Trans. Mach. Learn. Res. (2023)
40. Zeng, Y., Park, W., Mao, Z.M., Jia, R.: Rethinking the backdoor attacks' triggers: a frequency perspective. In: ICCV (2021)
41. Zhang, C., Bengio, S., Hardt, M., Recht, B., Vinyals, O.: Understanding deep learning (still) requires rethinking generalization. ACM Commun. (2021)
42. Zhang, J., et al.: Poison ink: robust and invisible backdoor attack. IEEE Trans. Image Process. (2022)

Trustworthy AI-Generated Content Based on Quality Assessment

DDRE: Decoupled Diffusion Reconstruction Error for AI-Generated Image Detection

Mengcheng Li[1,2] and Fei Chao[1,3](✉)

[1] School of Informatics, Xiamen University, Xiamen, China
limengcheng@stu.xmu.edu.cn, fec10@aber.ac.uk
[2] ByteDance Ltd., Beijing, China
[3] Department of Computer Science, Aberystwyth University, Aberystwyth, UK

Abstract. The growing diversity of generative models has made distinguishing AI-generated images increasingly challenging, especially under unknown generator scenarios. While diffusion reconstruction-based methods have shown promise in detecting generated content, a key limitation persists: the entanglement between artifact and image content distributions during reconstruction. In this paper, we propose **DDRE** (Decoupled Diffusion Reconstruction Error), a novel, training-free detection framework that explicitly disentangles these two distributions via a two-stage reconstruction process. By comparing reconstruction error maps from successive denoising stages and applying a simple norm-based ratio metric, DDRE effectively isolates generative artifacts. Furthermore, we introduce a *self-conditioning* strategy that leverages CLIP embeddings to guide reconstruction in the absence of prompts, enhancing the fidelity of inversion. To provide a more comprehensive evaluation, we propose **GenNEXT**, a benchmark that extends GenImage by reducing JPEG bias and incorporating more recent generative models. Extensive experiments on GenNEXT demonstrate that DDRE achieves state-of-the-art performance and exhibits strong generalization to previously unseen generators, all without requiring additional training.

Keywords: Image Forgery Detection · Artifact Disentanglement · Diffusion Inversion

1 Introduction

With the increasing diversity of image generators in terms of data distribution and network architecture, tasks such as image generation and editing have become significantly easier. Even individuals with no prior experience in AI can now generate high-quality images using simple prompts. Generative Adversarial Networks (GANs) [4] are widely used for generating realistic images, videos, and audio by learning data distributions through adversarial training. They have

© The Author(s), under exclusive license to Springer Nature Singapore Pte Ltd. 2026
J. Kittler et al. (Eds.): PRCV 2025, LNCS 16289, pp. 273–287, 2026.
https://doi.org/10.1007/978-981-95-5764-6_19

been successfully applied in fields such as image synthesis, super-resolution, style transfer, and deepfake synthesis. The application of diffusion models [6,17] has substantially advanced generative capabilities, leading to significant improvements in high-quality image synthesis, image editing, and personalized generation. The DiTs [22] departs from the conventional U-Net architecture commonly employed in diffusion frameworks and instead adopts a flow-matching training strategy, which further enhances the diversity of generated images.

The increasing diversity of model architectures and training data distributions has introduced significant security concerns. Generating a realistic image now requires only a simple prompt, yet accurately distinguishing generated images becomes highly challenging, particularly under unknown generator scenarios. Developing a model that can be efficiently deployed and is capable of detecting images produced by a wide range of previously unseen generators has become a key focus of current research.

Early efforts in generative image detection [8,21] focused on identifying artifacts from image-level statistics. During the rise of image-to-image (I2I) translation networks, simple CNN-based classifiers were sufficient to distinguish real from fake images. GAN-generated images often exhibit distinct frequency-domain artifacts, leading to the development of synthesis simulators and fingerprint-based detection methods [3,13,27]. Diffusion models, on the contrary, are trained on more diverse data and possess significantly larger model capacities. While diffusion introduces new challenges for detection, it also enables novel approaches: for example, recent work [24] has shown that AI-generated images are more robust to the denoising-reconstruction process of diffusion models. Follow-up studies further simplified detection pipelines via ablations or threshold-based classifiers to build lightweight and robust detectors [1,28].

However, an important theoretical issue remains underexplored: during reconstruction, the intrinsic distribution of the image often becomes entangled with the artifact distribution, leading to mixed representations in the feature maps. This entanglement imposes a fundamental limitation on detection performance. In this paper, we investigate the problem of disentangling artifact distributions from the intrinsic distribution of the image and propose DDRE. DDRE achieves artifact disentanglement and fine-grained conditional guidance through a two-stage reconstruction process and self-conditioning, enabling fast, training-free deployment using a single backbone. To evaluate DDRE, we introduce GenNEXT, an extended and refined version of GenImage that mitigates JPEG compression bias and incorporates a broader set of generative models. DDRE achieves state-of-the-art performance on GenNEXT, demonstrating strong generalization in detecting images from previously unseen generators.

Our main contributions are summarized as follows:

1. The proposed two-stage inversion reconstruction enables effective disentanglement of artifact distributions, leading to improved classification accuracy.
2. The self-conditioning mechanism enhances the quality of the reconstruction process by optimizing conditional guidance, thereby further boosting detection performance.

3. The training-free design simplifies the construction of generative image detection pipelines and enables rapid, lightweight classification of images from previously unseen generators.
4. GenNEXT offers reduced JPEG compression bias and comprehensive coverage of state-of-the-art generative models, providing a more reliable evaluation benchmark.

2 Related Work

2.1 Diffusion Models

Initiating from Gaussian noise, both diffusion models [2,6,16,18] and their more recent counterpart, flow matching models [9,10,19], leverage neural networks to iteratively predict the noise at each step. This process progressively eliminates noise to synthesize images that align with the target data distribution. DDPM [6] formulates the denoising procedure as Markovian processes. DDIM [18] employs deterministic denoising and a scheduler to skip timesteps during inference, reducing computation without retraining. Latent Diffusion Models (LDM) [16] compress the denoising process into a low-resolution latent space and perform transformations between the pixel space and latent space via a VAE, thereby further reducing resource consumption. Building upon LDM, frameworks such as Stable Diffusion 1.5 (SD1.5) and Stable Diffusion XL (SDXL) have furnished both industrial and academic communities with state-of-the-art pre-trained models. Recently, frameworks such as Stable Diffusion 3 (SD3) series and FLUX.1, leveraging flow matching training paradigms and the DiT network architecture, have pushed the quality of image generation to a new level [10,19].

2.2 AI-Generated Image Detection

As generative models gain the ability to produce increasingly realistic and stunning images, the detection of AI-generated images has become an unavoidable research topic. Early work [14] focused on identifying differences between AI-generated images and real-world images from image parameters and simple features. For images generated by image-to-image translation networks, simple CNNs [12] can suffice for classification. With the rise of GANs, Frank et al. [3] pointed out that images generated by GANs exhibit strong artifacts in the frequency domain. Furthermore, Zhang et al. [27], Ma et al. [11], and Yu et al. [25] have enhanced the detection capability for GAN-generated images through methods such as synthetic simulators and fingerprint detection. Since diffusion models have been widely adopted for image generation, the ability of a single detector to identify images generated by multiple unseen models has become increasingly important. RIGID [20] leverages the pre-trained DINOv2 [15] to extract more general artifact features. Recently, some researchers have focused on the improvement of general AI-generated image detection through diffusion reconstruction errors. Leveraging the capabilities of pre-trained diffusion models, they extract more refined artifact features during the noising-denoising process.

2.3 Diffusion Reconstruction-Based Detection

Diffusion models involve a forward noising process and a reverse denoising process, which transform images into noise and noise back into images, respectively. First discovered by Wang et al. [23], AI-generated images exhibit greater robustness to such reconstruction processes, whereas real-world images incur significantly higher reconstruction losses. This work employs error feature maps from inversion-reconstruction as inputs to ResNet for training AI-generated image detectors. LaER$\hat{2}$ [28] replaces the full inversion-based reconstruction process with single-step denoising and utilizes the Monte Carlo method to improve accuracy. SeDID [1] performs detailed ablation studies on the number of denoising steps and the starting steps of reconstruction, and proposes a threshold method to replace the ResNet detection head. To enhance the quality of reconstructed error features, FakeInversion [7] utilizes BLIP to identify prompts corresponding to images, which are then used to guide the inversion-based reconstruction process. Zhang et al. [26] further observed that scene images are not only non-robust to reconstruction but also to incorrect prompts during the reconstruction process, thus proposing ZeroFake. The aforementioned work aims to achieve multi-model general generative detection by extracting more refined artifact features. However, researchers have overlooked that the extracted artifact feature maps often contain the distribution of the image's own information, and such uncoupled features can interfere with the detector.

3 Method

Figure 1 illustrates the proposed DDRE method, which innovatively obtains the artifact distribution and image distribution during the two-stage reconstruction process, and decouples these two distributions through simple mathematical operations. During the reconstruction process, to improve the quality of error features, we propose a self-condition method that uses the image's own feature embedding to compensate for the text conditions missing due to prompt absence. Finally, after the feature maps of the two stages are decoupled by division and scalarized using the 1-norm, they can be directly used to discriminate AI-generated images through a threshold method.

3.1 Preliminaries

Latent Diffusion Models. Latent Diffusion Models (LDMs) introduce a pair of VAE encoder $\mathcal{E}$ and decoder $\mathcal{D}$ to compress operations from pixel space $\mathbb{R}^{H\times W\times 3}$ into the latent space $\mathbb{R}^{h\times w\times c}$. In the latent space, the forward process adds noise directly to the latent $\boldsymbol{z}_0$ at an arbitrary timestep, which is defined as:

$$\boldsymbol{z}_t = \sqrt{\bar{\alpha}_t}\boldsymbol{z}_0 + \sqrt{1-\bar{\alpha}_t}, \boldsymbol{\epsilon} \sim \mathcal{N}(\mathbf{0}, \mathbf{I}) \tag{1}$$

where $\{\alpha_t\}_{t=1}^{T}$ represents a set of predetermined variance schedules, and $\bar{\alpha}_t = \Pi_{i=1}^{t}\alpha_i$. In contrast, the reverse denoising process utilizes a U-Net architecture

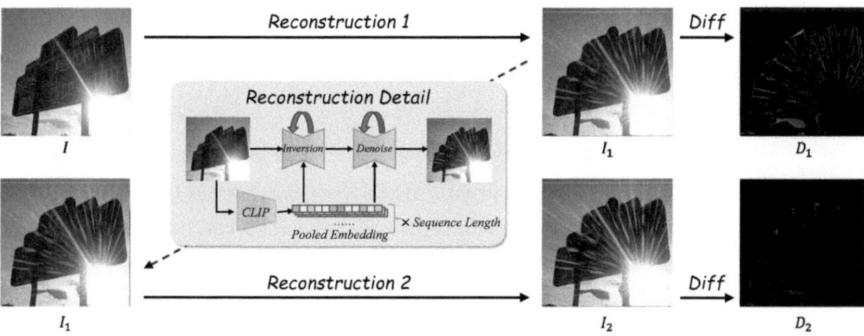

Fig. 1. Overview of the proposed DDRE framework. Given an input image $\boldsymbol{I}$, we perform a two-stage reconstruction using DDIM inversion and denoising, guided by self-conditioned CLIP embeddings. In the first reconstruction, the image is reconstructed as $\boldsymbol{I}_1$, and the corresponding difference map $\boldsymbol{D}_1$ captures a mixture of artifact and image distributions. The second reconstruction further produces $\boldsymbol{I}_2$ and a difference map $\boldsymbol{D}_2$ that predominantly reflects the image distributions. The scalar error ratio $\|\boldsymbol{D}_1\|_1/\|\boldsymbol{D}_2\|_1$ is used as a decision metric to discriminate between real and Generated images.

to progressively transform Gaussian noise into a clean latent image through iterative refinement:

$$\boldsymbol{z}_{t-1} = \frac{1}{\sqrt{\alpha_t}}\Big(\boldsymbol{z}_t - \frac{1-\alpha_t}{\sqrt{1-\bar{\alpha}_t}}\,\epsilon_\theta(\boldsymbol{z}_t, t, \boldsymbol{e})\Big) \tag{2}$$

where $\boldsymbol{e}_c = \tau_\phi(\mathcal{P})$ denotes a text encoder that converts the conditional text prompt $\mathcal{P}$ into an embedding. At time step $t = 0$, a decoder $\mathcal{D}$ decodes the latent space output $\boldsymbol{z}_0$ into the pixel space $\boldsymbol{x}_0 = \mathcal{D}(\boldsymbol{z}_0)$.

DDIM. Denoising Diffusion Implicit Models (DDIM) [18] offer a deterministic alternative to the traditional stochastic denoising diffusion probabilistic models (DDPM). The key difference between DDPM and DDIM lies in the reverse (denoising) process. While DDPM models this process as a stochastic Markov chain with learned noise predictions, DDIM reformulates it as a deterministic mapping:

$$\boldsymbol{z}_{t-1} = \sqrt{\frac{\bar{\alpha}_{t-1}}{\bar{\alpha}_t}}\,\boldsymbol{z}_t + \sqrt{\bar{\alpha}_{t-1}}\left(\sqrt{\frac{1}{\bar{\alpha}_{t-1}}-1} - \sqrt{\frac{1}{\bar{\alpha}_t}-1}\right)\epsilon_\theta(\boldsymbol{z}_t, t, \boldsymbol{e}) \tag{3}$$

DDIM Inversion. The denoising process typically begins with a random Gaussian noise and progressively generates the final image. In contrast, the inversion process aims to approximate the initial latent from a given image. Assuming that the predicted noise is approximately invariant over nearby time steps, Equation (3) can be reformulated as a function of z_{t-1} and $t-1$:

$$z_t = \sqrt{\frac{\bar{\alpha}_t}{\bar{\alpha}_{t-1}}}\, z_{t-1} + \sqrt{\bar{\alpha}_t}\left(\sqrt{\frac{1}{\bar{\alpha}_t} - 1} - \sqrt{\frac{1}{\bar{\alpha}_{t-1}} - 1}\right) \epsilon_\theta(z_{t-1}, t-1, e). \quad (4)$$

This constitutes the noising process of DDIM Inversion. A DDIM inversion and a DDIM denoising process together constitute a complete reconstruction pipeline, which aims to obtain a deterministic denoising starting point from a given image, enabling controlled editing and faithful reconstruction during the denoising process.

3.2 Two-Stage Reconstruction

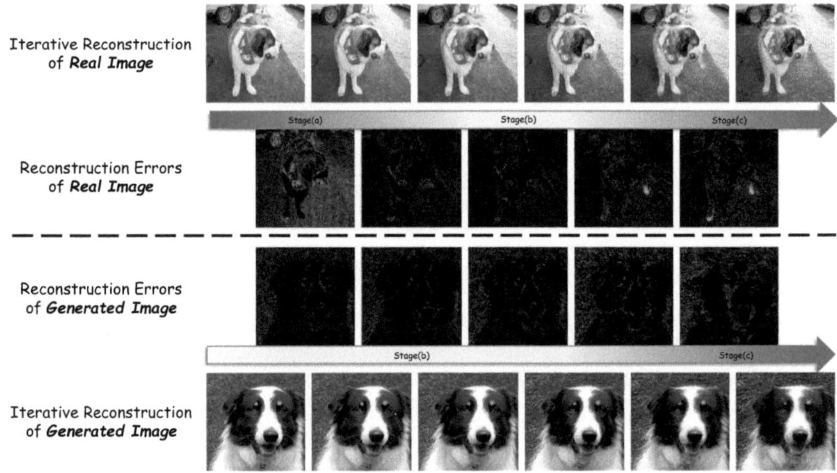

Fig. 2. The iterative reconstruction process and error maps exhibit distinct characteristics for real and generated images. For real image, a significant reconstruction error emerges during the first iteration. From the second iteration onward, the error stabilizes initially but gradually increases and becomes more stochastic as iterations proceed. In contrast, generated image display a relatively small and stable reconstruction error from the early stages of the iteration. However, similar to real images, the error also increases progressively over subsequent iterations. To facilitate a clearer visualization of the changes in the error maps, brightness enhancement was applied to the reconstructed error representations.

We propose a two-stage reconstruction framework designed to explicitly disentangle the artifact distribution. Through our observations, as illustrated in Fig. 2, we observe a particularly intriguing phenomenon when the inversion process is applied iteratively to real images: (a) The reconstruction error resulting from the first inversion-reconstruction cycle is the largest. (b) Beginning with the second reconstruction, the error decreases sharply and remains stable over subsequent iterations. (c) As the number of reconstruction iterations increases, the primary content of the image gradually deteriorates, and the corresponding error maps become increasingly stochastic in nature. When the same process is applied to AI-generated images, the phenomenon exhibits subtle changes: Stage (a) vanishes, and the process instead transitions directly into stage (b) from the very first iteration, subsequently progressing toward the distortion dynamics characterized by stage (c).

This phenomenon corroborates two hypotheses:

1. After undergoing a single reconstruction in stage (a), the distribution of real images becomes similar to that of AI-generated images.
2. AI-generated images are not entirely robust to the reconstruction process, and minor errors remain after reconstruction in stage (b).

Fig. 3. Reconstruction errors at stage (b) for different images. The magnitude and spatial distribution of the reconstruction errors differ across images. All error maps have been enhanced in brightness to improve visual clarity.

These minor errors stem from the texture and content of the images themselves and occur in the reconstruction of both AI-generated and real images. The error distribution in (a) is often mixed with the error distribution observed in (b). Previous work focused on extracting error features at stage (a), resulting in an impure error distribution. As shown in Fig. 3, due to differences in content and texture, the reconstruction errors at stage (b) vary significantly across different images. Therefore, we divide the errors at stage (a) by those at stage (b), which represents the pure artifact distribution. Specifically, after an image $\boldsymbol{I}$ is encoded into the latent space by a VAE, $\boldsymbol{z}_0 = \mathcal{E}(\boldsymbol{I})$ is obtained. The first-stage reconstruction of $\boldsymbol{z}_0$ is expressed as follows:

$$\boldsymbol{z}_T = Inversion(\boldsymbol{z}_0),\ \boldsymbol{z}_0' = Denoise(\boldsymbol{z}_T),\ \boldsymbol{I}_1 = \mathcal{D}(\boldsymbol{z}_0'),\ \boldsymbol{D}_1 = \boldsymbol{I}_1 - \boldsymbol{I}, \tag{5}$$

where $\boldsymbol{D}_1$ denotes the reconstruction error feature map of the first stage. Correspondingly, the reconstruction error of the second stage $\boldsymbol{D}_1$ is obtained through the following process:

$$\boldsymbol{z}'_T = Inversion(\boldsymbol{z}'_0),\ \boldsymbol{z}''_0 = Denoise(\boldsymbol{z}'_T),\ \boldsymbol{I}_2 = \mathcal{D}(\boldsymbol{z}''_0),\ \boldsymbol{D}_2 = \boldsymbol{I}_2 - \boldsymbol{I}_1. \tag{6}$$

Therefore, we obtain the final error feature value by dividing the L1 norm of the two feature maps:

$$d = \|\boldsymbol{D}_1\|_1 / \|\boldsymbol{D}_2\|_1 \tag{7}$$

Then we apply a threshold-based decision rule:

$$y = \begin{cases} Real, & d > \epsilon \\ Fake, & d < \epsilon \end{cases} \tag{8}$$

where ϵ denotes the segmentation threshold. If the error value is greater than the threshold, the image is considered non-robust to reconstruction and thus classified as a real image; otherwise, it is classified as an AI-Generated image.

3.3 Self-condition

As the inversion process is initiated from a given image, the corresponding prompt required to guide the reconstruction is inherently unavailable. A straightforward yet naive solution is to simply set the prompt to an empty input:

$$\boldsymbol{e}_\emptyset = \tau_\phi(\emptyset) \tag{9}$$

where $\emptyset$ denotes an empty string, serving as a placeholder for the missing prompt. Although this is the most widely adopted inversion procedure, the absence of prompts introduces a bias that causes the trajectories of inversion and denoising to deviate from the original distribution, thereby hindering the identification of AI-generated images based on reconstruction error. Prior studies have explored the use of BLIP to infer prompts from images in a reverse-mapping manner:

$$\boldsymbol{e}_{BLIP} = \tau_\phi(BLIP(\boldsymbol{x}_0)) \tag{10}$$

where $\boldsymbol{x}_0$ denotes the input image. However, the condition features are still compressed by discrete mapping, which inevitably leads to a loss of information. We adopt the image encoder of CLIP as the condition extractor to bypass prompts and directly extract continuous embeddings. Meanwhile, since the image encoder uses only one token to represent features, we replicate and pad it to meet the sequence length required for the condition input of diffusion:

$$\boldsymbol{e}_{self} = padding(CLIP(\boldsymbol{x}_0), max\_seqlen) \tag{11}$$

where $padding(\mathbf{e}, k)$ refers to replicating the feature $\mathbf{e}$ k times along the seqlen dimension. In this way, we preserve the continuous distribution from the image in the condition to adapt to the reconstruction process with high-precision requirements. The entire method is summarized in Algorithm 1.

Table 1. The L1 norm error values obtained on selected images from the SD1.5 subset of GenImage, using the SD1.5 backbone under a six-step DDIM schedule, with single-step noising and denoising at timestep $t = T$.

Image Source	Real Image (JPEG 96)	Fake Image (PNG)	Fake Image (JPEG 96)
image1	1.95×10^{-7}	-	-
image2	2.29×10^{-7}	-	-
image3	1.73×10^{-7}	-	-
image4	-	2.36×10^{-9}	1.31×10^{-7}
image5	-	2.35×10^{-9}	1.80×10^{-7}
image6	-	2.07×10^{-9}	1.55×10^{-7}

4 Experimentation

4.1 Dataset

Based on GenImage, we propose a new evaluation benchmark GenNEXT that includes AI-generated images from various generative models and eliminates artifacts introduced by JPEG compression. GenImage introduces a large-scale benchmark comprising over one million paired real and AI-generated images synthesized by state-of-the-art diffusion and GAN-based models. It enables rigorous evaluation of detection methods through cross-generator and degraded image classification tasks, simulating real-world challenges in generative image forensics. GenImage incorporates eight generators, including BigGAN, GLIDE, VQDM, Stable Diffusion V1.4 (SD1.4), Stable Diffusion V1.5 (SD1.5), ADM, Midjourney, and Wukong. The real images in GenImage are sampled from ImageNet. Consequently, the 1000 class labels from ImageNet are also adopted to condition the generative models for synthesizing fake images. In the test set,

Algorithm 1. DDRE: Dual-stage Diffusion Reconstruction for Detection

Require: Image $\boldsymbol{I}$, diffusion model $\mathcal{M}$, VAE encoder $\mathcal{E}$, decoder $\mathcal{D}$, CLIP encoder $\mathcal{C}$, threshold ϵ

Ensure: Predicted label $y \in \{\texttt{Real}, \texttt{Fake}\}$

$\boldsymbol{z}_0 \leftarrow \mathcal{E}(\boldsymbol{I})$
$e_{\text{self}} \leftarrow \text{padding}(\mathcal{C}(\boldsymbol{I}), \text{max\_seqlen})$
$\boldsymbol{z}_T \leftarrow \text{Inversion}(\boldsymbol{z}_0, \boldsymbol{e}_{\text{self}})$
$\boldsymbol{z}_0' \leftarrow \text{Denoise}(\boldsymbol{z}_T, \boldsymbol{e}_{\text{self}})$
$\boldsymbol{I}_1 \leftarrow \mathcal{D}(\boldsymbol{z}_0')$
$\boldsymbol{z}_T' \leftarrow \text{Inversion}(\boldsymbol{z}_0', \boldsymbol{e}_{\text{self}})$
$\boldsymbol{z}_0'' \leftarrow \text{Denoise}(\boldsymbol{z}_T', \boldsymbol{e}_{\text{self}})$
$\boldsymbol{I}_2 \leftarrow \mathcal{D}(\boldsymbol{z}_0'')$
$\boldsymbol{D}_1 \leftarrow \|\boldsymbol{I}_1 - \boldsymbol{I}_2\|_1, \boldsymbol{D}_2 \leftarrow \|\boldsymbol{I}_2 - \boldsymbol{I}_1\|_1$
$d \leftarrow \boldsymbol{D}_1 / \boldsymbol{D}_2$,
if $d > \epsilon$ **then**
  $y \leftarrow \texttt{Real}$
else
  $y \leftarrow \texttt{Fake}$
end if
return y

each class contains 6 real images and 6 generated images. For the SD1.5 generator, the number is slightly increased to 8 real and 8 generated images per class. In total, the 8 test subsets comprise 50,000 real images and 50,000 generated images.

Our GenNEXT benchmark extends the construction protocol of GenImage by incorporating three additional generators—Stable Diffusion 2 (SD2), Stable Diffusion 3 (SD3), and FLUX.1, thereby introducing more recent models, particularly those based on DiT, into the evaluation. In terms of data volume, we align with GenImage by allocating six real images and six generated images per class for each generator. Recently, several researchers [5] have noted that JPEG compression can introduce additional biases during dataset construction. In the case of GenImage, most real images are stored in JPEG format with a quality factor of 96, while all generated images are saved as lossless PNGs. This discrepancy may be more detrimental than previously assumed. In Table 1, our small-scale experiments suggest that this error may even lead to metric discrepancies of up to two orders of magnitude. Therefore, we compress the generated images in the original GenImage test set into JPEG format with a quality factor of 96. Subsequently, both the generated and real images are re-saved in PNG format to prevent the accumulation of compression-induced bias during multiple rounds of read and write operations in experiments. In summary, GenNEXT comprises 11 test subsets, with all images standardized to a unified compression quality. It serves as a low-bias evaluation benchmark encompassing a diverse set of generative models.

4.2 Experiment Setup

We selected SD1.5 as the unified backbone and employed DDIM as the denoising scheduler. In Sect. 4.4, we conduct a detailed ablation study on the backbone network and analyze the reasons why SD1.5 outperforms other backbones. We follow the denoising step configurations used in the compared methods. In cases where no specific investigation of the timesteps is conducted, we adopt the standard DDIM scheduler with 50 steps for denoising sampling. For each specific baseline model, we follow its original approach for computing the error-related feature values. Both DIRE and FakeInversion employ a ResNet-based classification network following the extraction of error-related features. For the sake of fair comparison and to focus our investigation on eliminating complex training procedures, we remove their classification networks and instead perform classification directly using a threshold-based approach. We observe that, among thresholding methods based on L1 and L2 norms, the L2 norm is more effective for single-pass reconstruction approaches such as DIRE and FakeInversion. Therefore, we employ the L2 norm as the scalarization method for error features in our threshold-based framework. We acknowledge that DIRE and FakeInversion achieve superior performance when their classification networks are retained. Our objective is to explore more effective feature extraction strategies during the reconstruction phase in the context of training-free and rapidly deployable models, rather than to diminish the contributions of previous research efforts. For each comparison method, we independently select an appropriate threshold, as both the backbone and the method itself can influence the choice of threshold. The experiments were performed on a single NVIDIA GeForce RTX 3090 GPU.

Table 2. Quantitative comparison on GenNEXT. The † denotes the removal of the classification network, and * indicates replacement with SD1.5 due to the use of alternative diffusion backbones.

Test Sets	Compared Methods					
	DDRE(Ours)	DIRE†*	SeDIDstat*	RIGID	ZeroFake*	FakeInv†
SD1.5	**90.69**	58.50	55.16	59.53	77.66	<u>89.79</u>
SD1.4	**90.58**	58.25	55.13	59.48	77.84	<u>89.64</u>
biggan	73.59	85.23	<u>85.58</u>	**86.44**	57.79	74.24
midjourney	**68.45**	60.12	65.07	<u>66.18</u>	55.07	55.32
wukong	**92.47**	54.35	50.42	63.14	79.73	<u>91.42</u>
vqdm	53.92	55.33	<u>72.54</u>	**83.29**	47.32	55.43
glide	<u>67.03</u>	64.80	**78.55**	65.08	57.72	65.76
adm	59.95	66.03	**78.48**	<u>78.12</u>	50.57	53.20
SD2	**72.41**	54.21	63.71	51.62	68.12	<u>70.12</u>
SD3	<u>67.90</u>	62.41	59.01	63.70	**71.45**	66.81
FLUX.1	**80.21**	67.70	71.77	72.14	70.52	<u>74.41</u>
avg ACC	**74.29**	62.45	66.86	68.07	64.89	<u>71.47</u>

4.3 Quantitative Results

We compare DDRE with previous methods across all 11 subsets of GenNEXT by computing classification accuracy to evaluate model performance. As shown in Table 2, DDRE achieves either the best or second-best results on multiple subsets and reaches state-of-the-art performance in terms of average accuracy. While DDRE achieves exceptionally high accuracy on several subsets, it approaches the performance of a random classifier on only two subsets. In contrast, the baseline methods exhibit near-random accuracy on 3 to 5 subsets, and in some extreme cases, even fall below random chance. Although DDRE adopts a latent diffusion model as its backbone, it demonstrates consistently strong performance across subsets generated by diffusion models, latent diffusion models, and DiT-based models, highlighting its superior generalization capability to unseen generators.

4.4 Ablations

We conducted comprehensive ablation studies to rigorously validate the effectiveness of our proposed method. As shown in Table 3, we first compare the

Table 3. Ablation on the Number of Stages and Norm Types

Norm	Stage Setting		
	1-stage	2-stage	3-stage
L1 Norm	67.24	**74.29**	64.03
	70.32	72.79	51.49

impact of two-stage reconstruction and norm type on detection performance. For the ablation study on the three-stage reconstruction strategy, we adopt a hierarchical error ratio as the scalarization method—specifically, the ratio between the error ratio of stages 1 and 2 and that of Stages 3 and 4, denoted as:

$$d_{\text{3-stage}} = \frac{\|\boldsymbol{D}_1\| \cdot \|\boldsymbol{D}_3\|}{\|\boldsymbol{D}_2\|^2} \tag{12}$$

where $\boldsymbol{D}_1$, $\boldsymbol{D}_2$, and $\boldsymbol{D}_3$ denote the error feature maps from the three reconstruction stages, respectively. The motivation behind this design is to further decouple the intrinsic distributional error of the image itself by incorporating the iterative change induced by stage (c), as discussed in Sect. 3.2. The ablation results demonstrate that the combination of the two-stage strategy and L1 norm yields the most effective error decoupling. Interestingly, while the L1 norm performs better in the two-stage setting, the L2 norm shows superior performance when the method degrades to a single-stage configuration. This observation supports our hypothesis that the proposed two-stage framework successfully decouples artifact distributions into a lower-order feature space, thereby reducing the need to introduce additional complexity during scalarization to enhance artifact-related features.

To verify the effectiveness of the Self-Conditioning method, we conduct a controlled comparison by keeping all other settings fixed and evaluating two conditions: using empty prompts and using prompts generated by BLIP. As shown in Table 4, the proposed Self-Conditioning strategy significantly improves the quality of conditional inputs, thereby enhancing the ability to distinguish AI-generated images.

In addition, we perform ablation on the backbone network. Although SD2 shares a similar architecture with SD1.5, differences in training data distribution lead to a degradation in detection performance. While DiT-based models such as SD3 and FLUX.1 benefit from higher-quality training data, the Flow-matching training paradigm currently lacks support for high-fidelity inversion, resulting in performance comparable to that of a random classifier. Based on these observations, we adopt SD1.5 as the backbone for all experiments (Table 5).

Table 4. Ablation on Conditioning Methods

Self-condition (DDRE)	w/o prompt	w/ BLIP
74.29	66.39	72.70

Table 5. Ablation on Backbones

SD1.5 (DDRE)	SD2	SD3	FLUX
74.29	68.46	54.62	56.05

5 Conclusion

In this work, we present DDRE, a novel, training-free framework for AI-generated image detection that explicitly disentangles artifact distributions from the intrinsic image content during the diffusion reconstruction process. By introducing a two-stage inversion-reconstruction strategy and a self-conditioning mechanism, DDRE effectively isolates generative artifacts and enhances reconstruction fidelity, thereby improving detection performance. Moreover, we propose GenNEXT, a refined benchmark that mitigates JPEG compression bias and incorporates a broader range of generative models, providing a more robust evaluation platform. Extensive experiments demonstrate that DDRE achieves state-of-the-art performance across a diverse set of unseen generators, validating its superior generalization capability. We believe this work provides new insights into understanding and leveraging diffusion-based reconstruction artifacts and offers a strong foundation for future research on robust and efficient generative content forensics.

In future research, we hope to see the development of more generalized models that can achieve consistently high detection accuracy across virtually all unknown generative models. Beyond using diffusion models as the backbone, alternatives such as DINOv2 also exhibit desirable properties for this task. Thus, exploring higher-quality backbones and more universally applicable reconstruction behaviors represents a promising research direction. Furthermore, enhancing the effectiveness of conditional guidance not only benefits the detection of AI-generated images but also contributes to improving performance in related tasks such as image editing. On the benchmarking side, in addition to mitigating JPEG compression artifacts, discrepancies in real-world image data distributions can also introduce substantial performance bias. Notably, differences among real-world datasets may account for a performance variation of 10–20%, which should not be overlooked.

References

1. Chen, Z., Liu, J., He, W., Zhang, Q.: SeDID: semantic diffusion for AI-generated image detection. arXiv preprint arXiv:2403.09167 (2024)
2. Dhariwal, P., Nichol, A.: Diffusion models beat GANs on image synthesis. Adv. Neural. Inf. Process. Syst. **34**, 8780–8794 (2021)
3. Frank, J., Eisenhofer, T., Schönherr, L., Fischer, A., Kolossa, D., Holz, T.: Leveraging frequency analysis for deep fake image recognition. In: International Conference on Machine Learning, pp. 3247–3258. PMLR (2020)
4. Goodfellow, I.J., et al.: Generative adversarial nets. Adv. Neural. Inf. Proc. Syst. **27** (2014)
5. Grommelt, P., Weiss, L., Pfreundt, F.J., Keuper, J.: Fake or JPEG? Revealing common biases in generated image detection datasets. In: Del Bue, A., Canton, C., Pont-Tuset, J., Tommasi, T. (eds.) European Conference on Computer Vision. LNCS, vol. 15644, pp. 80–95. Springer, Cham (2025). https://doi.org/10.1007/978-3-031-92089-9_6
6. Ho, J., Jain, A., Abbeel, P.: Denoising diffusion probabilistic models. Adv. Neural. Inf. Process. Syst. **33**, 6840–6851 (2020)
7. Huang, Y., Zhang, X., Wu, Y., et al.: FakeInversion: prompt-guided inversion for AI-generated image detection. arXiv preprint arXiv:2404.02369 (2024)
8. Li, L., et al.: Face X-ray for more general face forgery detection. In: Proceedings of the IEEE/CVF Conference on Computer Vision and Pattern Recognition, pp. 5001–5010 (2020)
9. Lipman, Y., et al.: Flow matching for generative modeling. In: International Conference on Machine Learning (ICML) (2023)
10. Liu, S., et al.: FLUX: flow matching for latent diffusion. arXiv preprint arXiv:2405.13722 (2024)
11. Ma, L., Wang, P., Wang, Y., et al.: A deepfake detector generalizing to unseen generative models using vision transformers. IEEE Trans. Pattern Anal. Mach. Intell. (2023)
12. Marra, F., Gragnaniello, D., Verdoliva, L., Poggi, G.: Detection of GAN-generated fake images over social networks. In: 2018 IEEE Conference on Multimedia Information Processing and Retrieval (MIPR), pp. 384–389 (2018)
13. Marra, F., Gragnaniello, D., Verdoliva, L., Poggi, G.: Inception forensics: learning dense representations for detection and localization of GAN-generated images. In: Proceedings of the IEEE/CVF Conference on Computer Vision and Pattern Recognition, pp. 6457–6466 (2019)
14. McCloskey, S., Albright, M.: Detecting GAN-generated imagery using saturation cues. In: IEEE International Conference on Computer Vision Workshops (ICCVW) (2019)
15. Oquab, M., Darcet, T., Moutakanni, T., et al.: DINOv2: learning robust visual features without supervision. arXiv preprint arXiv:2304.07193 (2023)
16. Rombach, R., Blattmann, A., Lorenz, D., Esser, P., Ommer, B.: High-resolution image synthesis with latent diffusion models. In: Proceedings of the IEEE/CVF Conference on Computer Vision and Pattern Recognition (CVPR), pp. 10684–10695 (2022)
17. Sohl-Dickstein, J., Weiss, E.A., Maheswaranathan, N., Ganguli, S.: Deep unsupervised learning using nonequilibrium thermodynamics. arXiv preprint arXiv:1503.03585 (2015)

18. Song, J., Meng, C., Ermon, S.: Denoising diffusion implicit models. In: International Conference on Learning Representations (ICLR) (2021)
19. Stability AI: Stable diffusion 3 (2024). https://stability.ai/news/stable-diffusion-3. Accessed 07 Jul 2025
20. Wang, Q., Liu, Y., Chen, Y., et al.: Rigid: reliable generalization for image deepfake detection via distillation. arXiv preprint arXiv:2307.05750 (2023)
21. Wang, S.Y., Wang, O., Zhang, R., Owens, A., Efros, A.A.: CNN-generated images are surprisingly easy to spot... for now. In: Proceedings of the IEEE/CVF Conference on Computer Vision and Pattern Recognition, pp. 8695–8704 (2020)
22. Wang, X., et al.: DIT: diffusion transformer. arXiv preprint arXiv:2212.09748 (2022)
23. Wang, X., Zhuang, B., et al.: Exposing AI-generated images via diffusion reconstruction. arXiv preprint arXiv:2309.09512 (2023)
24. Wang, Z., Chen, J., Jiang, W., Lu, H., Luo, P.: DIRE for diffusion-generated image detection. In: Proceedings of the IEEE/CVF International Conference on Computer Vision, pp. 22445–22455 (2023)
25. Yu, N., Davis, L.S., Fritz, M.: Attributing fake images to GANs: learning and analyzing GAN fingerprints. In: Proceedings of the IEEE/CVF International Conference on Computer Vision, pp. 7556–7566 (2019)
26. Zhang, H., Sun, K., Qiu, Z., et al.: ZeroFake: prompt-free zero-shot detection of AI-generated images. arXiv preprint arXiv:2405.12288 (2024)
27. Zhang, T., Kishore, V., Wu, F., Weinberger, K.Q., Artzi, Y.: Detecting face synthesis using convolutional neural networks and image quality assessment. In: Proceedings of the IEEE/CVF Conference on Computer Vision and Pattern Recognition, pp. 10917–10926 (2019)
28. Zhao, F., Zhang, H., Liu, B.: LaRE$\hat{2}$: lightweight and efficient reconstruction-based detection of AI-generated images. arXiv preprint arXiv:2403.18726 (2024)

Towards Trustworthy Document Information Extraction with Self-evaluation Mechanism

Haoyu Cao(✉), Anqi Gou, Rui Hu, and Haobin Cao

University of Science and Technology of China, Hefei 230026, Anhui, China
{caohaoyu,gouan7,be23011005,caohaobin2023}@mail.ustc.edu.cn

Abstract. Document Information Extraction (DIE) plays a crucial role in document understanding systems by identifying structured information from various documents with applications spanning academic research to industry. While recent end-to-end generative models have demonstrated promising results, their over-reliance on language information often leads to imbalanced multimodal integration and utilization, compromising the trustworthiness of extracted results. To address this issue, we present a novel trustworthy framework that integrates a self-evaluation mechanism to enhance the reliability of document information extraction. This mechanism allows the model to evaluate and identify its generated results, facilitating our model to enhance the utilization of visual information without reducing the ability to use language information, thereby utilizing the visual and language information in a balanced way. Besides, an algorithm is introduced to automatically generate negative samples for the self-evaluation mechanism during training. Moreover, to ensure the negative samples do not adversely affect the model's learning process, we elaborately design a simple joint training optimization strategy. Extensive evaluations across three benchmark datasets (Ticket, CORD, and SROIE) demonstrate our method's superiority, achieving F1-score improvements of 2.1% over OmniParser, 2.9% over Donut in CORD dataset.

Keywords: Document Information · Trustworthy Extraction · Self-Evaluation

1 Introduction

Document information extraction (DIE) aims to structured key-value pairs from various document images, including receipts, forms, contracts, business invoices, and academic papers, which attracts substantial attention across academia and industry [1–6]. This challenging problem needs accurate and reliable output

H. Cao—These authors contributed equally to this work.

Supplementary Information The online version contains supplementary material available at https://doi.org/10.1007/978-981-95-5764-6_20.

© The Author(s), under exclusive license to Springer Nature Singapore Pte Ltd. 2026
J. Kittler et al. (Eds.): PRCV 2025, LNCS 16289, pp. 288–301, 2026.
https://doi.org/10.1007/978-981-95-5764-6_20

(a) Incorrect result "SHAN ALAM"

(b) Incorrect result "University"

Fig. 1. Incorrect results generated from existing end-to-end document models. (a) Incorrect result "SHAN ALAM" compared to the correct result "SHAH ALAM" with the clear document image. (b) Incorrect result "University" compared to the correct result "Universiti", which is semantically coherent but factually incorrect. The examples clearly show that end-to-end document models do not utilize visual and language information in a balanced way.

results, which demands harmonious integration of visual and language information [7,8]. Previous multimodal pre-training approaches predominantly adopt a two-stage paradigm: 1)OCR-driven text extraction followed by, 2) joint text-image comprehension [1,3–6,9,10]. While effective, this methodology has two inherent limitations: First, cascaded OCR dependencies bring additional computing overhead. Second, error propagation from imperfect OCR results compromises downstream performance [2,11–14].

Emerging end-to-end alternatives [2,11–14] eliminate the need for preprocessing with OCR tools in recent years. Representative works like Donut [2], SeRum [12], and OmniParser [13] demonstrate the viability of unified architectures for multimodal document parsing. However, our community increasingly recognizes critical limitations when applying the generative models to vision-language tasks requiring balanced multimodal integration, such as document information extraction, image captioning and visual reasoning. As evidenced in Fig. 1(a) and (b), current models frequently produce vision-language inconsistencies, which generate either visually obvious errors or semantically coherent yet factually incorrect predictions. We assume this stems from autoregressive models' excessive reliance on language information priors during sequential decoding, resulting in suboptimal visual information utilization. This observation motivates our investigation into balanced multimodal fusion for robust document information extraction. To address these limitations, we propose a novel trustworthy framework that establishes dynamic equilibrium between visual and language modalities through three key innovations.

First, we introduce a self-evaluation mechanism that allows the model to critically assess its own predictions. Unlike conventional autoregressive approaches, our mechanism can enhance visual understanding without suppressing linguistic reasoning capabilities. Second, we develop an automated negative sample generation algorithm that synthesizes visually similar high-quality negative samples without manual annotation. Third, we elaborately design a joint training optimization strategy for training both the positive and negative samples, ensuring the model to critically assess its own predictions.

Our contributions are summarized as follows:

1) We propose a novel mechanism called self-evaluation for enhancing the utilization of visual information without reducing the ability to use language information, resulting in utilizing visual and language information in a balanced way.
2) A brand-new joint training optimization strategy is proposed in this paper to optimize positive and negative samples simultaneously, which prevents negative samples from adversely affecting the model's learning process.
3) We introduce an algorithm to automatically build high-quality negative samples that are visually similar to positive samples during training.
4) Experimental results demonstrate our method achieves state-of-the-art performance on document information extraction task.

2 Related Work

Traditional methods for document information extraction [15] usually include feature selection manually, which is insufficient for complex document images. In recent years, many pre-trained models have achieved great success in the document field because of their capabilities to learn multi-modal representations effectively [2,4–6,9,11,12,16]. These methods can generally be divided into two categories: OCR-dependent methods and OCR-free end-to-end methods.

OCR-Dependent Methods for DIE. The OCR-dependent methods usually first extract text from the document images relying on OCR tools. Next, the results from OCR tools and images are used as input to understand the document. LayoutLM [6] is the first model to propose a combination of text and layout embedded in BERT models for pre-training. LayoutLMv2 [5] integrated visual feature information into the pre-training process to improve the model's ability to understand the image. LayoutLMv3 [4] designed various pre-training tasks to learn better text/image representations and their alignment. GeoLayoutLM [9] proposed geometric pre-training tasks to enhance the ability of handling DIE. However, these works are computationally expensive, and their high dependence on OCR tools often makes these models suffer from errors originating from OCR engines and reading order problems [2,11,12].

OCR-Free End-to-End Methods for DIE. In contrast, another line of work aims to alleviate the need for OCR tools and deal with documents in an end-to-end way [2,11–13,16,17]. Donut [2] introduces a new end-to-end model to address the problems induced by the OCR-dependency. Dessurt [16] operates in an end-to-end manner with a single pass: text segmentation and recognition are learned implicitly. SCOB [11] utilizes character-wise contrastive learning with online text rendering to bridge the domain gap between visual document understanding and scene text understanding domains. SeRum [12] further converts document image understanding and recognition tasks into a local decoding process of the interested visual tokens. OmniParser [13] is a universal model that can simultaneously handle three parsing tasks: text spotting, document information extraction, and table recognition.

However, most existing end-to-end models for DIE simply apply the generative models' structure without sufficiently considering their weaknesses. Such a structure may overly rely on language information, resulting in the unbalanced utilization of visual and language information. In contrast, our method is equipped with a novel task directing our model to enhance the utilization of visual information without reducing the ability to use language information, which results in using the visual and language information in a balanced way. The balanced use of visual and language information helps improve the accuracy and robustness of our model.

3 Methodology

3.1 Overall Architecture

As shown in Fig. 2, our framework involves a vision encoder and query-text decoder, which is similar to existing works [2,12].

Vision Encoder aims to map the input document image $\mathbf{x} \in \mathbb{R}^{H \times W \times C}$ into a feature $\mathcal{F} \in \mathbb{R}^{h \times w \times d}$ which can be processed by subsequent modules. The feature $\mathcal{F}$ is further serialized into a set of embeddings. We utilize the Swin Transformer [18] with modifications. The Swin Transformer divides the input image $\mathbf{x}$ into non-overlapping patches, and applies Swin Transformer blocks consisting of a shifted window-based multi-head self-attention module and a two-layer MLP to these patches. Patch merging layers are subsequently applied to

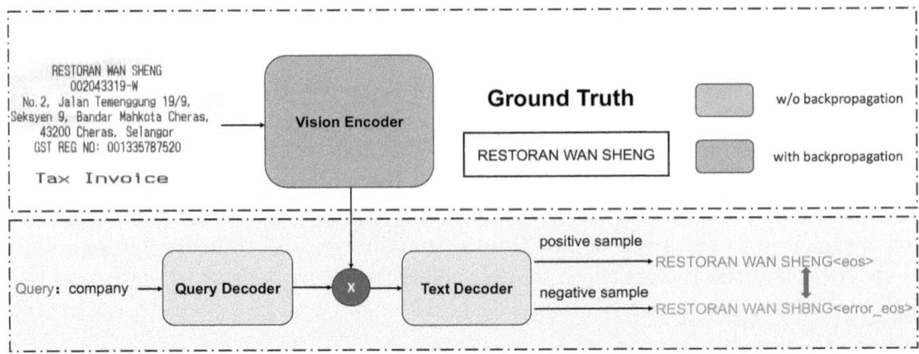

Fig. 2. The architecture of our proposed method. It is an end-to-end document model which aims to enhance the utilization of visual information without reducing the ability to use language information, resulting in the balanced utilization of visual and language information. An image and its corresponding query are the inputs of our model.

the patch tokens at each stage, and the output of the final Swin Transformer block is fed into the query-text decoder. The vision encoder also upsamples the feature map to a larger size for fine-grained mask area acquisition.

Query-Text Decoder consists of two sub-modules: the query decoder and the text decoder. The query decoder is a standard transformer decoder that utilizes the input queries and the image features to compute the per-segment embeddings. The goal of the text decoder is to decode the corresponding text token sequences, which generate text in an autoregressive manner by attending to the query embedding, previously generated tokens, and the encoded visual features.

3.2 Self-evaluation Mechanism

In order to enable a more balanced use of visual and language information, we've developed a self-evaluation mechanism. This approach involves appending a specific token to the end of text sequences to indicate correctness: $<eos>$ signifies a correct sequence (positive sample), while $<error\_eos>$ denotes an incorrect one (negative sample), with these incorrect sequences generated by a specific algorithm. This system trains the model to distinguish between positive and negative samples. For text lacking clear semantic coherence, the model must rely more heavily on visual information to differentiate visually similar results, as language alone is insufficient. Conversely, for semantically coherent texts, this self-evaluation task encourages the model to utilize both language and visual information, thereby enhancing its use of visual data without reducing its reliance on language. This balanced approach significantly improves the model's accuracy and robustness. During inference, our end-to-end model determines if a generated result is incorrect; if so, it appends an $<error\_eos>$ token; otherwise, it appends an $<eos>$ token. A specific example of our task is shown in Fig. 3.

Fig. 3. A specific example of our novel task and joint training scheme. For ground truth "SANYU STATIONERY SHOP", the positive sample is "SANYU STATIONERY SHOP<*eos*>", with all tokens participating in the gradient backpropagation and loss calculation. While the negative sample is "SANYO STATIONERY SHOP<*error_eos*>", with only "<*error_eos*>" participating in the gradient backpropagation and loss calculation.

3.3 Algorithm for Automatically Constructing Negative Samples

One challenge in training our task with both positive and negative samples is the difficulty of obtaining high-quality data. Positive samples can be constructed using ground truths, but currently, there are no available high-quality negative sample datasets. Generally, collecting and annotating datasets in the real world is impractical, as the number of negative samples corresponding to a positive sample can theoretically be infinite. This is why constructing negative samples using a common visually similar character table is not feasible, as negative samples are too huge for a similar character table to cover, which we will discuss in Sect. 4.4.

To provide a continuous supply of high-quality negative samples for our training, we propose an algorithm to automatically construct negative samples in this paper. Considering our self-evaluation task, we believe high-quality negative samples should be visually similar to positive samples. The algorithm for

Algorithm 1. Function *gen_negative_samples*()

```
Initialization gen_model, model
Get Image i, Query q, Epoch e, Max_epochs m
if e < m/3 then
    flag ← −1
else if m <= 2 * m/3 then
    flag ← 0.5
else
    flag ← 1
end if
Get prob ← random()
With torch.no_grad():
if prob > flag then
    gen_logits ← gen_model(i, q)
    negative_samples ← get_negative(gen_logits)
else
    gen_logits ← model(i, q)
    negative_samples ← get_negative(gen_logits)
end if
```

automatically constructing negative samples during training is presented in Algorithm 1. Specifically, we use a baseline model *gen_model* trained with only positive samples to obtain logits with image and query as inputs. And then we select the second candidate token to be the negative character. Next, we randomly replace the corresponding character in the ground truth with its negative character to obtain the incorrect text sequence, which is visually similar to the ground truth. Consequently, the incorrect text sequence and <*error_eos*> form a high-quality negative sample.

We divide the entire training process into three stages. In the first stage, only the *gen_model* is used to construct negative samples, enabling the model to generate high-quality negative samples. In the second stage, we use *gen_model* and *model* to generate negative samples with a probability of 0.5 each, aiming to increase the diversity of negative samples. In the third stage, we only use the *model* to generate negative samples, enabling the model to fully evaluate and identify its results. Experiments have shown the algorithm is capable of continually constructing high-quality negative samples during training, which we will further analyze in the ablation study in Sect. 4.4.

3.4 Joint Training Optimization Scheme

We elaborately design a joint training optimization scheme for training the positive and negative samples simultaneously. Our goal is to ensure that the negative samples do not have an adverse effect on the model's learning process. During the training phase, we implement a strategy that selectively blocks the gradient backpropagation of the text sequence within negative samples. Instead of backpropagating the entire sequence, only the gradient of the indicator <*error_eos*>, located at the end of the output result, is allowed to backpropagate. This approach prevents negative samples from adversely influencing the generation of correct results. In contrast, for positive samples, the gradients are backpropagated for all outputs, encompassing both the text sequence and the indicator *<eos>*. By incorporating this joint training optimization scheme, we enable the model to utilize the visual and language information in a balanced way using both positive and negative samples, while mitigating the potential negative impact of the latter. A specific example of our joint training optimization scheme is shown in Fig. 3. The loss of positive samples is defined as:

$$\mathcal{L}_{pos} = -\log P(y_T|\mathbf{i},\mathbf{q}) - \log P(y_I|\mathbf{i},\mathbf{q}) \tag{1}$$

where y_T and y_I respectively denote the ground truth of text sequence and *<eos>*. Besides, **i** and **q** respectively denote the document image and query as input. For positive samples, we use the complete text sequence along with the indicator at the end for gradient backpropagation and loss calculation. The loss of negative samples is expressed as:

$$\mathcal{L}_{neg} = -\log P(y_I|\mathbf{i},\mathbf{q}) \tag{2}$$

where y_I denotes the ground truth and *<error_eos>*. Besides, **i** and **q** respectively denote the document image and query as input. For negative samples, we only use the indicator at the end for gradient backpropagation and loss calculation. The total loss is given by:

$$\mathcal{L}_{total} = \mathcal{L}_{pos} + \mathcal{L}_{neg} \tag{3}$$

4 Experiments

In this section, we present a comprehensive experimental evaluation of our proposed model on the DIE task. To assess the effects of our model, we compare it with other methods. Experimental results show that our model achieves state-of-the-art performance on several public datasets in comparison with other end-to-end models.

4.1 Datasets and Metrics

We compare our method with other methods on various pubic datasets, including **CORD** [19], **Ticket** [20], and **SROIE** [21]. We employ the common metric, F1 score [2,5,10,12], to assess the model's performance. The F1 score is a harmonious average of precision and recall. Precision represents the model's capacity to accurately recognize positive instances, ensuring that it does not erroneously identify negative cases as correct. Recall evaluates the model's ability to recognize all positive cases, minimizing the chance of overlooking correct results. Consequently, a higher F1 score signifies that the model exhibits superior performance by achieving a balance between precision and recall.

Table 1. Comparisons with other models. ‡# parameters represents that OCR needs to be used.

	OCR	#Params	CORD [19]	Ticket [20]	SROIE [21]
			F1	F1	F1
SPADE [22]	✓	$93M + \alpha^{\ddagger}$	74.0	14.9	–
WYVERN [23]	✓	$106M + \alpha^{\ddagger}$	43.3	41.8	–
BERT [1]	✓	$86M + \alpha^{\ddagger}$	73.0	74.3	–
BROS [10]	✓	$86M + \alpha^{\ddagger}$	74.7	–	–
LayoutLM [6]	✓	$89M + \alpha^{\ddagger}$	78.9	–	–
LayoutLMv2 [5]	✓	$179M + \alpha^{\ddagger}$	78.9	87.2	61.0
LayoutLMv3 [4]	✓	$87M + \alpha^{\ddagger}$	80.2	–	77.7
TRIE [17]		–	–	–	82.1
Dessurt [16]		87M	82.5	–	84.9
Donut [2]		143M	84.1	94.1	83.2
DocParser [14]		70M	84.5	–	87.3
OmniParser [13]		–	84.8	–	85.6
SeRum-prompt [12]		136M	84.9	99.2	85.8
Ours		143M	**86.9**	**99.34**	**88.3**

Table 2. Effects of self-evaluation task. * represents our method has output results with both *<eos>* and *<error_eos>* indicators.

Tag	Model	F1	Precision	Recall
(a)	Donut [2]	83.2	83.2	83.2
(b)	SeRum-prompt [12]	85.8	85.8	85.8
(c)	Ours*	87.6	87.6	87.6
(d)	Ours	**88.3**	**89.7**	86.9

4.2 Implementation Details

We directly apply our method during the fine-tuning stage. Our model is initialized with the weights in Donut [2]. We utilize the Adam optimizer with an initial learning rate of 5×10^{-5} for all datasets, and incorporate a learning rate decay factor of 0.1 after every 10 epochs to enhance the model's performance. We set the batch size to 8 for CORD and Ticket, while the batch size for SROIE is 16. The input image resolution is set to 1600×1600. To ensure optimal performance and convergence of the model, we train all datasets for 100 epochs. We utilize the same generation mechanisms as SeRum-prompt [12], which uses the keys as queries and generates each value in parallel (Table 2).

4.3 Comparisons with Previous Approaches

We present a comparative evaluation of our proposed method with several previous approaches, including approaches that employ OCR tools as well as fully end-to-end methods. In the former, OCR tools are used to extract the text and position of the image. Approaches such as LayoutLMv3 [5] can produce satisfactory results when the OCR results are entirely accurate. We use the OCR engine API reported in Donut [2] and SeRum [12], including MS OCR and others, for consistency. Since our model is an end-to-end model, TRIE [17], Donut [2], Dessert [16], OmniParser [13] and SeRum [12] are our primary comparing targets. As shown in Table 1, our method achieves new state-of-the-art results on the three open benchmarks of document information extraction compared with other end-to-end document models. Especially for the SROIE dataset, which contains text sequences spanned across multiple lines with numerous characters, our method shows its superiority over other end-to-end document models. The results and comparisons demonstrate the effectiveness of our model for handling the DIE task.

Table 3. Ablation study for joint training optimization scheme in SROIE.

Tag	Our strategy	F1	Recall	Precision
(a)		85.9	82.3	89.9
(b)	✓	88.3	86.9	89.7

Table 4. Ablation study for our algorithm, which automatically constructs negative samples in SROIE.

Tag	Method	F1	Recall	Precision
(a)	Similar character table	86.8	85.7	87.8
(b)	Only gen_model	87.0	85.2	88.9
(c)	Only model	87.1	85.0	89.2
(d)	Our algorithm	88.3	86.9	89.7

4.4 Ablation Study

To further understand the effectiveness of the self-evaluation task, the joint training optimization scheme, and the algorithm to automatically construct negative samples, we conduct comprehensive experiments and thorough analyses.

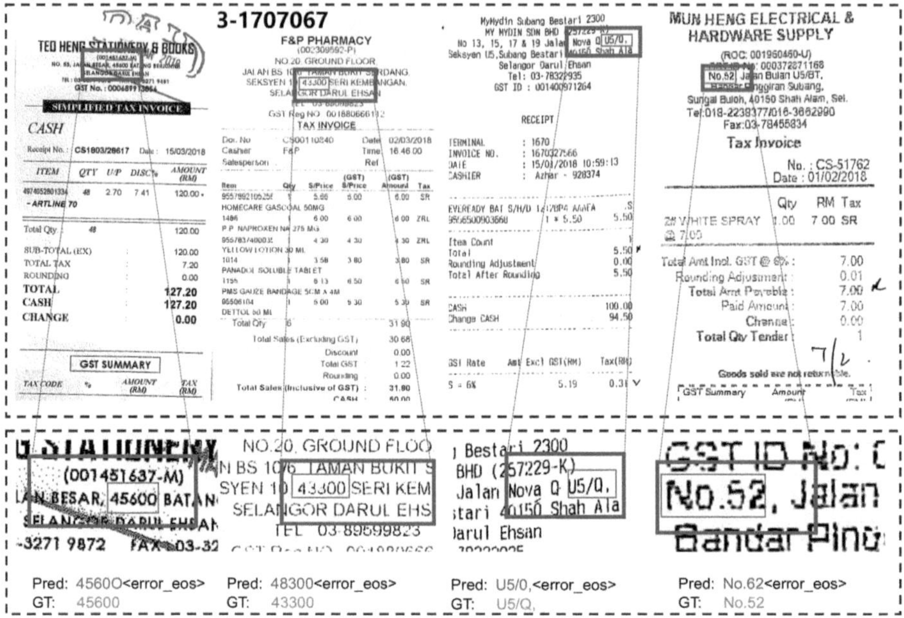

Fig. 4. The case study. Our method generates both the desired text sequence and the indicator simultaneously.

Effect of Self-evaluation Task. In order to alleviate the issue of unbalanced utilization of visual and language information in the majority of existing end-to-end models, we propose a novel task called self-evaluation that enhances the utilization of visual information without reducing the ability to use language information, consequently balancing visual and language information. This contributes to improving the accuracy, robustness, and reliability of the model in handling the DIE task. During inference, our method outputs results that the model deems correct based on the indicator. Once the model can identify its generated incorrect results, which are visually similar to correct results, it demonstrates that our model indeed enhances the utilization of visual information and balances the visual and language information. By comparing Tags (a) and (b) with (c) and (d), we observed that balancing the visual and language information improves the model's performance, especially in precision. Comparing Tags (c) and (d) reveals that our model has the capacity to identify its generated incorrect results, which are similar to the correct results. Additionally, the cases presented in Fig. 4 further demonstrate the effectiveness of the self-evaluation task, which helps the model identify incorrect results that are visually similar to correct results.

Effect of Joint Training Optimization Strategy. To ensure that negative samples do not have an adverse effect on the model's learning process, we have elaborately designed a joint training optimization scheme. During the training process, only the indicator at the end of the negative samples participates in gradient backpropagation and loss calculation. To figure out the effectiveness of the joint training optimization scheme, we conduct experiments with a normal training strategy where all results of negative samples participate in gradient backpropagation and loss calculation. As shown in Table 3, by comparing (a) and (b), the model using the joint training optimization scheme achieved an improvement of over 2.3% in F1 score, over 0.2% in precision, and especially over 4.0% in recall on the SROIE dataset. The comparison indicates that the negative samples indeed adversely affect the model to generate correct results. And the obvious decline in recall further demonstrates a reduction in the model's ability to generate correct results.

Effect of Algorithm for Generating Negative Samples. To evaluate our algorithm for automatically generating negative samples during training, we conducted ablation experiments on SROIE, comparing three methods: (a) random replacement using a visually similar character table, (b) using a baseline (gen) model throughout training, and (c) using the model itself during training. Tag (d) represents our proposed algorithm. As shown in Table 4, comparing Tags (a) with (b), (c), (d) demonstrates that using manually constructed visually similar character tables to construct negative samples makes it lack diversity, which is insufficient for training the model. By comparing Tag (b) and (d), we find that our algorithm improves the F1-score by 1.3%, suggesting that constructing negative samples using only a well-trained baseline model is inadequate. This method also results in a lack of diversity in negative samples, with fixed negative samples in each epoch. Comparing Tag (c) and (d), we find that our algorithm improves the F1-score by 1.2%, suggesting that constructing negative samples using only the model itself is suboptimal. This is because the model is far from converging during the initial training, yielding low-quality negative samples with poor performance. The results of our experiments confirm the effectiveness of our proposed algorithm to automatically construct negative samples.

5 Conclusion

We present an end-to-end document model that aims to better use visual information without reducing its ability to utilize language information. With our self-evaluation mechanism, it is capable of utilizing visual and information in a balanced way to improve the accuracy and robustness of the model. We introduce an algorithm to automatically construct high-quality negative samples during the training process. Moreover, we propose a brand-new joint training optimization scheme to prevent negative samples from adversely affecting the learning process of the model. Besides, the self-evaluation task can be easily employed in methods that utilize generative models. The generality of this task remains to be further explored. Moreover, our method shows potential in making end-to-end document models more trustworthy and reliable.

References

1. Hwang, W., et al.: Post-OCR parsing: building simple and robust parser via bio tagging. In: Workshop on Document Intelligence at NeurIPS 2019 (2019)
2. Kim, G., et al.: OCR-free document understanding transformer. In: Avidan, S., Brostow, G., Cissé, M., Farinella, G.M., Hassner, T. (eds.) European Conference on Computer Vision. LNCS, pp. 498–517. Springer, Cham (2022). https://doi.org/10.1007/978-3-031-19815-1_29
3. Tang, Z., et al.: Unifying vision, text, and layout for universal document processing. In: Proceedings of the IEEE/CVF Conference on Computer Vision and Pattern Recognition, pp. 19254–19264 (2023)
4. Huang, Y., Lv, T., Cui, L., Lu, Y., Wei, F.: LayoutLMv3: pre-training for document AI with unified text and image masking. In: Proceedings of the 30th ACM International Conference on Multimedia, pp. 4083–4091 (2022)
5. Xu, Y., et al.: LayoutLMv2: multi-modal pre-training for visually-rich document understanding. arXiv preprint arXiv:2012.14740 (2020)
6. Xu, Y., Li, M., Cui, L., Huang, S., Wei, F., Zhou, M.: LayoutLM: pre-training of text and layout for document image understanding. In: Proceedings of the 26th ACM SIGKDD International Conference on Knowledge Discovery & Data Mining, pp. 1192–1200 (2020)
7. Cui, L., Xu, Y., Lv, T., Wei, F.: Document AI: benchmarks, models and applications. arXiv preprint arXiv:2111.08609 (2021)
8. Long, S., He, X., Yao, C.: Scene text detection and recognition: the deep learning era. Int. J. Comput. Vis. **129**, 161–184 (2021)
9. Luo, C., Cheng, C., Zheng, Q., Yao, C.: GeoLayoutLM: geometric pre-training for visual information extraction. In: Proceedings of the IEEE/CVF Conference on Computer Vision and Pattern Recognition, pp. 7092–7101 (2023)
10. Hong, T., Kim, D., Ji, M., Hwang, W., Nam, D., Park, S.: BROS: a pre-trained language model focusing on text and layout for better key information extraction from documents. In: Proceedings of the AAAI Conference on Artificial Intelligence, pp. 10767–10775 (2022)
11. Kim, D., Kim, Y., Kim, D., Lim, Y., Kim, G., Kil, T.: SCOB: universal text understanding via character-wise supervised contrastive learning with online text rendering for bridging domain gap. In: Proceedings of the IEEE/CVF International Conference on Computer Vision, pp. 19562–19573 (2023)
12. Cao, H., et al.: Attention where it matters: rethinking visual document understanding with selective region concentration. In: Proceedings of the IEEE/CVF International Conference on Computer Vision, pp. 19517–19527 (2023)
13. Wan, J., et al.: OmniParser: a unified framework for text spotting, key information extraction and table recognition. arXiv preprint arXiv:2403.19128 (2024)
14. Dhouib, M., Bettaieb, G., Shabou, A.: DocParser: end-to-end OCR-free information extraction from visually rich documents. In: Fink, G.A., Jain, R., Kise, K., Zanibbi, R. (eds.) International Conference on Document Analysis and Recognition, vol. 14191, pp. 155–172. Springer, Cham (2023). https://doi.org/10.1007/978-3-031-41734-4_10
15. Shilman, M., Liang, P., Viola, P.: Learning nongenerative grammatical models for document analysis. In: Tenth IEEE International Conference on Computer Vision, ICCV'05, Volume 1, vol. 2, pp. 962–969. IEEE (2005)

16. Davis, B., Morse, B., Price, B., Tensmeyer, C., Wigington, C., Morariu, V.: End-to-end document recognition and understanding with Dessurt. In: Karlinsky, L., Michaeli, T., Nishino, K. (eds.) European Conference on Computer Vision, ECCV 2022. LNCS, pp. 280–296. Springer, Cham (2022). https://doi.org/10.1007/978-3-031-25069-9_19
17. Zhang, P., et al.: TRIE: end-to-end text reading and information extraction for document understanding. In: Proceedings of the 28th ACM International Conference on Multimedia, pp. 1413–1422 (2020)
18. Liu, Z., et al.: Swin Transformer: hierarchical vision transformer using shifted windows. In: Proceedings of the IEEE/CVF International Conference on Computer Vision, pp. 10012–10022 (2021)
19. Park, S., et al.: CORD: a consolidated receipt dataset for post-OCR parsing. In: Workshop on Document Intelligence at NeurIPS 2019 (2019)
20. Guo, H., Qin, X., Liu, J., Han, J., Liu, J., Ding, E.: EATEN: entity-aware attention for single shot visual text extraction. In: 2019 International Conference on Document Analysis and Recognition, ICDAR 2019, 20–25 September 2019, Sydney, Australia, pp. 254–259. IEEE (2019)
21. Huang, Z., et al.: ICDAR2019 competition on scanned receipt OCR and information extraction. CoRR abs/2103.10213 (2021)
22. Hwang, W., Yim, J., Park, S., Yang, S., Seo, M.: Spatial dependency parsing for semi-structured document information extraction. In: Zong, C., Xia, F., Li, W., Navigli, R. (eds.) Findings of the Association for Computational Linguistics, ACL/IJCNLP 2021, Online Event, 1–6 August 2021, vol. ACL/IJCNLP 2021, pp. 330–343. Association for Computational Linguistics (2021)
23. Hwang, A., Frey, W.R., McKeown, K.R.: Towards augmenting lexical resources for slang and African American English. In: Zampieri, M., Nakov, P., Ljubesic, N., Tiedemann, J., Scherrer, Y. (eds.) Proceedings of the 7th Workshop on NLP for Similar Languages, Varieties and Dialects, VarDial@COLING 2020, Barcelona, Spain (Online), 13 December 2020, pp. 160–172. International Committee on Computational Linguistics (ICCL) (2020)

Multimodal Applications of Large Language Models: From Robotics to Healthcare and Scientific Discovery

TrafXpert: Zero-Shot Road Anomaly Reasoning via Chain-of-Anomaly Thought

Jiaying Wu(✉), Liqi Yan, Siqi Song, and Yun Li

Hangzhou Dianzi University, Hangzhou, Zhejiang, China
23080806@hdu.edu.cn

Abstract. With the rapid development of intelligent transportation systems (ITS), the complexity and dynamics of urban traffic continue to increase, making traffic anomaly detection and analysis more and more important. Traditional traffic anomaly detection methods have disadvantages such as poor flexibility, limited detection range, and overly strong assumptions about data distribution. Existing vision-language models also exhibit deficiencies in local feature sensitivity, causal reasoning, and zero-shot generalization when applied to road anomaly detection. To tackle these challenges, this study introduces **TrafXpert**, a zero-shot road anomaly reasoning framework that pushes the boundaries of generalization and reliability in traffic anomaly detection. **First**, this framework innovatively combines image features extracted by a visual encoder with multi-source data to construct a conditional probability model, and realizes the preliminary judgment of traffic scene anomalies by calculating the posterior probability. **Second**, it uses large models to mark seed samples and then generate a large number of question-answering data in batches, and generates high-quality enhanced corpus by designing specific Prompts to standardize the output. **Third**, based on a specific model, it goes through stages of perception, judgment, and classification to achieve accurate identification and classification of traffic anomalies. This framework can quickly and accurately detect various types of traffic anomalies, providing a new solution for anomaly detection in the field of intelligent transportation. All models and datasets will be publicly available.

Keywords: Traffic Anomaly Detection · Multimodal Large Models · Zero-Shot Generalization · Deep Learning

1 Introduction

With the rapid development of ITS, the growing complexity and dynamics of urban traffic have made traffic anomaly detection increasingly critical. Anomalies like damaged road markings, potholes, spillage, congestion, and accidents severely threaten road safety and traffic efficiency [1], urging the urgent need for an intelligent method to efficiently and accurately identify multiple traffic anomalies in the ITS field [2] (Fig. 1).

© The Author(s), under exclusive license to Springer Nature Singapore Pte Ltd. 2026
J. Kittler et al. (Eds.): PRCV 2025, LNCS 16289, pp. 305–318, 2026.
https://doi.org/10.1007/978-981-95-5764-6_21

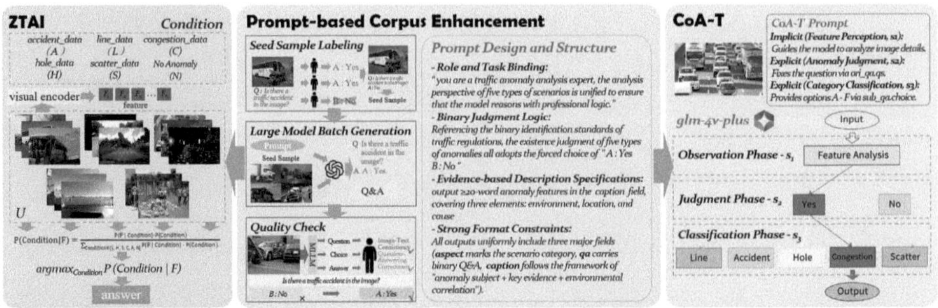

Fig. 1. Overall Framework of our Method. The diagram outlines a traffic anomaly detection workflow with three modules: ZTAI for Bayesian-based inference, Prompt-based Corpus Enhancement for dataset building, and CoA-T for step-by-step reasoning, enabling accurate and interpretable detection.

Traditional traffic anomaly detection methods mainly rely on rule-based algorithms, sensor-based detection, and statistical model-based detection [3], but these methods have many drawbacks: rule-based algorithms lack flexibility and are difficult to adapt to complex scenarios [4]; sensor-based detection has limited coverage and is susceptible to environmental interference [5]; statistical model-based detection has strong assumptions about data distribution and is difficult to cope with sudden anomalies [6].

With the development of Vision-Language Models (VLMs), their application in traffic anomaly detection offers new approaches to overcome the limitations of traditional methods [7]. Existing VLMs, such as ViLA [8], OmniVLM [9], GPT-4V [10], and CLIP [11], have made significant progress in tasks like image description generation, Visual Question Answering (VQA), and zero-shot object recognition [12]. However, several limitations remain: **1)** Current VLMs exhibit insufficient sensitivity to local subtle features, such as cracks in road markings or small-scale spillage [13]. **2)** In environments with multi-object interactions or traffic congestion, these models have limited causal reasoning capabilities [14], failing to accurately analyze the relationships between anomalies [15]. **3)** The application of existing zero-shot transfer learning methods in traffic scenarios also poses challenges [16,17].

To address the aforementioned challenges, this study proposes **TrafXpert**, a zero-shot reasoning framework designed to enable rapid and accurate detection of diverse road anomalies. By integrating advanced inference mechanisms, targeted corpus augmentation, and interpretable reasoning strategies, TrafXpert aims to push the boundaries of generalization and reliability in traffic anomaly detection. The specific methods are as follows:

First, we propose a Zero-shot Traffic Anomaly Inference (ZTAI) module extracts image features with a visual encoder, combines multi-source data, constructs a conditional probability model, calculates $P(\text{Condition}|\text{F})$and uses argmax to preliminarily detect traffic scene anomalies. **Second**, we use a Prompt-based Corpus Enhancement module to label seed samples, batch-generate Q&A data with a large model, conduct quality checks, design prompts, and standardize the output of the enhanced corpus. **Third**, we also put forward a Chain-of-Anomaly Thought (CoA-T) module, based on GLM-4v-plus, analyzes image features in the perception stage, determines anomaly presence in the judgment stage, and classifies anomalies into traffic scene types in the classification stage for accurate identification.

The main contributions of our study are as follows:

- Constructed RoadCompass, the first dataset covering 5D traffic indicators (road lines, scatter, accidents, potholes, congestion), enabling comprehensive VLM cognitive evaluation in traffic scenarios.
- Proposed a zero-shot transfer learning framework for traffic anomaly reasoning, enabling accurate multi-type anomaly identification without target-domain labeled data.
- Developed specific-anomaly and unified-classification Prompts, enhancing detection performance via format constraints and enabling cross-anomaly model evaluation.
- Introduced a two-stage reasoning strategy integrating CoT and ToT, boosting reasoning in complex scenes for zero-shot transfer learning applications.

2 Related Work

2.1 Vision-Language Models

In recent years, Vision-Language Models (VLMs) have made significant strides in uniting visual perception with linguistic reasoning through multimodal alignment. This capability has attracted considerable interest in autonomous driving (AD) and intelligent transportation systems (ITS). For example, ViLA [8] excels at fine-grained scene descriptions-capturing line cracks and obstacle layouts-via detailed visiontext alignment. OmniVLM [9] incorporates an adaptive environment module to robustly detect debris and potholes under rain, fog, or low-light conditions. GPT-4V [10], with its vast parameter count and world knowledge, delivers superior causal explanations in accident analysis. Meanwhile, CLIP [11]'s contrastive-learning framework builds an open-vocabulary visual space, reducing dependence on closed-set labels and opening paths for long-tail traffic event recognition.

Despite these advances, VLMs still struggle with detection of subtle local anomalies (e.g., fine line fissures or small scatters), causal inference in crowded or congested scenes, and zero-shot generalization to new risk categories. We therefore undertake a systematic evaluation of diverse VLM architectures on zero-shot traffic-scene understanding.

2.2 Zero-Shot Transfer Learning

Zero-shot transfer learning leverages pre-trained models to tackle unseen tasks or domains without additional tuning. CLIP first showed that a contrastively learned image-text embedding space can recognize tens of thousands of open-domain categories without fine-tuning, suggesting a route for detecting novel road obstacles. Subsequent work has extended this to dynamic environments: Florence [18] uses hierarchical concept disentanglement to improve detection under occlusion, and BLIP-2 [19] employs lightweight adapters for multimodal fusion to achieve state-of-the-art zero-shot question answering in low-light traffic scenes. OpenMask3D [20] adapts CLIP to 3D point clouds, enabling open-vocabulary obstacle segmentation-achieving 78.9% accuracy on unseen highway-construction debris.

Traffic scenes pose unique challenges for zero-shot methods: models must grasp abstract concepts like "congestion" without domain examples and distinguish visually similar classes (e.g., "pothole" vs. "shadow"). Here, we benchmark emerging large models-such as DeepSeek-Reasoner [21] and Qwen2.5-VL-72B-Instruct [22] on zero-shot analysis of traffic states, establishing new standards for domain adaptability.

2.3 Road-Condition Classification Dataset

High-quality datasets are essential for advancing traffic-scene research. Existing benchmarks (KITTI [23], BDD100K [24], Argoverse [25]) focus on object detection and trajectory prediction, offering limited coverage of road anomalies: BDD100K, for instance, annotates just 2.3% anomaly scenes and omits fine-grained line-wear labels. Specialized sets-Pothole-600 [26–28] and CrashD [29],targeting single anomaly types, while RoadDamageDataset [30] catalogs cracks and wear but only on Japanese roads. None span multiple anomaly dimensions concurrently.

To fill this gap, we introduce **RoadCompass**, the first dataset annotated across five traffic-state dimensions: **Hole**, **Lines**, **Congestion**, **Accident**, and **Scatters**. Collected under varied lighting, weather, and roadway conditions, RoadCompass delivers high-precision, fine-grained annotations to rigorously assess VLMs' multimodal cognition and reasoning in complex traffic environments.

3 Methods

3.1 ZTAI : Zero-Shot Traffic Anomaly Inference

We partition all traffic road image sets U into six mutually exclusive and exhaustive subsets based on anomaly types: road marking line damage L, road hole pit H, road spillage S, traffic congestion C, traffic accident A, and no anomaly N, satisfying the mutual exclusivity and exhaustiveness: $L \cup S \cup H \cup C \cup A \cup N = U$ and $L \cap S \cap H \cap C \cap A \cap N = \emptyset$. A single data point x is defined as a feature sequence of length n (each feature contains f-dimensional information, i.e., $x \in \mathbb{R}^{n \times f}$). For example, when $n = 200$ data packets and each packet has $f = 8$-dimensional features, it forms a 1600-dimensional high-dimensional feature space. For a labeled scenario d, the dataset contains m data points $X_d = \{x_1^d, x_2^d, \ldots, x_m^d\}$ and corresponding labels Y_d, while an unseen scenario $d \in U$ only has data points X_d without labels. [31,32]

Inference Model and Probability Framework. The zero-shot inference process is based on Bayes' theorem, realizing anomaly state inference through posterior probability calculation (this method is named ZTAI, i.e., Zero-shot Traffic Anomaly Inference). The formula is as follows:

$$P(\text{Condition}|\text{F}) = \frac{P(\text{F}|\text{Condition}) \cdot P(\text{Condition})}{\sum_{\text{Condition}\in\{L,H,S,C,A,N\}} P(\text{F}|\text{Condition}) \cdot P(\text{Condition})} \quad (1)$$

where: Condition represents road anomaly states (e.g., $\{L, H, S, C, A, N\}$); F is the feature of the input road image; $P(\text{Condition})$ is the prior probability of the anomaly state (based on historical data statistics, the prior probability of the normal scenario N is usually higher than that of the accident scenario A); $P(\text{F}|\text{Condition})$ is the likelihood function, representing the probability of the image appearing given the anomaly state; $P(\text{Condition}|\text{F})$ is the posterior probability, i.e., the probability of the anomaly state inferred from the image.

Inference Process and Formula Mapping. To show how the inference workflow aligns with Bayesian formula (1), we break it down as follows:

- **Image Encoding**: Extract the image feature vector F through a visual encoder, corresponding to the input of the likelihood function $P(\text{F}|\text{Condition})$ in the formula;
- **Joint Inference**: The model combines text prompts with image features, calculates the posterior probability of each state based on the Bayesian framework, and selects the state with the maximum posterior probability $\text{argmax}_{\text{Condition}} P(\text{Condition}|\text{F})$, corresponding to the binary decision (A/B) of qa.ans in the code;
- **Result Generation**: The caption field describes the inference basis of the posterior probability in natural language, such as " There is a 10-meter-long construction gravel spill on the road, possibly caused by a truck leak", corresponding to the semantic interpretation of $P(\text{Condition}|\text{F})$ in the formula.

This framework transforms zero-shot learning into a probability inference problem through Bayes' theorem, using the prior knowledge of pre-trained models (such as traffic rules and anomaly patterns) and the visual evidence of input images to achieve generalizable inference for unseen anomaly types.

3.2 Prompt-Based Corpus Enhancement

Corpus Construction Process. To systematically build high-quality traffic anomaly datasets, we design a three-stage corpus construction pipeline. This process balances human expertise for accuracy with large model efficiency for scale, ensuring both precision and coverage across anomaly scenarios.

- **Seed Sample Labeling**: Randomly select 20 high-resolution road images from each scenario, and three annotators independently complete the binary label ("A:Yes" or "B:No") for "whether an anomaly exists" and a scenario description of $\geq$ 20 words. Through cross-validation, samples with a tripartite consistency rate $\geq 90\%$ are screened as the seed set.
- **Large Model Batch Generation**: Based on similar images in public datasets, using the "few-shot Prompting" method, input the seed samples and custom templates into GPT-4o to automatically generate JSONL annotation records containing fields such as aspect, dataset, image_name, qa, and caption, with a scale of approximately 300–900 records per category.
- **Quality Check**: Batch-verify JSONL integrity via regex, randomly sample records for manual review against original images, correct mislabeled entries or misleading descriptions.

Prompt Design: Structured-Driven Professional Analysis. To make the model output meet the professional requirements of traffic anomaly analysis in terms of semantic accuracy and structural standardization, the Prompt design is constructed around four dimensions: "role setting, problem logic, evidence description, and format constraint".

- **Role and Task Binding**: Through the identity setting of "you are a traffic anomaly analysis expert", the analysis perspective of five types of scenarios is unified to ensure that the model reasons with professional logic.
- **Binary Judgment Logic**: Referencing the binary identification standards of traffic regulations, the existence judgment of five types of anomalies all adopts the forced choice of "A:Yes/B:No" (e.g., "Does a traffic accident exist in the image?"), eliminating ambiguities caused by open-ended questions.
- **Evidence-Based Description Specifications**: The model is required to output $\geq$ 20-word anomaly features in caption, covering three elements: environment, location, and cause, to build a standardized evidence chain.
- **Strong Format Constraints**: All outputs uniformly include three major fields (aspect marks the scenario category, qa carries binary Q&A, caption follows the framework of "anomaly subject + key evidence + environmental correlation"), and extra text/notes are disabled to ensure direct parsing by downstream systems.

3.3 CoA-T: Chain-of-Anomaly Thought

Traditional Direct Inference Method. In road anomaly detection tasks, traditional approaches prioritize computational efficiency by simplifying the process into a direct probability-maximization operation. When given an input road image x, these methods generate a classification result y^* using the formula below, aiming to produce an output in a single step:

$$y^* = \arg\max_y P(y \mid x) \tag{2}$$

While efficient, this "black-box" paradigm lacks interpretability. It fails to explain *how* visual features in the image lead to the final classification. For instance, in complex traffic scenarios, errors like misclassifying a hairline crack as a pothole become difficult to trace, and there is no clear pathway to refine the model's logic.

CoA-T: Chain-of-Anomaly Thought Framework. To address these limitations, we propose **CoA-T (Chain-of-Anomaly Thought)**, a structured reasoning mechanism that decomposes road anomaly detection into three sequential, human-like steps: *Feature Perception* → *Anomaly Judgment* → *Category Classification*. This transparency mirrors how humans analyze road anomalies in practice.

For an input image x, CoA-T does not directly output the final classification y. Instead, it breaks the reasoning process into a product of conditional probabilities across intermediate steps s_1, s_2, s_3, deriving results through step-by-step inference. The core mathematical formulation is:

$$P(y \mid x) = P(s_3 \mid x, s_2) \cdot P(s_2 \mid x, s_1) \cdot P(s_1 \mid x) \tag{3}$$

Step Roles Each intermediate step serves a distinct purpose in constructing a complete reasoning chain:

- s_1: Extracts low-level anomaly features from the input image (e.g., blurred lane markings, potholes), providing the foundational "clues" for subsequent analysis.
- s_2: Uses the features identified in s_1 to make a binary judgment: *Does an anomaly exist?* This converts visual clues into a simple yes/no decision.
- s_3: If s_2 confirms an anomaly, this step maps the anomaly to a specific category (e.g., `lines_data` for damaged lane markings, `hole_data` for potholes).

Generalized Reasoning CoA-T is not limited to three steps—it generalizes to n reasoning steps, ensuring the model's logic remains transparent and traceable. Mathematically, this step-by-step optimization is expressed as:

$$\{s_1^n, \ldots, s_n^n\} = \arg\max_{\{s_1^n, \ldots, s_n^n\}} \prod_{i=1}^{n} P(s_i \mid x, s_{<i}) \tag{4}$$

This structured design delivers two critical benefits:

- **Error Tracing**: Isolate errors to specific steps (e.g., if the final classification is flawed, check whether s_1 correctly extracted features).

- **Experimental Alignment**: s_1, s_2, s_3 align with implicit feature analysis, binary judgments (e.g., `ori_qa` questions), and category label mappings (e.g., `sub_qa` outputs), respectively.

By transforming the traditional "direct output" (opaque) approach into a step-by-step (transparent) reasoning framework, CoA-T enhances both the accuracy of road anomaly detection and the interpretability of model decisions—making it better suited for real-world traffic monitoring and safety applications.

4 Experiments

4.1 Experiment Settings

Datasets. We construct a multi-category road anomaly image dataset covering five major types of anomalies: **Lines**, **Congestion**, **Holes**, **Scatter**, and **Accidents**. The images are collected from public data platforms [33–35], encompassing diverse conditions such as different weather (sunny, cloudy), lighting (daytime, nighttime), and geographical environments (urban roads, wastelands, mountainous areas). During the annotation phase, we utilize GPT-4o [36] to perform automatic multimodal labeling on the images. To ensure high annotation quality, we incorporate a human verification process in which each annotation is cross-checked by multiple annotators. Inconsistent or ambiguous samples are either corrected or removed. The resulting annotations serve as the ground-truth references for subsequent model evaluation.

Implementation Details. We propose **TrafXpert**, a zero-shot anomaly detection framework built upon GLM-4v-Plus[37] as the base vision-language model. To comprehensively evaluate its generalizability, we also conduct zero-shot transfer experiments on several other representative vision-language models, including DeepSeek-VL-Reasoner [21], Qwen2.5-VL-72B-Instruct [22], GPT-4.1-nano [38], and Gemini-1.5-Flash [39]. All models are tested under a strict zero-shot setting without any task-specific fine-tuning. During inference, models are prompted to generate structured outputs from input images, consisting of a binary answer to the visual question and a concise caption summarizing the road scene. To ensure consistency and fair comparison, we design unified zero-shot prompt templates

Fig. 2. Examples of five traffic anomaly types and corresponding visual questions.

tailored to each anomaly type and model, guiding output generation through controlled natural language instructions (Fig. 2).

Evaluation. To assess the zero-shot performance of models across different tasks, we use accuracy as the primary evaluation metric. The evaluation procedure is as follows:

- Match the `image_name` field in the model output with the corresponding entry in the ground-truth annotation file;
- For successfully matched samples, compare the model-generated `answer` with the reference `answer` field;
- Compute accuracy as the proportion of correctly predicted samples over the total number of matched samples.

This evaluation protocol effectively measures model reasoning capabilities under different anomaly scenarios while avoiding interference from unmatched images, ensuring both objectivity and reproducibility of the experiment (Table 1).

4.2 Main Results

Table 1. Accuracy (%) of different vision-language models on five types of traffic anomaly detection tasks, with TrafXpert achieving the best overall performance compare to others.

Model	Line	Congestion	Pothole	Accident	Scatter
DeepSeek-Reasoner	65.99	69.40	50.62	49.94	49.15
Qwen2.5-VL-72B-Instruct	68.26	**98.17**	66.62	**81.08**	**93.42**
Gemini-1.5-Flash	49.17	81.65	74.67	50.61	78.47
GPT-4.1-nano-2025-04-14	**73.39**	89.13	**75.07**	59.36	41.67
TrafXpert(Ours)	**70.95**	**89.80**	**75.12**	**82.98**	**96.94**

Overall, Our TrafXpert exhibits the most consistent performance across all five perception tasks, with accuracy all above 70%. It achieves the highest accuracy of 96.94% in scatter detection, demonstrating strong adaptability in multi-task anomaly recognition. In traffic congestion detection, Qwen2.5-VL-72B-Instruct leads with 98.17%, also performing well on scatter (93.42%) and accident detection (81.08%), making it suitable for real-time traffic monitoring. GPT-4.1-nano-2025-04-14 excels in pothole detection (75.07%) and lane marking recognition (73.39%), highlighting strengths in fine-grained structure extraction. However, its scatter detection accuracy is only 41.67%, indicating challenges in modeling random or unstructured events. Gemini-1.5-Flash performs poorly in lane marking detection (49.17%), far below its performance on other tasks, revealing difficulty in recognizing narrow linear features. In contrast, DeepSeek-Reasoner shows moderate results (50–70%), with accident (49.94%), pothole (50.62%), and scatter (49.15%) detection accuracy near random chance, reflecting weaknesses in dynamic scene understanding.

TrafXpert consistently outperforms traditional models across all five anomaly detection tasks. Compared with KNN [40], PSPNet [41], Res50-Seg [42], Decision Tree [43], SAE [44], Enet-SAD [45], DANet [46], YOLOv8+DAT [47], and GMM+HSV [48], it achieves higher accuracy in each corresponding aspect, demonstrating superior robustness and classification capability (Fig. 3).

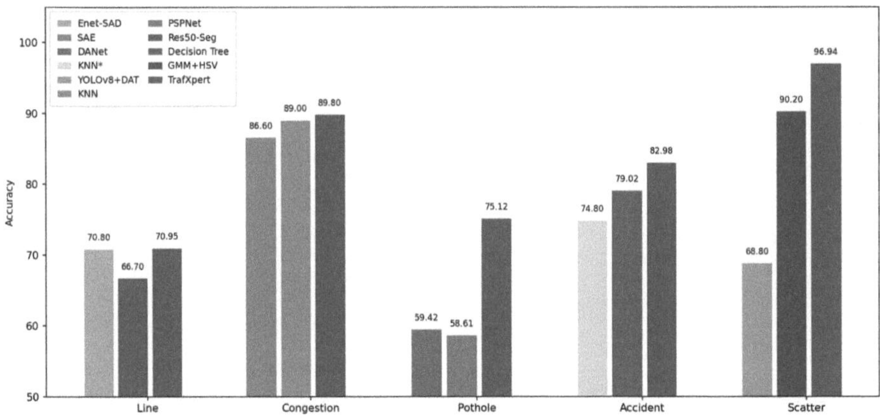

Fig. 3. Comparison between TrafXpert and traditional models. It can be observed that ours outperforms traditional models across all five aspects.

4.3 Ablation Study

To further enhance the performance of the model in multicategory anomaly detection tasks, we conducted an ablation study by incorporating a **task-of-thought with observation-judgment classification for traffic anomaly detection (CoA-T)** reasoning mechanism into the best-performing model, **TrafXpert**. Instead of performing direct one-step classification, the task is decomposed into two consecutive cognitive steps, mimicking the human reasoning process in complex visual understanding:

- **Primary Question:** *Is there any traffic anomaly in the image?*
- **Conditional Sub-question:** *If yes, what type of anomaly does it belong to?*

Experimental results show that CoA-T-based reasoning significantly improves model performance across multiple tasks. For instance, in traffic congestion detection, the accuracy increases from **89.80%** to **97.49%**. Similarly, accident and scatter detection tasks also see accuracy gains of approximately

2–3%. These results suggest that the explicit step-by-step reasoning path helps the model make more stable and accurate predictions, especially in ambiguous or uncertain scenarios (Fig. 4).

Q:Is there any abnormality on the road in this image?

(A) Yes (B) No

Sub_Q:What category does the anomaly belong to?

(A) Accident (D) Congestion

(B) Line (E) Hole

(C) Scatter (F) No abnormity

(a) CoA-T Question Structure

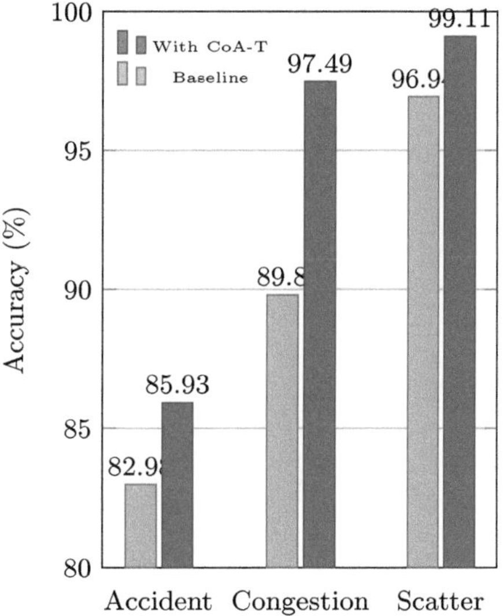

(b) Accuracy Improvement via CoA-T

Fig. 4. Illustration of CoA-T strategy and its impact on model performance.

5 Conclusion and Future Work

This study addresses the challenge of traffic anomaly detection in intelligent transportation systems. Analyzing the limitations of traditional methods and VLMs, we innovatively developed a zero-shot road anomaly reasoning framework. The ZTAI, Prompt-based Corpus Enhancement, and CoA-T modules enable preliminary judgment, data expansion, and precise classification, overcoming issues like inflexibility and low feature sensitivity.

Key achievements include: the RoadCompass dataset for evaluating VLMs in traffic; a zero-shot transfer learning paradigm for unlabeled data; improved reasoning performance via specific and unified Prompts; and enhanced reasoning in complex scenarios through a two-stage strategy.

Future research will be deepened and expanded in multiple dimensions:

- Integrate multi-source data such as infrared and millimeter-wave radar, and combine generative adversarial network algorithms to enhance the model's detection robustness in extreme environments such as rain, fog, and nighttime.

- Establish a dynamic mechanism for real-time data collection and annotation, and optimize the Prompt strategy through meta-learning to enhance the model's generalization ability in emerging scenarios such as autonomous vehicle failures.
- Expand the detection scenarios to special areas such as rural roads and expressways, analyze the differences in anomaly features under different road environments, and optimize cross-scenario transfer learning strategies.

Acknowledgements. This project is supported by Zhejiang Provincial Natural Science Foundation of China (NO. LQN25F020019), Fundamental Research Funds for the Provincial Universities of Zhejiang (NO. GK249909299001-033), and Zhiyuan Laboratory (NO. ZYL2024023).

References

1. Kong, H., Audibert, J.Y., Ponce, J.: Vanishing point detection for road detection. In: 2009 IEEE Conference on Computer Vision and Pattern Recognition, pp. 96–103. IEEE (2009)
2. Wang, T., et al.: M^2pt: multimodal prompt tuning for zero-shot instruction learning (2024)
3. Kong, H., Audibert, J.-Y., Ponce, J.: General road detection from a single image. IEEE Trans. Image Process. **19**(8), 2211–2220 (2010)
4. Lengyel, L.: Validating rule-based algorithms. Acta Polytech. Hung **12**, 59–75 (2015)
5. Kumar, H., et al.: Applications of nanotechnology in sensor-based detection of foodborne pathogens. Sensors **20**(7), 1966 (2020)
6. Qiao, T., Shi, R., Luo, X., Ming, X., Zheng, N., Yiming, W.: Statistical model-based detector via texture weight map: application in re-sampling authentication. IEEE Trans. Multimedia **21**(5), 1077–1092 (2018)
7. Liu, D., Cui, Y., Cao, Z., Chen, Y.: A large-scale simulation dataset: boost the detection accuracy for special weather conditions. In: 2020 International Joint Conference on Neural Networks (IJCNN), pp. 1–8 (2020)
8. Liu, Z., et al.: Efficient frontier visual language models. Nvila (2025)
9. Chen, W., Li, Z., Xin, S.: A token-compressed, sub-billion-parameter vision-language model for efficient on-device inference. Omnivlm (2024)
10. Yang, Z., et al.: The dawn of lmms: preliminary explorations with gpt-4v(ision) (2023)
11. Radford, A., et al.: Learning transferable visual models from natural language supervision (2021)
12. Yan, L., Han, C., Xu, Z., Liu, D., Wang, Q.: Prompt learns prompt: exploring knowledge-aware generative prompt collaboration for video captioning
13. Shtedritski, A., Rupprecht, C., Vedaldi, A.: What does clip know about a red circle? visual prompt engineering for vlms. In: Proceedings of the IEEE/CVF International Conference on Computer Vision, pp. 11987–11997 (2023)
14. Lan, L., Wang, X., Zhang, S., Tao, D., Gao, W., Huang, T.S.: Interacting tracklets for multi-object tracking. IEEE Trans. Image Process. **27**(9), 4585–4597 (2018)

15. Cui, Y., et al.: Dg-labeler and dgl-mots dataset: boost the autonomous driving perception. In: Proceedings of the IEEE/CVF Winter Conference on Applications of Computer Vision, pp. 58–67 (2022)
16. Dong, S., Feng, Y., Yang, Q., Huang, Y., Liu, D., Fan, H.: Efficient multimodal semantic segmentation via dual-prompt learning. In: 2024 IEEE/RSJ International Conference on Intelligent Robots and Systems (IROS), pp. 14196–14203. IEEE (2024)
17. Cao, W., et al.: A review on multimodal zero-shot learning. Wiley Interdisciplinary Rev. Data Min. Knowl. Disc. **13**(2), e1488 (2023)
18. Yuan, L., et al.: A new foundation model for computer vision. Florence (2021)
19. Li, J., Li, D., Savarese, S., Hoi, S.: Blip-2: bootstrapping language-image pre-training with frozen image encoders and large language models (2023)
20. Takmaz, A., Fedele, E., Sumner, R.W., Pollefeys, M., Tombari, F., Engelmann, F.: Openmask3d: open-vocabulary 3d instance segmentation. arXiv preprint arXiv:2306.13631 (2023)
21. Lu, H., et al.: Deepseek-vl: towards real-world vision-language understanding. arXiv preprint arXiv:2403.05525 (2024)
22. Bai, S., et al.: Qwen2. 5-vl technical report. arXiv preprint arXiv:2502.13923 (2025)
23. Vision meets robotics: The kitti dataset. Int. J. Robot. Res. **32**(11), 1231–1237 (2013)
24. Yu, F., et al.: Bdd100k: a diverse driving dataset for heterogeneous multitask learning. In: Proceedings of the IEEE/CVF Conference on Computer Vision and Pattern Recognition, pp. 2636–2645 (2020)
25. Chang, M.-F., et al.: Argoverse: 3d tracking and forecasting with rich maps. In: Proceedings of the IEEE/CVF Conference on Computer Vision and Pattern Recognition, pp. 8748–8757 (2019)
26. Fan, R., Ai, X., Dahnoun, N.: Road surface 3d reconstruction based on dense subpixel disparity map estimation. IEEE Trans. Image Process. **27**(6), 3025–3035 (2018)
27. Fan, R., Ozgunalp, U., Hosking, B., Liu, M., Pitas, I.: Pothole detection based on disparity transformation and road surface modeling. IEEE Trans. Image Process. **29**, 897–908 (2019)
28. Fan, R., Liu, M.: Road damage detection based on unsupervised disparity map segmentation. IEEE Trans. Intell. Transp. Syst. **21**(11), 4906–4911 (2019)
29. Lehner, A., et al.: 3d-vfield: adversarial augmentation of point clouds for domain generalization in 3d object detection. In: Proceedings of the IEEE/CVF Conference on Computer Vision and Pattern Recognition, pp. 17295–17304 (2022)
30. Arya, D., Maeda, H., Ghosh, S.K., Toshniwal, D., Sekimoto, Y.: Rdd2022: a multinational image dataset for automatic road damage detection. Geosci. Data J. **11**(4), 846–862 (2024)
31. Zhuang, J., et al.: See it, think it, sorted: large multimodal models are few-shot time series anomaly analyzers. arXiv preprint arXiv:2411.02465 (2024)
32. Xu, P., Zhu, X., Clifton, D.A.: Multimodal learning with transformers: a survey. IEEE Trans. Pattern Anal. Mach. Intell. **45**(10), 12113–12132 (2023)
33. Nienaber, S., Booysen, M.J., Kroon, R.S.: Detecting potholes using simple image processing techniques and real-world footage (2015)
34. Wen, L., et al.: A new benchmark and protocol for multi-object detection and tracking. Ua-detrac (2020)
35. Karim, F.: Clean & dirty road classification dataset. https://www.kaggle.com/datasets/faizalkarim/cleandirty-road-classification/data (2022)

36. Hurst, A., et al.: Gpt-4o system card. arXiv preprint arXiv:2410.21276 (2024)
37. Team GLM, et al.: Chatglm: a family of large language models from glm-130b to glm-4 all tools. arXiv preprint arXiv:2406.12793 (2024)
38. OpenAI. Gpt-4 technical report (2024)
39. Gemini Team, et al.: Gemini 1.5: unlocking multimodal understanding across millions of tokens of context. arXiv preprint arXiv:2403.05530 (2024)
40. Guo, G., Wang, H., Bell, D., Bi, Y., Greer, K.: Knn model-based approach in classification. In: On The Move to Meaningful Internet Systems 2003: CoopIS, DOA, and ODBASE: OTM Confederated International Conferences, CoopIS, DOA, and ODBASE 2003, Catania, Sicily, Italy, 3–7 November 2003. Proceedings, pp. 986–996. Springer (2003)
41. Yan, L., et al.: Psp net-based automatic segmentation network model for prostate magnetic resonance imaging. Comput. Methods Programs Biomed. **207**, 106211 (2021)
42. Jie, H., Xiong, Z., Wencai, X., Cao, K., Ruoyu, L., et al.: Lane detection based on lightweight convolutional neural networks. Laser Optoelectron. Progress **59**(10), 1015012–1015012 (2022)
43. Ying, L.U., et al.: Decision tree methods: applications for classification and prediction. Shanghai Arch. Psychiatry **27**(2), 130 (2015)
44. Tan, X., Zhou, Y., Zhao, L., Mei, Y.: Short-term traffic flow prediction based on sae and its parallel training. Appl. Intell. **54**(4), 3650–3664 (2024)
45. Lyu, H., Zhu, Z., Fu, S.: Enet-sad–a cnn-based lane detection for recognizing various road conditions. In: Third International Conference on Algorithms, Network, and Communication Technology (ICANCT 2024), vol. 13545, pp. 268–276. SPIE (2025)
46. Xue, H., Liu, C., Wan, F., Jiao, J., Ji, X., Ye, Q.: Danet: divergent activation for weakly supervised object localization. In: Proceedings of the IEEE/CVF International Conference on Computer Vision, pp. 6589–6598 (2019)
47. Jiang, Y.: Road damage detection and classification using deep neural networks. Disc. Appl. Sci. **6**(8), 421 (2024)
48. Chmelar, P., Benkrid, A., et al.: Efficiency of hsv over rgb gaussian mixture model for fire detection. In: 2014 24th International Conference Radioelektronika, pp. 1–4. IEEE (2014)

GenACT: Towards Unified Vision-Language-Action Co-training for Robot Manipulation

Jirong Liu and Cewu Lu(✉)

Shanghai Jiaotong University, Shanghai, China
{jirong,lucewu}@sjtu.edu.cn

Abstract. Vision-Language-Action models (VLAs) have emerged as a promising paradigm for building embodied agents, capable of acting in physical environments. Although often built from powerful Vision-Language models (VLMs), most existing VLAs cannot fully exploit the capacity of large foundation models, since they rely heavily on limited-scale action-only supervision. This narrow paradigm also limits their capabilities to leverage the internet-scale multimodal knowledge, thereby constraining their generalization capabilities. In this paper, we present **GenACT** (generative action transformer), a unified robot foundation model that moves beyond purely action-centric supervision and unifies modalities by tokenizing visual, language, and action into a shared discrete space. **GenACT** aims at unified vision-language-action co-learning which consists of two stages: (1) multimodal generative pretraining with a large language model and (2) multimodal action co-training. We adopt next token prediction as the training objective, where the model learns to predict future tokens across all modalities in a self-supervised manner, for a unified and flexible training paradigm. Hence, given language instruction and visual observation, the **GenACT** autoregressively generates action predictions. The experiments suggest that our training paradigm significantly benefits robot manipulation, and consequently **GenACT** achieves state-of-the-art (SOTA) manipulation performance on both simulation and real robot benchmarks. We also conduct thorough experiments to identify the key design choices.

Keywords: VLAs · Robot manipulation · Embodied Agent

1 Introduction

Building upon Vision-Language models (VLMs), Vision-Language-Action models (VLAs) aim to develop embodied agents that can perceive, understand, and act through sequential decision-making [1,3,12,17]. However, most current VLAs

Supplementary Information The online version contains supplementary material available at https://doi.org/10.1007/978-981-95-5764-6_22.

© The Author(s), under exclusive license to Springer Nature Singapore Pte Ltd. 2026
J. Kittler et al. (Eds.): PRCV 2025, LNCS 16289, pp. 319–333, 2026.
https://doi.org/10.1007/978-981-95-5764-6_22

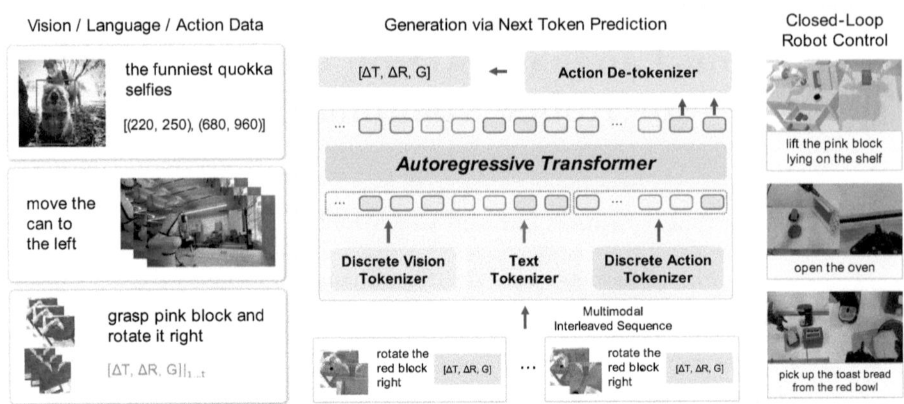

Fig. 1. We present **GenACT**, a fully-discrete robot foundation model empowered by vision-language-action co-training. **GenACT** unifies modalities by converting language, vision and action into a shared discrete token space and co-trains multimodal interleaved data and robot manipulation trajectories solely via next token prediction. Hence, **GenACT** shows SOTA performance on both simulation and real robot.

fail to achieve broader generalization and are prone to overfitting. One underlying cause is their reliance on labeled action data—a bottleneck that restricts scalability and generalization. Typically, VLAs are supervised only on the action modality [17], leading to significant degradation of multimodal capabilities despite initialization from pretrained VLMs [18]. Consequently, these VLAs struggle to retain the broader generalization capabilities of their parent models.

Furthermore, this narrow action-only training paradigm fails to fully exploit the vast capacity of large foundation models. Recent VLAs often employ lightweight action prediction heads as external modules to VLMs [1,17,18], which achieve commendable manipulation performance despite their modest parameter sizes, suggesting that low-level action prediction does not necessarily require large-scale parameters. Additionally, robot datasets exhibit significantly limited diversity compared to vision-language (VL) datasets [4,13]. Consequently, the vast capacity of large-scale foundation models remains underutilized in conventional VLA paradigms, as backbones typically collapse rapidly to fit only the training patterns, leading to significant loss of pretrained multimodal knowledge even though they are initialized from VLMs.

On the other hand, robot manipulation inherently demands strong spatial reasoning and temporal prediction capabilities [11,25,28]. However, most VLAs are not simultaneously pretrained on tasks that require these capabilities, such as visual grounding and video prediction. As a result, this limitation constitutes one major bottleneck for current VLA backbones as well.

These observations together lead to our central question: *Can we model vision, language and action in a unified generative manner, and can vision-language-action co-training benefit modern VLAs with increasingly larger param-*

eter scales by leveraging the world knowledge inherent in diverse multimodal data? To this end, we propose **GenACT**, a fully-discrete multimodal robot foundation model trained solely on next token prediction for vision-language-action co-training. The training pipeline consists of two stages: first, multimodal generative pretraining of an LLM-initialized transformer on large-scale curated VL datasets for VL alignment; second, multimodal action co-training that incorporates expert robot manipulation trajectories while retaining the model's multimodal capabilities through joint learning on full vision-language-action modalities.

Since robot manipulation trajectories are inherently formulated in an interleaved style, it can be modeled as a problem of generating multimodal-action interleaved sequences. Hence, we organize languages, vision, and actions as interleaved discrete tokens, facilitating next token prediction across the multimodal sequences. The fully discrete nature and casuality inherited from decoder-only large language models (LLMs) enables unified modeling of all modalities, flexible sequence construction, and simplified training. We opt for LLM initialization over VLMs as video prediction - a task proven beneficial for VLAs [28] - can be effectively modeled via next token prediction [26], enabling unified sequence modeling of vision, language, and action. We illustrate the overview in Fig. 1.

Experiments on both simulation and real robot demonstrate that vision-language-action co-training not only improves the model performance on seen manipulation tasks, but also significantly helps the model generalize to new environments and objects. In addition, we conduct ablation studies to identify key design choices.

We summarize our contributions as follows:

- We present **GenACT**, a robot foundation model that leverages a unified discrete input-output space and can be trained solely on next token prediction. **GenACT** supports easy co-training of VL tasks and robot manipulation thanks to the unified architecture.
- We validate that vision-language-action co-training effectively benefits robot manipulation learning with improved performance and data efficiency.
- **GenACT** achieves SOTA performance on both simulation and real robot benchmark, across various experimental settings, demonstrating strong manipulation performance.

2 Related Work

2.1 Vision-Language-Action Models

Recent research works have explored learning VLAs via finetuning vision-language models (VLMs) on multi-task robot dataset, thereby requiring minimal modification to the pretrained VLMs. For instance, RoboFlamingo [18] adds additional robot specific vision resampler and additional action head to prediction robot motion. RT-X [4] and OpenVLA [14] further scales up robot action learning by employing the large scale robot dataset Open-X [4]. Inspired by the recent progress in visual generation [24], π_0 [1] combines flow matching with VLMs and RDT-1B [19] trains a robot diffusion transformer from scratch.

The above works focus on building VLAs with minimal modifications to the VLMs. They often suggest using a separate continuous action prediction head and yield competitive manipulation performance. On the contrary, our work unifies action prediction and other VL tasks in a discrete manner, thereby leveraging the capacity of large foundation models and surpassing previous methods with decoupled action heads.

2.2 Co-training Action Data with Vision-Language Data

While much progress has been made in learning action generation with VLAs, an emerging line of research emphasizes improving their multimodal capabilities for better generalization through joint training with VL tasks. RT-2 [3] first demonstrates that incorporating general VL datasets enhances adaptation to novel objects. Alternatively, approaches like GR-1 [28], VPP [11] and LAPA [30] strengthen action representations from large-scale human video data, aiming to bridge the gap between human demonstrations and robotic execution. Further studies targeting high-level cognitive capabilities, such as task planning and spatial reasoning, incorporate specialized auxiliary objectives to enhance these skills, exemplified by π_0.5 [12] and Gemini Robotics [25].

Unlike these approaches, the fully-discrete nature of our approach enables the model to simply unify both multimodal understanding (spatial reasoning) and video prediction (future dynamics prediction)—two capabilities that are intuitively beneficial for VLAs but have not been effectively incorporated in previous models. This paradigm allows our model to flexibly handle a broader range of multimodal data, which not only expands the multimodal capacities available to VLAs but also contributes to improved performance of robot manipulation.

3 Multimodal Next Token Prediction

Given a token sequence $y = (y_1, ..., y_n)$, a causal transformer parameterized by θ models the probability of the sequence as:

$$P(y) = \prod_{i=1}^{n} P_\theta(y_i | y_{<i}), \tag{1}$$

The standard next token prediction objective optimizes the model by minimizing the cross entropy between the $P(y)$ and the empirical distribution of y.

To achieve next token prediction on multimodal sequences, a multimodal sample $x = (x_1, ..., x_m)$ can be tokenized by a unified tokenizer f, i.e. $y = f(x)$. The modality of x_j is one of the three modalities: vision, language, and action. And f employs the corresponding tokenizer (vision, language, and action) based on the modality of each x_j.

4 Approach

We present **GenACT** in this section. We start by introducing the modality tokenizer in Sect. 4.1. After that, we delve into the training paradigm of **GenACT** in Sect. 4.2. Please refer to the supplementary material for more data preparation and inference details.

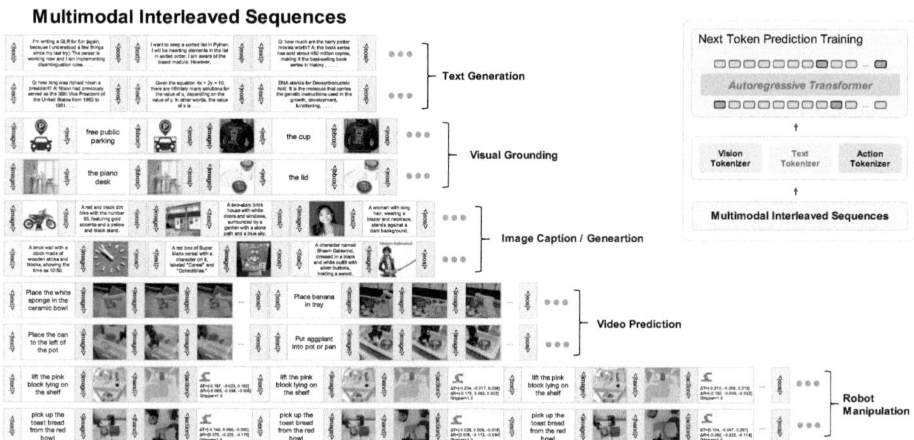

Fig. 2. Training pipeline of **GenACT**. We construct multimodal interleaved sequences by converting all modalities into a unified discrete token space and packing multiple samples to the maximum sequence length. Hence the model and various multimodal data can be trained simply via standard next token prediction. Currently, the training datasets include text generation, visual grounding, image caption, image generation, video prediction and robot manipulation.

4.1 Tokenization

We prepare tokenizers for images, texts and actions to tokenize them into a shared discrete space, which facilitates the unified training objective.

Text Tokenization. For language, we simply adopt the pretrained Qwen2.5 text tokenizer [29].

Vision Tokenization. For vision, we finetune a pretrained VQGAN checkpoint [5] on a mixed images sources, including robot datasets [4,21] and general VL datasets [7] to enhance its performance on robot data. The vision tokenizer discretizes the image with 16x spatial compression rate using a codebook size of 8192. After converting the images into discrete visual tokens by VQGAN, we flatten the visual token sequences and thus the images can be treated as 1D visual sentences. For instance, a 224×224 image can be converted to a visual token sequence with length 196.

Action Tokenization. Following [14], we discretize each dimension of robot actions into 256 bins, uniformly divided between the range $[-1, 1]$. Rather than employing the min-max boundary for normalization, we use the 1st and 99th quantile of action statistics from the training set to reduce the impact of outlier actions and enhance control granularity.

4.2 Vision-Language-Action Co-training

We train a transformer decoder initialized from the pretrained Qwen2.5-7B LLM to perform robot manipulation using standard next token prediction. We model robot manipulation as multimodal interleaved sequence generation.

Benefiting from the flexible sequence construction and simplified training, discrete token sequences are more suitable for learning interleaved generative tasks, such as image-to-text, text-to-image and image-text-to-action generation, by directly leveraging the sequence modeling capabilities of LLMs. Previous VLAs do not support this generation paradigm. The training paradigm of **Gen-ACT** offers a promising path towards building robot generalists and has the potential to unlock more multimodal capabilities.

We first train the LLM-initialized model on VL tasks for VL alignment. After that, we co-train the model using VL data and robot manipulation trajectories. To increase efficiency, we pack multiple samples into the maximum sequence length. The training process is shown in Fig. 2

Multimodal Generative Pretraining. Firstly, we curate large-scale VL datasets for VL alignment. VL tasks are constructed as interleaved sequences, leveraging the causality of autoregressive transformers. Specifically, we use the following data:

Text-Only. Text generation allows the robot to understand natural language instructions. Consequently, to preserve the LLMs' pretrained language capabilities, we utilize 2M textual sequences from a variety of natural language datasets [20,27]. We append a special token <|text|> to indicate the start of texts.

Image-Text. To align vision and language, we curate a large-scale image-text dataset, using re-annotated samples from [7,15]. In practice, we construct a visual caption task by placing the image before the text in a sequence. We use Qwen2.5-VL 32B to generate dense image captions. We use a special token <|image|> to indicate the start of images. We use 207M image-text pairs in total. A sample can be organized as (V_1, T_1), where V_1 represents visual observation and T_1 denotes the textual description.

Text-Image. This part shares the same dataset as the previous image-text setting, but with the sequence order reversed. Text-Image pairs represents text-conditioned image generation. A sample can be organized as (T_1, V_1).

Image-Text-Bounding Box. We further endow the model with the capability to generate bounding boxes. Intuitively, visual grounding helps the robots to locate the target objects. We represent the bounding box coordinates as "$(X_{top\ left}, Y_{top\ left}), (X_{bottom\ right}, Y_{bottom\ right})$" and normalize the coordinates within [0, 999]. We use a special token <|bbox|> for the start of bounding box coordinates. We use textual integers to tokenize bounding box coordinates. We train on a 10M subset of GRIT dataset [22]. A sample can be organzied as (T_1, V_1, T_{bbox}), where T_1 cotains the grounding reference, V_1 denotes image and T_{bbox} denotes the textual bounding box coordinates.

Text-Video. As suggested by [28], video data contains wealthy knowledge about temporal dynamics which can significantly improve robot manipulation. We therefore incorporate a curated video dataset built from open-source robot datasets and human activities datasets [4,6,8,9,13]. After data cleaning, we retain 2.3M high-quality videos, which cover diverse manipulation tasks and human activities. We treat each video frame as an independent image and the sequence is organized as a languaged-conditioned video prediction task, formulated as $(T_1, V_1, V2, ..., V_n)$, where the subfix n represents the timestep index.

Multimodal Action Co-training. In the second stage, we reduce the weight of the pretrained VL tasks and incorporate the robot manipulation datasets for action prediction learning.

Image-Text-Action. The sequence is formulated as interleaved image-text-action tuples temporally ranging from the beginning to the end of the manipulation tasks. In practice, we employ a sliding-window approach to enumerate all segment data across the complete trajectory for training efficiency. We use a special token <|action|> to indicate the start of actions. Additionally, since robot manipulation can be improved with multiview observation, we add a special token <|hand|> for the start of wrist camera observations. A manipulation trajectory can be formulated as $(T_1, V_1, H_1, A_1, T2, V2, H_2, A_2, ..., T_n, V_n, H_n, A_n)$, where A_n is the action at timestep n and H_n is the wrist camera image at timestep n.

5 Experiments

In this section, we first illustrate the supervision strategy and implementation details of **GenACT**. Then, we evaluate **GenACT** on both simulation and real robot benchmark. Finally, we conduct ablation studies in Sect. 5.4. We leave the implementation details in the supplementary material.

5.1 Supervision

Given that all modalities are converted into a unified discrete token space, we can apply the standard next token prediction loss straightforwardly. In addition, we

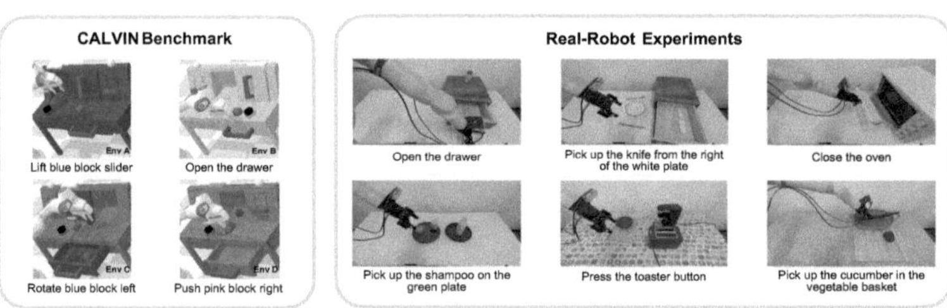

Fig. 3. CALVIN benchmark and real robot benchmark. Both benchmarks include various setups and manipulation skills.

pack the multimodal data into the maximum sequence length to maximize the training efficiency. Such a design choice results in a long sequence may consist of multiple data samples and we directly apply next token prediction training over the full sequence. We leave more details about sequence packing in the supplementary material.

In particular, during multimodal pretraining, we apply a weight of 0.2 to the visual token loss to avoid visual tokens dominating the learning process. During the multimodal action co-training stage, we only enable loss for the targeted modality relevant to each task except for the manipulation tasks. For example, we only activate vision loss for video prediction tasks and language loss for image caption tasks.

A notable exception is that we simultaneously activate action loss and vision loss for the manipulation tasks. Our ablation studies in Sect. 5.4 suggest that such a design choice is beneficial for robot manipulation because intuitively it prevents overfitting to the low-level action command and endows the model with the capability to infer the consequence of its action under the interleaved sequence formulation similar to the problem of world model [32].

Furthermore, we adopt classifer-free guidance (CFG) [10] during action learning, to enhance the model's capability of instruction following. In practice, we mask the language instruction of manipulation trajectories with a probability of 0.1 during training. We leave more details in the supplementary material.

5.2 Experimental Setup

To thoroughly evaluate **GenACT**'s performance, we benchmark it on both simulation tasks and real world robot experiments. Specifically, we choose a widely-used multi-task manipulation simulation benchmark CALVIN [21] and in-house real robot benchmark to evaluate our model. We show the overview in Fig. 3.

CALVIN Benchmark. CALVIN is a simulation benchmark for evaluating generalist robot policies, comprising 34 manipulation tasks across four scene settings, with 22,966 expert trajectories and language instructions. We report success rates for completing 1–5 consecutive tasks and the average number of tasks completed per trial over 1000 rollouts. Evaluations are conducted on split D, while models are trained on ABCD (multi-task learning) and ABC (unseen scene generalization). We use side and wrist cameras, a history window of 10 frames (9 past steps + current observation), and resize images to 224 × 224.

Real Robot Benchmark. Our real robot experiments are conducted on a 7-DoF Kinova Gen3 arm with a Robotiq 2F-85 gripper, using a Kinect Azure side camera and a RealSense D435 wrist camera. The models are trained on 105 tasks and over 70k in-house human teleoperation trajectories. We evaluate on 20 representative tasks involving skills such as `pick place`, `open`, `close`, `press button`, and `pour`. As in simulation, we test under both multi-task learning and generalization settings. The generalization setting includes 2 novel scenes with background changed and 20 novel target objects with distractors which are unseen during training. Each task is evaluated with 3 rollouts, and we report the average success rate. For fair comparison, baseline methods are finetuned on our training data. We use a history window of 8 frames during training and evaluation, and resize images to 224 × 224 resolution.

Baseline Methods. We consider several representative baseline methods on CALVIN benchmark with their reported performance. The strongest baseline VLA method is RoboVLMs [17]. The fundamental difference between **GenACT** and RoboVLMs is that RoboVLMs finetunes a VLM using an additional policy head, whereas **GenACT** processes all modalities within a unified autoregressive transformer and thus it supports flexible co-training of various multimodal data. Note that, we finetune OpenVLA [14], a commonly used VLA baseline on CALVIN.

For real robot experiments, we finetune π_0 [1] and OpenVLA [14] using the official finetuning recipe on our real robot data. π_0 is the SOTA conditioned policy based on flow matching whereas OpenVLA is a representative robot policy based on the next token prediction objective.

5.3 Experiment Results

Multimodal Generative Petraining and Unified Next Token Prediction Training surpasses current VLAs. As shown in Table 1, **GenACT** demonstrates strong and competitive multi-task learning performance on CALVIN Benckmark, compared against several representative baseline methods even without multimodal action co-training at the action learning stage (denoted as **GenACT w/ pretrain**). When trained on ABCD split and evaluated on D split, **GenACT** achieves an average executed length of 4.50 and a 5-task success rate of 80.9%, which is competitive to the SOTA method RoboVLMs. Note that, the average length indicates average number of tasks completed per rollout. It is evident that multimodal generative pretraining is effective for robot manipulation, since the model only achieves an average length of 2.35 if it is trained from scratch. Also, the results suggest that the precision loss caused by discrete action does not lead to significant performance drop. The precision loss introduced by

Table 1. Simulation performances on CALVIN benchmark, all models are trained on split ABCD/ABC, and evaluated on split D. **GenACT from scratch** represents the model trained on action prediction without multimodal pretraining, while **GenACT w/o co-train** indicates the model with only multimodal pretrain and without the multimodal action co-train stage. **GenACT w/ co-train** represents the full model with both training stages. **GenACT** surpasses previous models on both ABCD/ABC setting. *Avg.Len.* stands for average length.

Method	Train	Consecutive tasks success rates					*Avg. Len.*
		1	2	3	4	5	
RT-1 [2]		0.844	0.617	0.438	0.323	0.227	2.45
GR-1 [28]	ABCD	0.949	0.896	0.844	0.789	0.731	4.21
OpenVLA [14]		0.921	0.732	0.565	0.455	0.346	3.03
UP-VLA [31]		0.962	0.921	0.879	0.842	0.812	4.42
RoboVLMs [17]		0.967	0.930	0.899	0.865	0.826	4.49
GenACT from scratch		**0.804**	**0.603**	**0.426**	**0.323**	**0.221**	**2.35**
GenACT w/o co-train		**0.990**	**0.944**	**0.923**	**0.849**	**0.809**	**4.50**
GenACT w/ co-train		**0.992**	**0.966**	**0.931**	**0.883**	**0.830**	**4.61**
GR-1 [28]		0.854	0.712	0.596	0.497	0.401	3.06
Roboflamingo [18]	ABC	0.824	0.619	0.466	0.331	0.235	2.47
GR-MG [16]		0.968	0.893	0.815	0.727	0.644	4.04
UP-VLA [31]		0.928	0.865	0.815	0.769	0.699	4.08
RoboVLMs [17]		0.980	0.936	0.854	0.778	0.704	4.25
GenACT w/o co-train		**0.981**	**0.903**	**0.822**	**0.739**	**0.646**	**4.10**
GenACT w/ co-train		**0.989**	**0.935**	**0.871**	**0.804**	**0.738**	**4.37**

discrete action is tolerable compared to the controller error, which further highlights the simplicity and flexibility brought by this unified discrete framework. The same evidence can also be observed in real robot experiments shown in Fig. 4, where **GenACT w/o co-train** achieves a success rate of 65%, 45% and 50% across multi-task learning, unseen backgrounds, and unseen objects respectively which outperform the chosen baselines even without multimodal action co-training at the action learning stage.

Preserving Multimodal Knowledge via Co-training VL Data with Action Data at the Action Learning Stage is Essential for Boosting Robot Manipulation Performance, Especially for Generalization Experiments. Benefiting from the unified training, our model enables seamless co-training of various VL data with action data. This design preserves multimodal knowledge from pretraining, addressing the limitation of conventional VLA models that supervise only actions and thus suffer from multimodal capability forgetting. The generalization benefits are particularly evident in cross-domain evaluation. When trained on ABC splits and evaluated on the unseen D split, co-training VL data with action data (**GenACT w/ co-train**) demonstrates substantial improvements: average task length increases from 4.10 to 4.37, and 5-task success rate improves from 0.646 to 0.738. This improvement regarding unseen scene generalization highlights the critical role of multimodal capabilities—including spatial reasoning and future prediction provided by visual grounding and video prediction—in robot manipulation tasks. Similar generalization benefits extend to real robot experiments, where mutlimodal action co-training improves success rates by 5%, 15%, and 10% across multi-task learning, unseen backgrounds, and unseen objects respectively (Fig. 4). On the standard CALVIN benchmark setting (ABCD train split), **GenACT w/ co-train** achieves an average length of 4.61 and 5-task success rate of 83.0% as well. These results demonstrate our unified training pipeline effectively enables simple yet powerful co-training of diverse multimodal data, with particularly stronger generalization to unseen domains.

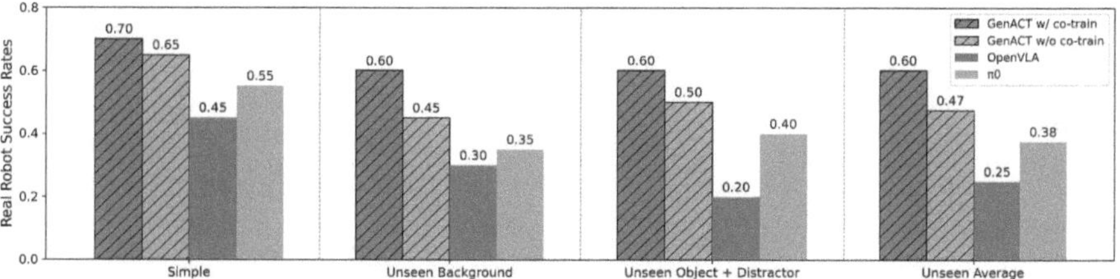

Fig. 4. GenACT surpasses baseline methods on both basic manipulation setting and generalization setting in real robot experiments. **GenACT w/ co-train** denotes model with multimodal action co-train whereas **GenACT w/o co-train** denotes model with only multimodal pretrain.

Table 2. Impact of Pretrain Settings on CALVIN Performance.

Setting	Train	Avg. Len.
Full Model	ABCD	4.61
w/o Image-Text Pairs		3.70
w/o Visual Grounding		4.28
w/o Video Prediction		4.35
Full Model	ABC	4.37
w/o Image-Text Pairs		3.22
w/o Visual Grounding		3.92
w/o Video Prediction		3.75

Table 3. Impact of Co-train Settings on CALVIN Performance.

Setting	Train	Avg. Len.
Full Model	ABCD	4.61
w/o Image-Text Pairs		4.59
w/o Visual Grounding		4.52
w/o Video Prediction		4.53
Full Model	ABC	4.37
w/o Image-Text Pairs		4.32
w/o Visual Grounding		4.24
w/o Video Prediction		4.15

5.4 Ablation Studies

Effectiveness of Individual Pre-trained VL Tasks. We conduct a study to evaluate the importance of each VL task by excluding each individual VL task from the whole training pipeline respectively. The results from Table 2 show that excluding each individual VL task from the whole training pipeline leads to a degradation in manipulation performance for both multi-task learning setting and unseen scene generalization setting. Notably, the image-text pairs—the largest data source (207M)—have the most significant impact on performance, causing a substantial drop from 4.61 to 3.70 (a decrease of 0.91) in the ABCD setting and from 4.37 to 3.22 (a decrease of 1.15) in the ABC setting. This dramatic performance degradation implies that image-text alignment represents a fundamental multimodal capability, and the sheer scale of this type of data further enhances learning. In contrast, visual grounding and video prediction tasks show more moderate impacts, with visual grounding reducing performance from 4.61 to 4.28 in ABCD setting and from 4.37 to 3.92 in ABC setting, while video prediction leads to drops from 4.61 to 4.35 and from 4.37 to 3.75, respectively. These results indicate that high-level tasks such as visual grounding and video prediction, while important, rely on the foundational capabilities such as image-text alignment. Also, video prediction proves more critical than visual grounding regarding unseen scene generalization (ABC) with a larger performance drop.

Effectiveness of Individual Co-train VL Tasks. We further study the necessity of each incorporated VL tasks at the multimodal action co-training stage and report the CALVIN performance in Table 3. Unlike the pretrain stage, the performance drop caused by excluding image-text pairs during the co-training stage is relatively minimal, with only a slight decrease from 4.61 to 4.59 (a drop of 0.02) in the ABCD setting and from 4.37 to 4.32 in the ABC setting. In contrast, removing visual grounding results in more noticeable drops from 4.61 to 4.52 in ABCD and from 4.37 to 4.24 in ABC, while excluding video prediction leads to decreases from 4.61 to 4.53 and from 4.37 to 4.15, respectively. This phenomenon indicates that during the co-training stage, spatial reasoning capabilities provided by visual grounding and the future dynamics prediction enabled by video prediction offer more direct benefits to robot manipulation than image-text alignment. This is because the larger-scale image-text pairs are better suited for the pretraining, where greater data volume is typically required to establish foundational multimodal representations, while the co-training stage benefits more from task-specific capabilities. Furthermore, the results suggest that the importance of different VL tasks varies between standard and generalization settings. In the standard setting (ABCD), removing visual grounding causes a larger performance drop while removing video prediction is more critical in the generalization setting (ABC).

Impact of Activating Vision Loss on Action Learning. As stated in Sect. 5.1, we simultaneously activate action loss and vision loss for the manipulation task. Such a design choice is motivated by endowing the model with the capability of inferring the outcomes of its action predictions under an interleaved vision-language-action sequence formulation. As shown in Table 4, activating vision loss in the action learning stage boosts model performance on both ABCD→D and ABC→D setting. Especially, we find that the model achieves the best performance with 0.2 vision loss weight (4.55→4.61) and the performance improvement is even larger on the unseen scene setting (4.13→4.37).

Table 4. Impact of Activating Vision Loss during Action Learning on CALVIN.

Vision Weight	Train	Consecutive tasks success rates					Avg. Len.
		1	2	3	4	5	
0.0	ABCD	0.994	0.940	0.925	0.861	0.810	4.55
0.1		0.991	0.952	0.929	0.860	0.814	4.57
0.5		0.989	0.950	0.931	0.864	0.817	4.58
0.2		**0.992**	**0.966**	**0.931**	**0.883**	**0.830**	**4.61**
0.0	ABC	0.962	0.894	0.835	0.762	0.701	4.13
0.1		0.987	0.910	0.855	0.784	0.729	4.29
0.5		0.991	0.900	0.841	0.769	0.720	4.22
0.2		**0.989**	**0.935**	**0.871**	**0.804**	**0.738**	**4.37**

Table 5. Data Efficiency and Scalability on CALVIN Benchmark

Method	Data	Avg.Len.
RoboVLMs	10%	2.52
GenACT	10%	3.10
RoboVLMs	500%	4.51
GenACT	500%	4.69

Table 6. Data Efficiency on Real Robot Benchmark

Method	Data	Success Rate
OpenVLA	10%	0.0
GenACT	10%	0.2
OpenVLA	50%	0.35
GenACT	50%	0.5

Data Efficiency and Scalability. We further evaluate data efficiency and scalability of **GenACT**. Table 5 demonstrates that on CALVIN, with only 10% of the data, **GenACT** achieves an average length of 3.10, outperforming RoboVLMs (2.52). At 500% data scale (script-generated), **GenACT** maintains its advantage with an average length of 4.69 versus RoboVLMs' 4.51. On the real robot benchmark, Table 6 suggests that **GenACT** reaches a success rate of 0.2 with 10% data, surpassing OpenVLA's 0.0, and further improves to 0.5 at 50% data, compared to OpenVLA's 0.35. These results highlight **GenACT's** superior data efficiency and scalability, which we attribute to its unified architecture and vision-language-action co-training. In contrast, by focusing solely on action supervision, methods including RoboVLMs and OpenVLA suffer from degradation of pretrained multimodal capabilities and fail to capitalize on the vast parameter space that could otherwise encode rich multimodal representations. This action-centric approach essentially underutilizes the model's capacity and makes the model prone to overfitting training data patterns, particularly when large-scale foundation models are trained on relatively small robot datasets. Additionally, they lack joint visual grounding and video prediction pretraining which are shown to be beneficial for robot manipulation in Table 2 and Table 3.

6 Conclusion and Limitations

GenACT is a fully-discrete robot foundation model that leverages a unified input-output space by tokenizing language, vision, and action as discrete tokens. This enables vision-language-action co-training via standard next token prediction over multimodal interleaved sequences. Our experiments demonstrate that **GenACT** achieves SOTA manipulation performance on both simulation and real robot benchmarks, with vision-language-action co-training data significantly improving robot manipulation. The main limitations include: 1) unexplored action tokenization methods such as FAST [23], and 2) limited video dataset size, preventing fully unleashing the power of video pretraining for dynamics learning.

References

1. Black, K., Brown, N., Driess, D., et al.: π_0: a vision-language-action flow model for general robot control (2024). https://arxiv.org/abs/2410.24164
2. Brohan, A., Brown, N., et al.: Rt-1: robotics transformer for real-world control at scale. In: arXiv preprint arXiv:2212.06817 (2022)
3. Brohan, A., Brown, N., et al.: Rt-2: vision-language-action models transfer web knowledge to robotic control. In: arXiv preprint arXiv:2307.15818 (2023)
4. Collaboration, O.X.E., et al.: Open X-embodiment: robotic learning datasets and RT-X models (2023). https://arxiv.org/abs/2310.08864
5. Esser, P., et al.: Taming transformers for high-resolution image synthesis. In: IEEE Conference on Computer Vision and Pattern Recognition (2021)
6. Fang, H.S., et al.: Rh20t: a comprehensive robotic dataset for learning diverse skills in one-shot. In: 2024 International Conference on Robotics and Automation
7. Gadre, S.Y., et al.: Datacomp: In search of the next generation of multimodal datasets. In: Conference on Neural Information Processing Systems (2023)
8. Goyal, R., et al.: " something something" video database for learning and evaluating visual common sense. In: International Conference on Computer Vision (2017)
9. Grauman, K., Westbury, A., et al.: Ego4d: around the world in 3,000 hours of egocentric video (2022). https://arxiv.org/abs/2110.07058
10. Ho, J., Salimans, T.: Classifier-free diffusion guidance (2022)
11. Hu, Y., et al.: Video prediction policy: a generalist robot policy with predictive visual representations, https://arxiv.org/abs/2412.14803

12. Intelligence, P., Black, K., et al.: $\pi_{0.5}$: a vision-language-action model with open-world generalization (2025). https://arxiv.org/abs/2504.16054
13. Khazatsky, A., et al.: DROID: a large-scale in-the-wild robot manipulation dataset. In: Proceedings of Robotics: Science and Systems (2024)
14. Kim, M.J., Pertsch, K., et al.: OpenVLA: an open-source vision-language-action model. In: 8th Annual Conference on Robot Learning (2024)
15. Kuznetsova, A., Rom, H., et al.: The open images dataset v4: Unified image classification, object detection, and visual relationship detection at scale. IJCV
16. Li, P., Wu, H., et al.: Gr-mg: leveraging partially-annotated data via multi-modal goal-conditioned policy. IEEE Robot. Autom. Lett. (2025)
17. Li, X., Li, P., et al.: Towards generalist robot policies: what matters in building vision-language-action models. arXiv preprint arXiv:2412.14058 (2024)
18. Li, X., Liu, M., et al.: Vision-language foundation models as effective robot imitators. arXiv preprint arXiv:2311.01378 (2023)
19. Liu, S., Wu, L., et al.: Rdt-1b: a diffusion foundation model for bimanual manipulation. arXiv preprint arXiv:2410.07864
20. Lozhkov, A., Ben Allal, L., von Werra, L., Wolf, T.: Fineweb-edu: the finest collection of educational content (2024). https://doi.org/10.57967/hf/2497
21. Mees, O., Hermann, L., Rosete-Beas, E., Burgard, W.: Calvin: a benchmark for language-conditioned policy learning for long-horizon robot manipulation tasks. IEEE Robot. Autom. Lett. (RA-L) **7**(3), 7327–7334 (2022)
22. Peng, Z., Wang, W., et al.: Kosmos-2: grounding multimodal large language models to the world. ArXiv **abs/2306.14824** (2023)
23. Pertsch, K., Stachowicz, K., et al.: Fast: efficient action tokenization for vision-language-action models (2025). https://arxiv.org/abs/2501.09747
24. Rombach, R., Blattmann, A., Lorenz, D., Esser, P., Ommer, B.: High-resolution image synthesis with latent diffusion models (2022)
25. Team, G.R., et al.: Gemini robotics: bringing ai into the physical world (2025). https://arxiv.org/abs/2503.20020
26. Wang, X., Zhang, X., et al.: Emu3: next-token prediction is all you need. arXiv preprint arXiv:2409.18869 (2024)
27. Weber, M., Fu, D.Y., et al.: Redpajama: an open dataset for training large language models. NeurIPS Datasets and Benchmarks Track (2024)
28. Wu, H., et al.: Unleashing large-scale video generative pre-training for visual robot manipulation. In: International Conference on Learning Representations (2024)
29. Yang, A., Yang, B., Zhang, B., Hui, B., Zheng, B., Yu, B., et al.: Qwen2.5 technical report. arXiv preprint arXiv:2412.15115 (2024)
30. Ye, S., Jang, J., Jeon, B., et al.: Latent action pretraining from videos (2024). https://arxiv.org/abs/2410.11758
31. Zhang, J., Guo, Y., et al.: Up-vla: a unified understanding and prediction model for embodied agent (2025). https://arxiv.org/abs/2501.18867
32. Zhu, F., Wu, H., Guo, S., Liu, Y., Cheang, C., Kong, T.: Irasim: learning interactive real-robot action simulators. arXiv:2406.12802 (2024)

Full-Lifecycle Data Governance for Embodied Intelligence

Chuanhou Liu, Ding Qi, and Cairong Zhao(✉)

Tongji University, Shanghai, People's Republic of China
{2011267,zhaocairong}@tongji.edu.cn

Abstract. With the development of embodied intelligence technology and the accelerated industrialization of humanoid robots, insufficient data supply has become the core bottleneck for industry breakthroughs. The efficient processing system of multi-source real robot and simulation data opens up new paths for model training, while facing challenges such as cross-modal fusion and scene generalization. To address this, this paper proposes a full-lifecycle data management scheme to construct a systematic dataset system: starting from scenario engineering, covering robot body selection, hierarchical task planning, multi-modal collection, and full-chain quality inspection, integrating simulation and real robot data to form a virtual-real feedback loop. Validation on mainstream VLA models ($\pi0$) shows that the dataset produced by this scheme performs outstandingly in data diversity, scene coverage, and annotation accuracy, meeting the high-quality data requirements of embodied intelligence models and providing underlying support for improving model robustness and generalization.

Keywords: Embodied Intelligence · Data Collection · Data Quality

1 Introduction

The current embodied intelligence industry is booming. Within the entire embodied intelligence system, data plays a foundational role: it serves as the fuel for driving models, the core driver for the operation and optimization of the entire system, the key input for the continuous optimization of models, and a critical factor in boosting model performance. With the iteration of embodied intelligence technologies and the accelerated industrialization of humanoid robots, insufficient data supply has become a core bottleneck restricting industrial breakthroughs. Although the collaborative processing of multi-source real robot data and simulation data has opened up new avenues for model training, challenges such as cross-modal feature fusion and generalization in complex scenarios remain to be addressed. To tackle this pain point, this paper proposes a full-lifecycle data collection and quality control scheme, and constructs a systematic dataset construction framework. Figure 1 illustrates the operational tasks of embodied intelligence data collection using heterogeneous robotic embodiments.

This scheme starts with scenario engineering setup, runs through core links such as dynamic selection of robotic embodiments, hierarchical task planning, multimodal data

© The Author(s), under exclusive license to Springer Nature Singapore Pte Ltd. 2026
J. Kittler et al. (Eds.): PRCV 2025, LNCS 16289, pp. 334–348, 2026.
https://doi.org/10.1007/978-981-95-5764-6_23

Fig. 1. Embodied Intelligence Data Collection. In various pre-set scenarios, various heterogeneous collection machines are used to collect embodied intelligence data.

collection, and full-link quality inspection and warehousing. It innovatively integrates physics engine simulation data and real-robot operation data to form a closed-loop of multi-source data with virtual-real mutual feedback. Verification results on mainstream VLA models (π0) show that the dataset generated by this scheme performs prominently in key indicators such as diversity of data dimensions, task scenario coverage, and semantic accuracy of annotations. It can effectively meet the stringent requirements for high-quality training data of embodied intelligence models, provide underlying data support for enhancing the decision-making robustness of models and generalization capabilities in complex tasks, and promote the critical leap of embodied intelligence from laboratory scenarios to industrial applications.

2 Related Works

Open X-Embodiment [1] is a key dataset for cross-embodiment learning in robotics. Led by Google DeepMind and developed in collaboration with 21 institutions, it integrates 60 datasets from 34 laboratories, covering 22 robotic embodiments (from single-armed manipulators to quadruped robots), with over 1 million trajectories, 527 skills (160,266 tasks). Data is stored in RLDS format [2], compatible with multimodal inputs and different action spaces, supporting loading by mainstream frameworks. Data from Franka robots accounts for the largest proportion, focusing mainly on "pick-and-place" tasks, covering long-tail skills such as "wiping", including elements of household scenarios, and has verified generalization potential through the PaLM model [3]. RT-X series models trained on it show outstanding performance: RT-1-X [4] achieves a 50% higher success rate, while RT-2-X [5] has approximately 3 times stronger generalization ability. The project open-sources the dataset, models and toolchains, laying the foundation for cross-embodiment research. Current challenges include: not covering robots with significant differences in sensory-drive modalities, lack of research on generalization to new robots, and no criteria for judging positive transfer. This work confirms the feasibility of cross-robot data fusion, advances the development of general intelligence, and provides a solution to address data fragmentation.

AgiBot World [6] is a large-scale embodied intelligence dataset led by Zhiyuan Robotics, aiming to address the challenges of data fragmentation and scenario generalization. It integrates 217 tasks performed by over 100 robots across 5 major scenarios (home, catering, etc.), containing over 1 million trajectories and nearly 3,000 h of data. Covering 87 skills and 106 sub-scenarios, it is 10 times the scale of Open X-Embodiment and 100 times in scenario diversity, with industrial-grade quality control ensuring data usability. The dataset is collected based on the AgiBot G1 platform, equipped with dual 7-DoF robotic arms, supporting millimeter-level operations and multimodal perception. 80% of the data consists of 60–150 s long-horizon tasks, including complex operations such as inserting memory modules. After pre-training, the GO-1 model [7] achieves a success rate of over 60% in complex tasks, 30% higher than that of Open X-Embodiment models, with stronger generalization ability. The dataset is open-sourced under the CC license [8], providing a full-process toolchain. It plans to release a Beta version and a global challenge, marking the first deep integration of real scenarios, hardware platforms, and quality control. It provides a benchmark for research such as dual-arm collaboration, promoting the leap of robot learning towards practical applications.

The above is the research of two leading enterprises in the field of embodied intelligence data. OXE's dataset is relatively fragmented, and it only uses arms for data collection without actual collection and verification on humanoid robot embodiments. AgiBotWorld's dataset has a single embodiment and lacks verification on heterogeneous humanoid robot embodiments. However, with the advancement of embodied intelligence technology, it is necessary to solve the problems of embodied intelligence data shortage and excessive costs caused by low-cost mass data collection of heterogeneous humanoid robots.

3 Full-Lifecycle Dataset Construction

3.1 Data Collection Tasks

Collection tasks are set according to the requirements of model training. These multi-source, multi-scenario embodied intelligence data, including real-robot and simulation data, mainly include methods such as teleoperation-collected real-robot data, production-accompanying collected real-robot data, and simulation-synthesized data. This paper mainly introduces two methods: teleoperation-based real-robot data collection and simulation-synthesized data collection.

The definition of minimum trainable data for datasets refers to a continuous action unit data, which includes several segments of free movements (such as approaching or moving away from objects), several skill actions (such as grasping, placing, inserting, pressing, etc.), and multi-modal data (global visual data, force feedback, joint data, etc. under the same timestamp, with the sensor frame rate not less than 15 Hz–30 Hz).

Collection tasks can be divided into short-sequence tasks and long-sequence tasks. A short-sequence task refers to an independent basic action, generally lasting between 20 to 40 s. Such collection tasks can be pre-annotated and then assigned to collectors for data collection. A long-sequence task refers to a continuous sequence of actions, usually ranging from several minutes to over ten minutes. After collection, such tasks need to be split into short-sequence tasks and annotated. Both types of tasks have their respective applicable collection scenarios and application requirements, but they will ultimately be served as a piece of data in the dataset in the form of short-sequence task segments.

Collection tasks are set according to different scenarios. As shown in Fig. 2, they are divided into several major application scenarios: industrial manufacturing, household services, catering services, supermarkets and pharmacies, and others. Each scenario is subdivided into different task lists, corresponding to the action sequences in the scenario, and each task requires collecting a certain amount of data.

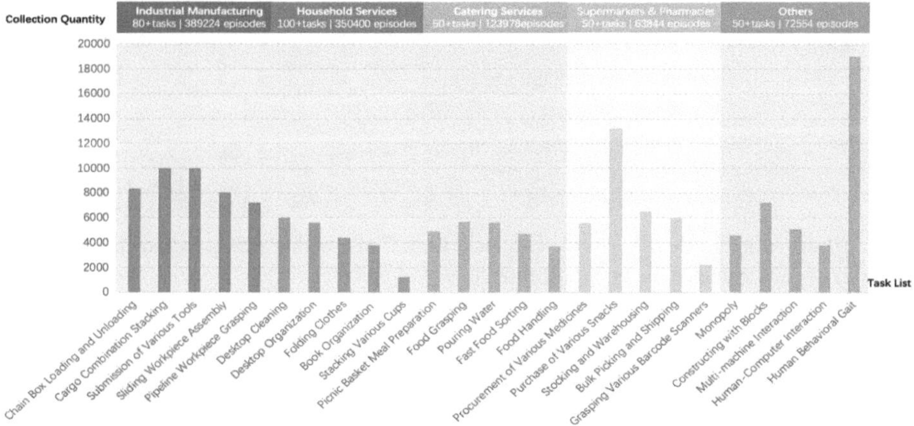

Fig. 2. Data Collection Tasks. For different scenarios, collection tasks and collection quantities are set.

3.2 Scenario Construction

Given that humanoid robots have not yet been commercially deployed, a training field needs to be built in advance for data collection and subsequent verification if data collection and follow-up validation are to be carried out. Training fields are divided into two categories: physical training fields and simulation training fields. A physical training field requires the construction of a physical space, where relevant materials are placed according to task requirements, and collection machines are operated to complete operational tasks. A simulation training field needs to build a virtual digital space and configure data assets with physical properties. Operational tasks in the digital space are completed by virtual robots through teleoperation or driven by large models.

Physical Scenario. Construct multiple common embodied intelligence application scenarios or directly use enterprises' existing work or production environments for non-disruptive data collection, such as factories, home settings, domestic services, kitchens and bathrooms, factories, medical facilities, offices, supermarkets, catering establishments, warehouses, and construction sites. In each scenario, rich props and task elements are arranged to simulate the complexity and diversity of the real world, providing lifelike environments for model testing, as shown in Fig. 3. Meanwhile, in terms of scenario quality, it is necessary to ensure the coverage of scenarios, such as task diversity (whether it covers typical tasks in the target domain). The cost of constructing physical scenarios and collecting real-robot data remains very high.

Fig. 3. Multi-task Physical Scenario Construction. Constructing rich scenarios helps achieve data diversity and enhance the generalization ability of models.

Simulation Scenario. Facing the data dilemma of embodied intelligence, to further reduce the cost of data collection, the path of generating synthetic data based on high-precision simulation has become an industry consensus. Internationally, NVIDIA's Omniverse and its Isaac Sim module [9] have supported the training of numerous embodied intelligent robots worldwide; Physical Intelligence (PI) has also open-sourced its $\pi 0$ model [10]. In China, Shanghai-based Songying Technology, relying on its independently developed ORCA—the first domestic physical AI system—and its sub-module ORCA Sim, has provided key support for the "brain" (both core and peripheral intelligence) training of robots in dozens of embodied intelligence teams. The simulation tool used in this paper is ORCA Sim [11], mainly because Songying can provide customized digital assets and the construction of simulation environments, and can integrate with data collection and processing workflows to meet the needs of mass data collection.

Using ORCA Sim, dynamic and interactive simulation scenarios can be constructed, as shown in Fig. 4.

Fig. 4. Simulation Scene Construction. Construct a virtual simulation environment and synthesize data through simulation.

3.3 Collection Robot Body Selection

Compared with OXE and AgiBot, multiple heterogeneous humanoid robot bodies will be used for data collection in terms of data acquisition. This is also the key difference from OXE, which mainly uses robotic arms, and AgiBot, which uses only a single body as the collection machine. Using multiple heterogeneous bodies can enhance the diversity of data collection.

Industry-recognized robot hardware bodies with comprehensive hardware capabilities are selected. Such robots should be able to accurately execute instructions output by the model, realize various complex operations, and provide reliable hardware support for model testing in real scenarios. Hardware parameters must meet actual task requirements and ensure long-term stable operation, such as technical parameters including arm span, load capacity, positioning accuracy, and end-effectors. In the scenario of robotic arms, smooth follow control (i.e., unobstructed online trajectory planning) [12] must be supported. Before testing, comprehensive calibration, debugging, and maintenance should be performed on the robots to ensure their hardware performance is in optimal condition, avoiding the impact of hardware issues on the accuracy of test results. As shown in Fig. 5, the currently used robot bodies and their proportions in dataset construction are displayed.

In the simulation environment, the application of these bodies in the simulation environment can be realized by importing their URDF [13] files.

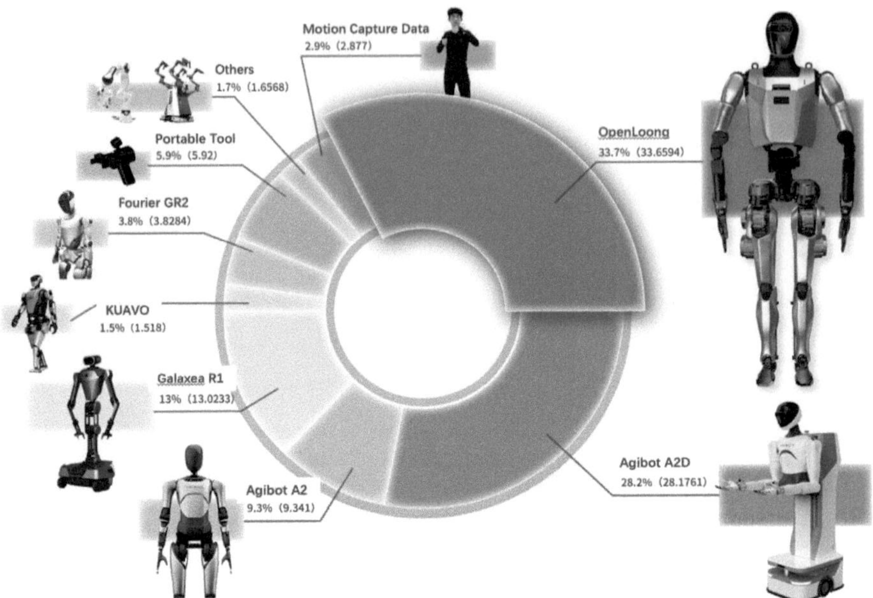

Fig. 5. Robot Bodies. Data is collected using different heterogeneous robot bodies. The proportions of data collection by each body are as above.

3.4 Data Collection and Processing Process

A complete data collection and processing process is crucial for improving the efficiency of data collection and data quality [14, 15]. Starting from the access of heterogeneous humanoid robot data collection bodies, data collection is initiated, and the collected data is monitored in real-time. The collected data is uploaded to the cloud for data cleaning (slicing, annotation, etc.) and data verification, followed by manual review to eliminate low-quality data, and finally deliver high-quality data that has passed the review. The complete data collection and processing process is shown in Fig. 6.

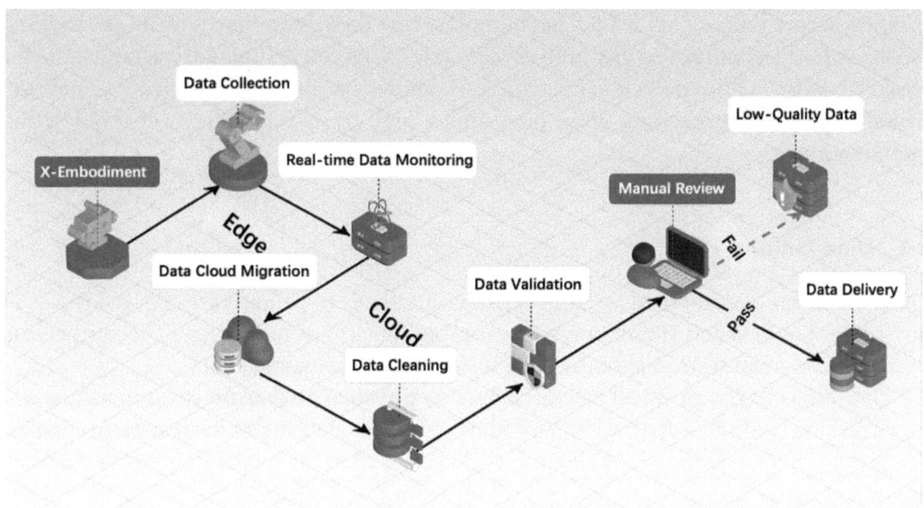

Fig. 6. Full Workflow of Data Processing. Through a complete data processing workflow, batch data collection and processing are realized to ensure the quality and efficiency of delivered data.

Data collection for embodied intelligence requires designing a complete workflow based on the characteristics of heterogeneous humanoid robots:

Preliminary Preparations Focus on Body Access and Adaptation: Resolve differences in communication protocols among robots of different brands through a standardized interface layer, and unify data formats of multi-source sensors such as vision and touch; dynamically configure sampling frequencies according to motion characteristics (1 kHz for high-speed movement, 100 Hz for static interaction), with spatiotemporal synchronization error controlled within 1 ms; preset safety boundaries and privacy desensitization rules, enabling automatic emergency stop when exceeding thresholds and real-time blurring of sensitive information such as human faces.

The Key Stage Lies in Dynamic Collection and Monitoring: Adopt the "edge + cloud" architecture to capture motion data such as robotic arm poses and plantar friction, generate 3D environmental point clouds combined with SLAM [16] technology, and upload key data via 5G with priority; monitor hardware status (battery, sensor online rate), data quality (joint angle jump) and scene safety through the dashboard. In case of anomalies, trigger local caching and remote troubleshooting to ensure data integrity and robot safety.

Data Governance Needs to Adapt to Physical Interaction Characteristics: Slice action sequences by behavioral units, and annotate action types, environmental attributes, and physical parameters; eliminate sensor drift data and fill in missing frames; verify data rationality based on kinematics and dynamics models, combine LSTM model [17] pre-screening with expert review, focus on evaluating action validity and generalization value, and eliminate data to feed back and optimize collection strategies.

Result Delivery Focuses on Data Application Value: Adopt time-series and graph databases to associate action-environment-effect data, and classify by quality (Level S includes scarce scenarios; Level A has complete core data); combine with model training feedback (such as improved grasping success rate) to targetedly increase data volume for weak scenarios. Ultimately, it achieves a 40% improvement in collection efficiency and a quality pass rate exceeding 95%, providing a high-precision dataset for robot action optimization.

3.5 Data Quality

Quality control of embodied intelligence datasets needs to balance the characteristics of physical robot data and simulation data, forming full-lifecycle synergy. The verification of data quality can be divided into three levels with increasing costs.

Data collected by physical robots centers on **physical authenticity**: joint torque and fingertip pressure recorded by sensors must strictly match the motion state (dynamics deviation $\leq 5\%$), and the time synchronization error of multi-modal data is < 1 ms (e.g., alignment between visual frames and robotic arm poses). It is necessary to cover both conventional scenarios (such as picking up objects on flat ground) and edge scenarios (such as operations in narrow spaces). The number of samples for a single action type should be ≥ 500 groups, and outliers should be filtered through sensor health monitoring (noise < 0.5 mV) to ensure the data can reflect the interaction rules of the real world.

Simulation-collected data emphasizes **model fidelity and controllability**: physical engine parameters (friction coefficient, gravity) must have an error $< 2\%$ compared with the real world, and the joint kinematics model should reproduce the mechanical characteristics of physical robots (e.g., moment of inertia deviation $< 5\%$). It supports batch generation of extreme scenarios (such as high-temperature or high-interference environments), with parameter gradients of no less than 10 levels for a single scenario (e.g., ground friction coefficients continuously adjustable from 0.1 to 0.8). It automatically generates semantic labels (e.g., "Reason for grasping failure: slippery contact surface") with a label accuracy of $\geq 98\%$. Meanwhile, it requires calibration with physical robot samples (e.g., correcting simulation curves using 100 sets of real gaits) to reduce virtual-real transfer errors.

The three levels of data quality verification each have distinct characteristics. **The first** is manual judgment through replay: by manually replaying data, one can intuitively determine whether the data meets expectations. This level has relatively low cost but low efficiency and strong subjectivity. **The second** is Real2Sim: replaying in a simulation environment and using the controllability of the simulation environment to verify the performance of data in virtual scenarios. The cost is higher than that of manual judgment, but it can more systematically detect issues such as data consistency. **The third** is Real2Sim2Real: replaying on another robot body and applying the data to another real robot to comprehensively verify the applicability of the data. This level has the highest cost, but the verification result is the most reliable.

A closed-loop verification mechanism must be established throughout the full lifecycle: In the collection phase, kinematic compliance verification is conducted (with joint angles not exceeding limits); In the processing phase, hardware drift is eliminated from physical robot data, and sensor noise simulation is added to simulation data; In the application phase, if the model's performance in physical robot testing degrades by more than 10%, simulation parameters shall be retrospectively optimized. The collaboration between the two types of data must meet the following requirements: extreme scenarios are supplemented by simulation, conventional scenarios are dominated by physical robot data, the overall effective sample rate is $\geq 95\%$, which supports the improvement of the generalization ability of the embodied intelligence model.

4 Experimental Evaluation

This paper mainly focuses on constructing the embodied intelligence dataset; the following experimental evaluation serves only as verification of the collected data.

Embodied intelligence large models: currently, mainstream representative open-source models include the OpenVLA model [18] jointly released by Stanford University, University of California, Berkeley, and Deepmind/Google; π0 of Physical Intelligence upgraded from the VLA model; RDT model [19] by TSAIL of Tsinghua University; and Seer model [20] by Shanghai AI Laboratory. This experimental evaluation mainly adopts the π0 model of Physical Intelligence as the base model, verifies data validity through fine-tuning of the collected data, and conducts deployment verification in the simulation environment.

4.1 π0 Model

The π0 model is the first open-source end-to-end VLA model released by Physical Intelligence in 2024. It aims to address the issues of multimodal fusion and cross-platform adaptation in general robot control. Trained on heterogeneous data from 7 robot platforms and 68 tasks, it can convert natural language instructions into continuous action sequences. The π0 adopts a pre-training-fine-tuning mode, based on flow matching and diffusion model architecture. It supports multi-task processing and long-range dependencies, and can adapt to generalized scenarios. Its pre-training phase integrates data from different robot platforms such as single-arm, dual-arm, and mobile manipulators, forming cross-embodiment training capability. The π0.5 model [21] is an upgraded version of π0, which significantly enhances open-world generalization capability through collaborative training on heterogeneous data (including network data and multi-environment robot data).

4.2 Evaluation Scheme

The short-term scheme involves testing the effect of different embodied intelligence datasets on a single model: specify multiple representative and diverse embodied intelligence datasets to be tested, and select one model. While keeping the model's initial parameters and training hyperparameters consistent, the model is trained using different embodied intelligence datasets respectively to ensure the comparability of the experiments. In this way, an in-depth exploration is conducted on the impact of different embodied intelligence datasets (including physical robot datasets, physical-synthetic mixed datasets, etc.) on the training effect of the same model.

The long-term scheme involves testing the effect of a single dataset on multiple models: specify an embodied intelligence dataset to be tested with typical characteristics, and select multiple models. These models are trained respectively using the same dataset to compare the performance differences of different models driven by the same embodied intelligence data, and analyze the adaptability and utilization efficiency of different models to the same embodied intelligence dataset.

This experiment adopts the short-term plan for verification, specifically using physical robot data, simulation data, and the combined approach of physical robot and simulation data for testing.

4.3 Task Design, Data Collection, and Model Fine-Tuning

Taking "opening the refrigerator, grasping and taking out the item, then closing the refrigerator" in the "household" scenario as the sample test task for this experiment, as shown in Fig. 7, the implementation plan is as follows:

Fig. 7. Task operation of opening the refrigerator, grasping and taking out the item, then closing the refrigerator in a household scenario.

The task objectives include requiring the robot to open the refrigerator door with the right hand, complete grasping from the refrigerator with the left hand and take out the designated item, and finally close the refrigerator door with the right hand;

Technical verification points include object state perception, trajectory planning for grasping, taking out, and opening/closing actions;

Definition of initial state includes environmental state: a closed refrigerator, where the robot maintains a sufficient distance from the refrigerator to allow it to perform tasks in this area; the item to be taken out is placed in the refrigerator;

Data collection: collect 500 pieces of data (2000 actions) using physical robots to complete the aforementioned task operation; synthesize 500 pieces of data (2000 actions) in the simulation environment to complete the aforementioned task operation.

Fine-Tuning Based on the π0 Base Model [22]:

- Select 500 pieces of data collected by physical robots to perform fine-tuning based on π0; the fine-tuned model is designated as π0-1.
- Select 500 pieces of data synthesized in simulation to perform fine-tuning based on π0; the fine-tuned model is designated as π0-2.
- Select 250 pieces of data collected by physical robots and 250 pieces of data synthesized in simulation to perform fine-tuning based on π0; the fine-tuned model is designated as π0-3.

4.4 Deployment Verification in the Simulation Environment and Experimental Results

Verification metrics include scores for four steps, with a total of 4 points:

1. Verification metrics include scores for four steps, with a total of 4 points.
2. Grasping the item: grasping the item from the refrigerator, awarded 1 point.
3. Taking out the item: taking the item out of the refrigerator, awarded 1 point.
4. Closing the refrigerator: closing the refrigerator door; awarded 1 point.

The score for each step is determined by the quality of completion: 1 point for success (no manual intervention required), 0 points for failure. The testing criteria are based on a total score of 4, with 10 independent task executions conducted to check the execution results.

Principles for calculating the number of failures include cases counted as failures: Failure in exception handling: when the system fails to automatically resolve the exception within the preset time ($\leq$5 s), resulting in the inability to continue the task; cases not counted as failures: Successful autonomous recovery (the system resolves the exception within the allowed time through established strategies and ultimately completes the task), non-destructive intervention (operators assist in resolving the exception through remote assistance without triggering hardware reset).

Experimental results are shown in Table 1. Using the fine-tuned model, validation and evaluation were conducted in the simulation environment, with success rates of completing four actions in **10 trials**.

Table 1. Fine-tuning data and verification results of fine-tuned models in the simulation environment

Model	π0-1	π0-2	π0-3
DataSet Type	Real Data	Synthetic Data	Real(50%)+Synthetic(50%)
Fine-tuning Data Volume	500	500	250+250
Open the refrigerator	10	10	10
Grasp items	9	8	8
Take out items	9	6	7
Close the refrigerator	9	6	7
Success rate	92.5%	75%	80%

Experimental results show the constructed embodied intelligence dataset is effective for models. Simulation validation has a high success rate: physical robot data is of the best quality, followed by the combination of physical and simulated synthetic data, while simulated synthetic data currently lags behind physical robot data.

5 Discussion, Limitations, and Future Work

The full-life-cycle data management and control scheme proposed in this paper addresses the issue of insufficient data supply in the field of embodied intelligence by integrating physical robot and simulation data, and constructing a closed loop of virtual-real mutual feedback. Starting with scene engineering, the scheme integrates multimodal collection, full-link quality inspection, and cross-ontology data collaboration. Verified on VLA models, the generated dataset has advantages in diversity, scene coverage, and annotation accuracy, supporting the improvement of the model's robustness and generalization ability. It highlights its key value: ensuring physical authenticity through physical robot data, compensating for shortcomings in collecting data for extreme scenarios with simulation data, forming an efficient supply mode of "relying on physical robots for regular scenarios and simulation for edge scenarios," and providing an implementable framework for solving the problems of cross-modal fusion and generalization in complex scenarios.

Although the scheme significantly improves dataset quality, it has three limitations: First, correction of simulation data relies on physical robot samples; when extreme scenarios lack corresponding data, virtual-real transfer error may exceed 8%. Second, in full-link quality inspection, Real2Sim2Real validation has high accuracy but high cost (requiring multiple heterogeneous robots), making it hard to popularize on a large scale. Third, hierarchical task planning has not covered dynamic interaction scenarios (e.g., response to sudden instructions in human-robot collaboration), and the dataset's support for high-complexity tasks needs improvement.

Future research can be advanced in three aspects: develop a reinforcement learning-based adaptive calibration algorithm for simulation parameters to reduce reliance on physical robot samples and improve virtual-real consistency in extreme scenarios; explore a "semi-automated verification" scheme that combines AI pre-screening with small-scale Real2Sim2Real validation, maintaining an effective sample rate of over 95% while reducing costs; expand task scenarios by introducing dynamic interaction data (such as sudden obstacle avoidance), optimize the annotation system to support finer-grained action semantic reasoning, and enhance the dataset's support for complex tasks. In addition, it is necessary to study the data migration mechanism for cross-brand robots to improve versatility in industrialization.

References

1. O'Neill, A., Rehman, A., Maddukuri, A., et al.: Open X-embodiment: robotic learning datasets and RT-X models: Open X-embodiment collaboration 0. In: 2024 IEEE International Conference on Robotics and Automation (ICRA), pp. 6892–6903. IEEE (2024)
2. Ramos, S., Girgin, S., Hussenot, L., et al.: RLDS: an ecosystem to generate, share and use datasets in reinforcement learning. arXiv preprint arXiv:2111.02767 (2021)
3. Anil, R., Dai, A.M., Firat, O., et al.: PaLM 2 technical report. arXiv preprint arXiv:2305.10403 (2023)
4. Brohan, A., Brown, N., Carbajal, J., et al.: RT-1: robotics transformer for real-world control at scale. arXiv preprint arXiv:2212.06817 (2022)
5. Brohan, A., Brown, N., Carbajal, J., et al.: RT-2: vision-language-action models transfer web knowledge to robotic control. arXiv preprint arXiv:2307.15818 (2023)
6. AgiBot-World. https://github.com/OpenDriveLab/Agibot-World. Accessed 30 June 2025
7. Bu, Q., Cai, J., Chen, L., et al.: AgiBot world Colosseo: a large-scale manipulation platform for scalable and intelligent embodied systems. arXiv preprint arXiv:2503.06669 (2025)
8. Kim, M.: The Creative Commons and copyright protection in the digital era: Uses of Creative Commons licenses. J. Comput.-Mediat. Commun. **13**(1), 187–209 (2007)
9. Isaac Sim Homepage. https://developer.nvidia.com/isaac/sim. Accessed 30 June 2025
10. Black, K., Brown, N., Driess, D., et al.: π0: a vision-language-action flow model for general robot control (2024). https://arxiv.org/abs/2410.24164
11. ORCA-SIM Homepage. https://github.com/andersondomingues/orca-sim. Accessed 30 June 2025
12. Bae, H., Kim, G., Kim, J., et al.: Multi-robot path planning method using reinforcement learning. Appl. Sci. **9**(15), 3057 (2019)
13. Ivanou, M., Mikhel, S., Savin, S.: Robot description formats and approaches. In: 2021 International Conference "Nonlinearity, Information and Robotics" (NIR), pp. 1–5. IEEE (2021)
14. Qi, D., Li, J., Peng, J., et al.: Fetch and forge: efficient dataset condensation for object detection. Adv. Neural. Inf. Process. Syst. **37**, 119283–119300 (2024)
15. Qi, D., Li, J., Gao, J., et al.: towards universal dataset distillation via task-driven diffusion. In: Proceedings of the Computer Vision and Pattern Recognition Conference, pp. 10557–10566 (2025)
16. Kim, P., Chen, J., Cho, Y.K.: SLAM-driven robotic mapping and registration of 3D point clouds. Autom. Constr. **89**, 38–48 (2018)
17. Yu, Y., Si, X., Hu, C., et al.: A review of recurrent neural networks: LSTM cells and network architectures. Neural Comput. **31**(7), 1235–1270 (2019)
18. Kim, M.J., Pertsch, K., Karamcheti, S., et al.: OpenVLA: an open-source vision-language-action model. arXiv preprint arXiv:2406.09246 (2024)

19. Liu, S., Wu, L., Li, B., et al.: RDT-1B: a diffusion foundation model for bimanual manipulation. arXiv preprint arXiv:2410.07864 (2024)
20. Tian, Y., Yang, S., Zeng, J., et al.: Predictive inverse dynamics models are scalable learners for robotic manipulation. arXiv preprint arXiv:2412.15109 (2024)
21. Intelligence, P., Black, K., Brown, N., et al.: $\pi_ {0.5} $: a vision-language-action model with open-world generalization. arXiv preprint arXiv:2504.16054 (2025)
22. Openpi. https://github.com/Physical-Intelligence/openpi. Accessed 30 June 2025

Co-BioBench and SDTL: Advancing Human-AI Collaboration in Open-Ended Scientific Discovery

Yifan Liu, Xinwei Wang, and Yin Zhang(✉)

College of Computer Science and Technology, Zhejiang University, Hangzhou, China
{yifan.liu,xinwei_wang,zhangyin98}@zju.edu.cn

Abstract. Achieving autonomous scientific discovery remains a formidable challenge for even the most advanced Large Language Models (LLMs). Seamlessly integrating LLMs into scientific workflows particularly by delineating the optimal boundary between human and machine capabilities to foster synergistic collaboration presents a complex, underexplored issue. To address this, we introduce Co-BioBench, a novel tool learning benchmark designed to assess LLM agents' ability to collaborate with human scientists in exploring open-ended scientific research domains. Derived from peer-reviewed bioinformatics literature, Co-BioBench encompasses 3,785 meta-tasks across 15 diverse research scenarios. Each scenario guides agents through the iterative process of refining an initial hypothesis to produce a scientifically robust study. Evaluations using Co-BioBench reveal a key limitation in current LLM agents: their inadequate proficiency in leveraging and orchestrating external tools. To overcome this, we propose SDTL, a fine-tuning framework tailored to complex tool-calling tasks. Utilizing a robust corpus generated during development, SDTL enhances a tool-augmented model's ability to retrieve, comprehend, and integrate diverse tools to achieve sophisticated objectives. Extensive experiments on Co-BioBench and other benchmarks confirm SDTL's efficacy, with fine-tuned models significantly outperforming recent state-of-the-art function-calling approaches.

Keywords: Tool Learning · Multi-Agent System · Bioinformatics

1 Introduction

Modern scientific research is increasingly conducted by assembling workflows built upon these pre-packaged, complex computational tools and libraries, effectively making them the bedrock of contemporary discovery. This reliance, while

This work was supported by the Zhejiang Provincial Natural Science Foundation of China under Grant No. LZ23F020009, the NSFC project (No. 62072399), the Fundamental Research Funds for the Central Universities (No. S20240030), MoE Engineering Research Center of Digital Library, China Research Centre on Data and Knowledge for Engineering Sciences and Technology.

© The Author(s), under exclusive license to Springer Nature Singapore Pte Ltd. 2026
J. Kittler et al. (Eds.): PRCV 2025, LNCS 16289, pp. 349–362, 2026.
https://doi.org/10.1007/978-981-95-5764-6_24

enabling sophisticated analyses, often necessitates learning extensive and complex documentation, potentially involving dozens of advanced parameters, for functions that may be needed only once or twice, a significant and unnecessary cognitive burden for researchers. This knowledge is frequently codified within computational tools, libraries, and APIs that underpin modern scientific workflows. Examples span multiple disciplines, including domain-specific libraries such as Python's BioPython and R's Bioconductor packages, as well as specialized resources such as the KEGG REST API for pathway analysis and The Cancer Genome Atlas (TCGA) for comprehensive cancer genomics data. While these tools provide pre-built functions that significantly simplify complex tasks, their effective application demands a deep understanding of their intended inputs, expected outputs, and inherent practical limitations.

Existing research on tool-augmented AI systems, such as pioneering efforts like ToolLLM [15] and SCIAGENT [14], has achieved significant advancements in enhancing general tool-handling capabilities across various domains. However, applying these approaches directly to the complexities of scientific tasks reveals substantial limitations. Most current frameworks are primarily designed for generic tool interaction and API calls, neglecting the deeply specialized demands inherent in scientific workflows. However, some existing tool-use benchmarks rely on task combinations that may not fully reflect authentic scientific research scenarios. While proficient in executing basic function calls, they frequently overlook the domain-specific intricacies, context-dependent constraints, and nuanced parameterization required for effective scientific tool use. Scientific discovery contexts typically necessitate the use of highly complex, domain-specific tools whose design and nomenclature are intricately tied to specialized knowledge. These tools often feature numerous parameters with strong interdependencies. Current AI systems often struggle with such contextually sensitive and scientifically informed parameter determination, highlighting a key gap in their capability to effectively act as scientific co-pilots.

To tackle the pivotal challenge of scientific tool function calls, we propose a novel data generation pipeline with a specialized fine-tuning framework. Our main contributions are threefold:

First, to generate a large-scale, bioinformatics tool learning benchmark that reflects authentic research scenarios, we introduce a two-agent system consisting of a Scientist Agent that extracts hypotheses from literature and a Co-pilot Agent responsible for selecting and executing the proper tools. This system simulates the collaborative and iterative nature of scientific inquiry, producing a high-quality benchmark Co-BioBench, derived from 15 representative scenarios in peer-reviewed bioinformatics literature. Co-BioBench is comprised of 3,785 meta-tasks. These tasks are structured into five main stages Data Acquisition, Data Curation, Core Analysis, Results Presentation, and Infrastructure/Auxiliary to cover the bioinformatics scientific discovery process.

Second, we propose a Scientific Discovery Tool Learning (SDTL) framework, a fine-tuning methodology designed to enhance an LLM's proficiency with the complex, multi-parameter tools common in science. SDTL first employs data augmentation techniques to compel the model to focus on rich function descriptions rather than ambiguous names, improving its semantic understanding. Afterwards, inspired by the Zone of Proximal Development (ZPD) from educational psychology, it implements a dynamic complexity assessment to evaluate the difficulties of training samples. SDTL ensures the model is consistently challenged with tasks that are slightly beyond its current capabilities, thereby maximizing learning efficiency and enhancing its ability to handle sparse documentation and make scientifically informed parameter choices.

Finally, we tested general LLMs, function-call optimized models, and our SDTL-finetuned models on Co-BioBench and NesTools. Experimental results demonstrate that SDTL significantly outperforms the examined LLM models, validating the effectiveness of the proposed multi-agent architecture and the fine-tuning methodology in calling scientific tools.

2 Related Works

2.1 Tool Learning

Recent research has significantly advanced the capabilities of Large Language Models (LLMs) as autonomous agents through function calling. State-of-the-art models such as IBM's Granite-FunctionCalling [1], APIGen [4], and ToolACE [13] have demonstrated remarkable performance on general-purpose benchmarks by leveraging high-quality, automatically generated datasets and multi-task learning frameworks. This progress has been supported by the development of comprehensive evaluation benchmarks like API-Bank [11] and Seal-Tools [16], which provide thousands of diverse APIs to test an agent's planning and retrieval proficiency. Building upon these foundations, researchers have explored various fine-tuning techniques. While these foundational works are crucial for advancing general agent capabilities, their primary focus has not been on optimizing for the unique complexities of specialized scientific domains, leaving this as an important area for further exploration. Our work builds on these foundations, but focuses on the specific hurdles encountered in scientific discovery.

2.2 AI in Bioinformatics

The application of AI agents in science is a burgeoning field. Pioneering systems like ChemCrow [3] for chemistry and SciAgent [14] for scientific reasoning have demonstrated the potential of tool-augmented LLMs to tackle complex research tasks. Within bioinformatics, agents such as AutoBa [20] have been developed to automate specific multi-omic analysis workflows. These efforts reveal a critical bottleneck: AI agents face difficulties in mastering the highly specialized, multi-parameter tools common in scientific software libraries. Addressing this challenge requires rigorous, domain-specific benchmarks. Recent work like ScienceAgentBench [5] has begun to tackle this by creating evaluation tasks derived from peer-reviewed publications. Our work, Co-BioBench, significantly expands on this direction by providing a large-scale benchmark with 3,785 meta-tasks meticulously curated from bioinformatics literature. Unlike benchmarks that focus on single-shot code generation, Co-BioBench is uniquely designed to evaluate an agent's ability to engage in the iterative scientific process simulating the back-and-forth hypothesis refinement that is central to real-world research.

To address the performance gaps revealed by such complex benchmarks, we propose SDTL, a fine-tuning framework that applies curriculum learning principles. The application of curriculum learning to enhance large models, particularly for code-related tasks, has shown promise in prior work like CodeRL [10], where models are trained on programming tasks of increasing difficulty to improve performance. Our SDTL framework adapts this concept specifically for scientific tool-use. Leveraging a dynamic complexity assessment inspired by the Zone of Proximal Development (ZPD) and domain-specific data augmentation, SDTL is designed to improve an agent's proficiency with complex scientific tools, which is currently a major barrier for autonomous scientific agents.

3 Data Generation Pipeline

3.1 Pipeline Overview

The proliferation of complex computational toolsets in scientific domains, particularly bioinformatics, presents a significant usability challenge for domain experts, often hindering research efficiency. AI agents, especially those built on Large Language Models (LLMs), offer a promising paradigm to bridge this gap by functioning as "Co-Pilots" for scientists. This Co-Pilot model, inspired by its success in software engineering, focuses on assisting with discrete, fundamental tasks, such as data gathering, processing, analysis, and visualization, rather than pursuing the less feasible goal of complete end-to-end automation of the scientific discovery process.

The development of such specialized agents, however, is critically dependent on the availability of high-fidelity training and evaluation data that encapsulates the nuances of real-world scientific workflows. To address this need, we introduce a multi-agent data generation pipeline designed to produce a rich corpus of human-AI interactions grounded in authentic scientific contexts. The significance of our framework lies in its commitment to scientific integrity; by deriving tasks directly from high-impact peer-reviewed academic literature, we ensure that the generated data accurately reflect genuine research questions and methodologies.

Central to our pipeline is an interactive, self-correcting loop between a Scientist Agent, which emulates a domain expert, and an Execution Agent. The Scientist Agent formulates a task, assesses the output, and provides targeted feedback for iterative refinement until a satisfactory solution is achieved, as detailed in Algorithm 1. The ultimate contribution of this process is the generation of a structured Co-Pilot Corpus. This corpus archives the entire interaction: the initial query, toolset, revision history, and final solution, creating an invaluable resource for training and benchmarking next-generation scientific AI assistants capable of complex reasoning and tool manipulation.

Algorithm 1. Corpus Data Generation with Iterative Refinement

1: **function** GENERATECORPUSDATA($\mathcal{P}, \mathcal{T}_{full}, S_g, N_{max}$)
2: Initialize Scientist Agent A_s, Co-pilot Agent A_c; History $H \leftarrow \emptyset$; Feedback $f \leftarrow$ NULL; *is_satisfactory* $\leftarrow$ FALSE; Counter $n \leftarrow 0$.
3: Toolset $\mathcal{T}_q \subseteq \mathcal{T}_{full}$ from literature $\mathcal{P}$.
4: *instruction* $\leftarrow q$ ▷ Initialize instruction with the base task
5: **while** $\neg$*is_satisfactory* **and** $n < N_{max}$ **do**
6: $n \leftarrow n + 1$
7: Append (*instruction*) to H.
8: $S_{exec} \leftarrow A_c$ :: ExecuteTask(*instruction*, $\mathcal{T}_q$) ▷ A_c attempts the task
9: Append (S_{exec}) to H.
10: *is_satisfactory* $\leftarrow A_s$ :: Evaluate(S_{exec}, S_g) ▷ A_s evaluates the result
11: **if** $\neg$*is_satisfactory* **then**
12: $f \leftarrow A_s$ :: GenerateFeedback(S_{exec}, S_g) ▷ Generate guidance for self-correction
13: *instruction* $\leftarrow (q, f)$ ▷ Revise task with feedback for the next turn
14: Append (f) to H.
15: **end if**
16: **end while**
17: dialogue_data $\leftarrow (q, \mathcal{T}_q, H, S_{exec})$. ▷ Archiving
18: **if** POSTINSPECTION(dialogue_data) **then** ▷ Quality Control
19: Add dialogue_data to the Co-pilot Corpus $\mathcal{C}$.
20: **end if**
21: **return** dialogue_data
22: **end function**

Before being added to the final corpus, each archived dialogue undergoes a rigorous Post-Inspection (Algorithm 1, line 17) to ensure accuracy, diversity, and complexity. For instance, we use a structured Chain of Thought (CoT) technique to guide the agent's iterative refinement, making the process more controllable.

3.2 Scientist Agent and Co-pilot Agent

Our data generation pipeline is driven by a collaborative, iterative cycle between a Scientist Agent and a Co-pilot Agent, as depicted in the workflow in Fig. 1. The Scientist Agent emulates a scientist, responsible for initiating tasks derived from scientific literature and evaluating the results. The Co-pilot Agent functions as a computational assistant, which strategizes and executes these tasks by reformulating them into a sequence of tool invocations. In our experiments, Qwen2.5-72B-Instruct and Qwen2.5-7B-Instruct were used as the Scientist Agent and Co-pilot Agent, respectively.

The interactive workflow begins when the Scientist Agent formulates and proposes a task. The Co-pilot Agent processes the request by invoking tools, and the Scientist Agent then evaluates the output against a ground-truth solution from the source paper. If the result is unsatisfactory, the Scientist Agent provides corrective feedback to guide a revised attempt, initiating a self-correction loop.

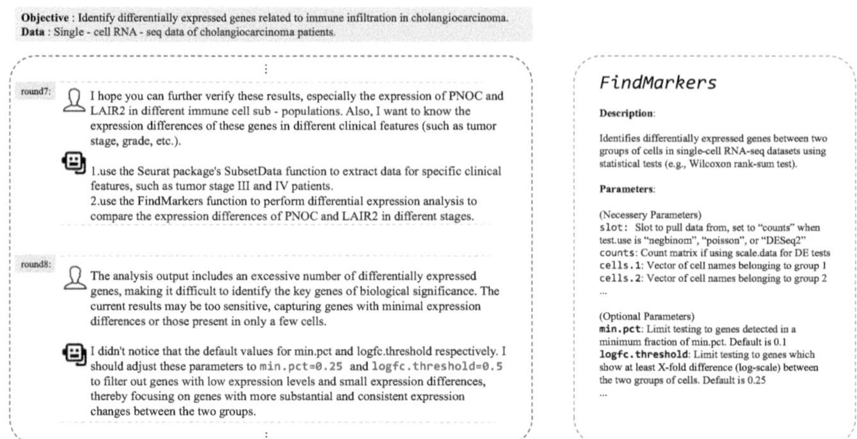

Fig. 1. Workflow for refining a data analysis task. The left plot shows a dialogue between a Scientist Agent and a Co-pilot Agent. The right plot shows a documentation for the *FindMarkers* tool used in this turn.

For instance, as shown in Fig. 1, an initial analysis yields an excessive number of differentially expressed genes. The Scientist Agent identifies that the default parameters are too sensitive and provides targeted feedback, instructing the Executor to adjust the `min.pct` to 0.25 and `logfc.threshold` to 0.5 to refine the results. This cycle repeats until a satisfactory outcome is achieved, at which point the entire dialogue, including the initial problem, the revision history, and the validated solution, is archived.

4 Scientific Discovery Tool Learning

To address the pivotal challenge of tool calling in scientific discovery tasks, which often involve domain-specific tools characterized by numerous parameters and incomplete functional descriptions, we introduce the Scientific Discovery Tool Learning (SDTL) framework. Existing approaches often struggle to generalize in such scenarios due to the intricate nature of tool parameterization. SDTL tackles this deficiency through a systematic training paradigm, the architecture of which is illustrated in Fig. 2. The framework incorporates three key components: Policy-Driven Difficulty Assessment, Pace-Adaptive Selection, and Difficulty-Guided Data Augmentation. The Policy-Driven Difficulty Assessment module analyzes and determines the complexity of different tool function calls. Subsequently, the Pace-Adaptive Selection mechanism dynamically selects sample batches with appropriate difficulty levels based on the model's prescription. These samples are then fed into the Difficulty-Guided Data Augmentation module, which generates augmented training data by manipulating function names, arguments, descriptions, and default values. The large language model (LLM) is then fine-tuned on these augmented samples, enhancing its ability to interpret and invoke tools with sparse or incomplete specifications, thereby reducing reliance on rigid function templates.

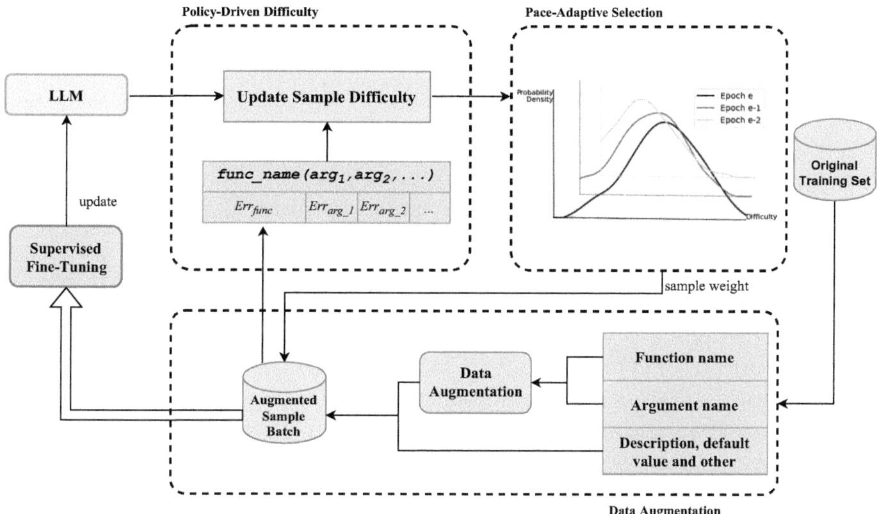

Fig. 2. SDTL Training Framework. Given function-calling data, the **Dynamic Complexity Assessor** (§4.2) evaluates the difficulty of each sample. Based on this assessment, the **Adaptive Sample Selection** module (§4.3) selects a training batch. This batch is then processed by the **Data Augmentation** module (§4.1) before being used to fine-tune the model. The model's training progress, in turn, dynamically updates the complexity assessment and sample weighting for subsequent iterations, creating a self-improving training loop.

4.1 Data Augmentation

In bioinformatics and related scientific fields, tools and functions frequently employ highly specialized naming conventions and domain-specific abbreviations. For instance, `seqinfo` and `seqinfo0`, both from the same R package, serve distinct roles in genomic data processing, yet their significance is equally critical. In addition, scientific tools often feature optional parameters such as convergence thresholds or normalization flags that influence outcomes, but are rarely explicitly emphasized by users. Consequently, models must deduce implicit task requirements from incomplete descriptions to achieve precise results.

A central obstacle in training function-calling models is fostering an understanding of a function's purpose through its description, rather than depending on terse or ambiguous identifiers like function or parameter names. Real-world tool naming varies unpredictably, and over-reliance on such labels risks severe generalization failures across domains. To counter this, SDTL explicitly shifts the model's focus toward function descriptions, mitigating overfitting to superficial naming patterns. Key strategies include:

- **Function Name Randomization**: Function names are substituted with placeholders (e.g., func_001) during training, compelling the model to depend exclusively on descriptive content.
- **Parameter Name Masking**: Parameter names are randomly obscured (e.g., temperature becomes param_3a) while preserving their descriptions, dissociating semantics from nomenclature.
- **Dynamic Description Expansion**: Domain knowledge is injected into function descriptions via templates (e.g., appending "This function requires [parameter] to be within [range], measured in [unit]"), elucidating implicit constraints.
- **Mandatory-Optional Parameter Mixing**: Optional parameters are sporadically omitted from input queries, necessitating inference of their relevance from descriptions.
- **Cross-Domain Style Transfer**: Training data are augmented by rewriting functions to emulate naming conventions from unrelated domains (e.g., adapting an R function to Python-style abbreviations), fostering robust generalization.

This augmentation strategy ensures that models accurately discern functional intent and adapt fluidly to diverse naming conventions, proving especially advantageous in scientific ecosystems where tools evolve swiftly and documentation standards fluctuate. By emphasizing description-driven reasoning over pattern memorization, SDTL lays a scalable foundation for deploying LLMs in real-world scientific workflows with dynamic, underspecified toolchains.

4.2 Dynamic Complexity Assessment

To intelligently guide the model's training, we employ a dynamic complexity assessment mechanism. This system evaluates the difficulty of each training sample in real-time based on the model's current performance, allowing the training curriculum to adapt as the model learns.

A sample's difficulty is defined as being inversely proportional to the model's confidence in predicting the correct tool call. For a given sample consisting of an input instruction x_i and the correct tool call sequence y_i (which includes the function name f and its parameters a_j), we calculate its complexity, $D(x_i, y_i)$, using the following formula:

$$D(x_i, y_i) = 1 - (P(f|x_i))^{\alpha} \cdot \prod_{j=1}^{n} P(a_j|x_i, f, a_1, \ldots, a_{j-1}) \tag{1}$$

α is a weighting factor that adjusts the importance of correctly identifying the function name. Essentially, samples that the model finds difficult to predict (i.e., yields a low probability for the correct sequence) are assigned a higher complexity score.

To ensure a stable and progressive learning curve, we introduce a regularization term, r_{θ_e}, which smooths out complexity changes between training iterations. This prevents the model from over-focusing on outlier difficult samples too early in training. The adjusted difficulty, D_{adj}, for iteration e is calculated as follows. β is a hyperparameter that controls the strength of the regularization:

$$r_{\theta_e} = \beta(D(x_i, y_i, \theta_{e-1}) - D(x_i, y_i, \theta_e)) \tag{2}$$

$$D_{\text{adj}}(x_i, y_i, \theta_e) = D(x_i, y_i, \theta_e) + r_{\theta_e} \tag{3}$$

This dynamic assessment provides a fine-grained difficulty score for each sample at every stage of training, enabling a more effective and efficient learning process.

4.3 Adaptive Sample Selection

After assessing the complexity of each sample, we adopt an adaptive sampling strategy to create a dynamic training curriculum. The goal is to intelligently select training batches that are optimally challenging for the model's current learning stage. This avoids inefficient training on overly simple examples or destabilizing the model by prematurely introducing excessively difficult ones.

At the beginning of each training epoch, we use the complexity scores calculated from the previous epoch to generate new sampling weights for each sample in the dataset. This is achieved by modeling the selection probability using a dynamic Gaussian distribution, where the complexity score itself is the random variable.

The sampling weight v for a sample (x_i, y_i) at epoch e is determined by its complexity score $D(x_i, y_i, \theta_{e-1})$ under the Gaussian distribution for that epoch, $N(\mu_e, \sigma_e)$, as defined by the formula:

$$v(x_i, y_i, e) = \frac{1}{\sigma_e\sqrt{2\pi}} \exp\left(-\frac{(D(x_i, y_i, \theta_{e-1}) - \mu_e)^2}{2\sigma_e^2}\right) \tag{4}$$

The key to this strategy is that the parameters of the Gaussian distribution, its mean (μ_e) and variance (σ_e^2), are not static. They are dynamically adjusted with each epoch to guide the curriculum, ensuring the model is presented with progressively more suitable challenges.

After calculating these weights for all samples, they are normalized and used to sample the training batch for the current epoch. This adaptive curriculum begins by exposing the model to a broad spectrum of difficulties and systematically progresses to focus on more challenging examples, thereby optimizing training efficiency and enhancing the model's final performance.

5 Co-bioBench

5.1 Dataset Overview

To address the existing gap in evaluating tool-calling models for scientific research, we introduce Co-BioBench, a novel and credible benchmark tailored to authentic bioinformatics challenges. This benchmark is meticulously designed to be extensible, supporting adaptation to a wide range of scientific tasks. Its structure is organized across five foundational domains of bioinformatics research: Data Acquisition, Data Wrangling, Core Analysis, Result Presentation, and Infrastructure/Auxiliary.

Co-BioBench comprises a comprehensive suite of problems, each paired with a curated set of corresponding tools to emulate genuine scientific workflows. We expect large language models (LLMs) to proficiently extract critical parameter information from extensive tool documentation and generate accurate call results for specified simulation scenarios. The overall composition of Co-BioBench underscores its depth and breadth, featuring a robust total of 3,785 questions and 671 functions (Table 1).

Table 1. The statistics of our benchmark. **Tasks**: Number of functions. **Tools**: The number of positive/negative functions in the toolset. **APP**: Average number of parameters per function call. **FPQ** (function per question): The number of derived positive functions from each question.

Domain	Tasks	Tools	APP	FPQ
Data Acquisition	773	58/79	2.75	1.89
Data Wrangling	1452	275/336	3.31	1.35
Core Analysis	473	154/181	4.14	1.43
Result Presentation	848	144/162	6.31	1.77
Infrastructure/Auxiliary	239	39/65	2.71	1.60
Total	**3785**	**670/823**	**3.94**	**1.58**

5.2 Dataset Annotation

To ensure the scientific rigor and validity of our benchmark, we invited several researchers specializing in bioinformatics and related disciplines to oversee the dataset annotation phase. This process involved a close collaboration between these domain experts and the Qwen2.5-72B-Instruct model. We curated a collection of peer-reviewed publications that provided open access to their code and data. The task annotation followed a structured four-step process: (1) For each publication, we identified scenarios involving tool calls and used the previously described framework for automated data collection. (2) To prevent models from finding simple shortcuts, negative functions were algorithmically generated from the collected positive functions. (3) Initial task descriptions and tiered evaluation criteria were automatically formulated based on agent dialogue histories. (4)

Crucially, our domain experts conducted a thorough manual review of these generated tasks. This final step assessed whether the tasks were scientifically sound and if standard tool calls could be uniquely inferred from the descriptions alone. From an initial pool of 5,714 tasks, 1,929 were discarded during this expert-led inspection, resulting in a final, validated set of 3,785 tasks.

6 Experiments

6.1 Experiment Settings

To evaluate the performance of AI agents in emulating scientific discovery workflows, we utilize a diverse set of baseline models. This set includes prominent commercially available closed-source models such as GPT-4o [9] and Claude-3.5-sonnet [2], as well as several widely used open-source and research models, specifically ChatGLM [7], Qwen2.5 [19], Hammer-7B [12], Llama3.1-70B [8], QWQ-32B [17], DeepSeek-R1 [6], Watt-tool-8B [18], and toolACE-8b [13]. Furthermore, our evaluation incorporates two fine-tuned models developed as part of this work: SDTL-qwen2.5-7B, fine-tuned on Qwen2.5-7B-Instruct, and SDTL-llama3.1-8B, fine-tuned on Llama3.1-8B-Instruct. To improve evaluation stability and account for potential variability in model outputs, we repeat each task with two independent runs for all experiments conducted with these baseline models.

6.2 Main Results

We evaluate agent performance using Completion Accuracy, a metric that measures whether an agent's final output meets predefined success criteria. In cases of execution failure, a fallback mechanism assesses the correctness of the generated tool-call path to award partial credit. The results, presented in Table 2, demonstrate the significant impact of our SDTL framework. Our fine-tuned models, SDTL-qwen2.5-7B (51%) and SDTL-llama3.1-8B (50%), are the only agents to surpass the 50% accuracy threshold, achieving state-of-the-art performance that exceeds much larger models like GPT-4o (46%) and DeepSeekR1-671B (47%). The powerful effect of our method is further highlighted by the 17-point absolute improvement of SDTL-qwen2.5-7B over its base model. While our approach sets a new performance benchmark, the overall difficulty of the tasks is evident, with "Core Analysis" remaining a notable bottleneck even for our top-performing agents, signaling a key challenge for future work.

6.3 Ablation Study

To investigate the contribution of each component within our proposed system, we conducted a thorough ablation study, with the results presented in Table 3. We established several configurations to systematically evaluate the impact of removing key elements from our full model. The **Full Framework** represents our complete proposed method, achieving the highest performance across all metrics.

Table 2. The main results of LLMs on Co-BioBench. The best results are in bold face and the second best are underlined.

Model Name	Data Acquisition	DataWrangling	CoreAnalysis	ResultPresentation	Infrastructure/Auxiliary	OverallAcc
Closed-source Models						
GPT-4o	51.68%	42.32%	42.31%	51.51%	47.72%	46.63%
claude-3.5-Sonnet	47.19%	43.65%	47.77%	49.36%	48.13%	46.45%
Open-source Base Models						
DeepSeekR1-671B	44.58%	**49.95%**	45.42%	48.54%	48.10%	47.85%
Qwen2.5-72B	46.07%	38.29%	35.10%	42.90%	43.81%	40.86%
QWQ-32B	48.28%	45.55%	44.29%	45.25%	47.64%	46.02%
Qwen2.5-32B	40.76%	44.20%	35.98%	36.67%	41.11%	40.59%
GLM-4-9B	41.08%	35.31%	26.04%	44.20%	39.95%	37.61%
Llama3.1-8B	40.00%	38.59%	37.08%	41.58%	40.26%	39.46%
Qwen2.5-7B	36.89%	29.67%	27.46%	42.45%	35.33%	34.09%
GLM-3-6B	13.50%	12.26%	8.84%	17.59%	13.20%	13.34%
Hammer-7B	35.14%	32.09%	38.69%	39.85%	37.13%	35.59%
Watt-tool-8B	31.72%	34.11%	26.15%	23.73%	30.68%	30.09%
toolACE-8b	26.11%	35.90%	23.35%	8.90%	24.63%	25.57%
SDTL-qwen2.5-7B	52.24%	48.75%	**49.27%**	**56.60%**	**54.55%**	**51.65%**
SDTL-llama3.1-8B	**54.26%**	47.54%	43.10%	56.21%	51.19%	50.53%

The **baseline** configuration utilizes the base Qwen2.5-7B-Instruct model without any of our proposed architectural or methodological enhancements, serving as a lower-bound reference. The **w/o multi-agent** setting removes the collaborative agent structure but retains the fine-tuned model and other components to isolate the impact of the agentic workflow. Finally, **w/o feedback loop** and **w/o Structured CoT** respectively remove the iterative refinement mechanism and the specialized chain-of-thought prompting to measure their individual contributions.

Table 3. Ablation study of our framework's components on the NesTools.

Configuration	Sel. F1	Order F1	Param. F1	Nest. F1	Avg F1
Full Framework	92.8	86.0	79.1	62.0	80.0
baseline	68.6 (↓24.2)	46.5 (↓39.5)	54.0 (↓25.1)	35.0 (↓27.0)	51.0 (↓29.0)
w/o multi-agent	69.2 (↓23.6)	48.7 (↓37.3)	58.6 (↓20.5)	41.4 (↓20.6)	54.5 (↓25.5)
w/o feedback loop	88.5 (↓4.3)	72.1 (↓13.9)	70.3 (↓8.8)	45.5 (↓16.5)	69.1 (↓10.9)
w/o Structured CoT	85.2 (↓7.6)	78.5 (↓7.5)	75.4 (↓3.7)	53.1 (↓8.9)	73.1 (↓6.9)

Our analysis reveals that every component plays a crucial role in the framework's success. The most significant performance degradation occurs when the entire framework is removed, as shown by the **baseline**, which underperforms the **Full Framework** by 29.0 points in Average F1 score. This highlights the overall effectiveness of our combined approach. The removal of the **multi-agent** architecture results in the largest performance drop among all ablated components (↓25.5 Avg F1), indicating that the agent-based structure is the most critical element for task decomposition and execution. The performance degradation is particularly severe for 'Order F1' and 'Nest. F1', demonstrating the multi-agent system's essential role in handling complex sequential and nested operations. The **feedback loop** is the second most vital component; its removal leads to a substantial 10.9-point drop in Avg F1. This shows that the ability to iteratively reflect and refine solutions is key to achieving high accuracy, especially for complex metrics like 'Nest. F1' (↓16.5). Lastly, removing **Structured CoT** results in a 6.9-point decrease in Avg F1, confirming that guiding the model's reasoning process with structured thinking is highly beneficial, even if its impact is more modest compared to the core architectural components. In summary, the ablation study confirms that all proposed components contribute positively, with the multi-agent system forming the backbone of our framework, augmented significantly by the feedback loop and Structured CoT.

7 Conclusion

In this work, we introduce Co-BioBench, a benchmark derived from peer-reviewed literature to evaluate language agents' ability to assist human scientists in open-ended bioinformatics discovery. Co-BioBench's meta-tasks simulate the iterative nature of scientific research and necessitate the use of external tools. Our evaluations reveal that while current large language models (LLMs) show potential, they struggle with complex tool orchestration, especially in core analysis and data visualization. To address these limitations, we propose SDTL, a fine-tuning framework using context-aware data augmentation and dynamic complexity assessment. SDTL demonstrably improves model proficiency in handling complex tool-calling with sparse specifications. Despite these gains, a significant performance gap remains across all models, underscoring the benchmark's complexity and highlighting key challenges for future research in developing capable AI scientific co-pilots.

References

1. Abdelaziz, I., et al.: Granite-function calling model: introducing function calling abilities via multi-task learning of granular tasks. arXiv preprint arXiv:2407.00121 (2024)
2. Anthropic: Claude 3.5 Sonnet Model Card Addendum (2024). Accessed 07 May 2025
3. Bran, A.M., et al.: ChemCrow: augmenting large-language models with chemistry tools (2023). https://arxiv.org/abs/2304.05376
4. Chen, Y., Gao, C., Zhu, M., Liao, Q., Wang, Y., Xu, G.: APIGen: generative API method recommendation (2024). https://arxiv.org/abs/2401.15843
5. Chen, Z., et al.: ScienceAgentBench: toward rigorous assessment of language agents for data-driven scientific discovery (2025). https://arxiv.org/abs/2410.05080
6. DeepSeek-AI, Guo, D., et al.: DeepSeek-R1: incentivizing reasoning capability in LLMs via reinforcement learning (2025). https://arxiv.org/abs/2501.12948

7. Team GLM, Zeng, A., et al.: ChatGLM: a family of large language models from GLM-130B to GLM-4 all tools (2024). https://arxiv.org/abs/2406.12793
8. Grattafiori, A., et al.: The Llama 3 herd of models. arXiv preprint arXiv:2407.21783 (2024)
9. Hurst, A., et al.: GPT-4o system card. arXiv preprint arXiv:2410.21276 (2024)
10. Le, H., Wang, Y., Gotmare, A.D., Savarese, S., Hoi, S.C.H.: CodeRL: mastering code generation through pretrained models and deep reinforcement learning (2022). https://arxiv.org/abs/2207.01780
11. Li, M., et al.: API-Bank: a comprehensive benchmark for tool-augmented LLMS (2023). https://arxiv.org/abs/2304.08244
12. Lin, Q., et al.: Robust function-calling for on-device language model via function masking. In: The Thirteenth International Conference on Learning Representations (2025)
13. Liu, W., et al.: ToolACE: winning the points of LLM function calling. arXiv preprint arXiv:2409.00920 (2024)
14. Ma, Y., et al.: SciAgent: tool-augmented language models for scientific reasoning (2024). https://arxiv.org/abs/2402.11451
15. Qin, Y., et al.: TooLLLM: facilitating large language models to master 16000+ real-world APIs arXiv:2307.16789 (2023). https://arxiv.org/abs/2307.16789
16. Santi, R.D., Joseph, F.A., Liniger, N., Mutti, M., Krause, A.: Geometric active exploration in Markov decision processes: the benefit of abstraction (2024). https://arxiv.org/abs/2407.13364
17. Qwen Team: QwQ-32B: the power of scaling RL (2025). https://qwenlm.github.io/blog/qwq-32b/
18. watt-ai: watt-ai/watt-tool-8B (2024). https://huggingface.co/watt-ai/watt-tool-8B. Accessed 07 May 2025
19. Yang, A., et al.: Qwen2.5 Technical report. arXiv preprint arXiv:2412.15115 (2024)
20. Zhou, J., et al.: Automated bioinformatics analysis via AutoBA (2023). https://arxiv.org/abs/2309.03242

GraphDance: A Semantics-Driven Framework for Authoring Narrative Data Video in Graph Structure

Zhiyuan Wu[1], Qishuo Bai[1], Yinuo Liu[2], and Xiaoju Dong[1(✉)]

[1] Department of Computer Science and Engineering, Shanghai Jiao Tong University, Shanghai, China
xjdong@sjtu.edu.cn

[2] SJTU Paris Elite Institute of Technology, Shanghai Jiao Tong University, Shanghai, China

Abstract. Narrative Data Videos (NDVs) are gaining traction as powerful information mediums by combining storytelling and visualization. Among the core elements of NDVs, graphs visualize abstract relational data, rendering complex relational narratives perceptible and comprehensible. However, existing NDV tools rarely focus on graphs. Moreover, their complex, manual authoring process poses a significant challenge for non-expert users, especially when dealing with unstructured narrative text. To address this gap, we propose GraphDance, a human-AI collaborative framework designed for the semi-automated authoring of graph NDVs from raw narrative text. We further develop an interactive system that, via a GUI, supports users in narrative text editing, animation intent annotation, and the fine-tuning of animation parameters. To evaluate GraphDance's effectiveness and practicality, we detail the graph NDV authoring process and conduct a mixed-methods user study. Results indicate that GraphDance enables users to easily and efficiently author graph NDVs, delivering a positive user experience. This work pioneers exploration into narration text-driven graph NDV authoring, providing a human-AI collaborative framework and a user-friendly interactive system. It also offers practical insights for this domain while pointing to future research on graph animation intent understanding, mechanisms, and user experience optimization.

Keywords: Narrative Visualization · Data Video · Knowledge Graph

1 Introduction

Narrative visualization has emerged as a pivotal tool in education [6], data journalism [15]. Narrative Data Videos (NDVs), as a form of narrative visualization, boost data appeal and comprehension by integrating visualizations, animations and audio [19]. The increasing demand for media immediacy underscores the importance of automating the production of rich audiovisual content for rapid

© The Author(s), under exclusive license to Springer Nature Singapore Pte Ltd. 2026
J. Kittler et al. (Eds.): PRCV 2025, LNCS 16289, pp. 363–378, 2026.
https://doi.org/10.1007/978-981-95-5764-6_25

consumption [22]. However, their authoring is resource-intensive, demanding specialized skills and manual work [20].

Graph NDVs combine dual strengths: intuitive visualization of abstract, complex relational data via graph structures, and clear conveyance of relationship evolution plus precise narrative guidance through dynamic animation. This potential, however, is largely untapped in current NDV authoring tools, which GraphDance aims to bridge. Existing tools create NDVs from structured data and require visualization to be prepared in advance [18,20]. Data Player [20] elegantly achieves the transformation from narration text and visual design inputs to NDVs, but it focuses on basic chart types like line and bar graphs, lacking support for more complex charts like graphs. With LLMs advancing text processing and semantic analysis [14], their reasoning strengths in narrative logic, open information extraction, and relation inference provide a promising way to support graph NDV authoring. We present GraphDance, a semantics-driven framework for semi-automatic graph NDVs authoring, which includes the modules: *Knowledge Graph Construction and Text Markup*, *Graph Animation Intent Annotation*, and *Multimodal Alignment and Graph NDV Creation*. The ultimate goal is to empower creators to readily author graph NDVs that clearly articulate narrative structure and the dynamic evolution of entity relationships. The main contributions are:

1. We propose GraphDance, a semantics-driven framework for semi-automatic graph NDV authoring, to enable efficient NDV authoring with narration text.
2. We design an extensible graph animation mechanism that aligns with narrative requirements.
3. We develop an interactive authoring system based on GraphDance, conduct a user study, and derive development recommendations for NDV authoring systems and key challenges in graph NDV authoring.

2 Related Work

2.1 Narrative Visualization

In 2010, Segel and Heer introduced the term *Narrative Visualization (NV)*, defining it as "an emerging class of visualizations that attempts to combine narratives with interactive graphics" [17]. The integration of narratives with interactive visualizations allows NV to enhance data exploration, rendering it more engaging and memorable.

Based on the driving relationship between narrative and visualization, relevant research falls into two main paradigms: *Narrative for Visualization(Nar4Vis)* and *Visualization for Narrative(Vis4Nar)*. *Nar4Vis* uses narrative techniques to effectively convey data insights, enhancing visualization comprehensibility and appeal [16]. For example, it uses narrative patterns and visual design to emotionally engage the audience [11], controls pacing to manage attention [16]. However, its data-driven nature restricts it from fully capturing the richness of qualitative narratives involving complex interactions and causal relationships [12].

Vis4Nar prioritizes visual elements for qualitative and interpretive narratives. This paradigm leverages charts, animations, and multimodal techniques to enhance narrative expressiveness and immersiveness. By addressing *5W1H* questions, *Vis4Nar* visualizes spatiotemporal contexts and causal relationships [9]. In this paradigm, visualization serves as a medium for conveying information, viewpoints, and emotions, transcending mere data discovery. However, existing work often relies on static visualizations or extensive manual intervention. Our research focuses on reducing this manual effort by leveraging human-AI collaboration to generate dynamic graph visualizations from unstructured narration text.

2.2 Data Video Authoring

Data videos are a multimodal narrative visualization form that integrates visual, motion, narrative, and audio elements to enhance information communication [2,17,19]. Research on data videos has focused on the design space, exploring effective creation and comprehension strategies. Tversky et al. [24] proposed the *Congruence and Apprehension Principles* for animated graphics, and subsequent work analyzed data video to identify key elements like visualization types, narrative structures, and phases [1,2]. Design spaces have also been proposed to formalize animated transition and pacing [23] and integrate animation with visual narrative strategies [21], and these refined design spaces and guidelines provide a crucial theoretical foundation for data video authoring tools.

Traditional video tools like Adobe After Effects and Premiere require substantial manual effort and have a steep learning curve for data video authoring. To lower this barrier, the visualization community has proposed high-level *Domain-Specific Languages (DSLs)* like Canis [8] and Vega-Lite [25], which simplify creation through programming interfaces. However, these DSLs still demand programming expertise, limiting their widespread adoption. To further lower the technical threshold, researchers have developed interactive UI tools. For instance, DataClips [3] allows users to assemble data clips without extensive expertise. CAST [7] offers interactive creation via dSVGs, and DataParticles [4] provides a block-based editor for animated unit visualizations. However, current data video tools mostly focus on basic charts (line, bar, pie charts), confining storytelling to data-driven insights and failing to effectively convey complex relational networks. Our work aims to support richer narratives that express dynamic entity relationships and event-based flows.

3 GraphDance

This section first details GraphDance's design goals and provides an overview of the framework, followed by introductions to its three main modules.

3.1 Design Goals

To ensure the expression of narrative intent, the semantic consistency of multimodal content, and ultimately achieve the expressive authoring of graph NDVs, we establish the following design goals:

- *G1: Semi-Automated NDV authoring.* Currently, authoring NDVs is inefficient and costly because it relies on a jumble of different tools. An integrated, semi-automated process could significantly lower the barrier to entry and boost efficiency.
- *G2: Intuitive Representation of Narrative Events & Relationships.* Narrative elements contain complex dynamics and structured relationships that traditional representations struggle to capture. Graph structures can clearly reveal these inherent connections and their evolution, enhancing the expression of the user's narrative intent.
- *G3: Interpretable Checks & Necessary Human Intervention Embedding.* LLMs can sometimes create inaccurate or inappropriate animations, which could harm credibility. To balance the efficiency of automation with the need for user control and accuracy, we can use interpretable checks and allow for essential human intervention.
- *G4: Rich & Extensible Animation Effects for Diverse Narrative Intents.* Existing tools, constrained by fixed templates and basic chart types, struggle to accommodate diverse narrative themes. A rich and extensible range of visual effects and dynamic graph animations can better match complex user narrative intentions.
- *G5: Semantic & Temporal Consistency in Multimodal Narrative.* Multimodal NDVs can be hard to understand if the content is not aligned. Using cross-modal semantic consistency rules can make the narrative more coherent and impactful.

3.2 Overview

The GraphDance framework comprises three collaborating modules: *Knowledge Graph Construction and Text Markup Module* extracts a knowledge graph (G2) from the narration text and performs initial markup. *Graph Animation Intention Annotation Module* automatically annotates animation intentions based on predefined animation rules (G4) and provides a user interface for fine-tuning (G3). *Multimodal Alignment and GraphNDV Creation Module* interprets the annotated text, integrates multimodal narrative content (G5) to generate a unified animation specification, and renders the NDV (G1).

As depicted in Fig. 1, three modules work collaboratively to achieve the authoring of graph NDVs from user-input narration text. First, the user inputs plain narration text (A). The system then uses an LLM to extract entities, relationships, and attributes from the text, which it saves as a JSON-formatted knowledge graph (B). At the same time, it outputs a *Markup Text* (C), which

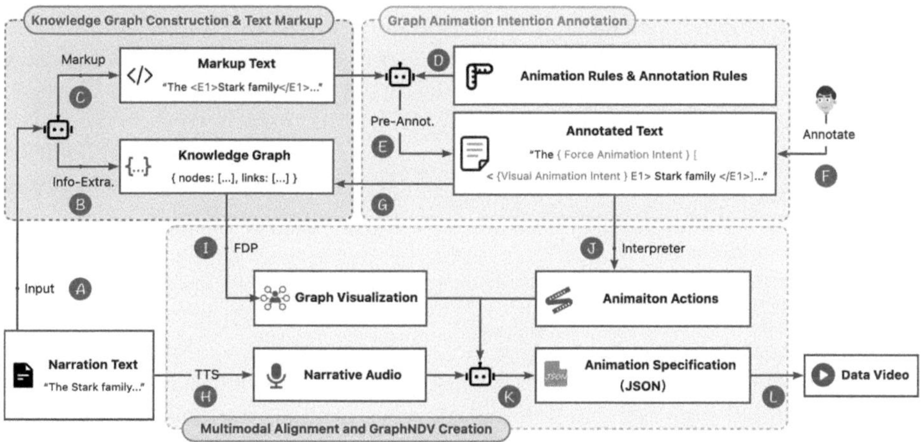

Fig. 1. GraphDance Framework Overview and Processing Pipeline.

is the basis for annotating animation intentions later on. Next, based on predefined graph animation and annotation rules (D), GraphDance automatically pre-annotates *Animations Intent* within the *Markup Text* (E). Users can then interactively modify or supplement the markup-corresponding entity relationships and entity-level animation intents. They can also annotate unit-level animation intent through a brushing interaction (F). Any changes made to entity relationship markup are automatically synchronized with the knowledge graph (G). Then, *Text-to-Speech (TTS)* technology generates the narrative audio and returns timestamps for each word, establishing the timeline (H). The knowledge graph is visualized as a node-link diagram using a force-directed layout algorithm (I). Subsequently, animations specified in the *Annotated Text* are interpreted to determine the animation actions (J). Finally, an LLM aligns the multimodal narrative content and generates the complete animation specifications (K), which are then used to render the final NDV (L).

3.3 Knowledge Graph Construction and Text Markup

GraphDance begins with the *Knowledge Graph Construction and Text Markup Module*, which automatically extracts structured information from the input narration text and generates *Markup Text*. Compared to prior NDV authoring systems [20], GraphDance internalizes the process of establishing text-to-visual links using an *Open Information Extraction (OpenIE)* pipeline, eliminating the need for users to provide pre-made visual charts.

Narrative Information Extraction. Narrative information extraction is the vital first step in constructing a narrative knowledge graph, converting raw text into structured data for dynamic visualizations. We employ a phased approach guided by the *5W1H* principle to clearly sequence events (Fig. 2A). Its hexa-tuple elements are the foundation of the narrative knowledge graph, offering a structured way to analyze event progression. We specifically guide LLMs to identify each entity's *EntityType* and *5W1HCategory*, extracting relationships and attribute descriptions. Following optimizations like entity disambiguation and relation canonicalization, this module outputs a structured knowledge graph in JSON format (Fig. 1B) and *Markup Text* for annotation (Fig. 1C).

Markup Text. Given the importance of establishing a fine-grained anchor between narration text and visual representation, we utilize *Markup Text* (Fig. 5D), a custom XML format that not only precisely associates phrases and words with relevant entities and relationships in the knowledge graph, but also maintains critical context and referential relationships. For instance, the tag <*E*1>*he*</*E*1> explicitly references a previously defined entity *E1*, preventing any loss of meaning. This method helps precisely identify the target elements for unit animations during the animation intent annotation phase. By preserving the semantic text-to-visual correspondence, it offers users a direct way to intervene and adjust. We explicitly define the output format of *Markup Text* via a few-shot prompt.

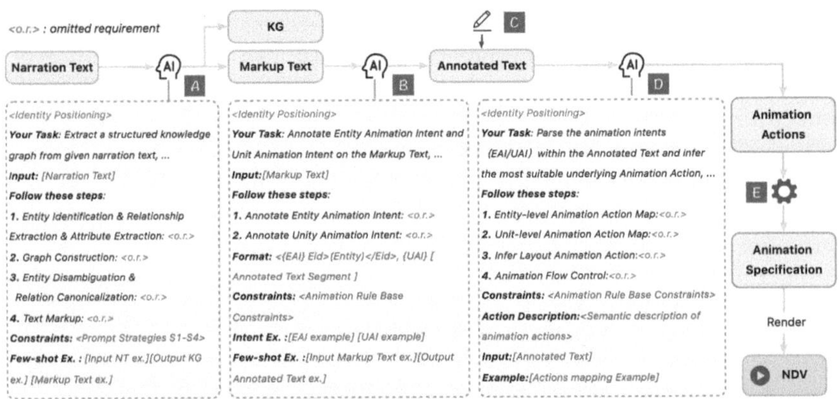

Fig. 2. GraphDance Workflow and Prompts: (A) KG Construction and Markup from Narration Text; (B) Animation Intent Pre-Annotation and (C) Manual Interactively adjust Annotated Text; (D) Animation Intent Interpretation; (E) Animation Specification Generation. DeepSeek-R1 model is used in this paper.

Prompt Strategies. Given common LLM challenges like hallucinations, inconsistencies, and over-inference, we utilize specific prompting strategies (Fig. 2A). *(S1) Source Anchoring.* We restrict the model to extract information solely from the input narration text, preventing it from generating fictitious entities or relationships by introducing external knowledge. *(S2) Explicit Prompt Reinforcement.* To ensure crucial information isn't overlooked in long texts, we explicitly guide the model to focus on extracting core ontological data (entities and relationships). *(S3) Source Constraint for Relation Extraction.* To avoid misinterpretation from over-generalization, we require the LLM to ground each extracted relationship with direct textual evidence from the narration. *(S4) Context Understanding and Optimizations.* We address name ambiguity and entity reference variations through context-based entity disambiguation, merging different mentions of the same entity. Concurrently, we perform relation canonicalization by merging semantically similar edge descriptions between identical nodes, preventing redundant edges.

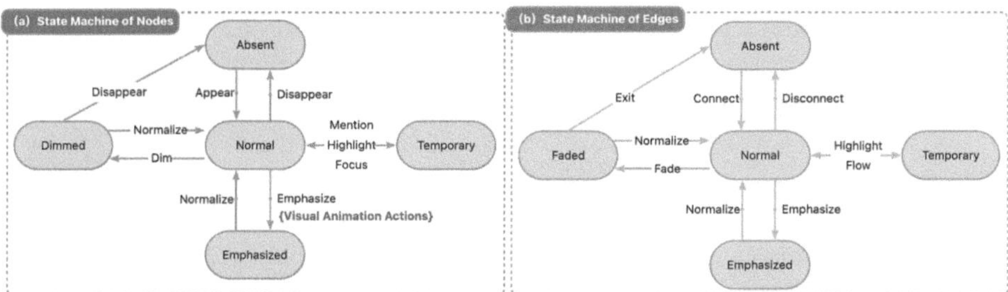

Fig. 3. Graph Elements State Machine. (a) State of Nodes. (b) State of Edges. *States* correspond to specific visual representations of elements, while *Animation Actions* between states define the visual animation effects (excluding positional changes) applied to the graph elements.

3.4 Graph Animation Intention Annotation

NDVs convert narratives into dynamic visuals, with animation intent as the key. However, a semantic gap exists between animation intentions expressed in natural language and the actual underlying animation actions executed. This module uses LLM semantic understanding to bridge this gap. It starts by pre-annotating animation intent on the *Markup Text*, offering users examples to ease the learning curve while allowing semantic-level intervention. Afterward, a user-friendly interface lets users confirm, modify, or add to the pre-annotations, including adjusting text-visual links and refining *Entity-level Animation Intent (EAI)*. The interface also supports brushing interactions for annotating *Unit-level Animation Intent (UAI)*. To avoid visual confusion, we design the animation mechanism by combining rule-based animation and state transition animation to control the visual animations. Additionally, we introduce *Layout Animation* within the *UAI* to drive element animations at the layout level.

Entity-Level Animation Intent. The synchronization of visual cues with auditory information effectively reduces cognitive load, making data easier for the audience to process and understand [5]. To capitalize on this advantage, GraphDance uses a state machine-based animation mechanism (Fig. 3) to control and interpret the animation intent, ultimately converting it into executable animation actions (Sect. 3.5). In graph NDV, a state is an abstract encoding of an entity's (nodes and edges) role and semantic information within a narrative. Each entity can only have one unique state at a time. This animation mechanism relies on a state's persistence and changes, which aligns with the narrative's need to maintain an entity's specific story state over a period of time.

Additionally, some animations serve only for temporary emphasis and need not alter a visual element's persistent state. For such brief, one-off visual effects, GraphDance introduces transient states in the state machine—these effects run briefly before restoring the element to its prior state. Specifically, we use the *<{EAI}Eid/Rid>* syntax to preserve the correspondence between an EAI and its Markup Element. The EAI specifies the animation intent that controls the visual properties of an element, such as "Highlight the node" or "Connect its related edges".

Unit-Level Animation Intent. Inspired by *Annotated Narration* [20], we use the syntax *"{UAI}[Narrative unit]"*, where the UAI specifies the unit's animation intent and the brackets *[]* delineate the animation scope. The duration of the animation is determined by the audio length of the text within the brackets, allowing users to control the pacing. The unit also includes multiple visual elements that participate in the specified animation action. For example, "*{let them light up}*[*<E1 > he</E1><R4>meets</R4><E5>Lena, the witch</E5>*]" would perform *Highlight* action on E1 and E5, and a *Connect* action on edge R4, making it appear from nothing.

In dynamic graph narratives, node position is crucial for highlighting key elements [13]. We introduce *Layout Animation* to capture this dynamism, complementing visual animation by expressing narrative flow through adjusted force-directed layout parameters. For instance, we can animate two nodes moving closer together to reflect a closer relationship between two characters in the narrative. Layout Animation runs in parallel with visual animations, as it only affects a node's position without altering its visual properties. In GraphDance, EAI expresses fine-grained semantic changes, while UAI captures relationships between multiple entities and overall state changes. We set the priority of EAI animation actions higher than UAI actions to prevent conflicts.

User Intervention and Fine-Tuning. While GraphDance leverages an LLM for pre-annotation, the complexity of natural language and inherent LLM limitations may lead to annotation errors or failure to capture nuanced narrative intent. To mitigate this issue, GraphDance provides a user-friendly interface (Sect. 4) for refining and confirming the pre-annotated text. Users can adjust the text-to-element links with markup and modify or add EAI and UAI at the semantic level. This gives users control over the final animation, ensuring it aligns with their creative vision and narrative goals.

3.5 Multimodal Alignment and GraphNDV Creation

GraphDance's ultimate goal is to generate viewable, dynamic graph NDV. As a key link between semantic annotations and NDV presentation, this final module first visualizes the knowledge graph as a node-link graph via a force-directed placement (FDP) algorithm. It then parses animation intent from the *Annotated Text*, translating it into specific animation actions for visual elements. Finally, these animations are synchronized with other narrative modalities to form a unified animation specification for the final graph NDV.

Animation Intent Interpretation. To bridge the semantic gap between natural language animation intent and executable animation actions, GraphDance introduces an intent interpreter. The interpreter maps EAI/UAI to the most appropriate animation actions using a semantic similarity strategy. Specifically, we provide a precise *Semantic Description* for each executable *Animation Action*. When Interpreter receives a user-annotated EAI/UAI, it matches the natural language animation intent with these predefined semantic descriptions, and deduces the most appropriate Animation Action. For example, the intent *Emphasize all family members* would be translated into a *Highlight* action and assigned to all corresponding nodes.

For UAI, the interpreter first identifies all entities mentioned within the brackets *[]* and assigns animation actions to these entities. Additionally, it synchronizes the animation duration with the audio duration of the text enclosed in the brackets. For layout animation, GraphDance identifies subject and object nodes list, inferring corresponding layout actions from the UAI's semantics. Finally, the interpreter automatically supplements missing animation actions according to state machine rules (e.g., adding an *Appear* action prior to a *Highlight*). It also prioritizes EAI over UAI, ensuring the execution of users' fine-grained control intentions takes precedence.

TTS and Force-Directed Graph Layout. NDVs derive expressive power from the tight integration of visual animation and spoken narration. We use Text-to-Speech (TTS) to convert narration text into an audio stream, with word timestamps serving as the synchronization baseline for multimodal content. The knowledge graph is visualized as a node-link graph via the force-directed layout algorithm (d3-force). By simulating virtual physical forces between nodes, this method effectively presents complex relationships while avoiding visual overlap. *Layout Animation* adjusts force model parameters like attraction, repulsion and iteration count to control node positions, enabling effects like nodes moving closer or farther apart.

Animation Modeling and Specification. To bridge the gap between multimodal narrative content and the final NDV, we design a declarative specification inspired by existing DSLs [10]. This specification (Fig. 4) unifies narration text, audio timestamps, element states and actions, animation details, and layout animations into a single structure—providing comprehensive instructions for NDV rendering.

```
{
  "metadata": {
    "narration_text": "The young knight Alan ..", // Full narration text
    "audio": [ // Audio timing information
      { "word": "The", "startTime": "0.32", "endTime": "0.58" },
      ...]
  },
  "elements": [{                        // Elements with actions
    "element_id": "E1",                 // Unique ID of the element
    "actions": []
  }, ...],                              // More elements
  "layout_animations": [{               // Force-directed layout animations
    "start_time": 3.0,                  // Animation start time (seconds)
    "duration": 2.0,                    // Animation duration (seconds)
    "animation_action": "Attract",      // Force animation action
    "subject_ids": ["E1"],              // IDs of affected elements
    "object_ids": ["E5"],
    "force_parameters": [               // Force parameters changes
      {"parameter": "attractionStrength", "target_value": 0.8},
      ...]
  }, ...]                               // More force-directed layout animations
}
```

```
"actions": [
  // Animation actions of the element
  {
    "start_time": 1.25,             // Animation start time (seconds)
    "duration": 0.5,                // Animation duration (seconds)
    "action": "Emphasize",          // Animation action
    "easing": "easeOutBack",        // Easing function
    "start_state": "Normal",        // State before this animation action
    "target_state": "Emphasized",   // State after this animation action
    "effects": [                    // Visual property changes
      {"channel": "scale", "from": 1, "to": 1.2},
      {"channel": "color", "from": "#3c66b2", "to": "#41a2cc"},
      ...
    ]
  },
  ...
  // More animations actions
]
```

Fig. 4. The Specification for graph NDVs consists of three components: Metadata (containing the narration text and audio timestamps), Elements and Actions (for each graph element, listing all animation actions and their parameters as expressed by the EAI and UAI), and Layout Animations (defining dynamic adjustments to the force-directed layout by controlling parameters over time to guide node movement).

4 Prototype System

Leveraging the GraphDance framework, we develop an intuitive authoring system (Fig. 5). This interface integrates the authoring workflow into three core functional panels. *Narrative & Annotate Panel* is located on the left, allowing users to input narration text (A) and configure *Text-to-Speech* parameters. After clicking the "Confirm Narration Text" button, the system then generates knowledge graph data (C) and audio timestamps (B). In the *Annotated Text* area below (D), users can perform automatic pre-annotation via the "PreAnnotate" button or manual annotation in "Edit" mode, adding entity-level (EAI) and unit-level (UAI) animation intents. *Graph & Timeline Panel* renders the knowledge graph on the canvas (E) (where animations are displayed) upon clicking "Draw". Its timeline below (F) provides a visual representation of all animation actions, enabling users to precisely adjust their timing by dragging and zooming. *Animation Panel* displays detailed information (G) of the selected entity (from either the canvas or the timeline) and a list of animation actions (H). It further allows users to modify animation parameters through these displayed options, granting complete control over the visual presentation of graph NDVs.

5 User Study

To evaluate the usability, effectiveness, and user experience of GraphDance and its authoring GUI, we conduct a mixed-methods user study, combining both qualitative and quantitative approaches. Our evaluation focused on three key

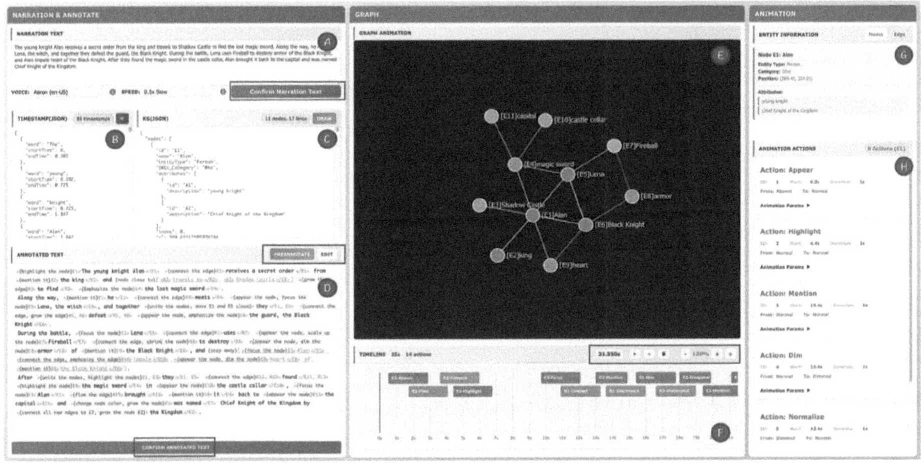

Fig. 5. GraphDance User Interface.

areas. (1) Usability and Ease of Use: Can users intuitively and efficiently utilize the GraphDance interface to complete NDV authoring tasks? (2) Effectiveness and Expressiveness: Can narrative intents be successfully translated into expressive and dynamic graph NDVs? (3) User Experience and Satisfaction: Are users satisfied with the overall workflow—including LLM-based automatic pre-annotation and visual editing?

5.1 Study Design and Procedure

We recruited 8 participants (P1–P8, 5 females and 3 males, aged 22–26) with no prior experience using GraphDance. Participants completed three progressive authoring tasks: *(1) Basic Task.* Construct a knowledge graph, draw a visualization, use the pre-annotation to add animation intents, and manually add one animation intent. *(2) Intermediate Task.* Author a character interaction-focused narrative, using EAI and UAI to annotate relationship connections and node layout changes. *(3) Advanced Task.* Author a complete graph NDV by leveraging all system features—including adjusting animation parameters to ensure full alignment with narrative intent.

The study procedure included a system introduction, warm-up exercise, task execution, questionnaire, and interview. Data collection encompassed two categories: *Objective Data*, which included task completion time and success rate for each task; and *Subjective Data*, which included post-task Likert scale questionnaires (assessing usability, controllability, effectiveness, and overall satisfaction) supplemented by semi-structured interviews for in-depth qualitative feedback. During the task execution phase, participants independently completed all authoring tasks following a brief system introduction and self-exploration period. No assistance was provided by researchers during this process to ensure the objectivity of the collected data.

Table 1. User Study Results: Task Performance and Questionnaire Averages

Pid	Time (min) & Success Rate			Average Questionnaire Scores			
	Task 1	Task 2	Task 3	Usability Q1–Q4	Control Q5–Q8	Effectiveness Q9–Q11	Satisfaction Q12–Q14
P1	2.5 (100%)	6.5 (100%)	10.0 (100%)	5.0	5.0	4.75	5.0
P2	3.5 (100%)	8.0 (100%)	12.5 (100%)	4.25	4.25	4.5	4.5
P3	3.0 (100%)	7.5 (100%)	14.0 (80%)	4.5	4.25	4.5	4.5
P4	2.5 (100%)	6.0 (100%)	11.0 (100%)	5.0	5.0	5.0	5.0
P5	4.0 (100%)	9.5 (90%)	16.0 (90%)	3.0	3.0	3.25	2.5
P6	3.0 (100%)	7.5 (100%)	12.0 (100%)	3.75	3.75	3.75	4.0
P7	3.0 (100%)	8.5 (100%)	13.0 (95%)	4.75	5.0	5.0	5.0
P8	4.5 (100%)	10.5 (85%)	18.5 (80%)	2.75	2.0	2.25	3.5
Avg.	**3.25 (100%)**	**8.0 (96.9%)**	**13.5 (93.1%)**	**4.13**	**4.03**	**4.13**	**4.25**

5.2 Results Analysis

(1) Task Completion Efficiency Analysis. Table 1 presents participant completion times (in minutes) for the three progressive tasks, with sub-100% success rates indicating minor animation issues (e.g., synchronization flaws). Participants completed the basic task quickly (avg. 3 min), demonstrating the system's ease of learning. However, intermediate task times increased significantly (avg. 8 min), revealing room to improve complex intent annotation and revision. This indicates the system has a low entry barrier, but complex narratives and layout animations require higher user proficiency. *(2) Usability and User Experience Evaluation.* Our quantitative Likert scale evaluation reveals high user ratings for GraphDance: usability (Q1–Q4, mean 4.13) and overall satisfaction (Q12–Q14, mean 4.25), indicating an intuitive interface and satisfying authoring experience. Notably, the LLM-powered pre-annotation feature (Q5) earned the highest mean score (4.5), confirming its effectiveness in reducing users' creative barriers. However, slight variations were observed in user ratings for animation control granularity (Q5–Q8) and overall satisfaction(Q12–Q14). For instance, one participant (P8) highlighted the inconvenience of the authoring interface lacking an animation action preview feature, which contributed to lower satisfaction score. *(3) Semi-Structured Interviews and Qualitative Findings.* Interview results confirmed GraphDance's strengths: users praised the LLM-driven pre-annotation for lowering creative barriers and saving time, found semantic intent annotation (e.g., "highlight") more intuitive than low-level parameters, and valued the timeline's control over animation rhythm. However, challenges were noted: LLM markup, while generally accurate, needed extensive manual correction for errors. Users also requested audio waveforms, finer-grained timeline control, and additional animation state mechanisms for complex narratives.

6 Discussion

6.1 Findings

Based on the design, development, and user study of the GraphDance framework, we draw the following key conclusions: *(1) Efficient Human-AI Collaboration and Low Barrier to Entry.* GraphDance balances creative efficiency and usability: user study results show participants completed basic tasks quickly, driven by the intuitive GUI and LLM-powered automatic pre-annotation. This feature's highest average score (4.5) confirms its value in lowering initial creative hurdles. *(2) LLM's Potential and the Need for Robust Rule Systems.* While LLMs excel at understanding and pre-annotating animation intents, their output is sometimes unpredictable. For instance, LLM frequently mistook "appear" for "highlight". This indicates LLMs alone are insufficient; a comprehensive, reliable rule system is essential to ensure predictable animation behavior and user control. *(3) The Challenge of Balancing Personalization and a General Animation Library.* Storytellers' unique styles create challenges for a one-size-fits-all animation library, highlighting the need for deeper user research to develop a versatile library that supports diverse storytelling approaches. *(4) Balancing Automation and User Control.* While automation greatly enhances efficiency, insufficient control remains a challenge: users consistently noted fine-tuning is critical to ensuring animation quality and alignment with their creative vision. This underscores the importance of robust user intervention mechanisms—such as timeline editing and parameter controls—to balance efficiency and controllability.

6.2 Limitations and Future Work

This research demonstrates the potential of an LLM-based human-AI collaboration model for narrative data visualization creation. However, the current framework and system have limitations that point to promising future research directions.

Limitations. *(1) Challenges in LLM Semantic Understanding and Animation Mechanisms.* The LLM's uncertainty in mapping animation intents necessitates a robust rule-based system for control. While our general rule set (e.g., highlight, connect) supports basic creation, it fails to fully accommodate highly personalized narrative expressions—limiting further gains in automation efficiency. *(2) Insufficient Exploration of Force-Directed Animation Control.* A key challenge persists in using force-directed algorithms for animation: how to effectively control force model parameters to both comply with physical laws and accurately convey complex narrative intents, requiring further in-depth research. *(3) Limitations of the User Study Sample.* Our user study included only eight participants, primarily from a specific age group. Thus, the generalizability of our findings needs validation via larger, more diverse user studies.

Future Work. *(1) Improve LLM Intent Understanding.* We will fine-tune LLMs and use few-shot learning to improve animation intent mapping accuracy, reducing reliance on rigid rules. A user feedback loop will continuously optimize the model with user corrections. *(2) Develop Advanced Interaction Tools.* We plan to enhance the GUI by adding an audio waveform overlay to the timeline, enabling precise audio-animation alignment. *(3) Explore Personalized Animation Rules.* We will conduct more user research to expand the animation rule library, allowing users to define and combine custom intents with basic actions for a personalized animation vocabulary. *(4) Optimize Force-Directed Animation Control.* We will explore advanced physical models and parameter control methods to make force-directed animations more expressive and aligned with narrative needs. *(5) Conduct a Large-Scale User Study.* We will recruit a larger, more diverse group of participants to validate the system's usability and effectiveness on a broader scale, gathering comprehensive data for future iterations.

7 Conclusion

This paper presents GraphDance, a framework exploring a human-AI collaboration model for the authoring of graph NDVs. GraphDance leverages an LLM to construct knowledge graphs and annotate/interpret animation intents, integrates a force-directed layout to enhance animation effects, and features a user-friendly GUI. The framework offers an effective collaboration model combining automation with user fine-tuning, providing practical insights into automated graph animation generation. A mixed-methods user study confirms GraphDance enables easy, efficient graph NDV authoring and delivers positive user experience.

References

1. Amini, F., Henry Riche, N., Lee, B., Hurter, C., Irani, P.: Understanding data videos: looking at narrative visualization through the cinematography lens. In: Proceedings of the 33rd Annual ACM Conference on Human Factors in Computing Systems, pp. 1459–1468 (2015)
2. Amini, F., Riche, N.H., Lee, B., Leboe-McGowan, J., Irani, P.: Hooked on data videos: assessing the effect of animation and pictographs on viewer engagement. In: Proceedings of the 2018 International Conference on Advanced Visual Interfaces, pp. 1–9 (2018)
3. Amini, F., Riche, N.H., Lee, B., Monroy-Hernandez, A., Irani, P.: Authoring data-driven videos with DataClips. IEEE Trans. Vis. Comput. Graph. **23**(1), 501–510 (2016)
4. Cao, Y., E, J.L., Zhu-Tian, C., Xia, H.: DataParticles: block-based and language-oriented authoring of animated unit visualizations. In: Proceedings of the 2023 CHI Conference on Human Factors in Computing Systems, pp. 1–15 (2023)
5. Cheng, H., Wang, J., Wang, Y., Lee, B., Zhang, H., Zhang, D.: Investigating the role and interplay of narrations and animations in data videos. Comput. Graph. Forum **41**, 527–539 (2022)

6. Firmansah, M.L.H.: Visualization and message design concepts of presenting statistical data through videos to improve understanding. Int. J. Multidisc. Sci. Arts **1**(1), 1–6 (2022)
7. Ge, T., Lee, B., Wang, Y.: CAST: authoring data-driven chart animations. In: Proceedings of the 2021 CHI Conference on Human Factors in Computing Systems, pp. 1–15 (2021)
8. Ge, T., Zhao, Y., Lee, B., Ren, D., Chen, B., Wang, Y.: Canis: a high-level language for data-driven chart animations. Comput. Graph. Forum **39**, 607–617 (2020)
9. Inoue, Y., Tsuruoka, K., Arikawa, M.: Spatio-temporal story mapping animation based on structured causal relationships of historical events. Int. Arch. Photogramm. Remote. Sens. Spat. Inf. Sci. **40**, 101–103 (2014)
10. McNutt, A.M.: No grammar to rule them all: A survey of JSON-style DSLs for visualization. IEEE Trans. Vis. Comput. Graph. **29**(1), 160–170 (2022)
11. Nowak, S., Bartram, L., Schiphorst, T.: A micro-phenomenological lens for evaluating narrative visualization. In: 2018 IEEE Evaluation and Beyond-Methodological Approaches for Visualization (BELIV), pp. 11–18. IEEE (2018)
12. Peng, H.: Quantifying narrative data in qualitative analysis: an abductive approach and interactive process. Acad. Manage. Proc. **2022**, 14953 (2022)
13. Perri, V., Scholtes, I.: HOTVis: higher-order time-aware visualisation of dynamic graphs. In: Auber, D., Valtr, P. (eds.) 28th International Symposium on Graph Drawing and Network Visualization, GD 2020, Vancouver, BC, Canada, 16–18 September 2020, Revised Selected Papers 28. pp. 99–114. Springer, Cham (2020). https://doi.org/10.1007/978-3-030-68766-3_8
14. Ren, M.: Advancements and applications of large language models in natural language processing: a comprehensive review. Appl. Comput. Eng. **97**, 55–63 (2024)
15. Rodríguez, M.T., Nunes, S., Devezas, T.: Telling stories with data visualization. In: Proceedings of the 2015 Workshop on Narrative & Hypertext, pp. 7–11 (2015)
16. Santos, C.Q., Silveira, M.S.: Design de visualizações narrativas interativas. Anais Estendidos do Simpósio Brasileiro sobre Fatores Humanos em Sistemas Computacionais, 2018, Brasil. (2018)
17. Segel, E., Heer, J.: Narrative visualization: telling stories with data. IEEE Trans. Vis. Comput. Graph. **16**(6), 1139–1148 (2010)
18. Shen, L., Li, H., Wang, Y., Luo, T., Luo, Y., Qu, H.: Data playwright: authoring data videos with annotated narration. IEEE Trans. Vis. Comput. Graph. (2024)
19. Shen, L., Li, H., Wang, Y., Qu, H.: Reflecting on design paradigms of animated data video tools. In: Proceedings of the 2025 CHI Conference on Human Factors in Computing Systems, pp. 1–21 (2025)
20. Shen, L., Zhang, Y., Zhang, H., Wang, Y.: Data player: automatic generation of data videos with narration-animation interplay. IEEE Trans. Vis. Comput. Graph. **30**(1), 109–119 (2023)
21. Shi, Y., Lan, X., Li, J., Li, Z., Cao, N.: Communicating with motion: a design space for animated visual narratives in data videos. In: Proceedings of the 2021 CHI Conference on Human Factors in Computing Systems, pp. 1–13 (2021)
22. Silva, C., Mota, M., Silva, T.: Automated production of audiovisual informative content. In: 2018 13th Iberian Conference on Information Systems and Technologies (CISTI), pp. 1–6. IEEE (2018)
23. Thompson, J., Liu, Z., Li, W., Stasko, J.: Understanding the design space and authoring paradigms for animated data graphics. Comput. Graph. Forum **39**, 207–218 (2020)

24. Tversky, B., Morrison, J.B., Betrancourt, M.: Animation: can it facilitate? Int. J. Hum Comput Stud. **57**(4), 247–262 (2002)
25. Zong, J., Pollock, J., Wootton, D., Satyanarayan, A.: Animated Vega-Lite: unifying animation with a grammar of interactive graphics. IEEE Trans. Vis. Comput. Graph. **29**(1), 149–159 (2022)

Perception and Intelligent Processing of Infrared Imagery

Tri-guided Hybrid Attention Network with Adaptive Top-K Channel and Body-Edge Spatial Modeling for Infrared Small Target Detection

Maoyong Li[1,2], Yingying Gao[1,2], Xuedong Guo[1,2], Lei Deng[1,2](✉), Mingli Dong[1,2], and Lianqing Zhu[1,2]

[1] Key Laboratory of the Ministry of Education for Optoelectronic Measurement Technology and Instrument, Beijing Information Science and Technology University, Beijing, China
dally211@163.com

[2] Beijing Laboratory of Optical Fiber Sensing and System, Beijing Information Science and Technology University, Beijing, China

Abstract. Infrared small target detection (IRSTD) plays a critical role in a wide range of applications, including precision strike, early warning systems, forest fire monitoring, and autonomous driving. However, it remains a challenging task due to low contrast, small target size, blurred boundaries, and complex background clutter. To address these issues, we propose a novel Tri-guided Hybrid Attention Network (TriHANet) that jointly exploits multi-scale structure awareness, adaptive channel selection, and spatial consistency modeling for robust and accurate detection. Specifically, we design a Tri-guided Hybrid Attention Module (TirHA) that integrates a Multi-Scale Perception Module (MSPM), an Adaptive Top-K Channel Self-Attention (ATCSA), and a Body-Edge Spatial Attention (BESA) mechanism. This module enables the network to extract structural features at multiple scales, dynamically suppress redundant channels, and enhance spatial responses along both the target body and contour. Furthermore, we introduce a Dynamic Alignment Feature Fusion (DAFF) module in the decoding stage to align multi-scale semantics and reinforce boundary consistency through hierarchical guidance. Extensive experiments on two benchmark datasets, SIRST and IRSTD-1K, demonstrate that our TriHANet significantly outperforms state-of-the-art methods in both quantitative metrics and qualitative visual performance. The results validate the effectiveness and generalization capability of the proposed approach in complex infrared imaging scenarios.

Keywords: IRSTD · Hybrid Attention Mechanism · Multi-Scale Structural Modeling

© The Author(s), under exclusive license to Springer Nature Singapore Pte Ltd. 2026
J. Kittler et al. (Eds.): PRCV 2025, LNCS 16289, pp. 381–394, 2026.
https://doi.org/10.1007/978-981-95-5764-6_26

1 Introduction

Infrared small target detection (IRSTD) aims to accurately identify tiny targets in infrared images under complex backgrounds [4]. Leveraging infrared systems with long-range detection, strong concealment, and robust anti-interference capabilities, this technology is widely used in precision guidance, forest fire monitoring, autonomous driving, and air defense [5]. However, due to long imaging distances and low resolution, small targets often appear with weak signals, minimal texture, and blurred contours, making them easily overwhelmed by background clutter [6]. Accurate detection is therefore crucial for these applications.

However, IRSTD faces two key challenges in practical applications [3]. First, the low contrast between targets and background poses a major difficulty. Infrared targets typically lack distinct textures and differ only slightly in brightness from their surroundings, making them difficult to distinguish using traditional feature extraction methods. This often results in the targets being overwhelmed by background interference, especially in complex scenes. Second, the inherent saliency of infrared small targets is weak—they are small, variably shaped, blurry-edged, and irregular, which leads to unstable and inconsistent feature representations.

Currently, two primary approaches are used to detect such targets: model-driven and data-driven methods. Model-driven approaches, based on different detection principles, are typically categorized into filter-based [7], local information-based [9], and global detection-based methods [24]. However, they often depend on prior knowledge and manual feature design, limiting their generalizability in complex or unknown scenarios. In contrast, data-driven methods based on convolutional neural networks (CNNs) automatically learn robust target features and have shown promising performance in recent years. These data-driven methods fall into two main categories: detection-based frameworks (e.g., SSD-ST [18], YOLOSR-IST [19]), which predict target positions through regression; and segmentation-based strategies (e.g., ACM [13], DNANet [20]), which achieve finer localization through pixel-level modeling.

Despite recent advances in IRSTD, performance is still constrained by fundamental limitations in feature modeling. Existing methods are constrained by two primary modeling limitations. First, channel attention mechanisms, such as SE-Net [1] and SKNet [2], rely on global pooling to generate channel descriptors. This coarse aggregation often suppresses vital target-related channels while preserving background noise, failing to adaptively select features in low-contrast conditions. Second, spatial modeling is often superficial; approaches that focus on edge enhancement [17] neglect the target's internal contextual consistency, which increases false positives from edge-like clutter and undermines detection integrity. These shortcomings highlight the need for a unified framework that cohesively integrates multi-dimensional cues to achieve fine-grained and robust target detection in complex environments.

To address these challenges, we propose a novel framework, the Tri-guided Hybrid Attention Network with Adaptive Top-K Channel and Body-Edge Spatial Modeling (TriHANet), which tackles both issues while achieving state-of-the-art performance. To overcome the limitations in channel and spatial dimension modeling, we design a Tri-guided Hybrid Attention Module (TriHA). This module integrates multi-scale structural guidance, adaptive Top-K channel selection, and a spatial modeling strategy combining target body and edge information, effectively enhancing the model's sensitivity and discriminative capability for target regions. Additionally, during feature decoding, the progressive transfer of high-level semantic features to shallow layers can lead to semantic gap, manifesting as incomplete foreground structures or blurred boundaries. To address this challenge, we introduce the Dynamic Alignment Feature Fusion Module (DAFF), which achieves semantic alignment and detail complementarity between features at different layers, thereby improving the model's ability to distinguish true targets from false alarms in complex backgrounds and enhancing overall scene understanding. In summary, the main contributions of this paper are as follows:

- We propose a novel hybrid attention network, TriHANet, for IRSTD, which unifies the modeling of channel-spatial and global-local information flows.
- We design TirHA, which integrates multi-scale structural information, adaptive Top-K channel self-attention mechanism, and body-edge spatial modeling strategy, enhancing the response capability to small target regions from both channel selectivity and spatial structure perception.
- We develop DAFF to mitigate the progressive gap of high-level semantic information during decoding. By achieving semantic alignment and detail complementarity across different feature levels, DAFF effectively enhances the integrity of foreground regions and the continuity of target boundaries.

2 Proposed Method

2.1 Overall Architecture

As depicted in Fig. 1, TriHANet employs an encoder-decoder architecture, comprising three primary components: the Encoder, TirHA, and DAFF. The encoder, built upon the ResNet architecture, consists of five stages designed to progressively extract multi-level semantic feature representations from input infrared images. To optimize computational efficiency for subsequent modules, a convolutional layer is incorporated after each encoding stage to standardize the channel dimensions of the output features. To enhance the network's sensitivity to small targets during cross-layer feature interactions, the TirHA module is integrated into the skip-connection pathways between stages. The TirHA module sequentially leverages three components—Multi-Scale Structural Perception Module (MSPM), Adaptive Top-K Channel Self-Attention (ATCSA), and Body-Edge Spatial Attention (BESA)—to guide the network toward focusing on highly discriminative regions, enabling precise modeling of critical target areas while effectively suppressing redundant background interference. In the decoder, three DAFF modules are introduced to progressively restore spatial resolution and generate refined target response maps. Finally, the fused decoder features are fed into the detection head to produce the ultimate prediction results.

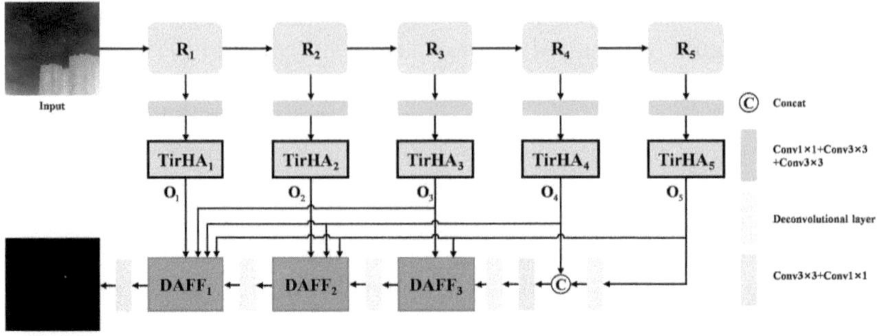

Fig. 1. Overall architecture of the proposed method.

2.2 Tri-guided Hybrid Attention Module

To address the challenges of response weakening and insufficient target-background separation in feature modeling for infrared small targets, we propose the TirHA, as illustrated in Fig. 2. This module is designed to enhance discriminative target regions in feature representations and suppress redundant background interference by focusing on structural perception, multidimensional selectivity, and target region modeling. TirHA comprises three components: MSPM, ATCSA, and BESA. These components collaboratively model critical responses and target structures across channel and spatial dimensions.

Multi-Scale Perception Module (MSPM). To address the challenges of varying target sizes and blurred edges in IRSTD, traditional single-scale convolutional operations often struggle to adapt to the spatial scale variations of targets, resulting in inadequate modeling of target structural information. To overcome this, we propose the MSPM as the front-end component of TriHA, designed to enhance the structural expressiveness of feature maps.

The overall architecture of MSPM, as depicted in the top-left corner of Fig. 2, consists of four parallel convolutional branches. The first branch employs a single 1×1 convolution to preserve the original information of the input features. The remaining branches ($j = 2, 3, 4$) each incorporate a Multi-Scale Feature Extraction Block (MFEB_i, $i = 1, 2, 3$). Each MFEB is composed of a 1×1 convolution, a $1 \times (2i - 1)$ convolution, a $(2i - 1) \times 1$ convolution, and a 3×3 dilated convolution with a dilation rate of $2i - 1$. By combining convolutional kernels of varying shapes within a single branch, MSPM effectively captures features of target regions with diverse shapes.

Furthermore, to enhance feature discriminability and expressiveness, we introduce a top-down information propagation mechanism. Specifically, the output of the j-th branch ($j = 1, 2, 3$) is fed into the $(j + 1)$-th branch to achieve progressive information transfer and enhancement. This design not only enriches cross-scale semantic representations but also encourages each branch to learn

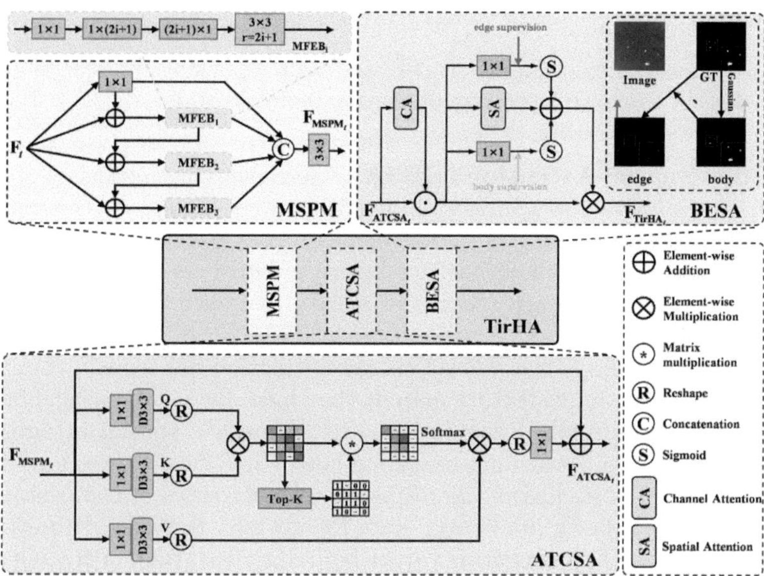

Fig. 2. Illustration of the TirHA. TirHA comprises three components: MSPM, ATCSA, and BESA.

complementary features through cascaded residual connections, thereby reducing feature redundancy and improving the overall efficiency and effectiveness of feature modeling. The formulation is presented as follows:

$$\mathrm{F}_{\mathrm{MSPM}_t} = \mathrm{Conv}_{3\times 3}\left(\mathrm{Concat}\left(s_1, s_2, s_3, s_4\right)\right). \tag{1}$$

Adaptive Top-K Channel Self-Attention (ATCSA). Traditional channel attention mechanisms (e.g., SE, SK) typically rely on linear compression strategies, such as global average pooling, to perform channel-wise statistics on feature maps. However, in scenarios with low signal-to-noise ratios and high intermixing of target features with background interference, these mechanisms struggle to effectively distinguish critical target channels from redundant background channels, often activating irrelevant regions and suppressing the response to weak targets. To address this, we propose the ATCSA, which introduces self-attention modeling in the channel dimension to explicitly enhance the most target-sensitive channels. Unlike traditional attention methods that depend on dense softmax operations, we propose a sparsification strategy that first applies Top-K selection to attention scores, retaining only the K most responsive channels. This approach increases the sparsity and discriminability of the attention distribution.

$$\mathrm{Attention}(\mathrm{Q},\mathrm{K},\mathrm{V}) = \mathrm{Softmax}(\tau_{\mathrm{k}}(\frac{\mathrm{QK}^{\mathrm{T}}}{\alpha}))\mathrm{V}, \tag{2}$$

$$\mathrm{F}_{\mathrm{ATCSA}_t} = \mathrm{W}_{1\times1}\mathrm{Attention}(\mathrm{Q},\mathrm{K},\mathrm{V}) + \mathrm{F}_{\mathrm{MSPM}_t}. \quad (3)$$

where $\mathcal{T}_{\mathbf{k}}$ denotes the learnable Top-K selection operator, and α is a scaling parameter used to control the size of matrix multiplication.

Body-Edge Spatial Attention (BESA). Given the characteristics of infrared small targets, such as low contrast, blurred boundaries, and diverse morphologies, precise spatial modeling of target regions is particularly critical. To address this, we propose BESA, which utilizes both the body region and edge contour of targets as complementary structural cues to enhance the expressiveness of spatial features.

The BESA module first applies a channel attention mechanism (CA) to preliminarily weight the input feature map. It then introduces two parallel branches, the Body Branch and the Edge Branch, to generate a spatial attention map under the supervision of learning-based guidance. Specifically, the Body Branch, guided by a Body Loss, learns the response characteristics of the overall target region, producing a body prediction map. Meanwhile, the Edge Branch, driven by Edge Loss, focuses on capturing target boundary features, generating an edge prediction map. To provide accurate supervision signals, we first apply Gaussian filtering to the original target ground-truth map to generate a body ground-truth map. The original ground-truth map is then subtracted from the body ground-truth map to obtain an edge ground-truth map for edge learning.

After obtaining the prediction maps from the Body Branch and Edge Branch, both are normalized using the Sigmoid function to generate a body weight map and an edge weight map, respectively. These are then integrated through element-wise summation to form an enhanced spatial attention map, which simultaneously encodes the consistency of the target's internal region and the continuity of its boundary structure. Finally, this enhanced attention map is element-wise multiplied with the channel-weighted feature map to achieve structural enhancement of spatial features.

$$f_t^{\mathrm{ca}} = CA(\mathbb{F}_{\mathtt{MSPM}_t}) \odot \mathbb{F}_{\mathtt{MSPM}_t}, \quad (4)$$

$$a_t^{\mathrm{pred}} = \mathrm{Sigmoid}(Com_{1\times1}(f_t^{\mathrm{ca}})) \oplus \mathrm{Sigmoid}(Com_{1\times1}(f_t^{\mathrm{ca}})) \oplus SA(f_t^{\mathrm{ca}}), \quad (5)$$

$$f_t^{\mathrm{eifa}} = a_t^{\mathrm{pred}} \otimes f_t^{\mathrm{ca}}. \quad (6)$$

where $\odot$ denotes channel-wise multiplication, $\oplus$ denotes element-wise summation, and $\otimes$ denotes element-wise multiplication. CA($\cdot$) and SA($\cdot$) represent the channel and spatial attention mechanisms, respectively.

2.3 Dynamic Alignment Feature Fusion Module

In IRSTD tasks, cross-layer feature fusion is crucial for achieving collaborative modeling of detail perception and semantic understanding. However, traditional feature fusion methods, such as static concatenation or simple weighting, struggle to accommodate the disparities in semantic expression and spatial distribution among features from different layers, often resulting in compromised target structures or excessive diffusion of foreground information. To address these issues, we propose DAFF, as illustrated in Fig. 3. DAFF employs a dual-channel attention mechanism guided by global perception to adaptively adjust the fusion strategy for features from different sources, thereby achieving unified modeling of structural alignment and semantic consistency.

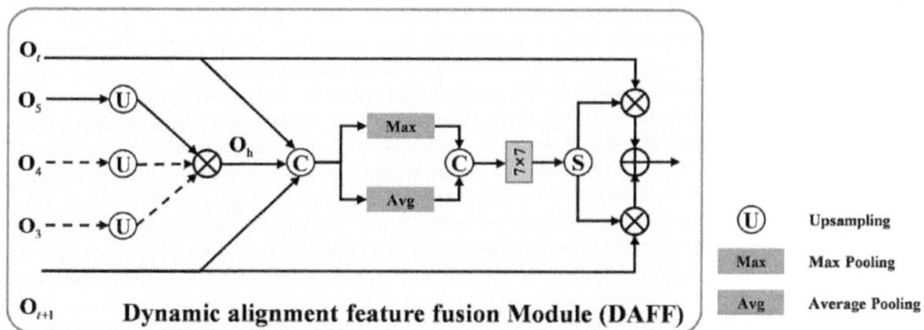

Fig. 3. Illustration of the DAFF.

The DAFF module leverages multi-scale semantic information to construct a spatial attention map through global statistical modeling, enabling adaptive enhancement of the current stage's features. Specifically, high-level semantic features (O_3, O_4, O_5) are first upsampled to match the spatial resolution of the current feature and fused via pixel-wise multiplication to generate a guidance feature map O_h. Subsequently, O_h is concatenated along the channel dimension with the current layer feature O_t and the adjacent lower-layer feature O_{t+1}, forming a multi-source fused feature. To extract discriminative spatial response information from the fused feature, DAFF applies both global average pooling and max pooling operations, followed by a 7×7 convolution to generate a dual-channel spatial attention map. Next, these aggregated features are transformed into N spatial attention maps using convolution. After Sigmoid activation, these attention maps are applied to O_t and O_{t+1}, enabling explicit modeling and dynamic weighted fusion of these local structural information components.

$$\widehat{\mathbf{SA}} = \text{Concat}\left(\text{Avg}\left(\text{Concat}(\mathbf{O}_t, \mathbf{O}_h, \mathbf{O}_{t+1})\right), \text{Max}\left(\text{Concat}(\mathbf{O}_t, \mathbf{O}_h, \mathbf{O}_{t+1})\right)\right), \tag{7}$$

$$\text{F}_{\text{DAFF}_t} = \mathbf{O}_t \odot \sigma(\mathbf{Conv}(\widehat{\mathbf{SA}})) + \mathbf{O}_{t+1} \odot (1 - \sigma(\mathbf{Conv}(\widehat{\mathbf{SA}}))). \tag{8}$$

where $\sigma(\cdot)$ denotes the sigmoid function, which produces the dynamic fusion weights.

3 Experiment

3.1 Datasets

To rigorously evaluate our method, we conducted experiments on two public benchmarks: SIRST [14] and IRSTD-1K [17]. SIRST, the inaugural benchmark in this field, provides 427 images of relatively simple sky and sea backgrounds with variable resolutions, while the more extensive IRSTD-1K dataset offers 1000 images representing more challenging and diverse scenarios (e.g., urban, mountains) at a fixed 512 × 512 resolution with precise pixel-level annotations. Adhering to their respective standard protocols for fair comparison, we partition SIRST with a 1:1 training-to-testing split and IRSTD-1K with an 8:2.

3.2 Evaluation Metrics

We adopt several widely used evaluation metrics, including Intersection over Union (IoU), Normalized IoU (nIoU), Probability of Detection (Pd), and False Alarm Rate (Fa). These metrics are formulated as follows:

$$IoU = \frac{TP}{T + P - TP}, nIoU = \frac{1}{N}\sum_{i=1}^{N} IoU_i, \tag{9}$$

$$PD = \frac{TP}{TP + FN}, FA = \frac{FP}{FP + TN}. \tag{10}$$

Where N represent the total number of samples, while T and P correspond to the total number of ground truth and predicted positive pixels, respectively. The quantities TP, FP, and FN indicate the numbers of true positives, false positives, and false negatives.

3.3 Experimental Settings

All model-driven methods were implemented in the MATLAB 2023 environment, while data-driven methods were trained and tested using the PyTorch framework. Experiments were conducted on a workstation equipped with an Intel i7-12700 CPU and an NVIDIA 4090D GPU.

For both the SIRST and IRSTD-1K datasets, all images and their corresponding labels were uniformly resized to a resolution of 512 × 512 pixels. To increase training diversity, random cropping to 480 × 480 pixels was further applied. During training, the Adam optimizer was employed with an initial learning rate of 0.001, a weight decay coefficient of 1×10^{-4}, and a batch size of 4. The total number of training epochs was set to 1500 for the SIRST dataset and 400 for the IRSTD-1K dataset. We employ a composite loss function that integrates Binary Cross-Entropy (BCE) loss [23], Soft-IoU loss [22], and F-measure (F-m) loss [21].

To validate the effectiveness of the proposed method, we compared it with 10 representative state-of-the-art algorithms, including five model-driven methods such as Top-Hat [7], LCM [8], MPCM [9], PSTNN [10], and TV-PCP [11], and five data-driven methods such as ACM [13], ALCNet [16], ISTDU-Net [15], DNANet [16], and SCTransNet [12].

3.4 Performance Comparison

Quantitative Results. Table 1 presents the performance comparison of 10 state-of-the-art methods on the SIRST and IRSTD-1K datasets across various evaluation metrics. The experimental results demonstrate that the proposed method achieves the best performance across all evaluation metrics on both datasets, showcasing a significant performance advantage.

Table 1. Performance Comparison of the Proposed Method and State-of-the-Art Approaches on SIRST and IRSTD-1K. The best results for each metric are marked in bold, while the second-best results are underlined.

Method	SIRST				IRSTD-1K				Params(M)	FLOPs (G)	FPS	
	Iou	nIou	Pd	Fa	Iou	nIou	Pd	Fa			CPU	GPU
Top-Hat [7]	24.45	5.624	38.82	349.9	7.743	11.28	43.48	1300	-	-	144	-
LCM [8]	0.630	2.599	85.75	8713	0.204	1.203	82.99	11450	-	-	3.8	-
MPCM [9]	0.147	5.015	48.20	1946	0.147	5.015	48.20	1946	-	-	35.73	-
PSTNN [10]	42.86	4.909	44.57	23.69	25.22	10.26	40.59	167.58	-	-	10.33	-
TV-PCP [11]	0.076	0.132	54.74	4225	0.080	0.163	45.31	3269	-	-	0.015	-
ACM [13]	68.66	69.42	90.49	30.80	60.97	57.71	91.58	61.78	0.398	0.402	-	99.16
ALCNet [14]	65.98	65.83	89.73	25.04	59.14	57.55	91.95	74.30	0.427	0.378	-	91.44
DNANet [16]	75.88	75.69	93.06	25.38	65.28	65.80	89.92	<u>12.96</u>	4.697	14.26	-	40.08
ISTDU-Net [15]	74.08	76.65	<u>95.39</u>	34.04	62.02	63.96	93.25	38.05	2.752	7.944	-	58.13
SCTransNet [12]	**78.82**	<u>77.48</u>	95.36	<u>15.33</u>	<u>70.35</u>	<u>68.22</u>	<u>93.35</u>	12.99	108.89	140.95	-	28.92
TriHANet	<u>78.77</u>	**78.86**	**96.35**	**14.53**	**71.42**	**68.43**	**94.56**	**12.22**	2.51	19.98	-	35.21

Overall, data-driven methods consistently outperform traditional model-driven methods. Across multiple evaluation metrics, data-driven methods exhibit stronger adaptability and stability. This disparity primarily stems from the fundamental differences between the two approaches: model-driven methods are typically handcrafted for specific scenes and target features, such as modeling target size, shape, or local contrast, and rely on predefined parameters. While such methods may perform well in simple backgrounds or scenarios with clear prior knowledge, they often fail in infrared images with complex backgrounds and diverse targets, particularly in controlling FA.

Notably, while improvements in Pd and Fa are evident, the increase in IoU is particularly significant. This performance advantage is primarily attributed to the proposed TirHA and DAFF. TirHA synergistically models features through multi-scale structural perception, explicit channel modeling, and spatial edge guidance, effectively enhancing the representation of low-contrast and blurred-boundary targets. Meanwhile, DAFF, guided by high-level semantic features, dynamically fuses information from different feature levels, strengthening the spatial response consistency of target regions. These designs fundamentally improve the model's ability to perceive target shapes and boundaries in complex scenes, leading to higher IoU and overall detection performance.

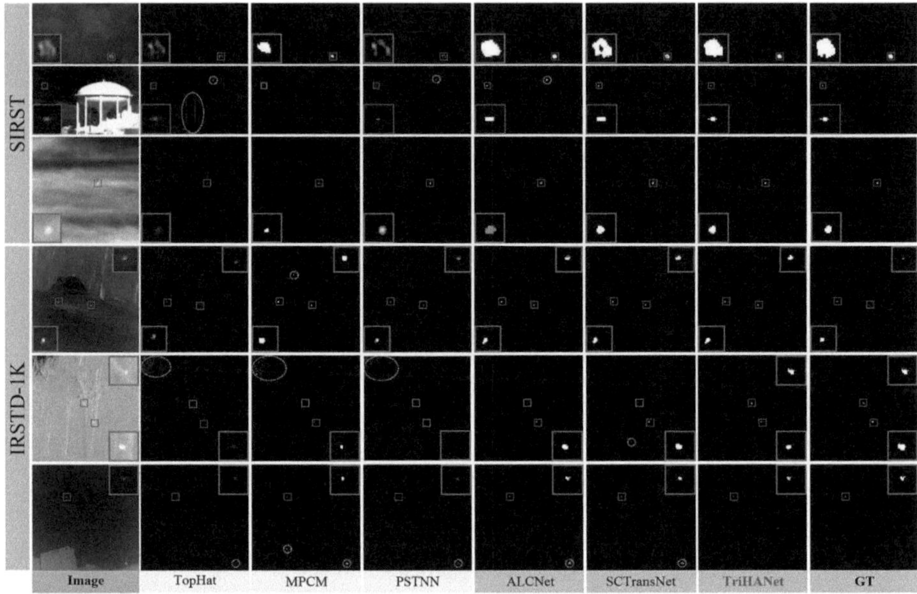

Fig. 4. Visualization results of various methods on representative samples from the SIRST and IRSTD-1K datasets. Correct detections are marked with red boxes, missed targets with blue boxes, and false alarms are highlighted by yellow ellipses.

Qualitative Results. As illustrated in Figs. 4 and 5, we select three representative and challenging samples from each of the SIRST and IRSTD-1K datasets for qualitative visual analysis. It can be clearly observed that TriHANet achieves significantly more accurate predictions of both the edge contours and internal structures of infrared small targets, not only reconstructing the shape and boundary of the targets more completely but also effectively suppressing false activations caused by background interference.

This performance benefits from the proposed TirHA. Specifically, MSPM extracts structural information at multiple scales, accommodating variations in target size and blurry boundaries. ATCSA further enhances channel-wise selectivity by dynamically suppressing redundant features and emphasizing target-relevant responses. BESA, through explicit supervision on the interior body and edge contour of the target, improves spatial focus, particularly contributing to consistent internal activation and coherent edge delineation.

In contrast, the Top-Hat method suffers from prominent missed detections and false alarms in multiple scenarios, revealing the limitations of traditional filtering-based approaches under noisy backgrounds and their lack of adaptability to complex semantic structures. Although MPCM enhances the brightness of small targets and improves PD to some extent, it fails to effectively differentiate between background and target context, resulting in a high rate of false positives. PSTNN, when exposed to low-contrast and high-brightness background clutter,

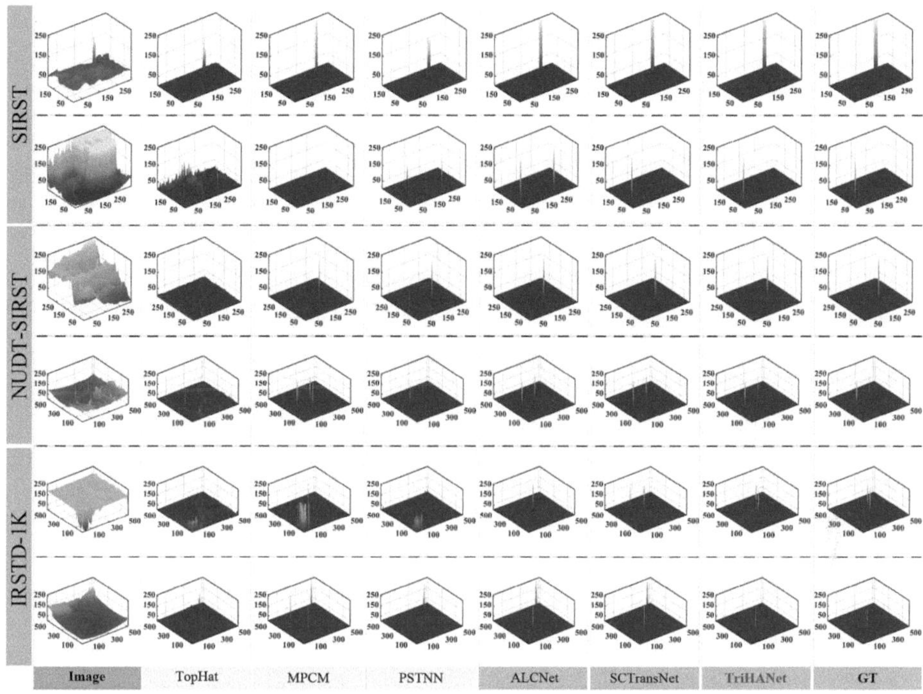

Fig. 5. 3-D visualization comparison of detection results via different methods.

also exhibits severe miss detection, indicating insufficient global modeling and poor recognition of target structure.

Compared to traditional model-driven approaches, data-driven methods demonstrate stronger adaptability and robustness in handling feature diversity. However, even among data-driven techniques, limitations remain under structurally complex scenarios. For instance, in the first-row scene, SCTransNet struggles with incomplete internal responses, lacking coherent shape reconstruction. In the fifth and sixth rows, ALCNet and SCTransNet both fail to avoid missed or false detections under cluttered backgrounds, highlighting insufficient spatial modeling of joint local-global semantics. In contrast, our decoder-integrated DAFF effectively leverages high-level semantic cues to guide shallow feature representations, enhancing the structural consistency and discriminative power within the target region.

3.5 Ablation Study

To further verify the effectiveness of the proposed modules, we conducted comprehensive ablation experiments on the IRSTD-1K dataset. Using UNet as the baseline, we progressively introduced MSPM, ATCSA, BESA, and DAFF. As shown in Table 2, the full version of our TriHANet consistently achieves the best performance across all evaluation metrics, highlighting the advantages of each component and their synergistic integration.

Table 2. Quantitative results. Ablation study on the d MSPM, ATCSA, BESA, and DAFF modules. the best results are bolded.

Model	IoU	nIoU	PD	FA
UNet	58.12	56.36	88.23	75.23
+MSPM	59.42	58.46	90.35	35.24
+ATCSA	64.42	61.39	91.36	25.71
+BESA	68.46	65.15	92.84	19.36
+DAFF	70.64	67.25	94.11	14.32
TriHANet	**71.42**	**68.43**	**94.56**	**12.22**

The addition of MSPM enables the network to capture richer structural representations of small targets, leading to improved shape awareness and enhanced localization, as reflected by noticeable gains in IoU and recall. With the integration of ATCSA, the model exhibits enhanced channel-wise discrimination, effectively boosting the response to target regions while suppressing irrelevant background activations. The inclusion of BESA strengthens spatial modeling by focusing simultaneously on the internal consistency and boundary continuity of target regions, thereby reducing false detections caused by ambiguous background structures. Finally, DAFF facilitates more accurate alignment and fusion of multi-scale features by leveraging high-level semantic guidance, which helps preserve fine boundary details and reinforce target integrity. Compared with the original UNet architecture, the complete TriHANet brings substantial improvements in PD and a remarkable reduction in FA, demonstrating the superiority and robustness of the proposed network design in addressing the challenging task of IRSTD.

4 Conclusion

In this paper, we propose TriHANet, a hybrid attention-based IRSTD framework that effectively tackles the challenges of low signal-to-noise ratio, scale variation, and structural ambiguity. By leveraging the TirHA module, our model achieves enhanced multi-scale feature perception, adaptive channel-wise attention, and fine-grained spatial modeling guided by body and edge priors. The inclusion of the DAFF module further improves multi-scale feature alignment and promotes consistent target representation during decoding. Extensive experiments demonstrate that each proposed component contributes significantly to the overall performance, and their integration leads to substantial gains over existing methods in terms of precision, recall, and IoU. The proposed framework offers a robust and scalable solution for real-world IRSTD tasks and provides a promising direction for future research in structure-aware attention modeling.

Acknowledgements. This work was supported by the project "Vision-guided Automatic Vehicle Refueling Hardware System Design" (No. 9162523202) and the Research Project of Beijing Municipal Natural Science Foundation (No. BJXZ2021-012-00046).

References

1. Hu, J., Shen, L., Sun, G.: Squeeze-and-excitation networks. In: Proceedings of the IEEE Conference on Computer Vision and Pattern Recognition, pp. 7132–7141 (2018)
2. Li, W., Wang, W., Hu, X., Yang, J.: Selective kernel networks. In: Proceedings of the IEEE/CVF Conference on Computer Vision and Pattern Recognition, pp. 510–519 (2019)
3. Yang, Z., Yu, H., Zhang, J., Tang, Q., Mian, A.: Deep learning based infrared small object segmentation: challenges and future directions. Inf. Fus. **118**, 103007 (2025)
4. Zhang, K., Ni, S., Yan, D., Zhang, A.: Review of dim small target detection algorithms in single-frame infrared images. In: 2021 IEEE 4th Advanced Information Management, Communicates Electronic and Automation Control Conference (IMCEC), vol. 4, pp. 2115–2120 (2021)
5. Zhao, M., Li, W., Li, L., Hu, J., Ma, P., Tao, R.: Single-frame infrared small-target detection: a survey. IEEE Geosci. Remote Sens. Mag. **10**(2), 87–119 (2022)
6. Kou, R., et al.: Infrared small target segmentation networks: a survey. Pattern Recogn. **143**, 109788 (2023)
7. Tom, V.T., Peli, T., Leung, M., Bondaryk, J.E.: Morphology-based algorithm for point target detection in infrared backgrounds. In: Signal and Data Processing of Small Targets 1993, vol. 1954, pp. 2–11. SPIE (1993)
8. Chen, C.L.P., Li, H., Wei, Y., Xia, T., Tang, Y.Y.: A local contrast method for small infrared target detection. IEEE Trans. Geosci. Remote Sens. **52**(1), 574–581 (2013)
9. Wei, Y., You, X., Li, H.: Multiscale patch-based contrast measure for small infrared target detection. Pattern Recogn. **58**, 216–226 (2016)
10. Zhang, L., Peng, Z.: Infrared small target detection based on partial sum of the tensor nuclear norm. Remote Sens. **11**(4), 382 (2019)
11. Wang, X., Peng, Z., Kong, D., Zhang, P., He, Y.: Infrared dim target detection based on total variation regularization and principal component pursuit. Image Vis. Comput. **63**, 1–9 (2017)
12. Yuan, S., Qin, H., Yan, X., Akhtar, N., Mian, A.: SCTransNet: spatial-channel cross transformer network for infrared small target detection. IEEE Trans. Geosci. Remote Sens. **62**, 1–15 (2024)
13. Dai, Y., Wu, Y., Zhou, F., Barnard, K.: Asymmetric contextual modulation for infrared small target detection. In: Proceedings of the IEEE/CVF Winter Conference on Applications of Computer Vision, pp. 950–959 (2021)
14. Dai, Y., Wu, Y., Zhou, F., Barnard, K.: Attentional local contrast networks for infrared small target detection. IEEE Trans. Geosci. Remote Sens. **59**(11), 9813–9824 (2021)
15. Hou, Q., Zhang, L., Tan, F., Xi, Y., Zheng, H.: ISTDU-Net: infrared small-target detection U-Net. IEEE Geosci. Remote Sens. Lett. **19**, 1–5 (2022)
16. Li, B., et al.: Dense nested attention network for infrared small target detection. IEEE Trans. Image Process. **32**, 1745–1758 (2022)

17. Zhang, M., Zhang, R., Yang, Y., Bai, H., Zhang, J., Guo, J.: ISNet: shape matters for infrared small target detection. In: Proceedings of the IEEE/CVF Conference on Computer Vision and Pattern Recognition, pp. 877–886 (2022)
18. Ding, L., Xu, X., Cao, Y., Zhai, G., Yang, F., Qian, L.: Detection and tracking of infrared small target by jointly using SSD and pipeline filter. Digit. Sig. Proc. **110**, 102949 (2021)
19. Li, R., Shen, Y.: YOLOSR-IST: a deep learning method for small target detection in infrared remote sensing images based on super-resolution and YOLO. Sig. Process. **208**, 108962 (2023)
20. Fu, J., et al. : Dual attention network for scene segmentation. In: Proceedings of the IEEE/CVF Conference on Computer Vision and Pattern Recognition, pp. 3146–3154 (2019)
21. Zhao, K., Gao, S., Wang, W., Cheng, M.-M.: Optimizing the F-measure for threshold-free salient object detection. In: Proceedings of the IEEE/CVF International Conference on Computer Vision, pp. 8849–8857 (2019)
22. Rahman, M.A., Wang, Y.: Optimizing intersection-over-union in deep neural networks for image segmentation. In: Bebis, G., et al. (eds.) ISVC 2016. LNCS, vol. 10072, pp. 234–244. Springer, Cham (2016). https://doi.org/10.1007/978-3-319-50835-1_22
23. Qin, X., Zhang, Z., Huang, C., Gao, C., Dehghan, M., Jagersand, M.: BASNet: boundary-aware salient object detection. In: Proceedings of the IEEE/CVF Conference on Computer Vision and Pattern Recognition, pp. 7479–7489 (2019)
24. Dai, Y., Wu, Y.: Reweighted infrared patch-tensor model with both nonlocal and local priors for single-frame small target detection. IEEE J. Sel. Top. Appl. Earth Obs. Remote Sens. **10**(8), 3752–3767 (2017)

GDTFusion: Gated Dual-Branch Attention Transformer Network for Infrared and Visible Image Fusion

Xuedong Guo[1,2], Maoyong Li[1,2], Yingying Gao[1,2], Lei Deng[1,2](✉), Mingli Dong[1,2], and Lianqing Zhu[1,2]

[1] Key Laboratory of the Ministry of Education for Optoelectronic Measurement Technology and Instrument, Beijing Information Science and Technology University, Beijing 100192, China
dally211@163.com

[2] Beijing Laboratory of Optical Fiber Sensing and System, Beijing Information Science and Technology University, Beijing 100192, China

Abstract. Infrared and visible image fusion aims to generate a composite image that simultaneously contains thermal radiation information from infrared images and fine texture details from visible images, thereby enabling high-resolution scene perception, target segmentation, and accurate detection under adverse weather and other complex environmental conditions. However, existing fusion methods generally struggle to simultaneously model local self-similarity and long-range dependencies within images, resulting in insufficient complementarity of features across multiple layers or modules, low information transmission efficiency, and ultimately, limited detail representation and suboptimal fusion performance. To address this issue, this paper proposes a novel infrared and visible image fusion algorithm, named GDTFusion, which integrates CNN with a Transformer architecture. The method is designed to fully exploit and fuse local structural features and global semantic information from the source images, enabling efficient cross-modal information interaction. First, an Interactive Gated Hybrid Attention (IGHA) module based on CNN is designed to extract high-quality visual features, effectively enhancing the texture representation, contrast, and color perception of the fused image. Second, a Transformer-based Multi-Scale Interactive Attention (TMSIA) module is designed to capture local details at different scales and long-range global dependencies, and then fuse them effectively, thereby enhancing the representation capability and integration efficiency of cross-modal features. Extensive comparative experiments were conducted on two public datasets, FMB and MFNet, and the results demonstrate that the proposed GDTFusion method is both effective and superior compared to several state-of-the-art infrared and visible image fusion approaches.

Supported by the project "Vision-guided Automatic Vehicle Refueling Hardware System Design" (No. 9162523202) and the Research Project of Beijing Municipal Natural Science Foundation (No. BJXZ2021-012-00046).

© The Author(s), under exclusive license to Springer Nature Singapore Pte Ltd. 2026
J. Kittler et al. (Eds.): PRCV 2025, LNCS 16289, pp. 395–409, 2026.
https://doi.org/10.1007/978-981-95-5764-6_27

Keywords: Image fusion · Interactive Gated Hybrid Attention · Multi-Scale Interactive · Transformer

1 Introduction

Different types of sensors capture information through their respective imaging modalities, enabling multi-level perception of the scene. Visible images exhibit significant advantages in texture representation, but their performance is easily affected by illumination conditions, weather, and occlusions. In contrast, infrared images provide stable thermal radiation information under complex lighting environments, yet suffer from limited texture detail. By leveraging the complementary characteristics of infrared and visible images through image fusion, more informative and higher-quality representations can be achieved, which effectively support a variety of downstream tasks such as object detection [1], semantic segmentation [2], scene understanding [3], and visual tracking [4].

With the advancement of research, a variety of infrared and visible image fusion methods have been proposed, which can be broadly categorized into traditional algorithm-based approaches and deep learning-based models. Traditional image fusion techniques encompass a variety of strategies, including transform domain-based methods [5], sparse representation-based methods [6], subspace-based methods [7], hybrid approaches [8], and other conventional methods [9]. However, traditional fusion methods often rely on manually designed activity-level measures and fusion rules, which introduce considerable subjectivity and significantly affect the final results. Moreover, because these algorithms extract information from the source images through predefined transforms, they tend to introduce redundant components, leading to sub-optimal and inefficient fusion results.

In recent years, the rapid advancement of deep learning techniques has led researchers to develop a variety of CNN-based image fusion methods. Currently, widely adopted deep image fusion techniques can be broadly categorized into four types: autoencoder (AE)-based methods [10], convolutional neural network (CNN)-based methods [11], Transformer-based methods [12], and generative adversarial network (GAN)-based methods [13]. However, AE-based fusion methods still rely on manually designed fusion strategies when integrating deep features, which limits their end-to-end learning capability [11]. GAN-based models face challenges during optimization, often resulting in fused images that are blurry and lack certain important features [14]. CNN-based methods are limited by their receptive field, making it difficult to capture global features; whereas Transformer-based methods lack convolutional inductive biases, which also hampers their ability to achieve optimal fusion results. In infrared and visible image fusion, the network is required to possess the capability to extract local features while simultaneously modeling global information [15]. Although Tang et al. [16] attempted to integrate CNN and Transformer architectures to capture both local and global features, the feature extraction processes remained independent of each other.

To address the above challenges, we propose a novel infrared and visible image fusion method, termed GDTFusion, which integrates CNN and Transformer architectures to jointly model local structures and global semantic features. This design enables deep and collaborative integration of cross-modal features. First, we design a Transformer-based Multi-Scale Interactive Attention (TMSIA) module that merges multi-scale convolutions with Transformer mechanisms within a single block, jointly modeling local structures at different scales and global contextual information to boost the representational power and integration efficiency of cross-modal features. Second, we design a CNN-based Interactive Gated Hybrid Attention (IGHA) module to extract critical visual features, thereby enhancing the fused image in terms of texture details, contrast, and color perception.

In summary, the main contributions of this paper are as follows:

1. We propose GDTFusion for infrared and visible image fusion, which integrates the local feature extraction capabilities of CNNs with the global dependency modeling strength of Transformers, enabling more effective feature complementarity and improved fusion performance.
2. We design a Transformer-based Multi-Scale Interactive Attention (TMSIA) module that effectively enhances the representation quality and fusion capability of cross-modal features by integrating local information at multiple scales with long-range global dependencies.
3. We design an Interactive Gated Hybrid Attention (IGHA) module that significantly enhances the fused image's ability to preserve texture details, improve visual contrast, and maintain accurate color perception.

2 Related Works

Over the past few decades, numerous image fusion algorithms have been proposed to meet the demands of effective image representation. These algorithms include transform domain-based methods [17], sparse representation-based methods [18], subspace-based methods [19], hybrid methods [20], and other conventional methods [21]. Chen et al. [22] proposed a target-enhanced multi-scale transform-based image fusion method, which effectively improves the fusion quality of infrared and visible images. Li et al. [23] proposed an image decomposition method based on multi-level Laplacian low-rank representation, which effectively enhances the structural and detail preservation in infrared and visible image fusion. Mitianoudis et al. [7] proposed pixel-level and region-level image fusion methods based on Independent Component Analysis (ICA) and Topographic Independent Component Analysis (TICA). Zhou et al. [24] proposed a fusion strategy based on visual saliency and hybrid features, which enhances detail preservation and target representation in infrared and visible image fusion. Ma et al. [21] proposed a fusion method that combines saliency detection with convolutional features to enhance salient targets and texture details in infrared and visible image fusion.

With the success of deep learning in image processing and computer vision, deep learning-based infrared and visible image fusion methods have seen rapid advancement. These methods can be broadly categorized into four types: autoencoder (AE)-based approaches [25], convolutional neural network (CNN)-based approaches [26], Transformer-based methods [27], and generative adversarial network (GAN)-based methods [28]. Li et al. [29] proposed a CNN-based image fusion method that effectively extracts and integrates feature information from infrared and visible images. Xu et al. [30] proposed an image fusion method based on the Transformer architecture, which enhances long-range dependency modeling and feature complementarity between infrared and visible images. Zhang et al. [31] proposed a generative adversarial network (GAN)-based image fusion method that improves structural preservation and target saliency in infrared and visible images.

3 Method

Overall Architecture. The overall architecture of the proposed GDTFusion model is illustrated in Fig. 1. It mainly consists of four blocks and a fusion head. Each block comprises an encoder, an IGHA module, and a TMSIA module. The encoder adopts the configuration from the SegFormer encoder [32]. The IGHA module suppresses background noise while significantly enhancing the fused image's representation in terms of texture details, visual contrast, and color perception, thereby improving the overall fusion performance of visible and infrared images. The TMSIA module enhances the model's ability to capture and interpret multi-scale image features by integrating local information at different scales with long-range global dependencies. This leads to more precise and comprehensive feature representations, further improving the quality of image fusion. Specifically, the input visible and infrared images are first passed through the encoder to extract essential features. These features are then refined by the IGHA module, which enhances texture details, contrast, and color perception. Subsequently, the TMSIA module integrates local information and global dependencies to generate enriched feature representations, which are fed into the next block. This process is repeated across four identical blocks. Additionally, the output of the TMSIA module in each block is forwarded to the Fusion Head. Finally, after processing through the Fusion Head, the model produces the fused output image that combines information from both the visible and infrared inputs.

Interactive Gated Hybrid Attention (IGHA) Module. In each block of the GDTFusion model, we embed an IGHA module, whose architecture is illustrated in Fig. 2. The IGHA module not only effectively suppresses background noise but also significantly enhances the representation of multimodal images in terms of texture details, visual contrast, and color perception. This facilitates more effective extraction of target information by the network and improves the discriminability and visual quality of the fused image.

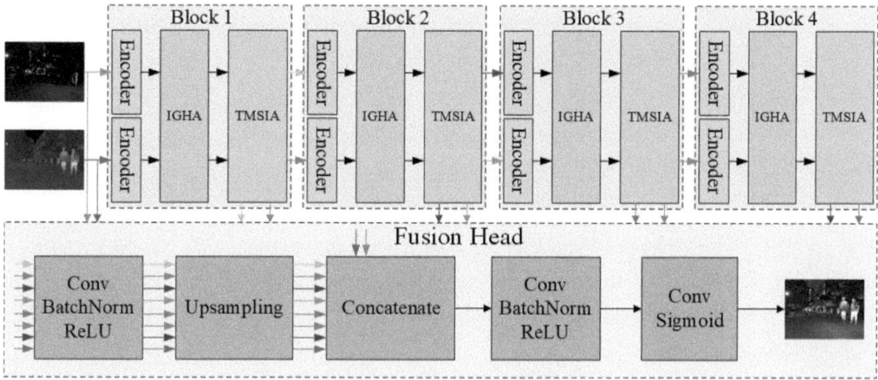

Fig. 1. Overall architecture of the proposed GDTFusion model. GDTFusion consists of four sequential blocks and one fusion head. Each block comprises an encoder, an Interactive Gated Hybrid Attention (IGHA) module, and a Transformer-based Multi-Scale Interactive Attention (TMSIA) module.

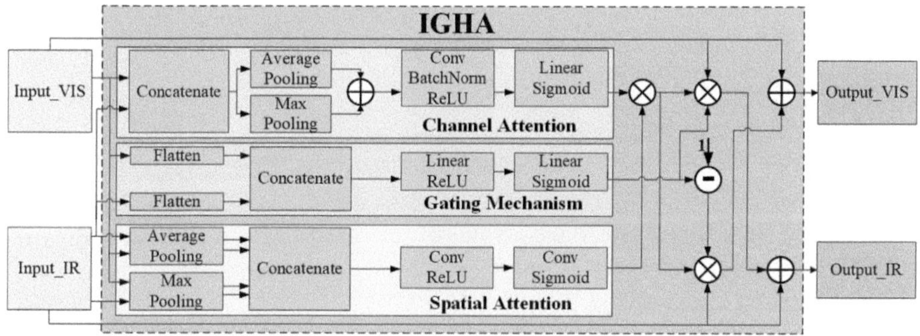

Fig. 2. Network architecture of the IGHA module. The IGHA module consists of three components: Channel Attention, Spatial Attention, and a Gating Mechanism.

As shown in Fig. 2, the IGHA module is mainly composed of three submodules: Channel Attention, Spatial Attention, and a Gating Mechanism. This module takes the visible features $Input\_VIS$ and infrared features $Input\_IR$ as inputs, aiming to emphasize informative cues from multi-source data while suppressing redundancy and background noise, thereby enhancing texture representation and perceptual quality in the fused image.

In the Channel Attention submodule, the visible features $Input\_VIS$ and infrared features $Input\_IR$ are first concatenated to obtain CA_{cat}. Then, CA_{cat} is passed through Average Pooling and Max Pooling operations separately to obtain CA_{AP} and CA_{MP}, respectively. These two outputs are subsequently added to produce CA_{add}. Next, CA_{add} is sequentially processed by a convolutional layer (Conv), batch normalization (BatchNorm), and a ReLU activation to produce CA_1. Finally, CA_1 is passed through a linear layer followed by a Sigmoid activation to obtain the channel attention output CA_{output}. The computation processes of CA_{add} and CA_{output} are as follows:

$$CA_{add} = AvgPool(CA_{cat}) + MaxPool(CA_{cat}) \tag{1}$$

$$CA_{output} = Sigmoid(Linear(ReLU(BN(Conv(CA_{add}))))) \tag{2}$$

where $Conv(\cdot)$ denotes a standard convolution operation, $BN(\cdot)$ denotes batch normalization, $ReLU(\cdot)$ denotes the rectified linear unit activation, $AvgPool(\cdot)$ denotes to AdaptiveAvgPool2d, and $MaxPool(\cdot)$ denotes to AdaptiveMaxPool2d.

In the Spatial Attention submodule, the visible features $Input\_VIS$ are first processed by Average Pooling and Max Pooling to obtain SA_{AP}^{VIS} and SA_{MP}^{VIS}, respectively. Similarly, the infrared features $Input\_IR$ are passed through Average Pooling and Max Pooling to produce SA_{AP}^{IR} and SA_{MP}^{IR}. These four feature maps are then concatenated to form SA_{cat}. Subsequently, SA_{cat} is sequentially passed through a convolutional layer and a ReLU activation to obtain SA_1. Then, SA_1 is further processed by another convolutional layer followed by a Sigmoid activation to produce the spatial attention output SA_{output}. The computation processes of SA_{output} is as follows:

$$SA_{output} = Sigmoid(Conv(ReLU(Conv(SA_{cat})))) \tag{3}$$

where $Conv(\cdot)$ denotes a standard convolution operation, $ReLU(\cdot)$ denotes the rectified linear unit activation.

In the Gating Mechanism, the visible features $Input\_VIS$ and infrared features $Input\_IR$ are first flattened to obtain GM_{fla}^{VIS} and GM_{fla}^{IR}, respectively. These flattened features are then concatenated to form GM_{cat}. Next, GM_{cat} is sequentially passed through a linear layer and a ReLU activation to obtain GM_1. Finally, GM_1 is processed by another linear layer followed by a Sigmoid activation to generate the gating factor GM_{output}. The computation processes of GM_{output} is as follows:

$$GM_{output} = Sigmoid(Linear(ReLU(Linear(GM_{cat})))) \tag{4}$$

where $ReLU(\cdot)$ denotes the rectified linear unit activation.

Finally, CA_{output} and SA_{output} are element-wise multiplied to obtain $CASA_{att}$. Then, $CASA_{att}[0]$, GM_{output}, and $Input\_VIS$ are multiplied together to generate IR_{att}, while $CASA_{att}[1]$, 1-GM_{output} and $Input\_IR$ are multiplied to obtain VIS_{att}. Finally, $Input\_VIS$ is added to VIS_{att} to produce $Output\_VIS$, and $Input\_IR$ is added to IR_{att} to produce $Output\_IR$. The detailed computation process is as follows:

$$IR_{att} = CASA_{att}[0] \times GM_{output} \times Input\_VIS \tag{5}$$

$$VIS_{att} = CASA_{att}[1] \times (1 - GM_{output}) \times Input\_IR \tag{6}$$

$$Output\_VIS = Input\_VIS + VIS_{att} \tag{7}$$

$$Output\_IR = Input\_IR + IR_{att} \tag{8}$$

The weighting coefficients extracted by the three attention mechanisms jointly contribute to feature reweighting and information selection, providing more discriminative and robust representations for subsequent feature fusion. This module effectively enhances the network's focus on texture details, salient targets, and edge regions, while reducing information conflicts between different modalities.

Transformer-Based Multi-Scale Interactive Attention (TMSIA) Module. In each block of the GDTFusion model, the features output by the IGHA module are fed into the TMSIA module, whose architecture is illustrated in Fig. 3. The TMSIA module integrates multi-scale convolution with Transformer mechanisms in a unified manner, effectively fusing local structures at different scales with global contextual information. This significantly enhances the representational capacity and integration efficiency of cross-modal features, thereby improving the fusion performance of visible and infrared images.

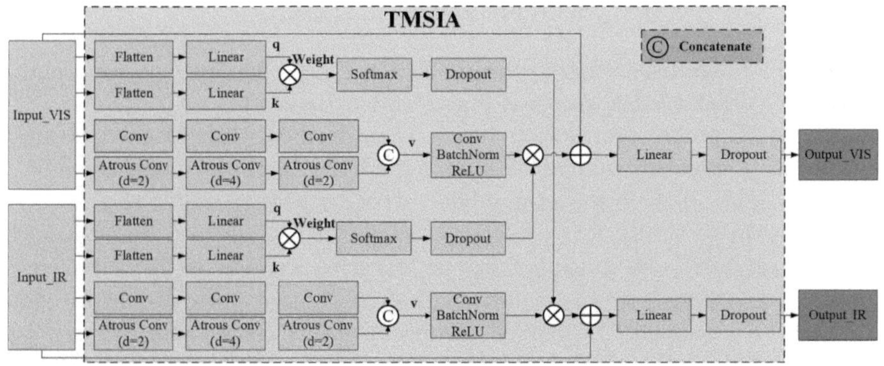

Fig. 3. Network architecture of the TMSIA module.

As shown in Fig. 3, the TMSIA module takes the visible features $Input\_VIS$ and infrared features $Input\_IR$ as inputs, which are processed separately through a global Transformer-based attention path and a multi-scale convolutional path. In the global Transformer-based attention path, $Input\_VIS$ is first flattened and passed through a linear layer to generate the query and key matrices, denoted as Q_{VIS} and K_{VIS}, respectively. Then, the attention weight matrix QK_{VIS} is computed based on the dot product of Q_{VIS} and K_{VIS}. Subsequently, dropout is applied to QK_{VIS} to obtain Att^{qk}_{VIS}, which helps prevent overfitting. The computation processes of Att^{qk}_{VIS} is as follows:

$$Att^{qk}_{VIS} = Dropout(Softmax(Q_{VIS} \times K_{VIS})) \tag{9}$$

In the multi-scale convolutional path, $Input\_VIS$ is first passed through three standard convolutional layers and then through three dilated convolutional layers with dilation rates of 2, 4, and 2, respectively. The outputs from these two branches are concatenated to form V_{VIS}. Finally, V_{VIS} is processed sequentially by a convolutional layer, batch normalization, and a ReLU activation to generate Att^{v}_{VIS}. The computation processes of Att^{v}_{VIS} is as follows:

$$Att^{v}_{VIS} = ReLU(BN(Conv(Input\_VIS))) \tag{10}$$

where $Conv(\cdot)$ denotes a standard convolution, $BN(\cdot)$ denotes batch normalization, $ReLU(\cdot)$ denotes the rectified linear unit activation.

When $Input\_IR$ is used as the input, the computation process is identical to that of $Input\_VIS$. The computation processes of Att^{qk}_{IR} and Att^{v}_{IR} are as follows:

$$Att^{qk}_{IR} = Dropout(Softmax(Q_{IR} \times K_{IR})) \tag{11}$$

$$Att^{v}_{IR} = ReLU(BN(Conv(Input\_IR))) \tag{12}$$

where $Conv(\cdot)$ denotes a standard convolution, $BN(\cdot)$ denotes batch normalization, $ReLU(\cdot)$ denotes the rectified linear unit activation.

Next, cross-modal information fusion is performed. Specifically, the multi-scale convolution feature map of the visible modality, Att^{v}_{VIS}, is multiplied by the attention weights of the infrared modality, Att^{qk}_{IR}, and then added to $Input\_VIS$ to obtain the fused visible featureAtt_{VIS}. Similarly, the infrared multi-scale convolution output Att^{v}_{IR} is multiplied by the attention weights of the visible modality Att^{qk}_{VIS}, and added to $Input\_IR$ to obtain the fused infrared feature Att_{IR}. Then, Att_{VIS} is sequentially passed through a linear layer and a dropout layer to produce $Output\_VIS$, while Att_{IR} undergoes the same process to generate $Output\_IR$. The computation processes of $Output\_VIS$ and $Output\_IR$ are as follows:

$$Output\_VIS = Dropout(Linear(Att_{VIS})) \tag{13}$$

$$Output\_IR = Dropout(Linear(Att_{IR})) \tag{14}$$

4 Experiments

Datasets. In our experiments, we use the publicly available FMB [33] and MFNet [34] datasets as the evaluation benchmarks. The FMB dataset consists of 1,500 pairs of images captured using an intelligent multi-band binocular imaging system with a resolution of 800 × 600. We use 1,220 pairs for training and 280 pairs for testing. The MFNet dataset is the first urban scene dataset with pixel-level annotations for infrared and visible image pairs. It consists of 1,569 paired images, of which 1,082 pairs are used for training and 362 pairs for testing.

Evaluation Metrics. In this work, we adopt five evaluation metrics for image fusion: Entropy (EN), Mutual Information (MI), Standard Deviation (SD), Visual Information Fidelity (VIF), and Qabf. These metrics comprehensively assess the fusion performance from the perspectives of information content, information preservation, contrast, visual fidelity, and overall perceptual quality.

Implementation Details. All experiments are conducted using the PyTorch framework on a system equipped with an Intel(R) Core(TM) i7-12700 CPU (16 GB RAM) and an NVIDIA GeForce RTX 4090 D GPU. During model training, the Adam optimizer is employed with a learning rate of 1e–4, and the batch size and number of epochs are set to 4 and 500, respectively.

Results and Analysis. To demonstrate the superiority of our method, we compare GDTFusion with six state-of-the-art (SOTA) fusion methods on two publicly available datasets, FMB and MFNet. The compared methods include DenseFuse [10], MDA [35], SeAFusion [36], KDFuse [37], MLFuse [38], and ICAFusion [39]. To ensure a fair comparison, all baseline methods are implemented using their default hyperparameters, with training and testing procedures strictly following the settings described in their original publications.

Quantitative Results. Table 1 presents the quantitative results of infrared and visible image fusion using seven network models on the two public datasets. In the table, the best performance for each metric is highlighted in red, while the second-best is highlighted in blue. As observed from the experimental results, the proposed method outperforms other network models on both the FMB and MFNet datasets, demonstrating a clear performance advantage.

On the FMB dataset, GDTFusion achieves the best performance on four metrics: EN, SD, VIF, and Qabf, and ranks second on the MI metric, demonstrating a significant overall advantage. An EN value of 7.0576 indicates that the fused image contains more information content. The SD value reaches 9.9753, suggesting higher image contrast and richer detail. VIF and Qabf reach 0.9605 and 0.6823, respectively, reflecting superior visual quality and improved structural perception. Although the MI value is slightly lower than that of KDFuse, it still remains at a high level, demonstrating good information preservation.

Table 1. Quantitative comparison of different methods in terms of EN, MI, SD, VIF, and Qabf on the FMB and MFNet infrared and visible image fusion datasets. The best results are highlighted in red, and the second-best results are shown in blue.

Model	FMB					MFNet				
	EN	MI	SD	VIF	Q_{abf}	EN	MI	SD	VIF	Q_{abf}
DenseFuse	6.3683	3.1788	8.1139	0.7133	0.3956	6.0886	3.0706	7.9288	0.7814	0.3881
MDA	6.3468	2.6395	8.5203	0.7467	0.4058	6.1067	2.6577	7.6937	0.7479	0.4101
SeAFusion	6.7037	3.8827	9.6530	0.9041	0.6498	6.3606	3.2152	7.9115	0.9221	0.5849
KDFuse	6.6484	4.0406	9.6617	0.9120	0.6579	6.4488	3.3401	7.8847	0.9018	0.6118
MLFuse	6.6656	3.2089	8.6910	0.8082	0.5412	6.4061	2.9213	8.0022	0.9205	0.5631
ICAFusion	6.6359	3.9556	8.8247	0.9470	0.6005	6.1614	4.0089	8.3451	0.9199	0.5226
GDTFusion	7.0576	3.9841	9.9753	0.9605	0.6823	6.9498	3.9378	9.2402	0.9359	0.6594

On the MFNet dataset, GDTFusion also achieves the best results on four metrics: EN, SD, VIF, and Qabf, with values of 6.9498, 9.2402, 0.9359, and 0.6594, respectively. These results further demonstrate the method's stable fusion performance across diverse scenarios. Additionally, GDTFusion ranks second in MI, just behind ICAFusion, indicating its strong ability to preserve source image information.

In summary, GDTFusion demonstrates superior fusion performance across both datasets, effectively extracting and integrating useful information from

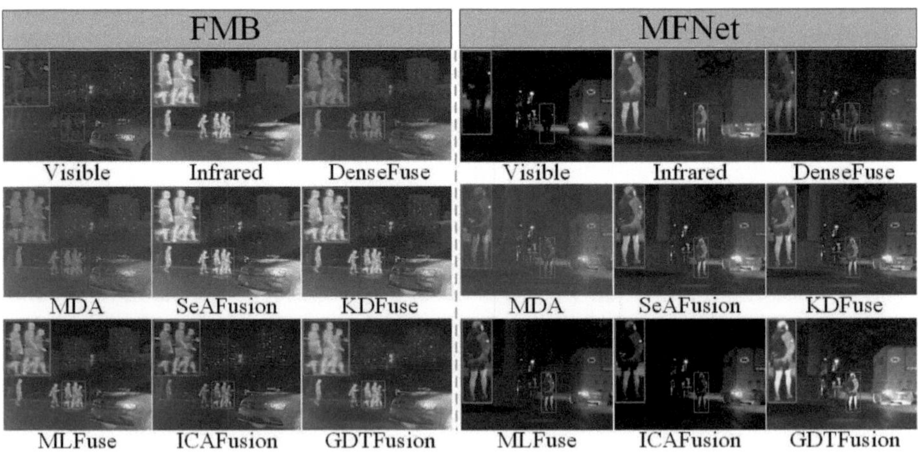

Fig. 4. Visual comparison between GDTFusion and six other SOTA fusion methods on the FMB and MFNet dataset. To facilitate a clearer comparison, texture-rich and salient regions in the images are locally enlarged and highlighted with red bounding boxes.

multimodal images. It outperforms existing methods in terms of information content, detail preservation, contrast enhancement, and overall visual quality.

Visual Results. Figure 4 show the visual fusion results of different methods on the FMB and MFNet public datasets, respectively, with the target regions enlarged and displayed at the top. It can be clearly observed that our proposed GDTFusion model outperforms other network models across both datasets, exhibiting superior fusion performance.

As shown in Fig. 4 on the FMB dataset, benefiting from the effective modeling and integration of salient target information by the IGHA and TMSIA modules, GDTFusion is capable of preserving the thermal targets from the infrared image while accurately fusing the rich textures and edge details from the visible image. Compared to other methods, it significantly suppresses common artifacts and blurring effects. GDTFusion maintains the clarity and brightness of salient targets while achieving better background detail restoration, resulting in a more natural and visually pleasing fusion outcome.

As shown in Fig. 4 on the MFNet dataset, under low-light nighttime conditions, GDTFusion delivers superior fusion performance compared to other methods. It not only highlights target contours but also accurately reconstructs headlight and environmental details, demonstrating its strong capability in handling complex scenarios. GDTFusion effectively preserves pedestrian thermal targets from the infrared image while integrating background details and luminance information from the visible image. The resulting fused images outperform methods such as DenseFuse, MDA, and SeAFusion in terms of structural clarity, contrast, and visual naturalness.

In summary, GDTFusion demonstrates outstanding fusion performance across a variety of complex scenarios. It effectively balances target perception from infrared images with fine detail preservation from visible images. This is attributed to the integration of the IGHA module, which precisely models local salient features, and the TMSIA module, which efficiently captures multi-scale global semantic information. Together, these components enable high-efficiency cross-modal feature collaboration and the generation of high-quality fused images.

Ablation Study. To validate the effectiveness of the key components in the proposed network architecture, we conduct ablation studies focusing on the roles of the IGHA and TMSIA modules in the image fusion process. Starting from the full GDTFusion model, we perform comparative experiments by removing each critical module individually. First, to evaluate the contribution of the IGHA module in suppressing redundant information and enhancing texture representation, we remove all IGHA modules from the network while retaining the TMSIA modules, forming a variant denoted as w/o IGHA. Then, to assess the capability of the TMSIA module in modeling global context and multi-scale semantic information, we remove all TMSIA modules and retain only the IGHA modules, forming another variant denoted as w/o TMSIA. The ablation results are presented in Table 2.

Table 2. Quantitative results of the ablation study on the FMB and MFNet datasets. The best results are highlighted in red.

Model	FMB					MFNet				
	EN	MI	SD	VIF	Q_{abf}	EN	MI	SD	VIF	Q_{abf}
w/o IGHA	5.8793	2.8858	8.8193	0.8581	0.5996	5.7208	3.0032	8.1535	0.8693	0.6097
w/o TMSIA	6.0349	3.2956	8.9136	0.8695	0.6098	6.0010	2.9366	8.8079	0.8934	0.6191
GDTFusion	7.0576	3.9841	9.9753	0.9605	0.6823	6.9498	3.9378	9.2402	0.9359	0.6594

Table 2 presents the ablation study results on the FMB and MFNet infrared-visible image fusion datasets. It can be observed that the complete GDTFusion model achieves the best performance across all five evaluation metrics on both datasets, fully validating the effectiveness of the proposed IGHA and TMSIA modules in the image fusion task.

Specifically, on the FMB dataset, GDTFusion achieves values of 7.0576, 3.9841, 9.9753, 0.9605, and 0.6823 for EN, MI, SD, VIF, and Qabf, respectively, significantly outperforming both variant models. When the IGHA module is removed (w/o IGHA), all metrics experience a noticeable decline—particularly EN drops from 7.0576 to 5.8793, and VIF falls to 0.8581—indicating the IGHA module's crucial role in enhancing image details and salient target features. In contrast, when the TMSIA module is removed (w/o TMSIA), although the MI value slightly exceeds that of w/o IGHA, the overall performance remains inferior to the full model, highlighting the importance of TMSIA in modeling global context and multi-scale semantic information.

A similar trend is observed on the MFNet dataset: GDTFusion outperforms the variant models across all metrics, with particularly strong performance in SD and VIF, which reflect image contrast and perceptual quality. In comparison, the w/o IGHA model shows significant drops in EN, MI, and VIF—falling to 5.7208, 3.0032, and 0.8693, respectively—demonstrating that the absence of local texture enhancement severely degrades image clarity and visual quality. Although the w/o TMSIA model preserves some structural information, its MI and Qabf values remain lower than those of the complete model, indicating that the lack of global semantic modeling hinders effective cross-modal feature fusion.

In summary, the experimental results on both datasets clearly demonstrate that the IGHA and TMSIA modules are indispensable for improving information preservation, detail clarity, and perceptual consistency in the fused images. Their complementary roles significantly enhance the overall performance of the fusion model, validating the effectiveness and generalizability of the proposed architectural design.

5 Conclusion

This paper proposes GDTFusion, an infrared and visible image fusion algorithm based on a hybrid CNN-Transformer architecture, aimed at addressing the challenges of preserving local features and modeling global information in multimodal fusion under complex environments. Specifically, we design an Interactive Gated Hybrid Attention (IGHA) module to enhance texture details, structural contrast, and color perception of the images. In addition, a Transformer-based Multi-Scale Interactive Attention (TMSIA) module is introduced to model cross-modal contextual information from local to global levels, thereby improving the structural consistency and information completeness of the fused images. Finally, high-quality fused images that retain both thermal radiation and fine texture details are generated through feature reconstruction. Extensive quantitative and visual comparison experiments were conducted on the publicly available FMB and MFNet datasets, along with ablation studies to evaluate the effectiveness of each module. The experimental results show that GDTFusion outperforms various state-of-the-art methods in terms of information preservation, detail enhancement, and visual perception, clearly demonstrating the superiority and practical applicability of the proposed approach in infrared and visible image fusion tasks.

References

1. Peng, D., Zhou, W., Pan, J., Wang, D.: MSEDNet: multi-scale fusion and edge-supervised network for RGB-T salient object detection. Neural Netw. **171**, 410–422 (2024)
2. Lv, Y., Liu, Z., Li, G.: Context-aware interaction network for RGB-T semantic segmentation. IEEE Trans. Multimedia **26**, 6348–6360 (2024)
3. Zhou, W., Gong, T., Lei, J., Yu, L.: DBCNet: dynamic bilateral cross-fusion network for RGB-T urban scene understanding in intelligent vehicles. IEEE Trans. Syst. Man Cybern. Syst. **53**(12), 7631–7641 (2023)
4. He, Y., Ma, Z., Wei, X., Gong, Y.: Knowledge synergy learning for multi-modal tracking. IEEE Trans. Circ. Syst. Video Technol. **34**(7), 5519–5532 (2024)
5. Tang, W., Liu, Y., Cheng, J., Li, C., Peng, H., Chen, X.: A phase congruency-based green fluorescent protein and phase contrast image fusion method in nonsubsampled shearlet transform domain. Microsc. Res. Tech. **83**(10), 1225–1234 (2020)
6. Liu, Y., Yang, X., Zhang, R., Albertini, M.K., Celik, T., Jeon, G.: Entropy-based image fusion with joint sparse representation and rolling guidance filter. Entropy **22**(1), 118 (2020)
7. Mitianoudis, N., Stathaki, T.: Pixel-based and region-based image fusion schemes using ICA bases. Inf. Fus. **8**(2), 131–142 (2007). Special Issue on Image Fusion: Advances in the State of the Art
8. Nie, R., Cao, J., Zhou, D., Qian, W.: Multi-source information exchange encoding with PCNN for medical image fusion. IEEE Trans. Circ. Syst. Video Technol. **31**(3), 986–1000 (2021)
9. Tan, M.J., Gao, S.B., Xu, W.Z., Han, S.C.: Visible-infrared image fusion based on early visual information processing mechanisms. IEEE Trans. Circ. Syst. Video Technol. **31**(11), 4357–4369 (2021)
10. Li, H., Wu, X.J.: DenseFuse: a fusion approach to infrared and visible images. IEEE Trans. Image Process. **28**(5), 2614–2623 (2019)
11. Tang, L., Yuan, J., Zhang, H., Jiang, X., Ma, J.: PIAFusion: a progressive infrared and visible image fusion network based on illumination aware. Inf. Fus. **83–84**, 79–92 (2022)

12. Tang, W., He, F., Liu, Y., Duan, Y., Si, T.: DATFuse: infrared and visible image fusion via dual attention transformer. IEEE Trans. Circ. Syst. Video Technol. **33**(7), 3159–3172 (2023)
13. Ma, J., Zhang, H., Shao, Z., Liang, P., Xu, H.: GANMcC: a generative adversarial network with multiclassification constraints for infrared and visible image fusion. IEEE Trans. Instrum. Meas. **70**, 1–14 (2021)
14. Zhao, F., Zhao, W., Yao, L., Liu, Y.: Self-supervised feature adaption for infrared and visible image fusion. Inf. Fus. **76**, 189–203 (2021)
15. Xing, M., Liu, G., Tang, H., Qian, Y., Zhang, J.: CFNet: an infrared and visible image compression fusion network. Pattern Recogn. **156**, 110774 (2024)
16. Tang, W., He, F., Liu, Y.: TCCFusion: an infrared and visible image fusion method based on transformer and cross correlation. Pattern Recogn. **137**, 109295 (2023)
17. Liu, S., Chen, J., Rahardja, S.: A new multi-focus image fusion algorithm and its efficient implementation. IEEE Trans. Circ. Syst. Video Technol. **30**(5), 1374–1384 (2020)
18. Zhu, Z., Yin, H., Chai, Y., Li, Y., Qi, G.: A novel multi-modality image fusion method based on image decomposition and sparse representation. Inf. Sci. **432**, 516–529 (2018)
19. Lu, Y., Wang, F., Luo, X., Liu, F.: Novel infrared and visible image fusion method based on independent component analysis. Front. Comp. Sci. **8**(2), 243–254 (2014). https://doi.org/10.1007/s11704-014-2328-2
20. Liu, Y., Liu, S., Wang, Z.: A general framework for image fusion based on multi-scale transform and sparse representation. Inf. Fus. **24**, 147–164 (2015)
21. Qin, X., Shen, J., Mao, X., Li, X., Jia, Y.: Robust match fusion using optimization. IEEE Trans. Cybern. **45**(8), 1549–1560 (2015)
22. Chen, J., Li, X., Luo, L., Mei, X., Ma, J.: Infrared and visible image fusion based on target-enhanced multiscale transform decomposition. Inf. Sci. **508**, 64–78 (2020)
23. Li, H., Wu, X.J., Kittler, J.: MDLatLRR: a novel decomposition method for infrared and visible image fusion. IEEE Trans. Image Process. **29**, 4733–4746 (2020)
24. Zhou, Z., Wang, B., Li, S., Dong, M.: Perceptual fusion of infrared and visible images through a hybrid multi-scale decomposition with Gaussian and bilateral filters. Inf. Fus. **30**, 15–26 (2016)
25. Xu, H., Zhang, H., Ma, J.: Classification saliency-based rule for visible and infrared image fusion. IEEE Trans. Comput. Imag. **7**, 824–836 (2021)
26. Wang, Z., Wang, J., Wu, Y., Xu, J., Zhang, X.: UNFusion: a unified multi-scale densely connected network for infrared and visible image fusion. IEEE Trans. Circ. Syst. Video Technol. **32**(6), 3360–3374 (2022)
27. Ma, J., Tang, L., Fan, F., Huang, J., Mei, X., Ma, Y.: SwinFusion: cross-domain long-range learning for general image fusion via Swin transformer. IEEE/CAA J. Autom. Sinica **9**(7), 1200–1217 (2022)
28. Ma, J., Yu, W., Liang, P., Li, C., Jiang, J.: FusionGan: a generative adversarial network for infrared and visible image fusion. Inf. Fus. **48**, 11–26 (2019)
29. Li, H., Wu, X.J., Kittler, J.: RFN-Nest: an end-to-end residual fusion network for infrared and visible images. Inf. Fus. **73**, 72–86 (2021)
30. Tang, W., He, F., Liu, Y.: YDTR: infrared and visible image fusion via Y-shape dynamic transformer. IEEE Trans. Multimedia **25**, 5413–5428 (2023)
31. Gao, Y., Ma, S., Liu, J.: DCDR-GAN: a densely connected disentangled representation generative adversarial network for infrared and visible image fusion. IEEE Trans. Circ. Syst. Video Technol. **33**(2), 549–561 (2023)

32. Xie, E., Wang, W., Yu, Z., Anandkumar, A., Alvarez, J.M., Luo, P.: SegFormer: Simple and efficient design for semantic segmentation with transformers. In: Ranzato, M., Beygelzimer, A., Dauphin, Y., Liang, P., Vaughan, J.W. (eds.) Advances in Neural Information Processing Systems, vol. 34, pp. 12077–12090. Curran Associates, Inc. (2021)
33. Liu, J., et al.: Multi-interactive feature learning and a full-time multi-modality benchmark for image fusion and segmentation. In: Proceedings of the IEEE/CVF International Conference on Computer Vision (ICCV), pp. 8115–8124 (2023)
34. Ha, Q., Watanabe, K., Karasawa, T., Ushiku, Y., Harada, T.: MFNet: towards real-time semantic segmentation for autonomous vehicles with multi-spectral scenes. In: 2017 IEEE/RSJ International Conference on Intelligent Robots and Systems (IROS), pp. 5108–5115 (2017)
35. Yang, G., Li, J., Lei, H., Gao, X.: A multi-scale information integration framework for infrared and visible image fusion. Neurocomputing **600**, 128116 (2024)
36. Tang, L., Yuan, J., Ma, J.: Image fusion in the loop of high-level vision tasks: a semantic-aware real-time infrared and visible image fusion network. Inf. Fus. **82**, 28–42 (2022)
37. Yang, C., Luo, X., Zhang, Z., Chen, Z., Jun, W.X.: KDFuse: a high-level vision task-driven infrared and visible image fusion method based on cross-domain knowledge distillation. Inf. Fus. **118**, 102944 (2025)
38. Lei, J., et al.: MLFuse: multi-scenario feature joint learning for multi-modality image fusion. IEEE Trans. Multimedia, 1–16 (2025)
39. Xu, M., Tang, L., Zhang, H., Ma, J.: Infrared and visible image fusion via parallel scene and texture learning. Pattern Recogn. **132**, 108929 (2022)

DCAPNet: A Contrast-Enhanced and Multi-scale Feature Fusion Network for Infrared Small Target Detection

Yingying Gao[1,2], Maoyong Li[1,2], Xuedong Guo[1,2], Lei Deng[1,2(✉)], Mingli Dong[1,2], and Lianqing Zhu[1,2]

[1] Key Laboratory of the Ministry of Education for Optoelectronic Measurement Technology and Instrument, Beijing Information Science & Technology University, Beijing, China

[2] Beijing Laboratory of Optical Fiber Sensing and System, Beijing Information Science & Technology University, Beijing, China

dally211@163.com

Abstract. Infrared Small Target Detection (IRSTD) plays a vital role in military surveillance and national defense. However, it remains a highly challenging task due to the small size of targets, low target-to-background contrast, and complex background clutter. To tackle these issues, we propose a novel detection framework, the Dual-branch Contrast-Attentive Pyramid Network (DCAPNet), which is designed to model the contrastive relationships between targets and background across multiple feature levels to improve detection performance.Specifically, the Multi-Contrast Dilation (MCD) module enhances weak target responses by leveraging multi-scale dilated convolutions to capture essential semantic cues. The Dual Contrast Enhance (DCE) module adopts a dual-branch architecture to emphasize local details and alleviate representation bottlenecks in low-texture regions. Moreover, the Contrast-Attention Fusion (CAF) module facilitates multi-scale semantic alignment and introduces an attention-guided mechanism to enhance edge perception while suppressing background interference. Extensive experiments on three publicly available IRSTD benchmarks, NUAA-SIRST, IRSTD-1K, and NUDT-SIRST, demonstrate that DCAPNet consistently outperforms state-of-the-art methods across various key evaluation metrics. These results validate the effectiveness, robustness, and generalization capability of the proposed method in complex infrared imaging scenarios.

Keywords: Infrared small target detection (ISTD) · Dual-branch structure · Contrast enhancement

1 Introduction

With the continuous advancement of infrared detection technology, its applications have become increasingly widespread in areas such as maritime early

© The Author(s), under exclusive license to Springer Nature Singapore Pte Ltd. 2026
J. Kittler et al. (Eds.): PRCV 2025, LNCS 16289, pp. 410–423, 2026.
https://doi.org/10.1007/978-981-95-5764-6_28

warning, infrared guidance, medical imaging, and nighttime reconnaissance [1–3]. Among these, Infrared Small Target Detection (IRSTD) has become a key focus due to its critical role in enabling precise target identification and early threat detection [4]. However, small targets in infrared images are typically tiny, dim, and exhibit low contrast against complex backgrounds, making them difficult to distinguish from clutter. They are easily obscured, missed, or confused with environmental noise, which greatly increases the challenge of detection. Therefore, enhancing the robustness and accuracy of infrared small target detection under complex conditions is both highly valuable and essential for practical applications.

In the early stages of infrared small target detection, research primarily relied on manually constructed scenes or simulated images. As the field progressed, mainstream methods have broadly fallen into two categories: traditional approaches based on prior knowledge and data-driven deep learning methods. Traditional prior-based methods typically leverage image priors—for example, filtering techniques use designed filter templates to suppress background clutter and noise [5–7]; visual perception models simulate the human eye's sensitivity to local contrast, edges, and brightness to enhance the saliency of target regions [8,9]; low-rank sparse decomposition transforms the detection problem into a matrix decomposition task to separate foreground and background [10–12], among others. Although these methods do not rely on large amounts of training data and are effective against moderate background interference, they often suffer from false alarms or missed detections in complex textured or dynamically changing scenes, exhibiting limited robustness and adaptability.

In recent years, data-driven deep learning methods have gained increasing attention and have significantly advanced the performance of infrared small target detection, owing to their powerful end-to-end feature learning capabilities. Liu et al. [13]. Were the first to introduce deep learning into this domain, proposing a convolutional neural network (CNN) based on multilayer perceptrons (MLPs). By employing a signal-to-noise ratio (SNR)-controlled sample generation strategy, their approach achieved substantial improvements in detection performance. Deep learning-based methods have since demonstrated superior robustness and generalization capabilities in complex background conditions. To address the imbalance between target and background features, Sun et al. [14]. proposed the RDIAN network and introduced the IRSTD dataset to mitigate the scarcity of publicly available infrared small target detection data. Furthermore, various approaches such as ALCNet [15], UIU-Net [16], and DNA-Net [17] introduced architectural innovations—including multi-scale feature processing, guided supervision, and dense connectivity—to enhance target discriminability, significantly improving the accuracy and stability of small target detection in infrared imagery.

Building upon these advancements, several studies have explored the integration of Transformer architectures to further enhance the model's representational capacity. For instance, GSTUnet [18] employs a gated structure to improve shape representation, while DMFNet [19]adopts a dual-encoder framework to strengthen cross-layer feature fusion. Additionally, innovative approaches based on graph neural networks (GNNs) have been proposed [20,21]. Among them, Shen et al. [22]. successfully incorporated GNNs into the IRSTD task, effectively addressing the limited receptive field problem inherent in conventional CNN-based models. Although recent deep learning methods have made progress in infrared small target detection, they still face three major challenges in real-world applications: (1) Traditional single-branch networks have limited feature representation capabilities, making it difficult to capture both high-level semantic information and low-level local details of small targets. (2) These networks often lose contrast information between targets and the background during feature extraction.(3) Under complex backgrounds, multi-branch feature fusion can introduce redundant information, weakening target representation and adversely affecting detection performance. To address the aforementioned challenges:

- We propose a novel architecture, DCAPNet, featuring an encoder composed of two key branches. The FSFE branch is designed to capture fine structural details and multi-scale semantic features of small targets, while the CAPE branch focuses on enhancing the contrast and saliency of target regions.
- To enhance the contrast information of small targets in infrared images, we propose the MCD module to strengthen edge and structural perception. Additionally, we introduce the DCE module to reinforce the network's ability to perceive contrast features of small targets.
- In the CAF module, we incorporate an Adapter and the ECA attention mechanism. The Adapter is designed to adjust the channel dimensions of the CAPE branch, enabling smooth feature fusion. Meanwhile, the ECA mechanism guides the CAF module by suppressing irrelevant information, thereby improving the model's robustness in detecting small targets within complex backgrounds.

2 Proposed Method

In Sect. 2, we first provide an overview of the overall architecture of DCAPNet. We then introduce its core components, including the MCD, DCE, and CAF modules. Finally, we describe the loss functions designed to further enhance the detection performance for infrared small targets.

2.1 Overall Architecture

To address the limitations of single-branch networks in feature extraction—such as the loss of fine-grained details, inadequate contrast modeling during the encoding stage, and limited representation of small targets in infrared imagery—we propose a novel detection framework named DCAPNet. As illustrated in Fig. 1, DCAPNet adopts an encoderdecoder structure inspired by UNet. It incorporates two specialized branches: the FSFE branch is responsible for extracting deep semantic features of small targets, while the CAPE branch emphasizes potential target boundaries and performs multi-scale contrast modeling to enhance the response of small targets in cluttered infrared backgrounds.

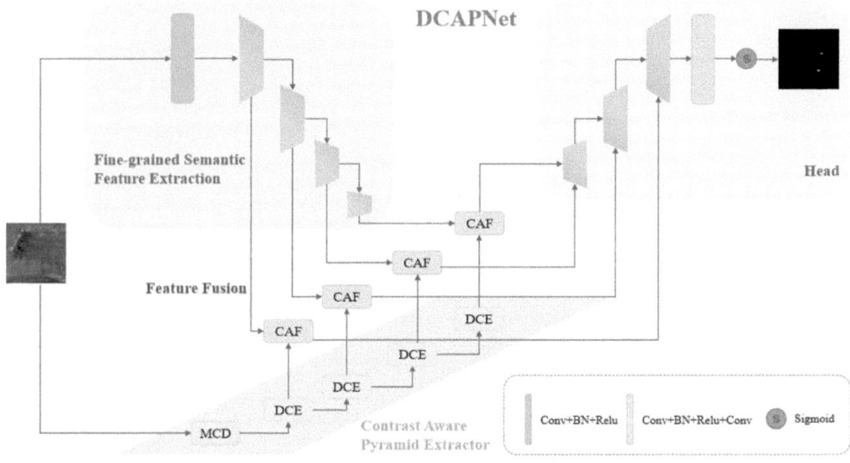

Fig. 1. The Overall Architecture of the Proposed DCAPNet.

To enable effective multi-scale collaboration and information complementation between the two branches, we introduce the CAF module. Specifically, the MCD module enhances edge and structural information in the FSFE branch; a lightweight Adapter aligns the channel dimensions of the CAPE branch; and the ECA attention mechanism guides feature fusion by adaptively amplifying responses in key channels. This design not only strengthens the representation of small target regions and their contrast against the background but also maintains a lightweight model architecture.

2.2 Multi-contrast Dilation Module

Conventional convolutions struggle to capture edge details and low-contrast regions of small targets in infrared images due to their fixed, limited receptive fields. Additionally, shallow features are often compressed during downsampling, weakening target saliency. To address this, we design the MCD module, which combines gradient-guided contrast, dilated, and standard convolutions to form a multi-scale, multi-directional feature stream. This enhances the network's ability to perceive target boundaries, structures, and local contrast.

Figure 2(a) illustrates the proposed MCD module, which consists of three parallel paths designed to enhance the network's feature extraction capability. The standard convolution branch employs a 3×3 convolution to preserve local spatial coherence and strengthen the representation of target details. Specifically, the output of the standard convolution branch can be expressed as:

$$F_{\text{std}}(i,j) = \sum_{m=-1}^{1} \sum_{n=-1}^{1} W_{m,n}^{\text{std}} \cdot F_{\text{back}}(i+m, j+n) \tag{1}$$

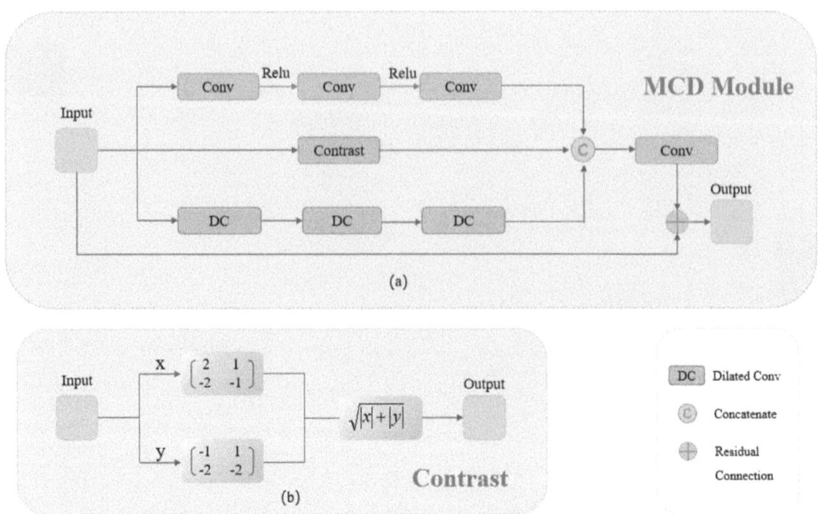

Fig. 2. Structure of the Multi-path Contrast Dilation Module.

where $F_{\text{std}}(i,j)$ represents the output feature at position (i,j) of the standard convolution branch. 85 Given the input feature map F_{back} and the convolution kernel weights W^{std}, 86 the output at (i,j) is computed by summing the element-wise products of the kernel weights $W^{\text{std}}_{m,n}$ 87 and the corresponding input features $F_{\text{back}}(i+m, j+n)$ within a 3×3 neighborhood, 88 where $m, n \in \{-1, 0, 1\}$. 89 This operation effectively performs a standard 2D convolution, capturing local spatial information from the input feature map.

As illustrated in Fig. 2(b), the contrast branch applies fixed differential convolution kernels (e.g., $[-1,1]$ and $[-2,2]$) to convolve feature maps along the x and y directions, enabling the extraction of edge and contrast information. The expression for the contrast branch is as follows:

$$F_{\text{edge}} = F_{\text{back}} + |F_{\text{back}} * K_x| + |F_{\text{back}} * K_y| \tag{2}$$

where K_x and K_y denote convolution kernels specifically designed to extract edge features along the horizontal and vertical directions, respectively.

The dilated convolution branch employs atrous convolutions with varying dilation rates to expand the receptive field, enabling the network to capture richer contextual cues around target regions.

$$F_{\text{dilate}} = \text{ReLU}\left(F_{\text{back}} *_{d=2} W_1 + F *_* \text{back} *_{d=4} W_2 + F_{\text{back}} *_{d=2} W_3\right) \tag{3}$$

The input feature map F_{back} is convolved with three convolution kernels W_1, W_2, and W_3 using dilated convolutions, where the notation $*_{d=k}$ denotes a convolution operation with a dilation rate of k.

Finally, features from all branches are concatenated along the channel dimension and fused using a 1×1 convolution. By collaboratively extracting multi-scale contrast information, the MCD module enhances the contrast information in infrared images.

2.3 Dual Contrast Enhance Module

Although the MCD module excels at enhancing the local feature representation of infrared small targets, it remains limited in handling weak contrast information within complex backgrounds. Specifically, MCD primarily emphasizes the expansion of multi-scale spatial receptive fields but exhibits insufficient capacity for extracting deep contrast features. Consequently, it struggles to comprehensively capture the multi-level contrast relationships between targets and their backgrounds. To overcome these limitations, this paper further proposes the DCE module, as illustrated in Fig. 3.

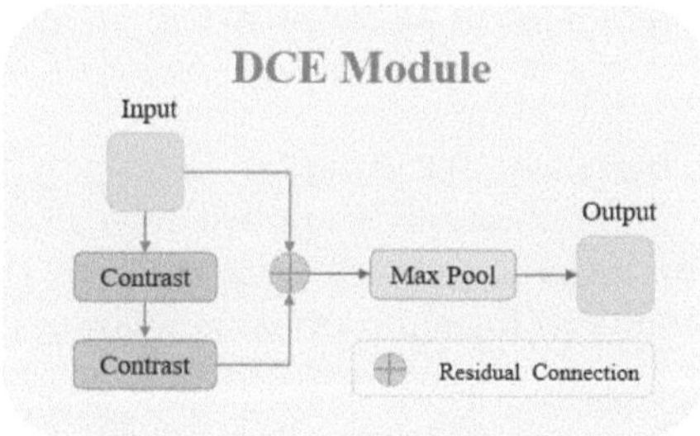

Fig. 3. Architecture of the Dual Contrast Enhance Module.

This module utilizes a two-stage sequential contrast convolution operation to progressively deepen feature representations and enhance the contrast between targets and backgrounds. Residual connections are then employed to fuse the enhanced features with the original input, which are subsequently integrated into the encoder. This design not only improves the detection accuracy of infrared small targets but also effectively enhances the model's generalization ability in complex background scenarios.

2.4 Contrast-Attention Fusion Module

Although the dual-branch structure enhances deep semantic features and shallow contrast details, it lacks effective attention guidance, causing deep features to struggle in focusing on target regions and thereby affecting detection accuracy. As shown in Fig. 4, we propose the CAF module to guide features to focus on target regions.

CAF takes as input the feature map from the FSEE branch, $F_{\text{back}} \in \mathbb{R}^{C\times H\times W}$, and the feature map from the CAPE branch, $F_{\text{cape}} \in \mathbb{R}^{C'\times H'\times W'}$. To ensure consistency in both channel dimensions and spatial resolution between

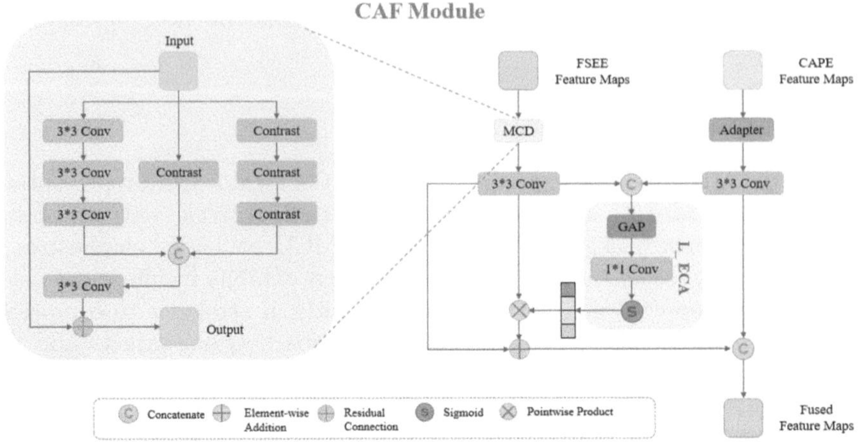

Fig. 4. Architecture of the Contrast-Attention Fusion Module.

the FSEE and CAPE branches, an Adapter is employed to perform feature alignment. First, a 1×1 convolution is applied for channel mapping, followed by bilinear interpolation to resize the feature map to the backbone's spatial dimensions. The mathematical formulation is as follows:

$$F'_{\text{cape}} = W_{\text{adapt}} * F_{\text{cape}}, \quad F'_{\text{cape}} \in \mathbb{R}^{C \times H' \times W'} \tag{4}$$

$$F''_{\text{cape}} = \text{Interp}_{\text{bilinear}}(F'_{\text{cape}}, H, W) \tag{5}$$

where W_{adapt} denotes the learnable convolutional kernel, and F'_{cape} represents the feature map after channel mapping. The resulting feature map F''_{cape} is aligned with the backbone feature map in both channel dimension and spatial resolution, providing a structurally consistent input for subsequent fusion operations. We integrate ECA into the CAF module to dynamically adjust channel weights, guiding feature fusion and improving the model's sensitivity to weak targets in complex scenes. ECA concatenates features from both branches, applies global average pooling on channels, and uses a 1D convolution to generate attention weights, which are then applied to the contrast branch. The formulation is as follows:

$$F_{\text{cat}} = \left[F_{\text{mcd}}; F''_{\text{cape}}\right] \in \mathbb{R}^{2C \times H \times W} \tag{6}$$

$$z_c = \frac{1}{H \cdot W} \sum_{i=1}^{H} \sum_{j=1}^{W} F_{\text{cat}}(c, i, j) \tag{7}$$

$$s_c = \sigma \left(\sum_{k=-\lfloor K/2 \rfloor}^{\lfloor K/2 \rfloor} w_k \cdot z_{c+k} \right) \tag{8}$$

$$F_{\text{attn}}(c,i,j) = s_c \cdot F''_{\text{cape}}(c,i,j) \tag{9}$$

Where c denotes the channel index ranging from 1 to $2C$ (due to concatenation doubling the channel count), and i, j represent the spatial row and column indices corresponding to height H and width W, respectively. z_c is the global average pooled value of channel c, and s_c is the channel attention weight obtained via a one-dimensional convolution followed by Sigmoid activation, used to recalibrate the feature responses. $F_{\text{attn}}(c,i,j)$ denotes the weighted feature at spatial position (i,j) in channel c of the CAPE branch.

2.5 Loss Function

To address the challenges of small size, weak features, and severe class imbalance in infrared small target detection, and to improve accuracy and robustness, we introduce a pixel-level binary soft-IoU loss [23] during training. Compared to the traditional IoU, the soft-IoU loss retains continuous probability outputs, enabling more effective guidance for network optimization in early training stages, thereby enhancing localization accuracy and detection robustness. It is defined as follows:

$$\mathcal{L}^{(k)}_{\text{SoftIoU}} = 1 - \frac{\sum_{i,j} \hat{y}^{(k)}_{i,j} \cdot y^{(k)}_{i,j}}{\sum_{i,j} \hat{y}^{(k)}_{i,j} + y^{(k)}_{i,j} - \hat{y}^{(k)}_{i,j} \cdot y^{(k)}_{i,j} + \epsilon} \tag{10}$$

where $\hat{y}^{(k)}_{i,j}$ denotes the predicted probability (ranging in $[0,1]$) of the pixel at position (i,j) in the k-th image, $y^{(k)}_{i,j}$ is the corresponding ground truth label (either 0 or 1), and ε is a small constant (e.g., 10^{-6}) added to prevent division by zero.

3 Experiment

3.1 Dataset and Implementation Details

To thoroughly assess the performance of the proposed method for infrared small target detection across various scenarios, experiments were conducted on three publicly available datasets: NUAA-SIRST [24], IRSTD-1K [25], and NUDT-SIRST [17]. These datasets encompass a wide range of target types and background conditions, providing both diversity and complexity for evaluation. For all experiments, each dataset is divided into training and testing subsets with an 8:2 ratio to ensure fairness and consistency. The proposed approach is developed using Python 3.12 and PyTorch 2.4.1. All training and inference are conducted on an NVIDIA GeForce RTX 4090 GPU with CUDA 12.1, utilizing the open-source BasicIRSTD toolbox.

The model is optimized using Adam with an initial learning rate of 0.001. A MultiStepLR scheduler is applied, decaying the learning rate by a factor of 0.1 at the 200th and 300th epochs. The training process spans 400 epochs with a batch size of 16.

3.2 Evaluation Metrics

To thoroughly evaluate the performance of the proposed DCAPNet in infrared small target detection, we conduct a comparative analysis with several state-of-the-art (SOTA) methods. The evaluation employs a set of widely recognized metrics, including PixAcc, mIoU, PD, and FA. The definitions and corresponding calculation formulas for these metrics are provided below:

$$\text{pixAcc} = \frac{|P \cap G|}{|G| + |B|} \tag{11}$$

$$\text{mIoU} = \frac{1}{C} \sum_{c=1}^{C} \frac{|P_c \cap G_c|}{|P_c \cup G_c|} \tag{12}$$

$$\text{PD} = \frac{N_{\text{TP}}}{N_{\text{GT}}} \tag{13}$$

$$\text{FA} = \frac{N_{\text{FP}}}{N_{\text{FP}} + N_{\text{TN}}} \tag{14}$$

where P denotes the pixels predicted as targets, G represents the ground-truth target region, and B is the background. $|P \cap G|$ counts the correctly predicted target pixels. For mIoU, C is the number of classes (usually 2), with P_c and G_c as the predicted and true pixels for class c. PD is the ratio of true positives N_{TP} to total targets N_{GT}, and FA is the ratio of false positives N_{FP} to all negative samples $N_{\text{FP}} + N_{\text{TN}}$.

Table 1. Performance Comparison of the Proposed Method and State-of-the-Art Approaches on NUAA-SIRST, IRSTD-1K, and NUDT-SIRST. The best results for each metric are marked in bold, while the second-best results are underlined.

Method	NUAA-SIRST				IRSTD-1K				NUDT-SIRST			
	mIoU(↑)	PixAcc(↑)	Pd(↑)	Fa (↓)	mIoU(↑)	PixAcc(↑)	Pd(↑)	Fa (↓)	mIoU(↑)	PixAcc(↑)	Pd(↑)	Fa (↓)
ALCNet	69.79	81.82	91.25	33.82	59.32	78.77	91.58	60.79	71.72	84.24	98.10	14.91
ACM	67.56	79.68	90.49	46.24	56.73	81.23	90.24	81.96	67.52	85.46	96.30	25.88
UIUNet	78.11	85.25	95.82	**18.36**	56.48	81.52	93.27	96.13	87.75	90.56	97.04	**2.44**
DNAnet	76.89	83.93	95.06	32.44	64.57	78.81	92.26	**24.82**	94.08	**96.39**	98.73	3.61
RDIAN	73.37	82.42	94.30	43.22	61.02	76.33	89.90	43.31	82.98	90.49	98.62	19.07
ISTDUNet	77.50	85.79	97.34	22.29	62.57	77.21	92.93	44.71	92.08	94.77	98.41	5.22
DCAPNet	**78.89**	**86.91**	**98.10**	21.54	**64.68**	**82.12**	**92.95**	47.69	**94.16**	96.24	**98.83**	3.03

Experimental results demonstrate that the proposed **DCAPNet** achieves state-of-the-art performance across multiple benchmarks, exhibiting strong detection accuracy and generalization. On the NUAA-SIRST dataset, DCAPNet achieves an mIoU of 78.89% and a Pd of 98.10%, outperforming UIUNet (78.11%/95.82%) and DNANet (76.89%/95.06%). It also achieves 94.16% mIoU and 98.83% Pd on NUDT-SIRST. While UIUNet and DNANet benefit from attention and fusion mechanisms, they remain limited in handling noise and background clutter. In contrast, our CAF module suppresses non-target responses through contrast-guided attention, enhancing accuracy and consistency. On the IRSTD-1K dataset, DCAPNet further demonstrates robustness with the best performance in mIoU (64.68%), pixel accuracy (82.12%), and Pd (92.95%). Although its false alarm rate (Fa) is slightly higher (47.69%) than DNANet (24.82%), it remains acceptable, showing that the dual-branch DCE module effectively enhances target-background discrimination. Overall, DCAPNet achieves a balanced trade-off among accuracy, robustness, and false alarm control, benefiting from the multi-scale modeling of MCD, the fine-grained contrast enhancement of DCE, and the focused attention of CAF (Table 1).

3.3 Visualization Analysis

We select two challenging images from each of the three datasets as input examples and visualize the final outputs of all methods, as shown in Fig. 5. In the visualizations, blue indicates correct predictions, while yellow highlights false alarms.

Across the three infrared datasets, targets are typically small, blurry, and low in contrast, making them vulnerable to interference from complex backgrounds. As shown in Fig. 5 (Row 1), ACM suffers from severe noise interference and missing edge information, resulting in poor detection performance. Methods such as ALCNet, RDIAN, and ISTDUNet also exhibit false alarms and enhanced background responses in multiple regions. In Fig. 5 (Row 7), although DNANet performs comparably to DCAPNet in complex scenarios, its lack of contrast modeling leads to frequent misclassification of background noise as targets under low-contrast conditions, increasing the false alarm rate. By comparison, DCAPNet achieves the best results among all seven methods. This improvement is attributed to the integration of the MCD and DCE modules, which enhance the response to weak targets, and the CAF module, which suppresses background interference and improves edge perception through multi-scale alignment and fusion. These results demonstrate that DCAPNet offers superior target sensitivity and background adaptability, confirming its effectiveness and robustness in ISTD.

3.4 Ablation Analysis

To validate the effectiveness of each module in the infrared small target detection task, we progressively incorporated the proposed MCD, DCE, and CAF modules into the baseline model and conducted ablation experiments across three public datasets. The results of these experiments are summarized in Table 2.

The comparisons between strategy (a) and strategies (b), (c), and (d) demonstrate that the individual introduction of MCD, CAF, or DCE results in consistent performance improvements across multiple datasets. For instance, incorporating only the CAF module in strategy (d) increases the mIoU on the NUAA-SIRST dataset from 72.90% to 75.12%, with the PixAcc improving by approxi-

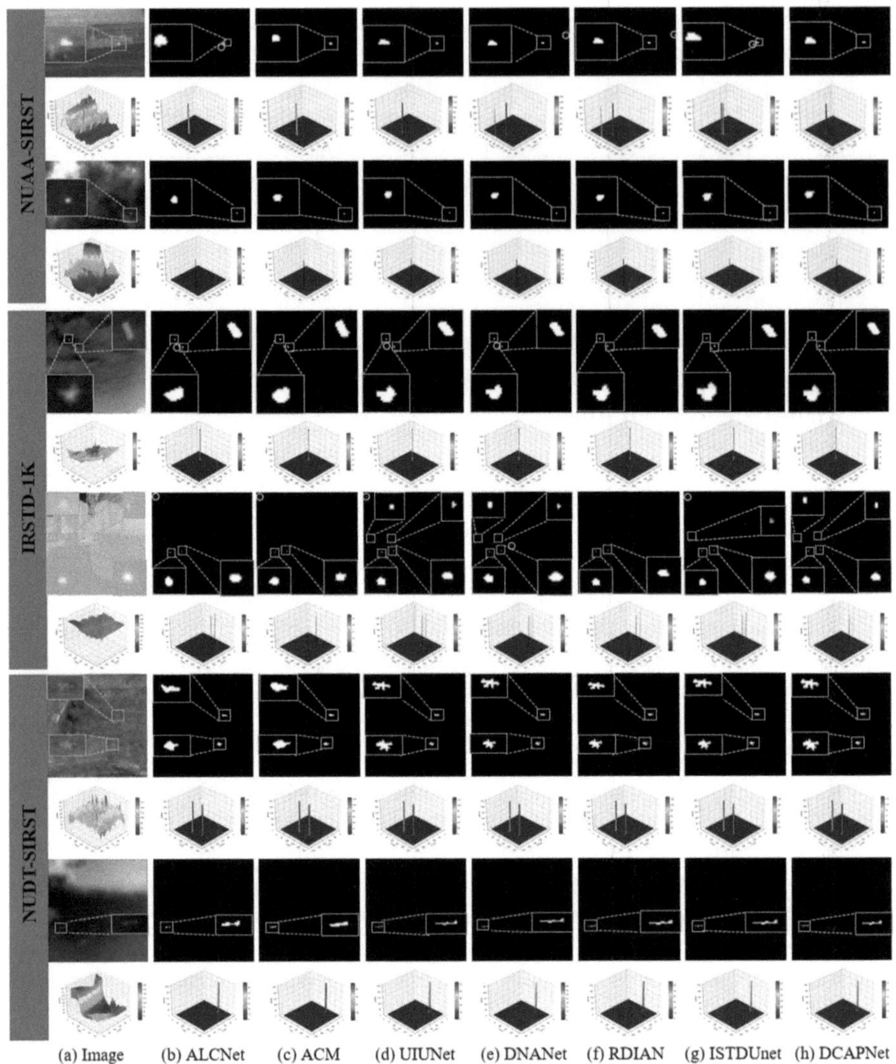

Fig. 5. Visual comparison of DCAPNet and six state-of-the-art methods on the NUAA-SIRST, IRSTD-1K, and NUDT-SIRST datasets.

mately 4% points. This highlights CAF's strong ability in global feature aggregation and suppression of background interference. Comparing (a) with (b), (c), and (d) shows that individually adding MCD, CAF, or DCE consistently improves performance across datasets. For example, in (d), the mIoU on NUAA-SIRST increases from 72.9% to 75.12%, and pixAcc improves by about 4% points, demonstrating CAF's strong ability in global feature fusion and background suppression. Comparing (a) and (b), adding MCD raises mIoU on IRSTD-1K from 53.63% to 56.67%, and improves NUDT-SIRST by 5.35 points, validating

Table 2. Quantitative ablation study assessing the impacts of core components MCD, DCE, and CAF

Strategy	MCD	DCE	CAF	NUAA-SIRST		IRSTD-1K		NUDT-SIRST	
				mIoU (↑)	pixAcc (↑)	mIoU (↑)	pixAcc (↑)	mIoU (↑)	pixAcc (↑)
(a)	×	×	×	72.90	81.89	53.63	74.73	84.36	88.58
(b)	✓	×	×	73.65	82.90	56.67	80.92	89.71	92.74
(c)	×	✓	×	72.05	82.21	55.47	76.93	86.22	89.05
(d)	×	×	✓	75.12	85.62	57.54	72.63	90.78	94.35
(e)	✓	✓	×	74.01	82.05	58.48	81.91	91.76	94.89
(f)	✓	×	✓	76.98	86.07	62.56	80.32	90.26	93.83
(g)	×	✓	✓	77.13	85.01	60.64	77.86	91.87	95.06
(h)	✓	✓	✓	**78.89**	**86.91**	**64.68**	**82.12**	**94.16**	**96.24**

MCD's effectiveness in highlighting small targets via contrast-sensitive features under complex backgrounds. From (e) and (g), although DCE shows limited gain on NUAA-SIRST, it improves mIoU on IRSTD-1K and NUDT-SIRST by 2.16% and 0.11%, respectively, indicating its suitability for edge enhancement of low-contrast, small targets. Comparing (b) and (f), introducing CAF increases NUAA-SIRST mIoU from 73.65% to 76.98%, showing that attention mechanisms and hierarchical alignment significantly boost spatial precision. In (h), DCAPNet achieves the best results across all three datasets, indicating these modules complement each other well in feature extraction, detail enhancement, and information fusion, effectively balancing small target perception and contrast modeling in complex scenes.

4 Conclusion

In this paper, we address the limitations of traditional single-branch networks in infrared small target detection, particularly their inability to effectively represent target features under complex backgrounds and their low sensitivity to target-to-background contrast. To overcome these challenges, we propose a novel detection framework—DCAPNet, which integrates three core modules: MCD, DCE, and CAF. These modules collaboratively reconstruct the contrast relationship between targets and backgrounds at the feature level, enhancing weak target responses while suppressing background clutter. Specifically, MCD adopts a multi-scale dilation strategy to amplify target signals and emphasize weak features. DCE employs a dual-branch structure to enhance shallow-layer local details, alleviating the representation bottleneck caused by weak textures. CAF performs multi-scale semantic alignment and contrast-aware attention fusion, improving the model's adaptability to complex backgrounds and its ability to perceive target boundaries. Extensive experiments on NUAA-SIRST, IRSTD-1K, and NUDT-SIRST demonstrate that DCAPNet consistently outperforms state-of-the-art methods in detection accuracy. Furthermore, the proposed method shows strong robustness and generalization capability, making it well-suited for infrared small target detection in complex real-world scenarios.

Acknowledgements. This work was supported by the project "Vision-guided Automatic Vehicle Refueling Hardware System Design" (No. 9162523202) and the Research Project of Beijing Municipal Natural Science Foundation (No. BJXZ2021-012-00046).

References

1. Deng, H., Sun, X., Liu, M., Ye, C., Zhou, X.: Small infrared target detection based on weighted local difference measure. IEEE Trans. Geosci. Remote Sens. **54**(7), 4204–4214 (2016)
2. Raghavan, K., Balasubramanian, S., Veezhinathan, K.: IR-GAN: improved generative adversarial networks for infrared breast image segmentation. Quant. Infrared Thermogr. J. **22**(1), 70–96 (2025)
3. Sheng, D., Jin, W., Wang, M., Yang, J.: Region-based self-segmentation guided diffusion model for thermal infrared to pseudo-color visible light image conversion. IEEE Access **13**, 47860–47873 (2025)
4. Danaci, K.I., Akagunduz, E.: A survey on infrared image & video sets. Multimed. Tools Appl. **83**(6), 16485–16523 (2024)
5. Zeng, M., Li, J., Peng, Z.: The design of top-hat morphological filter and application to infrared target detection. Infrared Phys. Technol. **48**(1), 67–76 (2006)
6. Gao, X., et al.: Infrared small target detection algorithm based on filter kernel combination optimization learning method. Infrared Phys. Technol. **139**, 105346 (2024)
7. Paris, S., Hasinoff, S.W., Kautz, J.: Local laplacian filters: edge-aware image processing with a Laplacian pyramid. ACM Trans. Graph. **30**(4), 68 (2011)
8. Chen, C.P., Li, H., Wei, Y., Xia, T., Tang, Y.Y.: A local contrast method for small infrared target detection. IEEE Trans. Geosci. Remote Sens. **52**(1), 574–581 (2013)
9. Han, J., Ma, Y., Huang, J., Mei, X., Ma, J.: An infrared small target detecting algorithm based on human visual system. IEEE Geosci. Remote Sens. Lett. **13**(3), 452–456 (2016)
10. Qin, Y., Bruzzone, L., Gao, C., Li, B.: Infrared small target detection based on facet kernel and random walker. IEEE Trans. Geosci. Remote Sens. **57**(9), 7104–7118 (2019)
11. Zhang, L., Peng, Z.: Infrared small target detection based on partial sum of the tensor nuclear norm. Remote Sens. **11**(4), 382 (2019)
12. Pang, D., Shan, T., Ma, Y., Ma, P., Hu, T., Tao, R.: LRTA-SP: Low rank tensor approximation with saliency prior for small target detection in infrared videos. IEEE Trans. Aerosp. Electron. Syst. (2024)
13. Liu, M., Du, H.y., Zhao, Y.j., Dong, L.q., Hui, M., Wang, S.: Image small target detection based on deep learning with snr controlled sample generation. Curr. Trends Comput. Sci. Mech. Autom. **1**(211-220), 1–2 (2017)
14. Sun, H., Bai, J., Yang, F., Bai, X.: Receptive-field and direction induced attention network for infrared dim small target detection with a large-scale dataset irdst. IEEE Trans. Geosci. Remote Sens. **61**, 1–13 (2023)
15. Dai, Y., Wu, Y., Zhou, F., Barnard, K.: Attentional local contrast networks for infrared small target detection. IEEE Trans. Geosci. Remote Sens. **59**(11), 9813–9824 (2021)

16. Wu, X., Hong, D., Chanussot, J.: UIU-Net: U-net in u-net for infrared small object detection. IEEE Trans. Image Process. **32**, 364–376 (2022)
17. Li, B., Xiao, C., Wang, L., Wang, Y., Lin, Z., Li, M., An, W., Guo, Y.: Dense nested attention network for infrared small target detection. IEEE Trans. Image Process. **32**, 1745–1758 (2022)
18. Zhu, Y., Ma, Y., Fan, F., Huang, J., Wu, K., Wang, G.: Towards accurate infrared small target detection via edge-aware gated transformer. IEEE J. Select. Topics Appl. Earth Observ. Remote Sens. (2024)
19. Guo, T., Zhou, B., Luo, F., Zhang, L., Gao, X.: DMFNet: dual-encoder multi-stage feature fusion network for infrared small target detection. IEEE Trans. Geosci. Remote Sens. **62**, 1–4 (2024)
20. Khemani, B., Patil, S., Kotecha, K., Tanwar, S.: A review of graph neural networks: concepts, architectures, techniques, challenges, datasets, applications, and future directions. J. Big Data **11**(1), 18 (2024)
21. Leus, G., Marques, A.G., Moura, J.M., Ortega, A., Shuman, D.I.: Graph signal processing: history, development, impact, and outlook. IEEE Signal Process. Mag. **40**(4), 49–60 (2023)
22. Shen, Y., Li, Q., Xu, C., Chang, C., Yin, Q.: Graph-based context learning network for infrared small target detection. Neurocomputing **616**, 128949 (2025)
23. Huang, Y., Tang, Z., Chen, D., Su, K., Chen, C.: Batching soft IoU for training semantic segmentation networks. IEEE Signal Process. Lett. **27**, 66–70 (2019)
24. Dai, Y., Wu, Y., Zhou, F., Barnard, K.: Asymmetric contextual modulation for infrared small target detection. In: Proceedings of the IEEE/CVF Winter Conference on Applications Of Computer Vision, pp. 950–959 (2021)
25. Zhang, M., Zhang, R., Yang, Y., Bai, H., Zhang, J., Guo, J.: ISNet: shape matters for infrared small target detection. In: Proceedings of the IEEE/CVF Conference on Computer Vision and Pattern Recognition, pp. 877–886 (2022)

Multimodal Brain-Computer Interfaces: Algorithms, Integration, Applications

Alzheimer's Disease Stage Classification Using Rs-fMRI: A Dual-Branch Model with Data Augmentation

Jianheng Zhou[1(✉)], Haoyuan Liang[2], Ruizhi Yang[3], and Tianyu Liu[4]

[1] Nanyang Technological University, Singapore, Singapore
934537084@qq.com
[2] Shanghaitech University, Shanghai, China
[3] Imperial College London, London, UK
[4] The University of Hong Kong, Hong Kong, Hong Kong SAR

Abstract. Resting state functional magnetic resonance imaging (rs-fMRI) can explain the connectivity of different regions in the human brain, and thus explain the disease through the different states of brain regions. However, fMRI imaging is complex, and understanding it usually requires a high threshold, while deep learning can enable more non-medical professionals to participate in auxiliary diagnosis research. Therefore, based on rs-fMRI data and deep learning methods, this paper attempts to achieve the classification of early stages Alzheimer's disease. We used the data from the Alzheimer's Disease Neuroimaging Initiative (ADNI) database. It contains 313 complete samples from 177 subjects. We used SPM12 to perform necessary preprocessing on the data, and then divided the data into 94 brain regions based on the AAL template. Subsequently, we calculated the graph theory coefficients for each brain region and applied the fisher-score to select important regions. Mixup data augmentation was then applied for generating more items. Finally, a dual-branch CNN-LSTM network was built to classify the obtained correlation coefficients. The model finally achieved good results of accuracy = 0.859 for the four stages prediction of Alzheimer's Disease (AD), Early Mild Cognitive Impairment (EMCI), Late Mild Cognitive Impairment (LMCI), and Cognitively Normal (CN).

Keywords: Resting-State fMRI · Dual-Branch Network · Alzheimer's Disease · Data Augmentation

1 Introduction

It was estimated that 35.6 million people lived with dementia worldwide in 2010, with numbers expected to almost double every 20 years, to 65.7 million in 2030 and 115.4 million in 2050 [10]. People have begun to pay more and more attention to the treatment of Alzheimer's disease patients [12]. Current treatments are focused on symptom management, although several trials are underway aimed

© The Author(s), under exclusive license to Springer Nature Singapore Pte Ltd. 2026
J. Kittler et al. (Eds.): PRCV 2025, LNCS 16289, pp. 427–437, 2026.
https://doi.org/10.1007/978-981-95-5764-6_29

at reducing brain pathology and its overall burden. The medical establishment needs to develop more effectively predictive methods.

Functional magnetic resonance imaging (fMRI) generates a dynamic representation of brain activity through a blood oxygen level dependent (BOLD) signal, which measures fluctuations in blood flow and volume [4]. fMRI studies in AD found tasks involving working memory, visuospatial skills, attention, semantic knowledge, and motor performance, while those with mild cognitive impairment involved attention and working memory. Resting state fMRI (rs-fMRI) provides insights into functional connections between intrinsic network structures associated with Alzheimer's disease lineages [13]. Although fMRI provides great prospect into pathophysiology, it would be difficult to take it for clinical use.

Nowadays, deep learning is widely applied in the medical field, which has spurred the development of predictive methods for Alzheimer's disease. Most research has focused on interpretation from a structural level using MRI or other imaging methods. However, the early stages of the disease often show less significant structural changes. These studies largely ignore the impact of the disease on the brain functional connectivity, which is precisely the strength of functional Magnetic Resonance Imaging (fMRI). Many researches indicated that connectivity and network integrity appear to decrease in healthy aging, but this decrease is accelerated in AD, with specific systems hit hardest, such as the default mode network (DMN) [2].

However, using fMRI also presents some challenges: **1) Useful information from fMRI is difficult to extract.** This is mainly due to its imaging mechanism. Compared to structural imaging, which directly reflects structural changes, it is often difficult to easily extract core information from the fMRI signal itself, requiring cumbersome data processing and feature calculation based on experience. **2) The amount of fMRI data for Alzheimer's disease is scarce.** Due to the difficulty of data acquisition and the limited number of related studies, the data volume is very scarce, which constrains the development of deep learning models in this field.

Our research introduces fMRI and addresses the aforementioned problems by introducing efficient and simple methods. Experiments have demonstrated that we achieved excellent results using a relatively simple feature selection method and a simple deep learning model, based on scarce data.

2 Research Survey

Previous research [6] attempted to integrate features from brain regions and subgraphs, subsequently employing multi-kernel support vector machines (SVM) for classification. To validate the proposed methodology, 28 normal control subjects and 38 patients with Alzheimer's disease participated in the study. The method achieved satisfactory classification accuracy, averaging 91.60%. Another study [7] utilized convolutional neural networks (CNN) for classifying stages of Alzheimer's disease, achieving an accuracy of 93% with a 3D fMRI dataset. In a similar study [5] demonstrated the effectiveness of deep learning techniques in early Alzheimer's detection. They applied an improved autoencoder to the classification task and finally got the 94.6% sensitivity for AD and MCI. Graph neural networks (GNNs) are also very suitable for fMRI research. Related study [1,15] combined the characteristics of time and space to design a spatial-temporal graph neural network (ST-GNN) for early diagnosis of Alzheimer's disease. In addition to the spatial structure of the graph, fMRI also has the characteristics of time series. A related study [11] combined CNN and LSTM, first using the Generative Adversarial Network (GAN) to enhance the data of the fMRI correlation matrix, then using CNN followed by LSTM to extract spatial features of the correlation matrix at different time points and then temporal features, achieving an accuracy rate of 93.5% for AD and CN binary classification and 75.5% for LMCI and EMCL binary classification. All these researches have proven that rs-fMRI is capable of Alzheimer's Disease Stage Classification.

However, these studies have some shortcomings, to varying degrees, such as some only performed binary classification while others were time-consumed and required high computational resource. Due to the complexity and high dimensionality of medical data, traditional machine learning methods have difficulty achieving good performance in the absence of complete data preprocessing. Although deep learning is capable of these tasks, the scarcity of medical data also means that the model cannot be fully trained, and may even overfit due to insufficient sample size. Especially for rs-fMRI data, most studies can only be carried out based on a small amount of data, and traditional data enhancement methods are difficult to apply, which brings huge challenges to related research. Therefore, we aim to design a simple but efficient deep learning model, achieve multi-classification and solve the problem of insufficient data. In this study, the method we designed can effectively make up for the above shortcomings.

3 Methodology

Figure 1 shows the entire process of our study. First, the raw rs-fMRI data is preprocessed, then the processed data will be mapped to the AAL2 template, followed by region selection and data augmentation. Finally, a classification model is built and trained to automatically classify disease stages.

3.1 Data Preprocessing

Our experimental data are from the ADNI2 database of the Alzheimer's Disease Neuroimaging Initiative (ADNI) database (adni.loni.usc.edu). The ADNI is a large, longitudinal study designed to develop clinical, imaging, genetic, and biochemical biomarkers for the early detection and tracking of Alzheimer's disease.

We selected 313 complete rs-fMRI records from 177 subjects. The number of each category is shown in Table 1. The equipment used to collect fMRI usually needs to be preheated to generate high-quality images, therefore the data of the first ten time points need to be removed for all samples as recommended. Then we

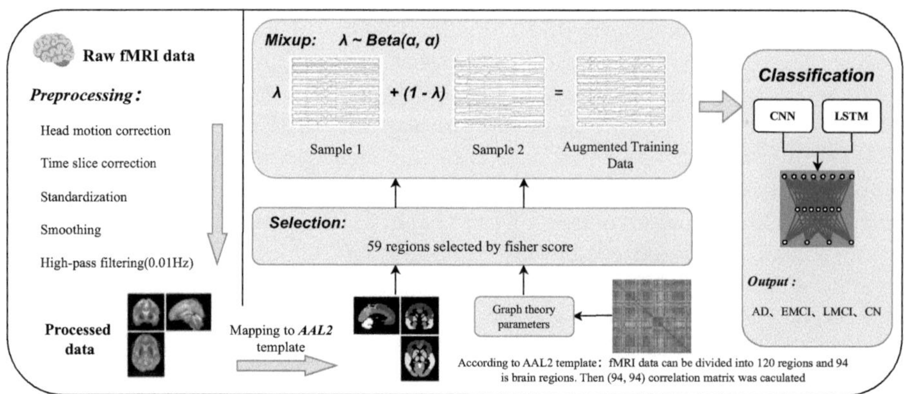

Fig. 1. Entire Workflow of Alzheimer's Disease Stage Classification Using rs-fMRI.

used SPM12 (Statistical Parametric Mapping, developed by the Wellcome Centre for Human Neuroimaging) to perform preprocessing operations on the fMRI data on the MATLAB platform, including head motion correction, time slice correction, standardization to the Montreal Neurological Institute (MNI) space, smoothing, high-pass filtering, and brain region division according to the AAL template. Except for the last step, the previous steps are common operations for preprocessing fMRI [3], and the last step is to better analyze the functional areas of the brain and analyze the impact of Alzheimer's disease on the brain from the perspective of functional areas. After completing basic preprocessing and brain partitioning, we obtained 94 brain regions divided based on the AAL template, with a total of 130 time points.

Table 1. Subjects of Each Class

Class	AD	CN	EMCI	LMCI
Count	60	88	96	69
Age	74.7 ± 7.4	74.8 ± 5.9	72.5 ± 6.1	72.3 ± 7.7

3.2 Brain Regions Selection

According to the AAL template, we finally got 94 regions of cerebrum but it is unexpected to use all of them because of the redundancy and computational cost. Here we screened brain regions by calculating graph theory parameters of each brain region and using the fisher-score feature selection method. By calculating the Pearson correlation coefficient between two regions, for 94 brain regions, 94*94 size of correlation matrix is calculated of each sample, which means the brain functional network of each subject are constructed. In order to remove weak connection, only those values on top 20% are kept [9]. In total 6 graph theory parameters were calculated in this study. All the parameters are calculated by BCT toolkit on MATLAB platform. For each parameter, we got a discrimination parameter for each region and selected the first 20 regions and then removed those repeated. Finally, 59 regions were considered significant.

$$F_j = \frac{\sum_{i=1}^{c} P(c_i) \cdot (\mu_{j,c_i} - \mu_j)^2}{\sum_{i=1}^{c} P(c_i) \cdot \sigma_{j,c_i}^2} \tag{1}$$

where F_j represents the fisher score. $P(\cdot)$ is the prior probability, μ_{j,c_i} is the average of feature X_j in the class C_i. μ_j is the average of feature X_j of all samples. σ_{j,c_i}^2 is the variance of feature X_j in the class C_i (Table 2).

Table 2. Graph theory parameters

Parameter	Formula	Note
Degree Centrality	$\deg(i) = \sum_{j=1}^{n} A_{ij}$	A_{ij}: Indicate whether node i and node j are connected
Betweenness Centrality	$C_B(i) = \sum_{s \neq i \neq t} \frac{\sigma_{st}(i)}{\sigma_{st}}$	σ_{st}: Number of shortest paths from node s to node t. $\sigma_{st}(i)$: Number of shortest paths through node i
Eigenvector Centrality	$C_E(i) = \frac{1}{\lambda} \sum_{j=1}^{n} A_{ij} C_E(j)$	λ: the maximum eigenvalue. $C_E(j)$: Eigenvector centrality of node j
Local Efficiency	$E_i = \frac{1}{k_i(k_i-1)} \sum_{j,j' \in N_i} \frac{1}{d(j,j')}$	$d(j,j')$: Shortest distance
PageRank Centrality	$C_{PR}(i) = \frac{1-d}{n} + d \sum_{j \in \mathrm{In}(i)} \frac{C_{PR}(j)}{\deg(j)}$	$\mathrm{In}(i)$: Set of all nodes pointing to node i. d: Damping factor
K-Core Centrality	The K-core value of a node i is the K value of the largest K-core of the node.	K-core: A subgraph in a graph where each node is connected to at least K nodes

3.3 Mixup Augmentation

A sample set that is too small will result in insufficient model training and the model will not be able to learn general classification knowledge. However, traditional data augmentation may not suitable for rs-fMRI data due to the similarity between different timepoints in the same subject, therefore data enhancement methods such as data noise addition and sliding window data extraction are not applicable. Those applied in images tasks are unable either because medical images or signals usually have clear anatomical structures, which are crucial for disease diagnosis. Improper enhancement operations may lead to the loss or distortion of this information (Fig. 2).

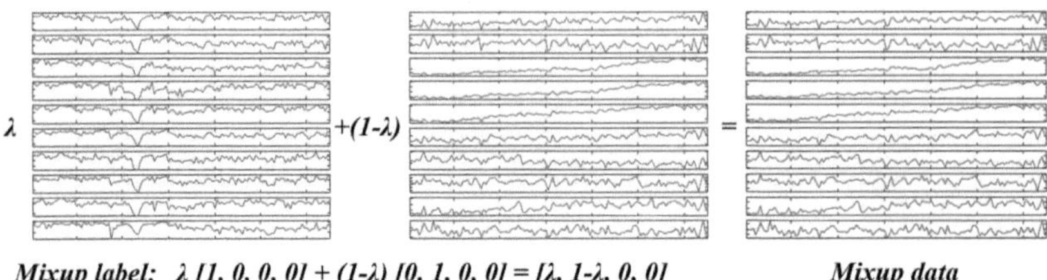

Fig. 2. ROI Signals Mixup. (Only shows the first 10 ROIs signals as example)

Mixup is a data augmentation method that aims to improve the generalization ability of the model by creating synthetic samples in the training data. Specifically, Mixup generates new samples by linearly interpolating the features and labels of two input samples. This process not only increases the diversity of the dataset, but also improves the robustness of the model by smoothing the decision boundary [14].

$$\begin{aligned} x_{\text{mix}} &= \lambda x_i + (1-\lambda)x_j \\ y_{\text{mix}} &= \lambda y_i + (1-\lambda)y_j \end{aligned} \tag{2}$$

where λ is generated by Beta distribution.

$$\lambda \sim \text{Beta}(\alpha, \alpha) \tag{3}$$

In this study, we applied the Mixup method twice. Once, after data preprocessing, the training set was expanded three times the original data set. The other time was combined with the method during training iterations, and the model training samples were expanded using this method for each batch of data. The advantage of this is that the training data can be expanded comprehensively and multiple times, eliminating the uncertainty caused by random data combination. A second Mixup can also be performed on the basis of the expanded data set to further fuse and produce smoother samples. At the same time, there is no need to store the expanded massive data in advance, because it is discarded after each iteration, saving memory space. One should be noted that the label should be transformed into one-hot format (Fig. 3).

3.4 Dual-Branch Network

Convolutional Neural Networks (CNN) is a deep learning model that is particularly good at processing data with grid structures, such as images, videos, and

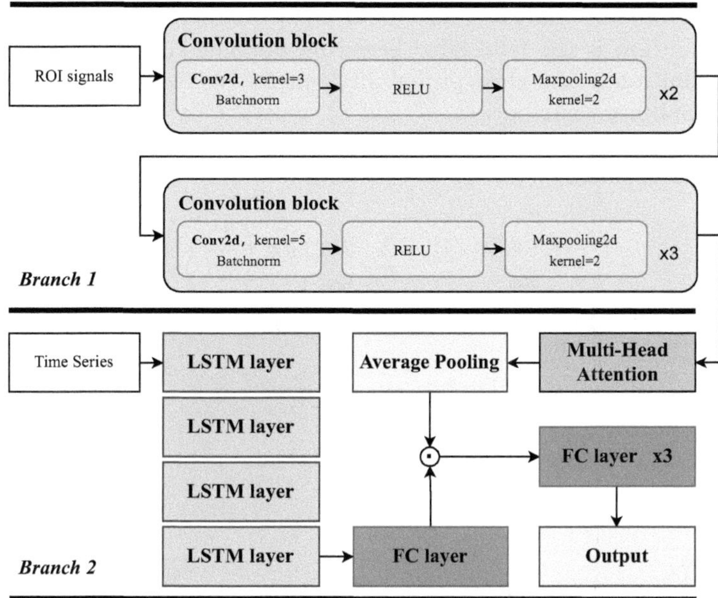

Fig. 3. Dual-Branch Network Architecture.

time series. CNN automatically extracts local features through convolutional layers, and gradually refines higher-level feature information through a multi-level structure. In the convolutional layer, the filter (convolution kernel) is convolved with the input data to extract features of different scales and levels. The pooling layer is used to reduce the spatial dimension of the feature map, reduce computational complexity, and prevent overfitting. Here, we use its characteristics to extract the spatial features of the brain area.

Long Short-Term Memory (LSTM) [8] is a special type of recurrent neural network (RNN) that can effectively process and predict time series data. LSTM controls the flow of information by introducing forget gates, input gates, and output gates, overcoming the gradient vanishing problem that traditional RNNs are prone to when processing long sequence data. LSTM can learn long-term dependencies and is very effective in modeling sequence data. Since rs-fMRI data has time dependency, we use the characteristics of LSTM to extract time series features here.

Each convolutional layer output is followed by batchnormalization and activated by Relu function. The first two fullyconnect layers are applied dropout layer for avoiding overfitting. Kullback-Leibler Divergence Loss (KLDivLoss) is a loss function based on Kullback-Leibler divergence (KL divergence), which is usually used to measure the difference between two probability distributions. In machine learning, KLDivLoss is often used for classification tasks, especially in multi-category classification, where the loss function is used to evaluate the difference between the probability distribution (predicted distribution) output by the model and the true label distribution (target distribution). Typically, the target distribution is the true label based on one-hot encoding, while the predicted distribution is the class probability output by the model. Assume there are two probability distributions P and Q, where P is the target distribution (usually the distribution of labels) and Q is the distribution of model outputs. KL divergence formula:

$$D_{\mathrm{KL}}(P \parallel Q) = \sum_i P(i) \log \left(\frac{P(i)}{Q(i)} \right) \tag{4}$$

In practical applications, KLDivLoss usually calculates the loss in the following way:

$$\mathrm{KLDivLoss} = -\sum_i p_i \log(q_i) \tag{5}$$

Based on Mixup augmentation, the model training applies Kullback-Leibler Divergence Loss as loss function.

4 Results

This experiment was conducted based on the NVIDIA GeForce RTX 3060 Laptop GPU. In this study, we randomly selected 16 subjects from each category as test set. Therefore, for the 4 classes classification 64 items were selected in total. The model was trained using 96 samples as every mini-batch size, with a total of 35 epochs in the training. And a strategy of adjusting the learning rate in stages was adopted. After completing two-thirds of the epochs, reduce the learning rate to the original 0.2 to prevent the model from failing to converge as the training progressed and continuing to oscillate near the optimal point, while also preventing the model from overfitting. The initial learning rate was set as 0.001. In each iteration of model training, the Mixup method is applied to augment the data again, generating fused data with the hyperparameter α equal to 0.4. Here we use comprehensive evaluation parameters, as follows:

$$\begin{aligned}
\mathrm{Accuracy} &= \frac{TP + TN}{TP + TN + FP + FN} \\
\mathrm{Recall} &= \frac{TP}{TP + FN} \\
\mathrm{Specificity} &= \frac{TN}{TN + FP} \\
\mathrm{Precision} &= \frac{TP}{TP + FP} \\
\mathrm{F1\ Score} &= 2 * \frac{\mathrm{Precision} * \mathrm{Recall}}{\mathrm{Precision} + \mathrm{Recall}} \\
\mathrm{AUC} &= \text{area under the ROC curve}
\end{aligned}$$

Table 3. Classification Results of Dual-Branch Model

	Rec	Spe	Pre	F1-score	AUC
AD	0.9375	0.8163	1.0	0.9677	0.99
CN	0.875	0.820	0.7778	0.8235	0.96
EMCI	0.8125	0.8235	0.8667	0.8387	0.87
LMCI	0.8125	0.8235	0.8125	0.8125	0.94
Average	0.8593	0.8208	0.8642	0.8606	0.94

For the test set, the accuracy we got equaled 85.94%. Other evaluation indicators are shown on the Table 3. The table indicates that for AD identification, the model got comprehensively good result, which is significant in clinical diagnosis.

In order to evaluate the effectiveness of this model and data processing, we also conducted simple ablation experiments to verify the advantages of the dual-branch network over the single-branch network, as well as the benefits of data augmentation and brain region selection. We performed four ablation schemes to verify the advantages of our method, including verification of the single-branch model under the same conditions, verification of data without data augmentation and brain region selection. Due to the high dimensionality of the data without brain region selection. Here, the number of training iterations was increased to 45 for verification. The graph shows the advantage of dual-branch network

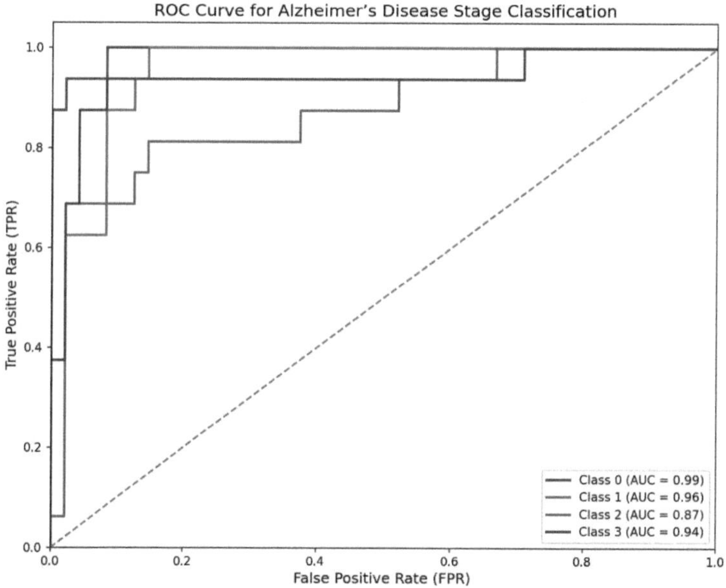

Fig. 4. ROC Curve for Alzheimer's Disease Stage Classification.

and significant improvement developed by Mixup data augmentation and brain regions selection (Figs. 4 and 5).

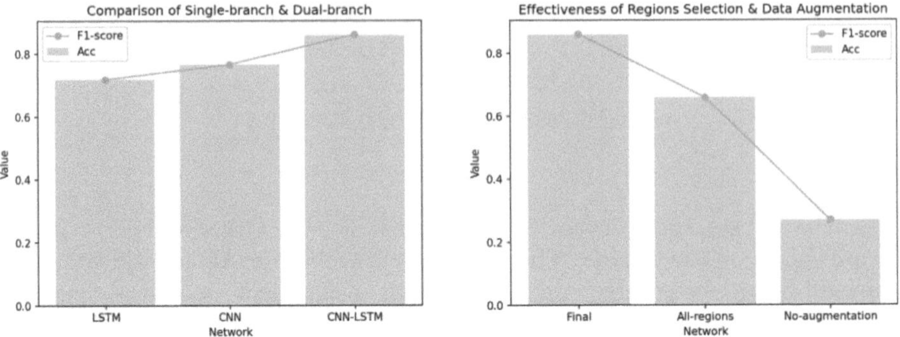

Fig. 5. Ablation Experiments. The left shows the improvement from dual-branch. The right shows the improvement from regions selection and data augmentation.

5 Discussion

According to the verification results in the previous chapter, we can find the positive effects of using a dual-branch network, brain region screening, and data enhancement. Compared with a single-branch network, a dual-branch network integrates different information in the data (time series information and spatial information). Since medical data has always been scarce and there are also some complex reasons that make it difficult to open source, data enhancement technology is also very useful. Here, with the help of the Mixup method, we have achieved a significant improvement in classification accuracy. In order to reduce the redundant effects of some irrelevant brain regions, we also performed a simple brain region screening, and the results show that this is also helpful to the results.

Most Alzheimer's disease research using fMRI data is based on the ADNI dataset. This significantly limits the field's development. Indeed, in reality, the cost and difficulty of acquiring fMRI data are far greater than for other common data. In this study, we introduced the Mixup data augmentation technique, originally designed for image classification, but experiments have shown that it also demonstrates excellent performance on fMRI data. This allows us to achieve performance comparable to that of complex models, even without performing complex feature computation on raw fMRI data. By simply selecting brain regions and using a simple network model, we can achieve performance comparable to that of complex models.

Although our model has achieved good results, there is still room for improvement. First, we did not select brain regions very strictly, and may have missed brain regions that are not significant on the surface but are very important for the diagnosis of Alzheimer's disease. Second, the Mixup method has some improved versions, such as Mixup combined with Transformer, which are the latest improvements worth trying. This is also our future in-depth research direction.

References

1. An, X., Zhou, Y., Di, Y., Han, Y., Ming, D.: A novel method to identify mild cognitive impairment using dynamic spatio-temporal graph neural network. IEEE Trans. Neural Syst. Rehabil. Eng. (2024)
2. Dennis, E.L., Thompson, P.M.: Functional brain connectivity using fMRI in aging and Alzheimer's disease **24**(1), 49–62. https://doi.org/10.1007/s11065-014-9249-6
3. Esteban, O., et al.: fMRIPrep: a robust preprocessing pipeline for functional MRI **16**(1), 111–116. https://doi.org/10.1038/s41592-018-0235-4
4. Fox, M.D., Raichle, M.E.: Spontaneous fluctuations in brain activity observed with functional magnetic resonance imaging. Nat. Rev. Neurosci. **8**(9), 700–711 (2007)
5. Guo, H., Zhang, Y.: Resting state fMRI and improved deep learning algorithm for earlier detection of Alzheimer's disease. IEEE Access **8**, 115383–115392 (2020)
6. Guo, H., Zhang, F., Chen, J., Xu, Y., Xiang, J.: Machine learning classification combining multiple features of a hyper-network of fMRI data in Alzheimer's disease. Front. Neurosci. **11**, 615 (2017)
7. Helaly, H.A., Badawy, M., Haikal, A.Y.: Deep learning approach for early detection of Alzheimer's disease. Cogn. Comput. **14**(5), 1711–1727 (2022)
8. Hochreiter, S., Schmidhuber, J.: Long short-term memory. Neural Comput. **9**(8), 1735–1780 (1997)
9. Khazaee, A., Ebrahimzadeh, A., Babajani-Feremi, A.: Identifying patients with Alzheimer's disease using resting-state fMRI and graph theory. Clin. Neurophysiol. **126**(11), 2132–2141 (2015)
10. Prince, M., Bryce, R., Albanese, E., Wimo, A., Ribeiro, W., Ferri, C.P.: The global prevalence of dementia: a systematic review and metaanalysis. Alzheimer's Dementia **9**(1), 63–75.e2 (2013). https://doi.org/10.1016/j.jalz.2012.11.007, https://www.sciencedirect.com/science/article/pii/S1552526012025319
11. Sun, H., Wang, A., He, S.: Temporal and spatial analysis of Alzheimer's disease based on an improved convolutional neural network and a resting-state fMRI brain functional network. Int. J. Environ. Res. Public Health **19**(8), 4508 (2022)
12. Sun, J., Han, J.D.J., Chen, W.: Exploring the relationship among Alzheimer's disease, aging and cognitive scores through neuroimaging-based approach. Sci. Rep. **14**(1), 27472 (2024)
13. Wierenga, C.E., Bondi, M.W.: Use of functional magnetic resonance imaging in the early identification of Alzheimer's disease. Neuropsychol. Rev. **17**, 127–143 (2007)
14. Zhang, H., Cisse, M., Dauphin, Y.N., Lopez-Paz, D.: mixup: beyond empirical risk minimization. arXiv preprint: arXiv:1710.09412 (2017)
15. Zhang, Y., Jiang, J., Ling, R., Wang, L., Jiang, J., Wang, M.: Early diagnosis and biomarkers of Alzheimer's disease based on spatio-temporal graph convolution network. In: 2023 45th Annual International Conference of the IEEE Engineering in Medicine & Biology Society (EMBC), pp. 1–4. IEEE (2023)

Exploring Identifiable Tokens for Text-Based Person Re-identification

Shuai Yan[1], Wentao Ma[2], Xiaoqian Wu[2], Pengfei Yuan[1], Feng Li[1], and Shan Zhao[1](✉)

[1] Hefei University of Technology, Hefei, China
{2023110523,yuanpengfei}@mail.hfut.edu.cn, {fengli,zhaoshan}@hfut.edu.cn
[2] Anhui Agricultural University, Hefei, China
wtma@ahau.edu.cn, xiaoqian@stu.ahau.edu.cn

Abstract. Text-based person re-identification aims to retrieve the matched persons' images given a textual query. Recently, the literature has widely-adopted the powerful CLIP to extract fine-grained visual/textual features for cross-modal alignment. Yet, they generally overlook the *seemingly similar characteristics* in person re-identification, namely, the visuals and descriptions of two persons may share many intersections (e.g., grey jacket, walking), potentially leading to false matches. This work presents a novel framework by carefully elaborating on the identifiable CLIP tokens for the explicit attention of matching. The token informativeness of local features is measured by the visual/textual entropy related to person clothing, posture, hairstyle, etc. Additionally, a triplet ranking loss function is incorporated to expand both intra-modal and inter-modal distances among different persons/descriptions. Experimental results on three datasets demonstrate the superiority of our proposal against prior baselines.

Keywords: Text-based person re-identification · Cross-modal retrieval

1 Introduction

Text-based person Re-identification (ReID) [14] is a fundamental and long-standing cross-modal retrieval task, which aims to retrieve the best matching personal image based on a given textual query. Since the potential applications in searching for suspects, locating lost children, etc., this technique is steadily garnering widespread attention in both academia and industry. Although various methods drive developments of this technique, yet, real-world practices of text-based person ReID are hindered by the semantic gap between text and image.

To cope with the semantic gap, existing methods for text-based person ReID roughly fall into three categories: 1) ***coarse-grained paradigm***, most

Supplementary Information The online version contains supplementary material available at https://doi.org/10.1007/978-981-95-5764-6_30.

© The Author(s), under exclusive license to Springer Nature Singapore Pte Ltd. 2026
J. Kittler et al. (Eds.): PRCV 2025, LNCS 16289, pp. 438–452, 2026.
https://doi.org/10.1007/978-981-95-5764-6_30

methods [14,23,36,40] separately extract image and text global features by the visual/textual pre-training backbone, then align them via a tailored matching loss in a joint embedding common space. Although this paradigm successfully captures global cross-modal correspondence, it fails to adequately mine fine-grained local features (e.g., pedestrian appearance and clothing); 2) ***fine-grained paradigm***, enables fine-grained cross-modal alignment by matching words with image patches [25,34,35]. However, this paradigm incurs additional inference time during computations across different modalities; 3) ***vision-language pre-training (VLP) paradigm***, has demonstrated remarkable performance on various cross-modal retrieval tasks. Among VLP methods [7,27,33,34], CLIP [22] stands out as one of the most prominent representatives, also demonstrating impressive results on text-based person ReID tasks.

Although CLIP-based methods have facilitated the development of text-based person ReID technique, the following challenges remain:

1. **Exploration of Identifiable Tokens.** Redundant token informativeness present in the visuals and descriptions of two persons may share many intersections (e.g., grey jacket, walking), potentially leading to false matches, while also affecting the efficiency of the model. Focusing on these overlapping tokens of information does not help us distinguish between different individuals. Thus, determining how to refinedly select identifiable tokens poses a challenge for the text-based ReID coupled with CLIP.
2. **Ignoring Intra-modal Sample Differences.** As semantic concepts in personal images are complex and diverse, it commonly exists in text-based person ReID benchmarks [5,14,42] that multiple text sentences can describe the same pedestrian from different views. Therefore, the multi-view text representations bring a challenge to only considering inter-modal distance: *semantic boundaries between texts to describe different personal images are potentially ambiguous.*

To tackle those tricky challenges, we propose a **CLIP** with identifiable **T**oken **C**onsistency model, called **CLIP-TC**, for text-based person ReID. Specifically, we design a token selection mechanism to refine tokens, focusing on those that contribute the most to local semantics, which involves estimating the importance of each token and realizing the purification of identifiable tokens (for Challenge 1). To regularize the joint embedding common space, we propose a token consistency matching, considering the inter- and intra-modal distance to align samples for visual/textual similarity and visual-textual correlation (for Challenge 2). Our contributions can be summarised as follows:

- We propose a CLIP-based token selection mechanism incorporating a scorer network to estimate the weight of all local tokens, which enhances pedestrian retrieval by optimizing the utilization of local informative features without introducing redundancy.
- To exploit distinctions in inter-/intra-modal samples, we propose a multi-modal token consistency matching loss, concurrently constraining both inter-

and intra-modal semantic distances, effectively enlarging differences among different persons/descriptions.
- On three public benchmarks of text-based person ReID, we evaluate CLIP-TC by comparison with state-of-the-art (SoTA) methods and a series of ablation studies, and the results demonstrate that our proposal can achieve leading performance.

2 Related Work

2.1 Text-Based Person ReID

Text-based person ReID is a cross-modal retrieval task that aims to identify a target person based on a given textual query. Li *et al.*.[14] first introduced text-based person ReID and established the benchmark dataset CUHK-PEDES. Subsequently, other large-scale datasets such as ICFG-PEDES[5] and RSTPReid [42] were proposed, driving the development of various methods to tackle this challenging task.

In the coarse-grained paradigm, many existing methods utilize ResNet-50 or ViT as the image encoder and LSTM or BERT as the text encoder. Several works [2,26,36] focus on improving feature extraction models and designing cross-modal matching losses to align global features across modalities. In contrast, the fine-grained paradigm emphasizes the exploitation and alignment of local features. Most approaches [5,14,20,29,31] employ techniques such as patch-word matching, body part division, and color-related information extraction to achieve this goal. Recently, the introduction of the VLP paradigm by Han *et al.*.[7], leveraging CLIP for text-based person ReID, has gained significant attention due to its powerful cross-modal alignment capabilities.

2.2 Vision-Language Pre-training

Vision-Language Pretraining (VLP) models are designed to enhance the joint understanding of images and natural language by leveraging large-scale visual and textual datasets for pretraining. In several single-stream approaches [12, 18,41], paired image-text inputs are processed together in a transformer network, where both modalities share the same parameters. Conversely, dual-stream methods [11,19,38] encode text and visual sequences independently, followed by a cross-encoder to integrate features from both modalities. Building on the success of CLIP, subsequent works have aimed to fully exploit its potential by bridging the modality gap between images and texts, facilitating more robust and comprehensive understanding in text-based person ReID.

Although current VLP methods like CLIP have made great strides in cross-modal tasks, they still exhibit certain limitations. First, many methods [9,11,12,18,19,37,41] are unable to distinguish between similar features in visual and textual modalities, which can result in incorrect matches. Second, these approaches often ignore intra-modal differences within the same modality,

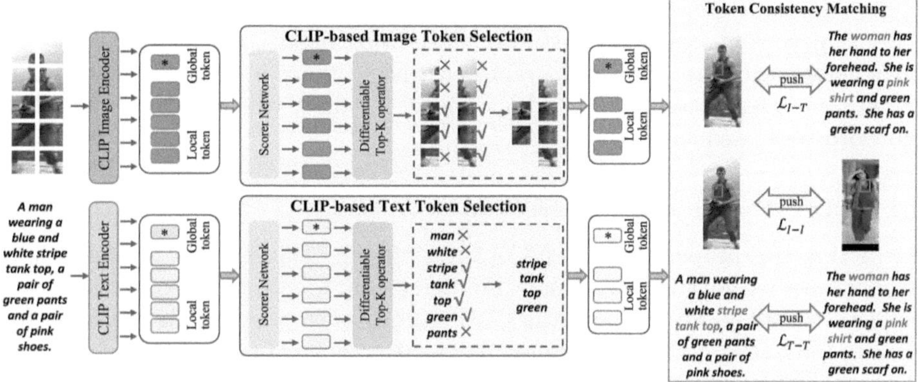

Fig. 1. Overview of our CLIP-TC model. It consists of three parts: visual-textual feature encoding, CLIP-based token selection and token consistency matching. Given image-text pairs, we first extract features by image and text encoders, then the CLIP-based token selection with a scorer network is used to select the Top-K key tokens. Finally, the tokens are sent to token consistency matching, bridging the semantic gap between text and image.

which affects the model's ability to distinguish between similar descriptions. To address these challenges, CLIP-TC introduces a refined token selection mechanism that maximizes the use of meaningful local features, minimizing interference from redundant information. Additionally, CLIP-TC improves inter-modal and intra-modal alignment by integrating a token consistency matching loss, significantly improving matching accuracy.

3 Method

3.1 Overview

As illustrated in Fig. 1, the overall structure consists of three key components: visual-textual feature encoding, CLIP-based token selection and token consistency matching.

Visual Feature Encoding. We use CLIP pre-trained ViT model as the image encoder. Specifically, given an image $I \in \mathbb{R}^{H \times W \times C}$, ViT first splits I into n non-overlapping image patches, then performs a linear projection to project them into 1D tokens $\{v_i\}|_{i=1}^{n}$. After adding a special [CLS] token to the sequence, the resulting token sequence is passed through a stack of transformer blocks to capture the interactions between tokens. This process generates the image-level global feature v_{cls} as well as the patch-level local features $\{v_1, v_2, \ldots, v_n\}$.

Textual Feature Encoding. We directly apply the CLIP text encoder to extract the text representation. That is, given a text query T, we first use byte pair encoding with a vocabulary size of 49152 to tokenize the text. By adding special tokens [SOS] and [EOS] at the start and end of query word sequence, the tokenized text sequence is fed into transformer blocks to capture the correlations between tokens. We let t_{eos} represent the sentence-level global feature and $\{t_1, t_2, \ldots, t_m\}$ represent the word-level local features, where m is the length of the word token sequence.

3.2 CLIP-Based Token Selection

Extracting the proper tokens and optimizing the utilization of local informative features without introducing redundancy help to accomplish the text-based person ReID task. We propose the CLIP-based token selection mechanism that aims to fully exploit the fine-grained information describing the appearance and clothing of pedestrians in images and texts, distinguishing between different pedestrians.

Scorer Network. The scorer network aims to generate importance scores for each token. We directly obtain global features from the [CLS] token. Therefore, when scoring, although we treat global and local tokens equally, we only select the required tokens from the local ones. Considering that the local features of different images may appear identical, relying solely on the highly scored local feature matching methods is insufficient to select local features that can effectively distinguish different identities. We attempt to leverage global information to enhance the distinctions between different local features. Specifically, given a sequence of image tokens $I = \{v_{cls}, v_1, v_2, \ldots, v_n\} \in \mathbb{R}^{(N+1)\times C}$, we first apply a fully connected network over I for dimension reduction to elaborate on the core features and reduce computation by the way, and output $I' = \{v'_{cls}, v'_1, v'_2, \ldots, v'_n\} \in \mathbb{R}^{(N+1)\times \frac{C}{2}}$. To leverage jointly global and local, we then concatenate v'_{cls} with each local token v'_i along the feature dimension C, and feed all the concatenated token features $\hat{v}$ to another fully connected network to generate the importance scores, which can be formulated as:

$$S_v = Softmax(\hat{v}) \in \mathbb{R}^{(N+1)}. \tag{1}$$

The score matrix S_v predicts a relevance score for each image token and formulates token selection as a ranking problem. Similarly to the image score matrix S_v, we calculate the text score matrix S_t using the same selection mechanism.

Information-Theoretic Token Selection. The scorer network aligns with the information bottleneck principle, aiming to select tokens that maximize mutual information with the global representation v_{cls}, while reducing redundancy among the original token set $\{v_i\}$. Formally, the token importance is quantified by mutual information value:

$$\text{InfoValue}(v_i) = I(v_i; v_{cls}) - \frac{1}{|Z|} \sum_{v_j \in Z} I(v_i; v_j), \tag{2}$$

where the first term $I(v_i; v_{cls})$ measures task relevance, quantifying how much information the local token v_i shares with the global feature v_{cls}, representing each token's unique contribution to the identification task. A higher value means that the token is carrying more valuable information. The second term $\frac{1}{|Z|}\sum_{v_j \in Z} I(v_i; v_j)$ penalizes redundancy, quantifying the average mutual information between the token v_i and the previously chosen tokens in set Z. A higher redundancy term implies that the token's information is covered by other tokens, thus decreasing its value and uniqueness. Practically, our scorer network embodies this principle by concatenating global and local token features, enabling it to effectively evaluate each token's marginal information contribution. The subsequent *Softmax* normalization highlights tokens that provide unique discriminative information essential for identification.

Differentiable Top-K Operator. Based on the image score matrix $S_v \in \mathbb{R}^{(N+1)}$ and the text score matrix $S_t \in \mathbb{R}^{(M+1)}$ extracted from the scorer network, we select the indices of the K_v highest image scores and the K_t highest text scores to identify the most salient tokens for person re-identification. Specifically, S_v contains importance scores for each image token, including the [CLS] token and N local patch tokens, while S_t contains importance scores for each text token, including the [EOS] token and M word tokens. These scores formulate token selection as a ranking problem, aiming to retain tokens that maximize discriminative information while minimizing redundancy, as outlined in the preceding section.

The selection process is defined as follows:

$$K_v = \text{Top-K}(S_v) \in \mathbb{R}^{(K_v)}, \tag{3}$$

$$K_t = \text{Top-K}(S_t) \in \mathbb{R}^{(K_t)}, \tag{4}$$

where K_v denotes the set of indices corresponding to the K_v highest scores in S_v, and K_t denotes the set of indices corresponding to the K_t highest scores in S_t. These indices identify the most informative image and text tokens, respectively, for downstream matching tasks.

To maintain positional consistency in outputs, the Top-K indices are aligned with the original input sequence order. Subsequently, the indices K_v are encoded as one-hot matrices $M_v \in \{0,1\}^{(N+1)\times K_v}$, enabling the extraction of batched tokens through matrix operations. The selected image tokens are obtained through:

$$I_{K_v} = M_v^T I \in \mathbb{R}^{K_v \times C}, \tag{5}$$

and text tokens via analogous operation:

$$T_{K_t} = M_t^T T \in \mathbb{R}^{K_t \times C}, \tag{6}$$

where each of M_v and M_t acts as a binary mask to aggregate tokens from the original sequence.

To enable end-to-end training with scorer network, we adopt a differentiable Top-K operator based on perturbed maximum methods [1], bypassing the non-differentiability of standard Top-K and one-hot operations. This approach can be equivalent to solve the optimal value of:

$$\arg\max_{M_v \in \mathcal{C}_v} \langle M_v, {S_v}^T \rangle, \arg\max_{M_t \in \mathcal{C}_t} \langle M_t, {S_t}^T \rangle, \tag{7}$$

where $\mathcal{C}_v$, $\mathcal{C}_t$ denote convex polytope constrains for image/text tokens.

The selected K_v image tokens and K_t text tokens are obtain through:

$$F(K_v) = \max_{M_v \in \mathcal{C}_v} \langle M_v, S_v^T \rangle, \tag{8}$$

$$F(K_t) = \max_{M_t \in \mathcal{C}_t} \langle M_t, S_t^T \rangle. \tag{9}$$

Following [4], we compute forward passes through perturbed optimizers and backward passes through implicit differentiation, ensuring gradient flow across the CLIP-based token selection module.

3.3 Token Consistency Matching

Similarity Calculation. Given image-level global feature v_{cls} and sentence-level global feature t_{eos}, we compute the global cross-modal similarity as follows:

$$S(v_{cls}, t_{eos}) = \frac{v_{cls}^T \times t_{eos}}{||v_{cls}|| \times ||t_{eos}||}. \tag{10}$$

Let $\{v_1, v_2, \ldots, v_{K_v}\}$ be the patch-level local features and $\{t_1, t_2, \ldots, t_{K_t}\}$ be the word-level local features selected in the previous section. We calculate the local similarity by aligning local features between the two samples:

$$S(v_i, t_j) = \frac{v_i^T \times t_j}{||v_i|| \times ||t_j||}. \tag{11}$$

Inter-modal Constraint Loss Function. Given an image-text pair (I, T), where I and T denote image candidate and text query, respectively. We calculate the triplet ranking loss [10] as follows:

$$\begin{aligned} \mathcal{L}_{I-T} = &\max(0, \delta - S(I,T) + S(I,T^-)) \\ &+ \max(0, \delta - S(I,T) + S(I^-,T)), \end{aligned} \tag{12}$$

where $S(\cdot)$ is the cross-modal similarity, and δ is a margin parameter to force the similarity in a positive pair (I, T) to be greater than that in negative pairs (I, T^-) and (I^-, T).

We find that using the triplet ranking loss alone is insufficient to constrain samples of the same modality for text-based person ReID. Therefore, we consider intra-modal sample differences by constraining both image-image pairs and text-text pairs of the same modality.

Visual Branch Constraint Loss Function. Similar to the triplet ranking loss, we first seek to construct a positive pair (I, I^+) and a negative pair (I, I^-) for each image I, where the positive pair represents the same person with the same ID, and the negative pair represents different individuals with different IDs. Given an image I as the anchor, we make other images in the same batch as the hard negative image I^-, and we encode the image I twice with random dropout according to [16] to get the positive image I^+. We define the visual branch constraint loss function as:

$$\mathcal{L}_{I-I} = \max(0, \delta_v - S(I, I^+) + S(I, I^-)), \quad (13)$$

where δ_v is margin parameter, which guarantees a gap between different images.

Text Branch Constraint Loss Function. We also construct a positive pair (T, T^+) and a negative pair (T, T^-) similar to the visual branch. Then, we define the text branch constraints loss function as:

$$\mathcal{L}_{T-T} = \max(0, \delta_t - S(T, T^+) + S(T, T^-)), \quad (14)$$

where δ_t is margin parameter, which guarantees a gap between different texts. We set δ_v equal to δ_t to constrain the gap and regularize the representations between the similarity distance of two images and the similarity distance of their corresponding texts. To ensure that the distance between an image and its corresponding text is smaller than the distance between images with similar semantics, we empirically set δ_v and δ_t greater than δ.

In summary, the final loss function can be directly calculated from all the above loss:

$$\mathcal{L} = \mathcal{L}_{I-T} + \mathcal{L}_{I-I} + \mathcal{L}_{T-T}. \quad (15)$$

4 Experiments

4.1 Datasets

To demonstrate the effectiveness of our proposal, we evaluate it on three text-based person ReID benchmarks, including CUHK-PEDES [14], ICFG-PEDES [5], RSTPReid [42].

- **CUHK-PEDES** [14] consists of a total of 40206 images and 80412 text descriptions from 13003 identities. Following the official experimental guidelines, the dataset is divided into a training set with 34054 images and 68126 text descriptions from 11003 identities, a validation set containing 3078 images and their corresponding captions from 1000 identities, and a test set with 3074 images and 6156 text descriptions.
- **ICFG-PEDES** [5] includes 54522 images from 4102 identities, with one textual description provided per image. According to the standard classification protocol, the dataset is split into a training set with 34674 images from 3102 identities and a test set with 19848 images from 1000 identities.
- **RSTPReid** [42] contains 4101 identities and 20505 images captured from multiple cameras, with each image annotated with two manually generated textual descriptions. The dataset is divided into a training set with 3701 identities, a validation set with 200 identities, and a test set with another 200 identities.

4.2 Evaluation Metrics

We measure the retrieval performance using the Recall at p (R@p, p=1, 5, and 10) metric, which is widely used in cross-modal person ReID tasks. R@p calculates the fraction of correct images among the top p retrieved images and higher is better. We also use the mean Average Precision (mAP) to reflect the mean rank of correct results in the retrieval ranking list.

Table 1. Comparison with other methods on CUHK-PEDES.

	Method	R@1	R@5	R@10	mAP
w/o VLP	GNA-RNN [14]	19.05	–	53.64	–
	Dual Path [40]	44.40	66.26	75.07	–
	CMPM/C [36]	49.37	71.69	79.27	–
	ViTAA [30]	55.97	75.84	83.52	–
	HGAN [39]	59.00	79.49	86.62	–
	SRCF [28]	64.04	82.99	88.81	–
	LBUL [32]	64.04	82.66	87.22	–
	SAF [13]	64.13	82.62	88.40	58.61
	TIPCB [3]	64.26	83.19	89.10	–
	CAIBC [31]	64.43	82.87	88.37	–
	C_2A_2 [21]	64.82	83.54	89.77	–
	LGUR [25]	65.25	83.12	89.00	–
	MGCN [6]	69.40	87.07	90.82	62.49
w/ VLP	PSLD [7]	64.08	81.73	88.19	60.08
	IVT [26]	65.59	83.11	89.21	–
	CFine [34]	69.57	85.93	91.15	–
	UniPT [24]	68.50	84.67	90.38	–
	EAIBC [43]	64.96	83.36	88.42	–
	CSKT [17]	69.70	86.92	91.80	62.74
	Our CLIP-TC	**72.17**	**88.37**	**92.84**	**64.11**

4.3 Implementation Details

All our experiments are conducted on a single NVIDIA Tesla A800 GPU. We initialize the image encoder and the text encoder with CLIP pre-trained weights from ViT-B/16. The dimensions of text embedding and image embedding are 512. All person images are resized to 256 $\times$ 128 and the max query text length is set to 77. The ADAM optimizer is used to optimize the entire model. We choose batch size and epoch of 128 and 60, respectively. The margin parameters in the loss function are set as δ=0.2, δ_v=0.3, δ_t=0.3 empirically.

Table 2. Comparison with other methods on ICFG-PEDES and RSTPReid.

	Method	ICFG-PEDES				RSTPReid			
		R@1	R@5	R@10	mAP	R@1	R@5	R@10	mAP
w/o VLP	Dual Path [40]	38.99	59.44	68.41	–	–	–	–	–
	CMPM/C [36]	43.51	65.44	74.26	–	–	–	–	–
	SSAN [5]	54.23	72.63	79.53	–	43.50	67.80	77.15	–
	SAF [13]	54.86	72.13	79.13	32.76	44.05	67.30	76.25	36.81
	TIPCB [3]	54.96	74.72	81.89	–	–	–	–	–
	SRCF [28]	57.18	75.01	81.49	–	–	–	–	–
	LGUR [25]	59.02	75.32	81.56	–	47.95	71.85	80.25	–
	ACSA [8]	–	–	–	–	48.40	71.85	81.45	–
	C_2A_2 [21]	–	–	–	–	51.55	76.75	85.15	–
	MGCN [6]	60.20	76.75	83.90	**37.56**	52.95	75.30	84.04	41.74
w/ VLP	IVT [26]	56.04	73.60	80.22	–	46.70	70.00	78.80	–
	CFine [34]	60.83	76.55	82.42	–	50.55	72.50	81.60	–
	UniPT [24]	60.09	76.19	82.46	–	51.85	74.85	82.85	–
	CSKT [17]	58.90	77.31	83.56	33.87	–	–	–	–
	EAIBC [43]	58.95	75.95	81.72	–	49.85	70.15	79.85	–
	PD [15]	60.93	77.96	84.11	36.44	56.65	77.40	84.70	45.27
	Our CLIP-TC	**62.15**	**78.96**	**84.74**	35.22	**59.20**	**80.40**	**87.30**	**45.54**

4.4 Comparisons with SoTA Methods

In this section, we compare our CLIP-TC with SoTA methods on three public benchmark datasets. We first evaluate the performance of our method on the most widely-used CUHK-PEDES, and Table 1 shows the retrieval results. Our CLIP-TC achieves 72.17%, 88.37%, 92.84%, and 64.11% of R@1, R@5, R@10, and mAP, which are comparable to previous models on all evaluation metrics. Although our CLIP-TC performs worse than recent SoTA methods on mAP, the improvements on R@1, R@5, and R@10 are particularly noticeable, which benefit from the CLIP-based token selection mechanism and token consistency matching.

Table 2 present the retrieval results on ICFG-PEDES and RSTPReid. Our model obtains better performance than other methods, which demonstrates that it is beneficial to select informative tokens and constraint the inter- and intra-modal distance. Compared with existing methods, our CLIP-TC can achieve considerable performance, with R@1 accuracy of 62.15% and 59.20% on ICFG-PEDES and RSTPReid, respectively. Specifically, CLIP-TC can achieve better performance on R@5 and R@10, with a significantly increase of 3.0% and 2.6% on RSTPReid, showcasing its ability to accurately identify more correct person images within a specified number of retrievals. Results on these datasets demonstrate the generalization of the proposed CLIP-TC.

Table 3. Ablation study on each component of CLIP-TC on CUHK-PEDES.

No.	Method	TTS	ITS	$\mathcal{L}_{I\text{-}T}$	$\mathcal{L}_{I\text{-}I}$	$\mathcal{L}_{T\text{-}T}$	R@1	R@5	R@10	mAP
0	Baseline						68.19	86.47	91.47	61.12
1	+TTS	✓					68.83	86.59	91.51	61.53
2	+ITS		✓				69.02	86.71	91.65	62.03
3	+TTS +ITS	✓	✓				69.75	86.66	91.63	62.17
4	+TTS +ITS+$\mathcal{L}_{I\text{-}T}$	✓	✓	✓			70.80	86.69	91.55	62.81
5	CLIP-TC	✓	✓	✓	✓	✓	72.17	88.37	92.84	64.11

4.5 Ablation Study

To quantify the contribution of each component in our CLIP-TC framework, we conduct an ablation study on CUHK-PEDES and report all results in Table 3. Baseline means using CLIP-ViT/16 image encoder and CLIP text encoder to extract features with the original InfoNCE loss. We perform the CLIP-based token selection separately for image features and text features, the performance is improved. When both adding text token selection and image token selection, performance is at its best. Comparison results with different Top-K settings can be found in the supplementary material. Replacing the standard InfoNCE loss with only the inter-modal constraint loss $\mathcal{L}_{I\text{-}T}$ boosts R@1 to 70.80%. Finally, our full CLIP-TC model using inter- and intra-model consistency matching achieves 72.17% R@1 and 64.11% mAP, an absolute gain of 1.37% R@1 over the inter-modal-only variant. These results clearly demonstrate that both token selection and intra-modal consistency matching contribute complementary benefits to text-based person ReID.

4.6 Qualitative Results

To verify the effectiveness of the proposed CLIP-TC, we employ t-SNE to visualize the distribution of textual and visual features in ten categories of data on the CUHK-PEDES test set. As shown in Fig. 2(a), we can see that textual features and corresponding visual features are at a great distance from each other. In addition, different classes of the same modality are not far apart enough. In Fig. 2(b), we visualize our method without intra-modal consistency matching. The model can aggregate semantically related features. However, inter-class separability characteristics are not enough. In Fig. 2(c), by equipping the baseline with all components, we can see that our CLIP-TC can greatly lessen the modality gap between image and text and the feature representations of different modalities are classified into several semantically different groups that are far apart. Due to space limitations, more qualitative results can be found in the supplementary material.

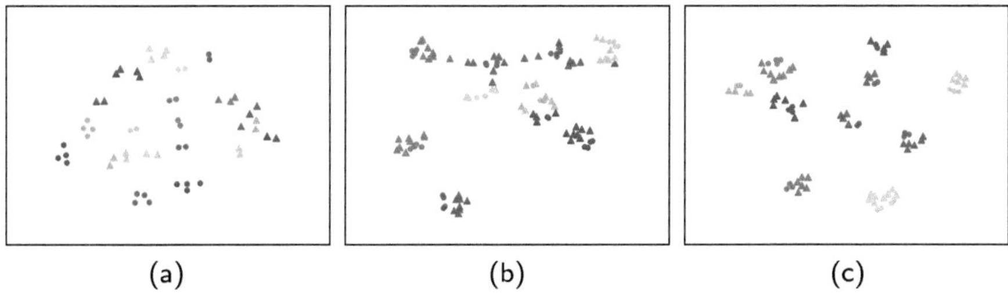

Fig. 2. t-SNE visualization of different kinds of image-text feature representations on CUHK-PEDES. Circles and triangles represent visual and textual features, respectively. The same color represents relevant semantics. (a) Baseline, (b) Without intra-modal consistency and (c) With intra-modal consistency.

5 Conclusions

In this paper, we propose the CLIP-TC model, designed to select identifiable tokens and learn a high-quality common embedding space. Our model enhances token informativeness by selecting identifiable CLIP tokens through an entropy-based mechanism that prioritizes fine-grained features, such as clothing, posture, and hairstyle, while a token consistency matching ensures robust alignment by widening both intra-modal and inter-modal distances in a high-quality common embedding space. The retrieval results surpass those of previous methods on three public benchmark datasets, providing evidence of the effectiveness of our proposal.

Acknowledgements. This work was supported in part by the National Natural Science Foundation of China under Grant 62302144, Grant 72188101, Grant 62307015, and Grant 62437002; and in part by the Fundamental Research Funds for the Central Universities under Grant JZ2024HGTB0251.

References

1. Berthet, Q., Blondel, M., Teboul, O., Cuturi, M., Vert, J.P., Bach, F.: Learning with differentiable pertubed optimizers. In: Advances in Neural Information Processing Systems, pp. 9508–9519 (2020)
2. Chen, Y., Huang, R., Chang, H., Tan, C., Xue, T., Ma, B.: Cross-modal knowledge adaptation for language-based person search. IEEE Trans. Image Process. **30**, 4057–4069 (2021)
3. Chen, Y., Zhang, G., Lu, Y., Wang, Z., Zheng, Y.: TIPCB: a simple but effective part-based convolutional baseline for text-based person search. Neurocomputing **494**, 171–181 (2022)
4. Cordonnier, J.B., Mahendran, A., Dosovitskiy, A., Weissenborn, D., Uszkoreit, J., Unterthiner, T.: Differentiable patch selection for image recognition. In: Proceedings of the IEEE/CVF Conference on Computer Vision and Pattern Recognition, pp. 2351–2360 (2021)

5. Ding, Z., Ding, C., Shao, Z., Tao, D.: Semantically self-aligned network for text-to-image part-aware person re-identification. arXiv preprint: arXiv:2107.12666 (2021)
6. Han, G., Lin, M., Li, Z., Zhao, H., Kwong, S.: Text-to-image person re-identification based on multimodal graph convolutional network. IEEE Trans. Multimedia (2023)
7. Han, X., He, S., Zhang, L., Xiang, T.: Text-based person search with limited data. arXiv preprint: arXiv:2110.10807 (2021)
8. Ji, Z., Hu, J., Liu, D., Wu, L.Y., Zhao, Y.: Asymmetric cross-scale alignment for text-based person search. IEEE Trans. Multimedia (2022)
9. Jia, C., et al.: Scaling up visual and vision-language representation learning with noisy text supervision. In: International Conference on Machine Learning, pp. 4904–4916. PMLR (2021)
10. Karpathy, A., Fei-Fei, L.: Deep visual-semantic alignments for generating image descriptions. In: Proceedings of the IEEE Conference on Computer Vision and Pattern Recognition, pp. 3128–3137 (2015)
11. Lei, J., et al.: Less is more: ClipBERT for video-and-language learning via sparse sampling. In: Proceedings of the IEEE/CVF Conference on Computer Vision and Pattern Recognition, pp. 7331–7341 (2021)
12. Li, G., Duan, N., Fang, Y., Gong, M., Jiang, D.: Unicoder-VL: a universal encoder for vision and language by cross-modal pre-training. In: Proceedings of the AAAI Conference on Artificial Intelligence, vol. 34, pp. 11336–11344 (2020)
13. Li, S., Cao, M., Zhang, M.: Learning semantic-aligned feature representation for text-based person search. In: ICASSP 2022-2022 IEEE International Conference on Acoustics, Speech and Signal Processing, pp. 2724–2728. IEEE (2022)
14. Li, S., Xiao, T., Li, H., Zhou, B., Yue, D., Wang, X.: Person search with natural language description. In: Proceedings of the IEEE Conference on Computer Vision and Pattern Recognition, pp. 1970–1979 (2017)
15. Li, W., Tan, L., Dai, P., Zhang, Y.: Prompt decoupling for text-to-image person re-identification. arXiv preprint: arXiv:2401.02173 (2024)
16. Liu, Y., Liu, H., Wang, H., Liu, M.: Regularizing visual semantic embedding with contrastive learning for image-text matching. IEEE Signal Process. Lett. **29**, 1332–1336 (2022)
17. Liu, Y., Li, Y., Liu, Z., Yang, W., Wang, Y., Liao, Q.: Clip-based synergistic knowledge transfer for text-based person retrieval. In: ICASSP 2024-2024 IEEE International Conference on Acoustics, Speech and Signal Processing (ICASSP), pp. 7935–7939. IEEE (2024)
18. Lu, J., Batra, D., Parikh, D., Lee, S.: VilBERT: pretraining task-agnostic visiolinguistic representations for vision-and-language tasks. In: Advances in Neural Information Processing Systems, vol. 32 (2019)
19. Luo, H., et al.: UniVL: a unified video and language pre-training model for multimodal understanding and generation. arXiv preprint: arXiv:2002.06353 (2020)
20. Ma, W., et al.: FedSH: towards privacy-preserving text-based person re-identification. IEEE Trans. Multimedia (2023)
21. Niu, K., Huang, L., Huang, Y., Wang, P., Wang, L., Zhang, Y.: Cross-modal co-occurrence attributes alignments for person search by language. In: Proceedings of the 30th ACM International Conference on Multimedia, pp. 4426–4434 (2022)
22. Radford, A., et al.: Learning transferable visual models from natural language supervision. In: International Conference on Machine Learning, pp. 8748–8763. PMLR (2021)
23. Sarafianos, N., Xu, X., Kakadiaris, I.A.: Adversarial representation learning for text-to-image matching. In: Proceedings of the IEEE/CVF International Conference on Computer Vision, pp. 5814–5824 (2019)

24. Shao, Z., Zhang, X., Ding, C., Wang, J., Wang, J.: Unified pre-training with pseudo texts for text-to-image person re-identification. In: Proceedings of the IEEE/CVF International Conference on Computer Vision, pp. 11174–11184 (2023)
25. Shao, Z., Zhang, X., Fang, M., Lin, Z., Wang, J., Ding, C.: Learning granularity-unified representations for text-to-image person re-identification. In: Proceedings of the 30th ACM International Conference on Multimedia (2022)
26. Shu, X., et al.: See finer, see more: implicit modality alignment for text-based person retrieval. arXiv preprint: arXiv:2208.08608 (2022)
27. Song, S., et al.: How to bridge the gap between modalities: survey on multimodal large language model. IEEE Trans. Knowl. Data Eng. (2025)
28. Suo, W., et al.: A simple and robust correlation filtering method for text-based person search. In: European Conference on Computer Vision, pp. 726–742. Springer (2022)
29. Wang, C., Zet al.: Hierarchical label-enhanced contrastive learning for Chinese NER. IEEE Trans. Neural Netw. Learn. Syst. (2025)
30. Wang, Z., Fang, Z., Wang, J., Yang, Y.: ViTAA: visual-textual attributes alignment in person search by natural language. In: European Conference on Computer Vision, pp. 402–420. Springer (2020)
31. Wang, Z., et al.: CAIBC: capturing all-round information beyond color for text-based person retrieval. In: Proceedings of the 30th ACM International Conference on Multimedia, pp. 5314–5322 (2022)
32. Wang, Z., et al.: Look before you leap: improving text-based person retrieval by learning a consistent cross-modal common manifold. In: Proceedings of the 30th ACM International Conference on Multimedia, pp. 1984–1992 (2022)
33. Wu, X., Ma, W., Guo, D., Zhou, T., Zhao, S., Cai, Z.: Text-based occluded person re-identification via multi-granularity contrastive consistency learning. In: Proceedings of the AAAI Conference on Artificial Intelligence, vol. 38, pp. 6162–6170 (2024)
34. Yan, S., Dong, N., Zhang, L., Tang, J.: Clip-driven fine-grained text-image person re-identification. arXiv preprint: arXiv:2210.10276 (2022)
35. Yan, T., et al.: FRCL-MNER: a finer grained rank-based contrastive learning framework for multimodal NER. IEEE Trans. Neural Netw. Learn. Syst. (2025)
36. Zhang, Y., Lu, H.: Deep cross-modal projection learning for image-text matching. In: Proceedings of the European Conference on Computer Vision, pp. 686–701 (2018)
37. Zhao, S., Hu, M., Cai, Z., Liu, F.: Dynamic modeling cross-modal interactions in two-phase prediction for entity-relation extraction. IEEE Trans. Neural Netw. Learn. Syst. **34**(3), 1122–1131 (2021)
38. Zhao, S., Wang, C., Hu, M., Yan, T., Wang, M.: MCL: multi-granularity contrastive learning framework for Chinese NER. In: Proceedings of the AAAI Conference on Artificial Intelligence, vol. 37, pp. 14011–14019 (2023)
39. Zheng, K., Liu, W., Liu, J., Zha, Z.J., Mei, T.: Hierarchical Gumbel attention network for text-based person search. In: Proceedings of the 28th ACM International Conference on Multimedia, pp. 3441–3449 (2020)
40. Zheng, Z., Zheng, L., Garrett, M., Yang, Y., Xu, M., Shen, Y.D.: Dual-path convolutional image-text embeddings with instance loss. ACM Trans. Multimed. Comput. Commun. Appl. **16**(2), 1–23 (2020)
41. Zhou, L., Palangi, H., Zhang, L., Hu, H., Corso, J., Gao, J.: Unified vision-language pre-training for image captioning and VQA. In: Proceedings of the AAAI Conference on Artificial Intelligence, vol. 34, pp. 13041–13049 (2020)

42. Zhu, A., et al.: DSSL: deep surroundings-person separation learning for text-based person retrieval. In: Proceedings of the 29th ACM International Conference on Multimedia, pp. 209–217 (2021)
43. Zhu, A., et al.: Improving text-based person retrieval by excavating all-round information beyond color. IEEE Trans. Neural Netw. Learn. Syst. (2024)

AMT-SNet: Adaptive Multi Scale Temporal-Spectral Network for Single-Channel EEG Sleep Stage Classification

Yutong Zheng, Ruiying Wang, Hanyu Wang, and Yuhui Du(✉)

Shanxi University, Taiyuan 030091, China
duyuhui@sxu.edu.cn

Abstract. Accurate sleep stage classification based on single-channel electroencephalogram (EEG) signals remains a fundamental challenge in automated sleep staging. Existing deep learning architectures may be limited by fixed receptive fields, sequential processing bottlenecks, and inadequate adaptation to inter-subject variability. We propose an Adaptive Multi Scale Temporal-Spectral Network (AMT-SNet) designed for efficient and accurate single-channel EEG-based sleep stage classification. Our method employs a dual-branch architecture with temporal-spectral feature extraction, subject-adaptive calibration, and component-wise training to achieve robust and personalized sleep stage classification. We evaluated our method on the Sleep-EDF-20 dataset for five-class sleep stage classification and further validated its generalization ability using the Sleep-EDF-78 dataset. The results on the Sleep-EDF-20 dataset demonstrate that AMT-SNet outperforms eight state-of-the-art models, achieving an accuracy of 85.8% and a macro F1-score of 79.4%. Furthermore, it exhibits strong generalization capability on the Sleep-EDF-78 dataset, setting new performance benchmarks for automated single-channel sleep stage classification. In summary, AMT-SNet offers an effective and generalizable approach for accurate and personalized single-channel sleep stage classification.

Keywords: Sleep stage classification · multi scale analysis · wavelet packet decomposition · phase-amplitude coupling

1 Introduction

Sleep is a fundamental physiological process that exerts a profound impact on cognitive function, productivity, and overall health [1]. The World Health Organization reports that approximately 27% of the global population experiences sleep disorders [2]. Sleep disorders not only increase the risks of cardiovascular disease and other serious health problems, but also impose significant economic costs, with the United States sleep disorder clinic market projected to grow from $9.2 billion to $16 billion between 2021 and 2028 [3]. According to the American Academy of Sleep Medicine (AASM), sleep cycles consist of three primary stages: wake (W), rapid eye movement (REM), and non-REM (NREM) (subdivided into stages NREM1 (N1), NREM2 (N2) and NREM3 (N3)) [4].

© The Author(s), under exclusive license to Springer Nature Singapore Pte Ltd. 2026
J. Kittler et al. (Eds.): PRCV 2025, LNCS 16289, pp. 453–467, 2026.
https://doi.org/10.1007/978-981-95-5764-6_31

An accurate classification of sleep stages is essential to understand sleep architecture and diagnose sleep disorders, as different stages play distinct physiological roles in cognitive restoration, memory consolidation, and hormonal regulation [5]. Emerging evidence indicates that precise monitoring of sleep stages facilitates targeted interventions, which can substantially improve sleep quality and overall health outcomes [6].

Currently, polysomnography (PSG) is recognized as the gold standard for assessing sleep architecture and diagnosing sleep disorders. This comprehensive method records various physiological signals, thereby enabling a detailed analysis of sleep processes and accurate classification of sleep stages. However, the complexity of data acquisition not only increases monitoring costs but also restricts the practical feasibility of implementing sleep monitoring in home settings. Although existing multi-channel electroencephalogram (EEG)-based approaches for sleep stage classification rely solely on electroencephalographic signals, they still face limitations in daily home environments, such as susceptibility to interference, limited wearing comfort, and inconsistent signal quality [7]. To address these challenges, single-channel EEG sleep monitoring has emerged as a particularly promising alternative, offering greater convenience and portability [8], which makes it a viable solution for home-based sleep assessment.

Furthermore, sleep monitoring based on single-channel EEG signals requires advanced and efficient sleep stage classification methods to ensure the accuracy and reliability of the classification results. Currently, existing deep learning approaches based on single-channel EEG for sleep stage classification still exhibit deficiencies. Convolutional neural network (CNN)-based approaches have evolved toward multi-scale architectures and deeper networks, with examples including ASSC [9] proposed by Khalili and Mohammadzadeh, which extracts multi-scale temporal features through parallel convolutional branches and integrates conditional random fields to model temporal dependencies, SingleChannelNet [10], proposed by Zhou et al., introduces an end-to-end framework incorporating multi-convolution blocks to enable multi-scale feature representation learning through parallel processing of multiple receptive fields, and FFTCN [11] by Bao et al., which utilizes temporal convolutional networks to perform feature fusion and effectively captures temporal patterns without relying on recurrent structures. However, these methods may have limitations in capturing long-range temporal dependencies, which are critical for sleep stage transitions and modeling complex inter-epoch relationships [12]. Long short term memory (LSTM)-based approaches have addressed temporal modeling through sophisticated architectures, such as DeepSleepNet [13] proposed by Supratak et al., which integrates CNN-based feature extraction with LSTM layers to capture temporal dependencies between consecutive time segments, TinySleepNet [14], proposed by Supratak and Guo, optimizes computational efficiency while preserving LSTM-based temporal modeling, Seo et al. proposed IITNet [15], which extracts sub-epoch level features via a ResNet-50 and captures both short-term intra-epoch patterns and long-term inter-epoch temporal dependencies using bidirectional LSTM. However, their sequential processing architecture may create computational bottlenecks that hinder parallelization and prolong training times. Attention-based approaches incorporated transformer architectures to better capture temporal dependencies, with examples including AttnSleep [16] by Eldele et al., which integrates multi-resolution CNN with adaptive feature recalibration and temporal context encoding utilizing multi-head attention mechanisms, and TSA-Net [17], proposed by Fu et al., employs a two-stream extractor for separate time and frequency domain processing, utilizing multi-head self-attention to capture feature dependencies. However, these methods still face challenges in terms of computational efficiency or robust generalization across diverse patient populations [18].

To address these limitations, we propose a novel Adaptive Multi Scale Temporal-Spectral Network (AMT-SNet), which makes four primary contributions.

(1) We propose a dual-branch multi-scale feature extraction architecture. The temporal branch integrates statistical behavior of local extrema (SBLE) analysis into inception modules, enabling the adaptive capture of temporal patterns across diverse time scales. Meanwhile, the spectral branch leverages wavelet packet transform enhanced by phase-amplitude coupling (PAC) module to specifically target cross-frequency interactions critical for sleep stage discrimination.
(2) We propose an adaptive calibration methodology that dynamically compensates for inter-subject variability and signal quality fluctuations. By integrating signal quality assessment with subject-specific feature adjustment mechanisms, this approach enables the model to sustain robust performance across diverse recording conditions and individual physiological characteristics.
(3) We propose a component-wise training strategy that first independently optimizes the dual-branch feature extraction modules using segment-level supervision, then integrates sequence learning through bidirectional gated recurrent units (BiGRU) with attention mechanisms to capture long-term sleep architecture patterns.
(4) We evaluate the model's performance on Sleep-EDF-20 and test its generalization capability on Sleep-EDF-78. Through comparison experiments with eight state-of-the-art models, the proposed model achieves superior performance in single-channel EEG sleep stage classification.

2 Method

Let $X = \{x_1, x_2, \cdots, x_n\}$ denote a continuous EEG recording that has been segmented into n consecutive time segments, where each $x_i \in \mathbb{R}^L$ represents a 30-s time segment containing L data points. Sleep stages generally do not transition abruptly; rather, they exhibit temporal continuity, which offers valuable contextual information for classification. Therefore, accurate classification necessitates modeling the temporal dependencies between adjacent time segments. This consideration leads to a mapping function defined as $f : \mathbb{R}^{L\times S} \rightarrow \{0, 1, 2, 3, 4\}$, , where the output corresponds to the five standard sleep stages (W, N1, N2, N3, and REM), and S denotes the number of consecutive time segments used for classifying the central time segment.

We then introduce the AMT-SNet, illustrated in Fig. 1, which comprises two core modules: (1) a feature extraction module that processes individual EEG time segments via parallel temporal and spectral branches to extract complementary neurophysiological features, and (2) a sequence learning module designed to capture temporal dependencies across consecutive sleep time segments by employing a BiGRU architecture augmented with a temporal attention mechanism.

We adopt a component-wise training strategy that sequentially trains the feature extraction and sequence learning modules. This approach tackles the challenges of training deep neural networks with multiple interdependent components by decomposing the training process into distinct phases, enabling each module to develop optimal representations for its specific task.

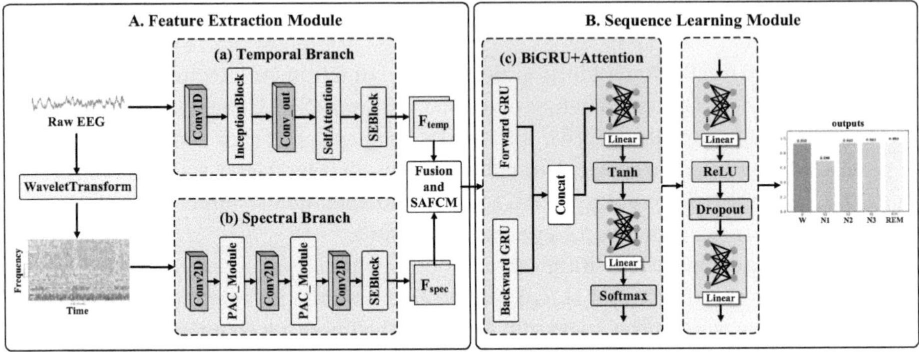

Fig. 1. Overall architecture of the proposed AMT-SNet.

2.1 Feature Extraction Module

The feature extraction module adopts a dual-branch architecture to capture the multifaceted characteristics of sleep EEG signals. Each 30-s time segment is processed in parallel through two complementary pathways: a temporal branch that identifies time-domain patterns via optimized convolutional operations, and a spectral branch that analyzes frequency components using wavelet transformations. This design allows for feature extraction by simultaneously characterizing both transient waveforms (e.g., sleep spindles and K-complexes) and spectral compositions (e.g., delta, theta, alpha, and sigma rhythms), which collectively distinguish between different sleep stages.

Temporal Branch. As depicted in Fig. 2, the temporal branch extracts time-domain features from raw EEG signals via a series of convolutional modules designed for sleep-specific pattern recognition.

Given an input EEG segment $x_i \in \mathbb{R}^L$, which represents a single 30-s time window comprising L data points, the signal is first processed through a convolutional layer with a small stride. This design choice helps maintain the high temporal resolution required for the detection of transient sleep events.

$$h_{initial} = MaxPool(ReLU(BN(Conv1D(x_i; \theta)))) \quad (1)$$

where $h_{initial}$ denotes the initial feature representation extracted from the raw input EEG, $Conv1D(\cdot; \theta)$ denotes the one-dimensional convolution operation with parameters θ (including a kernel size of 50, stride of 4, padding of 25, and 16 output channels), $BN(\cdot)$

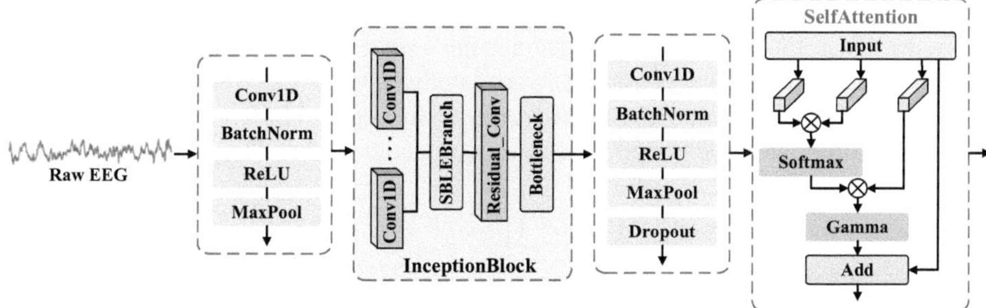

Fig. 2. The architecture of the temporal branch.

denotes the batch normalization layer, $ReLU(\cdot)$ denotes the rectified linear unit activation function, and $MaxPool(\cdot)$ denotes the max pooling operation.

The extracted features are subsequently processed through an Inception block that employs parallel convolutional filters with multiple kernel sizes, effectively captured sleep-specific patterns across various temporal scales. Specifically, the smaller kernels excel at detecting rapid transients and high-frequency oscillations, the medium-sized kernels are well-suited for identifying sleep spindles, and the larger kernels are tailored to extract slower phenomena such as K-complexes and delta waves, which are characteristic of deep sleep. The multi-scale feature extraction is formulated as:

$$h^{(k)} = ReLU(BN(Conv1D(h_{initial}; W_k, b_k))) \tag{2}$$

for $k \in \{1, 2, \cdots, K\}$, $h^{(k)}$ denotes the feature output from the k-th parallel convolutional branch within the Inception block, where W_k and b_k represent the weight matrix and bias vector of the k-th convolutional branch.

To enhance the temporal branch's capability for waveform capture, we introduce the SBLE module, which identifies local maxima and minima via adaptive thresholding. This approach is particularly effective for detecting patterns such as sleep spindles, which are characterized by clustered extrema, and slow waves, which exhibit prominent peaks and troughs.

$$E_{max}(t) = \begin{cases} 1 \; if \; a(t-1) < a(t) > a(t+1) \; and \; |a(t) - \mu_w| > \tau_{th} \\ 0 \; otherwise \end{cases} \tag{3}$$

$$E_{min}(t) = \begin{cases} 1 \; if \; a(t-1) > a(t) < a(t+1) and |a(t) - \mu_w| > \tau_{th} \\ 0 \; otherwise \end{cases} \tag{4}$$

where $a(t), a(t-1)$, and $a(t+1)$ denote the EEG signal amplitudes at time points $t, t-1$, and $t+1$, respectively, with t representing any moment during the EEG recording. μ_w denotes the local mean computed within a sliding window, and τ_{th} is an adaptive threshold parameter learned during training. The resulting extrema maps are then processed through specialized convolutional layers.

$$F_{SBLE} = ReLU(BN(Conv1D([E_{max}, E_{min}]; W_{SBLE}))) \tag{5}$$

where W_{SBLE} denotes the learnable weight parameters of the convolutional operation within the SBLE module, and F_{SBLE} denotes the output feature representation obtained by the SBLE module after processing the concatenated local maxima and minima maps.

The multi-scale features extracted from the Inception block are concatenated to construct a comprehensive temporal representation, denoted as $F_{temporal}$.

$$F_{temporal} = Concat\left(\left[h^{(1)}, h^{(2)}, \cdots, h^{(K)}\right]\right) \tag{6}$$

To enhance the discriminative capacity of temporal features, a self-attention mechanism is incorporated, which selectively focuses on the most salient temporal patterns relevant to sleep stage classification.

$$A = Softmax\left(\frac{QK^T}{\sqrt{d_k}}\right) \tag{7}$$

$$F_{attn} = \gamma \odot (AV) + F_{temporal} \tag{8}$$

where Q, K, and V denote the query, key, and value matrices, d_k represents the dimensionality of the key vectors, γ is a learnable gating factor that controls the contribution strength of the attention mechanism relative to the original temporal features, and $\odot$ denotes element-wise multiplication. The attention weights A enable the model to dynamically focus on temporally relevant patterns. F_{attn} denotes the attention-enhanced feature representation that combines weighted attention outputs with $F_{temporal}$.

The temporal branch concludes with a SEBlock that performs channel-wise recalibration by emphasizing the most discriminative feature channels.

$$z = GAP(F_{attn}) \tag{9}$$

$$s_{temporal} = \sigma(W_2 ReLU(W_1 z)) \tag{10}$$

$$F_{temporal}^{SE} = s_{temporal} \odot F_{attn} \tag{11}$$

where $GAP(\cdot)$ denotes global average pooling, z denotes the averaged global features extracted from the attention-enhanced representation, $\sigma(\cdot)$ denotes the sigmoid activation function, W_1 and W_2 are learnable parameters for channel recalibration, $s_{temporal}$ denotes the channel-wise recalibration weights, and $F_{temporal}^{SE}$ denotes the final output of the temporal branch after channel recalibration.

Spectral Branch. The spectral branch focuses on analyzing the frequency-domain characteristics of EEG signals, with particular attention to sleep-relevant spectral bands and their cross-frequency interactions. By utilizing wavelet packet decomposition, this branch constructs detailed time-frequency representations that effectively capture the dynamic spectral properties critical for sleep staging.

Initially, a sophisticated time-frequency representation is constructed by employing the discrete wavelet packet transform (WPT) with adaptive frequency band weighting.

$$W_{j,k}^{(l)} = \sum\nolimits_{n} a(m)\psi_{j,k}^{(l)}(m) \tag{12}$$

where $\psi_{j,k}^{(l)}(m)$ denotes the Daubechies-4 wavelet function at decomposition level $l = 5$, with scale parameter j and translation parameter k; $a(m)$ denotes the EEG signal amplitudes at time points m; and $W_{j,k}^{(l)}$ denotes the wavelet coefficients that quantify the frequency content at specific time locations. Compared to traditional Fourier-based methods, the WPT offers superior time-frequency localization, making it particularly well-suited for analyzing non-stationary sleep EEG signals.

The wavelet coefficients are subsequently organized into physiologically relevant frequency bands based on their corresponding frequency ranges.

$$W_b = \left\{ W_{j,k}^{(l)} : f_{j,l} \in F_b \right\} \tag{13}$$

where F_b denotes the frequency range associated with band b, corresponding to the delta, theta, alpha, sigma, and beta rhythms, $B = 5$ represents the total number of these rhythms; $f_{j,l} = f_s / \left(2^{j+1}\right)$ defines the center frequency at scale j and decomposition level l; and W_b denotes the wavelet coefficients corresponding to band b.

The resultant time-frequency representation is further enhanced through the application of adaptive frequency band weighting, thereby emphasizing clinically significant sleep rhythms.

$$W_{weighted} = \sum_{b=1}^{B} \alpha_b W_b \tag{14}$$

where α_b denotes the learnable weight assigned to the b-th frequency band, and $W_{weighted}$ represents the final weighted time-frequency representation.

A key innovation in the spectral branch is the PAC module, which models cross-frequency interactions across different frequency bands. This capability is particularly important for capturing the coordination between slow oscillations and faster rhythms across various sleep stages. The phase and amplitude components are extracted from frequency band representations using Hilbert transform analysis.

$$\phi_{b,low}(t) = angle\left(H\left(W_{b,low}(t)\right)\right) \tag{15}$$

$$A_{b,high}(t) = \left|H\left(W_{b,high}(t)\right)\right| \tag{16}$$

where $H(\cdot)$ denotes the Hilbert transform, $W_{b,low}$ denotes the lower frequency band coefficients, $angle(\cdot)$ extracts the instantaneous phase angle from the complex analytic signal, $\phi_{b,low}(\cdot)$ denotes the resulting instantaneous phase of the low-frequency oscillation, $W_{b,high}$ denotes the higher frequency band coefficients, and $A_{b,high}(\cdot)$ denotes the resulting instantaneous amplitude of the high-frequency oscillation.

The phase-amplitude coupling between frequency bands is subsequently calculated to quantify cross-frequency interactions.

$$PAC\left(b_{low}, b_{high}\right) = \left|\left\langle A_{b,high}(t) e^{i\phi_{b,low}(t)} \right\rangle_t\right| \tag{17}$$

The PAC module extracts phase information from lower-frequency components and amplitude information from higher-frequency components, models their coupling through specialized convolutional operations, and calculates the phase-amplitude coupling between frequency bands as $PAC(b_{low}, b_{high})$.

$$F_{PAC} = Conv2D\left(\left[\phi_{b,low}, A_{b,high}, PAC\left(b_{low}, b_{high}\right)\right]; W_{PAC}\right) \tag{18}$$

where F_{PAC} denotes the feature output from the PAC module. This mechanism effectively captures phenomena such as slow oscillation–spindle coupling during N2 sleep, delta-alpha coupling in light sleep transitions, and theta-gamma coupling in REM sleep.

The weighted frequency band representations are combined with PAC features to construct a comprehensive spectral representation, denoted as $F_{spectral}$.

$$F_{spectral} = Concat\left(\left[W_{weighted}, F_{PAC}\right]\right) \tag{19}$$

The spectral features are subjected to channel-wise recalibration through a SEBlock specifically designed for frequency-domain representations, and $F^{SE}_{spectral}$ denotes the final output of the spectral branch after channel recalibration.

$$F^{SE}_{spectral} = SE\left(F_{spectral}\right) = s_{spectral} \odot F_{spectral} \tag{20}$$

where the recalibration weights $s_{spectral}$ are computed as follows:

$$s_{spectral} = \sigma\left(W_{se2}ReLU\left(W_{se1}GAP\left(F_{spectral}\right)\right)\right) \tag{21}$$

Feature Fusion. The features from the temporal and spectral branches are subjected to global average pooling to generate fixed-dimensional feature vectors, after which these feature vectors are concatenated and passed through the subsequent layers.

$$F^{pool}_{temporal} = GAP\left(F^{SE}_{temporal}\right) \tag{22}$$

$$F^{pool}_{spectral} = GAP\left(F^{SE}_{spectral}\right) \tag{23}$$

$$F_{fused} = \left[F^{pool}_{temporal}; F^{pool}_{spectral}\right] \tag{24}$$

Subject-Adaptive Feature Calibration Module. To address inter-subject variability in EEG signal characteristics, we propose the subject-adaptive feature calibration module (SAFCM), which performs real-time signal quality assessment and adaptive feature calibration based on six key metrics.

The module evaluates the signal-to-noise ratio (SNR) through spectral analysis by comparing signal power in physiologically relevant frequency bands (0.5–30 Hz) with high-frequency noise components above 30 Hz. Variance stability (VS) is assessed using the coefficient of variation to measure signal consistency across time windows. Amplitude anomaly detection (AAD) employs interquartile range-based methods to identify signal outliers that may indicate artifacts or recording issues. Flatline detection (FD) evaluates electrode contact quality through the analysis of signal derivatives against adaptive thresholds. Additionally, the system monitors delta band relative power (DRP) to capture low-frequency sleep-related activity and alpha band relative power (ARP) to assess wake-related neural oscillations.

These quality metrics are processed through a multi-layer perceptron to generate subject-specific calibration factors.

$$q = MLP([SNR, VS, AAD, FD, DRP, ARP]) \tag{25}$$

$$F_{calibrated} = F_{fused} \odot (1 + \beta \cdot \tanh(q)) \tag{26}$$

where β is a learnable parameter that controls the calibration strength and determines the extent of adjustment, q represents the calibration vector generated by the quality assessment network, and $\tanh(\cdot)$ is employed to ensure bounded calibration factors.

During the first training phase, the calibrated features are passed through a final classification layer to generate segment-level predictions.

$$p_{epoch} = Softmax(W_{cls}F_{calibrated} + b_{cls}) \tag{27}$$

where $p_{epoch} = \left[p_{epoch}^{(1)}, p_{epoch}^{(2)}, \cdots, p_{epoch}^{(C)}\right]$ represents the probability distribution over C sleep stage classes for a single time segment.

Training Strategy. In the first training phase, the feature extraction module is trained independently using subject-specific EEG time segments without sequential context. This phase utilizes a weighted cross-entropy loss function to mitigate the class imbalance inherently present in sleep datasets.

$$L_{feature} = -\sum_{c=1}^{C} w_c \sum_{i=1}^{N} y_i^{(c)} \log\left(p_{epoch,i}^{(c)}\right) \tag{28}$$

where w_c denotes the weight assigned to class c, $y_i^{(c)}$ is the binary indicator for correct classification, $p_{epoch,i}^{(c)}$ is the predicted probability for class c of the i-th time segment from the feature extraction module, and N is the total number of training time segments.

2.2 Sequence Learning Module

The sequence learning module enhances classification accuracy by modeling temporal dependencies between consecutive sleep segments while incorporating physiological constraints related to stage transitions. By processing S consecutive segments centered on the target time segment, the module independently analyzes each time segment to generate corresponding feature vectors.

$$V = \left\{F_{calibrated}^{(i)}\right\}_{i=1}^{S} \tag{29}$$

where $F_{calibrated}^{(i)}$ denotes the calibrated feature vector for the i-th time segment in the sequence, and V represents the sequence of calibrated feature vectors.

Bidirectional Gated Recurrent. The feature sequence is processed by a BiGRU network to capture both past and future contextual information.

$$\vec{h}_t = GRU\left(F_{calibrated}^{(t)}, \vec{h}_{t-1}; \theta_{fwd}\right) \tag{30}$$

$$h_t^{\leftarrow} = GRU\left(F_{calibrated}^{(t)}, h_{t+1}^{\leftarrow}; \theta_{bwd}\right) \tag{31}$$

$$h_t = \left[\vec{h}_t; h_t^{\leftarrow}\right] \tag{32}$$

where θ_{fwd} and θ_{bwd} denote the learnable parameters of the forward and backward GRU units, respectively, $\vec{h}_t$ and $h_t^{\leftarrow}$ represent the forward and backward hidden states, respectively, and h_t denotes the concatenated output from both directional streams.

A temporal attention mechanism selectively focuses on the most relevant time segments to improve the classification accuracy of the central target time segment.

$$e_t = v_a^T \tanh(W_a h_t + b_a) \tag{33}$$

$$\alpha_t = \frac{\exp(e_{t_1})}{\sum_{t_2=1}^{V} \exp(e_{t_2})} \tag{34}$$

$$v = \sum_{t=1}^{V} \alpha_t h_t \tag{35}$$

where v_a, W_a, and b_a are learnable parameters of the attention mechanism, e_{t_1} denotes the attention score for the t_1-th time step, e_{t_2} denotes the attention score for the t_2-th time step, α_t represents the attention weight assigned to time t, and v denotes the context vector that captures relevant information from the entire sequence.

The learned attention weights dynamically adjust to emphasize time segments that are most informative for classifying the target time segment, which may vary depending on the sleep stage and transition patterns.

$$p_{final} = Softmax\left(W_{final} ReLU\left(W_{hidden} v + b_{hidden}\right) + b_{final}\right) \tag{36}$$

where W_{final}, W_{hidden}, b_{hidden}, and b_{final} denote the parameters of the final classification layers, and $p_{final} = \left[p_{final}^{(1)}, p_{final}^{(2)}, \cdots, p_{final}^{(C)}\right]$ represents the final probability distribution over sleep stage classes.

Training Strategy. Following the convergence of the feature extraction module, its parameters are frozen to preserve the learned feature representations. The sequence learning module is subsequently trained using sequences of consecutive time segments with a standard cross-entropy loss.

$$L_{sequence} = -\sum_{i=1}^{M} \sum_{c=1}^{C} y_i^{(c)} \log\left(p_{final,i}^{(c)}\right) \tag{37}$$

where M denotes the number of sequence samples, and $p_{final,i}^{(c)}$ is the predicted probability for class c of the i-th sequence from the sequence learning module.

3 Experiments

3.1 Datasets and Preprocessing

Our experimental evaluation was conducted on two widely-used public datasets: Sleep-EDF-20 and Sleep-EDF-78 [19]. We first assessed the model's performance on the Sleep-EDF-20 dataset, which includes polysomnographic recordings from 20 healthy individuals. Subsequently, we evaluated its generalization capability using a subset of data from the Sleep-EDF-78 dataset that was not included in Sleep-EDF-20. All recordings were manually annotated by sleep experts following the Rechtschaffen and Kales (R&K) criteria. Following standard preprocessing protocols established in prior sleep staging research, we extracted single-channel EEG signals from the Fpz-Cz electrode configuration, which has been shown to provide optimal discriminative information for automated sleep staging tasks [20].

All EEG signals were preprocessed using a standardized pipeline: (1) each 30-s time segment was sampled at 100 Hz, resulting in 3000 data points per time segment; (2) sleep periods were extracted by selecting data from 30 min before the first non-Wake stage to 30 min after the last non-wake stage, ensuring that the analysis focused on the relevant portions of sleep; and (3) sleep stages were mapped according to the AASM guidelines into five classes: W, N1, N2, N3, and REM. The unknown and movement stages were excluded from the subsequent analysis.

3.2 Experimental Setup

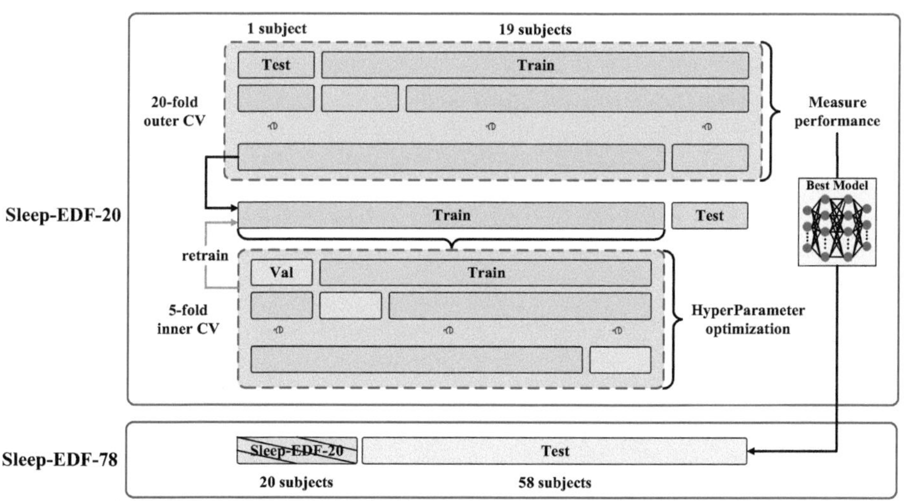

Fig. 3. The nested cross-validation framework.

To train our model using Sleep-EDF-20, we employed a nested cross-validation framework with 20-fold subject-wise cross-validation (Fig. 3). In the outer cross-validation, each of the 20 folds used one subject's complete sleep data as the test set, while the remaining 19 subjects constituted the training set, thereby preventing data leakage and ensuring cross-subject generalization assessment. For inner cross-validation within each outer fold, the 19-subject training set underwent an additional 5-fold cross-validation for hyperparameter optimization. Specifically, the 19 training subjects were randomly divided into five subsets, with four subsets used for internal training and one for validation during the grid search process. The hyperparameter space included sequence length for temporal context modeling, temporal kernel sizes for multi-scale feature extraction, and class weighting strategies to address sleep stage imbalance. Model performance was evaluated using the macro F1-score for each hyperparameter combination. Following optimal hyperparameter selection through inner cross-validation, the AMT-SNet model was retrained on the complete training set for each outer cross-validation run.

To evaluate the generalization capability of our approach, we conducted a test on the Sleep-EDF-78 dataset. From the 20 trained models corresponding to each outer cross-validation fold on Sleep-EDF-20, we selected the model achieving the highest macro-averaged F1-score as the best-performing configuration. This model was subsequently evaluated on the Sleep-EDF-78 dataset after excluding the 20 subjects that were common to the Sleep-EDF-20 dataset. This cross-dataset evaluation provides essential insights into the model's ability to generalize across different recording conditions, subject populations, and potential variations in sleep architecture patterns.

To evaluate model performance, we employed widely used evaluation metrics. Overall classification performance was assessed using accuracy, which measures the proportion of correctly classified time segments across all sleep stages, and the macro F1-score, which calculates the unweighted mean of F1-scores to ensure equal consideration of minority sleep stages. Additionally, per-class precision, recall, and F1-score were computed to evaluate performance at the individual sleep stage level, along with Cohen's kappa coefficient to quantify classification agreement while accounting for chance occurrence.

It is worth noting that these evaluation metrics and experimental configurations were consistently applied to our method, the comparative models, and ablation studies to ensure rigorous and fair performance assessment.

3.3 Ablation Studies and Comparison with State-of-the-Art Models

To evaluate the contribution of each component in AMT-SNet, we conducted ablation studies by systematically removing the Temporal Branch, Spectral Branch, SBLE Module, PAC Module, and Subject Calibration components to assess their individual impact on model performance. We implemented and evaluated eight state-of-the-art sleep staging models, including ASSC, SingleChannelNet, FFTCN, DeepSleepNet, TinySleepNet, IITNet, AttnSleep, and TSA-Net. The ablation analysis offers insights into the necessity and effectiveness of each architectural component, while the comparative evaluation establishes AMT-SNet's performance relative to existing methods across multiple benchmark datasets, demonstrating its capabilities in automated sleep stage classification tasks.

4 Results

The results of ablation studies on the Sleep-EDF-20 dataset are presented in Fig. 4 These results provide several key insights: (1) both the temporal and spectral branches make significant contributions, as their removal leads to accuracy reduces of 1.98% and 1.9%, respectively; (2) the PAC module contributes a 0.7% improvement in accuracy, thereby confirming its importance in capturing cross-frequency interactions; (3) the SAFCM module yields an 0.8% increase in accuracy, underscoring its effectiveness in addressing inter-subject variability. Collectively, these findings confirm that all modules are essential for optimal model performance and robustness.

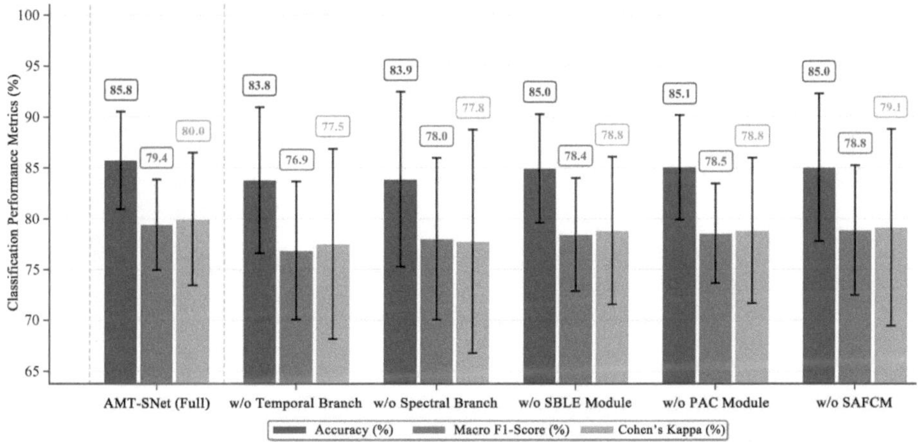

Fig. 4. The ablation results on the Sleep-EDF-20 dataset

As shown in Table 1, on the Sleep-EDF-20 dataset, AMT-SNet achieves the highest overall accuracy of 85.8% and a macro-averaged F1 score of 79.4%. On the Sleep-EDF-78 dataset, it attains an accuracy of 86.7% and a κ coefficient of 0.81. The consistently high performance across different datasets, along with robust κ values, indicates that AMT-SNet effectively captures the underlying patterns in single-channel EEG signals while maintaining generalization across diverse patient populations.

Table 1. The comparative experimental results

Model	Dataset	Overall metrics			F1 score per class				
		ACC	MF1	κ	W	N1	N2	N3	REM
ASSC [9]	Sleep EDF 20	80.3	73.8	0.72	87.0	36.0	85.0	82.0	79.0
SingleChannelNet [10]		81.8	<u>79.2</u>	0.77	88.0	**53.0**	82.0	84.0	**89.0**

(*continued*)

Table 1. (*continued*)

Model	Dataset	Overall metrics			F1 score per class				
		ACC	MF1	κ	W	N1	N2	N3	REM
FFTCN [11]		81.5	70.1	0.75	88.1	10.8	88.1	<u>88.4</u>	75.0
DeepSleepNet [13]		81.9	76.3	0.75	**89.9**	44.4	85.2	80.9	81.3
TinySleepNet [14]		83.9	78.9	0.78	87.8	<u>49.4</u>	87.9	87.1	82.7
IITNet [15]		82.5	76.0	0.76	85.0	41.6	86.7	84.9	82.1
AttnSleep [16]		<u>84.3</u>	78.7	<u>0.79</u>	89.6	45.4	**88.6**	**89.9**	80.1
AMT-SNet (Ours)		**85.8**	**79.4**	**0.80**	<u>89.7</u>	46.7	<u>88.2</u>	86.2	<u>86.3</u>
ASSC [9]	Sleep EDF 78	<u>83.8</u>	78.2	<u>0.78</u>	90.0	46.0	<u>88.0</u>	**83.0**	<u>84.0</u>
FFTCN [11]		81.9	71.4	0.73	**94.3**	40.5	81.5	75.7	64.8
TinySleepNet [14]		82.6	77.0	0.76	<u>92.4</u>	<u>47.9</u>	85.0	79.5	80.1
AttnSleep [16]		80.4	74.9	0.73	91.7	43.9	84.1	<u>81.7</u>	73.2
TSA-Net [17]		80.5	**75.5**	0.74	91.7	46.4	82.2	77.2	80.0
AMT-SNet (Ours)		**86.7**	<u>75.2</u>	**0.81**	91.7	**51.5**	**88.9**	56.6	**87.4**

Note: Bold values denote the highest performance metrics within each column, while underlined values indicate the second-best results.

5 Discussion

The primary challenge in single-channel EEG sleep staging lies in the effective capture of both fine-grained temporal-spectral patterns and long-range sequential dependencies, while simultaneously addressing inter-subject variability and signal quality fluctuations in sleep recordings. Our proposed AMT-SNet addresses these limitations through three key innovations: (1) a dual-branch multi-scale feature extraction framework that captures temporal patterns across diverse time scales via SBLE-enhanced inception modules and extracts spectral characteristics through wavelet packet decomposition with PAC module; (2) a subject-adaptive calibration mechanism that dynamically compensates for inter-subject variability and signal quality fluctuations by incorporating real-time signal quality assessment; (3) and a component-wise training strategy that optimizes the feature extraction and sequence learning modules independently. Experimental validation confirms the effectiveness of each component via ablation studies. Comparative results on the Sleep-EDF-20 and Sleep-EDF-78 datasets demonstrate that AMT-SNet outperforms eight state-of-the-art models, highlighting its generalization capability and practical value for automated sleep staging in clinical settings.

References

1. Gilley, R.R.: The role of sleep in cognitive function: the value of a good night's rest. Clin. EEG Neurosci. **54**(1), 12–20 (2023)

2. Gao, X., Qiao, Y.H., Chen, Q., Wang, C., Zhang, P.Z.: Effects of different types of exercise on sleep quality based on Pittsburgh Sleep Quality Index in middle-aged and older adults: a network meta-analysis. J. Clin. Sleep Med. **20**(7), 1193–1204 (2024)
3. Snopkowski, B., et al.: Impact of sleep disorders on cardiovascular diseases. J. Educ. Health Sport **20**(1), 45–52 (2023)
4. Malhotra, R.K., Avidan, A.Y.: Sleep stage scoring. In: Thomas, R.J., Bhat, S., Chokroverty, S. (eds.) Atlas of Sleep Medicine, pp. 125–163. Springer International Publishing, Cham (2023)
5. Strauss, M., et al.: Order matters: sleep spindles contribute to memory consolidation only when followed by rapid-eye-movement sleep. Sleep **45**(4), zsac022 (2022)
6. Navarro, M.J.M., Nicdao, J.A.I., Cruz, J.C.D.: machine learning based sleep phase monitoring using pulse oximeter and accelerometer. In: 2021 5th International Conference on Electrical, Telecommunication and Computer Engineering (ELTICOM), vol. 5, pp. 88–93. IEEE (2021)
7. Ding, L., Chen, B., Dai, Y., Li, Y.: A meta-analysis of the first-night effect in healthy individuals for the full age spectrum. Sleep Med. **89**, 159–165 (2022)
8. Markov, K., Elgendi, M., Menon, C.: EEG-based headset sleep wearable devices. npj Biosens. **1**(1), 12 (2024)
9. Khalili, E., Asl, B.M.: Automatic sleep stage classification using temporal convolutional neural network and new data augmentation technique from raw single-channel EEG. Comput. Methods Programs Biomed. **204** (2021)
10. Zhou, D.D., et al.: SingleChannelNet: a model for automatic sleep stage classification with raw single-channel EEG. Biomed. Sign. Process. Control **75** (2022)
11. Bao, J.M., et al.: A feature fusion model based on temporal convolutional network for automatic sleep staging using single-channel EEG. IEEE J. Biomed. Health Inform. **28**(11), 6641–6652 (2024)
12. Zhao, W., Jiang, X.L., Zhang, B.C., Xiao, S.X., Weng, S.J.: CTNet: a convolutional transformer network for EEG-based motor imagery classification. Sci. Rep. **14**(1) (2024)
13. Supratak, A., Dong, H., Wu, C., Guo, Y.K.: DeepSleepNet: a model for automatic sleep stage scoring based on raw single-channel EEG. IEEE Trans. Neural Syst. Rehabil. Eng. **25**(11), 1998–2008 (2017)
14. Supratak, A., Guo, Y.: TinySleepNet: an efficient deep learning model for sleep stage scoring based on raw single-channel EEG. In: 2020 42nd Annual International Conference of the IEEE Engineering in Medicine & Biology Society (EMBC), pp. 641–644. IEEE (2020)
15. Seo, H., Back, S., Lee, S., Park, D., Kim, T., Lee, K.: Intra-and inter-epoch temporal context network (IITNet) using sub-epoch features for automatic sleep scoring on raw single-channel EEG. Biomed. Signal Process. Control **61**, 102037 (2020)
16. Eldele, E., et al.: An attention-based deep learning approach for sleep stage classification with single-channel EEG. IEEE Trans. Neural Syst. Rehabil. Eng. **29**, 809–818 (2021)
17. Fu, G., Zhou, Y., Gong, P., Wang, P., Shao, W., Zhang, D.: A temporal-spectral fused and attention-based deep model for automatic sleep staging. IEEE Trans. Neural Syst. Rehabil. Eng. **31**, 1008–1018 (2023)
18. He, Z., et al.: Unified convolutional sparse transformer for disease diagnosis, monitoring, drug development, and therapeutic effect prediction from EEG raw data. Biology **13**(4), 203 (2024)
19. Kemp, B., Zwinderman, A.H., Tuk, B., Kamphuisen, H.A.C., Oberyé, J.J.L.: Analysis of a sleep-dependent neuronal feedback loop: the slow-wave microcontinuity of the EEG. IEEE Trans. Biomed. Eng. **47**(9), 1185–1194 (2000)
20. Moctezuma, L.A., Suzuki, Y., Furuki, J., Molinas, M., Abe, T.: GRU-powered sleep stage classification with permutation-based EEG channel selection. Sci. Rep. **14**(1) (2024)

EEG Graph Attention Network for Adaptive Spatiotemporal-Aware Emotion Recognition

Xiaolong Zhong, Fei Wu, Yoshiharu Hirano, and Gang Liu(✉)

The School of Electronic Information and Electrical Engineering, Shanghai Jiao Tong University, Shanghai 200240, China
liugang82@mail.sysu.edu.cn

Abstract. EEG-based emotion recognition is a pivotal enabler of affective brain–computer interfaces, yet existing approaches remain limited by biologically implausible modeling assumptions that undermine both accuracy and generalizability. Current graph and attention-based frameworks typically rely on static adjacency matrices or heuristic spatial priors, disregarding the dynamic and biophysically constrained nature of neural activity. To overcome these barriers, we present the EEG graph attention network (EGANet)—the first architecture to explicitly embed neurophysiological principles into an adaptive graph attention framework. EGANet introduces a spatial decay matrix derived from 3D Talairach coordinates to model inverse-square cortical potential attenuation, dynamically integrating physical distance constraints with learnable emotion-specific couplings. Complemented by rotary positional embeddings and a Hadamard product–based aggregation scheme, EGANet preserves electrode topology while capturing long-range spatiotemporal dependencies. Comprehensive evaluations on the DEAP, SEED, and FACED benchmarks demonstrate that EGANet establishes a new state of the art in EEG-based emotion recognition, delivering consistent gains in both accuracy and cross-dataset generalizability. These results highlight the transformative potential of neurophysiology-guided graph models in advancing robust, biologically grounded affective computing.

Keywords: EEG · emotion recognition · graph neural network · Transformer

1 Introduction

Electroencephalography (EEG) has emerged as a cornerstone neuroimaging modality, offering unparalleled millisecond-level temporal resolution for monitoring cortical dynamics through non-invasive scalp electrodes [1]. While its clinical utility spans epilepsy detection to sleep staging, recent advances have unlocked transformative applications in affective computing through EEG-based emotion recognition [2]. This paradigm shift addresses critical limitations of conventional emotion assessment methods – facial expression analysis suffers from voluntary masking, while speech prosody features exhibit cross-cultural variability [3]. By directly decoding valence and arousal states from cortical electrophysiology, EEG provides an objective window into emotional processing within the limbic-cortical loop.

© The Author(s), under exclusive license to Springer Nature Singapore Pte Ltd. 2026
J. Kittler et al. (Eds.): PRCV 2025, LNCS 16289, pp. 468–480, 2026.
https://doi.org/10.1007/978-981-95-5764-6_32

Current approaches to modeling EEG spatial relationships face several fundamental limitations that undermine their biological plausibility and computational efficiency. First, graph neural networks (GNNs) commonly employ static adjacency matrices based on Euclidean distances between electrodes, disregarding the neurophysiological principle of inverse distance-functional connectivity coupling [4]. This contradicts empirical evidence demonstrating that closer electrodes exhibit stronger signal correlations due to volume conduction effects - a phenomenon where electrical potentials propagate through cerebrospinal fluid and skull tissues, creating spatial smoothing [5]. By fixing connectivity weights through rigid graph structures, conventional GNNs fail to adapt to the dynamic nature of emotional neural responses where functional connectivity patterns reorganize across arousal states [6].

Second, while Transformer architectures have shown promise in capturing global dependencies, their canonical self-attention mechanisms often inadequately model the biophysical realities of EEG signals [7]. Prevailing methods treat electrodes as abstract graph nodes rather than biophysical measurement points constrained by volume conduction physics. This oversight manifests in two critical flaws: 1) Failure to account for individual head geometry variations that distort inter-electrode signal propagation, and 2) disregarding the physiological principle of nonlinear distance-dependent attenuation, whereby cortical source strength diminishes with increasing distance from scalp sensors. Such simplifications not only compromise the fidelity of spatial information but also inadvertently attenuate long-range cortico-limbic interactions that are crucial for emotion processing—for instance, frontal–parietal theta coherence during affective regulation [8]. Consequently, models trained on standardized electrode layouts demonstrate poor generalizability to real-world clinical recordings with customized montages.

Third, prevailing methods inadequately ground spatial embeddings in neuroanatomical reality, treating electrodes as abstract graph nodes rather than biophysical measurement points constrained by volume conduction physics. This oversight manifests in two critical flaws: 1) Failure to account for individual head geometry variations that distort inter-electrode signal propagation [9], and 2) Disregard for the physiological signal attenuation principle where cortical source strength decays quadratically with distance from scalp sensors [10]. Consequently, models trained on standardized electrode layouts demonstrate poor generalizability to real-world clinical recordings with customized montages [7].

To overcome these limitations, we introduce the EEG graph attention network (EGANet), a novel architecture that reconceptualizes spatiotemporal modeling for EEG-based emotion recognition by embedding neurophysiological priors into an adaptive graph attention framework. Central to EGANet is a spatial decay matrix that explicitly incorporates the inverse-square attenuation law of cortical potentials, parameterized by the 3D Talairach coordinates of EEG electrodes. This matrix adaptively modulates inter-channel connectivity by integrating physical distance constraints with learnable, emotion-specific functional couplings, thereby unifying static volume conduction effects with dynamic, state-dependent neural interactions. In addition, EGANet employs a spatiotemporal pattern encoder that leverages rotary positional embeddings in conjunction with a Hadamard product–based aggregation scheme to capture long-range inter-channel dependencies while retaining sensitivity to electrode topology. Collectively, these design choices enable EGANet to learn biologically grounded and cognitively meaningful representations of brain activity:

1. We design a novel spatial decay matrix that explicitly encodes the physical layout of EEG electrodes, offering a principled spatial prior for capturing inter-channel dependencies.
2. We introduce a graph attention mechanism grounded in neurophysiological principles, which enables the model to adaptively integrate physical distance constraints with learnable functional couplings, thereby yielding a biologically informed and cognitively meaningful spatiotemporal representation.
3. Extensive experiments on multiple benchmark EEG datasets demonstrate that EGANet significantly outperforms existing methods in both accuracy and computational efficiency, validating its effectiveness for EEG-based emotion recognition.

2 Related Work

Significant efforts have been made to enhance the performance of affective brain-computer interfaces (aBCIs), particularly through advancements in leveraging both the spatial and temporal characteristics of EEG signals [2]. Among these, GNNs have emerged as a dominant approach due to their ability to model inter-channel connectivity based on cortical topology, which enables more accurate emotion recognition through spatial information. For example, the dynamic graph convolutional neural network (DGCNN) [4] utilized backpropagation to iteratively refine global inter-channel connections, while the local-global graph network (LGGNet) [5] introduced graphical filtering layers to model both local brain activities and global interactions across functional areas. Additionally, the pyramidal graph convolutional network (PGCN) [11] explored multi-scale structural and functional connections embedded in graph nodes. The dynamic self-attention network (DySAT) generated adaptive node representations by incorporating local neighborhoods and dynamically weighted historical representations over time using temporal attention [8]. These models represent significant progress in capturing the temporal evolution of EEG signals; however, their effectiveness in integrating explicit spatial priors remains limited.

Attention mechanisms have gained popularity in aBCIs for modeling channel-wise dependencies. For example, Song et al. [12] proposed the compact convolutional Transformer (Conformer), which combines local convolutional features with global spatial relationships for EEG classification. Similarly, Tao et al. [13] introduced the attention-based convolutional recurrent neural network (ACRNN), which captures temporal dependencies by embedding extended self-attention into a recurrent neural network (RNN). The Emotion Transformer (EmT) [7] further extended this concept by integrating multi-view graph embeddings to model the complex cognitive processes underlying emotional states. Despite their success in capturing spatial and temporal relationships, these attention-based models are computationally expensive, limiting their scalability for real-time and large-scale EEG datasets. Efforts in fields such as natural language processing and computer vision have explored spatial priors and sparse attention mechanisms to reduce computational costs [14, 15], but these approaches have yet to fully adapt to EEG. Most methods neglect the explicit spatial structure of EEG electrodes, leading to suboptimal representations and inefficiencies.

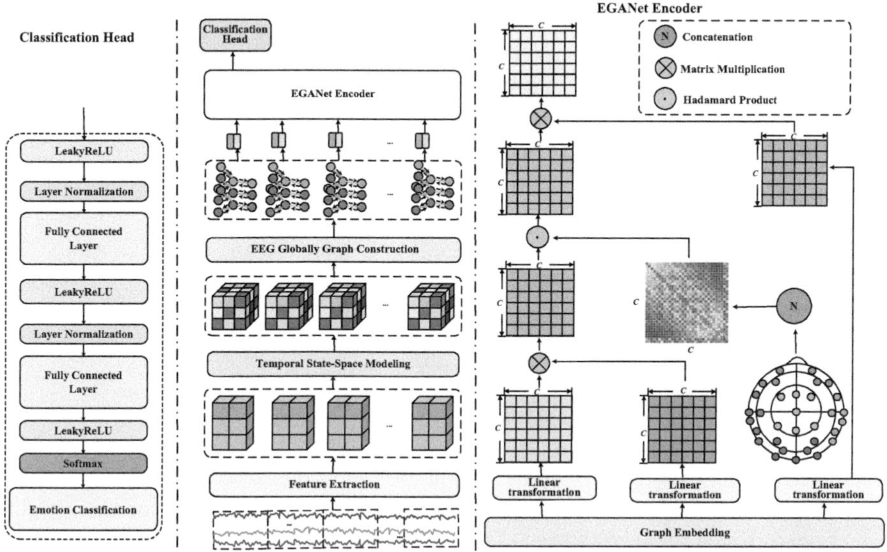

Fig. 1. The overview of the EGANet framework. The symbols '⊕' and '⊗' represent the concatenation and Hadamard product operators.

3 Methods

3.1 Temporal State-Space Modeling

The finite-duration impulse response filters with specific frequency bands—theta (4–8 Hz), alpha (8–14 Hz), beta (14–30 Hz), and gamma (30–47 Hz)—are employed to filter the EEG signals. The filtered EEG signals are then divided into K epochs using a non-overlapping Hamming window, each lasting 4 s, to extract differential entropy (DE) features [16]. For the mth trial with the nth participant, the DE feature of the pth band with the cth channel for the kth discrete EEG segment can be estimated as $u_{(k,m,n)}^{(c,p)} = 1/2 \cdot \log(2\pi \cdot e \cdot (\sigma_{(k,m,n)}^{(c,p)})^2)$, where $\sigma_{(k,m,n)}^{(c,p)}$ is the variance of the Gaussian random variable with the observations. These features of C channels across P bands are concatenated into a vector $\mathbf{u}_{(k,m,n)} = \left[u_{(k,m,n)}^{(1,1)}, \ldots, u_{(k,m,n)}^{(C,1)}; \ldots; u_{(k,m,n)}^{(1,P)}, \ldots, u_{(k,m,n)}^{(C,P)}\right]$, which is then passed to the temporal state-space module.

To model the inter-epoch stochastic processes of feature representations $\mathbf{u}_{(k,m,n)} \in \mathcal{R}^{CP}$ controlled by temporal-dependent hyperparameters, a linear dynamical system is employed to model real-valued $\mathbf{z}_{(k,m,n)} \in \mathcal{R}^{CP}$ using latent emotion states $\mathbf{u}_{(k,m,n)}$,

$$\mathbf{u}_{(k,m,n)}|\mathbf{u}_{(k-1,m,n)} \sim \mathcal{N}(\mathbf{u}_{(k,m,n)}|\mathrm{B}_1\mathbf{u}_{(k-1,m,n)}, \mathrm{B}_2), \tag{1}$$

$$\mathbf{z}_{(k,m,n)}|\mathbf{u}_{(k,m,n)} \sim \mathcal{N}(\mathbf{z}_{(k,m,n)}|\mathbf{B}_3\mathbf{u}_{(k,m,n)}, \mathrm{B}_4). \tag{2}$$

Equation (2) represents the emotion state dynamics, where $\mathbf{u}_{(k,m,n)}$ evolves according to the dynamic's matrix $\mathbf{B}_1 \in \mathcal{R}^{CP\times CP}$. Equation (3) describes the emotion observation model, where the observation $\mathbf{z}_{(k,m,n)}$ is generated from $\mathbf{u}_{(k,m,n)}$ via an emission matrix

$B_3 \in \mathcal{R}^{CP \times CP}$. These processes include process and observation noise, both modeled as zero-mean with covariance matrices B_2 and B_4, respectively. The causal features $\mathbf{z}_{(k,m,n)}$ can be updated with the spectral learning method [17].

3.2 EEG Globally Graph Construction

Following the temporal state-space modeling, each EEG instance $\mathbf{z}_{(k,m,n)}$ is represented as a graph $\mathcal{G} = \{\mathcal{V}, \mathcal{E}\}$, where the edge set $\mathcal{E}$ is captured by an adjacency matrix $\mathbf{A} \in \mathcal{R}^{C \times C}$. The entries $\mathbf{A}_{i,j}$ quantify the functional relationship between any two channels i and j within the channel set $\mathcal{V}$. By aggregating features $\{\mathbf{z}^c_{(k,m,n)} \in \mathcal{R}^P\}_{c=1}^C$ across all channels, a feature matrix characterizing the nodes' features on the graph is constructed as $\mathbf{Z}_{(k,m,n)} = [\mathbf{z}^{(1)}_{(k,m,n)}, \ldots, \mathbf{z}^{(C)}_{(k,m,n)}] \in \mathcal{R}^{C \times P}$.

Considering the topological network patterns of EEG dynamics and addressing the volume conduction effect induced by using the spatial covariance matrix $\mathbf{A}$, we design a graph relationship matrix $\mathbf{A}$ by normalizing the Euclidean metric $\hat{\mathbf{A}}$, computed based on the EEG nodes' prior locations from the international 10–20 system using the 3D Talairach coordinate representation [11],

$$\hat{\mathbf{A}}_{(i,j)} = \begin{cases} 0 & i = j \\ \frac{1}{(x_i - x_j)^2 + (y_i - y_j)^2 + (z_i - z_j)^2} & i \neq j \end{cases}, \tag{3}$$

$$\overline{\mathbf{A}} = \frac{\hat{\mathbf{A}} - \hat{\mathbf{A}}_{\min}}{\hat{\mathbf{A}}_{\max} - \hat{\mathbf{A}}_{\min}}, \ \mathbf{A} = \overline{\mathbf{D}}^{-1/2} \overline{\mathbf{A}\mathbf{D}}^{-1/2}. \tag{4}$$

Equation 3 represents the Euclidean measure using the 3D Talairach coordinates (x_i, y_i, z_i) and (x_j, y_j, z_j) of two channels i and j. In Eq. 4, the scaled matrix $\overline{\mathbf{A}}$ is obtained by applying Min-Max scaling and is further normalized using spectral graph theory [4] to ensure scale invariance. $\hat{\mathbf{A}}_{\max}$ and $\hat{\mathbf{A}}_{\min}$ are the minimum and maximum values of $\hat{\mathbf{A}}$. $\overline{\mathbf{D}}$ is the diagonal degree matrix of $\overline{\mathbf{A}}$, i.e., $\overline{\mathbf{D}}_{(c,c')} = \sum_c \overline{\mathbf{A}}_{(c,c')}$.

3.3 Global Spatial Pattern Encoder

To analyze inter-channel dependencies, we present a novel global spatial pattern encoder (SPE) module where the aggregation rule of the cth node features $\mathbf{z}^{(c)}_{(k,m,n)}$ selected from $\mathbf{Z}_{(k,m,n)}$ can be conceptualized as a random walk within this high-dimensional space. Specifically, this module aggregates all nodes within the specified cortical region to generate updated global node representations $\mathbf{h}^{(c)}_{(k,m,n)}$ by evaluating the occurrence magnitude of subsequent nodes along paths of fixed length to maintain global inter-channel dependencies,

$$\begin{aligned} \mathbf{h}^{(c)}_{(k,m,n)} &= \sum_{c'=1}^{C} \mathbf{A}_{(c,C-c')} (\mathbf{q}^{(c)}_{(k,m,n)}) (\mathbf{k}^{(c')}_{(k,m,n)})^{\mathrm{T}} \mathbf{v}^{(c')}_{(k,m,n)}, \\ \mathbf{q}^{(c)}_{(k,m,n)} &= \mathbf{R}_c \mathbf{z}^{(c)}_{(k,m,n)} \mathbf{\Theta}_Q, \\ \mathbf{k}^{(c')}_{(k,m,n)} &= \mathbf{R}_{c'} \mathbf{z}^{(c')}_{(k,m,n)} \mathbf{\Theta}_K, \\ \mathbf{v}^{(c')}_{(k,m,n)} &= \mathbf{z}^{(c')}_{(k,m,n)} \mathbf{\Theta}_V. \end{aligned} \tag{5}$$

Here $\boldsymbol{\Theta}_Q, \boldsymbol{\Theta}_K$, and $\boldsymbol{\Theta}_V \in \mathcal{R}^{P\times C}$ are transformation matrices used to perform linear transformations on the nodes. $\mathbf{R}_c \in \mathcal{R}^{C\times C}$ is a rotary matrix used to encode the relative positions of the EEG channels in a rotary position embedding manner [14]. Specifically, the C- dimensional feature space is divided into $C/2$ two-dimensional subspaces, as the rotation operation can be specified in a 2D plane. The rotation matrix $\mathbf{R}_c$ for the EEG features in the rth subspace and the cth channel can be defined as,

$$\mathbf{M}_{(r)}^{(c)} = \begin{bmatrix} \cos c\theta_r & -\sin c\theta_r \\ \sin c\theta_r & \cos c\theta_r \end{bmatrix},$$
$$\mathbf{R}_c = \begin{bmatrix} \mathbf{M}_{(1)}^{(c)} & & \\ & \ddots & \\ & & \mathbf{M}_{(C/2)}^{(c)} \end{bmatrix}. \tag{6}$$

Here, $\theta_r = 10000^{-2(r-1)/C}$, $r \in [1, 2, \ldots, C/2]$, defines the spatial resolution of the encoded embedding.

The graph retention mechanism, formulated in parallel following [14], is expressed as:

$$\mathbf{H}_{(k,m,n)} = (\mathbf{Q}_{(k,m,n)}(\mathbf{K}_{(k,m,n)})^{\mathrm{T}} \otimes \mathbf{A})\mathbf{V}_{(k,m,n)} \in \mathcal{R}^{C\times C}. \tag{7}$$

Here, $\mathbf{Q}_{(k,m,n)} = [\mathbf{q}_{(k,m,n)}^{(1)}, \ldots, \mathbf{q}_{(k,m,n)}^{(C)}]^{\mathrm{T}}$, $\mathbf{K}_{(k,m,n)} = [\mathbf{k}_{(k,m,n)}^{(1)} \ldots, \mathbf{k}_{(k,m,n)}^{(C)}]^{\mathrm{T}}$, and $\mathbf{V}_{(k,m,n)} = [\mathbf{v}_{(k,m,n)}^{(1)}, \ldots, \mathbf{v}_{(k,m,n)}^{(C)}]^{\mathrm{T}}$ represent the query, key, and value matrices, respectively. The symbol '$\otimes$' means the Hadamard product operation.

3.4 Overall Architecture of Graph Attention Network

These learned spatiotemporal features are flattened and then concatenated across all K time steps as a tensor $\mathbf{H}_{(m,n)} = [\sigma(\mathrm{FL}(\mathbf{H}_{(1,m,n)})); \sigma(\mathrm{FL}(\mathbf{H}_{(2,m,n)})); \ldots; \sigma(\mathrm{FL}(\mathbf{H}_{(K,m,n)}))]$. Where $\sigma(\cdot)$ is the LeakyReLU activation function and $\mathrm{FL}(\cdot)$ represents the flattening operation. Subsequently, $\mathbf{H}_{(m,n)}$ is concatenated across M trials from N participants as $\mathbf{H} = [\mathbf{H}_{(1,1)}; \ldots; \mathbf{H}_{(M,1)}; \mathbf{H}_{(1,2)}; \ldots; \mathbf{H}_{(M,2)}; \mathbf{H}_{(1,N)}; \ldots; \mathbf{H}_{(M,N)}]$. These concatenated representations serve as the input to the proposed EGANet, which incorporates the SPE followed by a stacked feed-forward network (FFN) to facilitate emotion classification. The classification process is formally represented as,

$$\mathbf{O} = \mathrm{softmax}(\sigma(\mathrm{LN}((\sigma(\mathrm{LN}(\mathbf{H})\mathbf{W}_1)))\mathbf{W}_2)) \tag{8}$$

where $\mathrm{LN}(\cdot)$ is the operator of layer normalization. $\mathbf{W}_1 \in \mathcal{R}^{CC\times D}$ and $\mathbf{W}_2 \in \mathcal{R}^{D\times E}$ are learnable parameter matrices the FFN, where D and E denote the dimensions of the hidden layer and the classification layer, respectively. The architecture of the proposed EGANet framework is illustrated in Fig. 1.

4 Experiments and Results

4.1 Datasets Descriptions

The DEAP dataset includes 32-channel EEG recordings from 32 participants, each viewing 40 one-minute music videos and rating arousal and valence on a 1–9 scale [18]. The SEED dataset consists of 62-channel EEG recordings from 15 participants across three sessions, with each session featuring 15 movie clips lasting ~4 min, annotated as positive, negative, or neutral [19]. The FACED dataset, designed for affective computing, contains 32-channel EEG signals from 123 participants, each viewing 28 clips (~66 s each) annotated across nine emotional categories (e.g., joy, anger, sadness, and neutral) [20].

EEG signals from DEAP, SEED, and FACED were down-sampled to 128 Hz, 200 Hz, and 250 Hz, respectively. Independent component analysis was applied to remove motion and ocular artifacts. Emotional categories for DEAP were binarized using a threshold of 5 on the 1–9 scale for arousal and valence. SEED used three categories (positive, negative, neutral), while FACED featured nine categories aligned with video annotations, enabling supervised machine learning with labeled EEG segments.

4.2 Implementation Details and Evaluation Metrics

We evaluate the generalization of EGANet with a leave-one-participant-out cross-validation strategy on the DEAP and SEED databases. For the FACED database, the subjects were divided into 10 folds (12 subjects for the first nine folds, and 15 for the 10th fold). Then, nine-fold subjects were used as the training sets, and the remaining subjects were used as the testing sets. The dimensions of the hidden layer and the classification layer in FFN are $D = 128$ and F, where F represents the number of categories. To derive conclusive outcomes, we computed averaged scores and standard deviation (std) from subject-generic experiments. Quantitative assessment was facilitated using key metrics, including accuracy (Acc) and weighted F1-score (F1), within the experimental context. All deep-learning models were trained in the PyTorch framework on a single NVIDIA RTX A4000 GPU, while the other shallow-learning models were tested using Python on an Intel i7 2.8 GHz CPU with 16 GB of memory. Since the limited number of samples may lead to overfitting, we introduced an L2 regularization term and dropout mechanism with a key probability of 0.6 into the error signal of every fully connected layer. To ensure fairness, all comparison methods were reimplemented and rigorously tuned within our experimental paradigm and data context. The reported results represent their optimal performance after thorough hyperparameter optimization.

4.3 Comparison with Deep-Learning Models

To thoroughly assess the effectiveness of the proposed EGANet, it is essential to compare its classification performance with existing state-of-the-art spatial and Transformer-based models. Such a comparison not only highlights the advantages of EGANet but also situates it within the broader advancements in EEG-based emotion recognition. The models selected for evaluation—EEGNet [6], generative adversarial network-based self-supervised data augmentation (GANSER) [21], ACRNN [13], DGCNN [4], DySAT [8], LGGNet [5], BPViT [22], Conformer [12], retentive network (RetNet) [14], and retentive network meet vision transformers (RMT) [15]—represent diverse methodologies spanning graph-based and attention-based approaches.

Table 1. Participant-averaged classification performance of the EGANet and modern deep learning models on DEAP database.

Classifiers	DEAP (2-class)			
	Valence		Arousal	
	Acc	F1	Acc	F1
EEGNet	0.5656(0.0907)	0.4130(0.1076)	0.5938(0.1492)	0.4542(0.1735)
GANSER	0.4781(0.0117)	0.3099(0.0132)	0.5314(0.0948)	0.3742(0.1047)
ACRNN	0.5889(0.0787)	0.4992(0.0920)	0.6167(0.1255)	0.5231(0.1309)
xLSTM	0.5680(0.0766)	0.6417(0.0795)	0.5752(0.1360)	0.6649(0.1360)
DGCNN	0.5614(0.0701)	0.5266(0.08146)	0.6082(0.0776)	0.5722(0.09152)
DySAT	0.5635(0.0682)	0.4856(0.0342)	0.5942(0.1407)	0.4624(0.0567)
LGGNet	0.5530(0.0970)	0.3833(0.0535)	0.5228(0.1404)	0.3591(0.0371)
BPViT	0.5656(0.0907)	0.3591(0.0371)	0.5891(0.1521)	0.3646(0.0646)
Conformer	0.5429(0.0754)	0.5627(0.0817)	0.5549(0.1150)	0.5804(0.1143)
RetNet	0.5525(0.0497)	0.5380(0.0581)	0.5423(0.0779)	0.5343(0.0769)
RMT	0.5757(0.0235)	0.4410(0.0314)	0.5732(0.0806)	0.4222(0.0120)
EGANet	**0.6473(0.0545)**	**0.6767(0.0616)**	**0.6545(0.0978)**	**0.6859(0.1151)**

Note: the standard deviation is listed in brackets. The optimal values are shown in boldface

The results in Tables 1 and 2 show that EGANet consistently achieves the highest F1-scores across the DEAP, SEED, and FACED datasets, demonstrating its ability to model spatiotemporal dependencies in EEG signals. On the SEED dataset, EGANet significantly outperforms graph-based models like DGCNN and LGGNet, which rely on static graphs, and attention-based models like RetNet and RMT, which lack explicit spatial priors. On the challenging FACED dataset, EGANet further proves its robustness by achieving the highest F1-score, outperforming models that struggle to generalize in complex multi-class scenarios.

Table 2. Participant-averaged classification performance of the EGANet and modern deep learning models on the SEED and FACED database.

Classifiers	SEED (3-class)		FACED (9-class)	
	Acc	F1	Acc	F1
EEGNet	0.5330(0.0707)	0.5076(0.0808)	0.3253(0.0375)	0.3226(0.0384)
GANSER	0.6756(0.0612)	0.6733(0.0616)	0.3870(0.0333)	0.3749(0.0368)
ACRNN	0.6642(0.0573)	0.6613(0.0589)	0.3477(0.0506)	0.3394(0.0474)
xLSTM	0.6360(0.0668)	0.6402(0.0680)	0.3507(0.0477)	0.3613(0.0444)
DGCNN	0.6820(0.0690)	0.6810(0.0695)	0.3393(0.0420)	0.3284(0.0367)
DySAT	0.6845(0.0635)	0.6742(0.0721)	0.3567(0.026)	0.3462(0.0332)
LGGNet	0.5831(0.0675)	0.5578(0.0743)	0.3808(0.0435)	0.3781(0.0444)
BPViT	0.6766(0.0630)	0.6757(0.0634)	0.3599(0.0353)	0.3468(0.0404)
Conformer	0.6591(0.0667)	0.6619(0.0665)	0.3718(0.0456)	0.3867(0.0450)
RetNet	0.6838(0.0671)	0.6813(0.0687)	0.3497(0.0385)	0.3410(0.0408)
RMT	0.6854(0.0683)	0.6855(0.0652)	0.3635(0.0384)	0.3524(0.0412)
EGANet	**0.7054(0.0609)**	**0.7074(0.0617)**	**0.4030(0.0418)**	**0.4181(0.0440)**

Note: the standard deviation is listed in brackets. The optimal values are shown in boldface

EGANet's exceptional performance stems from its use of a spatial decay matrix to explicitly model local and global dependencies based on the physical geometry of EEG electrodes. By integrating spatial priors while maintaining linear computational complexity, EGANet balances accuracy and efficiency, offering a scalable and robust solution for real-time and large-scale EEG applications. These results validate EGANet's innovative design and its contribution to advancing EEG-based emotion recognition.

4.4 Ablation Study

To systematically validate the effectiveness of each core component within EGANet, we conducted a rigorous series of ablation studies. By removing or replacing specific modules, we can quantitatively assess the contributions of the temporal state-space model (TSSM), the physics-grounded module (PGM), and the spatial pattern encoder (SPE) to the model's overall performance. The experiments were conducted on the DEAP, SEED, and FACED benchmark datasets, evaluating the following three model variants (Tables 3 and 4):

Table 3. Ablation study results on DEAP dataset.

Classifiers	DEAP (2-class)			
	Valence		Arousal	
	Acc	F1	Acc	F1
w/o PGM	0.6286(0.0690)	0.6475(0.0763)	0.6376(0.1086)	0.6529(0.0954)
w/o TSSM	0.6401(0.0732)	0.6721(0.0709)	0.6520(0.0925)	0.6806(0.1016)
w/o SPE	0.5780(0.0902)	0.5483(0.1231)	0.5975(0.0984)	0.5737(0.1029)
EGANet	**0.6473(0.0545)**	**0.6767(0.0616)**	**0.6545(0.0978)**	**0.6859(0.1151)**

Note: the standard deviation is listed in brackets. The optimal values are shown in boldface

Table 4. Ablation study results on SEED and FACED datasets.

Classifiers	SEED (3-class)		FACED (9-class)	
	Acc	F1	Acc	F1
w/o PGM	0.6862(0.0627)	0.6857(0.670)	0.3889(0.0515)	0.4033(0.0498)
w/o TSSM	0.7025(0.0618)	0.7065(0.0598)	0.3980(0.0387)	0.4087(0.0529)
w/o SPE	0.6854(0.0683)	0.6855(0.0652)	0.3635(0.0384)	0.3524(0.0412)
EGANet	**0.7054(0.0609)**	**0.7074(0.0617)**	**0.4030(0.0418)**	**0.4181(0.0440)**

Note: the standard deviation is listed in brackets. The optimal values are shown in boldface

Omitting the SPE resulted in the most pronounced decrease in accuracy across all datasets. On the DEAP arousal task, for instance, accuracy dropped from 0.6545 to 0.5483, while on the more complex FACED dataset it declined from 0.4030 to 0.3635. This substantial reduction highlights the critical importance of explicitly modeling inter-channel relationships using a graph-based framework. Without the SPE, the model loses the ability to capture topological information inherent in EEG signals, demonstrating that treating channels as an unstructured feature set leads to significant loss of information essential for emotion recognition.

Removing the PGM consistently impaired performance, confirming that incorporating biophysical priors provides a more robust representation than a purely data-driven functional connectivity graph. For example, on the DEAP valence task, accuracy decreased from 0.6473 to 0.6286. By encoding the physical geometry of electrodes, the PGM establishes a stable structural foundation that respects the biophysical nature of EEG signals, including volume conduction and distance-dependent attenuation. In contrast, a purely functional graph is more transient and susceptible to noise, highlighting the importance of grounding the model in physical principles for generalizable spatial representations.

Eliminating the TSSM produced a consistent, albeit modest, decrease in accuracy across datasets. On the SEED dataset, accuracy declined from 0.7054 to 0.7025. This result emphasizes the TSSM's role in capturing temporal dependencies, reflecting the dynamic evolution of emotional states over time. While the performance drop is less dramatic than that observed for spatial modeling, it demonstrates that explicitly modeling temporal dynamics enhances the model's sensitivity to continuous neural activity and contributes to more refined emotion classification.

5 Discussion

5.1 Visualization

The spatial distribution of EEG power across four frequency bands (theta, alpha, beta, and gamma) for various emotional states, as illustrated in Fig. 2, reveals distinct neural activity patterns associated with emotions. Positive emotions, such as joy and amusement, exhibit increased beta and gamma power in the frontal and parietal regions, indicative of active emotional engagement. In contrast, negative emotions, including sadness, anger, and fear, are characterized by elevated theta power in frontal regions, reflecting emotional regulation processes. High-arousal emotions (e.g., anger and fear) are linked to increased gamma activity, while low-arousal states (e.g., sadness and neutral) correspond to heightened theta and alpha activity.

These observations highlight the critical role of spatial and spectral information in distinguishing emotional states. Frequency-specific and region-dependent features provide valuable insights into the neural dynamics of emotional processing. These results further emphasize the need to incorporate both spatial relationships and frequency-specific features into EEG-based emotion recognition models to enhance classification accuracy and better capture the complexity of neural responses to emotional stimuli.

5.2 Modal Complexity

To further investigate the computational complexity of EGANet, we calculated the number of parameters and the floating-point operations (FLOPs) required for a single forward pass of the full EGANet model as follows: (1) Parameter Count: The EGANet model contains approximately 49K parameters. (2) FLOPs: A single forward pass involves approximately 184K floating-point operations (FLOPs). Compared to other state-of-the-art models in EEG emotion recognition, EGANet has a relatively lower parameter count and fewer FLOPs. This efficiency makes it particularly well-suited for deployment in resource-constrained environments, while still achieving competitive performance.

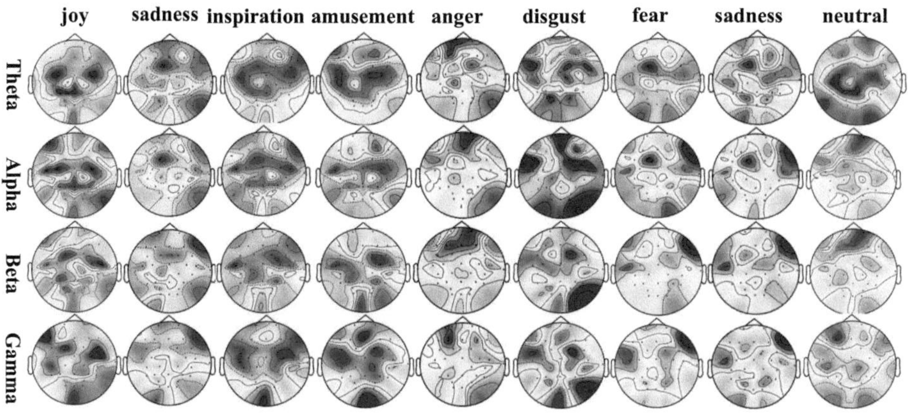

Fig. 2. Spatial distribution of the EEG power with four frequency bands (theta, alpha, beta, and gamma) averaged from all EEG segments and participants within FACED database.

6 Conclusion

This paper introduces EGANet, a novel framework for EEG-based emotion recognition that leverages a spatial decay matrix to explicitly model inter-channel relationships. By capturing both local and global dependencies, EGANet enhances EEG representation accuracy and interpretability while maintaining linear computational complexity for scalability and real-time applications. Experiments on benchmark datasets demonstrate its superior performance in recognition accuracy and efficiency compared to state-of-the-art methods.

However, EGANet faces limitations, including reliance on fixed electrode layouts, limited adaptability across datasets, and underexplored temporal dynamics and cross-frequency interactions. Future research will address these limitations by extending EGANet to adapt to diverse electrode layouts, integrating spatial, temporal, and spectral modeling, and exploring multimodal approaches that combine EEG with other physiological signals. We also plan to optimize EGANet for deployment on wearable and mobile platforms, paving the way for real-time applications in aBCIs.

References

1. Craik, A., He, Y., Contreras-Vidal, J.L.: Deep learning for electroencephalogram (EEG) classification tasks: a review. J. Neural Eng. **16**(3), 031001 (2019)
2. Zhang, J., Yin, Z., Chen, P., et al.: Emotion recognition using multi-modal data and machine learning techniques: a tutorial and review. Inf. Fusion **59**, 103–126 (2020)
3. Bänziger, T., Grandjean, D., Scherer, K.R.: Emotion recognition from expressions in face, voice, and body: the Multimodal Emotion Recognition Test (MERT). Emotion **9**(5), 691–704 (2009)
4. Song, T., Zheng, W., Song, P., et al.: EEG emotion recognition using dynamical graph convolutional neural networks. IEEE Trans. Affect. Comput. **11**(3), 532–541 (2020)
5. Ding, Y., Robinson, N., Tong, C., et al.: LGGNet: learning from local-global-graph representations for brain–computer interface. IEEE Trans. Neural Netw. Learn. Syst. **PP**, 1–14 (2023)

6. Lawhern, V.J., Solon, A.J., Waytowich, N.R., et al.: EEGNet: a compact convolutional neural network for EEG-based brain–computer interfaces. J. Neural Eng. **15**(5), 056013 (2018)
7. Ding, Y., Tong, C., Zhang, S., et al.: EmT: a novel transformer for generalized cross-subject EEG emotion recognition, arXiv preprint arXiv:2406.18345 (2024)
8. Sankar, A., Wu, Y., Gou, L., et al.: DySAT: deep neural representation learning on dynamic graphs via self-attention networks. In: Proceedings of the 13th International Conference on Web Search and Data Mining, Houston, TX, USA, pp. 519–527 (2020)
9. Zhang, G., Etemad, A.: Spatio-temporal EEG representation learning on Riemannian manifold and Euclidean space. IEEE Trans. Emerg. Top. Comput. Intell. **8**(2), 1469–1483 (2024)
10. Gong, P., Jia, Z., Wang, P., et al.: ASTDF-Net: attention-based spatial-temporal dual-stream fusion network for EEG-based emotion recognition. In: Proceedings of the 31st ACM International Conference on Multimedia, Ottawa ON, Canada, pp. 883–892 (2023)
11. Jin, M., Du, C., He, H., et al.: PGCN: pyramidal graph convolutional network for EEG emotion recognition. IEEE Trans. Multimedia (2024)
12. Song, Y., Zheng, Q., Liu, B., et al.: EEG conformer: convolutional transformer for EEG decoding and visualization. IEEE Trans. Neural Syst. Rehabil. Eng. **31**, 710–719 (2023)
13. Tao, W., Li, C., Song, R., et al.: EEG-based emotion recognition via channel-wise attention and self attention. IEEE Trans. Affect. Comput. **14**(1), 382–393 (2023)
14. Yutao Sun, L.D., et al.: Retentive Network: A Successor to Transformer for Large Language Models (2023)
15. Fan, Q., Huang, H., Chen, M., et al.: RMT: retentive networks meet vision transformers, arXiv preprint arXiv:2309.11523 (2023)
16. Zheng, W.L., Zhu, J.Y., Lu, B.L.: Identifying stable patterns over time for emotion recognition from EEG. IEEE Trans. Affect. Comput. **10**(3), 417–429 (2019)
17. Buesing, L., Macke, J.H., Sahani, M.: Spectral learning of linear dynamics from generalised-linear observations with application to neural population data. Adv. Neural Inf. Process. Syst. **25** (2012)
18. Koelstra, S., Muhl, C., Soleymani, M., et al.: DEAP: a database for emotion analysis using physiological signals. IEEE Trans. Affect. Comput. **3**(1), 18–31 (2012)
19. Zheng, W.L., Lu, B.L.: Investigating critical frequency bands and channels for EEG-based emotion recognition with deep neural networks. IEEE Trans. Auton. Mental Develop. **7**(3), 162–175 (2015)
20. Chen, J., Wang, X., Huang, C., et al.: A large finer-grained affective computing EEG dataset. Sci. Data **10**(1), 740 (2023)
21. Beck, M., Pöppel, K., Spanring, M., et al.: xLSTM: extended long short-term memory, arXiv preprint arXiv:2405.04517 (2024)
22. Beyer, L., Zhai, X., Kolesnikov, A.: Better plain ViT baselines for ImageNet-1k (2022)

Efficient Computation and Practical Application of Visual Models

I Can Still Steal Your Encoder: A Defense-Penetrating Encoder-Stealing Attack

Rongbin Xiao[1], Changyu Dong[1(✉)], Jie Zhang[2], Yan Pang[1], Zihan Xie[1], and Han Wu[3]

[1] Guangzhou University, Guangzhou, China
{rongbin.xiao,zihan.xie}@e.gzhu.edu.cn, changyu.dong@gmail.com
[2] University of Bath, Bath, UK
jz2558@bath.ac.uk
[3] University of Southampton, Southampton, UK
H.Wu@soton.ac.uk

Abstract. The rise of Encoder-as-a-Service (EaaS) has made pre-trained encoders accessible for various AI tasks, but this has introduced significant security concerns, particularly with model stealing attacks. While defenses like the B4B mechanism [6] have been proposed to protect against such attacks, we reveal critical vulnerabilities in B4B's strategies. B4B employs techniques such as embedding space coverage estimation, cost-based perturbation, and embedding transformations to thwart attackers. However, we introduce the first defense-penetrating attack that bypasses these protections. Our attack effectively circumvents all three defense mechanisms, enabling attackers to steal high-quality encoders with minimal degradation in performance. Extensive experiments show that the stolen encoder performs almost as well as the original, highlighting the weaknesses in B4B and similar defenses. Our work exposes significant gaps in the security of EaaS systems and calls for more robust, active defense strategies against model stealing.

Keywords: Model Stealing · Defense-Penetrating Attack · Representation Learning

1 Introduction

Recent advancements in artificial intelligence (AI) and deep learning (DL) have led to the widespread adoption of representation learning techniques, which train encoders through either supervised [25] or unsupervised [13,28] methods. These encoders extract rich and versatile features, enabling superior performance across a wide range of downstream tasks. However, the cost of training powerful encoders is prohibitively high. As a result, high-performance encoders are typically pre-trained by leading AI companies with substantial computational resources and are shared for commercial use through cloud-based platforms,

© The Author(s), under exclusive license to Springer Nature Singapore Pte Ltd. 2026
J. Kittler et al. (Eds.): PRCV 2025, LNCS 16289, pp. 483–501, 2026.
https://doi.org/10.1007/978-981-95-5764-6_33

a model known as Encoder-as-a-Service (EaaS). EaaS represents a significant evolution from traditional Machine-Learning-as-a-Service (MLaaS). Instead of providing downstream classifiers as cloud services, EaaS enables customers to query APIs for feature embeddings generated by pre-trained encoders. These feature embeddings (representations) are then used to train or test customer-specific classifiers. Leading technology companies, such as OpenAI, Google, have capitalized on this trend by offering embedding APIs for text and image data.

Despite the convenience and accessibility offered by EaaS, the deployment of these services raises significant security concerns, particularly in the context of model stealing attacks (MSAs) [19,26]. MSAs aim to replicate the parameters or functionality of a victim model by leveraging its outputs through continuous queries. Successful MSAs not only pose a threat to the intellectual property of the victim model but can also serve as a stepping stone for further attacks, such as adversarial attacks [12], backdoor attacks [16], and membership inference attacks [24]. Previous studies on stealing attacks targeting encoders, i.e. encoder-stealing attacks [7,17,23] have highlighted that encoders are more vulnerable than classifiers [11,21,27]. This increased vulnerability stems from the fact that encoders produce high-dimensional embeddings, which inherently expose more internal details of the model.

In response to these threats, defenses against encoder-stealing attacks have been developed. However, most of these approaches are reactive in nature. These reactive defenses do not actively prevent encoder theft but focus on post-theft detection using techniques such as watermarking [5,18] or performing dataset inference [8] to identify stolen copies. By the time theft is detected, the damage has already been done.

In practice, active defense mechanisms that thwart stealing attempts are more desirable. Early active defenses [7,17] used simple perturbation strategies to reduce the effectiveness of model stealing attacks, but they also significantly degraded the encoder's performance, making them unsuitable for real-world deployment. Recently, the B4B mechanism was proposed by [6]. This state-of-the-art (SOTA) defense presents a big step forward, disrupting the attacker's ability to extract sensitive representations while maintaining the encoder's utility for legitimate users.

That said, our thorough investigation reveals that the B4B mechanism is not as robust as claimed. It is vulnerable to exploitation and circumvention by adversaries. Its vulnerability has remained largely unexposed because existing attacks focus primarily on scenarios without defenses in place. In this paper, we introduce the first defense-penetrating attack that undermines the key strategies employed by B4B. The B4B mechanism is built on three core principles: (1) It adds Gaussian noise to the output embeddings, with the goal of misleading the adversary's model training and degrading the performance of stolen models. (2) To maximize utility for legitimate users, it continuously monitors queries and establishes a cost function to penalize malicious users. (3) To prevent evasion through Sybil attacks, it applies transformations to embeddings, ensuring that each user's embedding differs significantly from others. However, we demonstrate that all three of these defense strategies can be easily circumvented or nullified.

In summary, our work makes the following contributions:

- We identified critical vulnerabilities in existing active defenses against encoder-stealing attacks, demonstrating that these defenses are not as secure as claimed. This highlights a significant security risk for EaaS systems that rely on these defenses.
- We introduced the first defense-penetrating attack for encoder stealing. While our focus is on the B4B defense mechanism, the attack is broadly applicable to other defense strategies.
- We conducted extensive experiments to evaluate the effectiveness of our attack. The results show that the stolen encoder performs almost as well on downstream tasks as one taken without any defense mechanisms in place.

2 Related Work

Encoder-Stealing Attacks. Model stealing attacks [15,26] aim to replicate the parameters or functionality of a victim model $f_v(x;\theta)$. To achieve this, an adversary queries the victim model with a set of inputs and collects the corresponding outputs. These query-response pairs are then used as training data to construct a stolen model $f_s(x;\theta)$. Literatures [7,17] show that model stealing targeting encoders is also feasible and effective. Attackers aim to replicate the victim encoder by training a local copy that produces representations similar to those of the victim model. Two primary training strategies are employed for encoder stealing: (1) direct alignment of representations via Mean Squared Error (MSE) loss between the victim and the stolen encoder; and (2) self-supervised training with a contrastive loss, such as InfoNCE [20] or SoftNN [10], using the victim encoder's outputs as pseudo-labels. Recent works, such as StolenEncoder [17], have further optimized the attack process by exploiting the observation that victim encoders generate similar outputs for augmented views of the same image. This allows attackers to minimize queries to the victim encoder by augmenting a single input locally and training the stolen encoder on these augmentations. Cont-Steal [23] utilizes contrastive learning techniques to enhance stealing performance by aligning the stolen embedding of an image with its target embedding and distancing embeddings of different images, achieving superior accuracy of downstream tasks compared to conventional attack methods against encoders.

Encoder-Stealing Defenses. Most of the existing defenses are reactive. They employ techniques such as watermarking [5,18], and attempt to embed unique patterns into the victim encoder. Subsequently, watermark verification can determine if a suspect encoder contains a specific watermark embedded by the victim. Similarly, dataset inference [9] leverages the unique data distribution of the victim's training set to distinguish stolen encoders from independently trained ones.

These reactive methods, however, are limited to post-hoc detection rather than proactively preventing attacks.

Early active defenses, such as those proposed by [7,17], attempt to perturb or truncate the outputs of the victim encoder to disrupt the attacker's training process. These methods introduce noise into the stolen embeddings, making them less effective for training the stolen model. However, such approaches often degrade the quality of the representations provided to legitimate users, rendering them impractical for real-world applications. In contrast to these simple defenses, the B4B defense [6] introduces bucket occupancy tracking and noise injection mechanisms, designed to minimally impact legitimate users while thwarting attackers. Despite these improvements, our work shows that current defenses, including B4B, remain vulnerable to more sophisticated attack strategies.

3 Overview of the B4B Defense

Model stealing attacks aim to replicate the functionality of a victim model f_v trained on a dataset D_v. In this scenario, the attacker has black-box access to the victim model and constructs a stealing dataset $D_s = \{q_i, f_v(q_i)\}_{i=1}^{n}$, consisting of queries q_i and their corresponding outputs $f_v(q_i)$ returned by the victim model. This dataset is then used to train a stolen model f_s. Model stealing attacks have been demonstrated against various types of models, including classifiers and encoders. Specifically, when the victim model is an encoder, such attacks are referred to as encoder-stealing attacks.

B4B is an active defense framework designed to counter encoder-stealing attacks, offering protection to encoders while minimizing disruption for legitimate users. It is based on the observation that malicious queries from adversaries tend to be more diverse than those from benign users. As a result, embeddings for malicious queries span a much larger part of the embedding space compared to those used by legitimate users focused on specific downstream tasks. Building on this insight, B4B is composed of three primary components: Coverage Estimation, Cost-based Perturbation, and Per-User Representation Transformations. Each component plays a vital role in detecting and penalizing adversaries, all while preserving the experience of legitimate users.

Coverage Estimation. B4B utilizes Locality Sensitive Hashing (LSH) based on random projection [2,22] to approximate the portion of the embedding space covered by each user. A locality sensitive hash function $\mathcal{H}$ maps inputs into 2^n buckets, ensuring that similar items are assigned to the same bucket with high probability. For a given embedding space $\mathcal{E}$, and each query q_i submitted by a user U, B4B hashes the embedding $r_i = f_v(q_i)$ using $\mathcal{H}$ and counts the number of non-empty buckets. This count represents the embedding space coverage for the user, denoted as $\tilde{\mathcal{E}}_f^U$. As the number of queries grows, $\tilde{\mathcal{E}}_f^U$ increases, and B4B posits that the coverage for benign users grows more slowly compared to that of malicious users.

Cost-based Perturbation. B4B adds Gaussian noise into the returned embedding to the user:

$$\hat{r} = r + \mathcal{N}(0, \sigma^2),$$

where $\hat{r}$ represents the noise-injected embedding. To effectively prevent encoder theft while minimizing the impact on legitimate users, the noise magnitude is dynamically adjusted using a cost function:

$$\mathcal{C}_{\lambda,\alpha,\beta}(\tilde{\mathcal{E}}_f^U) = \lambda \times \left(\exp^{\ln \frac{\alpha}{\lambda} \times \tilde{\mathcal{E}}_f^U \times \beta^{-1}} - 1\right).$$

In B4B, the standard deviation of the Gaussian noise, σ, is set to $\mathcal{C}_{\lambda,\alpha,\beta}(\tilde{\mathcal{E}}_f^U)$. As a result, users with higher embedding space coverage $\tilde{\mathcal{E}}_f^U$ are penalized with noisier embeddings, increasing the deterrence for malicious users.

Per-User Transformations against Sybil Attacks. Since the noise introduced increases with embedding space coverage, adversaries can bypass this by using Sybil attacks, where they create multiple fake accounts (i.e. Sybils), each submitting only a small number of queries. As a result, the coverage remains low, and so does the noise. To counter this, the B4B defense assigns a distinct transformation T_U to each user. The output embeddings are passed through these transformations before being returned to the user. The goal of the transformation is to preserve legitimate utility while preventing the pooling of embeddings across different users. Concrete instantiations of transformations for B4B include Affine, Padding, Shuffle, and Binary. These transformations can be flexibly combined, further broadening the possible transformations applied to each user.

4 The Defense-Penetrating Attack

In this section, we present our Defense-Penetrating Attack. The attack comprises three key strategies: A1: embedding space coverage reduction; A2: noise reduction; and A3: embedding unification. Figure 1 shows an overview of our Defense-Penetrating Attack. The design details of each strategy are outlined below.

4.1 A1: Embedding Space Coverage Reduction

B4B estimates the coverage of the user embedding space $\tilde{\mathcal{E}}_f^U$ by counting the proportion of occupied hash buckets through LSH, and adding a greater penalty

Table 1. Downstream Task Accuracy of Stolen Encoder for Different Downscaling Parameters at 50k Query Cost in SimSiam.

	4×4	8×8	16×16	32×32	48×48	96×96
CIFAR10	48.530	57.730	67.190	**67.980**	59.120	31.270
STL10	42.338	48.613	53.588	57.400	**58.025**	28.375

to user embeddings as bucket occupancy increases. From an adversary's perspective, the objective is to find queries whose embeddings are more likely to be clustered into fewer buckets, thereby reducing the added penalty.

There might be many adversarial strategies that can achieve embedding space coverage reduction. Here we focus on a simple strategy, downscaling, which proved effective in our tests. In particular, we first resize a query image to a lower resolution, then convert the lower resolution image back to the original size. The rationale behind this is that downscaling constrains the input space, which in turn limits the output to a smaller sub-space of $\mathcal{E}$. Ultimately, this increases the probability that two embeddings fall into the same bucket.

The effectiveness of downscaling is illustrated in Fig. 2. Here the original query images are from ImageNet (224×224). We can see that downscaling can effectively decrease bucket occupancy. Moreover, a smaller resolution results in a slower increase in bucket occupancy. In Fig. 3, we show a t-SNE plot for the embedding space. We can see that with a smaller downscaling parameter (4×4), the occupancy is smaller than that of a larger parameter (32×32), which is in turn smaller than that with no downscaling.

When the downscaling parameters are set too small, the added noise is reduced; however, the representations become overly concentrated in the embedding space, significantly restricting the portion of the space that the stolen encoder can effectively capture. Conversely, when the parameters are set too large, the added noise severely impacts the stolen encoder's ability to fit the cor-

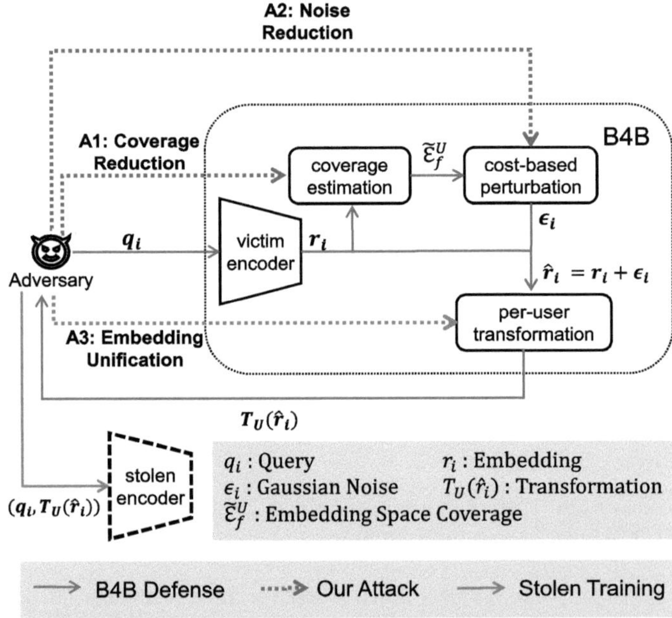

Fig. 1. Overview of Defense-Penetrating Attack against B4B.

rect representations. Both scenarios result in poor performance on downstream tasks, as demonstrated in Table 1. Consequently, for subsequent encoder-stealing experiments in Sect. 5.2, we selected image downscaling parameters of 32×32 and 48×48 to compare with the conventional attack.

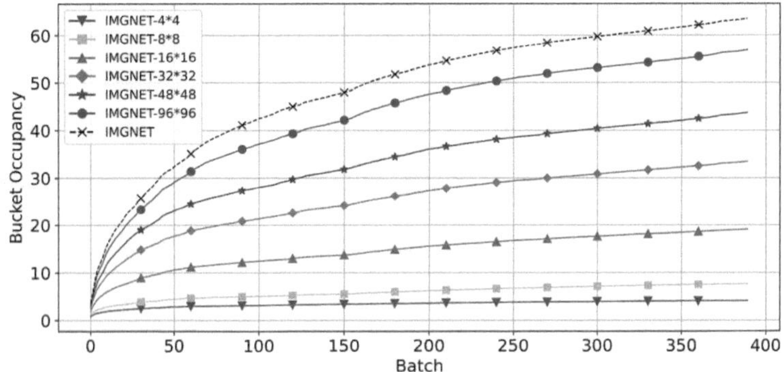

Fig. 2. Bucket Occupancy for Different Downscaling Parameters. The x-axis represents the batch being queried, and the y-axis represents the bucket occupancy.

4.2 A2: Noise Reduction

B4B adds Gaussian noise from $\mathcal{N}(0, \sigma^2)$ to output embeddings. Since the mean of the noise is 0, a well-known method to reduce the noise is for each query q_i, repeatedly query it n times to get $\hat{r}_i^1, \cdots, \hat{r}_i^n$, and obtain $\bar{r}_i = \frac{1}{n}\sum_{j=1}^{n} \hat{r}_i^j = r_i + \mathbb{E}_{\epsilon \sim \mathcal{N}(0,\sigma^2)}(\epsilon)$. However, this will reduce the number of effective queries to $1/n$ of the budget. The encoder obtained by the adversary may not perform well due to fewer queries.

Our strategy to counter the problem is based on two insights: (1) the level of noise increases monotonically; (2) up to a scale, small noise does not have a negative impact on training. The details are as the following:

1. At the very beginning of the attack, the adversary queries a sentinel sample q_0, and obtains the embedding r_0. Note that r_0 is without any noise because $\tilde{\mathcal{E}}_f^U$ is lazily updated after answering a batch (default: 256) of queries. The adversary then queries distinct samples, records the returned embeddings, and keeps track of the number of queries.
2. At the beginning of the b-th batch, the adversary queries the sentinel sample q_0 again, and obtains the corresponding $\hat{r}_0^b$. It then compute $\epsilon_b = \hat{r}_0^b - r_0$ and the current standard deviation $\sigma_b = \|\epsilon\|_2$. if σ_b is less than a pre-chosen threshold σ_τ, the adversary keeps querying distinct samples in this batch; otherwise, the adversary repeatedly queries each sample n times and records the average of the n embeddings returned. In later batches, the adversary does not need to query q_0 again since the level of noise will not decrease.

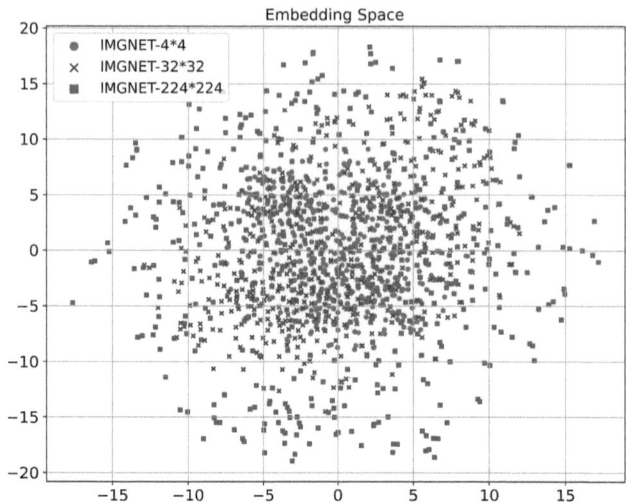

Fig. 3. **t-SNE Plot for Three Downscaling Parameters.**

3. The adversary repeats step 2 until the budget is exhausted, then trains an encoder using the (query, answer) pair accumulated during the query process.

To determine the threshold σ_τ, we notice that the noise $\epsilon \in \mathbb{R}^m$ is a random vector where each component ϵ_i follows a normal distribution, specifically $\epsilon_i \sim N(0, \sigma^2)$. Consequently, $\frac{\epsilon_i^2}{\sigma^2} \sim \chi^2(1)$ and $\sum_{i=1}^{m} \frac{\epsilon_i^2}{\sigma^2} \sim \chi^2(m)$. Our goal is to find σ_τ such that the L2 norm of the noise vector, $\|\epsilon\|$, is less than a constant α with a large probability $1 - \mathcal{P}$, i.e.

$$P(\|\epsilon\| < \alpha) = P\left(\sum_{i=1}^{m} \frac{\epsilon_i^2}{\sigma^2} < \frac{\alpha^2}{\sigma^2}\right) \geq 1 - \mathcal{P}_\tau.$$

Therefore σ_τ can be calculated by using the χ^2 inverse cumulative distribution function $\sigma_\tau = \frac{\alpha}{\sqrt{\text{chi2inv}(1-\mathcal{P}_\tau, m)}}$. We notice that σ_τ is related to α. Intuitively, the value of α determines the level of noise, and its impact on downstream tasks depends on the L2 norm of the embeddings. Hence, we define α relatively as $\alpha = \mathcal{R} \times \|r_0\|$ where r_0 is the embedding of the sentinel sample. Then σ_τ can be determined by hyperparameters $\mathcal{P}_\tau$ and $\mathcal{R}$.

Generalize to other active defenses. The noise reduction strategy can be generalized to other active defense mechanisms. For example, Feature Poisoning [17] and random perturbation [7] inject random noise from certain distributions into the output embeddings. Both of them can be penetrated in a similar way, i.e., by estimating the norm of noise and reducing the noise by repeated queries.

4.3 A3: Embedding Unification

To defend against potential Sybil attacks, B4B applies distinct transformations T_U to the embeddings of different users. However, we found that these transformed embeddings can be easily unified, thereby undermining the defense mechanism. More specifically, the adversary can first choose a Sybil U_0, then for other sybils U_i the adversary finds a transformation F_i such that $F_i(T_i(r)) \approx T_0(r)$. Then the embeddings obtained by each Sybil can still be pooled together for training the stolen encoder. In the main text, we focus on illustrative examples of Affine and Binary operations, while systematically presenting padding and shuffle methodologies in Appendix A.2.

Affine. The Affine transformation is defined as $T_i(r) = a_i \odot r + b_i$, where $\odot$ is the Hadamard product. B4B chooses random (a_i, b_i) for each U_i. In this case, $F_i(y) = m_i \odot y + c_i$ can be obtained as the following:

1. When U_0 is created, it queries x_1, x_2 and obtains $y_0^1 = T_0(r_1) = a_0 \odot r_1 + b_0$ and $y_0^2 = T_0(r_2) = a_0 \odot r_2 + b_0$, where $r_i = f_v(x_i)$.
2. When U_i is created, it sends the same x_1, x_2 and obtains $y_i^1 = a_i \odot r_1 + b_i$ and $y_i^2 = a_i \odot r_2 + b_i$.
3. The adversary computes and records $m_i = \frac{y_0^1 - y_0^2}{y_i^1 - y_i^2} = \frac{a_0}{a_i}$, $c = y_0^1 - m_i \odot y_i^1 = b_0 - m_i \odot b_i$

It is easy to see that $F_i(T_i(r)) = m_i \odot (a_i \odot r + b_i) + c_i = a_0 \odot r + m_i \odot b_i + b_0 - m_i \odot b_i = T_0(r)$.

Binary. The Binary transformation maps the original representation r into a binary vector based on a random partition of the embedding space. Specifically, B4B chooses n random pair$\{(a_i^j, b_i^j)\}_{j=1}^n$ for user U_i, where each a_i^j is a vector of the same dimension as the embedding r, and b_i^j is a scalar value. It also defines a binarization function $B(r, a_i^j, b_i^j) = \text{Sign}(a_i^j \cdot r + b_i^j)$ where Sign returns 1 for positive value and 0 for non-positive value. The returned binarized embedding of r is $T_i(r) = B(r, a_i^1, b_i^1) || \cdots || B(r, a_i^n, b_i^n)$. Note that this binarization process is lossy and has a greater impact on legitimate users' performance than other transformations. It is more difficult to invert because it is non-linear. That said, we developed an effective probabilistic algorithm for unifying binarized embeddings for different uses. Experimental results show that this algorithm achieves a 99.88% success rate. The details of the algorithm are as follows:

1. When U_0 is created, it queries t samples $x_1, \cdots, x_t$ and obtains $y_0^1, \cdots, y_0^t$, where $y_0^j = T_0(f_v(x_j))$ are binarized embedding.
2. When U_i is created, it queries the same t samples and obtains $y_i^1, \cdots, y_i^t$.
3. Build a lookup table L from U_i's binarized embedding to U_0's: for each index j, record $L[j] = (z_0, z_1)$, such that

$$z_b = \arg\max_{\beta \in \{0,1\}} \sum_{k=1}^{t} \mathbb{1}(y_i^k[j] = b \wedge y_0^k[j] = \beta), b \in \{0, 1\}.$$

Here (z_0, z_1) stores the most likely value of $y_0^k[j]$ when $y_i^k[j]$'s value is 0 or 1.

4. Then $F_i(y)$ is defined as: for each j, if $y[j] = 0$, set $y[j] = L[j][0]$; else set $y[j] = L[j][1]$.

Generalize to other transformations. In general, our strategy can be summarized as querying the same (or related) samples by different users, and then finding the correlations. For any linear transformation, a perfect unification transformation F_i such that $F_i(T_i(r)) = T_0(r)$ can always be found by solving a set of linear equations after a sufficient number of queries. For non-linear transformations, we notice that the non-linearity should not impact legitimate users too much and the transformations are often deterministic. Therefore, although the details may vary, a good approximation can often be found so that $F_i(T_i(r)) \approx T_0(r)$ with a high probability.

4.4 Putting Them Together

While we introduce the strategies individually, they can be used in conjunction to achieve the best result. For example, A1 can reduce the rate of noise growth, however, the embedding space coverage still increases and eventually renders the query results unusable after a certain number of queries. Therefore, A1 can be used with A2 so that the noise reduction process can be applied to later queries. For A3, ideally, the adversary can create an unlimited number of Sybils so that the query results are also noise-free. However, in practice, this might not be possible due to real-world constraints. If the number of Sybils is limited, then the adversary can use A1 and/or A2 to reduce the noise when necessary.

5 Empirical Evaluation

5.1 Experimental Setup

Following the experimental setup for B4B, we utilize two widely-used encoder frameworks, SimSiam [4] and DINO [1], as the victim encoder. Pre-trained models for both frameworks are directly downloaded from their official repositories. The SimSiam encoder produces output representations with a dimensionality of 2048, while the DINO encoder generates 1536-dimensional representations. Hyperparameters for the B4B defense were set according to the calibrated values provided in the original paper.

For the stealing attack, the attacker has black-box access to the victim encoder. The stolen encoder adopts a ResNet-50 [14] as the backbone, with its fully connected layer modified to accommodate different embedding dimensions. We use ImageNet-100k as the query dataset and employ the InfoNCE [3] loss function to train the stolen encoder. To evaluate the performance of the stolen encoder, we utilize multiple downstream classification tasks, including FashionMNIST, CIFAR10, SVHN, STL10, and IMGNET-C10 (sample 10 random classes on ImageNet). Compared to the B4B setup, we add IMGNET-C10 as an additional evaluation dataset to assess the accuracy of the stolen encoder in high-resolution downstream tasks. Detailed experimental settings and hyperparameters are provided in Appendix B.

5.2 Evaluation of Our Attack Strategies

In this section, we report the experiment results using SimSiam as the victim encoder; DINO results are in Appendix D.

Embedding Space Coverage Reduction. We conducted an end-to-end analysis using two downscaling parameters, 32 and 48, at query budgets of 50k and 100k. The effectiveness of stealing is measured by the accuracy of downstream classifiers, whose inputs are pre-processed with the stolen encoder. The results are summarized in Table 2. We can see that downscaling effectively circumvents the B4B defense mechanism and facilitates the theft of encoders. In all cases, the accuracy of downstream tasks increases when downscaling is used.

We can observe that when B4B is in place, the effectiveness of attack without downscaling declines when query budgets increase, due to excessive noise added to later query results. In contrast, with downscaling, the added noise is relatively low, allowing the performance of the stolen encoder to improve as the query count increases.

In addition, we observe that for low-resolution images (FashionMNIST, CIFAR10, SVHN), stealing with ImageNet data downscaled to 32×32 in the presence of B4B even outperforms the results of stealing with the original ImageNet data when there is no defense. We attribute this to downscaling makes the queries more concentrated so that the output representations are closer to those of the low-resolution images in the embedding space (as visualized in Fig. 3), enabling more information to be extracted. However, this advantage comes at the cost of reduced effectiveness in high-resolution embedding spaces, as reflected by the lower classification accuracy on the IMGNET-C10 downstream task. This reveals a possible attack optimization strategy that is overlooked in the literature, i.e., adaptively choosing query data according to the downstream task.

Noise Reduction Noise reduction involves three hyperparameters: $\mathcal{R}$, $\mathcal{P}_\tau$, and the repetition n. The values of $\mathcal{R}$ and $\mathcal{P}_\tau$ determine the noise standard deviation threshold σ_τ, and n specifies the number of repeated queries used to reduce noise once the mechanism is activated. In our experiments, we fix $\mathcal{P}_\tau = 0.05$, $n = 8$, and vary the hyperparameter $\mathcal{R}$ to assess its impact on attack performance. The downstream task accuracies are summarized in Table 3. In the table, we also show $\mathcal{N}_{td}$, which denotes the number of queries that occur before the noise reduction mechanism is activated. The final number of effective queried samples $\mathcal{N}_q$ can be calculated using the following formula:

$$\mathcal{N}_q = \frac{T - \mathcal{N}_{td}}{n} + \mathcal{N}_{td},$$

where T represents the total query budget, from the results, we observe a significant improvement in the accuracy of the downstream task accuracy. This shows that our attack greatly reduces the effectiveness of the B4B defense. Moreover, compared to downscaling, noise reduction does not hinder the effective learning

Table 2. Downstream Task Accuracy of Stolen Encoder Using A1 in SimSiam. QUERIES stands for the number of queries used for stealing. DEFENSE indicates whether the victim encoder has deployed B4B. DOWNSCALING column shows the downscaling parameters.

QUERIES	DEFENSE	DOWN-SCALING	F-MNIST	CIFAR10	SVHN	STL10	IMGNET-C10
50K	NONE	w/o	81.910	62.580	46.370	62.738	71.000
	NONE	32×32	82.950	69.180	48.248	58.050	52.000
	B4B	w/o	49.920	48.140	35.126	34.025	**56.600**
	B4B	32×32	**82.400**	**67.980**	**47.565**	**57.400**	48.600
	B4B	48×48	78.540	59.120	35.867	58.025	47.800
100K	NONE	w/o	83.510	66.580	52.443	68.750	76.000
	NONE	32×32	85.710	76.530	57.518	63.800	56.200
	B4B	w/o	36.540	15.420	19.587	15.900	16.600
	B4B	32×32	**84.780**	**74.190**	**55.336**	**62.575**	**55.200**
	B4B	48×48	64.370	41.610	26.318	42.700	43.000

Table 3. Downstream Task Accuracy of Stolen Encoder Using A2 in SimSiam. The ATTACK column lists the adversarial attack methods, where CONV denotes the conventional attack [7], and A2 means noise reduction is used. $\mathcal{N}_{td}$ is the number of queried samples when triggering the noise reduction mechanism. We fix the hyperparameter $\mathcal{P}_\tau = 0.05$, $n = 8$ while varying $\mathcal{R}$.

QUERIES	ATTACK	DEFENSE	$\mathcal{R}$	$\mathcal{N}_{td}$	F-MNIST	CIFAR10	SVHN	STL10	IMGNET-C10
50K	CONV	NONE	N/A	N/A	81.910	62.580	46.370	62.738	71.000
	CONV	B4B	N/A	N/A	49.920	48.140	35.126	34.025	56.600
	A2	B4B	0.1	9216	**78.540**	53.130	37.458	52.813	62.000
			0.3	13120	77.720	56.040	38.829	55.175	65.800
			0.5	15680	78.080	**56.790**	38.810	**56.375**	**66.000**
			0.7	17408	78.360	56.570	**41.272**	54.025	65.400
			1.0	28352	77.950	56.040	40.174	54.613	63.200
100K	CONV	NONE	N/A	N/A	83.510	66.580	52.443	68.750	76.000
	CONV	B4B	N/A	N/A	36.540	15.420	19.587	15.900	16.600
	A2	B4B	0.1	9216	79.460	56.700	38.795	55.575	**68.000**
			0.3	13120	79.780	**56.880**	41.395	53.688	63.600
			0.5	15680	**79.900**	56.760	40.220	**56.900**	64.200
			0.7	17408	79.680	58.500	**44.426**	56.513	65.000
			1.0	28352	77.770	54.300	39.486	52.888	66.800

of the stolen encoder within the high-resolution embedding space. This results in improved classification accuracy in the downstream task of IMGNET-C10.

Table 4. Downstream Task Accuracy of Stolen Encoder Utilizing Sybil Attack in SimSiam. The query budget is set to 100k and is evenly split across all users.

DATASET	USER						
	1	2	4	8	16	32	64
F-MNIST	36.540	61.560	81.220	83.090	83.800	83.570	84.060
CIFAR10	15.420	45.130	61.810	62.370	64.340	66.450	65.240
SVHN	19.587	30.501	47.960	43.289	50.884	49.927	47.760
STL10	15.900	40.038	56.250	65.025	67.338	68.600	67.650
IMGNET-C10	16.600	56.800	67.600	74.000	77.400	77.200	77.400

Embedding Unification. We simulate Sybil attacks with embedding unification and measure the performance of the stolen encoder under varying numbers of attacker users. For Affine, Padding, and Shuffle transformations, the embeddings can be perfectly unified, and the downstream task accuracies are reported in Table 4. We observed a significant increase in downstream task classification accuracy as the number of users increased from 1 to 8. However, as the user count continued to rise, the accuracy began to plateau. This plateauing can be explained by the exponential cost function of the B4B defense. When the number of users increased from 1 to 8, the total query budget was distributed among them, leading to a reduced query volume and, consequently, lower bucket occupancy. This reduction resulted in less noise applied to each user's output representations. As the user count increased further, the penalty imposed by the cost function became negligible, essentially rendering its impact on the representations insignificant, which resulted in relatively stable downstream task accuracy. For the Binary case, we assess the effectiveness of Sybil attacks with embedding unification by calculating the average L1 distance between stolen and victim encoder embeddings (results in Appendix C).

6 Conclusions

In this work, we have highlighted critical vulnerabilities in existing defense mechanisms against model stealing attacks in the context of Encoder-as-a-Service systems. Specifically, we demonstrated that the B4B defense, while a promising approach, is not as robust as previously claimed. Our proposed defense-penetrating attack successfully bypasses B4B's key strategies, including perturbation, query monitoring, and embedding transformations, allowing attackers to extract high-quality representations with minimal performance loss. Through extensive experimentation, we have shown that the stolen encoder performs nearly as well as the original model, underlining the significant weaknesses in current defense strategies. These findings highlight the necessity for enhanced security measures in the rapidly evolving landscape of AI services. They also suggest that a reassessment of current defense frameworks may be beneficial in addressing the increasing sophistication of emerging threats.

Acknowledgements. This work was supported in part by the National Key Research and Development Program of China under Grant 2023YFB2704300, in part by the Guangzhou Basic and Applied Basic Research Foundation under Grant 2024A03J0324, and in part by the Science and Technology Projects in Guangzhou 2024 Guangzhou School (Institute) Enterprise Joint Funding Project under Grant 2024A03J0166.

A The Defense-Penetrating Attack

A.1 Spherical Variance After Downscaling

The relationship between downscaling and clustering of embeddings can also be observed in Table 5. Here we normalize embeddings into unit vectors, and then calculate the corresponding spherical variance, which serves as an indicator of the degree of clustering of points on a hypersphere. We can see that a smaller downscaling parameter yields a lower spherical variance, indicating greater point clustering.

Table 5. Spherical Variance for Different Downscaling Parameters.

Downscaling	4×4	16×16	32×32	96×96	224×224
Spherical Variance	0.04602	0.12658	0.18371	0.30190	0.34512

A.2 Embedding Unification of Residual Transformations

Padding. The Padding transformation in B4B is defined as choosing a random fixed-length vector ρ_i for each user U_i, then $T_i(r) = r||\rho_i$, where $||$ means concatenation. Unifying this transformation is relatively straightforward:

1. When U_i is created, it queries x_1, x_2 and obtains $y_i^1 = T_i(r_1) = r_1||\rho_i$ and $y_i^2 = T_i(r_2) = r_2||\rho_i$. The adversary finds and records ρ_i that is the longest common vector at the end of y_i^1 and y_i^2.
2. $F_i(y)$ is defined as removing ρ_i from y then appending ρ_0 to the result (or simply every user including U_0 removes ρ_i).

Shuffle. The Shuffle transformation in B4B is defined as choosing a random permutation π_i for each user U_i, then $T_i(r) = \pi_i(r)$. Unifying this transformation is also easy:

1. When U_0 is created, it queries x and obtains $y_0 = \pi_0(r)$, where $r = f_v(x)$.
2. When U_i is created, it queries the same x and obtains $y_i = \pi_i(r)$.
3. The permutation $\pi_0 \circ \pi_i^{-1}$ can be constructed as an index mapping table L, by iterating through each index j and find k such that $y_i[j] = y_0[k]$, then record $L[j] = k$.
4. $F_i(y)$ is defined as: outputting a new vector such that the $y[j]$ is moved to the k-th position in the new vector, where $k = L[j]$.

B Details on Experimental Setup

B.1 Hyperparameter Settings for B4B Defense Mechanism

The hyperparameters for the B4B defense mechanism include the number of buckets in the LSH and the coefficients λ, α, and β in the cost function. We follow the calibrated hyperparameter values provided in the original B4B paper. Specifically, the number of buckets is set to 2^{12}, consistent with the B4B configuration. For experiments with the SimSiam architecture, the cost function hyperparameters are set as $\lambda = 10^{-6}$, $\alpha = 1$, and $\beta = 0.6$. For experiments with the DINO architecture, the hyperparameters are adjusted to $\lambda = 10^{-6}$, $\alpha = 1000$, and $\beta = 0.6$. The α value is increased by a factor of 1000 for DINO due to its representation norms being approximately 10^3 times larger than those of SimSiam.

B.2 Training Details of the Stolen Encoder

The architecture of the stolen model is also kept consistent with that used in the B4B defense. Specifically, we use ResNet-50 as the backbone and modify its fully connected layer to accommodate different representation output dimensions. The stealing dataset is a subset of ImageNet-1k, containing 100 examples per class. The stolen model is trained using the InfoNCE loss function for 150 epochs, with a batch size of 256. The learning rate is initialized to 0.1 and decays linearly to 0 over the course of training.

B.3 Training Details of the Downstream Classifier

We evaluate the performance of the stolen encoder on five downstream datasets: FashionMNIST, CIFAR10, SVHN, STL10, and IMGNET-C10. These datasets include both simple and complex tasks, providing a comprehensive assessment of the stolen encoder's capabilities. Table 6 summarizes the details of these downstream datasets. For the classification training of downstream tasks, the ResNet-50 backbone is frozen, and only the parameters of the added linear classifier are optimized. Each task is trained for 100 epochs, with a batch size of 256. The learning rate is initialized to 0.1 and decays linearly to 0 throughout the training process.

C Evaluation of Binary's Unification

The results, presented in Table 7, demonstrate that as the number of users increases, the L1 distance decreases. This signifies that the stolen encoder becomes increasingly similar to the victim encoder. These findings suggest that (1) embeddings from multiple users can be effectively unified by our algorithm and utilized collectively to train the stolen encoder, and (2) the Sybil attack successfully mitigates the noise introduced by B4B in the embedding process (Table 8, 9 and 10). Consequently, our attack proves to be effective.

Table 6. Dataset Specifications. IMGNET-C10 is a custom subset of ImageNet containing 10 randomly sampled classes. Each class contains 1000 training samples and 300 testing samples. The ImageNet dataset is a complex dataset with variable resolution, so we resized the resolution to 224 in our downstream classification experiment.

DATASET	CLASS	RESOLUTION	TRAIN	TEST
F-MNIST	10	$1 \times 28 \times 28$	60,000	10,000
CIFAR10	10	$3 \times 32 \times 32$	50,000	10,000
SVHN	10	$3 \times 32 \times 32$	73,257	26,032
STL10	10	$3 \times 96 \times 96$	5,000	8,000
IMGNET-C10	10	$3 \times 224 \times 224$	10,000	3,000

Table 7. The Average L1 Distance Between the Binary Embeddings Generated by the Stolen Encoder and the Victim Encoder under Sybil Attack in SimSiam. The query cost is set to 100k and is evenly split across all users.

DATASET	USER						
	1	2	4	8	16	32	64
F-MNIST	1620.40	831.71	203.55	5.93	4.96	4.26	4.27
CIFAR10	1440.97	375.85	73.98	4.04	4.47	3.66	3.16
SVHN	1350.33	221.24	114.85	6.93	5.92	5.49	4.70
STL10	1482.12	750.10	44.63	4.61	4.72	4.55	4.17
IMGNET-C10	395.21	342.58	46.63	35.74	40.61	33.88	23.15

D Results for DINO

Table 8. Downstream Task Accuracy of Stolen Encoder Using A1 in DINO. QUERIES stands for the number of queries used for stealing. DEFENSE indicates whether the victim encoder has deployed B4B. DOWNSCALING column shows the downscaling parameters.

QUERIES	DEFENSE	DOWN-SCALING	F-MNIST	CIFAR10	SVHN	STL10	IMGNET-C10
50K	NONE	w/o	89.490	76.040	67.014	78.863	83.000
	NONE	32×32	89.700	74.670	67.701	67.763	55.600
	B4B	w/o	86.050	62.270	43.047	62.975	38.000
	B4B	32×32	**89.450**	**75.140**	**67.939**	**68.438**	**58.800**
	B4B	48×48	87.240	65.680	60.391	64.812	55.400
100K	NONE	w/o	90.580	79.110	72.388	83.175	87.200
	NONE	32×32	90.590	80.540	72.568	71.800	63.400
	B4B	w/o	86.610	61.680	39.478	63.138	27.000
	B4B	32×32	**90.650**	**80.120**	**71.458**	**72.800**	**62.000**
	B4B	48×48	85.680	61.340	50.196	59.313	47.000

Table 9. Downstream Task Accuracy of Stolen Encoder Using A2 in DINO. The ATTACK column lists the adversarial attack methods, where CONV denotes the conventional attack, and A2 means noise reduction is used. $\mathcal{N}_{td}$ is the number of queried samples when triggering the noise reduction mechanism. We fix the hyperparameter $\mathcal{P}_{\tau} = 0.05$, $n = 8$ while varying $\mathcal{R}$.

QUERIES	ATTACK	DEFENSE	$\mathcal{R}$	$\mathcal{N}_{td}$	F-MNIST	CIFAR10	SVHN	STL10	IMGNET-C10
50K	CONV	NONE	N/A	N/A	89.490	76.040	67.014	78.863	83.000
	CONV	B4B	N/A	N/A	86.050	62.270	43.047	62.975	38.000
	A2	B4B	0.1	7260	88.630	65.830	57.621	66.138	67.800
			0.3	8288	88.320	66.360	57.925	**68.375**	65.000
			0.5	9537	88.630	67.320	59.027	67.863	65.000
			0.7	10164	88.580	**67.490**	58.920	68.050	**71.800**
			1.0	11253	**88.770**	65.720	**59.223**	67.413	65.800
100K	CONV	NONE	N/A	N/A	90.580	79.110	72.388	83.175	87.200
	CONV	B4B	N/A	N/A	87.200	61.680	39.478	63.138	27.000
	A2	B4B	0.1	7260	88.830	67.040	54.648	**68.325**	66.000
			0.3	8288	89.710	**69.000**	57.011	68.275	66.000
			0.5	9537	88.150	66.970	55.789	67.438	**66.400**
			0.7	10164	**88.880**	67.100	**57.545**	67.863	55.800
			1.0	11253	88.200	67.560	56.684	67.775	61.600

Table 10. Downstream Task Accuracy of Stolen Encoder Utilizing Sybil Attack in DINO. The query budget is set to 100k and is evenly split across all users.

DATASET	USER						
	1	2	4	8	16	32	64
F-MNIST	88.610	86.980	88.470	90.560	90.210	90.810	90.460
CIFAR10	61.680	66.970	73.140	77.860	78.520	78.840	78.970
SVHN	39.478	50.038	57.084	69.645	69.645	72.772	72.837
STL10	63.138	67.888	75.312	81.738	82.575	82.963	82.650
IMGNET-C10	27.000	58.800	77.400	84.800	84.800	87.000	87.800

References

1. Caron, M., et al.: Emerging properties in self-supervised vision transformers. In: Proceedings of the IEEE/CVF international conference on computer vision, pp. 9650–9660 (2021)
2. Charikar, M.S.: Similarity estimation techniques from rounding algorithms. In: Proceedings of the thiry-fourth annual ACM symposium on Theory of computing, pp. 380–388 (2002)
3. Chen, T., Kornblith, S., Norouzi, M., Hinton, G.: A simple framework for contrastive learning of visual representations. In: International conference on machine learning, pp. 1597–1607. PMLR (2020)

4. Chen, X., He, K.: Exploring simple siamese representation learning. In: Proceedings of the IEEE/CVF conference on computer vision and pattern recognition, pp. 15750–15758 (2021)
5. Cong, T., He, X., Zhang, Y.: Sslguard: a watermarking scheme for self-supervised learning pre-trained encoders. In: Proceedings of the 2022 ACM SIGSAC Conference on Computer and Communications Security, pp. 579–593 (2022)
6. Dubiński, J., Pawlak, S., Boenisch, F., Trzcinski, T., Dziedzic, A.: Bucks for buckets (b4b): active defenses against stealing encoders. Adv. Neural Inf. Proc. Syst. **36** (2024)
7. Dziedzic, A., Dhawan, N., Kaleem, M.A., Guan, J., Papernot, N.: On the difficulty of defending self-supervised learning against model extraction. In: International Conference on Machine Learning, pp. 5757–5776. PMLR (2022)
8. Dziedzic, A., et al.: Dataset inference for self-supervised models. Adv. Neural. Inf. Process. Syst. **35**, 12058–12070 (2022)
9. Dziedzic, A., et al.: Dataset inference for self-supervised models. Adv. Neural. Inf. Process. Syst. **35**, 12058–12070 (2022)
10. Frosst, N., Papernot, N., Hinton, G.: Analyzing and improving representations with the soft nearest neighbor loss. In: International conference on machine learning, pp. 2012–2020. PMLR (2019)
11. Gong, X., Chen, Y., Yang, W., Mei, G., Wang, Q.: Inversenet: augmenting model extraction attacks with training data inversion. In: IJCAI, pp. 2439–2447 (2021)
12. Goodfellow, I.J., Shlens, J., Szegedy, C.: Explaining and harnessing adversarial examples. In: International Conference on Learning Representations (ICLR) (2015)
13. He, K., Fan, H., Wu, Y., Xie, S., Girshick, R.: Momentum contrast for unsupervised visual representation learning. In: Proceedings of the IEEE/CVF conference on computer vision and pattern recognition, pp. 9729–9738 (2020)
14. He, K., Zhang, X., Ren, S., Sun, J.: Deep residual learning for image recognition. In: Proceedings of the IEEE conference on computer vision and pattern recognition, pp. 770–778 (2016)
15. Karmakar, P., Basu, D.: Marich: A query-efficient distributionally equivalent model extraction attack. Adv. Neural Inf. Proc. Syst. **36** (2024)
16. Li, Y., Jiang, Y., Li, Z., Xia, S.T.: Backdoor learning: a survey. IEEE Trans. Neural Netw. Learn. Syst. **35**(1), 5–22 (2022)
17. Liu, Y., Jia, J., Liu, H., Gong, N.Z.: Stolenencoder: stealing pre-trained encoders in self-supervised learning. In: Proceedings of the 2022 ACM SIGSAC Conference on Computer and Communications Security, pp. 2115–2128 (2022)
18. Lv, P., et al.: SSL-WM: a black-box watermarking approach for encoders pre-trained by self-supervised learning. In: 31st Annual Network and Distributed System Security Symposium, NDSS 2024, San Diego, California, USA, February 26 - March 1, 2024 (2024)
19. Oliynyk, D., Mayer, R., Rauber, A.: I know what you trained last summer: a survey on stealing machine learning models and defences. ACM Comput. Surv. **55**(14s), 1–41 (2023)
20. Oord, A.v.d., Li, Y., Vinyals, O.: Representation learning with contrastive predictive coding. arXiv preprint arXiv:1807.03748 (2018)
21. Orekondy, T., Schiele, B., Fritz, M.: Knockoff nets: stealing functionality of black-box models. In: Proceedings of the IEEE/CVF conference on computer vision and pattern recognition, pp. 4954–4963 (2019)
22. Paulevé, L., Jégou, H., Amsaleg, L.: Locality sensitive hashing: a comparison of hash function types and querying mechanisms. Pattern Recogn. Lett. **31**(11), 1348–1358 (2010)

23. Sha, Z., He, X., Yu, N., Backes, M., Zhang, Y.: Can't steal? cont-steal! contrastive stealing attacks against image encoders. In: Proceedings of the IEEE/CVF Conference on Computer Vision and Pattern Recognition, pp. 16373–16383 (2023)
24. Shokri, R., Stronati, M., Song, C., Shmatikov, V.: Membership inference attacks against machine learning models. In: 2017 IEEE symposium on security and privacy (SP), pp. 3–18. IEEE (2017)
25. Szegedy, C., Vanhoucke, V., Ioffe, S., Shlens, J., Wojna, Z.: Rethinking the inception architecture for computer vision. In: Proceedings of the IEEE conference on computer vision and pattern recognition, pp. 2818–2826 (2016)
26. Tramèr, F., Zhang, F., Juels, A., Reiter, M.K., Ristenpart, T.: Stealing machine learning models via prediction APIs. In: 25th USENIX security symposium (USENIX Security 16), pp. 601–618 (2016)
27. Yuan, X., et al.: Data-free hard-label robustness stealing attack. In: Proceedings of the AAAI Conference on Artificial Intelligence. vol. 38, pp. 6853–6861 (2024)
28. Zhu, L., et al.: Vision mamba: efficient visual representation learning with bidirectional state space model. In: International Conference on Machine Learning (ICML) (2024)

MusoMamba: Mamba-Based Multimodal Ultrasound Image Mutual Learning for Breast Tumor Segmentation

Jiahui Huang[1], Yuchen Jiang[2], Jiaxin Huang[3], Mingdu Zhang[1], Jufeng Yang[4], Qiong Wang[5], Xiaoqing Pei[3], and Yan Pang[5](✉)

[1] Guangzhou University, Guangzhou, China
[2] Macau University of Science and Technology, Macau, China
[3] Sun Yat-sen University Cancer Center, Guangzhou, China
[4] Nankai University, Tianjin, China
[5] Guangdong Provincial Key Laboratory of Computer Vision and Virtual Reality Technology, Shenzhen Institute of Advanced Technology, Chinese Academy of Sciences, Shenzhen, China
yanpang@siat.ac.cn

Abstract. Multimodal ultrasound imaging, combining B-mode ultrasound, shear wave velocity, and shear wave time, plays a crucial role in breast tumor diagnosis by providing detailed insights into tumor characteristics. However, challenges such as inter-modal feature misalignment and attention drift complicate accurate segmentation due to variations in how each modality captures tissue properties. To address issues, we propose the MusoMamba framework and the MUB2025 dataset. MusoMamba enhances segmentation accuracy through bidirectional alignment and region-specific feature enhancement, utilizing the Modality-Collaborative Learning and Modality-Guided Enhancement modules. The MUB2025 dataset, comprising paired images across the three modalities from 506 cases, supports detailed analysis and model training. MusoMamba achieves strong results on MUB2025, with a 72.67% Dice Similarity Coefficient and a 39.42 mm HD95, improving DSC by 3.24% and reducing HD95 by 5.37 mm over the second-best framework. These advancements demonstrate MusoMamba's potential to enhance segmentation accuracy in clinical settings.

Keywords: Mamba · B-mode ultrasonography · Shear-wave elastography · Multimodal learning · Breast tumor segmentation

This work was supported by the NSFC Key Project U23A20391, in part by the Regional Joint Fund of Guangdong (GuangdongâĂŞHong KongâĂŞMacao Research Team Project) under Grant 2021B1515130003 and the Guangdong Natural Science Foundation under Grant 2025A1515010276; in part by Shenzhen Science and Technology Program (JCYJ20241202152803005 & KJZD20240903102717023).

© The Author(s), under exclusive license to Springer Nature Singapore Pte Ltd. 2026
J. Kittler et al. (Eds.): PRCV 2025, LNCS 16289, pp. 502–515, 2026.
https://doi.org/10.1007/978-981-95-5764-6_34

Fig. 1. Divergent ultrasound modalities of breast tumor with tumor boundaries highlighted in red. (Color figure online)

1 Introduction

Breast tumor is a significant health threat and the most common malignancy among women [12,13,15,32], with approximately 310,720 women expected to be diagnosed with breast cancer in 2024. Ultrasound imaging [8,22,26], valued for its non-invasive, cost-effective, and accessible qualities, providing reliable insights into tumor size, extent, and characteristics. Ultrasound technology employs two primary modalities for breast tumor evaluation: Conventional B-mode Ultrasound (BUS) [14,27] and Shear Wave Elastography (SWE) [9,11,29]. As illustrated in Fig. 1, BUS generates high-resolution anatomical images that reveal essential tumor characteristics, including size, shape, and internal structure, which are crucial for evaluating tumor morphology, and boundaries. Complementing BUS, SWE provides diagnostic insights into tissue stiffness using two core parameters: Shear Wave Velocity (SWV) and Shear Wave Time (SWT). SWV measures the speed of shear waves in tissues, with a color gradient indicating red for high and blue for low. On the other hand, SWT measures the wave propagation time, with faster speeds in stiffer tissues (shown in red) and slower speeds in softer tissues (shown in blue). These modalities together enable clinicians to integrate insights from BUS, SWV, and SWT, facilitating more accurate identification of specific breast tumor regions in diagnostic settings [17,19].

However, a primary challenge in the identification of breast tumor regions by ultrasound is the **lack of publicly available multi-modality ultrasound data sets of breast tumors**. Most existing datasets [1] [23] provide only single-modality imaging, typically limited to BUS, restricting the scope of research focused on breast tumor segmentation. Multi-modality datasets that include SWT, SWV, and BUS are essential for achieving higher segmentation accuracy, as each modality contributes unique and complementary information about tissue characteristics [10]. In addition to the necessity for multi-modality datasets, current multi-modal medical segmentation frameworks [2–4,28,30,31], demonstrate significant promise in processing high-resolution, multi-modal medical images. However, challenges such as **inter-modal feature misalignment** and **attention drift** arise when these frameworks are applied to multi-modality breast tumor ultrasound images incorporating SWT, SWV, and BUS. Specifically, inter-modal feature misalignment can occur due to inherent uncertainties in shear wave elastography. For example, artifacts may sometimes result in tumors exhibiting lower elastic coefficients than surrounding tissues, as depicted in Case 2 of Fig. 1 (b). This discrepancy can lead to significant alignment issues across modalities. Normally, tumor tissues exhibit higher elastic coefficients than normal tissues, evident from the SWT and SWV readings in Case 1 and Case 3 of Fig. 1 (a)(c). In addition, the RGB values of the colored regions in SWV and SWT exceed those in BUS, which causes the standard dot-product attention [3,28,30] weights to lean towards the colored regions. This attention drift may obscure critical details in grayscale BUS images, which are vital for accurate tumor segmentation and clinical evaluations.

Addressing the challenges above, we present two significant contributions. To address the scarcity of comprehensive multimodal datasets, a curated 2D multimodal ultrasound breast tumor dataset, MUB2025, is tailored for segmentation tasks. This dataset includes paired ultrasound images from 506 breast tumor cases, spanning three modalities: SWV, SWT, and BUS. By integrating these modalities into a single dataset, MUB2025 aims to enhance segmentation accuracy and promote more extensive research into multimodal diagnostic techniques for breast cancer. In addition, we propose a framework named MusoMamba, which integrates a Modality-Collaborative Learning (MCL) module and a Modality-Guided Enhancement (MGE) module, aimed at addressing the critical challenges of feature misalignment and attention drift. The MCL module enhances mutual learning between modalities, using coupling functions within selective state spaces to facilitate bidirectional gradient propagation. Meanwhile, the MGE module introduces a correlation-driven attention mechanism to dynamically adjust attention weights, ensuring that each modality's contribution aligns with its clinical relevance. On the MUB2025 dataset, MusoMamba achieves a Dice Similarity Coefficient (DSC) of 72.67% and a Hausdorff Distance (HD95) of 39.42 mm, outperforming the second-best framework, MoSID [3], by 3.24% in DSC and reducing HD95 by 5.37 mm.

2 Method

2.1 Framework

The overall architecture of MusoMamba is illustrated in Fig. 2. The proposed framework primarily employs modality-specific encoders for feature extraction and integrates MCL modules for feature alignment. As a complementary measure for effective signal enhancement, it adopts a multimodal fusion method with MGE modules to allocate attention for adaptively weighing modality-specific contributions. A shared decoder is then used to generate multi-scale segmentation outputs to support deep supervision [18].

Encoder. As shown in Fig. 2 (a), three modality-specific encoders are employed to extract features from the three modalities, respectively. Concretely, given multimodal ultrasound images $\{x_m | x \in \mathbb{R}^{H \times W \times C}, m \in \{\text{SWT}, \text{SWV}, \text{BUS}\}\}$, where H, W and C denote height, width, and number of channels, respectively. A set of modality encoders $\{E_m\}$ are employed to extract modality-specific multi-scale features $\{f_m^i | i \in \{1, 2, 3, 4, 5\}\} = E_m(x_m)$. Each modality encoder is progressively divided into 5 stages. The first stage uses convolutional layers with a

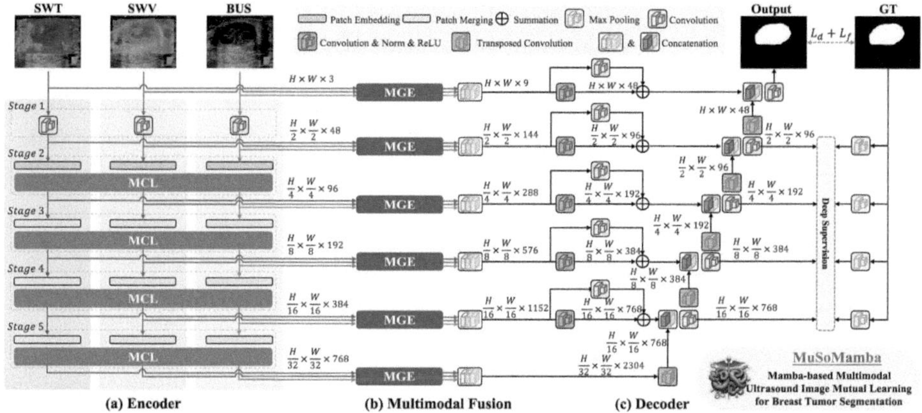

Fig. 2. An overview of MusoMamba framework. The MCL module are used to establish an information exchange channel between modalities. The MGE module is constructed to allocate attention for quantifying the contribution of modalities.

kernel of 7 × 7, a padding size of 3, and a stride of 2 for 2× downsampling. The second stage uses patch embedding layers with a 2 × 2 patch size for further 2× downsampling, and the MCL modules are used to provide enhanced visual modeling effects. Subsequently, each stage consists of patch merging layers for 2× downsampling and MCL modules for higher-level feature extraction and cross-modal mutual learning.

Multimodal Fusion. Given the multi-scale features $\{f_m^i\}$, the MGE module is constructed to model pixel-level correlations across modalities. To exploit the nonlinear relationship between modalities, the feature maps output by MGE are concatenated along the channel dimension as spatially-enhanced features:

$$f_C^i = f_{\mathrm{SWT}}^i \copyright f_{\mathrm{SWV}}^i \copyright f_{\mathrm{BUS}}^i, \tag{1}$$

where © represents the channel-wise concatenation. Once concatenated, f_C^i undergoes fusion processing through a convolution with residual connections.

$$f_F^i = \mathcal{C}(f_C^i) \oplus \sigma(\eta(\mathcal{C}(f_C^i))), \tag{2}$$

where $\mathcal{C}(\cdot)$ represent convolution using 3 × 3 kernels, $\oplus$ represents summation, σ represents ReLU activation, and η represents instance normalization.

Decoder. MusoMamba follows the classic U-shaped architectures [16] [20]. Given the skip connection features f_F^i from the i-th stage and the output features $\hat{f}_F^{i+1}$ of the $i+1$-th up-sample block, the segmentation map output by the i-th up-sample block is:

$$y^i = \mathcal{P}(f_F^i \copyright \hat{f}_F^{i+1}), \tag{3}$$

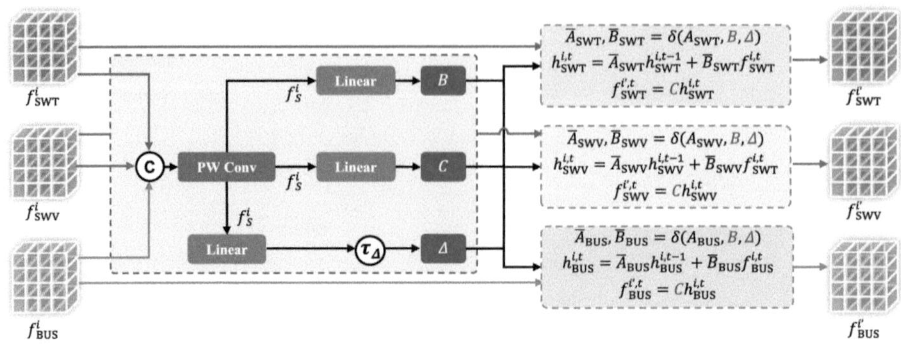

Fig. 3. Illustration of the MCL Module. Multiple state space modes are bridged by coupling functions to encourage mutual propagation of gradients.

where $\mathcal{P}(\cdot)$ represents 1×1 pointwise convolution. The output feature of the i-th up-sample block is:

$$\hat{f}^i_F = \mathcal{T}(\mathcal{P}(f^i_F \copyright \hat{f}^{i+1}_F)), \tag{4}$$

where $\mathcal{T}(\cdot)$ represents transpose convolution.

2.2 Modality-Collaborative Learning Module

Considering the uncertainty of feature alignment between different modalities, the MCL module integrates a novel coupling function that serves as a bridge connecting multiple state-space models (SSMs) [6] [7] [25], as shown in Fig. 3. In principle, the selective scan mechanism of Mamba [5] exploits the input dependencies of the system matrices B, C, and Δ to achieve context awareness. Building on this foundation, the MCL module fuses all input features to enable each SSM to leverage information from every available modality:

$$i_S = \mathcal{P}(f^i_{\mathrm{SWT}} \copyright f^i_{\mathrm{SWV}} \copyright f^i_{\mathrm{BUS}}), \tag{5}$$

where f^i_S represents the feature map that integrates all modal knowleage. Next, B, C, and Δ are derived from f^i_S to establish rigorous dependencies with all modalities:

$$B = \mathcal{F}_B(f^i_S),\ C = \mathcal{F}_C(f^i_S),\ \Delta = \tau_\Delta(\mathcal{F}_\Delta(f^i_S)). \tag{6}$$

where τ_Δ denotes the Softplus activation function. Subsequently, zero-order hold (ZOH) is adopted to generate the discretized sequence:

$$\bar{A}_m, \bar{B}_m = \delta(A_m, B, \Delta), \tag{7}$$

where $\delta(\cdot)$ denotes discretization process [6]. Given the knowledge-integrated $\bar{A}_m$, $\bar{B}_m$ and C matrices, SSMs are applied independently to each modal branch:

$$f^{i',t}_m = C h^{i,t}_m,\ h^{i,t}_m = \bar{A}_m h^{i,t-1}_m + \bar{B}_m f^{i,t}_m, \tag{8}$$

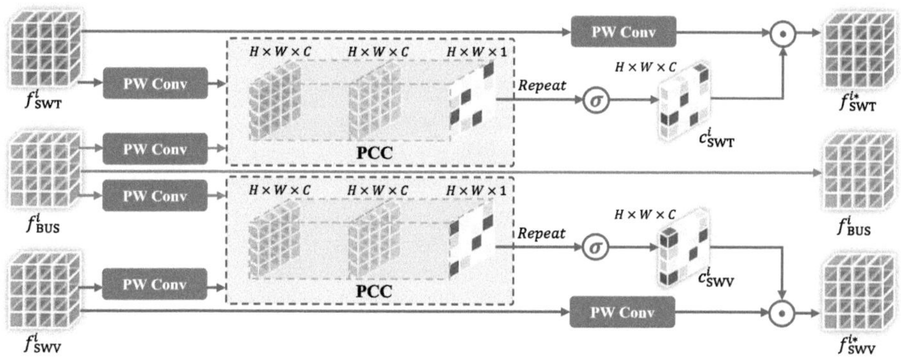

Fig. 4. Illustration of the MGE Module. Distinct branches process specific imaging modalities.

where the hidden sequence h_m^i transforms the input sequence f_m^i into the output sequence $f_m^{i'}$. By explicitly conditioning the interactions between features, MCL fosters robust mutual alignment across modalities.

2.3 Modality-Guided Enhancement Module

Considering that images of different modalities possess complementary and specific knowledge, the MGE module customizes dedicated branches for different modalities to generate region-sensitive features, as shown in Fig. 4. Using the Pixel-Wise Pearson Correlation Coefficient (PCC) operator to allocate attention to specific regions of different modalities, MGE is enabled to evenly integrate available modality features.

Given the feature maps of three modalities f_{SWT}^i, f_{SWV}^i, and f_{BUS}^i, the MGE module provides tailor-made pipelines for f_{SWT}^i and f_{SWV}^i, while f_{BUS}^i is used as supplementary information without any processing. Specifically, PCC is employed to compute the correlation of f_{SWT}^i and f_{SWV}^i with f_{BUS}^i.

$$c_{\mathrm{SWT}}^i, c_{\mathrm{SWV}}^i = \sigma(\mathrm{PCC}(\mathcal{P}(f_{\mathrm{SWT}}^i), \mathcal{P}(f_{\mathrm{BUS}}^i))), \sigma(\mathrm{PCC}(\mathcal{P}(f_{\mathrm{SWV}}^i), \mathcal{P}(f_{\mathrm{BUS}}^i))), \quad (9)$$

where c_{SWT}^i and c_{SWV}^i represent the correlation maps from f_{SWT}^i, f_{SWV}^i respectively. ReLU activation $\sigma(\cdot)$ is then introduced to further enhance the high correlation regions and weaken the low correlation regions. Specifically, the proposed PCC operator is implemented by calculating the pixel-wise Pearson correlation coefficient. For two input feature maps f_1 and f_2 with channel dimension C, given a pixel set $\{(p_{1,k}, p_{2,k}) | p_{1,k} \in f_1, p_{2,k} \in f_2, k \in C\}$, the PCC operator is defined as follows:

$$\mathrm{PCC}(f_1, f_2) = \frac{\sum (p_{1,k} - \bar{p_1}) (p_{2,k} - \bar{p_2})}{\sqrt{\sum (p_{1,k} - \bar{p_1})^2 \sum (p_{2,k} - \bar{p_2})^2}}. \quad (10)$$

This correlation coefficient-driven attention mechanism, by calculating linear correlation degrees, effectively prevents the attention weights derived from traditional dot-product attention for two feature maps from concentrating on color regions (with larger RGB values).

The generated correlation maps are then multiplied pixel by pixel with the corresponding feature maps to condition the pixel-granular contribution:

$$f^{i*}_{\text{SWT}}, f^{i*}_{\text{SWV}} = c^{i}_{\text{SWT}} \odot \mathcal{P}(f^{i}_{\text{SWT}}), c^{i}_{\text{SWV}} \odot \mathcal{P}(f^{i}_{\text{SWV}}). \tag{11}$$

Unlike the dot product attention mechanism, which may cause attention to drift to specific color areas due to the larger RGB values of color images, this correlation-driven approach measures the strength and direction of linear relationship between modalities rather than simply the product of two values.

2.4 Loss Function

MusoMamba is trained at multiple scales with deep supervision [18] at $\frac{1}{2}$, $\frac{1}{4}$, $\frac{1}{8}$ and $\frac{1}{16}$ resolutions, and max pooling is used to downsample the ground truth to each scale. The training loss at each scale is a combination of the dice loss $\mathcal{L}_d$ and the focal loss $\mathcal{L}_f$. The dice loss [21] is employed as the primary loss function, focal loss [24] is incorporated to adjust to varying class frequencies.

3 Experiments and Results

3.1 Dataset

The MUB2025 dataset was meticulously compiled from diagnostic imaging of 506 breast cancer patients receiving neoadjuvant therapy at *** University and *** Hospital between October 2016 and May 2023. This dataset utilized a Siemens Acuson S2000 ultrasound diagnostic device with a 9L4 linear array probe, operating at a frequency range of 4.0âĂŞ9.0 MHz, to guarantee high-resolution image acquisition. The dataset encompasses images from three distinct modalities: BUS, SWV, and SWT, with each image initially captured at a resolution of 838 × 666 pixels. For BUS, the parameters were set to an ultrasonic frequency of 8.0 MHz with a mechanical index of 1.3 and a dynamic range of 65, capturing 47 frames per second. Following BUS, SWE was conducted, maintaining the dynamic range but adjusting the mechanical index to 1.5 and reducing the frame rate to 13 frames per second to focus on elastographic data collection. For uniformity in training and analysis, images were resized to a resolution of 352 × 352 pixels. Ground-truth annotations for the dataset were performed by expert ultrasound physicians with over five years of clinical experience, strictly following the Breast Imaging Reporting and Data System (BI-RADS) guidelines established by the American College of Radiology (ACR). The concordant tumor manifestation across three modalities warrants the shared utilization of ground truth data annotated on the BUS. The dataset is structured with a training-validation split of 8:2, comprising 405 training cases and 101 validation cases.

Table 1. Performance comparative analysis of different network architectures for breast tumor segmentation on the MUB2025 datasets.

Methods	DSC(%)↑	mIOU(%)↑	SEN(%)↑	SPE(%)↑	ASD(mm) ↓	HD95(mm)↓
Robust-Mseg [2]	62.22	48.38	74.85	96.24	23.80	60.39
MAML [31]	55.41	42.12	71.66	95.01	26.49	66.38
RFNet [4]	64.37	51.34	73.89	96.59	21.78	57.74
NestedFormer [28]	67.27	53.71	74.02	97.10	19.26	57.56
MmFormer [30]	67.68	54.26	73.06	97.67	16.74	48.86
MoSID [3]	69.43	56.60	71.67	**98.20**	14.06	44.79
MusoMamba (ours)	**72.67**	**60.43**	**76.26**	98.18	**12.33**	**39.42**

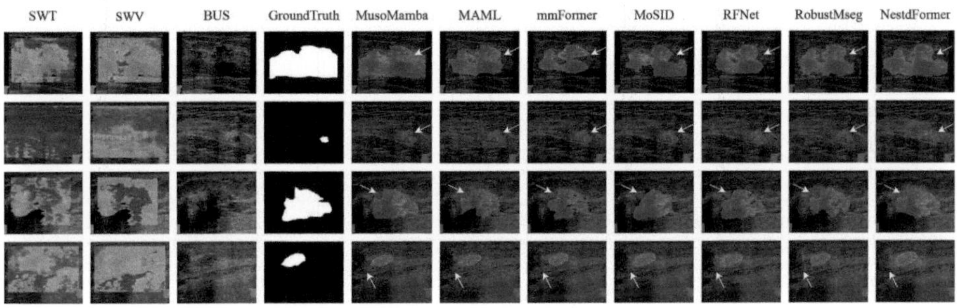

Fig. 5. Error map visualizations on the MUB2025 datasets. The correct segmentation regions and detection errors are visualized in green and red, respectively. (Color figure online)

3.2 Implementation Details

The MusoMamba is implemented on NVIDIA 4090 GPUs. Training incorporates data augmentation with random horizontal and vertical flips at a 20% probability. The model undergoes training for 150 epochs, with a batch size of 8 per GPU and an initial learning rate of 0.001. Optimization is achieved using the AdamW optimizer with a weight decay of 0.05.

3.3 Results and Analysis

Segmentation Results. Table 1 shows that MusoMamba outperforms other approaches in six crucial metrics for tumor segmentation: Dice Similarity Coefficient (DSC), Hausdorff Distance 95% (HD95), Mean Intersection over Union (mIOU), Specificity (SPE), Sensitivity (SEN), and Average Surface Distance (ASD). MusoMamba achieves the highest DSC score of 72.67%, exceeding the second-best model, MoSID [3], by 3.24%, indicating a more accurate delineation of tumor boundaries. For HD95, MusoMamba records the lowest value at 39.42 mm, improving by 5.37 mm over MoSID's 44.79 mm. Additionally, MusoMamba achieves the highest scores in mIOU at 60.43% and SPE at 98.18%. Its

SEN score of 76.26% and ASD of 12.33 mm further support its robustness, establishing MusoMamba as a consistent and effective solution for breast tumor segmentation across all evaluated metrics. The qualitative visualization presented in Fig. 5 underscores the superior segmentation performance of MusoMamba. Specifically, MusoMamba excels in delineating smoother lesion areas, as illustrated in the fourth row, where it closely matches the ground truth, unlike other methods that often misidentify or incorrectly segment these areas. In scenarios involving long lesions, shown in the first rows, MusoMamba precisely segments the areas of the lesion with precise edge definition, while competing models struggle with blurred edges and inaccurate outlines.

Table 2. Segmentation performance analysis of ablation studies on the MUB2025 dataset.

Methods	DSC(%)↑	mIOU(%)↑	SEN(%)↑	SPE(%)↑	ASD(mm) ↓	HD95(mm)↓
Baseline	68.62	55.29	75.05	97.45	16.07	46.33
MCL only	69.88	56.85	73.57	97.80	14.90	44.53
MGE only	68.97	55.62	**76.82**	97.24	16.92	44.53
MusoMamba (ours)	**72.67**	**60.43**	76.26	**98.18**	**12.33**	**39.42**

Ablation Studies. The effectiveness of the MCL module and the MGE module are validated through the experimental setup shown in Fig. 2. The baseline model initially records a DSC of 68.62% and an HD95 of 46.33 mm. With the incorporation of the MCL module, there is a notable improvement in DSC by 1.26% and a reduction in HD95 by 1.8 mm, underscoring the MCL module's capability to foster feature interactions and integrate knowledge across modalities. Further enhancements are observed with the MGE module, which improves Sensitivity (SEN) by 1.77% over the baseline. When both the MCL and MGE modules are integrated from the beginning of the study, they collectively yield substantial gains across all evaluation metrics, including a 5.14% increase in mIOU and a 3.74 mm decrease in ASD, demonstrating the architecture's comprehensive ability to optimize segmentation outcomes effectively.

Modality Ablation Studies. As shown in Fig. 6, MusoMamba demonstrates outstanding segmentation performance across six modality combinations of SWT, SWV, and BUS. The framework consistently outperforms state-of-the-art methods [2,4,28,30,31] [3] under most modality combination settings, highlighting its efficient integration and processing capabilities. Notably, MusoMamba maintains robust results even with single-modality inputs: except for partial SPE measurements, its metrics surpass the second-ranked MoSID [3] in almost all scenarios. This performance underscores its reliability and robustness under conditions with limited multimodal interaction. Additionally, when one modality

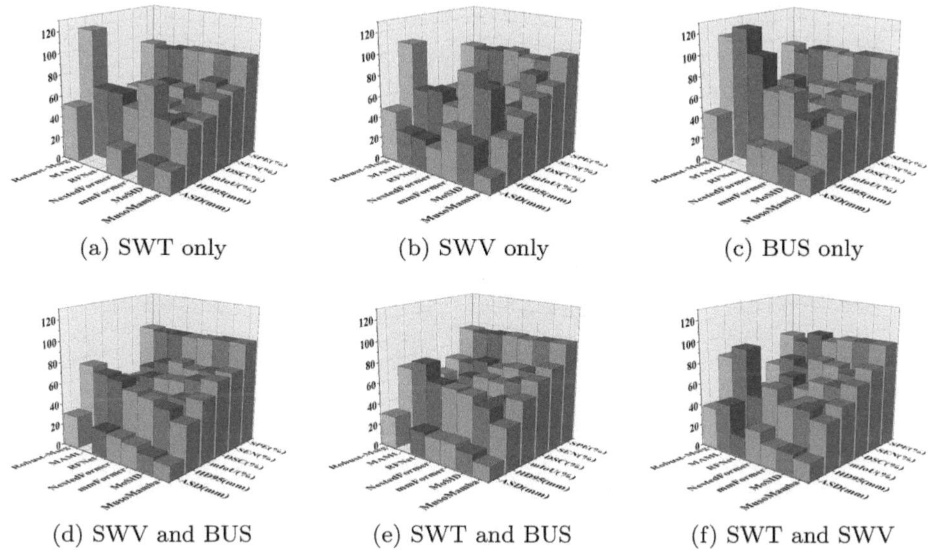

(a) SWT only (b) SWV only (c) BUS only

(d) SWV and BUS (e) SWT and BUS (f) SWT and SWV

Fig. 6. Comparison of modal ablation experiment results on the MUB2025 dataset, where missing results indicate infinity.

is missing, MusoMamba achieves optimal results across all evaluation metrics, as illustrated in Fig. 6(d), 6(e), and 6(f). These findings validate that MusoMamba can effectively integrate and analyze correlations among features from different modalities.

Explanation of Feature Misalignment. As shown in Fig. 7 (a), different colors are used to represent the different distributions of breast tissue in SWT and SWV, where the greater the tissue density, the brighter the color. For example, red, yellow, and green represent lesion tissue, and blue represents normal breast tissue. In BUS, black represents lesion tissue, which corresponds to the bright colors in SWT and SWV. However, in practical imaging of SWT and SWV, the fat, muscle, and fibrous tissue surrounding the lesion have brighter colors because their density exceeds that of normal breast tissue. These areas cannot correspond to the features of BUS, that is, feature misalignment.

Explanation of Attention Drift. As shown in Fig. 7 (a), the RGB values in the colored regions of SWV and SWT are larger than those in grayscale BUS. This disparity results in the attention weights derived from the dot products are disproportionately influenced by the colored regions. To demonstrate this, we implemented a variant called MusoMamba-dp with a standard dot-product cross-attention module instead of our MGE module. As shown in the top row of Fig. 7(b), the attention of MusoMamba-dp is concentrated in the colored regions in stage 1 and drifts more deterioratingly to a few pixels in stage 3.

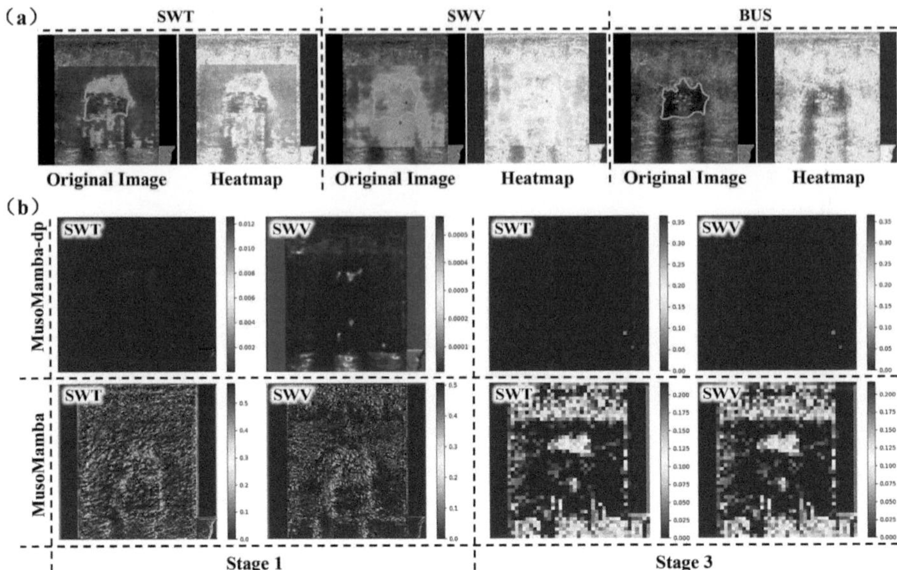

Fig. 7. . (a) Multimodal ultrasound images with the tumor circled in pink and the corresponding heatmaps. (b) Attention maps of MusoMamba-dp and MusoMamba in stage 1 and 3. (Color figure online)

Table 3. Performance analysis of breast tumor segmentation between MusoMamba-dp based on dot product attention mechanism and MusoMamba based on correlation coefficient driven attention mechanism on MUB2025 dataset.

Methods	DSC(%)	mIOU(%)	SEN(%)	SPE(%)	ASD(mm)	HD95(mm)
MusoMamba-dp	70.28	57.39	78.28	97.40	15.49	46.14
MusoMamba	72.87	60.53	76.32	98.26	12.25	39.36

Evidence of Responses to Challenges. 1) To address feature misalignment, the MCL module implements a collaborative selective scan mechanism to align modal features through cross-modal gradient propagation. As evidenced Fig. 7(b), the attention maps for SWT and SWV differ in stage 1 (without MCL, left side), but closely resemble each other in stage 3 (with MCL, right side). 2) To address the attention drift issue of MusoMamba-dp as shown in the top row of Fig. 7(b), the MGE module introduces correlation-driven attention, which measures the strength and direction of the linear relationship between two features. As evidenced in the bottom row of Fig. 7(b), fine-grained attention distribution reflecting tissue contours can be observed in the attention map of MusoMamba. More comparisons are shown in Table 3.

4 Conclusion

This paper introduces the MUB2025 dataset and the MusoMamba framework. The MUB2025 dataset addresses the need for extensive multimodal imaging data, while MusoMamba tackles specific issues like inter-modal feature misalignment and attention drift. Together, they improve segmentation accuracy and demonstrate significant improvements in key performance metrics. These contributions highlight the potential of integrated approaches to advance breast tumor diagnostics and treatment, promising improved clinical outcomes. Moving forward, we plan to expand our dataset to include larger patient cohorts, further refining our models to handle an even broader range of clinical scenarios.

References

1. Al-Dhabyani, W., Gomaa, M., Khaled, H., Fahmy, A.: Dataset of breast ultrasound images. Data Brief **28**, 104863 (2020)
2. Chen, C., Dou, Q., Jin, Y., Chen, H., Qin, J., Heng, P.-A.: Robust multimodal brain tumor segmentation via feature disentanglement and gated fusion. In: Shen, D., et al. (eds.) MICCAI 2019. LNCS, vol. 11766, pp. 447–456. Springer, Cham (2019). https://doi.org/10.1007/978-3-030-32248-9_50
3. Chen, Q., et al.: Modality-specific information disentanglement from multi-parametric mri for breast tumor segmentation and computer-aided diagnosis. IEEE Trans. Med. Imaging (2024)
4. Ding, Y., Yu, X., Yang, Y.: Rfnet: region-aware fusion network for incomplete multi-modal brain tumor segmentation. In: Proceedings of the IEEE/CVF International Conference on Computer Vision, pp. 3975–3984 (2021)
5. Gu, A., Dao, T.: Mamba: Linear-time sequence modeling with selective state spaces. arXiv preprint arXiv:2312.00752 (2023)
6. Gu, A., Goel, K., Ré, C.: Efficiently modeling long sequences with structured state spaces. arXiv preprint arXiv:2111.00396 (2021)
7. Gu, A., et al.: Combining recurrent, convolutional, and continuous-time models with linear state space layers. Adv. Neural. Inf. Process. Syst. **34**, 572–585 (2021)
8. Huang, J.X., et al.: Nomogram based on us and clinicopathologic characteristics: axillary nodal evaluation following neoadjuvant chemotherapy in patients with node-positive breast cancer. Clin. Breast Cancer **24**(6), e452–e463 (2024)
9. Huang, J.X., et al.: Shear wave elastography combined with molecular subtype in early prediction of pathological response to neoadjuvant chemotherapy in patients with breast cancer: a prospective study. Acad. Radiol. **30**(7), 1270–1280 (2023)
10. Huang, J.X., et al.: Comparing shear wave elastography of breast tumors and axillary nodes in the axillary assessment after neoadjuvant chemotherapy in patients with node-positive breast cancer. Radiol. Med. (Torino) **129**(8), 1143–1155 (2024)
11. Huang, J.X., et al.: Enhancing detection of high-level axillary lymph node metastasis after neoadjuvant therapy in breast cancer patients with nodal involvement: a combined approach of axilla ultrasound and breast elastography. Radiol. Med. (Torino) **130**(1), 121–131 (2025)
12. Huang, J.X., et al.: Elastography-based ai model can predict axillary status after neoadjuvant chemotherapy in breast cancer with nodal involvement: a prospective, multicenter, diagnostic study. Int. J. Surg. **111**(1), 221–229 (2025)

13. Huang, J.X., et al.: The development and validation of a risk stratification system for assessing axillary status after neoadjuvant therapy in node-positive breast cancer: a multicenter, prospective, observational study. Int. J. Surg. **111**(6), 3731–3741 (2025)
14. Huang, J.X., et al.: Deep learning model based on dual-modal ultrasound and molecular data for predicting response to neoadjuvant chemotherapy in breast cancer. Acad. Radiol. **30**, S50–S61 (2023)
15. Huang, Q., Chen, Y., Liu, L., Tao, D., Li, X.: On combining biclustering mining and adaboost for breast tumor classification. IEEE Trans. Knowl. Data Eng. **32**(4), 728–738 (2019)
16. Isensee, F., Jaeger, P.F., Kohl, S.A., Petersen, J., Maier-Hein, K.H.: nnu-net: a self-configuring method for deep learning-based biomedical image segmentation. Nat. Methods **18**(2), 203–211 (2021)
17. Jiang, M., et al.: Radiomics model based on shear-wave elastography in the assessment of axillary lymph node status in early-stage breast cancer. Euro. Radiol., 1–13 (2022)
18. Lee, C.Y., Xie, S., Gallagher, P., Zhang, Z., Tu, Z.: Deeply-supervised nets. Artifi. Intell. Statist., 562–570 (2015)
19. Li, B., et al.: Investigation of correlation between shear wave elastography and lymphangiogenesis in invasive breast cancer and diagnosis of axillary lymph node metastasis. BMC Cancer **24**(1), 409 (2024)
20. Ma, J., Li, F., Wang, B.: U-mamba: Enhancing long-range dependency for biomedical image segmentation. arXiv preprint arXiv:2401.04722 (2024)
21. Milletari, F., Navab, N., Ahmadi, S.A.: V-net: fully convolutional neural networks for volumetric medical image segmentation. In: 2016 Fourth International Conference on 3D Vision (3DV), pp. 565–571. Ieee (2016)
22. Mo, Y., et al.: Hover-trans: anatomy-aware hover-transformer for roi-free breast cancer diagnosis in ultrasound images. IEEE Trans. Med. Imaging **42**(6), 1696–1706 (2023)
23. Pawłowska, A., et al.: Curated benchmark dataset for ultrasound based breast lesion analysis. Scientific Data **11**(1), 148 (2024)
24. Ross, T.Y., Dollár, G.: Focal loss for dense object detection. In: Proceedings of the IEEE Conference on Computer Vision and Pattern Recognition, pp. 2980–2988 (2017)
25. Smith, J.T., Warrington, A., Linderman, S.W.: Simplified state space layers for sequence modeling. arXiv preprint arXiv:2208.04933 (2022)
26. Tan, J., et al.: A flexible and fully autonomous breast ultrasound scanning system. IEEE Trans. Autom. Sci. Eng. **20**(3), 1920–1933 (2022)
27. Trepanier, C., Huang, A., Liu, M., Ha, R.: Emerging uses of artificial intelligence in breast and axillary ultrasound. Clin. Imaging **100**, 64–68 (2023)
28. Xing, Z., Yu, L., Wan, L., Han, T., Zhu, L.: NestedFormer: nested modality-aware transformer for brain tumor segmentation. In: Wang, L., Dou, Q., Fletcher, P.T., Speidel, S., Li, S. (eds.) MICCAI 2022. LNCS, vol 13435. Springer, Cham (2022). https://doi.org/10.1007/978-3-031-16443-9_14
29. Yin, Z., Li, G.Y., Zhang, Z., Zheng, Y., Cao, Y.: Swenet: a physics-informed deep neural network (pinn) for shear wave elastography. IEEE Trans. Med. Imaging (2023)
30. Zhang, Y. et al. mmFormer: multimodal medical transformer for incomplete multimodal learning of brain tumor segmentation. In: Wang, L., Dou, Q., Fletcher, P.T., Speidel, S., Li, S. (eds.) MICCAI 2022. LNCS, vol 13435. Springer, Cham (2022). https://doi.org/10.1007/978-3-031-16443-9_11

31. Zhang, Y., et al.: Modality-aware mutual learning for multi-modal medical image segmentation. In: de Bruijne, M., et al. (eds.) MICCAI 2021. LNCS, vol. 12901, pp. 589–599. Springer, Cham (2021). https://doi.org/10.1007/978-3-030-87193-2_56
32. Zheng, X., et al.: Deep learning radiomics can predict axillary lymph node status in early-stage breast cancer. Nat. Commun. **11**(1), 1236 (2020)

Dual-SAM: Prompt-Enhanced Dual-Branch Adaptation of Vision Foundation Models for Semi-supervised Medical Image Segmentation

Wei Zhou[1], Shuru Song[1], Zhiyong Zheng[1], Guilin Guan[1], and Jun Qiang[2(✉)]

[1] Shenyang Aerospace University, Shenyang 110136, China
[2] Department of Imaging Center, The First Affiliated Hospital, and College of Clinical Medicine of Henan University of Science and Technology, Luoyang 471003, China
hkdyfyfskqj@163.com

Abstract. Semi-Supervised Learning (SSL) enhances medical image segmentation by leveraging unlabeled data to alleviate the scarcity of annotated samples. Although vision foundation models (e.g., the Segment Anything Model, SAM) demonstrate strong generalization and feature extraction capabilities, their integration with SSL remains underexplored. To address this, we propose a novel dual-branch SSL-SAM framework that enables iterative pseudo-label refinement through a co-training mechanism, harnessing labeled and unlabeled data. For enhanced segmentation precision, we introduce Cross-Path Prompt Fusion (CPF), which facilitates dynamic interaction between prompt-based segmentation paths, enhancing feature representation. Additionally, we develop Frequency Enhanced Pseudo-label Filtering (FEPF), a denoising strategy that suppresses high-frequency noise while preserving anatomical boundaries, improving pseudo-label reliability. Comprehensive experiments on four medical image datasets demonstrate that our approach consistently outperforms existing SSL and SAM-based methods, particularly in data-scarce scenarios. Code is available at: https://github.com/Heirudy/Dual-SAM.

Keywords: Vision Foundation Models · Semi-Supervised Learning · Medical Image Segmentation · Adaptive Prompt Learning

1 Introduction

Medical image segmentation is critical for clinical decision-making, supporting tasks such as lesion detection and surgical planning [1]. Traditional supervised models, such as U-Net [2] and DeepLab [3], rely on extensive labeled data, which is often limited in medical imaging. Semi-Supervised Learning (SSL) mitigates this constraint by leveraging unlabeled data to enhance model generalization. Approaches like pseudo-labeling [4], consistency regularization [5],

© The Author(s), under exclusive license to Springer Nature Singapore Pte Ltd. 2026
J. Kittler et al. (Eds.): PRCV 2025, LNCS 16289, pp. 516–529, 2026.
https://doi.org/10.1007/978-981-95-5764-6_35

and contrastive learning [6] have demonstrated success. However, these methods typically require task-specific architectures and careful pseudo-label optimization, limiting their adaptability across diverse anatomical structures and imaging modalities [7].

The Segment Anything Model (SAM) [8], pre-trained on large-scale natural image datasets, introduces a paradigm shift with its prompt-based segmentation and few-shot learning capabilities. Unlike conventional models that require extensive supervised fine-tuning, SAM generalizes across diverse tasks with minimal labeled data, making it promising for medical image segmentation. However, its direct application is challenged by domain gaps and the need for precise prompts, which limit its reliability in medical imaging. Recent studies have explored SAM-SSL integration to address data scarcity. Zhang et al. [9] applied consistency regularization to refine SAM-generated pseudo-labels, while Xu et al. [10] introduced a SAM-guided matching framework using point and bounding box prompts. Keuth et al. [11] and Chen et al. [12] further refined SAM's outputs into pseudo-ground truth to improve model training.

Despite these advancements, key challenges remain: (1) Existing methods lack iterative pseudo-label refinement, limiting the ability to fully exploit unlabeled data; (2) Prompt-based segmentation remains suboptimal, as standard point and bounding box inputs often result in over- or under-segmentation; and (3) Pseudo-labels are prone to noise, where boundary ambiguities and artifacts degrade segmentation accuracy, particularly in complex medical images.

To overcome these limitations, we present a dual-branch SSL framework that combines SAM with a co-training setup, utilizing a shared SAM encoder with parallel decoders for iterative pseudo-label refinement. To improve prompt accuracy, we introduce Cross-path Prompt Fusion (CPF), which combines global structural information with local anatomical features, allowing mask- and point-based prompts to interact dynamically for enhanced feature representation. Additionally, we develop Frequency Enhanced Pseudo-label Filtering (FEPF), which applies frequency-domain analysis and adaptive mean filtering to suppress high-frequency noise while preserving anatomical boundaries. Experimental results demonstrate that our framework significantly improves segmentation accuracy and robustness, particularly in data-scarce scenarios.

Main contributions: 1. A novel dual-branch SSL SAM architecture that enables iterative refinement of pseudo-labels, enhancing the use of both labeled and unlabeled data through a co-training setup. 2. The CPF mechanism combining global and local anatomical cues, refining prompts for precise segmentation of fine-grained structures. 3. The FEPF strategy that reduces pseudo-label noise while preserving anatomical boundaries, improving label quality.

2 Method

We propose Dual-SAM, a semi-supervised dual-branch segmentation framework that leverages a shared SAM encoder and parallel decoders for iterative pseudo-label refinement. The Cross-Path Prompt Fusion (CPF) module enhances segmentation by exchanging and refining mask and point prompts between branches, while the Frequency Enhanced Pseudo-label Filter (FEPF) suppresses noise through frequency-domain analysis. The training set D comprises a small labeled set $D^l = \{(x_i^l, y_i^l)\}_{i=1}^M$ and a larger unlabeled set $D^u = \{x_j^u\}_{j=1}^N$, where $x_i^l, x_j^u \in \mathbb{R}^{H\times W}$ are input images, and $y_i^l \in \{0,1\}^{H\times W\times C}$ is the ground truth for C categories.

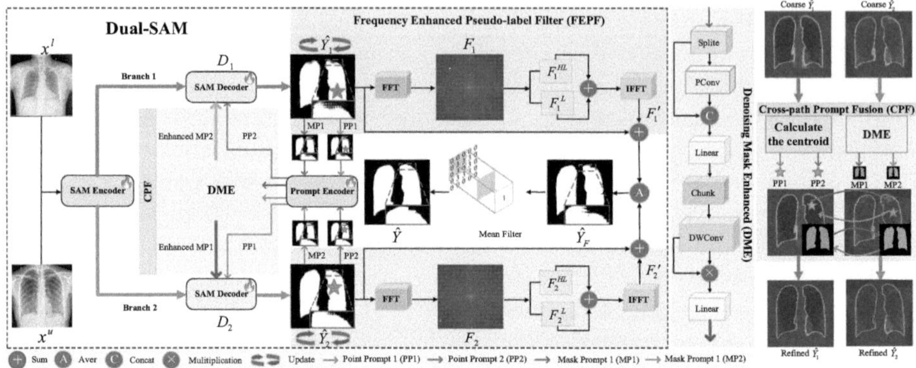

Fig. 1. Overview of the proposed Dual-SAM framework. Dual-SAM adopts a three-stage pipeline comprising a shared SAM encoder and two decoders that collaboratively refine pseudo-labels. Initially, each decoder generates segmentation hypotheses, which are mutually enhanced through Cross-Path Prompt Fusion (CPF) using exchanged mask- and point-based prompts. The fused outputs are then denoised by the Frequency-Enhanced Pseudo-label Filtering (FEPF) module to suppress noise while preserving anatomical boundaries. The final refined mask supervises both branches in an iterative co-training loop, enabling robust and accurate semi-supervised segmentation under limited annotations.

2.1 Dual-Branch SAM Architecture

Semi-supervised adaptation of SAM faces two key limitations under low-label regimes: (1) confirmation bias from unreliable pseudo-labels, and (2) overfitting due to lack of diversity in segmentation hypotheses. To overcome these, we propose a dual-branch SAM architecture designed to promote hypothesis diversity and collaborative refinement. As shown in Fig. 1, our framework consists of a shared encoder E (adapted from ViT in SAM) and two independently initialized decoders, D_1 and D_2. These decoders generate distinct predictions $(\hat{Y}_1, \hat{Y}_2)$ for unlabeled samples. Their diversity mitigates the bias that commonly arises in single-branch SSL setups, especially in complex anatomical regions. To enhance interaction while preserving independence, we propose a **Cross-Path Prompt Fusion (CPF)** strategy. Specifically, predictions from each decoder are encoded into task-aware prompts and exchanged between branches, enabling mutual correction without parameter sharing. This acts as an implicit regularizer that stabilizes learning and prevents collapse to trivial solutions. Subsequently, the two refined predictions are fused using a **Frequency-Enhanced Pseudo-label Filtering (FEPF)** module, which suppresses noise in the frequency domain while retaining anatomical boundary integrity. The fused pseudo-label $\hat{Y}$ serves as supervision for the next training iteration. The proposed dual-branch architecture leverages the complementary strengths of the two decoders, facilitating more diverse and accurate segmentation hypotheses while addressing the inherent challenges of few-shot learning and SSL.

2.2 Cross-Path Prompt Fusion (CPF)

SAM's point prompts offer coarse localization but lack shape precision, while mask prompts rely on segmentation quality for boundary delineation. These limitations hinder SAM's effectiveness, especially in complex semi-supervised segmentation tasks. Additionally, the traditional approach of single-path self-prompting for unlabeled data restricts the learning process to a single trajectory.

In response, we propose Cross-path Prompt Fusion (CPF), a novel bidirectional prompting mechanism that integrates point and mask prompts for mutual refinement. By leveraging the complementary strengths of both prompt types, CPF facilitates knowledge exchange between the decoders, allowing each to refine the other's predictions. Specifically, the coarse outputs from each decoder iteratively refine the prompts of the other, enhancing feature representations and improving boundary precision. This cross-path interaction ensures that the decoders learn from each other's predictions, leading to more robust and accurate segmentation. In addition to CPF, we introduce Denoising Mask Enhancement (DME), a dual-stream module designed to further enhance feature representation. DME utilizes Partial Convolutions (PConv) to suppress background noise and Depthwise Separable Convolutions (DConv) to extract spatially discriminative features, significantly improving segmentation performance. The gating mechanism in DME adaptively selects and fuses the most relevant features, enabling the model to focus on critical information while filtering out noise (see right side of Fig. 1). Together, CPF and DME form a powerful iterative refinement process, progressively enhancing segmentation accuracy and boundary precision. The CPF mechanism steps are detailed in Algorithm 1.

2.3 Frequency Enhanced Pseudo-Label Filter (FEPF)

Traditional filtering either over-smooths details or retains artifacts, compromising segmentation reliability. To address this, we propose Frequency Enhanced Pseudo-Label Filtering (FEPF), a frequency-domain approach that refines pseudo-labels by selectively suppressing noise while preserving anatomical boundaries. FEPF decomposes pseudo-labels into low-frequency components (F_1^L, F_2^L) capturing global structures and high-frequency components encoding fine details and noise. Instead of discarding high-frequency content, which

Algorithm 1. Cross-path Prompt Fusion (CPF)

Inputs: Image I; Two segmentation branches: Branch A and Branch B.
Output: Refined pseudo-masks Y_A and Y_B.
Step 1: Initial coarse predictions from both branches
Coarse mask $Y_A \leftarrow A$.predict(I)
Coarse mask $Y_B \leftarrow B$.predict(I)
Step 2: Prompt generation from coarse outputs
Point prompt $PP_A \leftarrow$ ComputeCentroids(Y_A)
Mask prompt $MP_A \leftarrow$ DenoiseMask(Y_A)
Point prompt $PP_B \leftarrow$ ComputeCentroids(Y_B)
Mask prompt $MP_B \leftarrow$ DenoiseMask(Y_B)
Step 3: Cross-path prompt exchange
Prompts for Branch A: $P_A \leftarrow \{PP_B, MP_B\}$
Prompts for Branch B: $P_B \leftarrow \{PP_A, MP_A\}$
Step 4: Prompt-guided refinement decoding
Refined mask $Y_A \leftarrow A$.decode(I, P_A)
Refined mask $Y_B \leftarrow B$.decode(I, P_B)
Return: Refined pseudo-masks Y_A, Y_B

risks boundary loss, we extract mid-to-low-frequency edge features (F_1^{HL}, F_2^{HL}) to refine boundaries while mitigating noise. The refined pseudo-label is reconstructed via inverse Fourier transform and fused with the original prediction through a residual connection. Finally, dual-branch averaging and mean filtering further suppress residual noise, yielding cleaner and more reliable segmentation outputs.

In this study, we introduce a FEPF loss, correcting the fusion output $\hat{Y}$ against the ground truth Y_L, formulated as:

$$\mathcal{L}_{FEPF} = \frac{1}{2}[\mathcal{L}_{dice}(\hat{Y}, Y_L) + \mathcal{L}_{ce}(\hat{Y}, Y_L)] \quad (1)$$

where $\mathcal{L}_{dice}$ and $\mathcal{L}_{ce}$ denote the Dice coefficient loss and the cross-entropy loss individually.

By integrating frequency-domain transformations, residual connections, and dual-branch refinement, FEPF significantly outperforms conventional filtering techniques, particularly in complex, low-contrast medical images, achieving a superior balance between noise suppression and edge fidelity. Detailed experimental comparisons are presented in the experiments section.

2.4 Loss Function

The total loss comprises three constituent parts: supervised loss, unsupervised loss, and FEPF loss.

In the case of labeled data, the supervised loss is defined by:

$$\mathcal{L}_{sup} = \alpha \left[\mathcal{L}_{\text{dice}}(\hat{Y}_1, Y_L) + \mathcal{L}_{dice}(\hat{Y}_2, Y_L)\right] + \beta \left[\mathcal{L}_{\text{ce}}(\hat{Y}_1, Y_L) + \mathcal{L}_{ce}(\hat{Y}_2, Y_L)\right] \quad (2)$$

where $\alpha = 0.8$ and $\beta = 0.2$ as suggested by [13].

For unlabeled data, we adopt a cross-pseudo supervision strategy [14], enhanced with low-frequency pseudo-labels:

$$\mathcal{L}_{unsup} = \frac{1}{2}[\mathcal{L}_{dice}(\hat{Y}_1, \hat{Y}) + \mathcal{L}_{ce}(\hat{Y}_1, \hat{Y}) + \mathcal{L}_{dice}(\hat{Y}_2, \hat{Y}) + \mathcal{L}_{ce}(\hat{Y}_2, \hat{Y})] \quad (3)$$

Finally, the total loss function integrates all components as:

$$\mathcal{L}_{total} = \mathcal{L}_{\mathrm{sup}} + \lambda_1 \mathcal{L}_{un\,\mathrm{sup}} + \lambda_2 \mathcal{L}_{FEPF} \quad (4)$$

where λ_1=λ_2=0.5 are empirically set weights.

3 Experiments

3.1 Experimental Setup

Datasets and Metrics. We assess our approach utilizing four openly accessible datasets: CHASE [15], Chest X-ray [16], Kvasir-SEG [17], and ACDC [18]. CHASE (28 retinal images) is split into 20 training and 8 testing samples. Chest X-ray (704 images) is randomly divided into 504 training and 200 testing samples. Kvasir-SEG (1,000 endoscopy images) is split 7:1:2 for training, validation, and testing. ACDC (100 cardiac MRIs) is split into 70 training, 10 validation, and 20 testing samples. For 2D segmentation, we report IoU, Dice, Accuracy (Acc), Specificity (Sp), and Sensitivity (Se); for 3D tasks, we use Dice, ASSD, HD95, and ASD.

Implementation Details. We adopt the pre-trained SAM ViT-B model, fine-tuned using LoRA (rank = 4) on an RTX 4090 GPU. Optimization uses ADAMW (β_1= 0.9, β_2= 0.999) with Gaussian warm-up from 0.4 and a peak learning rate of 0.001 under a pre-heat and exponential decay schedule. During inference, outputs from both branches are fused. Images are resized to 10241024 (CHASE, Chest X-ray) or 512512 (ACDC). Training samples include 10 from CHASE, 2 from Chest X-ray, and 1 from ACDC.

3.2 Comparison with State-of-the-Art Methods

We benchmark our method against 17 state-of-the-art semi-supervised segmentation models, including classical baselines (UNet [19], TransUnet [20], MT [21], UAMT [22], CPS [14], URPC [23], EM [24], R-Drop [25], DAN [26], BSNet [5], ABDNet [27], EVIL [28], MTNet [29]) and SAM-based variants (MedSAM [30], CPC-SAM [13], Semi-SAM [9], SP-SAM [31]). As shown in Table 1, SAM-based methods generally outperform traditional ones, with our model consistently achieving the best results. On CHASE, our method achieves the highest IoU (65.11) and Dice (78.86), outperforming CPC-SAM and BSNet, and significantly surpassing SP-SAM (22.88 IoU) via cross-path prompt refinement. On Chest X-ray, with only 2 labels, our model achieves 84.84 IoU and 91.80 Dice, outperforming CPC-SAM and avoiding the performance collapse seen in

Table 1. Comparison of 17 state-of-the-art segmentation methods across four public datasets. Both traditional and SAM-based models are included. SP-SAM is excluded from ACDC due to multi-class segmentation (denoted as -). The best results are marked in red.

Method	CHASE					Chest X-ray					Kavsir-SEG					ACDC			
	10 Labeled					2 Labeled					7 Labeled					1 Labeled			
	IoU	Dice	Se	Sp	ACC	IoU	Dice	Se	Sp	ACC	IoU	Dice	Se	Sp	ACC	Dice	JC	HD95	ASD
Unet	60.07	75.05	43.25	98.11	96.78	59.97	74.98	70.19	70.19	94.32	20.36	33.83	29.88	90.70	80.62	47.06	36.96	41.87	20.18
TransUNet	63.61	77.76	60.25	97.79	96.95	83.32	90.90	94.40	95.56	95.27	48.36	65.19	64.75	93.26	88.54	66.94	53.18	28.63	9.32
MT	56.38	72.21	83.99	96.71	95.91	55.16	71.10	59.07	97.64	88.00	33.87	50.60	40.41	96.16	86.92	54.82	42.92	50.84	20.88
UAMT	61.61	76.24	79.66	98.03	96.87	54.27	70.36	60.22	96.34	87.31	23.17	37.62	53.18	74.26	70.76	50.72	39.06	56.44	22.68
CPS	59.84	74.88	76.97	98.27	96.82	50.58	67.18	57.72	95.30	85.90	29.33	45.36	33.30	97.31	86.70	54.70	43.12	48.62	19.40
URPC	60.85	75.66	80.11	97.87	96.75	59.40	74.53	61.97	98.56	89.41	21.88	35.91	30.81	91.90	81.77	48.22	37.41	47.69	19.99
EM	62.26	76.74	79.66	98.00	96.91	26.99	42.51	27.69	99.14	81.27	19.72	32.94	21.01	98.69	85.81	50.36	38.24	59.27	25.89
R-Drop	61.01	75.78	77.36	98.20	96.89	23.01	37.41	23.61	99.13	80.25	29.74	45.84	33.29	97.63	86.96	54.10	41.78	57.70	23.77
DAN	61.42	76.10	80.61	97.74	96.75	22.22	36.36	23.13	98.64	79.76	25.25	40.31	28.39	97.52	86.06	55.39	43.53	32.45	10.73
BSNet	65.09	78.86	82.24	98.23	98.23	68.81	81.52	94.84	87.39	89.25	49.61	66.32	63.07	94.61	89.38	33.58	24.17	47.69	27.65
ABDNet	59.75	74.80	80.61	97.65	96.58	60.63	75.49	76.49	91.28	87.58	25.75	40.95	38.27	90.33	81.70	44.87	33.46	8.25	1.76
EVIL	60.29	75.22	81.01	98.17	96.82	69.15	81.76	74.54	97.40	91.69	21.58	35.50	28.31	93.80	82.95	56.42	45.94	23.69	6.63
MTNet	61.31	76.02	80.09	97.85	96.78	82.27	90.27	95.58	98.30	97.66	38.79	55.90	49.69	94.42	87.00	65.50	50.85	20.20	6.10
MedSAM	59.52	74.62	82.24	97.57	96.53	80.59	89.25	93.34	94.73	94.38	64.36	78.32	72.30	97.55	93.36	56.12	42.18	4.85	1.59
SP-SAM	22.88	37.23	43.25	94.01	90.81	66.35	79.77	76.12	95.11	90.38	31.26	47.63	79.23	69.51	71.12	-	-	-	-
Semi-SAM	40.22	57.37	60.25	96.66	94.37	52.08	68.49	85.69	78.49	80.29	26.75	42.21	59.82	75.45	72.86	41.70	29.66	56.00	23.58
CPC-SAM	64.54	78.45	87.95	97.56	96.96	83.54	91.03	93.48	96.04	95.40	62.40	76.84	67.46	98.39	93.26	79.96	68.04	13.90	4.43
Dual-SAM	65.11	78.86	86.58	97.78	97.08	84.84	91.80	95.63	95.76	95.73	68.61	81.38	82.25	96.05	89.38	80.66	69.22	16.24	5.05

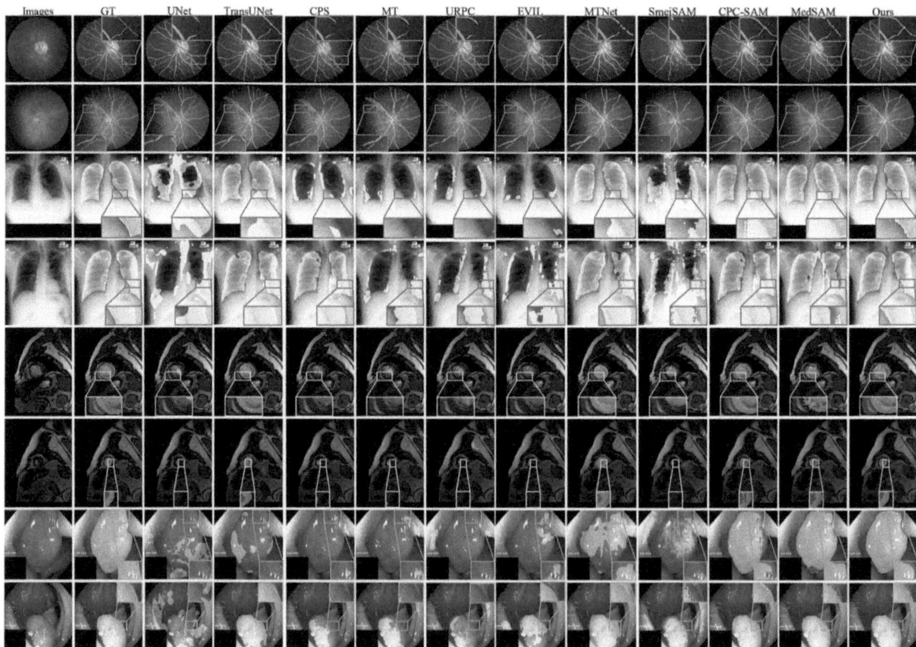

Fig. 2. Visualization of segmentation results our approach against baselines on representative samples from four public datasets.

Semi-SAM (52.08 IoU) under sparse supervision, thanks to robust dual-branch pseudo-labeling. On Kvasir-SEG, our method improves IoU and Dice by 4.25 and 3.06 over MedSAM, demonstrating strong generalization from just 7 labeled samples. FEPF enhances boundary accuracy and suppresses artifacts. On ACDC, our approach achieves the best Dice (80.66) and JC (69.22) with only one labeled case, highlighting FEPF's effectiveness in refining pseudo-labels and improving multi-class structure delineation. Qualitative results (Fig. 2) confirm our model's ability to produce cleaner boundaries and smoother contours under extreme data scarcity.

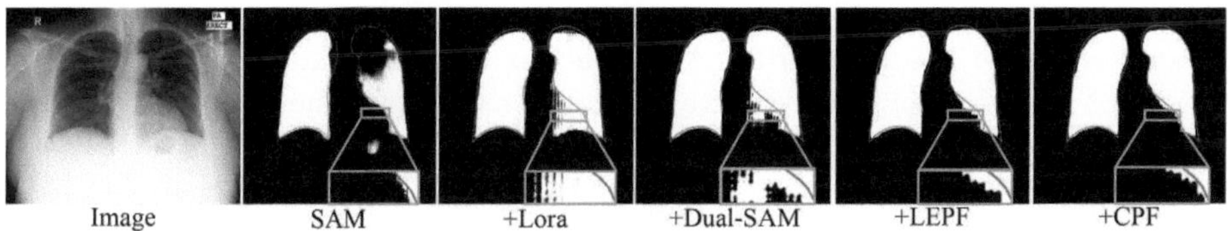

Fig. 3. Visualization of ablation results on Chest X-ray. GT is outlined in red. (Color figure online)

3.3 Ablation Study

To evaluate the effectiveness of our proposed modules, we conduct an ablation study on the Chest X-ray dataset, examining the individual contributions of LoRA, dual-branch architecture, FEPF, and CPF within the Dual-SAM framework. Comparisons are made against the baseline SAM model, with quantitative results shown in Table 2 and qualitative visualizations in Fig. 3.

Table 2. Ablation study of key components in our method on the Chest X-ray dataset. The best results are highlighted in red.

SAM	LoRA	Dual-branch	FEPF	CPF	Iou	Dice	Se	Sp	Acc
✓					80.01	88.89	90.36	95.68	94.35
✓	✓				80.30	89.07	92.66	94.87	94.32
✓	✓	✓			82.84	90.61	95.08	95.07	95.07
✓	✓	✓	✓		84.24	91.44	95.27	95.64	95.54
✓	✓	✓	✓	✓	**84.86**	**91.81**	**95.73**	**95.73**	**95.73**

Effectiveness of LoRA. To assess the contribution of LoRA, we conduct ablation experiments on the Chest X-ray dataset, as shown in Table 2. While the overall improvements in IoU and Dice are moderate, LoRA notably boosts sensitivity (**+2.30%**), a critical metric in identifying subtle or low-contrast lesions. This indicates LoRA's strength in enhancing fine-grained feature representation, especially in clinically challenging regions. Moreover, when integrated into the dual-branch architecture, LoRA yields a marked increase in both IoU and Dice, highlighting its synergistic effect in improving structural precision. These results demonstrate that LoRA effectively boosts fine-grained feature representation with minimal computational cost.

Effectiveness of Dual-Branch Architecture. As seen in Table 2, the introduction of Dual-branch architecture results in an improvement of 2.54% in IoU and 1.54% in Dice score compared to the baseline SAM model. This increase in performance demonstrates the advantage of having two independent branches in the architecture, which allow for more accurate and robust segmentation, particularly in complex regions. To validate the effectiveness of the proposed dual-branch architecture and demonstrate that the decoders do not prematurely converge to suboptimal solutions, we visualized the training process at 50-epoch intervals (Fig. 4).

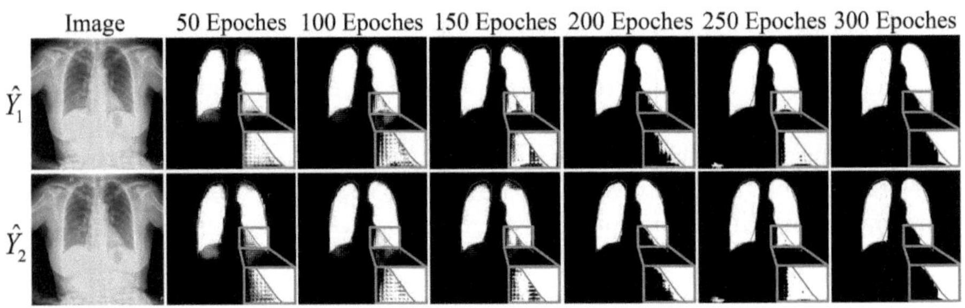

Fig. 4. Visual comparison of predicted masks from two decoders at different training stages, showcasing segmentation refinement over time.

The visualizations show that as training progresses, the model continues to refine its predictions, yielding sharper boundaries and progressively improved segmentation performance. This indicates that, despite identical architectures, the decoders maintain diverse prediction patterns and avoid rapid convergence to trivial local optima.

Effectiveness of FEPF. We integrate FEPF, which refines the segmentation boundaries by enhancing the quality of pseudo-labels through frequency-based filtering. When FEPF is added to the framework, the IoU increases to 84.24 and the Dice score improves to 91.44. This result underscores the importance of

FEPF in improving boundary precision and overall segmentation quality, particularly in challenging regions where boundaries may be unclear or ambiguous.

To further validate the performance of the FEPF module, we compare it with the traditional Haar wavelet-based pseudo-label refinement method. As shown in Table 3, while wavelet-based refinement offers a slight improvement in Dice score on the CHASE dataset, FEPF consistently outperforms wavelets across multiple datasets, including Chest X-ray, Kvasir-SEG, and ACDC. Specifically, FEPF achieves superior performance in metrics like HD95, ASD, and sensitivity, demonstrating its ability to preserve boundaries, particularly in complex and challenging anatomical scenarios.

Table 3. Fourier vs. Wavelet-based pseudo-label refinement in FEPF.

Dataset	Fourier Transform				Wavelet Transform			
	Iou	Dice	Se	Acc	Iou	Dice	Se	Acc
CHASE	65.1	78.86	86.58	97.00	65.70	79.30	81.81	97.31
Chest X-ray	84.84	91.08	95.63	95.73	84.08	91.35	94.25	95.54
Kavsir-SEG	68.61	81.38	82.25	93.76	62.13	76.64	65.76	93.35
	JC	Dice	HD95	ASD	JC	Dice	HD95	ASD
ACDC	69.22	89.66	16.24	5.05	64.63	77.30	21.82	6.99

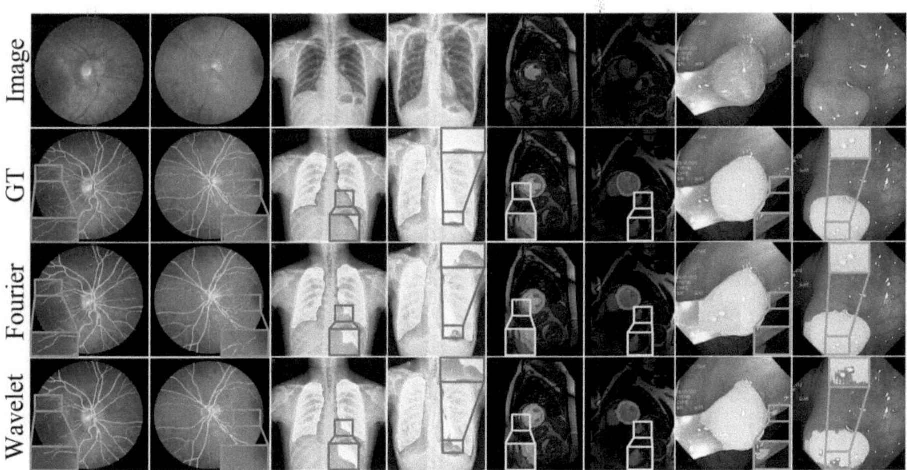

Fig. 5. Comparative visualization of Fourier vs. Wavelet in FEPF.

Visually, as illustrated in Fig. 5, FEPF effectively suppresses noise and enhances boundaries, especially in low-contrast or occluded regions. In contrast, wavelet filtering often leaves residual artifacts, leading to blurry or inconsistent boundaries. These qualitative results further highlight the structural fidelity of FEPF and demonstrate the advantages of our proposed frequency-enhanced pseudo-label refinement over traditional methods.

Effectiveness of CPF. When CPF is incorporated into the model, we observe the highest performance across all evaluation metrics. IoU and Dice scores reach 84.86 and 91.81, respectively. CPF enables the two decoders to share coarse mask information, facilitating mutual refinement. This cross-branch communication allows the model to better utilize complementary features, leading to enhanced segmentation results. The inclusion of CPF thus demonstrates its critical role in boosting performance by enabling better cooperation between the decoders.

Computational Complexity and Runtime Efficiency. We also assess the computational efficiency of Dual-SAM by comparing its FLOPs, parameters, FPS, and GPU usage against several other methods, as shown in Table 4. Despite incorporating computationally expensive components like CPF and FEPF, Dual-SAM remains efficient, with 378.85G FLOPs and 94.12M parameters. It achieves 16.13 FPS, a significant improvement over MedSAM (5.06 FPS) and TransUNet (8.91 FPS). The increase in FLOPs is justified by the additional refinement paths tailored for sparse labels, which result in improved segmentation accuracy and efficiency. Dual-SAM strikes an optimal balance between computational cost and performance, outperforming both traditional and SAM-based methods in terms of FPS, while maintaining a competitive level of complexity and GPU usage.

Table 4. Runtime and complexity comparison.

Methods	FLOPs(G)	Params(M)	FPS(s)	GPU(GB)
Unet	48.05	1.81	130.50	4.20
TransUNet	522.61	93.23	8.91	23.54
SAM	374.27	90.35	14.36	17.21
MedSAM	371.99	90.49	5.06	19.19
Semi-SAM	98.60	9.45	43.54	9.79
Dual-SAM	378.85	94.12	16.13	23.40

Clinical Application. To demonstrate the clinical applicability of our method, we evaluate its performance in cardiac function analysis on the ACDC dataset, which is specifically designed for the assessment of cardiac MRI in clinical settings. As summarized in Table 5, our approach achieves the highest Dice scores across three key anatomical structures, the Left Ventricle (LV), Right Ventricle

(RV), and Myocardium (Myo), surpassing all baselines in segmentation accuracy. Furthermore, our method provides superior estimates of critical diagnostic indicators, including Left Ventricular End-Diastolic Volume (LVEDV), Right Ventricular End-Diastolic Volume (RVEDV), and Myocardial mass (MYMass). Notably, our results exhibit the strongest correlations with expert-derived ground truths (e.g., Corr = 0.9947 for LVEDV, Corr = 0.9489 for RVEDV, Corr = 0.9663 for MYMass), demonstrating a clear advantage over existing methods and underscoring the potential of our approach for reliable clinical deployment.

Table 5. Comparison of cardiac structure segmentation and clinical diagnostic indicators calculation on the ACDC dataset.

Method	LV(Dice)	RV(Dice)	Myo(Dice)	LVEDV(ml)	Corr	RVEDV(ml)	Corr	MYMass(g)	Corr
UNet	79.44	69.59	64.67	139.23	0.8820	127.51	0.7818	99.16	0.8424
TransUNet	85.57	61.20	67.81	142.68	0.9876	154.43	0.7589	110.06	0.9106
MTNet	84.50	69.30	56.12	119.60	0.9267	125.46	0.7207	138.35	0.7476
MedSAM	70.78	45.62	43.53	91.99	0.8575	73.24	0.8559	108.57	0.8609
Dual-SAM	91.21	86.95	77.95	135.65	0.9947	156.76	0.9489	137.42	0.9663

4 Conclusion and Future Work

In this study, we propose Dual-SAM, an innovative semi-supervised adaptation of SAM designed for medical image segmentation, incorporating three main innovations: (1) A dual-branch architecture that facilitates mutual learning to optimize the utilization of unlabeled data, enhancing segmentation performance. (2) The CPF module, which refines feature representations through cross-branch prompt fusion, improving fine-grained texture depiction and anatomical structure modeling. (3) The FEPF module, which integrates frequency- and spatial-domain processing to enhance pseudo-label reliability and boundary awareness. Extensive experiments validate Dual-SAM's effectiveness, demonstrating superior segmentation accuracy, strong correlation with clinical ground truths across key diagnostic indicators, and robust generalization in semi-supervised settings. Future work will focus on extending Dual-SAM to broader semi-supervised learning tasks, optimizing clinical applicability, and addressing real-world medical imaging challenges.

Acknowledgments. This work is supported in part by grants from the National Natural Science Foundation of China (Nos. 62302488 and 62571349) and Zhejiang Provincial Natural Science Foundation of China (LQ23F010007).

References

1. Xia, Q., et al.: A comprehensive review of deep learning for medical image segmentation. Neurocomputing, 128740 (2024)
2. Zhu, W. et al.: SelfReg-UNet: self-regularized unet for medical image segmentation. In: Linguraru, M.G., et al. Medical Image Computing and Computer Assisted Intervention – MICCAI 2024. MICCAI 2024. LNCS, vol. 15008. Springer, Cham (2024). https://doi.org/10.1007/978-3-031-72111-3_56
3. Yang, J., Jun, T., Zhang, X., Shaoqing, Yu., Zheng, X.: Tse deeplab: an efficient visual transformer for medical image segmentation. Biomed. Signal Process. Control **80**, 104376 (2023)
4. Thompson, B.H., Di Caterina, G., Voisey, J.: Pseudo-label refinement using superpixels for semi-supervised brain tumour segmentation. In: 2022 IEEE 19th International Symposium on Biomedical Imaging (ISBI), pp. 1–5. IEEE (2022)
5. He, A., Li, T., Yan, J., Wang, K., Huazhu, F.: Bilateral supervision network for semi-supervised medical image segmentation. IEEE Trans. Med. Imaging **43**(5), 1715–1726 (2023)
6. Shen, N., Tingfa, X., Huang, S., Feng, M., Li, J.: Expert-guided knowledge distillation for semi-supervised vessel segmentation. IEEE J. Biomed. Health Inform. **27**(11), 5542–5553 (2023)
7. Li, W., Bian, R., Zhao, W., Weijin, X., Yang, H.: Diversity matters: cross-head mutual mean-teaching for semi-supervised medical image segmentation. Med. Image Anal. **97**, 103302 (2024)
8. Kirillov, A., et al.: Segment anything. In: Proceedings of the IEEE/CVF International Conference on Computer Vision, pP. 4015–4026 (2023)
9. Zhang, Y., Yang, J., Liu, Y., Cheng, Y., Qi, Y.: Semisam: enhancing semi-supervised medical image segmentation via sam-assisted consistency regularization. In: 2024 IEEE International Conference on Bioinformatics and Biomedicine (BIBM), pp.3982–3986. IEEE (2024)
10. Xu, G., Qian, X., Shao, H.C., Luo, J., Lu, W., Zhang, Y.: A sam-guided and match-based semi-supervised segmentation framework for medical imaging. arXiv preprint arXiv:2411.16949 (2024)
11. Keuth, R., et al.: Sam carries the burden: a semi-supervised approach refining pseudo labels for medical segmentation. arXiv preprint arXiv:2411.12602 (2024)
12. Chen, S., Lin, L., Cheng, P., Tang, X.: Aslseg: adapting sam in the loop for semi-supervised liver tumor segmentation. In: 2024 IEEE International Symposium on Biomedical Imaging (ISBI), pp. 1–5. IEEE (2024)
13. Miao, J., Chen, C., Zhang, K., Chuai, J., Li, Q., Heng, P.-A.: Cross prompting consistency with segment anything model for semi-supervised medical image segmentation. In: International Conference on Medical Image Computing and Computer-Assisted Intervention, pp. 167–177. Springer (2024)
14. Chen, X., Yuan, Y., Zeng, G., Wang, J.: Semi-supervised semantic segmentation with cross pseudo supervision. In: Proceedings of the IEEE/CVF Conference on Computer Vision and Pattern Recognition, pp. 2613–2622 (2021)
15. Fraz, M.M., et al.: An ensemble classification-based approach applied to retinal blood vessel segmentation. IEEE Trans. Biomed. Eng. **59**(9), 2538–2548 (2012)
16. Chowdhury, M.E.H., et al.: Can ai help in screening viral and covid-19 pneumonia? IEEE Access **8**, 132665–132676 (2020)
17. Jha, D., et al.: Kvasir-SEG: a segmented polyp dataset MultiMedia Modeling, pp. 451–462 (2020)

18. Bernard, O., et al.: Deep learning techniques for automatic mri cardiac multi-structures segmentation and diagnosis: is the problem solved? IEEE Trans. Med. Imaging **37**(11), 2514–2525 (2018)
19. Ronneberger, O., Fischer, P., Brox, T.: U-Net: convolutional networks for biomedical image segmentation. In: Navab, N., Hornegger, J., Wells, W.M., Frangi, A.F. (eds.) MICCAI 2015. LNCS, vol. 9351, pp. 234–241. Springer, Cham (2015). https://doi.org/10.1007/978-3-319-24574-4_28
20. Chen, J., et al.: Transunet: rethinking the u-net architecture design for medical image segmentation through the lens of transformers. Med. Image Anal. **97**, 103280 (2024)
21. Antti Tarvainen and Harri Valpola. Mean teachers are better role models: Weight-averaged consistency targets improve semi-supervised deep learning results. *Advances in neural information processing systems*, 30, 2017
22. Yu, L., Wang, S., Li, X., Fu, C.-W., Heng, P.-A.: Uncertainty-aware self-ensembling model for semi-supervised 3d left atrium segmentation. In: Shen, D., et al. (eds.) MICCAI 2019. LNCS, vol. 11765, pp. 605–613. Springer, Cham (2019). https://doi.org/10.1007/978-3-030-32245-8_67
23. Luo, X., et al.: Efficient semi-supervised gross target volume of nasopharyngeal carcinoma segmentation via uncertainty rectified pyramid consistency. In: de Bruijne, M., et al. (eds.) MICCAI 2021. LNCS, vol. 12902, pp. 318–329. Springer, Cham (2021). https://doi.org/10.1007/978-3-030-87196-3_30
24. Vu, T.-H., Jain, H., Bucher, M., Cord, M., Pérez, P.: Advent: adversarial entropy minimization for domain adaptation in semantic segmentation. In: Proceedings of the IEEE/CVF Conference on Computer Vision and Pattern Recognition, pp. 2517–2526 (2019)
25. Lijun, W., et al.: R-drop: regularized dropout for neural networks. Adv. Neural. Inf. Process. Syst. **34**, 10890–10905 (2021)
26. Zhang, Y., Yang, L., Chen, J., Fredericksen, M., Hughes, D.P., Chen, D.Z.: Deep adversarial networks for biomedical image segmentation utilizing unannotated images. In: Descoteaux, M., Maier-Hein, L., Franz, A., Jannin, P., Collins, D.L., Duchesne, S. (eds.) MICCAI 2017. LNCS, vol. 10435, pp. 408–416. Springer, Cham (2017). https://doi.org/10.1007/978-3-319-66179-7_47
27. Chi, H., Pang, J., Zhang, B., Liu, W.: Adaptive bidirectional displacement for semi-supervised medical image segmentation. In: Proceedings of the IEEE/CVF Conference on Computer Vision and Pattern Recognition, pp. 4070–4080 (2024)
28. Chen, Y., et al.: Evidence-based uncertainty-aware semi-supervised medical image segmentation. Comput. Biol. Med. **170**, 108004 (2024)
29. Zhong, L., Luo, X., Liao, X., Zhang, S., Wang, G.: Semi-supervised pathological image segmentation via cross distillation of multiple attentions and seg-cam consistency. Pattern Recogn. **152**, 110492 (2024)
30. Ma, J., He, Y., Li, F., Han, L., You, C., Wang, B.: Segment anything in medical images. Nat. Commun. **15**(1), 654 (2024)
31. Wu, Q., Zhang, Y., Elbatel, M.: Self-prompting large vision models for few-shot medical image segmentation. In: Koch, L., et al. (eds.) Domain Adaptation and Representation Transfer. DART 2023. LNCS, vol. 14293. Springer, Cham (2024). https://doi.org/10.1007/978-3-031-45857-6_16

DAWA: Dynamic Ambiguity-Wise Adaptation for Real-Time Domain Adaptive Semantic Segmentation

Taorong Liu[1], Zhen Zhang[1], Liang Liao[2], Jing Xiao[3(✉)], and Chia-Wen Lin[4]

[1] School of Computer Science, Wuhan University, Wuhan, China
{cameltr,zhangzhent}@whu.edu.cn

[2] Hangzhou Institute of Technology, Xidian University, Xi'an, China
liaoliang01@xidian.edu.cn

[3] School of Artificial Intelligence, Wuhan University, Wuhan, China
jing@whu.edu.cn

[4] Department of Electrical Engineering and the Institute of Communications Engineering, National Tsing Hua University, Hsinchu, Taiwan
cwlin@ee.nthu.edu.tw

Abstract. Test-time domain adaption (TTDA) for semantic segmentation aims to adapt a segmentation model trained on a source domain to a target domain for inference on-the-fly, where both efficiency and effectiveness are critical. However, existing TTDA methods either rely on costly frame-wise optimization or assume unrealistic domain shifts (*e.g.*, night→snow), resulting in poor adaptation efficiency and continuous semantic ambiguities. To address these challenges, we propose a real-time framework for TTDA semantic segmentation, called **Dynamic Ambiguity-Wise Adaptation (DAWA)**, which adaptively detects domain shifts and dynamically adjusts the learning strategies to mitigate continuous ambiguities in the test time. Specifically, we introduce the Dynamic Ambiguous Patch Mask (DAP Mask) strategy, which dynamically identifies and masks highly disturbed regions to prevent error accumulation in ambiguous classes. Furthermore, we present the Dynamic Ambiguous Class Mix (DAC Mix) strategy that leverages vision-language models to group semantically similar classes and augment the target domain with a meta-ambiguous class buffer. Extensive experiments on widely used TTDA benchmarks demonstrate that DAWA consistently outperforms state-of-the-art methods, while maintaining real-time inference speeds of approximately 40 FPS.

Keywords: Domain adaptation · Real time · Semantic segmentation

1 Introduction

Semantic segmentation aims to annotate images at the pixel level to provide crucial information for various applications, especially in safety-critical fields such

© The Author(s), under exclusive license to Springer Nature Singapore Pte Ltd. 2026
J. Kittler et al. (Eds.): PRCV 2025, LNCS 16289, pp. 530–545, 2026.
https://doi.org/10.1007/978-981-95-5764-6_36

as autonomous driving. While state-of-the-art segmentation models [2,12,30] excel in clear weather due to abundant annotations, they often fail in dynamic environments that undergo rapid changes during practical driving, where the distribution of ongoing captured vision data continuously shifts due to factors like changing lighting and weather. Unsupervised domain adaptation (UDA) has emerged as a promising approach for transferring learning-based models from labeled data distributions to unlabeled data. However, current UDA methods [1,9,14,16] are primarily tailored for static target domains and rely on offline training, making them unsuitable for handling continuous domain changes (Fig. 1).

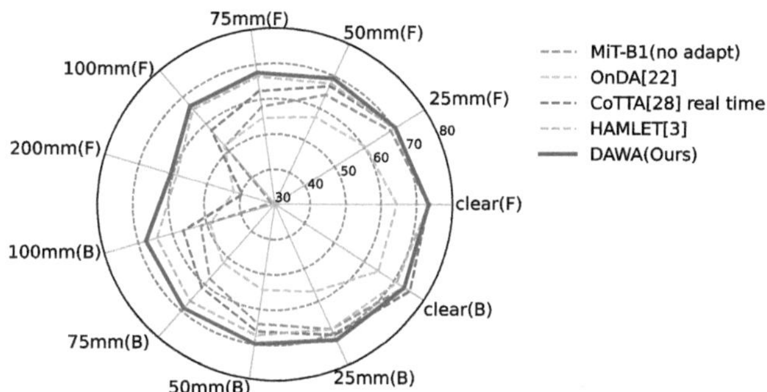

Fig. 1. Performance comparison of online adaptation methods on the Increasing Storm [22]. We plot mIoU (%) achieved on each rainy intensity (*i.e.*, clear, 25 mm, 50 mm, 75 mm, 100 mm, 200 mm) of single domains. "F" represents forward adaptation (from *clear* to 200 mm), while "B" denotes backward adaptation (from 200 mm to *clear*).

These challenges have led to the emergence of more demanding tasks, such as Test-Time Domain Adaptation (TTDA) [7,28,31], which involves rapidly fine-tuning models during test time to handle the changing data distribution in real-world scenarios. Despite its potential for on-site adaptation, TTDA faces significant limitations. For instance, continuously performing backpropagation on a per-frame basis incurs high computational costs and can reduce the overall framerate to meet the demands of continuous adaptation, resulting in a slower system. Additionally, optimizing on a per-frame basis for online adaptation could increase the risk of catastrophic forgetting of previous domains without enhancing adaptive performance. Furthermore, existing TTDA methods typically conduct adaptation on domain shift datasets [25] that deviate from realistic distributions (*e.g.*, day→night→rain→snow), which inadequately reflects real-world scenarios involving abrupt distribution shifts (*e.g.*, sudden rainstorms).

To address these issues, researchers have recently introduced Online Domain Adaptation (OnDA) [3,22], which reduces computation by automatically detecting domain changes to trigger adaptation only when necessary. To mitigate catastrophic forgetting, OnDA employs a replay buffer to retain source knowledge while adapting to new domains. This paradigm leverages gradual environmental shifts during deployment without requiring pre-associated data. However, we observe that existing OnDA still struggle with continuous ambiguity among visually similar classes under dynamic adverse conditions. As depicted in Fig. 2, when encountering sudden rainfall, the state-of-the-art method, *i.e.*, HAMLET [3], makes consistent errors in distinguishing such classes (*e.g., road* and *wall*). This suggests that the model transfers incorrect knowledge from prior domains, degrading performance in the current one.

We identify two key factors underlying this issue: (1) **Dynamic environmental disruptions** induce regional noise, blurring decision boundaries between ambiguous classes without explicit spatial suppression. This permits error propagation from noisy patches to dominate the learning; (2) **Semantic ambiguity persistence** between visually similar classes is reinforced by continuous domain shifts, as existing methods rely on rigid class relationship assumptions that mismatch evolving semantic contexts. This leads to pseudo-label error accumulation due to random cross-domain augmentation. Although approaches [3,22] employ a domain indicator and adaptive self-training, their adaptation suffers from two critical limitations: (1) Absence of spatial-aware noise suppression permits ambiguous patches to distort feature learning; (2) Lack of semantic contextual relationship modeling fails to resolve persistent inter-class ambiguity, perpetuating a cycle of confirmation bias.

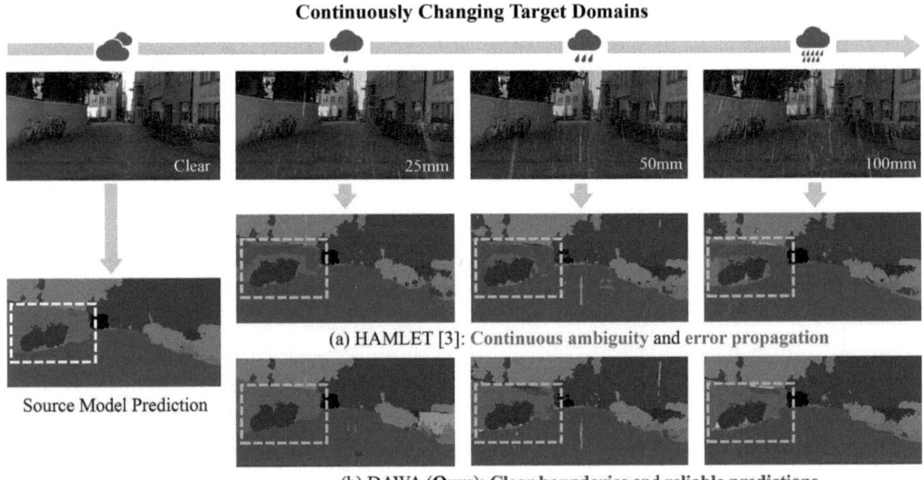

Fig. 2. Challenge posed by visually similar classes under continuous adverse weather during online adaptation. Under sudden rainfall, rain streaks cause certain classes (*e.g., road* and *wall*) to become easily ambiguous. While HAMLET [3] struggles with segmentation errors and error propagation under these conditions, our method robustly mitigates class ambiguity, yielding sharper boundaries and more reliable predictions.

In this work, we propose Dynamic Ambiguity-Wise Adaptation (DAWA), a real-time framework for domain shift detection and model adaptation that explicitly addresses ambiguity and uncertainty arising from environmental disturbances and continuous distribution shifts. The key idea is to enhance model robustness by focusing on ambiguous regions and classes that frequently occur in dynamic target domains. To this end, we introduce two core components: Dynamic Ambiguous Patch Mask (DAP Mask) and Dynamic Ambiguous Class Mix (DAC Mix). Specifically, in DAP Mask, inspired by [37], we analyze high-frequency energy distributions to identify semantically disturbed regions. A dynamic binary mask is generated to suppress these ambiguous patches, guiding the model to learn more stable representations from cleaner areas and mitigating error accumulation in uncertain classes. In DAC Mix, we leverage the semantic reasoning capabilities of Vision-Language Models (VLMs) [11,20] to construct a meta-ambiguous class buffer capturing semantically related class groups. Based on this buffer, we perform ambiguity-aware class mix, preserving contextual coherence and reducing confusion among visually similar classes. To summarize, our contributions are as follows:

(1) We propose Dynamic Ambiguity-Wise Adaptation (DAWA), a reliable framework tailored for TTDA semantic segmentation, which explicitly identifies and handles ambiguous regions and classes to enhance real-time adaptation.
(2) DAWA incorporates two novel modules to enhance adaptation: (i) DAP Mask leverages high-frequency energy analysis to identify highly disturbed regions and suppress error accumulation in ambiguous classes; and (ii) DAC Mix, a dynamic augmentation strategy guided by vision-language models that groups semantically related classes and augments the target domain with a meta-ambiguous class buffer to improve semantic disambiguation.
(3) Extensive experiments demonstrate the superior performance of our framework across various dynamic scenarios, achieving state-of-the-art results in segmentation accuracy while maintaining approximately 40 FPS.

2 Related Work

UDA for Semantic Segmentation. UDA aims to leverage labeled data from the source domain to develop a high-performing model for unlabeled data in the target domain. Common approaches include learning domain-invariant features via adversarial training [6], style transfer [5,32,33], similarity mining [35], and self-training with pseudo-labels [8,36]. Recently, many researchers have explored the domain adaptation from *normal* to *adverse* weather [1,17,23]. It is highly relevant for practical scenarios such as automated driving. However, these methods typically assume static target domains and rely on offline training, making them unsuitable for dynamic environments with continuous domain shifts.

Test-Time Domain Adaptation. TTDA addresses adaptation during test-time deployment without access to source domain data. Common strategies include generating pseudo-source data [19], freezing the final model layers [15], entropy minimization [27], and prototypes adaptation [29]. A notable advancement is Continual Test-Time Adaptation (CoTTA) [28], which adopts a weighted augmentation-averaged mean teacher framework and has inspired many follow-up works [13,18,31]. However, these methods still perform adaptation on a per-frame basis, resulting in high adaptation cost. Furthermore, widely used TTDA benchmarks (e.g., ACDC [25], day→night→rain→snow) often diverge from real-world conditions, limiting the practicality of the results.

To address this issue, OnDA [3,22] has been proposed to focus on more realistic and complex scenarios. Unlike TTDA, OnDA handles continuous, unpredictable domain shifts without clear boundaries between domains. OnDA [22] adopts self-training through coordinated static and dynamic teachers to enable online adaptation while mitigating forgetting, but at the cost of high computational overhead. HAMLET [3] introduces a hardware-aware modular training framework to reduce time cost. However, it overlooks the challenge posed by visually similar classes affected by continuous domain scenes.

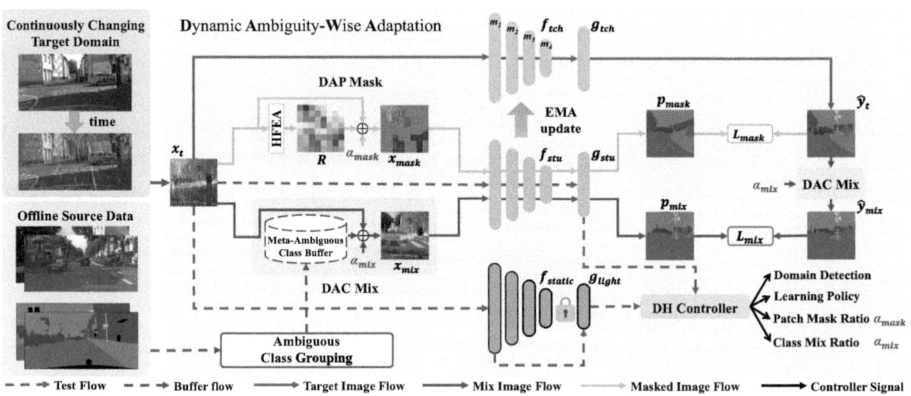

Fig. 3. The overview of our proposed DAWA. DAWA aims to detect and adapt to domain changes in real-time from the DH Controller, while simultaneously mitigating the ambiguity by DAP Mask and reducing the uncertainty by DAC Mix that arises from external environmental factors and continuous distribution shifts.

3 Proposed Method

3.1 Problem Formulation

In TTDA for semantic segmentation, a pretrained segmentation model $f_\theta : \mathbf{x} \rightarrow y$ is deployed in an open-world setting with streaming test data from potentially shifting and unknown target domains. Unlike traditional TTDA, OnDA is to enable efficient adaptation by dynamically detecting domain transitions and updating parameters only when necessary. It addresses *non-uniform*, *discontinuous* temporal flows where each segment t_i may belong to a distinct domain

$\mathcal{D}_{t_i}$, reflecting realistic scenarios with implicit transitions and varying domain durations. Thus, OnDA must decide not only *how* but also *when* to adapt.

At each time segment t_i, the model f_θ processes a target sample $\mathbf{x}_{t_i}$ through three steps: (i) detecting domain changes via a signal-based mechanism, (ii) generating a prediction $\hat{y}_{t_i}$, and (iii) updating the model if stability is confirmed. In the next segment t_{i+1}, the model receives a new sample $\mathbf{x}_{t_{i+1}}$, potentially from a new domain $\mathcal{D}_{t_{i+1}}$ and without access to prior data, highlighting the online nature of the setting.

3.2 Framework Overview

We introduce **DAWA**, a reliable and real-time framework tailored for TTDA semantic segmentation. As shown in Fig. 3, DAWA detects and adapts domain shifts in real-time through the Dynamic Hyper-parameter (DH) controller, while simultaneously mitigating the ambiguity of visually similar classes by Dynamic Ambiguous Patch Mask (DAP Mask) and reducing the uncertainty and noisy label during training by Dynamic Ambiguous Class Mix (DAC Mix).

Specifically, DAWA consists of a teacher network ϕ_{tch}, a student network ϕ_{stu}, and a static teacher encoder f_{static} paired with a lightweight decoder g_{light}. The network's backbone f is a modular encoder [3] incorporating four distinct modules: $f = m_4 \circ m_3 \circ m_2 \circ m_1$. To handle unforeseen domain shifts, we employ a DH Controller that dynamically adjusts relevant hyper-parameters in response to detected changes and optimizes training efficiency. To improve the model's ability to handle ambiguous classes, we propose a DAP Mask strategy, which utilizes High-Frequency Energy Analysis (HFEA) to identify and emphasize ambiguous regions within scenes. Furthermore, DAC Mix is introduced to integrate a meta-ambiguous class buffer through the knowledge of the vision language model on the source data into the target scene to mitigate high uncertainty and noisy labels during online adaptation while reducing training costs and speeding up the adaptation process. Finally, we leverage a masked loss $\mathcal{L}_{\text{mask}}$ to promote prediction consistency and a mixed loss $\mathcal{L}_{\text{mix}}$ to enhance training robustness, effectively handling continuous domain changes under adverse conditions.

3.3 Dynamic Ambiguous Patch Mask

Previous methods [10] often use ***random*** masking with a ***fixed*** ratio, which potentially neglects certain classes and introduce noise by ignoring scene-specific characteristics. However, the mask ratio should adapt to the evolving target domain. Inspired by [37], we observe that high-frequency components indicate scene disturbance, where severe interference reduces model confidence in ambiguous classes. Therefore, we employ HFEA to measure disturbance levels and dynamically adjust the mask ratio based on domain-specific features, which reduces the impact of noisy regions and guides the model to focus on clearer areas, improving contextual understanding and prediction accuracy.

High Frequency Energy Analysis. In Fourier spectral decomposition, low-frequency components represent smooth regions, while high-frequency components correspond to rapid intensity changes [37] (*e.g.*, edges, textures, noise). High frequency is more focused on harsh areas, which are more prone to continuous class confusion segmentation errors across continuous domain shifts. Thus, we divide the target image into $N \times N$ grids $\mathbf{c}_{i,j}$ and estimate the disturbance level of the current scene using the Fast Fourier Transform to calculate the high-frequency energy ratio $R_{i,j}$ in a certain area. This process can be defined as:

$$R_{i,j} = \frac{\sum_{(u,v)\in \mathrm{HF}} \log\left(|\mathrm{FFT}(\mathbf{c}_{i,j})_{uv}| + \epsilon\right)}{\sum_{(u,v)} \log\left(|\mathrm{FFT}(\mathbf{c}_{i,j})_{uv}| + \epsilon\right)}, \tag{1}$$

$$\mathcal{M}_{i,j} = \begin{cases} 1 & \text{if } R_{i,j} \geq \text{percentile}(\mathcal{R}, \alpha_{\text{mask}}) \\ 0 & \text{otherwise} \end{cases}, \tag{2}$$

where $\mathrm{FFT}(\mathbf{c}_{i,j})_{uv}$ denotes the value calculated by the Fast Fourier Transform of the grid $\mathbf{c}_{i,j}$ at the frequency coordinates (u, v) in the frequency domain. i and j denote the rows and columns of the patch indices. HF represents the specified high-frequency region, with (u, v) values indicating the range of high-frequency components. ϵ is a small constant used to prevent negative infinity in logarithmic calculations. percentile$(\mathcal{R}, \alpha_{\text{mask}})$ refers to the value below which a given percentage α_{mask} of the $R_{i,j}$ in the set $\mathcal{R}$. After sorting the energy of certain regions, we generate masks for the top α_{mask} of all regions. α_{mask} is the ratio of the mask, whose value is determined by the DH Controller.

Dynamic Mask Operation. By element-wise multiplying the mask $\mathcal{M}$ from HFEA, we obtain the masked target image x_{mask} with the target image x_{t}:

$$x_{\text{mask}} = \mathcal{M} \odot x_{\text{t}}. \tag{3}$$

Therefore, the model is encouraged to learn contextual relationships of ambiguous classes from the continuously changing domains, providing additional cues for robust segmentation of classes with similar local appearances.

3.4 Dynamic Ambiguous Class Mix

Effective data augmentation during online adaptation is critical for mitigating prediction uncertainty and model robustness. While ClassMix [21] demonstrates promise through cross-domain class-wise mixing, it still suffer from *static* mixing ratios and inadequate handling of semantic ambiguity in dynamic scenes. Meanwhile, unlike context-aware mix strategy [34], Our DAC Mix addresses this by leveraging Vision-Language Models (VLMs) to automatically discover **semantic ambiguity** and eliminate manual heuristics while ensuring scalability.

Ambiguous Class Grouping. We leverage VLMs' exceptional capability in capturing high-level relationships between visual patterns and linguistic concepts to uncover structured ambiguity among classes. Specifically, GPT-4o [11] is employed not for manual heuristics but to automatically construct a hierarchical semantic structure of frequently confused classes in segmentation scenarios. Formally, these ambiguous class groups are defined as:

$$A_g = C_1, C_2, ..., C_N, \tag{4}$$

where$A_g$represents an ambiguous class group and $C_n$corresponds to its constituent fine-grained classes. This structured approach enables more effective ambiguity-aware data augmentation compared to conventional methods.

Meta-ambiguous Class Buffer. Building on the semantic groupings, we design a Meta-Ambiguous Class Buffer for context-preserving augmentation. The process begins by randomly selecting an initial class from either domain's label map, then expanding it to include all contextually associated classes within its semantic group (e.g., *Traffic Sign*, *Traffic Light*, and *Pole*). Following [34], we generate a binary mask marking these classes' pixels as 1 (others as 0):

In this way, the Meta-Ambiguous Class Buffer stores a contextually extended class set reflecting semantic associations, along with a binary mask indicating their spatial distribution. This enables realistic mixing of class-wise content from the target domain, reinforcing the model's understanding of ambiguous classes and promoting domain-consistent scene structures for better adaptation.

Dynamic Mix Operation. In the mixing operation, the target pseudo labels p_{t} and source labels y_{s} are mixed based on a ratio α_{mix}. A binary mask $\mathcal{M}_{\mathrm{mix}}$ is used to determine which regions of the target image x_{t} are replaced by the source image x_{s}, generating the mixed image x_{mix} and label $\hat{y}_{\mathrm{mix}}$ as follows:

$$x_{\mathrm{mix}} = \mathcal{M}_{\mathrm{mix}} \odot x_{\mathrm{s}} + (1 - \mathcal{M}_{\mathrm{mix}}) \odot x_{\mathrm{t}}, \tag{5}$$

$$\hat{y}_{\mathrm{mix}} = \mathcal{M}_{\mathrm{mix}} \odot y_{\mathrm{s}} + (1 - \mathcal{M}_{\mathrm{mix}}) \odot \hat{y}_{\mathrm{t}}, \tag{6}$$

By including α_{mix}, the ratio between the source and target images can be flexibly adjusted to meet the needs of different scenarios.

3.5 Dynamic Hyper-Parameter Controller

Unforeseeable changes in the target domain occur when the model encounters target data streams during deployment. Therefore, we extend [3] to adjust the mask ratio α_{mask} and mix ratio α_{mix} dynamically during online adaptation.

Domain Detection. To identify target domain shifts, we compute the cross-entropy loss between the predictions of g_{stu} and g_{light} as a measure of domain distance. This measurement of domain distance improves as the g_{stu} continuously adapts over time. A domain shift is detected when the distance change exceeds a minimum threshold. We define $A_T^{(i)}$ as a denoised signal through bin-averaging calculated from the distance. Domains are modeled as discrete steps of $A_T^{(i)}$:

$$B_0 = A_0, \qquad B_i = \begin{cases} A_i & \text{if} \, |B_{i-1} - A_i| > z \\ B_{i-1} & \text{otherwise} \end{cases}, \tag{7}$$

where B is the discretized signal and z is the minimum distance used to identify new domains. A domain change is detected if the signed amplitude of the domain shifts $\Delta B_i = |B_i - B_{i-1}| > z$.

Learning Policy. Upon detecting a domain shift, the number of adaptation iterations L is determined by $L = K_l \frac{|\Delta B_i|}{z}$, where $|\Delta B_i|$ measures the shift magnitude relative to a threshold z, and K_l is a scaling factor for adaptation intensity. The value of K_l depends on the model's proximity to the source domain:

$$K_l = \begin{cases} K_l^{\max} & \text{if } \Delta B_i \geq 0, \\ K_l^{\min} + \frac{(B_i - B_{\text{source}})(K_l^{\max} - K_l^{\min})}{B_{\text{hard}} - B_{\text{source}}} & \text{otherwise} \end{cases}, \tag{8}$$

where B_{source} and B_{hard} denote the closest and furthest states from the source domain, respectively. $K_l^{\min}$ and $K_l^{\max}$ define the range of adaptation iterations.

The learning rate η is linearly decayed during adaptation, with its initial value K_η dynamically adjusted by:

$$K_\eta = K_\eta^{\min} + \frac{(B_i - B_{\text{source}})(K_\eta^{\max} - K_\eta^{\min})}{B_{\text{hard}} - B_{\text{source}}}. \tag{9}$$

Here, $K_\eta^{\min}$ and $K_\eta^{\max}$ correspond to easier and harder domain shifts, respectively, enabling adaptive learning based on shift severity.

Patch Mask Ratio. We leverage domain knowledge to control the mask ratio based on the domain distance from the source domain during online adaptation.

$$\alpha_{\text{mask}} = \alpha_{\text{mask}}^{\min} + \frac{(B_{\text{i}} - B_{\text{source}})(\alpha_{\text{mask}}^{\max} - \alpha_{\text{mask}}^{\min})}{B_{\text{hard}} - B_{\text{source}}}, \tag{10}$$

where $\alpha_{\text{mask}}^{\min}$ is the value of α_{mask} assigned when the network is close to the source domain. and $\alpha_{\text{mask}}^{\max}$ is, respectively, opposite in meaning to $\alpha_{\text{mask}}^{\min}$.

Class Mix Ratio. The class mix ratio during adaptation is also based on the domain knowledge:

$$\alpha_{\text{mix}} = \alpha_{\text{mix}}^{\min} + \frac{(B_{\text{i}} - B_{\text{source}})(\alpha_{\text{mix}}^{\max} - \alpha_{\text{mix}}^{\min})}{B_{\text{hard}} - B_{\text{source}}}, \tag{11}$$

where α_{mix} is the percentage of source classes used during adaptation, and $\alpha_{\text{mix}}^{\min}$ is the value of α_{mix} assigned when the network is close to the source domain. and $\alpha_{\text{mix}}^{\max}$ is, respectively, opposite in meaning to $\alpha_{\text{mix}}^{\min}$.

3.6 Overall Optimization

Once the DH Controller detects domain changes and returns the training signal, the model enters the online training.

For x_{mask}, the masked prediction can only utilize limited information from the unmasked regions. We refer to [10] for consistency prediction constraints, utilizing mask consistency loss $\mathcal{L}_{\text{mask}}$:

$$\mathcal{L}_{\text{mask}} = -\sum_{j=1}^{H\times W}\sum_{c=1}^{C}\hat{y}_t^{(i,j,c)}\log\phi_{\text{stu}}(x_{\text{mask}}^{(i,j,c)}), \tag{12}$$

where $\hat{y}_{\text{t}}$ represent the quality weighted pseudo-labels predicted by the teacher network ϕ_{tch} on the target image x_{t}. Additionally, for the mixed image, we constrain the mixed pseudo-label loss $\mathcal{L}_{\text{mix}}$ using mixed pseudo-labels $\hat{y}_{\text{mix}}$ obtained from the DAC Mix:

$$\mathcal{L}_{\text{mix}} = -\sum_{j=1}^{H\times W}\sum_{c=1}^{C}\hat{y}_{\text{mix}}^{(i,j,c)}\log\phi_{\text{stu}}(x_{\text{mix}}^{(i,j,c)}). \tag{13}$$

The teacher network ϕ_{tch} is implemented as an EMA teacher [26]. The total loss $\mathcal{L}$ is : $\mathcal{L} = \mathcal{L}_{\text{mix}} + \mathcal{L}_{\text{mask}}$.

Table 1. Quantitative comparison against relevant methods on Increasing Storm [22]. For each configuration, we report mIoU (%) and framerate per second (FPS). Type "T" indicates the test time adaptation method, while "O" refers to the online adaptation method. The best two scores are indicated by **bold** and underline.

Methods	Type	clear		25 mm		50 mm		75 mm		100 mm		200 mm	h-mIoU (%)			FPS
		F	B	F	B	F	B	F	B	F	B	F	F	B	All	
DeepLab-V2																
(A) No Adapt	–	64.5	–	57.1	–	48.7	–	41.5	–	34.4	–	18.5	37.3	–	–	39.4
(B) OnDA [22]	O	64.5	64.8	60.4	57.1	57.3	54.5	54.8	52.2	52.0	49.1	42.2	54.2	55.1	54.6	6.7
Segformer-B1																
(C) No Adapt	–	73.4	–	68.8	–	64.2	–	58.0	–	51.8	–	31.2	57.8	–	–	60.8
(D) TENT [27]	T	73.0	72.8	68.5	68.6	64.5	64.8	59.7	60.2	54.5	54.8	35.9	56.2	63.6	59.9	10.0
(E) TENT+Replay Buffer	T	73.0	72.8	68.5	68.6	64.5	64.8	59.7	60.2	54.4	54.7	35.8	56.1	63.6	59.9	7.8
(F) CoTTA [28]	T	72.5	74.4	69.5	70.9	65.9	68.2	66.1	64.7	64.6	63.5	57.2	65.6	68.1	66.8	0.6
(G) CoTTA *real-time*	T	73.3	**75.4**	70.3	70.6	66.9	66.4	62.5	61.4	57.6	56.9	39.7	59.2	65.5	62.3	27.0
(H) SVDP [31]	T	**75.8**	74.9	**71.4**	71.3	68.6	69.3	66.2	67.1	63.7	64.4	51.1	65.1	69.2	66.9	0.04
(I) HAMLET [3]	O	73.4	71.0	69.9	68.8	67.7	67.5	66.6	66.4	65.5	64.6	58.9	66.7	67.6	67.1	**46.3**
(J) DAWA (Ours)	O	73.4	73.5	70.4	**71.6**	**68.9**	**70.0**	**67.6**	**69.1**	**66.1**	**66.4**	**60.6**	**67.6**	**70.0**	**68.7**	40.7

Table 2. Quantitative comparison on Increasing Fog [24]. We report mIoU(%) and FPS. The best score is indicated by **bold**.

Methods	clear		600 m		300 m		150 m	h-mIoU (%)			FPS
	F	B	F	B	F	B	F	F	B	All	
(A) OnDA [22]	64.9	65.4	63.8	62.7	61.7	59.5	51.6	60.0	62.4	61.0	6.4
(B) HAMLET [3]	73.4	72.8	71.3	71.3	69.1	69.5	66	69.8	71.2	70.4	**42.0**
(C) DAWA	**73.4**	**73.3**	**71.6**	**72.0**	**69.9**	**70.0**	**66.6**	**70.3**	**71.6**	**70.9**	38.6

4 Experimental Results

4.1 Experimental Settings

Datasets. We set Cityscapes dataset [4] under *clear* weather conditions as the source domain. The experiments are carried out on the Increasing Storm [22] and Increasing Foggy Cityscapes [24], which are a semi-synthetic benchmark with 2,975 training images and 500 validation images and apply synthetic rain and fog at different intensities and visibilities. The main benchmark, Increasing Storm [22], presents a pyramidal intensity profile. We selected rainy domains with the intensity of {25 mm, 50 mm, 75 mm, 100 mm, 200 mm} and foggy domains with {600 m, 300 m, and 150 m} visibility as experimental domains.

Implementation Details. The online models were trained using AdamW with $\beta_1 = 0.9$, $\beta_2 = 0.999$, and weight decay 0.01. Following [3], the hyper-parameters in the DH Controller are: $\alpha = 0.1$, $K_l = 750$, $K_\eta^{\min} = 1.5 \times 10^{-4}$, $K_\eta^{\max} = 6 \times 10^{-5}$, $K_l^{\min} = 187$, $K_l^{\max} = 562$, $\alpha_{\text{mix}}^{\min} = 0.5$, $\alpha_{\text{mix}}^{\max} = 0.75$, $\alpha_{\text{mask}}^{\min} = 0.3$ and $\alpha_{\text{mask}}^{\max} = 0.7$. We use $B_{\text{source}} = 0.8$, $B_{\text{hard}} = 2.55$ for the rainy and foggy scenarios. During the DAP Mask stage, the mask patch size is 64, and ϵ is set to 1×10^{-7} to prevent negative infinity in logarithmic calculations. The evaluation metrics are mIoU(%), FPS, and the harmonic mean (h-mIoU(%)) over domains to present the overall adaptation performance. All models were trained on an RTX 4090 GPU.

4.2 Performance Comparison

Quantitative Comparison. Table 1 and Table 2 provides a comparison of **DAWA** with other relevant methods under Increasing Storm and Increasing Fog. Columns "F" indicate forward adaptation from *clear* to 200mm, while columns "B" show backward adaptation. Columns "All" show the all adaptation. The h-mIoU refers to the overall harmonic mean. Methods are categorized into different backbones. Type "T" and "O" indicates test time adaptation and online adaptation.

Our proposed DAWA (J) emerges as a standout method, particularly in its handling of backward adaptation scenarios. Unlike other methods, DAWA not only avoids catastrophic forgetting but also improves performance as it focuses

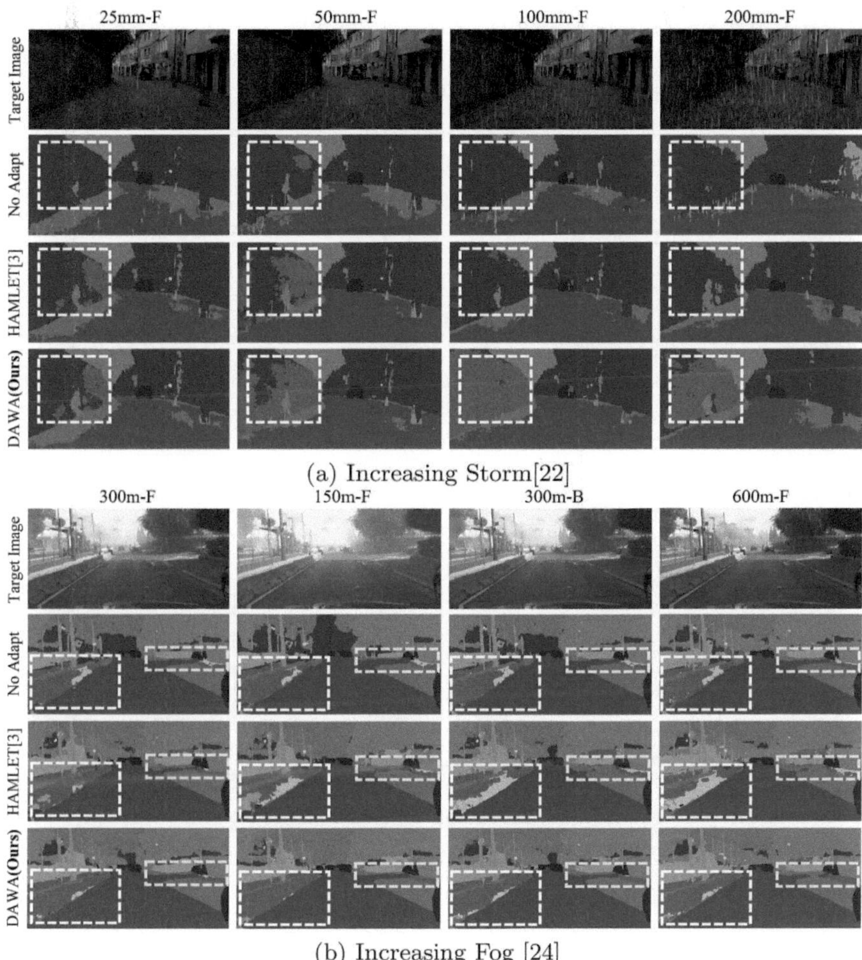

Fig. 4. Qualitative comparisons on (a) Increasing Storm [22] and (b) Increasing Fog [24] among source model (No Adapt), HAMLET [3] and DAWA.

on ambiguous regions. This is evident in its consistent performance in backward scenarios, where it surpasses even its forward adaptation results. With an FPS of 40, DAWA achieves an excellent balance between accuracy and efficiency, making it a strong candidate for real-time applications.

Qualitative Comparison. Figure 4 present continuous qualitative comparisons in dynamic target domains, featuring results from the pre-trained model, HAMLET, and DAWA. In rainy scenes (Fig. 4(a)), the pre-trained model struggles due to its clear-weather training, and while HAMLET improves upon it, it still misclassifies ambiguous classes like *wall* and *building*. DAWA, by contrast, better exploits contextual cues to yield more accurate results. Under foggy conditions

(Fig. 4(b)), HAMLET has difficulty with classes like *terrain* and *wall*, whereas DAWA maintains stronger performance. However, both methods fail in extreme fog where distant objects are severely obscured. Overall, DAWA shows superior adaptability to adverse weather by mitigating continuous ambiguities.

Table 3. Ablation studies of the effect of components on Increasing Storm [22]. For each configuration, we report the mIoU(%) and FPS. Best scores are indicated by **bold**.

	Components		clear		25 mm		50 mm		75 mm		100 mm		200 mm	h-mIoU (%)			FPS
	DAC Mask	DAC Mix	F	B	F	B	F	B	F	B	F	B	F	F	B	All	
(A)	No Adapt		73.4	–	68.8	–	64.2	–	58.0	–	51.8	–	31.2	57.8	–	–	60.8
(B)	✓	–	73.4	68.7	69.2	67.4	66.8	66.2	64.3	63.8	62.5	63.6	56.8	65.1	65.9	65.4	37.5
(C)	–	✓	73.4	73.0	70.1	71.0	67.5	68.5	66.6	67.3	64.6	65.1	59.4	66.6	68.9	67.6	**45.0**
(D)	✓	✓	**73.4**	**73.5**	**70.4**	**71.6**	**68.9**	**70.0**	**67.6**	**69.1**	**66.1**	**66.4**	**60.6**	**67.6**	**70.0**	**68.7**	40.7

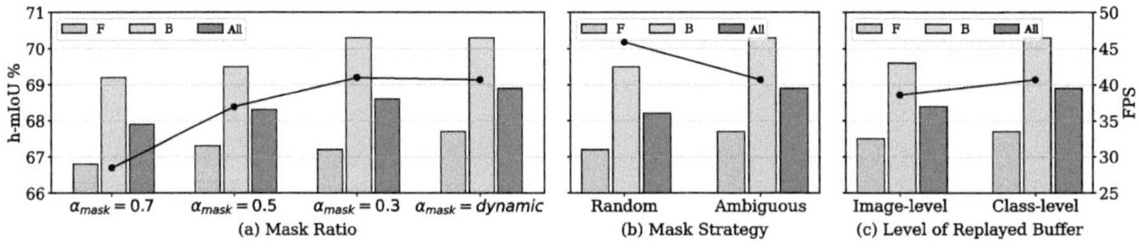

Fig. 5. Ablation studies on (a) mask ratio, (b) mask strategy, and (c) replayed buffer. We report FPS (black line) and h-mIoU (%) for forward (F), backward (B), and total (T) adaptation.

4.3 Ablation Study

Effect of Components. Table 3 presents each component's contribution under the Increasing Storm [22]. While the source model (A) shows limited performance, independently adding DAP Mask (B) or DAC Mix (C) improves mIoU with moderate FPS reduction. (D) combines both components, achieving the best overall performance with over 40 FPS. Despite a small FPS drop, the trade-off remains acceptable, demonstrating that DAP Mask and DAC Mix effectively balance accuracy and efficiency for practical deployment.

Design of DAP Mask. To evaluate the DAP Mask, we study the effect of mask ratio and masking strategy. Figure 5(a) shows that fixed mask ratios yield suboptimal results, while the dynamic ratio delivers the best performance. In Fig. 5(b), ambiguous masking on easily confused areas significantly outperforms random masking. In conclusion, These results confirm the effectiveness of the DAP Mask in enhancing adaptation by focusing on ambiguous regions.

Levels of Replayed Buffer. We also conducted experiments to demonstrate the superiority of our proposed meta-ambiguous class buffer. As shown in Fig. 5(c), the class-level (meta-ambiguous) buffer achieves higher FPS and better accuracy. This is because image-level replay can introduce excessive interference with current learning. Overall, the meta-ambiguous class buffer proves more suitable for online domain adaptation.

Table 4. Comparison of different mix strategies on Increasing Storm. We report mIoU (%) of 200 mm, all mIou and FPS. Best scores are indicated by bold.

Methods	Main Idea	200 mm	All	FPS
ClassMix [21]	Random Augmentation	59.1	67.5	**41.0**
CAMix [34]	Context Awareness	60.2	68.3	40.6
DAC Mix (Ours)	Semantic Ambiguity	**60.6**	**68.7**	40.7

Different Mix Strategies. As shown in Table 4, our DAC Mix outperforms random mix [21] and context-aware mix [34] methods, achieving the highest All mIoU of 68.7 while maintaining a competitive FPS of 40.7. This highlights the superiority of semantic ambiguity guidance in online adaptation.

5 Conclusion

In this study, we present the Dynamic Ambiguity-Wise Adaptation (DAWA) for solving real-time domain adaptive semantic segmentation under adverse weather conditions. DAWA address the challenge of ambiguous classes by continuous domain shifts that arise in online environments with DAP Mask and DAC Mix. Experiments on OnDA benchmarks show that DAWA achieves state-of-the-art performance, highlighting its competitiveness. Future work may explore extending these strategies to other complex scenarios, further improving its adaptability and performance.

Acknowledgement. This work was supported by the National Natural Science Foundation of China (62371351, 62202349), the Young Elite Scientists Sponsorship Program by CAST (2023QNRC001), and the Fundamental Research Funds for the Central Universities (ZYTS25036).

References

1. Brüggemann, D., Sakaridis, C., Truong, P., Van Gool, L.: Refign: align and refine for adaptation of semantic segmentation to adverse conditions. In: WACV, pp. 3174–3184 (2023)

2. Chen, L.C., Papandreou, G., Kokkinos, I., Murphy, K., Yuille, A.L.: DeepLab: semantic image segmentation with deep convolutional nets, atrous convolution, and fully connected CRFs. IEEE Trans. Pattern Anal. Mach. Intell. **40**(4), 834–848 (2017)
3. Colomer, M.B., et al.: To adapt or not to adapt? Real-time adaptation for semantic segmentation. In: ICCV, pp. 16548–16559 (2023)
4. Cordts, M., et al.: The cityscapes dataset for semantic urban scene understanding. In: CVPR, pp. 3213–3223 (2016)
5. Dundar, A., Liu, M.Y., Yu, Z., Wang, T.C., Zedlewski, J., Kautz, J.: Domain stylization: a fast covariance matching framework towards domain adaptation. IEEE Trans. Pattern Anal. Mach. Intell. **43**(7), 2360–2372 (2020)
6. Ganin, Y., et al.: Domain-adversarial training of neural networks. J. Mach. Learn. Res. **17**(59), 1–35 (2016)
7. Guo, Z., Jin, T.: Smoothing the shift: towards stable test-time adaptation under complex multimodal noises. In: ICLR (2025)
8. Hoyer, L., Dai, D., Van Gool, L.: DAFormer: improving network architectures and training strategies for domain-adaptive semantic segmentation. In: CVPR, pp. 9924–9935 (2022)
9. Hoyer, L., Dai, D., Van Gool, L.: HRDA: context-aware high-resolution domain-adaptive semantic segmentation. In: ECCV, pp. 372–391 (2022)
10. Hoyer, L., Dai, D., Wang, H., Van Gool, L.: MIC: masked image consistency for context-enhanced domain adaptation. In: CVPR, pp. 11721–11732 (2023)
11. Hurst, A., et al.: GPT-4o system card. arXiv preprint arXiv:2410.21276 (2024)
12. Jain, J., Li, J., Chiu, M.T., Hassani, A., Orlov, N., Shi, H.: OneFormer: one transformer to rule universal image segmentation. In: CVPR, pp. 2989–2998 (2023)
13. Lee, S., Kim, N., Kang, J., Oh, S.J., Kwak, S.: DiCoTTA: domain-invariant learning for continual test-time adaptation. arXiv preprint arXiv:2504.04981 (2025)
14. Li, M., Xie, B., Li, S., Liu, C.H., Cheng, X.: VBLC: visibility boosting and logit-constraint learning for domain adaptive semantic segmentation under adverse conditions. In: AAAI, vol. 37, pp. 8605–8613 (2023)
15. Liang, J., Hu, D., Feng, J.: Do we really need to access the source data? Source hypothesis transfer for unsupervised domain adaptation. In: ICML (2020)
16. Liao, L., Chen, W., Xiao, J., Wang, Z., Lin, C.W., Satoh, S.: Unsupervised foggy scene understanding via self spatial-temporal label diffusion. IEEE Trans. Image Process. **31**, 3525–3540 (2022)
17. Liao, L., et al.: Only a few classes confusing: Pixel-wise candidate labels disambiguation for foggy scene understanding. In: AAAI, vol. 37, pp. 1558–1567 (2023)
18. Liu, J., et al.: Continual-MAE: adaptive distribution masked autoencoders for continual test-time adaptation. In: CVPR, pp. 28653–28663 (2024)
19. Liu, Y., Zhang, W., Wang, J.: Source-free domain adaptation for semantic segmentation. In: CVPR, pp. 1215–1224 (2021)
20. Ma, P., Rietdorf, L., Kotovenko, D., Hu, V.T., Ommer, B.: Does VLM classification benefit from LLM description semantics? In: AAAI (2025)
21. Olsson, V., Tranheden, W., Pinto, J., Svensson, L.: ClassMix: segmentation-based data augmentation for semi-supervised learning. In: WACV, pp. 1369–1378 (2021)
22. Panagiotakopoulos, T., Dovesi, P.L., Härenstam-Nielsen, L., Poggi, M.: Online domain adaptation for semantic segmentation in ever-changing conditions. In: ECCV, pp. 128–146 (2022)
23. Rizzoli, G., Caligiuri, M., Shenaj, D., Barbato, F., Zanuttigh, P.: When cars meet drones: hyperbolic federated learning for source-free domain adaptation in adverse weather. In: WACV, pp. 1587–1596 (2025)

24. Sakaridis, C., Dai, D., Van Gool, L.: Semantic foggy scene understanding with synthetic data. Int. J. Comput. Vision **126**(9), 973–992 (2018)
25. Sakaridis, C., Dai, D., Van Gool, L.: ACDC: the adverse conditions dataset with correspondences for semantic driving scene understanding. In: ICCV (2021)
26. Tarvainen, A., Valpola, H.: Mean teachers are better role models: Weight-averaged consistency targets improve semi-supervised deep learning results. In: NIPS, vol. 30 (2017)
27. Wang, D., Shelhamer, E., Liu, S., Olshausen, B., Darrell, T.: Tent: fully test-time adaptation by entropy minimization. In: ICLR (2021)
28. Wang, Q., Fink, O., Van Gool, L., Dai, D.: Continual test-time domain adaptation. In: Proceedings of Conference on Computer Vision and Pattern Recognition (2022)
29. Wang, W., et al.: Dynamically instance-guided adaptation: a backward-free approach for test-time domain adaptive semantic segmentation. In: CVPR, pp. 24090–24099 (2023)
30. Xie, E., Wang, W., Yu, Z., Anandkumar, A., Alvarez, J.M., Luo, P.: SegFormer: simple and efficient design for semantic segmentation with transformers. In: NIPS, vol. 34, pp. 12077–12090 (2021)
31. Yang, S., et al.: Exploring sparse visual prompt for domain adaptive dense prediction. In: AAAI, vol. 38, pp. 16334–16342 (2024)
32. Yang, Y., Soatto, S.: FDA: Fourier domain adaptation for semantic segmentation. In: CVPR, pp. 4084–4094. IEEE (2020)
33. Zhong, X., et al.: Bat: Bi-alignment based on transformation in multi-target domain adaptation for semantic segmentation. In: ICASSP, pp. 1–5 (2023)
34. Zhou, Q., et al.: Context-aware mixup for domain adaptive semantic segmentation. IEEE Trans. Circuit Syst. Video Technol. **33**(2), 804–817 (2022)
35. Zhu, H., Yuan, J., Zhong, X., Liao, L., Wang, Z.: Find gold in sand: fine-grained similarity mining for domain-adaptive crowd counting. IEEE Trans. Multimedia **26**, 3842–3855 (2024)
36. Zou, Y., Yu, Z., Liu, X., Kumar, B., Wang, J.: Confidence regularized self-training. In: ICCV, pp. 5982–5991 (2019)
37. Zou, Z., Yu, H., Huang, J., Zhao, F.: FreqMamba: viewing mamba from a frequency perspective for image deraining. In: ACM MM (2024)

Adaptive Mixture of Experts for Cross-Domain Medical Image Segmentation with Vision Foundation Models

Qifei Wang[1], Yuefeng Zhao[1], Bolin Chen[1], Nai Zhou[2], Qianqian Tao[1], and Nannan Hu[1](✉)

[1] School of Physics and Electronics, Shandong Normal University, Jinan 250358, China
hunan246@sdnu.edu.cn
[2] Quan Cheng Laboratory, Jinan 250100, China

Abstract. Although vision foundation models like SAM2 excel at natural image segmentation, their direct application to medical image segmentation faces severe domain gap challenges due to unique imaging principles, complex noise characteristics, and specialized semantic requirements. We propose AMoE-SAM2UNet, a cross-domain medical image segmentation framework that integrates an Adaptive Mixture of Experts Decoder (AMoE-Decoder) with the SAM2 encoder. The AMoE-Decoder comprises three specialized expert modules: the Multi-Scale Adaptive Expert (MSAE) captures lesion scale variations through parallel dilated convolutions and adaptive fusion operations; the Boundary Refinement Expert (BRE) sharpens blurred boundaries by enhancing high-frequency information via wavelet transform; and the Foreground Enhancement Expert (FEE) leverages multi-branch convolutions and spatial-channel attention to enhance foreground-background discrimination, addressing low contrast and complex background. Moreover, a lightweight gating network dynamically combines expert outputs based on input characteristics. Extensive experiments on five diverse medical imaging modalities—dermoscopy (ISIC 2017), ultrasound (TN3K), endoscopy (ClinicDB), CT (COVID), and histology (GLAS)—demonstrate that AMoE-SAM2UNet achieves consistent Dice coefficient improvements ranging from 1.8% to 3.2% over the SAM2-UNet baseline and outperforms existing state-of-the-art methods by margins of 2.5% to 3.4%, validating the effectiveness of adaptive mixture-of-experts for medical vision foundation model adaptation.

Keywords: Medical Image Segmentation · Segment Anything Model · Mixture of Experts

1 Introduction

Medical image segmentation serves as the cornerstone of modern clinical practice, providing crucial quantitative information for disease diagnosis, treatment

© The Author(s), under exclusive license to Springer Nature Singapore Pte Ltd. 2026
J. Kittler et al. (Eds.): PRCV 2025, LNCS 16289, pp. 546–559, 2026.
https://doi.org/10.1007/978-981-95-5764-6_37

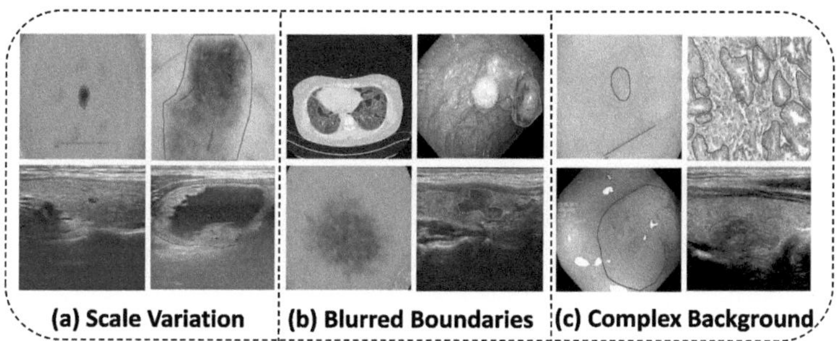

Fig. 1. Key challenges in medical image segmentation. (a) scale variation of lesions, (b) blurred lesion boundaries, and (c) lesions in complex background conditions, with red, green, and blue annotations marking the respective lesion regions. (Color figure online)

planning, and prognosis evaluation through precise delineation of anatomical structures and pathological regions. With the advancement of deep learning techniques, encoder-decoder architectures represented by UNet [20] and their numerous variants [2,4,14] have achieved remarkable success across various medical image segmentation tasks. In recent years, vision foundation models (VFMs) pre-trained on large-scale datasets, such as Segment Anything Model (SAM) [9] and its successor SAM2 [18,25], have garnered significant attention due to their powerful few-shot generalization capabilities and adaptation potential for diverse visual tasks, bringing new possibilities to the field of medical image segmentation.

Despite their success in natural images, when these foundation models are directly applied to medical image segmentation, their performance often falls short of expectations. This is primarily attributed to the fundamental differences between medical and natural images in terms of imaging principles, noise characteristics, target morphology, and semantic complexity [3,19,23]. Specifically, the core challenges that foundation models face in the medical domain include enormous size variations of lesions or anatomical structures, blurred target boundaries, and difficulties in distinguishing foreground from background under complex imaging conditions characterized by low contrast, high noise, or artifact interference, as shown in Fig. 1.

Researchers have explored various adaptation strategies to address the cross-domain challenges, including Parameter-Efficient Fine-Tuning (PEFT) [8,23] and architectural modifications [3,5,25] have achieved notable improvements. However, these methods primarily focus on enhancing feature extraction or optimizing overall architecture, with decoder components still employing generic designs that lack specialized mechanisms to systematically address medical imaging challenges. The Mixture of Experts (MoE) architecture offers significant potential for enhancing model capacity and adaptability by dynamically invoking specialized expert modules for specific sub-problems. While recent works have applied MoE to medical image segmentation [11,15,24,26], they predominantly target task-specific requirements, feature combination strategies, or modality differences, without providing a systematic expert framework directly tailored to the core challenges of medical imaging.

To address these challenges, we propose a novel AMoE-Decoder framework. We integrate the AMoE-Decoder with SAM2's powerful Hiera encoder to construct AMoE-SAM2UNet. This decoder operates through a core AMoE Block at each decoding stage, internally integrating three expert modules specifically designed to address the core challenges in medical image segmentation. The MSAE employs parallel convolutions with different dilation rates followed by adaptive feature fusion operations to address the extreme scale variations of targets. The BRE utilizes discrete wavelet transform to decompose features, thereby enhancing high-frequency boundary information and reconstructing features to sharpen blurred tissue boundaries. The FEE leverages multi-branch convolutions to extract diversified features and combines spatial and channel attention mechanisms to strengthen effective identification of foreground targets. Additionally, we design a lightweight adaptive gating network that dynamically computes the contribution weights of each expert based on the intrinsic characteristics of input features, enabling the network to adaptively focus on the primary challenges faced by the current input, thereby achieving more precise and efficient medical image segmentation. Our major contributions are summarized as follows:

- We propose AMoE-SAM2UNet, a novel AMoE-Decoder framework that systematically adapts foundation models to core medical imaging challenges.
- We design a core AMoE Block with three specialized experts—the MSAE for scale variations, the BRE for blurred boundaries, and the FEE for foreground enhancement—dynamically weighted by a lightweight gating network.
- Extensive experiments on five public datasets across diverse medical imaging modalities (ISIC 2017, TN3K, ClinicDB, COVID, and GLAS) demonstrate that our model achieves superior performance over existing methods.

2 Related Work

2.1 Development of Medical Image Segmentation Methods

Medical image segmentation has evolved from classical convolutional neural network (CNN) architectures to advanced vision foundation models (VFMs). The encoder-decoder paradigm, established by UNet [20] and its variants [14], laid the groundwork for the field. This was subsequently enhanced by Transformer-based architectures [2,4,16,17], which improved global context modeling. More recently, VFMs have introduced new opportunities, with SAM [9] demonstrating powerful zero-shot capabilities and SAM2 [18] achieving superior performance with its advanced Hiera backbone. Methods like SAM2-UNet [25] have pioneered the combination of SAM2's encoder with classical UNet decoders, validating the effectiveness of frozen pre-trained encoders. However, whether in traditional deep learning models or foundation models, their decoder designs predominantly adhere to generic principles, lacking specialized mechanisms to systematically address the core challenges inherent in medical imaging.

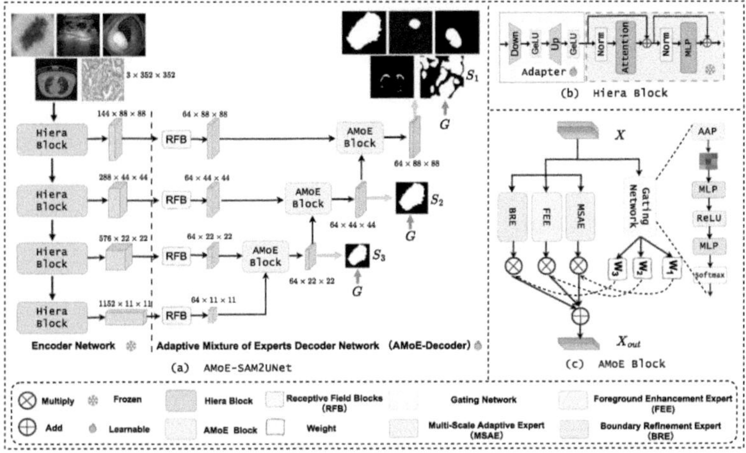

Fig. 2. The architecture of AMoE-SAM2UNet.

2.2 Mixture of Experts in Medical Image Segmentation

Mixture of Experts (MoE) models have demonstrated significant potential in enhancing model capacity and adaptability through their ability to dynamically invoke different experts for specific sub-problems, and have been widely applied in medical image analysis. Wu et al. [24] specifically designed boundary, spatial, and global experts for polyp segmentation. Luo et al. [11] innovatively applied MoE concepts to UNet skip connections to optimize information transfer. Patcher [15] and MORSE [26] applied stochastic expert selection to multi-scale decoder representations. Although these MoE methods have each made advances, they typically focus on specific task requirements, feature combination strategies, or particular architectural components, lacking a systematic framework that directly targets the universal core challenges of medical imaging.

3 Method

3.1 Overall Architecture

As shown in Fig. 2(a), the proposed AMoE-SAM2UNet architecture employs an encoder-decoder framework that integrates the powerful feature extraction capability of the SAM2 pre-trained encoder with a novel AMoE-Decoder specifically tailored for medical image segmentation. The encoder backbone utilizes frozen Hiera Blocks from SAM2 (as shown in Fig. 2(b)) [21], which transforms input images of size $H \times W \times 3$ into hierarchical feature representations across four stages, producing feature maps with channel dimensions of $\{144, 288, 576, 1152\}$ at spatial resolutions of $\{H/4, H/8, H/16, H/32\}$, respectively. To adapt the frozen encoder for medical imaging tasks while preserving learned representations, lightweight adapter modules are integrated before each Hiera block,

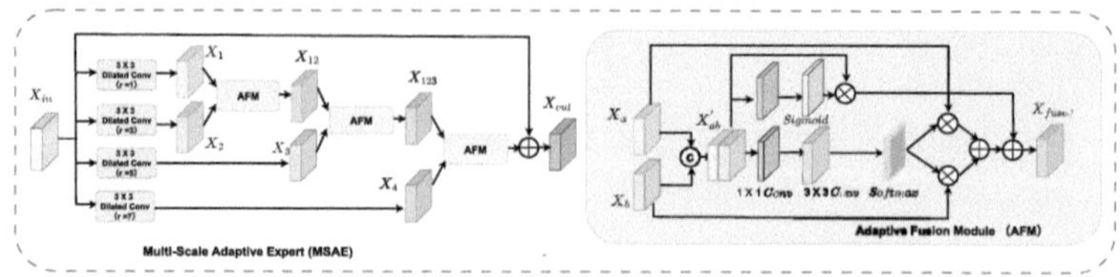

Fig. 3. Architecture of the Multi-Scale Adaptive Expert (MSAE).

following a parameter-efficient fine-tuning paradigm. Receptive Field Blocks (RFB) [10] then process the encoder outputs, applying 1×1 convolutions to unify all feature channels to 64 dimensions, creating standardized input for the decoder network. The core innovation of our work lies in the AMoE-Decoder, where standard decoder blocks are replaced with the proposed AMoE Blocks ((as shown in Fig. 2(c)).

3.2 Adaptive Mixture of Experts Decoder (AMoE-Decoder)

The AMoE-Decoder progressively upsamples encoder features through four decoding stages, each equipped with an AMoE Block that replaces conventional convolutional operations. As illustrated in Fig. 2(c), each AMoE Block processes incoming features through three parallel expert branches—MSAE, BRE, and FEE—whose outputs are dynamically combined by a lightweight gating network. Skip connections from corresponding encoder stages are integrated before each AMoE Block, preserving fine-grained spatial information. The following subsections detail the design of each expert module and the gating mechanism.

Multi-scale Adaptive Expert (MSAE). Medical imaging encompasses targets with extreme scale variability, from microscopic lesions to large anatomical structures, requiring sophisticated multi-scale processing strategies. The MSAE module, illustrated in Fig. 3, employs a hierarchical fusion architecture that adaptively integrates features across multiple receptive fields.

The MSAE module initially processes the input features X_{in} into four parallel branches using 3×3 dilated convolutions with dilation rates $r \in \{1, 3, 5, 7\}$:

$$X_i = \text{DilatedConv}_{3\times 3}(X_{in}, r_i), \quad i \in \{1, 2, 3, 4\} \tag{1}$$

Each AFM integrates features from two scales using dynamic feature selection. For input features X_a and X_b, the AFM first concatenates them to obtain $X^{'}_{ab}$ and processes through two parallel branches. One branch uses 1×1 convolution followed by sigmoid activation to generate excitation weights, while the other branch employs 1×1 and two 3×3 convolutions with softmax to produce fusion weights. The AFM output is computed as:

$$\text{AFM}(X_a, X_b) = \text{Softmax}(\text{Conv}(X^{'}_{ab})) \otimes [X_a; X_b] \oplus \sigma(\text{Conv}(X^{'}_{ab})) \otimes X^{'}_{ab} \tag{2}$$

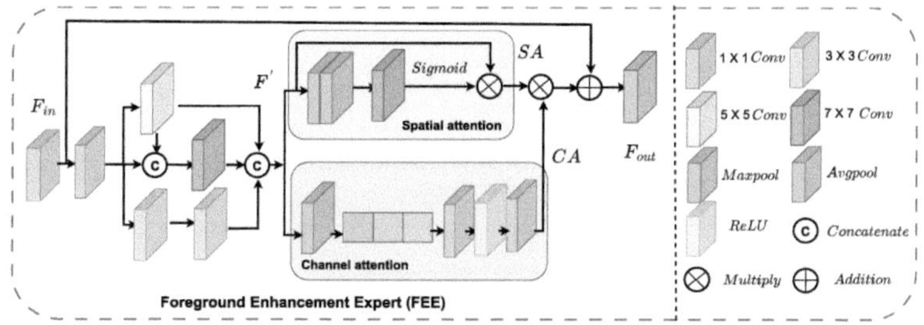

Fig. 4. Architecture of the Foreground Enhancement Expert (FEE).

where σ is the sigmoid function, $\oplus$ denotes element-wise addition and $\otimes$ represents element-wise multiplication.

The hierarchical fusion follows a progressive strategy:

$$X_{out} = X_{in} \oplus \text{AFM}(\text{AFM}(X_{12}, X_{123}), X_4) \tag{3}$$

where $X_{12} = \text{AFM}(X_1, X_2)$ and $X_{123} = \text{AFM}(X_{12}, X_3)$. This progressive fusion strategy ensures that features from all scales contribute meaningfully to the final representation.

Foreground Enhancement Expert (FEE). Distinguishing foreground targets from complex backgrounds remains a fundamental challenge in medical image segmentation, particularly when dealing with low-contrast regions or heterogeneous tissue structures. The FEE module, depicted in Fig. 4, employs a multi-scale feature extraction strategy combined with dual-attention mechanisms to selectively enhance salient foreground features while suppressing background noise.

The FEE module processes input features F_{in} through parallel multi-scale convolutions:

$$F' = \text{Concat}[\text{Conv}_{3\times3}(F_{in}), \text{Conv}_{5\times5}(F_{in}), \text{Conv}_{7\times7}(F_{in})] \tag{4}$$

Subsequently, two parallel attention mechanisms are applied. Spatial attention generates location-aware weights through max pooling and average pooling operations followed by sigmoid activation, while channel attention produces channel-wise recalibration weights through global average pooling followed by 1×1 convolution and ReLU activation:

$$\begin{aligned} SA &= \sigma(\text{Conv}([\text{MaxPool}(F'); \text{AvgPool}(F')])) \\ CA &= \text{ReLU}(\text{Conv}_{1\times1}(\text{GAP}(F'))) \end{aligned} \tag{5}$$

The final output integrates attention-refined features with the original input through residual connection:

$$F_{out} = F_{in} \oplus ((F' \otimes SA) \otimes CA) \tag{6}$$

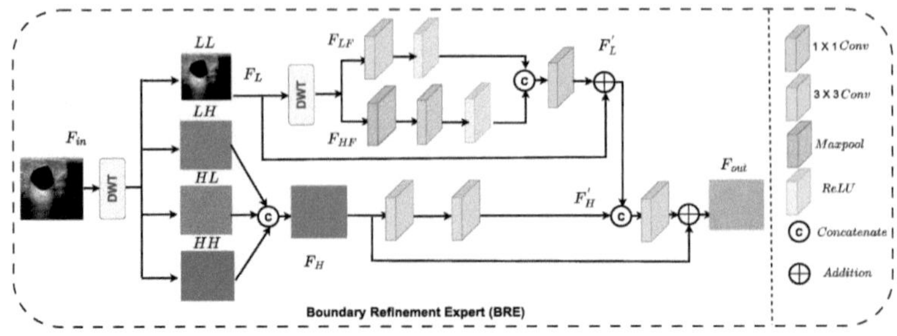

Fig. 5. Architecture of the Boundary Refinement Expert (BRE).

Boundary Refinement Expert (BRE). To address indistinct tissue boundaries in medical images, we propose the BRE module that uses Discrete Wavelet Transform (DWT) for frequency-domain enhancement, as shown in Fig. 5.

The BRE module employs a hierarchical wavelet decomposition strategy. First, input features F_{in} are decomposed using DWT to obtain four frequency subbands. Then, for the low-frequency pathway f_{L_path}, the approximation component $F_L = LL$ undergoes further wavelet decomposition to extract nested frequency information:

$$\text{DWT}(F_{in}) = \{LL, LH, HL, HH\}, \quad \text{DWT}(F_L) = \{F_{LF}, F_{HF}\} \tag{7}$$

These components are processed through separate sub-pathways where F_{LF} passes through 3×3 convolution and ReLU activation, while F_{HF} is processed through max pooling, 1×1 convolution, and ReLU activation. The processed components are then concatenated and combined with the original low-frequency features via residual connection:

$$F'_L = F_L \oplus \text{Concat}(\text{ReLU}(\text{Conv}_{3\times3}(F_{LF})), \text{ReLU}(\text{Conv}_{1\times1}(\text{MaxPool}(F_{HF})))) \tag{8}$$

For the high-frequency pathway f_{H_path}, the three detail subbands $\{LH, HL, HH\}$ are concatenated to form F_H and processed through 3×3 convolution to obtain F'_H. The dual-pathway outputs are fused and combined with original high-frequency features:

$$F_{out} = F_H \oplus \text{Conv}_{3\times3}(\text{Concat}(F'_L, F'_H)) \tag{9}$$

This nested wavelet processing design enables effective boundary enhancement by hierarchically extracting both structural context and edge details at multiple frequency scales, improving segmentation accuracy in regions with ambiguous boundaries.

Lightweight Gating Network. To dynamically integrate specialized knowledge from the three expert modules, we employ a lightweight adaptive gating network within each AMoE block. As shown in Fig. 2(c), the gating network processes input features X through adaptive average pooling to generate a global descriptor, which is then transformed by a compact MLP followed by softmax to produce three normalized weights w_1, w_2, and w_3 for MSAE, FEE, and BRE respectively, where $\sum_{i=1}^{3} w_i = 1$.

The final output is computed as a weighted combination of expert outputs:

$$X_{out} = w_1 \cdot X_{MSAE} + w_2 \cdot X_{FEE} + w_3 \cdot X_{BRE} \tag{10}$$

This adaptive weighting mechanism enables the network to emphasize the most relevant expert processing strategy—scale variation, foreground-background disambiguation, or boundary refinement—on a per-input basis, enhancing segmentation accuracy and adaptability to diverse medical imaging scenarios.

Loss Function. Our composite loss function $\mathcal{L}_{total}$ integrates segmentation accuracy with balanced expert utilization. The primary segmentation loss combines weighted Intersection over Union loss ($\mathcal{L}_{wIoU}(G, S_k)$) and weighted Binary Cross-Entropy loss ($\mathcal{L}_{wBCE}(G, S_k)$) for each decoder output S_k against ground truth G. Deep supervision is applied by summing losses across all decoder stages to enhance gradient flow at multiple scales.

To address expert utilization imbalance in mixture-of-experts architectures, we introduce an Expert Variance loss $\mathcal{L}_{EV}$ that promotes balanced activation across the MSAE, BRE, and FEE modules:

$$\mathcal{L}_{EV} = \frac{1}{N} \sum_{i=1}^{3} (u_i - \bar{u})^2 \tag{11}$$

where u_i represents the normalized utilization frequency of the i-th expert module during training, $\bar{u} = \frac{1}{3} \sum_{i=1}^{3} u_i$ is the mean utilization, and N is the number of experts. This loss prevents convergence to a subset of experts and ensures effective contribution from each specialized module.

The final training objective is:

$$\mathcal{L}_{total} = \sum_{k} (\mathcal{L}_{wIoU}(G, S_k) + \mathcal{L}_{wBCE}(G, S_k)) + \lambda \cdot \mathcal{L}_{EV} \tag{12}$$

where λ is a hyperparameter that balances segmentation accuracy against expert utilization diversity, guiding the model towards precise segmentation while maintaining effective learning dynamics within the AMoE framework.

4 Experiments

4.1 Datasets and Settings

To evaluate our AMoE-SAM2UNet, we utilize five publicly available medical datasets: (1) ISIC 2017 [6] contains 2,000/150/600 training/validation/test

Table 1. Comparison with State-of-the-Art Methods on Five Benchmark Datasets.

Dataset	Metric	**Ours**	Compared State-of-the-Art Models						
			UNet [20]	AttUNet [14]	TransUNet [4]	SwinUNet [2]	SAMed [27]	MedSAM [12]	SAM2-UNet [25]
ISIC	Dice↑	**0.929**	0.847	0.856	0.893	0.886	0.895	0.904	0.901
	IoU↑	**0.877**	0.741	0.762	0.784	0.773	0.786	0.805	0.804
	HD95↓	**6.63**	13.21	12.57	11.53	10.95	10.34	7.68	7.94
TN3K	Dice↑	**0.845**	0.765	0.781	0.805	0.812	0.826	0.817	0.824
	IoU↑	**0.726**	0.659	0.674	0.701	0.713	0.715	0.712	0.709
	HD95↓	**8.23**	13.89	11.23	10.43	9.75	9.32	9.80	9.96
ClinicDB	Dice↑	**0.935**	0.841	0.851	0.867	0.854	0.902	0.899	0.906
	IoU↑	**0.833**	0.732	0.742	0.767	0.749	0.813	0.796	0.818
	HD95↓	**7.28**	12.13	11.44	10.31	10.75	9.58	9.89	9.27
COVID	Dice↑	**0.837**	0.736	0.754	0.779	0.763	0.795	0.801	0.818
	IoU↑	**0.728**	0.621	0.645	0.668	0.657	0.694	0.705	0.717
	HD95↓	**7.68**	16.34	14.87	12.73	11.83	9.56	8.91	8.82
GLAS	Dice↑	**0.948**	0.927	0.928	0.937	0.916	0.913	0.924	0.931
	IoU↑	**0.902**	0.873	0.880	0.889	0.861	0.857	0.879	0.884
	HD95↓	**5.12**	6.67	6.42	6.24	6.87	6.73	5.94	5.36

images for melanoma segmentation from dermoscopy images. (2) TN3K [7] comprises 3,493 ultrasound images from 2,421 patients for thyroid nodule segmentation, split into 2,879 training and 614 testing images. (3) ClinicDB [1] includes 612 colonoscopy images for polyp segmentation with uniform 288×384 dimensions. (4) COVID [13] contains 1,277 CT images for lung infection segmentation, divided into 894 training and 383 testing images. (5) GLAS [22] consists of 165 H&E stained histological images for colorectal gland segmentation, with 85 training and 80 testing images.

All experiments were implemented using PyTorch on one NVIDIA GeForce RTX 4090 GPU. The model was fine-tuned using pretrained SAM2-Hiera-Large weights with Adam optimizer (learning rate: 0.001, weight decay: 0.0001, batch size: 12, epochs: 40). Performance was evaluated using Dice Coefficient (Dice), Intersection over Union (IoU), and 95th percentile Hausdorff Distance (HD95).

4.2 Comparison With State-of-the-Art Methods

We compare our proposed method with seven other state-of-the-art medical image segmentation methods, including two CNN-based methods (UNet [20], AttUNet [14]), two Transformer-based methods (TransUNet [4], SwinUNet [2]), and three vision foundation model-based methods (SAMed [27], MedSAM [12], SAM2-UNet [25]).

Quantitative Evaluation. Table 1 presents quantitative comparisons across five benchmark datasets. Our method consistently outperforms state-of-the-art approaches, achieving Dice scores of 0.929, 0.845, 0.935, 0.837, and 0.948 on ISIC, TN3K, ClinicDB, COVID, and GLAS datasets respectively. Compared to the strongest baseline SAM2-UNet, our approach demonstrates substantial improve-

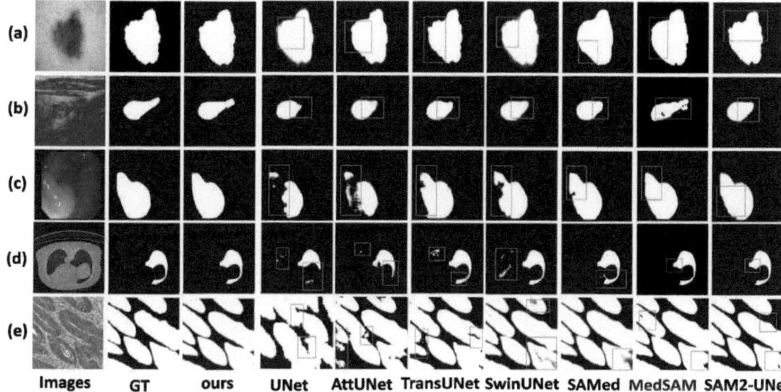

Fig. 6. Qualitative results of our proposed method and other state-of-the-art methods.

ments of 2.8%, 2.1%, 2.9%, 1.9%, and 1.7% in Dice scores while achieving superior boundary precision with HD95 reductions of 16.5%, 17.3%, 21.5%, 12.9%, and 4.5% respectively across the five datasets. The consistent improvements across diverse medical imaging modalities—dermoscopy, ultrasound, endoscopy, CT, and histology—validate the effectiveness of our adaptive mixture of experts strategy in handling varied anatomical structures and imaging characteristics.

Qualitative Evaluation. Figure 6 demonstrates visual segmentation performance across challenging medical scenarios. Our method excels in handling diverse imaging challenges: accurately segmenting irregular skin lesions with ambiguous boundaries (row a) and small-scale lesions (row b), detecting polyps with complex morphology that comparative methods struggle with (row c), precisely delineating anatomical structures in chest CT scans (row d), and maintaining structural integrity in complex histological images (row e). While existing approaches often produce fragmented results with boundary artifacts (highlighted in red boxes), our AMoE-SAM2UNet consistently generates smooth, anatomically consistent segmentation masks across all imaging modalities. The superior performance in challenging cases involving scale variations, tissue contrast changes, and complex anatomical structures validates the effectiveness of our adaptive mixture of experts in learning modality-specific representations while maintaining cross-domain generalization.

4.3 Ablation Studies

Expert Module Ablation. We conduct ablation studies to validate the effectiveness of each expert module in our proposed AMoE-SAM2UNet across five medical datasets. Table 2 presents the systematic analysis of different module combinations.

Each expert module demonstrates distinct contributions across different imaging scenarios. The Multi-Scale Adaptive Expert (MSAE) excels in handling irregular lesion boundaries, achieving substantial Dice improvements, most

Table 2. Ablation study on expert modules of AMoE-SAM2UNet across five medical datasets.

Expert Modules			ISIC 2017			TN3K			ClinicDB			COVID			GLAS		
MSAE	BRE	FEE	Dice↑	IoU↑	HD95↓	Dice↑	IoU↑	HD95↓	Dice↑	IoU↑	HD95↓	Dice↑	IoU↑	HD95↓	Dice↑	IoU↑	HD95↓
×	×	×	0.901	0.804	7.94	0.824	0.709	9.96	0.906	0.818	9.27	0.818	0.717	8.82	0.931	0.884	5.36
✓	×	×	0.913	0.847	7.35	0.831	0.715	9.21	0.918	0.824	8.76	0.825	0.721	8.47	0.938	0.889	5.25
×	✓	×	0.908	0.841	7.15	0.829	0.712	9.43	0.921	0.827	8.12	0.823	0.719	8.31	0.942	0.892	5.21
×	×	✓	0.906	0.838	7.58	0.827	0.711	9.67	0.915	0.821	8.95	0.821	0.718	8.59	0.936	0.887	5.28
✓	✓	×	0.920	0.856	6.95	0.837	0.719	8.87	0.927	0.831	7.89	0.831	0.724	8.15	0.944	0.896	5.18
✓	×	✓	0.918	0.853	7.21	0.834	0.717	9.02	0.924	0.828	8.43	0.829	0.722	8.37	0.943	0.894	5.22
×	✓	✓	0.916	0.851	6.87	0.836	0.718	8.79	0.929	0.829	7.73	0.827	0.721	8.23	0.939	0.889	5.26
✓	✓	✓	**0.929**	**0.877**	**6.63**	**0.845**	**0.726**	**8.23**	**0.935**	**0.833**	**7.28**	**0.837**	**0.728**	**7.68**	**0.948**	**0.902**	**5.12**

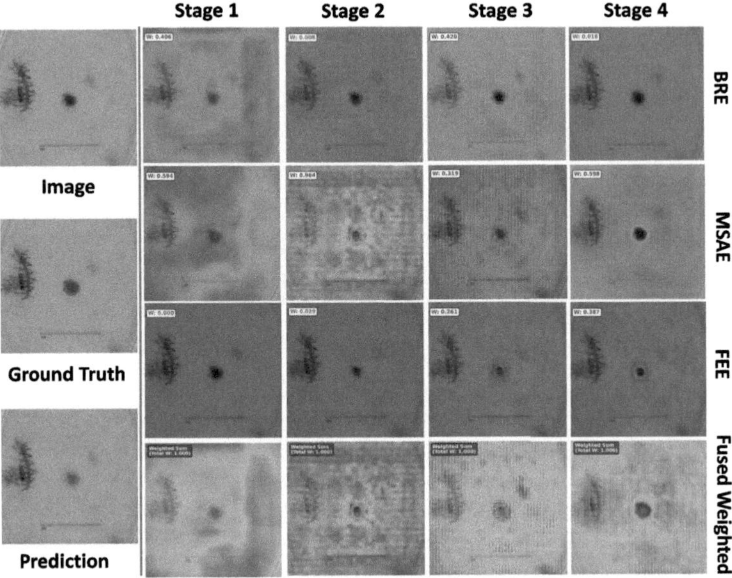

Fig. 7. Visualization of expert activation heatmaps across decoder stages for a representative ISIC sample.

notably on ISIC 2017 (+0.012, from 0.901 to 0.913) and consistent gains across other datasets. The Boundary Refinement Expert (BRE) shows specialized strength in enhancing segmentation precision, particularly effective on ClinicDB (+0.015, from 0.906 to 0.921) and GLAS datasets where boundary accuracy is critical. The Foreground Enhancement Expert (FEE) provides consistent but moderate improvements across all datasets, demonstrating its role in robust target identification under varying contrast conditions.

The synergistic effects become evident when combining multiple experts. The MSAE+BRE combination yields superior performance compared to individual experts, achieving Dice scores of 0.920 on ISIC 2017 and 0.927 on ClinicDB. Similarly, the BRE+FEE combination demonstrates strong capabilities, partic-

Table 3. Ablation study on loss function components of AMoE-SAM2UNet.

Loss Components				ISIC 2017			TN3K			ClinicDB			COVID			GLAS		
$\mathcal{L}_{IoU}$	$\mathcal{L}_{BCE}$	$\mathcal{L}_{DS}$	$\mathcal{L}_{EV}$	Dice↑	IoU↑	HD95↓	Dice↑	IoU↑	HD95↓	Dice↑	IoU↑	HD95↓	Dice↑	IoU↑	HD95↓	Dice↑	IoU↑	HD95↓
✓	✓	×	×	0.902	0.841	7.89	0.821	0.698	9.45	0.918	0.812	8.34	0.814	0.703	8.97	0.935	0.883	5.67
✓	✓	✓	×	0.919	0.862	7.15	0.834	0.714	8.76	0.928	0.825	7.81	0.826	0.714	8.34	0.942	0.894	5.31
✓	✓	✓	✓	**0.929**	**0.877**	**6.63**	**0.845**	**0.726**	**8.23**	**0.935**	**0.833**	**7.28**	**0.837**	**0.728**	**7.68**	**0.948**	**0.902**	**5.12**

ularly effective on TN3K (0.836) and GLAS (0.939) datasets. Most importantly, the complete AMoE-Decoder configuration (MSAE+BRE+FEE) achieves optimal performance across all datasets. This validates the complementary nature of our expert modules and confirms that their adaptive integration maximizes segmentation performance across diverse medical imaging scenarios.

Expert Activation Analysis. To understand the stage-specific behavior of our AMoE-Decoder, we visualize expert activation patterns across different decoder stages. Figure 7 presents feature activation heatmaps and expert weight distributions for a representative ISIC sample. The analysis reveals distinct specialization patterns: MSAE dominates in early stages (Stage 2: 0.964) for multi-scale feature extraction, BRE becomes prominent in middle stages (Stage 3: 0.420) for boundary refinement, and FEE gradually increases toward final stages (Stage 4: 0.387) for foreground enhancement. This stage-specific expert utilization validates our design rationale that different segmentation sub-tasks require specialized processing at different decoding levels.

Loss Function Ablation. Table 3 presents ablation studies on our composite loss function components across five datasets. The baseline configuration with weighted IoU and BCE losses achieves reasonable performance, while adding deep supervision ($\mathcal{L}_{DS}$) yields significant improvements by enhancing multi-level feature learning across decoder stages (e.g., Dice increases from 0.902 to 0.919 on ISIC 2017). The complete loss function with expert variance regularization ($\mathcal{L}_{EV}$) achieves optimal results by ensuring balanced expert utilization and preventing expert collapse, demonstrating that proper regularization is crucial for maximizing the effectiveness of our mixture-of-experts architecture.

5 Conclusion

In this paper, we presented AMoE-SAM2UNet, an innovative architecture that enhances foundation models for medical image segmentation through an Adaptive Mixture of Experts Decoder (AMoE-Decoder). The AMoE-Decoder integrates three specialized expert modules: MSAE for multi-scale adaptation, BRE for boundary refinement, and FEE for foreground enhancement, dynamically coordinated by a lightweight gating mechanism. Extensive experimental evaluations on five public datasets (ISIC 2017, TN3K, ClinicDB, COVID, and GLAS) demonstrate that AMoE-SAM2UNet consistently outperforms both SAM2-UNet baseline and state-of-the-art methods, validating the effectiveness of our expert design and the potential of mixture-of-experts strategies in bridging the gap between general-purpose foundation models and specialized medical image analysis requirements.

Acknowledgements. The work was supported by the National Natural Science Foundation of China under Grant Nos. 42271093 and 62376034, and by the Natural Science Foundation of Shandong Province under Grant No. ZR2024QF060.

References

1. Bernal, J., Sánchez, F.J., Fernández-Esparrach, G., Gil, D., Rodríguez, C., Vilariño, F.: WM-DOVA maps for accurate polyp highlighting in colonoscopy: validation vs. saliency maps from physicians. Comput. Med. Imaging Graph. **43**, 99–111 (2015)
2. Cao, H., et al.: Swin-Unet: Unet-like pure transformer for medical image segmentation. In: Karlinsky, L., Michaeli, T., Nishino, K. (eds) ECCV 2022, Part III. LNCS, vol. 13803, pp. 205–218. Springer, Heidelberg (2022). https://doi.org/10.1007/978-3-031-25066-8_9
3. Chen, C., et al.: MA-SAM: modality-agnostic SAM adaptation for 3d medical image segmentation. Med. Image Anal. **98**, 103310 (2024)
4. Chen, J., et al.: Transunet: Rethinking the u-net architecture design for medical image segmentation through the lens of transformers. Med. Image Anal. **97**, 103280 (2024)
5. Cheng, J., et al.: SAM-med2D. arXiv preprint arXiv:2308.16184 (2023)
6. Codella, N.C., et al.: Skin lesion analysis toward melanoma detection: a challenge at the 2017 international symposium on biomedical imaging (ISBI), hosted by the international skin imaging collaboration (ISIC). In: ISBI, pp. 168–172. IEEE (2018)
7. Gong, H., et al.: Multi-task learning for thyroid nodule segmentation with thyroid region prior. In: ISBI, pp. 257–261 (2021)
8. Hu, E.J., et al.: LoRA: low-rank adaptation of large language models. ICLR **1**(2), 3 (2022)
9. Kirillov, A., et al.: Segment anything. In: Proceedings of the IEEE/CVF International Conference on Computer Vision, pp. 4015–4026 (2023)
10. Liu, S., Huang, D., et al.: Receptive field block net for accurate and fast object detection. In: Proceedings of the European Conference on Computer Vision (ECCV), pp. 385–400 (2018)
11. Luo, Z., Zhu, X., Zhang, L., Sun, B.: Rethinking U-net: task-adaptive mixture of skip connections for enhanced medical image segmentation. In: Proceedings of the AAAI Conference on Artificial Intelligence, vol. 39, pp. 5874–5882 (2025)
12. Ma, J., He, Y., Li, F., Han, L., You, C., Wang, B.: Segment anything in medical images. Nat. Commun. **15**, 654 (2024)
13. Ma, J., et al.: Towards data-efficient learning: a benchmark for Covid-19 CT lung and infection segmentation. Med. Phys. **48**(3), 1197–1210 (2021)
14. Oktay, O., et al.: Attention U-net: learning where to look for the pancreas. arXiv preprint arXiv:1804.03999 (2018)

15. Ou, Y., et al.: Patcher: patch transformers with mixture of experts for precise medical image segmentation. In: Wang, L., Dou, Q., Fletcher, P.T., Speidel, S., Li, S. (eds.) MICCAI 2022. LNCS, vol. 13435, pp. 475–484. Springer, Cham (2022). https://doi.org/10.1007/978-3-031-16443-9_46
16. Pang, Y., et al.: Online self-distillation and self-modeling for 3d brain tumor segmentation. IEEE J. Biomed. Health Inform. 1–13 (2025)
17. Pang, Y., et al.: Slim UNETR: scale hybrid transformers to efficient 3D medical image segmentation under limited computational resources. IEEE Trans. Med. Imaging **43**(3), 994–1005 (2024)
18. Ravi, N., et al.: SAM 2: segment anything in images and videos. arXiv preprint arXiv:2408.00714 (2024)
19. Reynaud, H., Gomez, A., Leeson, P., Meng, Q., Kainz, B.: EchoFlow: a foundation model for cardiac ultrasound image and video generation. arXiv preprint arXiv:2503.22357 (2025)
20. Ronneberger, O., Fischer, P., Brox, T.: U-net: convolutional networks for biomedical image segmentation. In: Navab, N., Hornegger, J., Wells, W.M., Frangi, A.F. (eds.) MICCAI 2015. LNCS, vol. 9351, pp. 234–241. Springer, Cham (2015). https://doi.org/10.1007/978-3-319-24574-4_28
21. Ryali, C., et al.: Hiera: a hierarchical vision transformer without the bells-and-whistles. In: International Conference on Machine Learning, pp. 29441–29454. PMLR (2023)
22. Sirinukunwattana, K., et al.: Gland segmentation in colon histology images: the GlaS challenge contest. Med. Image Anal. **35**, 489–502 (2017)
23. Wu, J., et al.: Medical SAM adapter: adapting segment anything model for medical image segmentation. Med. Image Anal. **102**, 103547 (2025)
24. Wu, Z., Xiong, X., Chen, Y., Li, S., Chen, H.: MoE-polyp: shifting more attention to small polyp segmentation via mixture-of-experts. In: Proceedings of the 6th ACM International Conference on Multimedia in Asia, p. 1 (2024)
25. Xiong, X., et al.: SAM2-UNet: segment anything 2 makes strong encoder for natural and medical image segmentation. arXiv preprint arXiv:2408.08870 (2024)
26. You, C., Dai, W., Min, Y., Staib, L., Duncan, J.S.: Implicit anatomical rendering for medical image segmentation with stochastic experts. In: Greenspan, H., et al. (eds.) MICCAI 2023. LNCS, vol. 14222, pp. 561–571. Springer, Cham (2023). https://doi.org/10.1007/978-3-031-43898-1_54
27. Zhang, K., Liu, D.: Customized segment anything model for medical image segmentation. arXiv preprint arXiv:2304.13785 (2023)

Understanding Surgical Triplet Videos Through Transferable Visual Models from Natural Language Supervision

Yunhao Li[1], Aoying Wang[1], Yu-Xi Xie[2], Qiong Wang[1], Xiucai Ye[3], Patrizia Savi[4], Ying Hu[1], and Yan Pang[1](✉)

[1] Guangdong Provincial Key Laboratory of Computer Vision and Virtual Reality Technology, Shenzhen Institute of Advanced Technology, Chinese Academy of Sciences, Shenzhen, China
yanpang@siat.ac.cn
[2] South China University of Technology, Guangzhou, China
[3] Department of Computer Science, University of Tsukuba, Tsukuba, Japan
[4] Department of Electronics and Telecommunications , Politecnico di Torino, Turin, Italy

Abstract. Surgical triplet video understanding is essential for accurately recognizing and classifying surgical actions in real-time video data, enabling improved surgical planning and support. However, the recognition of surgical video triplets is particularly influenced by the varying frequency and duration of specific actions. Furthermore, the similarity in motion trajectories across various surgical actions presents another issue in video-based fine-grained surgical action recognition, complicating the differentiation of similar actions. To address these challenges, we propose a new comprehensive paired image-text surgical activity event dataset (SAE), consisting of 90,500 pairs of images and text depicting surgical actions. Additionally, we introduce TriClip, a novel dual-branch contrastive multimodal framework, which effectively bridges the gap between visual and textual modalities in surgical action recognition. By leveraging transferable visual models from natural language supervision, TriClip was evaluated using the CholecT45 dataset, where it achieved an SOTA average precision of 42.1%, setting a new state-of-the-art in the field of surgical action recognition.

Keywords: Surgical activity recognition · Vision-language modeling

1 Introduction

Video-driven fine-grained surgical action recognition seeks to accurately identify specific surgical activities within each frame of a video [36]. This technology

This work was supported by the Natural Science Foundation of China under Grant U23A20391 & 62576335, in part by the Guangdong Natural Science Foundation under Grant 2025A1515010276; in part by Shenzhen Science and Technology Program (JCYJ20241202152803005 & KJZD20240903102717023); and in part of Guangzhou Science and Technology Plan Project under Grant 2024D03J0010.

© The Author(s), under exclusive license to Springer Nature Singapore Pte Ltd. 2026
J. Kittler et al. (Eds.): PRCV 2025, LNCS 16289, pp. 560–573, 2026.
https://doi.org/10.1007/978-981-95-5764-6_38

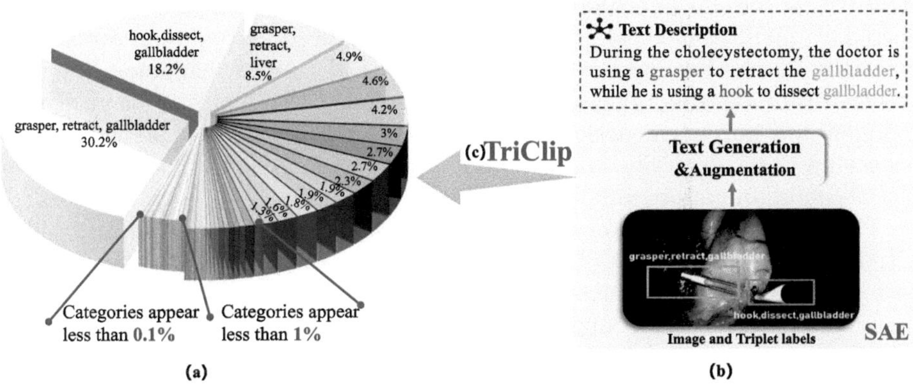

Fig. 1. A challenges and contributions summary: a. Surgical video triplet recognition varies due to different frequencies and durations of actions in procedures. b. The SAE dataset pairs images with text to balance recognition of surgical actions from activity videos. c. TriClip effectively links visual and textual elements in surgical recognition actions.

provides essential context-aware support to surgeons during procedures, thus enhancing safety within the operating room [25]. In addition to its immediate application in surgical settings, this technology serves a significant role in surgical archives, postoperative recovery, and medical education [10]. Among its various functions, triplet recognition—formalizing surgical activities as a triplet of <*instrument, verb, target*>—has emerged as a particularly nuanced approach. This task is conceptualized as a multi-label image classification problem, where multiple actions may occur concurrently within a single frame, enabling a more detailed and accurate understanding of activities.

Despite advancements, current methods [6,7,21,26,28,29,37] often overlook the difference in surgical actions prevalent in clinical procedures. Surgical video triplet identification is influenced by the frequency and duration of actions—certain actions occur more often than others [13,14,38]. For instance, as demonstrated in Fig. 1a, the triplet <*grasper, retract, gallbladder*> is often encountered, whereas <*grasper, pack, gallbladder*> manifests less frequently, distinguished solely by the action in question. This imbalance can lead methods to prioritize common pairs, like <*grasper, retract*>, neglecting significant pairs such as <*grasper, pack*>. This disparity may hinder the system's ability to recognize the full range of surgical activities, affecting its practical utility.

In order to alleviate the imbalance observed in surgical actions, we present a comprehensive paired image-text **S**urgical **A**ctivity **E**vent, SAE, derived from original surgical activity videos. This dataset is constructed through the extraction of key action frames, predicated upon their frequency of occurrence within the video content. Subsequently, advanced large vision models (LVMs) [2,31,33] are utilized to generate precise textual descriptions that correspond to these identified frames. As illustrated in Fig. 1b, to ensure clinical accuracy, the generated textual content undergoes a meticulous review and refinement process conducted by qualified medical professionals. This nuanced textual representation—especially for the less frequently occurring surgical actions—enhances the comprehension of these actions and aids in equalizing the representation of both common and infrequent actions. In total, The SAE consists of 90,500 pairs of images and text depicting surgical actions. Each image is associated with sentences containing approximately 30 words on average.

The similarity in motion trajectories of surgical actions complicates video-based fine-grained recognition. Actions like <*grasp, cut, dissect*> show similar patterns. Grasping uses an instrument to seize the organ; cutting requires precise tissue segmentation; dissecting involves gradually removing target tissue. Despite functional differences, these actions' trajectories overlap, hindering recognition systems' ability to differentiate them using standard imaging. This convergence creates a challenge in accurately identifying surgical actions, obstructing fine-grained recognition in practical environments.

To address this issue, we introduce **TriClip**, a dual-branch contrastive multimodal framework designed to differentiate similar surgical actions in fine-grained semantic spaces. TriClip has two branches: one extracts visual semantics from surgical video frames, and the other extracts textual semantics from corresponding descriptions. We incorporate a prompt learner using visual information to enhance the alignment between these modalities. By entering medical image-text pairs, TriClip effectively distinguishes between actions like *cutting* and *dissecting*, aligning their descriptions while clearly differentiating them from other actions *grasping*. TriClip was evaluated on the CholecT45 dataset, achieving an average precision (AP) of 42.1%, establishing a new SOTA in surgical action recognition. The main contributions are:

- The SAE dataset addresses surgical action recognition imbalance with video data, featuring LVM-generated textual descriptions validated by medical experts for better recognition of underrepresented actions.
- TriClip, a dual-branch contrastive multimodal framework, connects visual and textual modalities in surgical action recognition.
- TriClip achieves SOTA fine-grained action distinction on the CholecT45 dataset.

2 Related Work

2.1 Surgical Workflow Analysis

Laparoscopic surgery involves a complex intra-abdominal environment, including challenges such as smoke, instrument specular reflections, occlusions, and multi-instrument collaboration, which make visual scene understanding particularly difficult. Early studies mainly focused on single-task analysis of specific surgical scene components, such as instrument detection [1,5,30], instrument and tissue segmentation [17,19,24], or surgical phase recognition [12,18]. Although these approaches have achieved progress in their respective sub-tasks, the independence among tasks often leads to a lack of modeling of semantic relationships between different entities in the surgical scene, thus limiting the ability to comprehensively capture high-level surgical semantics.

To address this, Twinanda et al. [35] proposed EndoNet, a convolutional neural network architecture for laparoscopic video analysis that simultaneously performs surgical phase recognition and instrument presence detection. This work was one of the first to implement multi-task learning in laparoscopic surgery videos. Building on this, Czempiel et al. [8] introduced TeCNO, a multi-task framework based on temporal convolutional networks that further improves the accuracy of phase recognition and instrument detection by modeling temporal context. These studies demonstrate that incorporating multi-task learning mechanisms can more effectively capture the multi-dimensional semantic information inherent in surgical procedures.

However, these approaches focus primarily on high-level procedural cues (e.g., surgical phases and tool usage), and often overlook the fine-grained semantic interactions among instruments, actions, and targets, which are critical for deeper understanding and decision support in surgery.Recently, researchers begain to formalize surgical activities as surgical triplets consisting of instrument–verb–target, aiming to jointly model the interactions between instruments, actions, and target tissues. This enables a more comprehensive representation of the semantic structure of surgical behavior. Such a task is typically formulated as a Multi-Label Image Classification (MLIC) problem, where the model is required to predict multiple semantic labels for each video frame and capture their interrelations.Despite this,The triplet components exhibit complex semantic dependencies, which traditional multi-label classification methods struggle to explicitly model. This limitation hinders further improvements in model performances.

2.2 Triplet Recognition for Surgical Understanding

The Cholec45 [28] dataset with surgical triplet annotations was introduced, which formalizes surgical activities into triplets <*instrument, verb, target*>. This formulation enables a more detailed modeling of the interactions between surgical instruments and anatomical structures, thereby facilitating a deeper understanding of surgical semantics and promoting fine-grained analysis of surgical activities.Tripnet [26] was the first model to directly recognize surgical triplets from endoscopic videos by leveraging class activation guidance (CAG), where instrument activation maps guide the recognition of verbs and targets. Building on this, Nwoye et al. [28]which leverages the attention mechanism in Transformers to model the interactions between instruments, actions, and targets. Considering the temporal nature of surgical procedures, Sharma et al. [34] extended RDV with a temporal modeling variant named RiT, which captures the evolution of surgical actions across video frames through a temporal attention mechanism (TAM).While the above methods are capable of identifying instruments, verbs, and targets from single video frames and establishing their semantic associations, they overlook the severe class imbalance in this task. Accurately recognizing tail classes remains a major challenge. To address this, Gui et al. [14] proposed the MT4MTL-KD framework in 2023, which incorporates a multi-teacher knowledge distillation strategy to mitigate the scarcity of tail-class samples. In 2024, they further introduced TERL [13], which integrates contrastive learning with semantic enhancement to significantly improve the recognition performance of tail classes.Despite these advances, challenges persist in real-world surgical scenarios. Actions like grasp, cut, and dissect share similar motion patterns, making fine-grained recognition more challenging, which in turn reduces model representation quality and recognition accuracy.

2.3 Large Vision Models in Surgical

Large vision–language models (VLMs) have emerged rapidly in the analysis of surgical scenarios, leveraging cross-modal pretraining to mitigate the scarcity of annotated surgical video data and to enhance models' understanding of semantic and temporal structures in complex operating environments. Within multitask learning frameworks for laparoscopic and robotic surgery videos, VLMs are frequently employed as generic semantic priors or prompt-generation modules to enrich feature representations and improve generalization. Yuan et al. introduced PeskaVLP [39], which incorporates a hierarchical knowledge-augmentation strategy on surgical training videos to enforce both clip-level and procedure-level semantic consistency, achieving state-of-the-art performance on zero-shot scenario understanding and cross-modal retrieval tasks. Li et al. trained LLaVA-Surg [20] on an automatically constructed Surg-QA dataset, realizing open-ended question answering on surgical videos for the first time and yielding a 20%-point improvement in zero-shot answer accuracy over general-purpose multimodal models. Honarmand et al. further extended contrastive learning in VidLPRO [15] by adding video–text matching and masked-language modeling objectives, capturing fine-grained temporal dynamics and semantic alignments in laparoscopic and robotic surgery. Moreover, SurgVLP [40] leverages hundreds of hours of surgical lecture footage to achieve unsupervised cross-modal alignment, providing transferable representations for instrument detection, phase recognition, and triplet-relation extraction. These studies demonstrate that coupling large vision–language models with domain-specific surgical knowledge not only significantly improves the accuracy of traditional recognition tasks but also lays a solid foundation for interactive surgical assistance systems, automatic report generation, and decision-support in procedural workflows.

3 Method

3.1 Paired Image-Text Surgical Activity Event Dataset Generation

The SAE dataset significantly advances surgical activity recognition by providing high-quality paired image-text data. Derived from CholecT45, it offers action frames selected based on frequency in surgical videos, capturing both

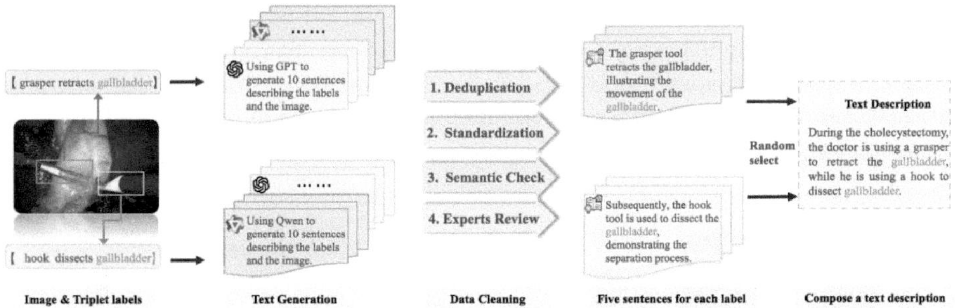

Fig. 2. Illustration of the data processing workflow. Overview of the construction pipeline for the proposed new comprehensive paired image-text surgical activity event (SAE) dataset. Surgical images are first annotated with instrument-verb-target triplets (e.g., <*grasp, cut, dissect*>). Second, Large language models are used to generate multiple candidate sentences per triplet. These candidates undergo cleaning process—deduplication, standardization, semantic validation, and expert review—to ensure accuracy and consistency.

common and rare actions. This balance is crucial for training models to recognize a wide variety of surgical actions, including infrequent yet vital ones. Additionally, SAE's precise textual descriptions improve the understanding of visual content, making it a key resource for research and the development of reliable systems for real-time surgical assistance.

Figure 2 illustrates that SAE generation follows a systematic method for creating high-quality image-text pairs for surgical action recognition model training. The first step extracts key action frames from the CholecT45 dataset, with resolutions from 480 × 854 to 1080 × 1920 pixels, based on frame frequency. For each label-image triplet, we use Qwen2.5VL-72B [3] and GPT-4o [16] to generate ten descriptive sentences, clarifying relationships among surgical instruments, actions, and targets in the images. These sentences are cleaned through deduplication, standardization, semantic checks, and review by clinicians to ensure accuracy and compliance with medical standards. From the ten descriptions, we select the five most representative, and one is chosen to create a comprehensive description for each triplet. This process results in high-quality, semantically consistent image-text pairs for the SAR dataset, aiding effective training for surgical action recognition systems. The SAE contains 90,500 image-text pairs, with varying sentence lengths per image, averaging around 30 words per sentence.

3.2 Dual-Branch Contrastive Multimodal Framework

Framework Overview. As a dual-branch contrastive multimodal framework, TriClip is designed to differentiate similar surgical actions within fine-grained semantic spaces. This framework consists of two branches: one for extracting visual semantics from surgical video frames using a ViT-based vision encoder [11] and the other for extracting textual semantics from corresponding descriptions using a BERT-based text encoder [9]. To enhance the alignment between these modalities, TriClip incorporates a prompt learner that utilizes visual information to guide the learning process of textual representations. By entering the medical image-text pairs from the SAE, TriClip efficiently differentiates between actions that share similar traits, enhancing the precision of detailed surgical action recognition (Fig. 3).

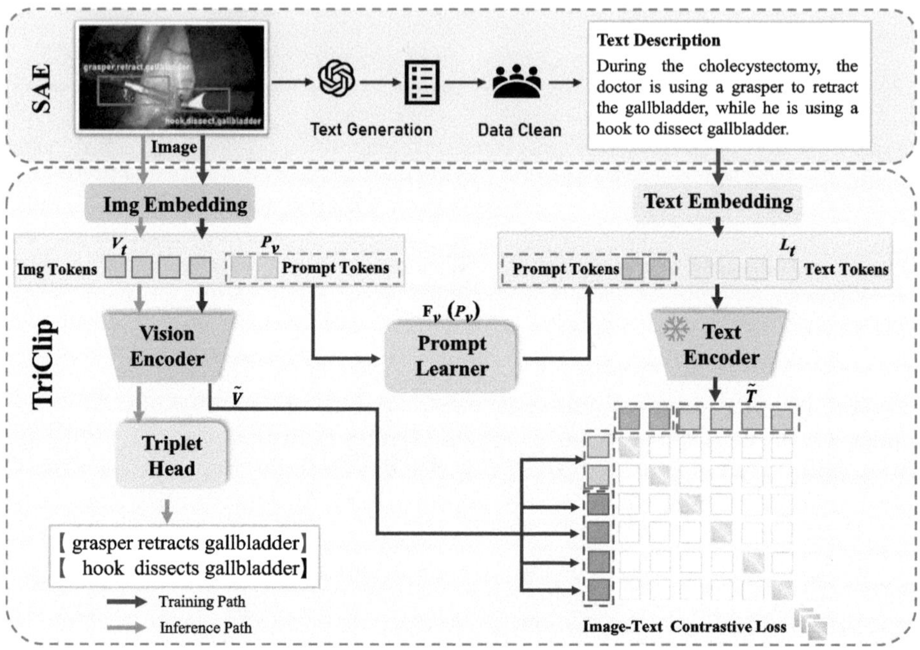

Fig. 3. Top: Paired image-text SAE. Bottom: Overview of the proposed a dual-branch contrastive multimodal framework TriClip. TriClip consists of an image branch and a text branch. TriClip enriches only the vision encoder with learnable prompt tokens to enhance image representations. These visual prompts are then projected into the text token space by a Prompt Learner, ensuring semantic alignment across modalities.

Prompt Learner. Establishing a solid alignment between visual and textual modalities is key to success in tasks involving video-driven fine-grained surgical action recognition, particularly in the context of recognizing surgical actions. Thus, a bidirectional prompt learner is introduced to steer the language modality's learning through visual cues, strengthening the connection between visual and textual representations. This approach promotes a more cohesive representation of both modalities across various surgical actions, enabling the model to grasp the subtle relationships between surgical actions and their corresponding descriptions.

The first step in the prompt learner is the alignment of visual and textual information at the token level. This is achieved by appending **trainable vision**

prompt tokens to the original image tokens before inputting them into the vision encoder. Specifically, the image tokens $\mathbf{V}_t \in \mathbb{R}^{N_t}$, which represent the visual features of the surgical video frames, are augmented with $\mathbf{P}_v \in \mathbb{R}^{N_v}$, the vision prompt tokens in Eq. 1.

$$\tilde{\mathbf{V}} = [\mathbf{P}_v \| \mathbf{V}_t] \in \mathbb{R}^{N_v + N_t} \tag{1}$$

where $\tilde{\mathbf{V}}$ represents the combined sequence of vision prompt tokens and image tokens, where $\|$ denotes the concatenation operation. N_v is the number of vision prompt tokens, and N_t is the number of original image tokens. The vision prompt tokens are learnable and allow the model to inject additional semantic context into the image tokens, enabling the vision encoder to capture more nuanced and discriminative visual features. This enhanced input facilitates a more detailed understanding of the visual modality, which is essential for recognizing fine-grained surgical actions.

In order to enhance the alignment between visual and textual modalities, a transfer function, F_v, is then introduced to map visual knowledge into the linguistic domain. It serves to bridge the gap between the vision and language branches, thus facilitating a mutual exchange of information. In this step, the vision prompt tokens, represented as $\mathbf{P}_v$, are transformed by the transfer function F_v into a text-compatible space, as outlined in Eq. 2.

$$\tilde{\mathbf{T}} = [F_v(\mathbf{P}_v) \| \mathbf{L}_t] \in \mathbb{R}^{N_l + N_t} \tag{2}$$

where $\tilde{\mathbf{T}}$ represents the combined sequence of the transformed vision prompt tokens and the original text tokens, where $\mathbf{L}_t \in \mathbb{R}^{N_t}$ denotes the original text tokens (i.e., the textual descriptions of surgical actions). The transfer function $F_v(\mathbf{P}_v)$ maps the vision prompt tokens $\mathbf{P}_v$ from the visual space to a text-compatible space of dimension N_l, where N_l is the number of text-compatible vision tokens. By appending these transformed vision prompt tokens to the original text tokens, the model ensures alignment and integration of both modalities before being processed by the language encoder. This bidirectional alignment enables mutual gradient propagation, allowing the model to refine textual features based on visual information, and vice versa. Consequently, this mechanism strengthens the synergy between the visual and language modalities, enhancing the model's overall performance in fine-grained recognition tasks.

Surgical Action Prediction. Surgical action prediction trains models to identify and classify surgeons' actions during procedures using visual and textual data. An image and text encoder are jointly trained to align image and text embeddings for matched surgical frames and descriptions while minimizing similarity for mismatched pairs. This creates a well-defined multi-modal embedding space, utilizing a symmetric cross-entropy loss as shown in Eq. 3.

$$\mathcal{L}_{\text{CLIP}} = -\frac{1}{2N}\sum_{i=1}^{N}\left[\log\frac{\exp(\text{sim}(\mathbf{v}_i,\mathbf{t}_i)/\tau)}{\sum_{j=1}^{N}\exp(\text{sim}(\mathbf{v}_i,\mathbf{t}_j)/\tau)} + \log\frac{\exp(\text{sim}(\mathbf{t}_i,\mathbf{v}_i)/\tau)}{\sum_{j=1}^{N}\exp(\text{sim}(\mathbf{t}_i,\mathbf{v}_j)/\tau)}\right] \tag{3}$$

where N is the batch size, and the summation is taken over all image-text pairs in the batch. This contrastive loss function encourages the model to learn a joint embedding space where semantically related images and texts are closer, while non-matching pairs are pushed apart. The symmetric loss $\mathcal{L}_{\text{CLIP}}$ maximizes the similarity between matched image-text pairs while concurrently minimizing the similarity between mismatched pairs within the joint embedding space. This loss function is computed utilizing cosine similarity, $\text{sim}(\cdot,\cdot)$, between the i-th image and its corresponding text embeddings, denoted as $\mathbf{v}_i$ and $\mathbf{t}_i$, respectively. In this context, $\mathbf{v}_i \in \mathbb{R}^{d_v}$ and $\mathbf{t}_i \in \mathbb{R}^{d_t}$ signify the embedding vectors for the image and text in the i-th pair, where d_v and d_t indicate their respective dimensions. The temperature parameter $\tau = 0.01$ is employed to regulate the scale of similarity values, thereby ensuring stable gradients during training.

In addition to cross-entropy loss, we employ a classification loss $\mathcal{L}_{\text{cls}}$ to make final action prediction. The overall objective function combines the contrastive loss $\mathcal{L}_{\text{CLIP}}$ with the classification loss $\mathcal{L}_{\text{cls}}$ through weighted sum in Eq. 4.

$$\mathcal{L}_{\text{total}} = \lambda_1\mathcal{L}_{\text{CLIP}} + \lambda_2\mathcal{L}_{\text{cls}} \tag{4}$$

where $\lambda_1 = 0.5$ and $\lambda_2 = 1$ are hyperparameters.

4 Experiments

4.1 Evaluation Dataset and Metrics

The CholecT45 dataset consists of 45 video sequences of laparoscopic cholecystectomy at one frame per second, totaling 90,500 frames and 137,900 annotated instances. It features six categories of surgical instruments, ten action classes, and fifteen anatomical targets, which surgical experts condensed into 100 triplet labels. Each frame includes relevant triplet labels for the procedure. Performance is evaluated using average precision (AP) metrics. AP_{IVT} (Instrument-Verb-Target) measures the model's understanding of surgical actions through triplet classification accuracy. AP_{IV} (Instrument-Verb) assesses the model's connection between instruments and actions, while AP_{IT} (Instrument-Target) evaluates the matching of instruments with their targets. Further metrics AP_I, AP_V, and AP_T measure the recognition of instruments, actions, and targets. AP_{IVT} is the primary metric, comprehensively assessing triplet classification accuracy.

Implementation Details. TriClip is trained on 8 NVIDIA V100 32 GB GPUs using a batch size of 96 per GPU. We use the AdamW optimizer [23] with a learning rate of $1e-3$, weight decay $1e-2$. The pre-trained model, CLIP-B/16 [32], has an image size of 224 and is trained for 20 epochs with random resized crops for data augmentation. We followed the official 5-fold cross-validation split [27]. Following [13], fold 1 is utilized to perform ablation studies.

Table 1. Performance Comparison on CholecT45 dataset using the official five-fold cross-validation split. The best scores are **bold**.

Method	AP_I	AP_V	AP_T	AP_{IV}	AP_{IT}	AP_{IVT}
Tripnet [26]	89.9±1.0	59.9±0.9	37.4±1.5	31.8±4.1	27.1±2.8	24.4±4.7
Attention Triplet [28]	89.1±2.1	61.2±0.6	40.3±1.2	33.0±2.9	29.4±1.2	27.2±2.7
Rendezvous [28]	89.3±2.1	62.0±1.3	40.0±1.4	34.0±3.3	30.8±2.1	29.4±2.8
ConceptNet-ViT [4]	88.3±1.4	65.1±3.9	43.8±3.1	33.7±3.2	33.4±3.2	30.6±1.9
RiT [34]	88.6±2.6	64.0±2.5	43.4±1.4	38.3±3.5	36.9±1.0	29.7±2.6
TDN [6]	91.2±1.9	65.3±2.8	43.7±1.6	–	–	33.8±2.5
RDV [22]	91.8±1.8	66.3±1.4	45.5±1.9	42.7±4.6	42.2±1.9	35.0±3.2
MT4MTL-KD [14]	93.9±2.0	73.8±2.0	52.1±5.2	46.5±3.4	46.2±2.3	38.9±1.6
TERL [13]	**94.5**±2.2	74.0±1.6	52.9±4.9	**47.6**±5.2	46.3±2.1	40.4±2.4
TriCLIP	94.1±1.4	**75.1**±2.0	**57.4**±6.8	46.5±1.5	**48.8**±2.5	**42.1**±1.4

4.2 Performance

Table 1 shows a comparison of triplet recognition accuracy (AP) on the CholecT45 dataset. TriCLIP achieves outstanding joint triplet accuracy of 42.1%. For AP_{IT}, TriCLIP scores 48.8%, surpassing the second-best model, TERL [13], by 2.5%. Additionally, our model obtains AP_V and AP_T scores of 75.1% and 57.4%, respectively, which are 1.1% and 4.5% higher than TERL. These findings indicate that developing a suitable text description dataset and applying a multimodal training approach can significantly address class imbalance issues, thereby improving triplet recognition accuracy.

4.3 Ablation Study

Number of Prompt Tokens. We conduct ablation experiments to validate the effectiveness of TriClip. The impact of the number of prompt tokens is analyzed in Table 2(a). The results demonstrate that increasing them initially enhances performance, with the highest AP_{IVT} score of 42.0% achieved using 4 tokens. However, further increasing those tokens to 8 or 16 does not consistently improve performance. While the AP_{IV} score slightly increases from 4 tokens to 16 tokens, the AP_{IT} and AP_{IVT} scores remain relatively stable or even decrease marginally.

Ablation on Backbones of TriClip. The choice of backbone architecture impacts the performance of TriClip illustrated in Table 2(b). Among the evaluated backbones, CLIP-B/16 [32] achieves the highest AP_{IVT} score, demonstrating its effectiveness in integrating visual and textual modalities. Although CLIP-L/14 exhibits the best AP_{IV} and AP_{IT} scores, 47.3%, and 49.0%, respectively, its AP_{IVT} performance is slightly lower. In contrast, CLIP-B/32 shows inferior performance across all metrics, underscoring the importance of selecting an appropriate backbone to achieve optimal results.

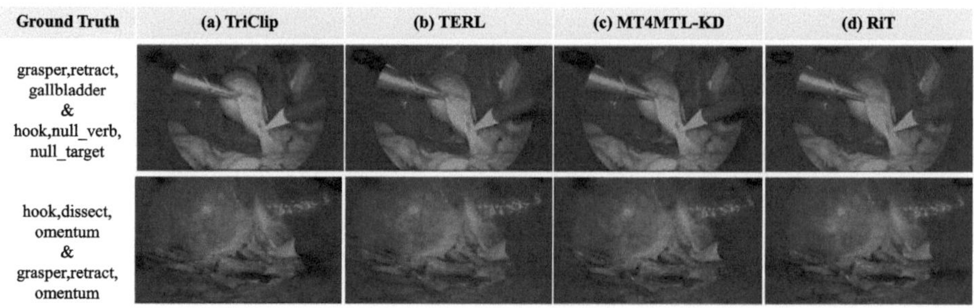

Fig. 4. Heatmap Comparison of different approaches in surgical video triplets. Note: Red indicates increased activation, and blue indicates reduced activation. (Color figure online)

Table 2. Ablation studies examine prompt tokens and backbone architectures. Best results are bolded, and TriCLIP instances are highlighted gray.

T45	AP_{IV}	AP_{IT}	AP_{IVT}
2	35.2	37.3	35.5
4	46.9	**48.9**	**42.0**
8	46.8	48.5	41.8
16	**47.5**	48.5	41.9

(a) Number of prompt tokens

T45	AP_{IV}	AP_{IT}	AP_{IVT}
CLIP-B/32	45.2	47.6	40.8
CLIP-B/16	46.9	48.9	**42.0**
CLIP-L/14	**47.3**	**49.0**	41.8

(b) Comparison of Backbones

Visualization. The heatmap comparison in Fig. 4 illustrates the performance of TriClip in surgical video triplet recognition. TriClip shows increased activation in key areas corresponding to surgical actions, notably in recognizing complex triplets like grasper, retract, gallbladder, and hook. Compared to other methods, TriClip demonstrates superior performance, with stronger activation in relevant regions, indicating more accurate identification of the surgical actions. In contrast, TERL [13], MT4MTL-KD [14], and RiT [34] show reduced activation or misalignment. This performance reflects TriClip's ability to better capture fine-grained details in surgical action recognition.

5 Conclusion

The SAE dataset addresses imbalance in surgical action recognition through expert-validated LVM-generated descriptions, enhancing recognition of under-represented actions. TriClip, our dual-branch contrastive multimodal framework, links visual and textual modalities to improve accuracy. This work advances surgical triplet video understanding, with potential applications in real-time assistance and education.

References

1. Abdulbaki Alshirbaji, T., Jalal, N.A., Möller, K.: Surgical tool classification in laparoscopic videos using convolutional neural network. Curr. Direct. Biomed. Eng. **4**(1), 407–410 (2018)
2. Bai, J., et al.: Qwen-VL: a frontier large vision-language model with versatile abilities. arXiv preprint arXiv:2308.12966 (2023)
3. Bai, S., et al.: Qwen2. 5-VL technical report. arXiv preprint arXiv:2502.13923 (2025)
4. Ban, Y., et al.: Concept graph neural networks for surgical video understanding. IEEE Trans. Med. Imaging (2023)
5. Bodenstedt, S., et al.: Real-time image-based instrument classification for laparoscopic surgery. arXiv preprint arXiv:1808.00178 (2018)
6. Chen, Y., He, S., Jin, Y., Qin, J.: Surgical activity triplet recognition via triplet disentanglement. In: Greenspan, H., et al. (eds.) MICCAI 2023. LNCS, vol. 14228, pp. 451–461. Springer (2023). https://doi.org/10.1007/978-3-031-43996-4_43
7. Cheng, Y., Liu, L., Wang, S., Jin, Y., Schönlieb, C.B., Aviles-Rivero, A.I.: Why deep surgical models fail?: revisiting surgical action triplet recognition through the lens of robustness. In: Chen, H., Luo, L. (eds) TML4H 2023. LNCS, vol. 1393, pp. 177–189. Springer, Cham (2023). https://doi.org/10.1007/978-3-031-39539-0_15
8. Czempiel, T., et al.: TeCNO: surgical phase recognition with multi-stage temporal convolutional networks. In: Martel, A.L., et al. (eds.) MICCAI 2020. LNCS, vol. 12263, pp. 343–352. Springer, Cham (2020). https://doi.org/10.1007/978-3-030-59716-0_33
9. Devlin, J., Chang, M.W., Lee, K., Toutanova, K.: BERT: pre-training of deep bidirectional transformers for language understanding. In: Proceedings of the 2019 Conference of the North American Chapter of the Association for Computational Linguistics: Human Language Technologies, Volume 1 (long and Short Papers), pp. 4171–4186 (2019)
10. Ding, X., Li, X.: Exploring segment-level semantics for online phase recognition from surgical videos. IEEE Trans. Med. Imaging **41**(11), 3309–3319 (2022)
11. Dosovitskiy, A., et al.: An image is worth 16×16 words: transformers for image recognition at scale. arXiv preprint arXiv:2010.11929 (2020)
12. Garrow, C.R., et al.: Machine learning for surgical phase recognition: a systematic review. Ann. Surg. **273**(4), 684–693 (2021)
13. Gui, S., Wang, Z.: Tail-enhanced representation learning for surgical triplet recognition. In: Linguraru, M.G., et al. (eds.) MICCAI 2024. LNCS, vol. 15011, pp. 689–699. Springer, Cham (2024). https://doi.org/10.1007/978-3-031-72120-5_64
14. Gui, S., Wang, Z., Chen, J., Zhou, X., Zhang, C., Cao, Y.: MT4MTL-KD: a multi-teacher knowledge distillation framework for triplet recognition. IEEE Trans. Med. Imaging (2023)
15. Honarmand, M., Jamal, M.A., Mohareri, O.: VidLPRO: a video-language pre-training framework for robotic and laparoscopic surgery. arXiv preprint arXiv:2409.04732 (2024)
16. Hurst, A., et al.: GPT-4o system card. arXiv preprint arXiv:2410.21276 (2024)
17. Jha, D., et al.: Exploring deep learning methods for real-time surgical instrument segmentation in laparoscopy. In: 2021 IEEE EMBS International Conference on Biomedical and Health Informatics (BHI), pp. 1–4. IEEE (2021)
18. Katić, D., et al.: LapOntoSPM: an ontology for laparoscopic surgeries and its application to surgical phase recognition. Int. J. Comput. Assist. Radiol. Surg. **10**, 1427–1434 (2015)

19. Kletz, S., Schoeffmann, K., Benois-Pineau, J., Husslein, H.: Identifying surgical instruments in laparoscopy using deep learning instance segmentation. In: 2019 International Conference on Content-Based Multimedia Indexing (CBMI), pp. 1–6. IEEE (2019)
20. Li, J., et al.: LLaVA-surg: towards multimodal surgical assistant via structured surgical video learning. arXiv preprint arXiv:2408.07981 (2024)
21. Li, Y., Xia, T., Luo, H., He, B., Jia, F.: MT-FIST: a multi-task fine-grained spatial-temporal framework for surgical action triplet recognition. IEEE J. Biomed. Health Inform. (2023)
22. Liu, D., Hu, A., Shah, M., Xu, C.: Surgical triplet recognition via diffusion model. arXiv preprint arXiv:2406.13210 (2024)
23. Loshchilov, I., Hutter, F.: Decoupled weight decay regularization. In: International Conference on Learning Representations, pp. 1–18 (2019)
24. Maier-Hein, L., et al.: Can masses of non-experts train highly accurate image classifiers? In: Golland, P., Hata, N., Barillot, C., Hornegger, J., Howe, R. (eds.) MICCAI 2014. LNCS, vol. 8674, pp. 438–445. Springer, Cham (2014). https://doi.org/10.1007/978-3-319-10470-6_55
25. Maier-Hein, L., et al.: Surgical data science for next-generation interventions. Nat. Biomed. Eng. **1**(9), 691–696 (2017)
26. Nwoye, C.I., et al.: Recognition of instrument-tissue interactions in endoscopic videos via action triplets. In: Martel, A.L., et al. (eds.) MICCAI 2020. LNCS, vol. 12263, pp. 364–374. Springer, Cham (2020). https://doi.org/10.1007/978-3-030-59716-0_35
27. Nwoye, C.I., Padoy, N.: Data splits and metrics for benchmarking methods on surgical action triplet datasets. arXiv preprint arXiv:2204.05235 (2022)
28. Nwoye, C.I., et al.: Rendezvous: attention mechanisms for the recognition of surgical action triplets in endoscopic videos. Med. Image Anal. **78**, 102433 (2022)
29. Pang, Y., et al.: Slim UNETR: scale hybrid transformers to efficient 3D medical image segmentation under limited computational resources. IEEE Trans. Med. Imaging **43**(3), 994–1005 (2023)
30. Primus, M.J., Schoeffmann, K., Böszörmenyi, L.: Instrument classification in laparoscopic videos. In: 2015 13th International Workshop on Content-Based Multimedia Indexing (CBMI), pp. 1–6. IEEE (2015)
31. Radford, A.: Improving language understanding by generative pre-training (2018)
32. Radford, A., et al.: Learning transferable visual models from natural language supervision. In: International Conference on Machine Learning, pp. 8748–8763. PMLR (2021)
33. Radford, A., et al.: Language models are unsupervised multitask learners. OpenAI blog **1**(8), 9 (2019)
34. Saurav, S., Nwoye, C.I., Didier, M., Nicolas, P.: Rendezvous in time: an attention-based temporal fusion approach for surgical triplet recognition. Int. J. Comput. Assist. Radiol. Surg. **18**, 1053–1059 (2023)
35. Twinanda, A.P., Shehata, S., Mutter, D., Marescaux, J., De Mathelin, M., Padoy, N.: EndoNet: a deep architecture for recognition tasks on laparoscopic videos. IEEE Trans. Med. Imaging **36**(1), 86–97 (2016)
36. Wagner, M., et al.: Comparative validation of machine learning algorithms for surgical workflow and skill analysis with the heichole benchmark. Med. Image Anal. **86**, 102770 (2023)
37. Xi, N., Meng, J., Yuan, J.: Chain-of-look prompting for verb-centric surgical triplet recognition in endoscopic videos. In: Proceedings of the 31st ACM International Conference on Multimedia, pp. 5007–5016 (2023)

38. Yamlahi, A., et al.: Self-distillation for surgical action recognition. In: Greenspan, H., et al. (eds.) MICCAI 2023. LNCS, vol. 14228. pp. 637–646. Springer, Cham (2023). https://doi.org/10.1007/978-3-031-43996-4_61
39. Yuan, K., Navab, N., Padoy, N., et al.: Procedure-aware surgical video-language pretraining with hierarchical knowledge augmentation. Adv. Neural. Inf. Process. Syst. **37**, 122952–122983 (2024)
40. Yuan, K., et al.: Learning multi-modal representations by watching hundreds of surgical video lectures. arXiv preprint arXiv:2307.15220 (2023)

Author Index

© The Editor(s) (if applicable) and The Author(s), under exclusive license
to Springer Nature Singapore Pte Ltd. 2026
J. Kittler et al. (Eds.): PRCV 2025, LNCS 16289, pp. 575–577, 2026.
https://doi.org/10.1007/978-981-95-5764-6

MIX
Papier aus verantwortungsvollen Quellen
Paper from responsible sources
FSC® C105338

If you have any concerns about our products,
you can contact us on
ProductSafety@springernature.com

In case Publisher is established outside the EU,
the EU authorized representative is:
Springer Nature Customer Service Center GmbH
Europaplatz 3, 69115 Heidelberg, Germany

Printed by Libri Plureos GmbH
in Hamburg, Germany